'Anyone looking to get up to speed on the state of the art in research on political parties needs to read this book. Written by a stellar cast of experts, it tells you where we are now and where things are heading. A truly invaluable collection'.

—**Tim Bale**, *Queen Mary University of London, UK*

'The editors have expertly curated a compelling collection of chapters which address classic research questions in the study of party politics, alongside contributions that reflect new research foci, international analysis via regional studies, and research design and methods. All of the chapters present a state of the art, reconsider key conceptual debates, explore empirical approaches, and outline future research agendas. Such an approach offers the reader clear links to "seminal" and pioneering literature complemented by more critical studies, provides for a comparative approach, and highlights debates among party scholars with regard to methodological and empirical stances. The *Routledge Handbook of Political Parties* tells those interested in party politics what they need to critically study in party types, families, systems, and party change; it reviews party responses to critical contemporary issues such as gender inequality, European integration, the environment, and immigration; and is attuned to the study of political parties beyond established, Western democracies. Accessible and yet comprehensive, the *Routledge Handbook of Political Parties* is a fine resource for students, the interested public, and scholars alike'.

—**Sarah Childs**, *University of Edinburgh, UK*

'This book is a must read for any serious scholar of political parties. It will be a very welcome addition to the libraries of scholars who study political parties. It includes many of the top scholars in the field and has a very coherent organisation, including definitional chapters, party as organisation, party ideology and party systems as well as exemplary types of parties. I will certainly be relying heavily on the contributions in this book in my own work and will be using it in my classes at the graduate and undergraduate levels'.

—**John Ishiyama**, *University Distinguished Research Professor and Chair, University of North Texas, USA*

THE ROUTLEDGE HANDBOOK OF POLITICAL PARTIES

The Routledge Handbook of Political Parties provides a systematic and comprehensive overview of the study of political parties provided by leading experts in the field.

In an era of widespread political disillusionment, political parties are often the main targets of citizen dissatisfaction, yet they are the key institutions that make democracy work. Analysing political parties in unrivalled depth and breath, with comparative thematic chapters throughout, as well as a dedicated section on political parties and party politics in specific country and regional settings, this handbook examines and illuminates the key questions around: how parties organise; how their ideologies have evolved over time; their relationship with society; how they differentiate themselves and how they respond to new social, economic, and political developments.

The Routledge Handbook of Political Parties is essential reading and an authoritative reference for scholars, students, researchers, and practitioners involved in and actively concerned about research in the study of political parties, party systems, and party politics.

Neil Carter is Professor of Politics at the University of York, UK.

Daniel Keith is Senior Lecturer in Politics at the University of York, UK.

Gyda M. Sindre is Senior Lecturer in Politics at the University of York, UK.

Sofia Vasilopoulou is Professor of European Politics at King's College London and Honorary Professor at the University of York, UK.

THE ROUTLEDGE HANDBOOK OF POLITICAL PARTIES

Edited by Neil Carter, Daniel Keith, Gyda M. Sindre and Sofia Vasilopoulou

LONDON AND NEW YORK

Designed cover image: © Getty Images

First published 2023
by Routledge
4 Park Square, Milton Park, Abingdon, Oxon OX14 4RN

and by Routledge
605 Third Avenue, New York, NY 10158

Routledge is an imprint of the Taylor & Francis Group, an informa business

© 2023 selection and editorial matter, Neil Carter, Daniel Keith, Gyda M. Sindre and Sofia Vasilopoulou; individual chapters, the contributors

The right of Neil Carter, Daniel Keith, Gyda M. Sindre and Sofia Vasilopoulou to be identified as the authors of the editorial material, and of the authors for their individual chapters, has been asserted in accordance with sections 77 and 78 of the Copyright, Designs and Patents Act 1988.

All rights reserved. No part of this book may be reprinted or reproduced or utilised in any form or by any electronic, mechanical, or other means, now known or hereafter invented, including photocopying and recording, or in any information storage or retrieval system, without permission in writing from the publishers.

Trademark notice: Product or corporate names may be trademarks or registered trademarks, and are used only for identification and explanation without intent to infringe.

British Library Cataloguing-in-Publication Data
A catalogue record for this book is available from the British Library

ISBN: 978-0-367-20874-5 (hbk)
ISBN: 978-0-367-62000-4 (pbk)
ISBN: 978-0-429-26385-9 (ebk)

DOI: 10.4324/9780429263859

Typeset in Bembo
by Apex CoVantage, LLC

CONTENTS

List of tables xii
List of figures xiii
Notes on contributors xiv
Acknowledgements xxi

    Introduction 1
    Neil Carter, Daniel Keith, Gyda M. Sindre and Sofia Vasilopoulou

PART 1
Definitions and party evolution 7

  1 Party change beyond the 'classical models?' The role of agency, context and democracy 9
    Oscar Mazzoleni and Reinhard Heinisch

  2 Parties and partisanship in political theory 20
    Alfred Moore

  3 Party systems and party system change 30
    Zsolt Enyedi and Fernando Casal Bértoa

PART 2
Party as an organisation 43

  4 Party organisation 45
    Anika Gauja

5	Party membership *Susan E. Scarrow and Paul D. Webb*	56
6	Party finance *Daniela R. Piccio*	68
7	Party institutionalisation *Nicole Bolleyer*	78
8	Political parties and social movements *Myrto Tsakatika*	90
9	Political parties and gender *Tània Verge*	101

PART 3
Party ideology and party families   **113**

10	Cleavage politics in the twenty-first century *James Dennison and Sophia Hunger*	115
11	The far right *Daphne Halikiopoulou*	125
12	The centre-right: Christian Democrats, Conservatives and Liberals *Marija Taflaga*	137
13	Liberal parties *Caroline Close and Thomas Legein*	149
14	Social democracy *Björn Bremer*	161
15	Radical left parties *Daniel Keith and Luke March*	173
16	Green parties *Neil Carter*	185

PART 4
Party competition and representation — 197

17 Party strategies: valence versus position — 199
    Agnes Magyar, Sarah Wagner and Roi Zur

18 Issue competition and agenda setting — 211
    Christoffer Green-Pedersen

19 Niche parties and party competition — 221
    Markus Wagner

20 Parties in government and in coalitions — 232
    Zachary Greene and Despina Alexiadou

21 Parties and representation — 243
    Jae-Jae Spoon

22 Personalisation and political parties — 254
    Helene Helboe Pedersen

PART 5
Contemporary issues and challenges — 267

23 Populism and parties — 269
    Stijn van Kessel

24 Parties and climate change — 280
    Conor Little

25 Parties and immigration — 291
    Pontus Odmalm

26 Parties and European integration — 301
    Sofia Vasilopoulou

27 Parties, issues and gender — 312
    Hilde Coffé, Miki Caul Kittilson, Bonnie M. Meguid and Ana Catalano Weeks

28 Post-conflict political parties 323
    Carrie Manning and Gyda M. Sindre

29 Clientelism and political parties 334
    Sergiu Gherghina and Clara Volintiru

PART 6
Regional comparisons **347**

30 Political parties in Russia and post-Soviet states 349
    Neil Robinson

31 Political parties in East Asia 360
    Ko Maeda

32 Political parties in Southeast Asia 371
    Andreas Ufen

33 Political parties in Latin America 382
    Saskia P. Ruth-Lovell

34 Political parties in Sub-Saharan Africa 392
    Matthijs Bogaards

35 Political parties in North Africa 403
    Lise Storm

36 Political parties in the Arab Middle East 414
    Hendrik Kraetzschmar and Valeria Resta

37 Political parties in India 426
    Indrajit Roy and Maya Tudor

PART 7
Methods for estimating party preferences **437**

38 Text analysis of party manifestos 439
    Daniela Braun

39	Voting advice applications *Frederico Ferreira da Silva and Diego Garzia*	450
40	Expert surveys in party research *Maurits J. Meijers and Nina Wiesehomeier*	466

Index 478

TABLES

19.1	Definitions of niche parties and nicheness	222
30.1	CPSU successor parties and presidential parties	351
31.1	Major parties of South Korea and Taiwan in presidential elections	361
36.1	Political parties and elections in the Arab Middle East	415
36.2	Principal Islamist movement parties in the Arab Middle East	419
38.1	Policy domains in the MARPOR and EM coding schemes	441
38.2	Coding example (based on the Euromanifestos coding scheme)	442
39.1	Continuous statements and dimensions of political competition (2009–2019)	453
39.2	Paired comparisons by dimension and election year: EU Profiler/euandi, CHES, and CMP	457
40.1	Overview of relevant expert surveys in party research	468

FIGURES

5.1	Self-identified party members as per cent of respondents of World Values Survey Wave 7 (2017–2020)	59
7.1	Configurations of the internal dimension of party institutionalisation	82
9.1	Interplay between gender and party	102
9.2	The vertical ladder of recruitment and the supply and demand model	106
14.1	Average vote share of centre-left and centre-right parties in 22 countries from 1945 to 2020	163
17.1	Party positions in three-party competition	201
22.1	Illustration of theoretical model explaining personalisation or personalised politics	259
27.1	Gender differences (male/female voter ratio) in voting behaviour for different party families, Europe 1985–2018 (Loess Smoothing)	313
27.2	Share of women in parliamentary party by party family, Europe 1980–2018 (Loess Smoothing)	317
29.1	Types of clientelism	335
39.1	Party positions on the socioeconomic left-right, EU integration, and GALTAN dimensions, by party family (2009–2019)	454

CONTRIBUTORS

Despina Alexiadou is Chancellor's Fellow and Senior Lecturer at the University of Strathclyde. She is the author of *Ideologues, Partisans and Loyalists: Ministers and Policymaking in Parliamentary Cabinets* published by Oxford University Press and various articles on the role of the executive on policy outcomes in OECD countries.

Fernando Casal Bértoa is Associate Professor in the School of Politics and International Relations at the University of Nottingham. He was awarded the 2017 Gordon Smith and Vincent Wright Memorial Prize, the 2017 AECPA Prize for the Best Article, and the 2018 Vice-Chancellor Medal of the University of Nottingham for 'exceptional achievements'.

Matthijs Bogaards is Associate Professor in the Department of Political Science at the Central European University, Vienna. Before, he was Full Professor of Political Science at Jacobs University Bremen. His research and teaching interest is in comparative politics, with a special interest in democratisation, democracy in divided societies, ethnic conflict, and African politics.

Nicole Bolleyer is Chair of Comparative Political Science at the Geschwister Scholl Institute of Political Science, LMU Munich. She is the author of several monographs including *New Parties in Old Party Systems: Patterns of Persistence and Decline in Seventeen Democracies* (Oxford University Press 2013) and *The State and Civil Society: Regulating Interest Groups, Parties and Public Benefit Organizations in Contemporary Democracies* (Oxford University Press 2018). Her research has appeared in a wide range of leading journals such as *Comparative Political Studies*, *Journal of Politics*, and the *European Journal of Political Research*.

Daniela Braun is Assistant Professor in Comparative Politics at the LMU Munich and co-directs the Euromanifestos project. Her research interests include European Union politics, party politics, public opinion, and political behaviour. Her work has been published, for example, in the *European Journal of Political Research*, *European Union Politics*, and *Party Politics*.

Björn Bremer is Senior Researcher at the Max Planck Institute for the Study of Societies. His research lies at the intersection of comparative politics, political economy, and political behaviour. He is particularly interested in the politics of macroeconomic policies, welfare state politics, and the political consequences of economic crises.

Neil Carter is Professor of Politics at the University of York. He has published widely on UK party politics, green politics, and environmental policy, including *The Politics of the Environment: Ideas, Activism, Policy* (Cambridge University Press, 2018, 3rd edition).

Caroline Close is Professor in Political Science at the *Université libre de Bruxelles* and affiliated to the *Centre d'étude de la vie politique* (CEVIPOL). Her research interests include party politics, elections, representation, and democratic innovations. She has recently published her work in *Party Politics*, *Acta Politica*, *Parliamentary Affairs*, and *Political Studies*.

Hilde Coffé is Professor in Politics at the University of Bath. Her main research interests include public opinion, political behaviour, political representation, and gender and politics.

James Dennison is Researcher at the University of Stockholm and part-time Professor at the Migration Policy Centre of the European University Institute in Florence. His interests include political attitudes and behaviour and quantitative methods.

Zsolt Enyedi is Professor at the Political Science Department of Central European University, working on party politics and political attitudes. He was the 2003 recipient of the Rudolf Wildenmann Prize and the 2004 winner of the Bibó Award. Currently he is Leverhulme Visiting Professor at the University of Oxford.

Frederico Ferreira da Silva is currently SNSF Senior Researcher at the University of Lausanne. He obtained his PhD degree in Social and Political Sciences from the European University Institute in 2019. He works on elections, public opinion, and voting behaviour. He is the co-author of *Leaders Without Partisans* (ECPR Press, 2021).

Diego Garzia is Assistant Professor of Political Science at the University of Lausanne and Permanent Visiting Fellow at the Robert Schuman Centre for Advanced Studies in Fiesole. He works on political parties, elections, and political behaviour in comparative perspective. He holds Eccellenza Professorial Fellowship of the Swiss National Science Foundation, 2020–2024.

Anika Gauja is Professor of Politics in the School of Social and Political Sciences, University of Sydney. Her research focuses on party membership, and how political parties adapt to social, institutional, and technological change. She is the author of *Party Reform* (OUP, 2017).

Sergiu Gherghina is Associate Professor in Comparative Politics at the Department of Politics and International Relations, University of Glasgow. His research interests lie in party politics, legislative and voting behaviour, democratisation, and the use of direct democracy.

Christoffer Green-Pedersen is a professor of political science at Aarhus University. His research focuses on party competition, agenda setting, and public policy. He has recently published *The Reshaping of West European Party Politics* with OUP.

Zachary Greene is Reader at the University of Strathclyde and Co-Convenor of the Elections, Public Opinion and Parties section of the PSA. His research examines the role of intra-party politics in elections and government. Find more about his research at zacgreene.com and the Norface network-funded EUINACTION project at www.euinaction.eu/home.

Daphne Halikiopoulou (PhD, LSE) is Professor of Comparative Politics at the University of York. She researches the far right, populism, and nationalism in Europe. Her work appears in the *European Journal of Political Research*, *West European Politics*, *Journal of Common Market Studies*, and the *European Political Science Review*. She is joint Editor-in-Chief of *Nations and Nationalism*.

Reinhard Heinisch is Professor of Comparative Austrian Politics and Chair of the Department of Political Science at the University of Salzburg. His research is centred on comparative populism, parties, and democracy. He recently edited with O. Mazzoleni and C. Holtz-Bacha, *Political Populism: Handbook on Concepts, Questions and Strategies of Research* (2021).

Sophia Hunger is a post-doctoral research fellow at the WZB Berlin Social Science Center. Her research interests include party competition, political protest, and the role of challenger parties. Methodologically, she takes a broad interest in quantitative methods, with a particular focus on text-as-data approaches.

Daniel Keith is Senior Lecturer in Politics at the University of York. He has coedited the volumes *Europe's Radical Left From Marginality to Mainstream* (2016) (with Luke March) and the *Palgrave Handbook of Radical Left Parties in Europe* (forthcoming, with Fabien Escalona and Luke March).

Miki Caul Kittilson is Professor in the School of Politics and Global Studies at Arizona State University. Her comparative research focuses on political behaviour, political parties, and women's representation in government. Her most recent co-authored book is *Reimagining the Judiciary: Women's Representation on High Courts Worldwide* (OUP, 2021)

Hendrik Kraetzschmar is Associate Professor in the Comparative Politics of the MENA at the University of Leeds. His research focuses on electoral, associational, and party politics in the Middle East and North Africa. He is the editor of several books, including *Islamists and the Politics of the Arab Uprisings* (EUP 2018) and *Opposition Cooperation in the Arab World* (Routledge 2012).

Thomas Legein is a PhD student in Political Science at the *Centre d'étude de la vie politique* (CEVIPOL) of the *Université libre de Bruxelles*. His research interests include party organisational dynamics, their evolution, and political representation. He is also actively involved in the Political Party Database Project (PPDB).

Conor Little is Lecturer in the Department of Politics and Public Administration at the University of Limerick. His interests include representative politics and public policy, especially climate policy. His research has appeared in *Environmental Politics*, the *International Political Science Review*, the *Journal of European Public Policy*, *Party Politics*, and *West European Politics*.

Ko Maeda is Associate Professor of Political Science at the University of North Texas. His main research interests include party competition, electoral systems, and political institutions. His work has appeared in journals, such as the *Journal of Politics* and the *British Journal of Political Science*.

Contributors

Agnes Magyar is a PhD candidate in the Department of Government at the University of Essex. Her research focuses on electoral behaviour and negativity in politics.

Carrie Manning is Professor of Political Science at Georgia State University in Atlanta. She is the author of three books, including *The Making of Democrats: Elections and Party Development in Post-War Bosnia, El Salvador and Mozambique* (2008), and several articles in journals including *Comparative Politics*, *Journal of Democracy*, and *Party Politics*.

Luke March is Professor of Post-Soviet and Comparative Politics at University of Edinburgh. His publications include *The Communist Party in Post-Soviet Russia* (2002), *Radical Left Parties in Europe* (2011), *Europe's Radical Left: From Marginality to the Mainstream* (edited with Daniel Keith, 2016), and *The European Left Party* (2019) (with Richard Dunphy).

Oscar Mazzoleni is Professor in Political Science and Director of the Research Observatory for Regional Politics at the University of Lausanne. His research interests are on political parties, populism, and regionalism. He has co-edited with R. Heinisch *Understanding Populist Organization: The Radical Right in Western Europe* (2016).

Bonnie M. Meguid is Associate Professor of Political Science at the University of Rochester. Her work focuses on political party strategy and voting behaviour in advanced industrial democracies. Her publications include *Party Competition Between Unequals* (Cambridge UP, 2008) and articles in *American Political Science Review*, *Comparative Politics*, and *Electoral Studies*.

Maurits Meijers is Assistant Professor of Comparative Politics at Radboud University Nijmegen. His research focuses on questions concerning political representation. His work has been published in outlets such as the *Journal of Politics* and *Comparative Political Studies*. He is an initiator of the Populism and Political Parties Expert Survey.

Alfred Moore is Senior Lecturer in the Department of Politics at the University of York. He works on contemporary political theory, and he is the author of *Critical Elitism: Deliberation, Democracy, and the Politics of Expertise* (2017, CUP). He has written widely on topics in democratic theory.

Pontus Odmalm is Senior Lecturer in Politics at the University of Edinburgh. His research interests include parties, elections, and the politics of migration in Europe. He is the author of 'From governmental success to governmental breakdown: how a new dimension of conflict tore apart the politics of migration of the Swedish centre-right' (2021), *Journal of Ethnic and Migration Studies* (with Marie Demker) and *The European Mainstream and the Populist Radical Right* (2017) (co-edited with Eve Hepburn).

Helene Helboe Pedersen is Professor in Political Science at Aarhus University. She is PI of a four-year research project investigating personalisation of representation. The project is funded by the Independent Research Fund Denmark and results are published in *European Journal of Political Research*, *West European Politics*, *Party Politics*, and other places.

Daniela R. Piccio is Assistant Professor at the Department of Cultures, Politics and Society of the University of Turin. Her main research and teaching interests include political representation, party organisations, and political finance regulation in national and comparative perspective.

Valeria Resta is Adjunct Professor at the Catholic University of the Sacred Heart in Milan and at Bocconi University. Her research focuses on the functioning of political parties in authoritarian and transitional settings in the Arab World. She is the co-editor of the *Routledge Handbook on Political Parties in the Middle East and North Africa* (2020). Her research also appears in *Politics and Religion* and in the *Italian Political Science Review*.

Neil Robinson is Professor of Comparative Politics at the University of Limerick. His research is primarily on Russian and post-Soviet politics. His recent publications include *Contemporary Russian Politics* (Polity, 2018) and *Comparative European Politics: Distinctive Democracies, Common Challenges* (with Rory Costello, Oxford University Press, 2021).

Indrajit Roy is Senior Lecturer in Global Development at the University of York. He is the editor of the multidisciplinary volume on India's 2019 elections titled *Passionate Politics: Democracy, Development and India's 2019 General Elections* with Manchester University Press.

Saskia P. Ruth-Lovell is Assistant Professor at the Department of Political Science, Radboud University, Nijmegen, the Netherlands. Her research specialises on comparative politics, clientelism, populism, and Latin American studies. She has published articles, among others, in *The Journal of Politics*, *Political Studies*, and *Latin American Politics and Society*.

Susan E. Scarrow is Moores Professor of Political Science at the University of Houston, Texas. Her recent publications include *Beyond Party Members: Changing Approaches to Partisan Mobilization* (Oxford University Press, 2014) and *Organizing Political Parties: Representation, Participation and Power* (OUP, 2017).

Gyda M. Sindre is Senior Lecturer in Politics at the University of York. Her research mainly focuses on post-war party politics, democratisation, and peacebuilding. In addition to several journal articles, she is the co-editor of *The Effects of Rebel Parties on Governance, Democracy and Stability After Civil Wars: From Guns to Governing* (Routledge)

Jae-Jae Spoon is Professor of Political Science and Director of the European Studies Center at the University of Pittsburgh. Her research focuses on electoral behaviour and party competition and has been published by the *Journal of Politics* and the *British Journal of Political Science*, among others. She is currently the co-editor of the *Journal of Elections, Public Opinion and Parties*.

Lise Storm is Senior Lecturer in Middle East Politics and Director of the Center for Middle East Politics at the University of Exeter. She is the co-editor of *The Routledge Handbook of Political Parties in the Middle East and North Africa* (2020) and has authored several journal articles on political parties, democratisation, and the state of democracy in the Middle East and North Africa.

Marija Taflaga is Lecturer and Director of the Australian Politics Studies Center at The Australian National University. Her research focuses on Australian politics in comparative context, specifically political parties' relationship with parliament and the executive and the career paths of political elites.

Myrto Tsakatika is Senior Lecturer in Politics at the University of Glasgow. Her research focuses on radical left parties in comparative perspective, populism, particularly in Southern

Europe and European Union politics and public policy. In addition to several journal articles, she is the co-editor of *Transformations of the Radical Left in Southern Europe* (Routledge, 2013).

Maya Tudor (PhD) is Associate Professor at the Blavatnik School of Government at the University of Oxford. Her research investigates the origins of stable, democratic, and effective states across the developing world, with a particular emphasis upon South Asia. She is the author of *The Promise of Power* (Cambridge University Press, 2013).

Andreas Ufen (PhD) is Senior Research Fellow at the German Institute for Global and Area Studies, Hamburg, and an adjunct professor of political science at the University of Hamburg. His main research interests are political parties, democratisation, political Islam, and populism in Southeast Asia, especially in Indonesia and Malaysia.

Stijn van Kessel is Senior Lecturer in European Politics at Queen Mary University of London. His main research interests are populism, Euroscepticism, and pro-European activism. He is a joint convenor of the ECPR Standing Group on *Extremism & Democracy* and a joint editor of the Routledge *Extremism & Democracy* book series.

Sofia Vasilopoulou (PhD, LSE) is Professor of European Politics at King's College London and Honorary Professor at the University of York. Her research is at the intersection of Comparative Politics and Political Behaviour. She studies the causes and consequences of political dissatisfaction among the public and the ways in which this is channelled through party strategies and party competition.

Tània Verge is Full Professor of Politics and Gender at Universitat Pompeu Fabra, Barcelona. Her main areas of research are the gendered underpinnings of political parties and parliaments and the resistance to the adoption and implementation of gender equality policy.

Clara Volintiru is Associate Professor at the Bucharest University of Economic Studies. She has been involved in various international research projects in the field of behavioural studies, good governance, informal exchanges, electoral clientelism, and political economy.

Markus Wagner is Professor in the Department of Government at the University of Vienna. His research focuses on the role of issues and ideologies in voting behaviour and party competition and has been published in journals such as the *American Journal of Political Science* and *Journal of Politics*.

Sarah Wagner is a PhD candidate in the Department of Government at the University of Essex. Her doctoral research is externally funded by the Foundation of German Business (SDW) through Germany's Federal Ministry for Education and Research. Her research interests are in electoral strategies of political parties, vote choice, and political participation.

Paul Webb is Professor of Politics at the University of Sussex. His recent publications include *Organizing Political Parties: Representation, Participation and Power* (Oxford University Press, 2017) and *Footsoldiers: Political Party Membership in the 21st Century* (Routledge, 2019). He is Editor of the journal *Party Politics*.

Ana Catalano Weeks is Assistant Professor in Comparative Politics at the University of Bath. She studies the causes and consequences of women's inclusion in politics, with a focus on party politics in OECD democracies. Her work is published in journals including *Comparative Political Studies*, *European Political Science Review*, and *Political Behavior*.

Nina Wiesehomeier is Assistant Professor of Comparative Politics at the School of Global and Public Affairs, IE University, Spain. Her research interests cover issues of political representation. Her work has appeared in journals such as the *Journal of Politics* and *Public Opinion Quarterly*. Nina is the coordinator of the Political Representation, Executives, and Political Parties Survey.

Roi Zur is Lecturer (Assistant Professor) in the Department of Government at the University of Essex. He studies voting behaviour, electoral strategies of political parties, and political institutions. His work has been published in the *British Journal of Political Science*, *Political Behavior*, *European Journal of Political Research*, and others.

ACKNOWLEDGEMENTS

We, the editors, would like to thank Andrew Taylor and Sophie Iddamalgoda of Routledge Taylor and Francis Group, who supported us designing this handbook. We are grateful for their help in organising and developing this project. We would also like to thank colleagues in the Department of Politics at the University of York for their support and especially James Reeves for his excellent editorial assistance. Most of all, we thank all of the contributors for their responsiveness to our requests, patience, and for producing such valuable and interesting contributions to studying research on political parties.

INTRODUCTION

Neil Carter, Daniel Keith, Gyda M. Sindre and Sofia Vasilopoulou

> *Political parties created democracy . . . modern democracy is unthinkable save in terms of political parties.*
>
> (Schattschneider 1942, 1)

Political parties are the key institutions that make democracy work. By aggregating policy preferences, they are the intermediaries between citizens' preferences on the one hand, and parliaments and the state on the other hand (Dalton 1985; Katz and Mair 1995; Powell 2004). Without parties fulfilling these functions, a democracy can hardly exist. Moreover, although the global trend of democratisation (Huntington 1993) did not necessarily lead to fully fledged democracies being established across the globe, political parties remain the cornerstone of democratic political systems. However, contemporary changes related to deindustrialisation, globalisation, mediatisation, technological and demographic change have been associated with an era of widespread political disillusionment with parties being one of the main targets of citizen dissatisfaction. This discontent may be observed not only in the ever-decreasing levels of party membership and the significant decline of mainstream parties but also in the rise of new parties and candidates whose core purpose is to challenge dominant models of party organisation, interest aggregation and representation. Do these developments entail the end of the party, as we know it? Not necessarily. Political parties are organisations in constant flux, partly responding to challenges related to socio-demographic, political and technological developments. At the same time, they are also political agents themselves whose actions shape the political environment. Political parties choose how to organise and how to mobilise. They also choose how to compete with other parties in their respective systems and which political issues to prioritise in order to gain votes and access to office. These decisions have significant implications for political representation and the functioning of contemporary democracies. In this context, research on political parties has moved on from studying parties' 'crises of existence' to exploring parties' resilience and adaptation (Gauja and Kosiara-Pedersen 2021).

The study of political parties is one of the most advanced sub-fields in political science and, more broadly, in the social sciences. An earlier *Handbook of Party Politics* edited by Richard Katz and William Crotty (2006) remains an invaluable resource on what is a rich and complex field which spans many areas. Yet it is outdated considering the tremendous changes at the social, party and party system levels since the mid-2000s. In this context, there is a need to take stock of how far research has come and significant advances in studying political parties beyond Europe and the USA.

In this handbook, we provide an in-depth exploration of the key issues and debates in the study of political parties. We asked leading scholars in the field to review the state of the research across a wide range of important areas. The chapters are comparative and address changes over time. Each chapter analyses the main debates on the topic, and highlights areas of 'cutting-edge' research as well as gaps in the literature to give recommendations for avenues for future research. Therefore, in addition to providing a systematic overview of key debates in the field, each chapter in this handbook seeks to set a future research agenda by identifying key questions that require investigation in further research. We expect that these recommendations will be useful to both scholars and students alike.

A handbook of political parties: rationale and structure

A number of key debates have emerged in the literature on political parties as scholars have asked: What is the role of parties in democracies? How do parties organise? How have their ideologies evolved over time? How do parties compete and in what ways has party competition changed over time? How do they respond to new social, economic and political challenges? To what extent are political parties different outside the established democracies of the Global North? How do political parties react to and tackle new political challenges facing contemporary democracies? And finally, what are the different approaches to studying political parties and party preferences?

These core questions have informed the structure of our handbook. While we retain a focus on key 'traditional' party politics topics, such as party internal organisation, ideological values and beliefs and party strategies, we also pay particular attention to new and emerging topics in the field as well as questions of methodology. The handbook is divided into seven parts: (1) definitions and evolution, (2) party as an organisation, (3) party ideology and party families, (4) party competition and representation, (5) contemporary issues and challenges, (6) regional comparisons and (7) methods for estimating party preferences.

Definitions and evolution

Part 1 includes three chapters which investigate questions addressed in the literature on the evolution of parties and their role in democracy. More specifically, it asks: how useful are abstract models (such as the cadre and cartel party models) for explaining the role of parties in established democracies? How have scholars tried to theorise the relationship between parties and concepts such as deliberative democracy? Do parties fulfil an effective representative role? How has research understood the role of cleavages in structuring party systems in democratic political systems? In doing so, the chapters highlight research which suggests that parties in democratic systems have not converged on a single model. They show how research on Western Europe has often lacked relevance to the experience of new democracies. The chapters identify areas for further research to investigate the conditions under which abstract models developed to understand political parties apply; to test the assumptions and ideas of key theories more fully; and to assess the scope to connect empirical and normative research on political parties.

The party as an organisation

The second part opens by exploring the continuing fascination of party scholars with the way party organisations have changed and adapted over time, and how power is distributed within parties and its practical implications. It asks what party organisations look like and what they do, and examines the conceptual tools and models party scholars have developed to analyse those questions. A key theme running through the chapters is whether parties are static or dynamic organisations. The chapters highlight advances made in understanding important changes taking place within party organisations. These include changes relating to parties' links with social movements, digital technology and social media which are transforming the nature of political participation. However, the chapters highlight debates surrounding new models such as the digital party and even the memberless party. Most parties also remain membership-based, so this part continues by exploring the many different definitions of a party member, why people join parties, why some are more active than others and why members are still important to parties despite the problems they might bring.

The chapters in this part highlight not just advances in the study of party organisation but also the need for future research to address empirical gaps, particularly in 'hard to reach' informal areas of party organisations and on the role of inequalities within party organisations. These gaps are particularly relevant when scholars have criticised the gendered lens of 'mainstream' party scholarship for limiting its capacity to address questions of representation and to explore how processes of party change have been constrained by the stickiness of informal rules – for example as they undermined implementation of reforms aimed at inclusion (e.g. Kenny et al. 2022). This part also identifies opportunities for theoretical development through moving beyond regional divides and greater dialogue with other disciplines. Several chapters suggest that the increasing online presence of political parties requires the development of not just new data but also new methodological approaches.

Party ideology and party families

The third part examines research on party families. The opening chapter analyses the development of cleavage theory and considers whether it still has contemporary relevance in understanding recent changes to party systems in Europe and beyond. It assesses the 'new' cleavages based on reactions to globalisation and the extent to which they reflect the growing importance of differences over cultural issues rather than economic issues. The remaining chapters look at work on six major party families, including the far right, centre-right, liberal, social democratic, radical left and green party families, each addressing a common set of questions. They start by asking how each party family has been conceptualised by examining its origins, identifying common ideological principles (although several chapters also outline the existence of different subgroups within the party family) and highlighting the major challenges that the party family faces. The chapters move on to explore research that explains the electoral performance of different party families and discuss debates surrounding the key sociodemographic characteristics and attitudinal trends in their electorates. The chapters explore research on the parties' ability to participate in government and the policies they deliver when they get there. Moreover, chapters on green, far right and radical left party families assess the wider impact of their development on mainstream parties and the party system. Each chapter finishes by asking what challenges the party family currently faces.

This part highlights the unevenness of comparative research on party families, with some literatures being more developed (e.g. the far right) than others (e.g. liberal and radical left parties). Chapters highlight reasons for wider comparative research to pay more sensitivity to the diversity evident within some party families. Although some party families have a weak presence beyond particular regions (e.g. Europe), several chapters identify opportunities to incorporate a wider range of parties into future research.

Party competition and representation

The fourth part on party competition examines core issues in the field related to different party strategies. It addresses the question of whether parties strategically emphasise positions or valence and discusses the electoral consequences of this choice. Another aspect of party competition relates to political issues and the extent to which political parties compete by emphasising certain issues rather than others. Part 4 then zooms in on the niche party, which has been the subject of a growing literature. This part explores how different types of parties behave in the electoral arena, what their strategies are and how they may differ; as well as the implications of such differences for understanding contemporary party politics. It further investigates the roles parties play in government, and the challenges for achieving collective action in multi-party systems. It explores important questions including: How constrained are parties by electoral promises? How do parties make policy in coalition cabinets? How do coalition agreements and portfolio allocation affect government policy? This part also considers parties as agents on representation. Specifically, do parties listen to voters and do voters listen to parties? It focuses on the dynamic aspect of representation, that is, responsiveness, and the ways in which this varies across different types of parties and contexts. The last chapter in this part explores the cutting-edge topic of personalisation, that is, whether political individuals become increasingly important relative to collective political actors such as political parties, cabinets and parliaments.

This part points to the need for future research to understand how different party strategies interact with each other, including position, valence, issue competition and framing, and personalisation. It points to opportunities to explore this interaction taking into consideration different party types, their government status and position in the party system, as well as using different types of observational and experimental research designs.

Contemporary issues and challenges

This part examines contemporary issues and challenges that are often considered cross-cutting of the more traditional typologies and approaches to the study of political parties. Three of the chapters analyse specific *features* of parties that have emerged as particularly relevant in recent years, that is, populism, conflict and clientelism. The remaining four chapters investigate how political parties relate to and are influenced by specific policy fields. These chapters reflect on some of the most pressing issues of our times, namely climate change, immigration, gender and (for European parties), the European Union (EU), respectively. The chapter on populism discusses the most common approaches to conceptualising populism, the conditions underlying populist parties' success or failure, and the implications of populism for political competition and liberal democracy. The chapter on post-conflict political parties draws attention to a set of political parties that have traditionally not been part of mainstream party research, namely political parties with backgrounds as armed movements. These types of parties provide opportunities to test existing party theory and provide a basis for analysing party formation in contemporary settings that have experienced civil wars. The chapter on clientelism provides a conceptual clarification of the term, explains how political parties use clientelism in advanced and new democracies, and outlines the most common consequences of clientelism for democracy.

The policy-focused chapters highlight how parties adapt to and engage with new issues and themes. The chapter on climate change focuses on the explanations of parties' climate policy preferences and parties' influence on climate policies. It highlights the need for research on the role of parties and their leaders in shaping public attitudes towards climate change. The chapter on immigration discusses the ways in which mainstream parties engage with issues of immigration and integration, noting how this policy field remains characterised by contradictions and tensions. In a similar fashion, the chapter on the EU outlines the scholarly debates on defining party responses to European integration, showing how the issue of Europe has entered electoral politics and domestic party competition in European countries. The chapter on gender similarly examines the dynamics of gender differences in the electorate and their implications for political parties.

Regional comparisons

We acknowledge that the literature on political parties is complex and often over-reliant on the study of parties in advanced industrialised democracies. To address this, part 6 enriches the handbook with an analysis of political parties and party politics in specific regions/countries of the world outside the Global North with individual chapters on Russia and post-Soviet States, East Asia, Southeast Asia, India, the Middle East, North Africa, Sub-Saharan Africa and Latin America. Each chapter provides a detailed overview of the main trends and characteristics of political parties in the specific region. In post-colonial regions, such as Southeast Asia, India, the Middle East and Sub-Saharan Africa, many political parties have their roots in anti-colonial struggle rather than other socio-economic cleavages. At the same time, regime change and the global trend of democratisation have led to the formation of new parties that have quickly become dominant.

The chapters in this part also ask whether traditional concepts derived from party theory are relevant to the study of political parties beyond advanced Western democracies. While some regions, such as Latin America, already feature prominently within comparative studies and theory development, parties in regions such as the Middle East and North Africa have received less systematic attention. The chapters highlight that political parties in regions classically described as semi-democratic or 'democratising' are structured by different social, economic and historical logics from those in advanced democracies, which lead several of the authors to call for attention to new concepts and benchmarks in analysis of political parties. The chapters further highlight new opportunities to study and theorise central themes such as populism, clientelism and personalisation – as well as party formation, party institutionalisation and party system change across a wide range of contemporary electoral systems.

Methods for estimating party preferences

The last part includes three chapters which examine several established methods for estimating party preferences, including text analysis, voting advice applications and expert surveys. The three chapters provide an overview of each method and associated methodological challenges. They examine the application of the method in key texts in the field. They also present some key comparative projects that collect data on political parties in systematic and rigorous ways and make them accessible to the academic community. All chapters explore the merits and limitations of each method as well as its complementarity with other approaches. They finally make recommendations for further development and data generation, including the different ways in which researchers can increase the reliability of data and address problems of bias and comparability. They also point to the need to link different fields of research drawing upon and linking different datasets and methodological approaches.

References

Dalton, R.J. (1985) 'Political parties and political representation: Party supporters and party elites in nine nations', *Comparative Political Studies*, 18(3), p267–299.

Gauja, A. and Kosiara-Pedersen, K. (2021) 'Decline, adaptation and relevance: political parties and their researchers in the twentieth century', *European Political Science*, 20(1), p123–138.

Huntington, S.P. (1993) *The Third Wave: Democratization in the late twentieth century*. Norman: University of Oklahoma Press.

Katz, R. and Crotty, W. (2006) *Handbook of Party Politics*. London, Thousand Oaks and New Delhi: Sage.

Katz, R. and Mair, P. (1995) 'Changing models of party organization and party democracy: The emergence of the cartel party', *Party Politics*, 1(1), p5–28.

Kenny, M., Bjarnegård, E., Lovenduski, J., Childs, S., Evans, E. and Verge, T. (2022) 'Reclaiming party politics research', *European Political Science*, 20(1), p123–138.

Powell, G.B. Jr. (2004) 'Political representation in comparative politics', *Annual Review of Political Science*, 7, p273–296.

Schattschneider, E.E. (1942) *Party Government*. New York: Holt, Rinehart, and Winston.

PART 1

Definitions and party evolution

1
PARTY CHANGE BEYOND THE 'CLASSICAL MODELS?' THE ROLE OF AGENCY, CONTEXT, AND DEMOCRACY

Oscar Mazzoleni and *Reinhard Heinisch*

In recent decades, research on political parties in established democracies has focused primarily on the so-called legitimacy crisis of parties, as reflected in declining voter turnout, growing anti-party sentiment, and other forms of citizen dissatisfaction (Webb 2005; Mair 2013). In their assessment of traditional or mainstream parties, scholars are divided between optimistic and pessimistic views: some emphasise the problems of established parties, especially in Western democracies (e.g. Ignazi 2017), while others focus more on the ability of parties to adapt and survive (e.g. Dalton, Farrell and McAllister 2011). Meanwhile, a strand of literature has emerged that focuses on new cleavages and new parties that are often seen as oppositional or outsiders – including those that become members of a democratic government (McDonnell and Newell 2011). What this last strand of research teaches us is that the relative instability of a party system does not necessarily imply a weakening of established democracy as such, and that party dynamics should not be limited to looking only at the long-established or mainstream parties.

As a result, the research agenda is divided into one strand that seeks to understand both the decline of old parties and their survival, while another focuses on both the emergence and growth of non-mainstream parties. Regardless of the focus, the evolution of political parties remains one of the most important topics in political science. The scholarly attention devoted to party change is limited to established Western democracies, and extends to new democracies and party systems elsewhere. The spread of electoral democracy since the 1990s has greatly expanded the scope of party democracy: while this has confirmed the crucial role of political parties in contemporary democracy, new party systems have proved more diverse and volatile. These dynamics have also led to more contextualised approaches to party transformation by taking into account the variation in sociocultural and political environments as well as the diversity of organisational patterns. The new party systems also entail more complex relationships with democracy, as evidenced by the increasing number of electoral democracies reverting to neo-authoritarian regimes even in Central and Eastern Europe (CEE) (Diamond 2015; Levitsky and Ziblatt 2018). The link between party and democracy does not imply a one-sided relationship. Parties do adapt to the changing characteristics of democratic competition, but parties can also change and sometimes subvert democratic rules and practices.

The aim of this chapter is to provide a critical review of current debates on party transformation and its relationship to democracy. First, we discuss the need for a dynamic understanding of political parties and how recent developments challenge the classical party models. Then, we focus on the role of the environment in party change. The subsequent section grapples with the trade-off between parsimony and complexity when we try to explain party responses to an increasingly diverse environment. Next, we analyse briefly the relationship between democracy and party change, leading to a discussion on party change in CEE and its implication for party evolution more generally. The final section provides conclusions and suggestions for a future research agenda.

Towards a dynamic understanding of political parties

In recent decades, a vast literature has been devoted to shedding light on the multifaceted transformation of old parties and the emergence of new ones in contemporary democracies. This encompasses developments including the steep erosion of voter loyalty, declining membership, falling voter turnout, increased fragmentation, and weakening legitimacy across democratic systems (see e.g. van Biezen, Mair and Poguntke 2012; Poguntke, Scarrow and Webb 2016). Yet, despite these debates about the decline of political parties, their continued relevance in the electoral arena and in representative institutions is also apparent and undoubtedly linked to their ability to adapt and endure.

In attempting to understand party adaptability, research in comparative politics has largely relied on model-oriented approaches. These have been inspired by or derived directly from the work of well-known party researchers such as Maurice Duverger, Otto Kirchheimer, Richard S. Katz, and Peter Mair. Their respective model-oriented approaches focused on issues of party organisation and its development, ideology and manifestos, voter support, party system change, and the role of parties in government. The core assumption here was that a party's environment both conditions and constrains its ability to adapt. In this context, scholars have identified a set of sequential models linked by evolutionary change with the most relevant being the cadre party, mass party, catch-all party, and cartel party.

The starting point, as emphasised by Duverger (1963), is the cadre party. It was followed by the mass party, characterised by a strong ideology, mass membership, and a clearly identifiable constituency defined by social class, religious affiliation, and/or ethnicity. According to Kirchheimer, the catch-all party represents a transformation of the mass party into a more centralised and flexible organisation that targets a much more heterogeneous constituency in terms of ideology and policy offerings. Within it, the role of the leadership group grew in importance at the expense of the role of ordinary party members. These developments were directly related to the transformation of western democratic societies from industrial to late- and post-industrial economies, leading to the emergence of a large and amorphous middle class (Kirchheimer 1966).

The next stage of party development was the cartel party, best known from the work of Katz and Mair (1995, 2018). In their view, party organisations became less rooted in civil society and increasingly dependent on the state. They argued that 'colluding parties become agents of the state and employ the resources of the state to ensure their own collective survival' (Katz and Mair 1995, 5). As a result, parties can draw on public resources to professionalise their organisations and become less dependent on grassroots membership and activism. One of the correlates of this thesis is that 'challenger' parties, if they want to compete successfully, cannot escape this functional logic and have little choice but to mimic cartelisation if they want to participate in government. In this context, cartel parties tend to converge in their political orientation because they compete in an electoral market conditioned by external pressures emanating from supranational governance and transnational economic integration. The analytical strength of the cartel party thesis is its relatively clear narrative, which provides an overarching explanation for both the decline of parties (in terms of weaker ties to voters, members, and activists) (van Haute and Gauja 2015) and the adaptation of parties (to the state). It can also explain developments within democratic political systems, including the fact that public subsidies to political parties have gradually increased in all democracies worldwide since the 1960s (Scarrow 2007).

Despite these strengths, the cartel model approach is being challenged from a variety of perspectives. Cross-national research and in-depth individual case studies have shown that cartelisation and attempts by parties to control the state have not necessarily prevented the emergence of new parties and their successful competition. Rather, cartelisation may have even contributed to an increasing polarisation of the party system (Aucante and Dézé 2008; Krouwel 2012; Enroth and Hagevi 2018). Moreover, the cartel party model has been questioned from a theoretical perspective because of its underlying 'linear-evolutionary' assumption (e.g. Koole 1996; Kitschelt 2000). Another criticism has been that the model provides a descriptive, step-by-step account of change but does not develop adequate explanations for the mechanism by which parties would change.

Alternative views of party development result from other themes in comparative party research. The first highlights the 'life cycle' of parties, inspired by Michels and his 'iron law of oligarchy' as the 'best known' example of how parties change in the direction of a more centralised and elite-oriented organisation (Harmel 2002, 121). In life cycle approaches, the goal has been to understand the trajectory of parties from their inception to their consolidation. Indeed, this approach has played an important role in tracing the institutionalisation of parties and explaining their ability to integrate into the party system (Bolleyer 2013; Harmel and Svasand 2019). Another view, rooted in the work of Panebianco (1988) and Harmel and Janda (1994), which appears less deterministic, emphasises the ability of parties, including traditional parties, to implement organisational reforms and revise issue positions to avert electoral defeat. Here, the role of leadership, perceptions of party leaders, and dominant intraparty coalitions are seen as 'key intervening variables' that play the critical role in enabling necessary reforms (Gauja 2017). The focus on party formation and the central role of party leadership has allowed researchers to better understand the social origin of parties outside the parliamentary arena as well as the emergence of political entrepreneurs acting as change agents and political architects of parties. In this view, new parties, such as anti-establishment, anti-system, entrepreneurial, movement parties, and digital parties, have increasingly become the focus of research as they tend to build relationships with the state and the media that differ from those of mainstream parties (Schedler 1996; Heinisch and Mazzoleni 2016; Gerbaudo 2019; Zulianello 2019; De Vries and Hobolt 2020).

The nature of party change and its environment

The approaches to party development discussed here serve as a reminder that important disagreements persist in the research community. Scholars studying party development differ on the nature of party change, the choice of dependent variables (model, institutionalisation, reform), and how to integrate environmental challenges into explanatory frameworks.

What is party change? Despite the widespread consensus that parties generally do not just passively endure their fate, scholars disagree over what it means to say that the party itself plays an active role in initiating change. This is not a trivial conceptual problem and was expressed by Peter Mair when he noted that political parties are in a 'state of almost permanent change', which makes the search for an 'essence' or 'identity' of a party virtually impossible (1997, 50). This fact has led to the assertion that the concept of party change may be elusive and therefore irrelevant (Mair 1997, 54). To the extent that we accept that parties actively face challenges, what does it mean for parties to 'change', 'transform', 'adapt', or 'evolve'? These terms do not have a uniform meaning, so this semantic uncertainty reflects the diversity of conceptualisations and approaches that characterise the literature.

Mair argues for the need to distinguish change tout court from certain aspects of change and from predetermined criteria against which these aspects can be interpreted (1997, 49). Indeed, parties may change gradually or discretely; such changes may be marginal or may greatly alter a party's organisation, ideology, constituency, and role in government. But under what conditions does party evolution really go beyond 'permanent flux' and manifest itself as party change? Parties may change their system of candidate selection, perhaps moving towards more personalised and candidate-oriented electoral competition (Poguntke and Webb 2005; Cross, Katz and Pruysers 2018; Rahat and Kenig 2018). Or parties may seek to modify the rules of the game, such as the electoral system (Mair, Müller and Plassner 2004). Organisationally, new intraparty dynamics may lead to greater or lesser complexity, changing size, and changing efficiency, or parties may change the distribution of power and representation (Harmel 2002, 138). Nevertheless, the nature of party change remains theoretically unclear, since there is almost always some kind of change taking place within parties, as in any organisation. It can be particularly difficult to determine the conditions under which particular changes such as a change of leadership become significant or decisive in shaping a party's development or in affecting its chances of survival.

There is a broad consensus that, in long-established parties, change typically follows electoral decline. However, there are some situations in which party leaders have tried to anticipate the crisis and avoid it by acting in time (Mair, Müller and Plassner 2004). Moreover, it is not always clear how and why environmental changes influence party change. Scholars generally agree that social, economic, and technological transformations pose crucial challenges to party competition with existential consequences for individual parties. So far, the literature has mainly identified exogenous factors as being strongly linked with parties entering a crisis. These include the loss of authority of traditional institutions and secularisation (Norris and Inglehart 2019), the disappearance of traditional class-based milieus, the erosion of socialist and communist ideologies after the fall of the Berlin Wall, and, crucially, the impact of globalisation and European integration, which challenge the monopoly of the nation-state in policy-making but also patterns of party competition (Hooghe and Marks 2018). However, the difficulty in accounting for such diverse economic, social, and cultural transformations, as well as the increasing role of the state in party mobilisation (Mendilow and Phélippeau 2018), within a shared theoretical conceptualisation, seems to limit systematic assessments.

Explaining party change: between parsimony and complexity

The recent literature on party evolution reflects a growing tension between analytical parsimony and complexity. Scholars are hardly able to account for the complexity of political parties and the myriad facets evident in their development. This highlights also the empirical difficulty of observing internal party dynamics 'for real' and not just 'on paper' (Borz and Janda 2020, 6). There also seems to be a growing awareness of the risks inherent in parsimonious and thus simplistic models. Thus, newer research on parties is driven less by formal and more by hybrid theories of change that largely turn away from the classical party models. This newer literature appears sceptical not only about the capacity of traditional scholarship to adequately account for party change empirically but also about the heuristic strength and thus validity of parsimonious theoretical frameworks. Accordingly, research that tries to understand specific cases of party change using models operating at a considerable level of abstraction must necessarily neglect important empirical observations. For some, these omissions render an analysis at best dissatisfying and at worst invalid. By contrast, the alternative approach to party research relies heavily on case studies, a method often neglected by scholarship for the difficulty in generalising findings to an entire class of phenomena. Yet, according to Bale (2012, 4), this alternative mode of inquiry also yields important empirical benefits, such as the opportunity to focus simultaneously on long time horizons and large sets of indicators related to change and its causes. Moreover, this approach is more attentive to factors that are novel or inconsistent with the classical models of party change and would normally be excluded from analysis, including 'anticipated reactions, unfinished business, non-electoral shocks, path-dependency, spillover, and long-term secular social change' (Bale 2012, 316).

As the usefulness of abstract heuristic party models for understanding contemporary party change has come under scrutiny, scholars are also reassessing the validity of such frameworks when applied to parties historically. In a new appraisal of the 'golden age' of mass parties in Western Europe in 1950s and 1960s, Scarrow (2015) shows that only a few parties corresponded to the mass party model with the committed and broad grassroots organisation that Duverger and Kirchheimer had extolled in their classic works. The need for scholarship to become more sensitive to spatial and temporal variation and more cautious when applying model-based approaches was underscored by research conducted by Webb, Pogunkte and Scarrow (2017). In their comparative analysis of 17 democratic systems in Europe, Israel, and Australia, they stress the need to pay 'more attention' to the 'appropriateness and limits' (2017, 315) of approaches based upon party models and caution us that the 'multifaceted universe of political parties in the twenty-first century' does not correspond to these models (2017, 319).

Generally speaking, the major studies of party change in a cross-national and diachronic perspective, containing country cases from the Middle East, South America, Southern Europe, and Western Europe, have shown not just several common trends but also relevant differences both between the democratic systems per se and between parties within individual countries (Dalton and Wattenberg 2000). Rahat and Kenig provide evidence of a decline in partisanship across 12 indicators and show that there is a considerable variation:

> [P]arty adaptation is characteristic of some countries, while party decline is characteristic of others. A more complex formulation of this thesis might be that we see a continuum of more or less successful cases of adaptation and sharp declines at the extreme ends if parties either fail to adapt at all or react excessively.
>
> *(2018, 91)*

Furthermore, it is worth noting that Rahat and Kenig (2018) are less interested in party evolution than the ability of parties to respond to critical situations. In doing so, they shift our view of party dynamics from an evolutionary and teleological perspective to a multi-layered and pluralistic understanding. This clearly highlights the limit of a rationale based on overarching and subsequent party models.

Which kind of democracy?

Attempts to move beyond evolutionary approaches to party change have also emerged from studies on the relationship between parties and democracy. The literature on party evolution implies a fundamental tension about the conception of democracy that political parties should address. In the classical tradition of comparative party politics, democracy is conceptualised as a matter of competition between parties, ideally 'led by responsible teams of leaders who ultimately converge on a single national will or interest from the center' (Katz and Mair 2018, 171). However, the relationship of parties to democracy concerns not only their external connection to the political system but also their internal functioning and organisation, which grants varying degrees of democratic agency to the grassroots membership. Parties are a means by which socially heterogeneous people enter into political engagement and are socialised into democratic behaviour; yet party organisation seems to follow Michel's 'iron law of oligarchy', which runs counter to the participatory principle of democracy. In recent decades, as the 'crisis' of parties became more salient, the principle of popular participation and its particular perspective on democracy has driven new research on party development, focusing in particular on intra-party democracy (Cross and Katz 2013; Gauja 2017; Borz and Janda 2020).

Incidentally, internal party democracy and new forms of participation are also seen as an alternative way for parties to survive, which differs from the strategy of relying on state subsidies (Ignazi 2020). Meanwhile, the question of the stability of democratic regimes and the role that political parties play in them are gaining relevance. Between the 1970s and 1990s, the shift to electoral democracy that characterised an increasing number of regimes worldwide changed how the relationship between political parties and democracy was viewed. This historical shift challenged the traditional division between the study of parties in established democracies and elsewhere. As electoral democracies proliferated, new democracies appeared to converge with established ones. More recently, however, the evolution of several new democracies has taken a turn towards authoritarianism, and some of the explanations for the deconsolidation of electoral democracy have pointed to the role of political parties. Because they have the ability to either change or subvert democratic rules, this trend is not limited to certain regions. Some parties promote representative democracy, its rules, and its practices, while in others they seem to play an opposite role, creating space for corruption and authoritarian tendencies (Lawson 2007).

Beyond established democracies: Central and Eastern Europe

The evolution of party systems in CEE provides new benchmarks for established theoretical perspectives that mainly emerged in Western democracies. For a long time, party systems in CEE were expected to emulate the relatively stable, highly differentiated, and institutionalised party systems in Western Europe. Recent developments, however, seem to contradict this assumption (Lane and Ersson 2007; Enyedi and Bértoa 2018).

Although CEE shares significant historical, political, and sociocultural similarities with Western Europe, it also has crucial differences that are theoretically and empirically important for understanding party dynamics in general. Shaped by the transition from communism to post-communism (Kitschelt et al. 1999, Evans 2006), the initial parties that emerged did not conform to Kirchheimer's (1966) notion of an organisation with close ties to a mass electorate. The first elections resembled plebiscites in which the newly formed parties had to navigate valence issues. In response, parties effectively 'diluted their original ideologies in order to widen their voter base' (Sikk 2018, 106). Some parties became what Innes (2002, 88) called 'instant catch-all parties' and appeared to lack a natural constituency (Schöpflin 1993; van Biezen 2005).

This failure was politically costly once the deep organisational roots of the former communists enabled them to come back politically by exploiting voter disillusionment with the reform process (Webb and White 2007, 7). In response, the major right-wing parties competed by either pushing for more market liberalism or focusing on sociocultural issues (Buštíková and Kitschelt 2009; Pirro 2015). While left-wing parties became eastern versions of liberal social democrats, the mainstream right moved further to the right, advocating illiberal and Eurosceptic positions (Riishøj 2004; Minkenberg 2017). In contrast, leftist parties, especially in Russia and the Balkans, pursued a 'national-patriotic' strategy which replaced Marxist-Leninist doctrine with an appeal to nationalist and nativist sentiments, with the aim of building a broader coalition (Bozoki and Ishiyama 2002, 4–6).

Where the mainstream right did not adapt successfully (Henderson 2008, 121–122), they were outmanoeuvred by political entrepreneurs, often touting their business credentials or communication skills, an example of which is the surge of the Czech party ANO2011 (Tomšič and Prijon 2013). A high level of personalisation and leadership concentration are significant features of these parties in CEE (Gherghina, Miscoiu and Sorina 2021) which ensures the prominent position of party leaders and their networks but weakens party institutionalisation. This makes parties 'disconcertingly fluid' and contributes to 'porous boundaries between the radical right and the mainstream right' (Minkenberg 2015, 34). The resulting greater ideological extremism and higher electoral volatility compared to Western Europe undermine established parties in CEE and favour new ones (Savage 2016), which are often formed just before elections (Sikk 2018, 106). These new parties quickly disappear if they do not develop viable survival strategies such as mastering the strategic use of propaganda and discursive frames (Minkenberg 2017; Pytlas 2018). Over time, successful new parties also develop organisational links with their supporters and collude to exclude new parties from coalition formation (Savage 2016). Another important strategy is engineering a 'symbiosis with the state' (Sikk 2018, 106), since all countries in the region have introduced public funding for political parties (Kopecký 2006).

Yet other strategies involve forms of state capture of which Hungary (Fazekas and Tóth 2016), Poland (Kozarzewski and Bałtowski 2016), and to a lesser extent Serbia (Bochsler and Juon 2020) are the best-known cases. There, the leader coordinates vast patronal and partisan networks that exert control over the judiciary, national financial institutions, the national media, and education institutions. Shaped by the context of transition and post-transition, fluid social structures, and the weakness of civil society, the organisational characteristics of parties in CEE spring from their development paths (Evans 2006, 258).

Conclusions and avenues for further research

Comparative party research focusing on established democracies, particularly in Western Europe, has provided a large body of theoretical insights and empirical evidence on both the decline and survival of mainstream parties. While there is broad consensus that parties are not passive organisations at the mercy of global transformations, government subsidies, declining traditional membership, and new media logics, research suggests that the adaptability of parties and the manner of active change varies widely. Since the 2000s, scholars have become increasingly aware of the need to think about party dynamics beyond a linear evolutionary approach, which means considering the relevance of the sociocultural, political, and institutional context and the crucial role of strategies in party transformation. If a traditional or mainstream party endures despite the decline of its constituency, it is because it adapts and avoids a predetermined path. Thus, such a party might implement intraparty democratic reforms or strengthen its leadership. On the whole, party dynamics in established democracies converge less than expected on any particular party model, such as the cartel party.

Although ideal types remain important from an analytical perspective and serve a heuristic purpose, this does not mean that all parties are expected to converge in a single type of party organisation. The ascendance of new parties in established democracies arguably challenges the idea of convergent trajectories as well. Short-lived or permanent, new parties may vary in the extent to which they are shaped by the dominant ideological or organisational characteristics of their party system. Instead, they may follow original paths, taking advantage of new environmental opportunities (such as digital parties) and become more or less influential in the face of new or old competitors. The availability of data from large cross-country studies and the opportunity to empirically test theoretical assumptions about individual parties in different contexts represent not only an advance in our knowledge but also a challenge to the evolutionary perspective, giving room for a pluralistic view of the paths that parties take.

The growing awareness of the multiplicity of party transformation is also a consequence of the spread of electoral democracy to other parts of the world, prompting researchers to address the role of party change in connection with new democracies. Until relatively recently, the literature on party transformation focused almost exclusively on the major Western European democracies, where there was a strong legacy of the mass party. While interest in established democracies continues, there is growing attention on new democracies, especially in CEE, which is driven by questions of how and to what extent conceptualisations developed in Western Europe also apply to new party systems. Party change is also receiving attention outside Europe, which provides us with an even broader comparative perspective and a richer source of empirical data.

Focusing on party dynamics beyond established Western democracies also allows for new questions to be asked regarding the interconnection of democratic regimes. Political parties are a necessary instrument of democracy and there is no evident practical alternative. Yet parties do not necessarily have to work with, or for these democratic rules, neither do they have to change in accordance with them. Taking into account the diversity of settings and legacies around the world, the relationship between party organisations and democracy needs to be considered a two-way process. Sometimes a party adapts to external pressures by pursuing intraparty democratisation and responds with increasing openness towards members. In other cases, a party survives by reducing party competition and curtailing democratic rules both in its internal organisation and in the party system as a whole. Political parties are a strong link to democracy, but they also face particular opportunities and constraints as they compete for power which may also make them a factor in democratic deconsolidation.

While scholars are more aware of the complexity of party organisations and their relationship to democracy, internal dynamics continue to pose the greatest empirical challenge to researchers. One of the most commonly recognised problems is in assessing the trade-off between established party organisations' 'natural inclination' against discrete change (Harmel 2002, 119) and emerging positions in favour of change. Similarly, the tension between intraparty grassroots participation and decision-making by the party leadership remains understudied. Despite widespread scepticism of Michels' iron law of oligarchy, the empirical evidence is not sufficiently strong that we might refute or even ignore his thesis.

The issue of party change poses methodological problems regarding access to party data. In many ways, intraparty dynamics represent a 'secret garden of politics' (Gallagher and Marsh 1987). While programmatic and ideological changes enacted by parties along with their effect on the party system and government are well documented and thus easier to study, the interactions among members, activists, staff, leaders, candidates, MPs, and government officials are difficult to investigate, as we still lack robust data on these relationships. Cross-national datasets represent a great advance in our understanding of party behaviour and organisation. Examples of quantitative data, such as those contained in the Political Party Database Project (Poguntke, Scarrow and Webb 2016), as well as qualitative historically oriented and ethnographic sources (Faucher-King 2005; Bale 2012; Weikert 2019), are important complements to gaining a deeper and more dynamic understanding of intraparty relations. Similarly, qualitative methodological approaches are well suited to measuring intraparty perceptions and gaining insights into the behaviour of individuals and groups.

Finally, we must come to terms with the realisation that not only intraparty relations but also the relationship between voters and parties is still something of a black box (Werner 2020). What forms of representation do voters want? Do they want to be constantly involved or left alone by parties? Do they prefer that campaign promises are fulfilled in principle even if fulfilling promises brings about unpopular policies (Thomson et al. 2017)? Do voters value responsiveness over accountability or are they more likely to favour a balance (Bardi, Bartolini and Trechsel 2014)? While all of these questions have yet to be empirically resolved, they send cues that influence party behaviour, which in turn affects voter behaviour and party competition. This calls for a perspective on party change that is dynamic, conceptually open to new possibilities, and attentive to both environment and agency.

References

Aucante, J. and Dézé, A. (2008) *Les systèmes de partis dans les démocraties occidentales. Le modèle du parti-cartel en question.* Paris: Presses de Science Po.

Bale, T. (2012) *The Conservatives since 1945: The drivers of party change.* Oxford: Oxford University Press.

Bardi, L., Bartolini, S. and Trechsel, A.H. (2014) 'Responsive and responsible? The role of parties in twenty-first century politics', *West European Politics*, 37(2), p235–52.

Bochsler, D. and Juon, A. (2020) 'Authoritarian footprints in Central and Eastern Europe', *East European Politics*, 36(2), p167–187.

Bolleyer, N. (2013) *New Parties in old party systems: Persistence and decline in seventeen democracies.* Oxford: Oxford University Press.

Borz, G. and Janda, K. (2020) 'Contemporary trends in party organization: Revisiting intra-party democracy', *Party Politics*, 26(1), p3–8.

Bozoki, A. and Ishiyama, J. (2002) *The communist successor parties of Central and Eastern Europe.* New York: M.E. Sharpe.

Buštíková, L. and Kitschelt, H. (2009) 'The radical right in post-Communist Europe. Comparative perspectives on legacies and party competition', *Communist and Post-Communist Studies*, 42(4), p459–483.

Cross, W.P. and Katz, R.S. (eds.) (2013) *The challenges of intra-party democracy.* Oxford: Oxford University Press.

Cross, W.P., Katz, R.S. and Pruysers, S. (eds.) (2018) *The personalization of democratic politics and the challenge for political parties.* London: ECPR Press.

Dalton, J.R. and Wattenberg, M.P. (eds.) (2000) *Parties without partisans: Political change in advanced industrial democracies.* Oxford: Oxford University Press.

Dalton, R.J., Farrell, D. and McAllister, I. (2011) *Political parties and democratic linkage: How parties organize democracy.* Oxford: Oxford University Press.

De Vries, C.E. and Hobolt, S.B. (2020) *Political entrepreneurs: The rise of challenger parties in Europe.* Princeton: Princeton University Press.

Diamond, L. (2015) 'Facing up to the democratic recession', *Journal of Democracy*, 26(1), p141–155.

Duverger, M. (1963) *Political parties: Their organization and activity in the modern state.* New York: Wiley.

Enroth, H. and Hagevi, M. (eds.) (2018) *Cartelisation, convergence or increasing similarities? Lessons from parties in parliament.* London: ECPR Press.

Enyedi, Z. and Casal Bértoa, F. (2018) 'Institutionalization and de-institutionalization in post-communist party systems', *East European Politics and Societies*, 32(3), p422–450.

Evans, G. (2006) 'The social bases of political divisions in post-Communist Eastern Europe', *Annual Review of Sociology*, 32(1), p245–270.

Faucher-King, F. (2005) *Changing parties: An anthropology of British political party conferences.* Basingstoke: Palgrave Macmillan.

Fazekas, M. and Tóth, I.J. (2016) 'From corruption to state capture: A new analytical framework with empirical applications from Hungary', *Political Research Quarterly*, 69(2), p320–334.

Gallagher, M. and Marsh, M. (1987) *Candidate selection in comparative perspective: The secret garden of politics.* London: Sage.

Gauja, A. (2017) *Party reform. The causes, challenges, and consequences of organizational change.* Oxford: Oxford University Press.

Gerbaudo, P. (2019) *The digital party. Political organisation and online democracy.* London: Pluto Press.

Gherghina, S., Miscoiu, S. and Sorina, S. (2021) 'How far does nationalism go? An overview of populist parties in Central and Eastern Europe' in Heinisch, R., Holtz-Bacha, C. and Mazzoleni, O. (eds.) *Political populism. Handbook on concepts, questions and strategies of research*. Baden-Baden: Nomos Verlags, pp. 239–256.

Harmel, R. (2002) 'Party organizational change: competing explanations?' in Luther, K.R. and Rommel, F.M. (eds.) *Political parties in the new Europe: Political and analytical challenges*. Oxford: Oxford University Press, pp. 119–143.

Harmel, R. and Janda, K. (1994) 'An integrated theory of party goals and party change', *Journal of Theoretical Politics*, 6(3), p259–87.

Harmel, R. and Svasand, L. (eds.) (2019) *Institutionalisation of political parties: Comparative cases*. London: ECPR Press.

Henderson, K. (2008) 'Exceptionalism or convergence? Euroscepticism and party systems in Central and Eastern Europe' in Szczerbiak, A. and Taggart, P. (eds.) *Opposing Europe? The comparative party politics of Euroscepticism*, vol. 2. Oxford: Oxford University Press, pp. 103–126.

Heinisch, R. and Mazzoleni, O. (2016) *Understanding populist party organisation. The radical right in Western Europe*. London: Palgrave.

Hooghe, L. and Marks, G. (2018) 'Cleavage theory meets Europe's crises: Lipset, Rokkan, and the transnational cleavage', *Journal of European Public Policy*, 25(1), p109–135.

Ignazi, P. (2017) *Party and democracy. The uneven road to party legitimacy*. Oxford: Oxford University Press.

Ignazi, P. (2020) 'The four knights of intra-party democracy: A rescue for party delegitimation', *Party Politics*, 26(1), p9–20.

Innes, A. (2002) 'Party competition in post-Communist Europe: The great electoral lottery', *Comparative Politics*, 35(1), p85–104.

Katz, R.S. and Mair, P. (1995) 'Changing models of party organization and party democracy. The emergence of the Cartel Party', *Party Politics*, 1(1), p17–21.

Katz, R.S. and Mair, P. (2018) *Democracy and the cartelization of political parties*. Oxford: Oxford University Press.

Kirchheimer, O. (1966) 'The transformation of the Western European party system', in LaPalombara, J. and Weiner, M. (eds.) *Political parties and political development*. Princeton: Princeton University Press, pp. 177–201.

Kitschelt, H. (2000) 'Citizens, politicians, and party cartelization: Political representation and state failure in post-industrial democracies', *European Journal of Political Research*, 37, p149–179.

Kitschelt, H., Mansfeldova, Z., Markowski, R. and Tóka, G. (1999) *Post-Communist party systems: Competition, representation, and inter-party cooperation*. Cambridge: Cambridge University Press.

Koole, R. (1996) 'Cadre, catch-all or cartel. A comment on the notion of cartel party', *Party Politics*, 2(4), p507–523.

Kopecký, P. (2006) 'Political parties and the state in post-Communist Europe: The nature of symbiosis', *Journal of Communist Studies and Transition Politics*, 22(3), p251–273.

Kozarzewski, P. and Bałtowski, M. (2016) 'Formal and real ownership structure of the Polish economy: State-owned versus state-controlled enterprises', *Post-Communist Economies*, 28(3), p405–419.

Krouwel, A. (2012) *Party transformations in European democracies*. New York: State University of New York Press.

Lane, J.E. and Ersson, S. (2007) 'Party system instability in Europe: Persistent differences in volatility between West and East?', *Democratization*, 14(1), p92–110.

Lawson, K. (2007) 'When parties dedemocratize', in Lawson, K. and Merkl, P.H. (eds.) *When parties prosper: The uses of electoral success*. Boulder: Lynne Rienner, pp. 353–66.

Levitsky, S. and Ziblatt, Z. (2018) *How democracies die*. New York: Crown.

Mair, P. (1997) *Party system change: approaches and interpretations*. Oxford: Oxford University Press.

Mair, P. (2013) *Ruling the void. The hollowing-out of Western democracy*. London: Verso.

Mair, P., Muller, C.W. and Plassner, F. (2004) *Political parties and electoral change: Party responses to electoral markets*. London: Sage.

McDonnell, D. and Newell, J.L. (2011) 'Outsider parties in government in Western Europe', *Party Politics*, 17(4), p443–452.

Mendilow, J. and Phélippeau, E., (eds.) (2018) *Handbook of political party funding*. Cheltenham: Elgar Publishing.

Minkenberg, M. (2015) 'Profiles, patterns, process. Studying the East European radical right in its political environment', in Minkenberg, M. (ed.) *Transforming the transformation? The East European radical right in the political process.* London: Routledge, pp. 27–56.

Minkenberg, M. (2017) *The radical right in Eastern Europe: Democracy under siege?* New York: Springer.

Norris, P. and Inglehart, R. (2019) *Cultural backlash. Trump, Brexit, and authoritarian populism.* Cambridge: Cambridge University Press.

Panebianco, A. (1988) *Political parties: organization and power.* Cambridge: Cambridge University Press.

Pirro, A.L. (2015) *The populist radical right in Central and Eastern Europe: Ideology, impact, and electoral performance.* London: Routledge.

Poguntke, T., Scarrow, S.E., Webb, P.D. et al. (2016) 'Party rules, party resources and the politics of parliamentary democracies: How parties organize in the 21st century', *Party Politics*, 22(6), p661–678.

Poguntke, T. and Webb, P. (2005) *The presidentialization of politics.* Oxford: Oxford University Press.

Pytlas, B. (2018) 'Populist radical right mainstreaming and challenges to democracy in an enlarged Europe' in Herman, L. and Muldoon, J. (eds.) *Trumping the mainstream: The conquest of democratic politics by the populist radical right.* London: Routledge, pp. 179–198.

Rahat, G. and Kenig, O. (2018) *From party politics to personalized politics? Party change and political personalization.* Oxford: Oxford University Press.

Riishøj, S. (2004) 'Europeanisation and euro-scepticism. Experiences from Poland and the Czech Republic', *Středoevropské politické studie/Central European Political Studies Review* 4/4, [online]. Available at: www.cepsr.com/clanek.php?ID=211 (Accessed 2 May 2021)

Savage, L. (2016) 'Party system institutionalization and government formation in new democracies', *World Politics*, 68(3), p499–537.

Scarrow, S.E. (2007) 'Political finance in comparative perspective', *Annual Review of Political Science*, 10, p193–210.

Scarrow, S.E. (2015) *Beyond party members: Changing approaches to partisan mobilization*, Oxford: Oxford University Press.

Schopflin, G. (1993) *Politics in Eastern Europe: 1945–92*, Oxford: Blackwell.

Schedler, A. (1996) 'Anti-political-establishment parties', *Party Politics*, 2(3), p291–312.

Sikk, A. (2018) 'Political parties and party organisations', in Fagan, A. and Kopecký P. (eds.) *Routledge handbook of East European politics.* London: Routledge, pp. 100–112.

Thomson, R., Royed, T., Naurin, E., Artés, J. et al. (2017) 'The fulfilment of parties' election pledges: A comparative study on the impact of power sharing', *American Journal of Political Science*, 61(3), p527–542.

Tomšič, M. and Prijon, L. (2013) 'Person-based politics in Italy and Slovenia: Comparing cases of leadership's individualisation', *International Journal of Social Science*, 64, p237–248.

van Biezen, I. (2005) 'On the theory and practice of party formation and adaptation in new democracies', *European Journal of Political Research*, 44(1), p147–174.

van Biezen, I., Mair, P. and Poguntke, T. (2012) 'Going, going, . . . gone? The decline of party membership in contemporary Europe', *European Journal of Political Research*, 51(1), p24–56.

van Haute, E. and Gauja, A. (2015) *Party members and activists.* London: Routledge.

Webb, P.D. (2005) 'Political parties and democracy: The ambiguous crisis', *Democratisation*, 12(5), p633–650.

Webb, P.D., Poguntke, T. and Scarrow, S.E. (2017) *Organizing political parties. Representation, participation, and power.* Oxford: Oxford University Press.

Webb, P.D. and White, S. (2007) *Party politics in new democracies.* Oxford: Oxford University Press.

Weikert, J.J. (2019) 'Inside two parties: Ethnographic analysis of partisan differences in political candidate recruitment', *SAGE Research Methods Cases*. [online]. Available at: www.doi.org/10.4135/9781526473004 (Accessed 26 September 2021).

Werner, A. (2020) 'Representation in Western Europe: Connecting party-voter congruence and party goals', *The British Journal of Politics and International Relation*, 22(1), p122–142.

Zulianello, M. (2019) *Anti-system parties: From parliamentary breakthrough to government.* London: Routledge.

2
PARTIES AND PARTISANSHIP IN POLITICAL THEORY

Alfred Moore

[A]lthough the literature of democratic theory is immense, it has developed largely without reference to the richness and complexity of empirical studies of political parties, and . . . although scholars of parties often make introductory reference to their centrality to modern democracy, they rarely go beyond this to consider the distinctions among varieties of normative democratic theories.

(Katz 2006, 44)

From the point of view of political theory, there are at least three reasons for the lack of engagement between democratic theory and empirical scholarship on parties. The first is a disciplinary division of labour between 'normative' and 'empirical' theory, the former taken up by political philosophers, the latter by political scientists (Shapiro 2002, 597; van Biezen and Saward 2008). This has led to the growth of 'two cultures' of democratic theory (Sabl 2015), which address different problems and have different aims, and often proceed without mutual engagement or understanding.

The second has been the relative marginalisation of questions of institutional design in political theory since at least 1970s in favour of general theories of justice – Rawls, for instance, ends a brief discussion of parties and 'regulated rivalry' in the democratic political process by noting that these questions 'belong to political sociology' (Rawls 1999, 199) – a trend lamented by Waldron (2016, 1–22). The third is a tendency among democratic theorists in particular to focus their energies on forms of mobilisation and engagement beyond party politics, such as social movements for justice and recognition (Young 2000), contestatory and 'counter-democratic' institutions focused on the executive (Rosanvallon 2008), and various ways of involving ordinary citizens in political decision processes without the mediation of parties, from Citizens' Assemblies (Pearse and Warren 2008) to randomly selected 'tribunes of the plebs' with veto powers (McCormick 2011, 170–188). Democratic reform has often been imagined outside of or even against party politics.

Since the mid-2000s (though with important precursors), a small but thriving literature has emerged in political theory engaging the theme of parties and partisanship, which is to say, parties as an organisational form and partisanship as a 'civic ideal' (White and Ypi 2016, 4). In this chapter, I survey this literature, taking up where earlier surveys (Johnson 2006; Katz 2006) leave off.[1] Some of this work has been motivated by a desire to bridge the gap between the 'two cultures' of democratic theory by formulating normatively significant distinctions, such as between 'partisans who help advance the principle of political pluralism [and] those who do not' in ways that are usable in empirical studies (Herman 2017, 740). In the final section, I discuss some arguments around party reform that draw on substantive engagement between political theorists and party scholars of the sort recommended by van Biezen and Saward (2008). However, it is important to recognise that the majority of the new political theory of parties and partisanship does not have the aim of – and should not be read as – trying to straightforwardly 'bridge the gap' between disciplinary subfields, or manufacture conceptual tools to help empirical researchers. As Sabl observes, 'separate vocations exist for a reason. Empirical and normative students of democracy will never think exactly the same way, nor should they. But each can learn from the other without becoming the other' (Sabl 2015, 356).

The role of this survey, accordingly, is to situate this emerging theoretical work in the context of its own distinctive questions and aims. I will begin in section one with the theme of parties and deliberation, not only because many of the new theorists of partisanship have focused on norms and practices of partisan debate and persuasion but also because the relative neglect of parties in democratic theory is often ascribed to the dominance of a particular understanding of deliberative democracy. Many of the theorists of parties and partisanship set out to challenge and reframe theories of public deliberation and public reason, or to articulate a role for parties and partisanship within those theories. The second section turns to the theme of participatory agency and what Muirhead and Rosenblum (2012) call 'partisan connection'. The central theoretical problem addressed here is that of unity and the integration of the political community, and the central underlying concern is with the conditions under which partisan and party competition might bind a political community together, and when it might drive such a community apart. I will also discuss the ethics of political competition, and debates around the role of ethos and institutions in constraining partisan conduct. I conclude in section three with a comment on new directions and unsolved problems. Here I highlight the question of party reform, and show how such debates intersect with debates in party scholarship about the (supposed) crisis of party democracy (Katz and Mair 1995; Mair 2013).

Parties and deliberation

In recent political theory, the democratic value of parties has often been framed in terms of their role in promoting public deliberation, broadly construed as debate, justification, and persuasion oriented to processes of collective decision. This is perhaps surprising. The field of deliberative democracy has tended to define itself against a model of 'competitive' or 'aggregative' democracy. Elster, in an influential essay, framed a contrast between 'politics as the aggregation of given preferences and politics as the transformation of preferences through rational discussion' (Elster 1997, 4), and later elaborations of deliberative democracy have been steady in their opposition to the idea that 'democratic politics is nothing other than a competition between private interests and preferences' (Young 2000, 22). Party politics has typically been associated with this 'aggregative' model of politics, and has accordingly received little positive attention from deliberative democrats. The index of the recent Oxford Handbook of Deliberative Democracy (Bächtiger et al. 2018), for instance, gives no entry for partisanship, but one entry for the Quakers; there are eight entries for 'political parties', but they are only mentioned in four of the book's 57 chapters.

Yet a range of scholars within the deliberative democratic tradition have suggested that parties – understood in a very general sense as 'political organisations that connect citizens to government by coordinating citizens for electoral purposes' (Johnson 2006, 2) – can serve as 'a vehicle for rather than an alternative to public persuasion and debate' (Johnson 2006, 4). Thus, Manin, an influential figure in the early theoretical development of deliberative democracy, argued that deliberation is essential to democratic legitimacy, and parties are 'essential to deliberation' (Manin 1987, 357). Deliberation is crucial to democratic legitimacy because, '[i]n the last analysis, a political decision is legitimate because it has been able to win the approval of the majority *at the conclusion of a process of free confrontation among various points of view*' (Manin 1987, 359; my emphasis). Moreover, the 'existence of political parties is essential for deliberation' insofar as their function is to develop, defend, and communicate rationales and justifications that can be understood and endorsed by the people at large: 'The parties face each other, and the process of argumentation is submitted to the arbitration of all' (Manin 1987, 357). Goodin, similarly, treats parties as the means by which law acquires a 'collective *ratio*', which is to say, a public justification that can be recognised by those subject to the law. It is through the articulation of competing platforms that citizens are able to appreciate such a ratio and manifest their consent to one of them by way of the vote (Goodin 2008, 214–217).

Deliberative democracy is often associated with restrictions on the sorts of reasons that can properly be advanced in public deliberation, and these restrictions have been used to define the kinds of rationales that parties should ideally produce. Bonotti, building on Rawls' (2005) account of public reason, is perhaps the most demanding: 'parties and partisans have a duty to present and justify their claims on the basis of *reasons that all citizens could accept*' (Bonotti 2017, 100; my emphasis). White and Ypi (2016, 3) slightly soften the demand: they define the 'genuine' or 'ethical' partisan as one who is committed to persuading others through 'the appeal to reasons that can be generally shared'. Put negatively, the ethical partisan should make claims 'that cannot be reduced to the interests of one sector or group in society' and which are thus 'plausibly generalisable' or at least not 'systematically exclusive' (White and Ypi 2016, 21, 24). Muirhead, however, overtly avoids the demand for reasons all could accept, arguing rather that partisans should offer reasons that 'appeal broadly – if not from an abstract moral commitment to democratic principles, then from strategic or prudential concerns' (Muirhead 2006, 719). Manin rejects the ideal of unanimity implicit in 'reasons all can accept' and prefers to describe universality as a 'horizon' that is never achieved: what party democracy ensures is a sort of 'competition for generality', an incentive to make claims that appeal to *more* people, not to *all* people. For Rosenblum, partisanship involves a 'responsibility for telling a comprehensive public story about the economic, social and moral changes of the time' (Rosenblum 2008, 358), at the same time as it makes available to the partisan a story with greater cohesiveness and durability than any individual could probably muster. Rosenblum's idea of parties as needing to develop a 'comprehensive story' is less demanding and rationalistic than the idea of parties providing a 'ratio' that could be accepted by all (Rosenblum 2008, 553). While there are important differences between the idea of parties as giving 'reasons all could accept' and the idea that they should tell 'comprehensive stories', these theorists share an idea of parties as agents of public deliberation.

One role of parties within the process of public deliberation is to simplify and organise arguments, reducing the complexity of the field of argument in the way that a chess player narrows down the range of credible moves so as to focus attention most effectively (Manin 1987, 357), and thereby helping people locate proposals in the 'space of public political reasons' (Rummens 2012, 33). This deliberative function implies a 'division of justificatory labour' (Bonotti 2017, 124–151). The thought here is that the normative demands on individual citizens implied by, for instance, a Rawlsian conception of public reason, are too demanding. We cannot expect citizens themselves to articulate their claims using reasons that could be accepted by all. But we perhaps could expect parties to elevate and filter partial perspectives and concerns such that whatever people choose will plausibly amount to a generalisable reason for political consent. The role of parties is to take our selfish and short-sighted claims, and reflect them back to us in a filtered form. Parties, then, can serve public reason by way of relieving individual citizens of the demanding burdens of judgement, and helping them 'relate comprehensive doctrines and values to widely shared political principles' (Bonotti 2017, 100; see also Muirhead and Rosenblum 2006).

Developing the idea of a justificatory division of labour, White and Ypi talk of the epistemic contribution of partisanship as levelling the kind of epistemic problems ordinary people have making sense of complex social arrangements (White and Ypi 2016, 91–2). Through partisan practice in the form of party conventions, branch meetings, assemblies, protests, websites, and meetings, 'sophisticated judgments and the sometimes esoteric terms of political justification cease to be available only to minority elites and may become part of a joint intellectual stock, available to other citizens and in turn reworked by them' (White and Ypi 2016, 92). Those participating in such forums thus become part of collective enterprises that elevate their understanding of complex issues. Such participation also has the effect of bringing them into contact with others who, while broadly on the same team, have quite different backgrounds and perspectives. This means at the individual level that active partisans are often required to compromise and 'trim' their convictions in order to stand with others, a distinct virtue of partisanship that is neither demanded nor cultivated by those who reject partisan commitments (Muirhead 2006, 719). Rather than associating independence with intellectual activity and self-reliance, theorists of partisanship have thus recast the political 'independent' as epistemically weak and morally 'weightless' (Rosenblum 2008, 348). Far from being the passive recipients of party lines, the partisan is here presented as someone forced to engage with others across disagreement and take responsibility for collective positions. In this way, such theorists have sought, as Rosenblum puts it, to 'chip away at the moral high ground claimed by Independents' (Rosenblum 2008, 322).

The rediscovery of parties has dovetailed with the re-evaluation of rhetoric in democratic theory (Garsten 2011). Parties do not simply discover and respond to existing preferences, but play an important role in transforming and shaping preferences, and creating cleavages. This dimension of competitive democracy was portrayed by Schumpeter (2003 [1943]) as a sort of manipulation, likening it to advertising. But Disch, in her 'mobilisation' conception of representation, emphasises that citizens have agency within this process. The unavoidable problem is that 'citizens' capacity to form preferences depends on the self-interested communications of elites' (Disch 2011, 101). Elite-led political communication serves at the same time to 'inform' (the sort of epistemic role discussed by White and Ypi) and to 'recruit' them to 'positions that work to elites' own advantage in an interparty struggle for power' (Disch 2011, 100–1). She thus rejects the model of deliberation which 'requires deliberators to argue their case in terms with which all reasonable people could agree' (Disch 2011, 110), and introduces instead a normative distinction between rhetoric that 'provokes thinking' and rhetoric that merely 'tap[s] prejudice' (Disch 2011, 111), echoing Chambers' (2009) distinction between 'deliberative' and 'plebiscitary' rhetoric. In support of the potentials of 'deliberative rhetoric', Disch cites research in political psychology claiming that competition can foster judgement by 'prompt[ing] people to think twice about their preferences' (Disch 2011, 103) and raising the 'odds that germane considerations will be publicised and discussed' (Chong and Druckman 2007, 652). Competition between parties, even when it is conducted through manipulative appeals, can have the side-effect of stimulating the judgement of citizens.

Democratic theory has tended to set up an unhelpful dichotomy between a 'competitive' or 'aggregative' model of democracy and a 'deliberative' model of democracy. The growing attention to parties and processes of party competition has begun to break down this dichotomy. For all the differences between the adversarial deliberative theory of Manin and the Rawlsian tradition of public reason liberalism, parties are now increasingly recognised within democratic theory as a crucial institution for making, communicating, and contesting political justifications.

The partisan connection

While it is commonly recognised that parties may have democratic value as 'vehicles for deliberation' (Johnson 2006), for some theorists the primary emphasis should be placed on the 'partisan connection' (Muirhead and Rosenblum 2012). This emphasis intersects more closely with party scholarship that frames parties as bridging the gap between disparate individuals and the formal institutions of government and linking the state and civil society. However, the focus of the new theorists of partisanship is on the normative dimensions of such a partisan connection. From this point of view, the primary virtues of partisanship are loyalty, commitment, and an enduring attachment to or identification with a collective project. Partisanship can promote an 'active democratic ethos', bringing 'motivational and epistemic resources' (White and Ypi 2016, 77–8) to principled 'projects'. Associative practices not only help to advance common projects but also develop new dispositions of loyalty, solidarity, collective responsibility, and pride in the achievements of a collective 'we' (White and Ypi 2016, 89). The good partisan is motivated by a strong commitment to a shared political project and to the goal of winning elected office in order to further that project.

The 'partisan connection' draws attention to citizens as agents or participants rather than as choosers. It is of course clear that many – possibly most – citizens would not be party members or strongly identify with a partisan project. This is reflected in much of the theorising about virtues, duties, and obligations of voters, which implicitly assumes that they ought ideally to be informed and impartial judges of the claims and appeals of competing elites. As J. S. Mill put it, the clash of arguments driven by one-eyed partisans serves to inform the judgement of the 'calmer and more disinterested bystander' (Mill 1989, 53). But the recent political theory work surveyed here seeks to build out from the experience of the committed partisan, which is not typically an experience of freely choosing from a menu of options or impartially judging a range of proposals. Thus, Rosenblum reads party identification as not straightforwardly a matter of choice, but rather of social integration. Quoting Walzer, she says that party identification involves 'loyalty to particular people, the sense of being at home with these people, the richness of a received tradition, and the longing for generational continuity' (Rosenblum 2008, 341). The point of this normative reframing of party identification is to change the relevant expectations and ideals with which we approach democratic citizenship: we should be neither surprised nor disappointed to find that many people do not choose their party following a reasoned and informed assessment of the consistency of the competing platforms with their values and preferences.

By focusing on the partisan connection, these theorists address the problem of social unity and integration. One central claim in this literature is that the 'regulated rivalry' (Rosenblum 2008) that manifests in party competition can (under certain conditions) serve to strengthen social integration and stability. As Urbinati puts it, in representative democracy, 'discord becomes a stabilising factor, an engine of the entire political process. It becomes the bond that holds together a society that has no visible center' (Urbinati 2006, 32). Parties are vehicles for a sort of 'pluralism without foundations' (Rosenblum 2008, 365). But how does the integration of partisans with their parties serve the integration of society as a whole? How do loyalty and solidarity within the partisan group translate into social cohesion and stability?

As we saw earlier, Bonotti in particular emphasises that parties help individual citizens relate their own values to more fully articulated accounts of political justice, and White and Ypi, similarly, think that partisanship is valuable because it generates political justifications that can form the basis for political consent. But Muirhead worries that parties understood as 'justificatory projects' cannot sustain the partisan connection: 'the most important function parties serve is found in the way they sustain sociological legitimacy. This happens not through philosophic justification, but rather through mobilisation' (Muirhead 2019, 85). Rosenblum similarly emphasises the integrative dimension of the more or less 'coherent stories' that parties tell about the 'economic, social, and moral changes of the time' (Rosenblum 2008, 358). Partisans are bound to the state through their attachment to a party: the party links the particular and the general in order to tell a story of 'what the nation requires' (Rosenblum 2008, 360). It is thus important for Rosenblum that parties are purely political identity groups, rather than drawing their identity from ethnicity, religion, or social position (Rosenblum 2008, 347). Rather than acquiring identity through parties, 'alternative political identities', perhaps deriving from given social, economic, or cultural identities, 'push forcefully in the other direction[s] of contraction and fragmentation' (Rosenblum 2008, 360).

The idea of framing parties less as a means of organising the options between which voters might choose, and more as a vehicle for agency and identification, has led some theorists to revisit the democratic theory of the early twentieth-century Austrian legal theorist Hans Kelsen.[2] Kelsen held that the 'people' can only be construed through a plurality of groups, comprising individuals integrated into 'associations based on their various political goals' (Kelsen 2013, 36). The political party, defined as an organisation 'which brings like-minded individuals together in order to secure them actual influence in shaping public affairs' (Kelsen 2013, 35), is thus central to Kelsen's normative account of democracy. Proportional representation, Kelsen thought, is crucial in order to accurately reflect the support for divergent groupings, and parliament is to be understood as the site where, through a process of compromise, the majority comes into being.

Much of the recent attention to Kelsen's work on parties and democracy has focused on his ambiguous notion of compromise. On the one hand, White and Ypi comment that for Kelsen

> all political conflict is reduced to a conflict of group interests, and the only way to resolve such conflicts is to give them political representation in hope that the democratic process itself will adjudicate between them in a freedom-preserving manner.
>
> *(White and Ypi 2016, 153)*

If this is the case, then democratic politics would indeed (as Przeworski 2010, 7051, observes) seem to reduce to pure bargaining. Yet it is not clear that Kelsen does reduce political conflict to interest conflict: he defines parties, after all, as groups of the 'like-minded', and, as Baume (2018, 434) observes, frames the conflictual nature of politics as a confrontation of diverging beliefs and opinions (Baume 2018, 434). On the other hand, if the point is to defend parliamentary deliberation ('argument and counter-argument') as the means for sorting multiple groups into a majority through some more principled compromise, then what might that process of principled compromise look like? As Knight and Schwartzberg (2020) note, the conceptualisation of fair bargaining and principled compromise is a pressing question for democratic theory today.

Kelsen's ideas have also been pushed in a new direction by advocates of intra-party democracy. Drawing on Kelsen, Wolkenstein argues that parties enable participatory agency. To say that citizens can connect their agency to collective decisions, there must be (1) some causal connection between their actions and general laws and policies, and (2) they must be able to perceive outcomes as traceable to themselves (Wolkenstein 2019, 341–2). These conditions can be fulfilled separately. You might perceive yourself to be an agent if you identify organically with the leader, as in Laclau's populist democracy, but you have no causal influence over decisions. Or you might actually have causal influence, but be unable to perceive it, as, in Wolkenstein's view, is the case with the European Union, where member states tend to decide issues in line with domestic public opinion, but citizens do not perceive much of a connection. Political parties enable the fulfilment of these conditions: it is through identification with parties as collective agents that individuals are able both to effect a small measure of contributory causal agency and to *perceive* their agency. This leads him to the further claim: if part of the democratic value of parties is to give their supporters a 'sense of agency', then this implies a measure of internal party democracy, and specifically intra-party deliberation.

The relationship between partisan connection and social integration has led to a focus on the ethics of partisanship, and in particular, the proper limits to the conduct of partisan struggle. The most common and obvious point is that 'partisans do not look to liquidate, erase, or permanently disorganise the opposition or represent them as public enemies' (Rosenblum 2008, 363). With this standard in mind, Muirhead and Rosenblum (2020) have recently argued that some right-wing political rhetoric has stepped over the line, and that the 'new conspiracism' adopted by some politicians and media outlets presents political opponents as enemies. Shapiro focuses less on political rhetoric and more on the effects of pursuing partisan advantage through redistricting, altering voting laws, and other ways (within the rules) of trying to permanently disorganise the opposition. He regards appeals to the ethos of party leaders as useless, and suggests that the solution lies with tough and impartial referees: 'Politicians can no better enforce their own compliance with the rules of the competitive game than can firms enforce theirs', and thus concludes that judicial review is necessary to 'protect the rules of the game' (Shapiro 2003, 73, 75). Yet this approach faces its own challenges. One is that in the USA at least, the Supreme Court has historically tended to erode rather than protect the conditions of political democracy (Dahl 2006, 59), a trend continued in the 2013 Shelby County v. Holder decision, which struck down key provisions in the 1965 Voting Rights Act. A second challenge is that it is hard to imagine rules of partisan conduct being enforced in time to make a difference to an actual political campaign. Bagg and Tranvik (2019) on this basis conclude that some sort of self-restraint in the process of electioneering is necessary to a functioning democracy (see also Beerbohm 2016). Third, and perhaps most fundamentally, the rules of the game are themselves a proper part of politics. White and Ypi thus suggest that sometimes protecting pluralism will require 'departing from institutional arrangements as they are' and that 'the concept of partisanship must retain space for the extraordinary and the disruptive' (White and Ypi 2016, 27). There are risks in politicising procedures, but they are 'not sufficient to make consent to them a defining characteristic of partisanship' (White and Ypi 2016, 28). There is no way, it seems, to avoid the demand for some measure of ethical or normative self-restraint if competitive politics is to survive over the long run.

Conclusions and avenues for further research

As political theorists have turned their attention to parties and partisanship, they have brought with them a distinctive set of normative concerns. Some of these concerns reflect movements within normative political theory, such as debates within democratic theory between rationalist and rhetorical accounts of deliberation. Others involve fundamental democratic problems, such as the generation of social integration and the peaceful management of conflict, rivalry, and difference. Much of the new work on parties, as we have seen earlier, sets out to articulate the place of parties and partisanship within a range of different approaches to democratic theory.

Among the new areas of research in this field that have emerged in recent years concerns the limits of partisanship: the question of when and why parties should be banned. This question has been largely neglected (though see Bader 1999) and is 'ripe for attention by democratic theorists' (Rosenblum 2008, 453). There are also questions about whether, and if so, how, religious and ethnic parties can find a legitimate place in systems in which partisans are supposed to 'compete for generality', or generate 'comprehensive narratives' or justifications that are not 'systematically exclusive'. Bonotti (2017, 119) argues that religious parties are legitimate to the extent that they present their demands in terms all reasonable people could accept, and are not if they do not. However, this leaves open the more interesting question of when and how religious parties move from being primarily confessional to secular and 'properly' partisan, as is arguably the case in the development of some Christian democratic parties in Europe in the nineteenth century.

Another emerging line of inquiry focuses on institutional reform, marking a practical step beyond simply rehabilitating or developing an 'appreciation' (Rosenblum 2008) of parties within fields of political theory that have either ignored or maligned them. One line of thought focuses on the organisation of parties within legislatures, and in particular the question of party discipline. Thus, Leydet argues that one way to generate the possibility of persuasion inside the legislative chamber is by 'allowing a significant level of dissidence within parliamentary parties' (Leydet 2015, 237). In order to keep wavering backbenchers on side, even majority governments have to make real arguments and address real counter-arguments, as in the UK parliamentary debate in 2013 on intervention in Syria (which the Conservative-led coalition government lost). Bhatia takes up Leydet's insight in the context of constitutional provisions against party defection, such as India's law compelling legislators to vote with their party. The stricter the coercive measures to enforce party discipline, the less party leaders need to 'engage with their views' (Bhatia 2020, 261). Furthermore, where there is strict party discipline, party positions appear rather like black boxes. When we can see the diverse traditions, normative premises, interpretations, and arguments from which the group position was forged, it makes it easier to 'find arguments within an adversary's perspective' and to 'explore an issue from premises entirely different from their own' (Bhatia 2020, 267). This line of research focuses on the ways dissenters within majority ruling parties can extract justifications and even concessions from the party leadership, which they hold to be a much more plausible mechanism of accountability than public opinion or the anticipation of sanction at the polls.

Although, as noted in the introduction, we should not read recent political theory on parties as a response to – or directly in service of – empirical scholarship on parties, on the question of party reform, there are clear points of intersection. For instance, building on claims about the weakening of the connection between parties and civil society (Katz and Mair 1995), some theorists have begun to explore the idea that parties might be 'resuscitated' by 'deliberative intraparty democracy' (Invernizzi-Accetti and Wolkenstein 2017, 97; see also Teorell 1999; Biale and Ottonelli 2019; Wolkenstein 2019). Intra-party deliberation is geared towards enticing 'critical citizens' (as Pippa Norris calls them) back to party politics from their social movements by 'allowing partisans [party members] to debate policy and more general visions for the polity' (Invernizzi-Accetti and Wolkenstein 2017, 97). These proposals for party reform (further developed in Wolkenstein 2020) are also normatively informed, emphasising the importance of participatory agency to the production of democratic legitimacy. There are empirical doubts about the effectiveness of such proposals (Katz 2013), as well as counter-arguments for 'restor[ing the] authority' of parties by reversing a trend towards greater intra-party democracy

(Rosenbluth and Shapiro 2018, 23), but this line of work offers just one model for engagement and conversation between normative theory and party scholarship. Another model for such engagement is provided by attempts to develop middle-range concepts through which the concerns articulated in normative theories of democracy can be made usable in empirical political analysis (see Herman 2017; Wolkenstein and Wratil 2021). Thus, some have begun to heed the call for political theorist and party scholars to talk to each other (van Biezen and Saward 2008).

Notes

1. I am restricting this chapter to debates in normative political theory, for reasons of space, though a parallel interest in parties can be seen in the history of political thought (see, for instance, Skjonsberg 2021).
2. Kelsen's *Essence and Value of Democracy* was re-published in a new English translation in 2013 with an introduction by Invernizzi-Accetti and Urbinati, and has been a focus of several recent works on parties in political theory (Baume 2018; Ragazzoni 2018; Wolkenstein 2019).

References

Bächtiger, A., Dryzek, J., Mansbridge, J. and Warren, M.E. (eds.) (2018) *The Oxford handbook of deliberative democracy*. Oxford: Oxford University Press.

Bader, V. (1999) 'Religious pluralism: Secularism or priority for democracy?', *Political Theory*, 27(5), p597–634.

Bagg, S. and Tranvik, I. (2019) 'An adversarial ethic for campaigns and elections', *Perspectives on Politics*, 17(4), p973–987.

Baume, S. (2018) 'Rehabilitating political parties: An examination of the views of Hans Kelsen', *Intellectual History Review*, 28(3), p425–449.

Beerbohm, E. (2016) 'The ethics of electioneering', *The Journal of Political Philosophy*, 24(4), p381–405.

Bhatia, U. (2020) 'Cracking the whip: the deliberative costs of strict party discipline', *Critical Review of International Social and Political Philosophy*, 23(2), p254–279.

Biale, E. and Ottonelli, V. (2019) 'Intra-party deliberation and reflexive control within a deliberative system', *Political Theory*, 47(4), p500–526.

Bonotti, M. (2017) *Partisanship and political liberalism in diverse societies*. Oxford: Oxford University Press.

Chambers, S. (2009) 'Rhetoric and the public sphere. Has deliberative democracy abandoned mass democracy?', *Political Theory*, 37(3), p323–350.

Chong, D. and Druckman, J. (2007) 'Framing public opinion in competitive democracies', *American Political Science Review*, 101(4), p637–55.

Dahl, R. (2006) *A preface to democratic theory. Expanded edition*. Chicago: Chicago University Press.

Disch, L. (2011) 'Toward a mobilization conception of democratic representation', *The American Political Science Review*, 105(1), p100–114.

Elster, J. (1997) 'The market and the forum: Three varieties of political theory', in Bohman, J. and Rehg, W. (eds.) *Deliberative democracy: Essays on reason and politics*. Cambridge: MIT Press, pp. 3–34.

Garsten, B. (2011) 'The rhetorical revival in political theory', *Annual Review of Political Science*, 14, p159–80.

Goodin, R.E. (2008) *Innovating democracy: Democratic theory and practice after the deliberative turn*. Oxford: Oxford University Press.

Herman, L.E. (2017) 'Democratic partisanship: From theoretical ideal to empirical standard', *American Political Science Review*, 111(4), p738–754.

Invernizzi-Accetti, C. and Wolkenstein, F. (2017) 'The crisis of party democracy, cognitive mobilization, and the case for making parties more deliberative', *American Political Science Review*, 111(1), p97–109.

Johnson, J. (2006) 'Political parties and deliberative democracy?', in Katz, R. and Crotty, W. (eds.) *The handbook of party politics*. London: Sage, pp. 47–50.

Katz, R.S. (2006) 'Party in democratic theory', in Katz, R.S. and Crotty, W. (eds.) *The handbook of party politics*. London: Sage, pp. 34–46.

Katz, R.S. (2013) 'Should we believe that improved intra-party democracy would arrest party decline?', in Cross, W.P. and Katz, R.S. (eds.) *The challenges of intra-party democracy*. Oxford: Oxford University Press.

Katz, R.S. and Mair, P. (1995) 'Changing models of party organization and party democracy: The Emergence of the Cartel Party', *Party Politics*, 1(1), p5–28.
Kelsen, H. (2013 [1929]). *The essence and value of democracy*. Plymouth: Rowman & Littlefield Publishers.
Knight, J. and Schwartzberg, M. (2020) 'Institutional bargaining for democratic theorists (or how we learned to stop worrying and love haggling)', *Annual Review of Political Science*, 23, p259–276.
Leydet, D. (2015) 'Partisan legislatures and democratic deliberation', *The Journal of Political Philosophy*, 23(3), p235–260.
Mair, P. (2013) *Ruling the void: The hollowing of western democracy*. London: Verso.
Manin, B. (1987) 'On legitimacy and political deliberation', *Political Theory*, 15(3), p338–368.
McCormick, J.P. (2011) *Machiavellian democracy*. Cambridge: Cambridge University Press.
Mill, J.S. (1989) *'On liberty' and other writings*. Cambridge: Cambridge University Press.
Muirhead, R. (2006) 'A defense of party spirit', *Perspectives on Politics*, 4(4), p713–727.
Muirhead, R. (2019) 'Partisan justification', *Political Theory*, 47(1), p82–89.
Muirhead, R. and Rosenblum, N.L. (2006) 'Political liberalism vs. "The great game of politics": The politics of political liberalism', *Perspectives on Politics*, 4(1), p99–108.
Muirhead, R. and Rosenblum, N.L. (2012) 'The partisan connection', *California Circuit Law Review*, 3, p99–112.
Muirhead, R. and Rosenblum, N.L. (2020) 'The political theory of parties and partisanship: Catching up', *Annual Review of Political Science*, 23(1), p95–110.
Pearse, H. and Warren, M.E. (eds.) (2008) *Designing deliberative democracy: The British Columbia citizen's assembly*. Cambridge: Cambridge University Press.
Przeworski, A. (2010) 'Consensus, conflict, and compromise in western thought on representative government', *Procedia Social and Behavioral Sciences*, 2, p7042–7055.
Ragazzoni, D. (2018) 'Political compromise in party democracy: An overlooked puzzle in Kelsen's democratic theory', in Rostboll, C.F. and Scavenius, T. (eds.) *Compromise and disagreement in contemporary political theory*. New York: Routledge, pp. 95–112.
Rawls, J. (1999) *A theory of justice, revised edition*. Cambridge: Belknap Press of Harvard University Press.
Rawls, J. (2005) *Political liberalism, expanded edition*. New York: Columbia University Press.
Rosanvallon, P. (2008) *Counter-democracy: Politics in an age of distrust*. Cambridge: Cambridge University Press.
Rosenblum, N. (2008) *On the side of the angels. An appreciation of parties and partisanship*. Princeton: Princeton University Press.
Rosenbluth, F.M. and Shapiro, I. (2018) *Responsible parties: Saving democracy from itself*. New Haven: Yale University Press.
Rummens, S. (2012) 'Staging deliberation: The role of representative institutions in the deliberative democratic process', *The Journal of Political Philosophy*, 20(1), p23–44.
Sabl, A. (2015) 'The two cultures of democratic theory: Responsiveness, democratic quality, and the empirical-normative divide', *Perspectives on Politics*, 13(2), p345–365.
Schumpeter, J. (2003 [1943]). *Capitalism, socialism and democracy*. London: Routledge.
Shapiro, I. (2002) 'Problems, methods, and theories in the study of politics, or what is wrong with political science and what to do about it', *Political Theory*, 30(4), p596–619.
Shapiro, I. (2003) *The state of democratic theory*. Princeton: Princeton University Press.
Skjonsberg, M. (2021) *The persistence of party: Ideas of harmonious discord in eighteenth-century Britain*. Cambridge: Cambridge University Press.
Teorell, J. (1999) 'A deliberative defence of intra-party democracy', *Party Politics*, 5(3), p363–382.
Urbinati, N. (2006) *Representative democracy: Principles and genealogy*. Chicago: The University of Chicago Press.
Van Biezen, I. and Saward, M. (2008) 'Democratic theorists and party scholars: Why they don't talk to each other, and why they should', *Perspectives on Politics*, 6(1), p21–35.
Waldron, J. (2016) *Political theory: Essays on institutions*. Cambridge and London: Harvard University Press.
White, J. and Ypi, L. (2016) *The meaning of partisanship*. Oxford: Oxford University Press.
Wolkenstein, F. (2019) 'Agents of popular sovereignty', *Political Theory*, 47(3), p338–362.
Wolkenstein, F. (2020) *Rethinking party reform*. Oxford: Oxford University Press.
Wolkenstein, F. and Wratil, C. (2021) 'Multidimensional representation', *American Journal of Political Science*, 65(4), p862–876.
Young, I.M. (2000) *Inclusion and democracy*. Oxford: Oxford University Press.

3
PARTY SYSTEMS AND PARTY SYSTEM CHANGE

Zsolt Enyedi and Fernando Casal Bértoa

The analysis of party systems is the study of political parties and their relations. The latter component, the interactions of parties, constitutes the core of the system-concept. As formulated most sharply by Sartori[1]: 'a party system is precisely the system of *interactions* resulting from inter-party competition' (1976, 44, own italics). This definition implies that party system analysis must go beyond the review of the characteristics of individual parties and that there must be some continuity in the set of actors and in their interactions, otherwise the term 'system' would not apply.[2] In other words, when we talk about interactions in this context, we must mean recurring, predictable interactions.

Since systematic party system studies emerged in the 1950s, they have constituted a core research programme within the larger field of comparative politics. These studies encompass the analysis of regular patterns of party politics in different dimensions, especially ideology, organisation, linkages to society, and competitive strategies, and in different fields, especially in electoral, parliamentary, and governmental arenas. The first generations of studies (Duverger 1954; Dahl 1966; Lipset and Rokkan 1967; Daalder 1987) typically had a qualitative approach and focused on the study of consolidated Western democracies (cf. Mair and Smith 1990; Broughton and Donovan 1999). The end of the Cold War, with the emergence of new fragile democracies, and advancements in quantitative techniques enabled the proliferation of large-N studies and a more global perspective (e.g. Pelizzo and Nwokora 2018).[3]

The literature on party systems and party system change can be further divided into several sub-literatures. The first focuses on the representative function of parties, and discusses party system change through the lens of changing relations between parties, social groups, and group-specific interests and attitudes. The second is concerned with the degree of dispersion of power within the party system. This approach emphasises the size of political parties as the main indicator of their influence and focuses on the number of parties in party systems. The third examines the way parties behave vis-à-vis each other, contrasting more or less competitive or consensual and more or less ideological or pragmatic modes of behaviour. The fourth body of work thinks of parties as actors standing for distinct positions in an ideological spectrum. The final line of research discusses the institutionalisation of party politics, and it either focuses on the stabilisation of voting preferences (the volatility approach) or on the stabilisation of inter-party relations (the closure approach).

Many publications on party systems aim at creating ideal-typical models and then assign real-life cases to their respective theoretical categories. Such studies do not necessarily address the issue of change, at least not explicitly. But because change is typically understood as a shift from one type to another (Mair 2006), the various classifications and typologies can assist us in analysing change. Alternatively, change can be conceptualised in a quantitative way. In this case, types are disregarded, and the focus is on the differences in degree. In the case of fragmentation or institutionalisation, for example, the movement of party systems on the continuum between the minimum and maximum values can be understood as a form of party system change. The rest of the chapter provides a critical discussion of the various research traditions and identifies key examples of quantitative and qualitative studies on party system transformation. We conclude by reflecting on the need for interaction-based indices of party system dynamics that can also 'travel' across regions.

The social and attitudinal aspect

The first major theoretical approach studies how socio-political cleavages play a vital role in providing both the support bases and the rationale of parties. In this literature, party politics is seen as structured around social conflicts. The paradigmatic example of this approach is Lipset and Rokkan's (1967) highly influential study about the consolidation of West European party systems.

In this approach, voters identify their interests and develop their party preferences on the basis of their sociological position (class, religion, ethnicity, urban/rural occupation/residence, etc.) and the values associated with them. The existence of social cleavages leads to enduring electoral alignments. When societies lack well-organised societal cleavages, party systems become susceptible to the swings associated with personality politics (Evans and Whitefield 1993).

Some analysts (Zuckerman 1975; Knutsen 1988; Enyedi 2008; Deegan-Krause and Enyedi 2010), while recognising that enduring cleavages do structure party systems, argue that these cleavages can be political rather than sociological in origin and that elite agency may have a crucial role in shaping the contours of social alignments. Ecclesiastical elites influence the boundaries of religious groups, socialist ideologues shape working-class identities, and parties can maintain conflicts across generations even if the original socio-demographic underpinning of these conflicts has faded away.

The Lipset and Rokkan's 'freezing hypothesis' suggested that the loyalties of the electorate and the parties are anchored by few structural divides. While this analysis may have been in line with the social reality in the 1960s, many subsequent developments pointed in the opposite direction: towards 'dealignment' and general de-structuration in party politics. The decline of the blue-collar working class, the process of globalisation and secularisation, and the even more general shift towards individualisation and detachment from social groups decreased the role of large socio-structural blocs in determining the behaviour of voters and parties.

The fundamental alternative to dealignment is 're-alignment'. The term re-alignment typically refers to the successions of various distinct socio-political configurations: long spells of stability divided by periods of critical junctures (Hooghe and Marks 2018). Such junctures occur when new conflicts lead to novel alliances among social groups. In multi-party systems, the transitions from one configuration to another usually entail the emergence of new parties that do not fit into old conflict-patterns. In two-party systems, on the other hand, the same parties may have a continuous existence while radically changing electorates and programmatic positions.

The literature discussing the transformations of American party politics also identifies periodic realignments that separate different successive party systems from each other (Sundquist 1983; Burnham 1986). One of the most spectacular shifts turned the Democratic Party from the party of white Southerners into the representative of the African-American community. The New Deal reforms of President Roosevelt, and the subsequent refusal of Republicans to support civil rights, led to a new alignment, one that is still shaping electoral behaviour.

Of course, given that social processes are cumulative in nature, the sociological approach also finds gradual changes in what social interests parties represent, and many authors consider the secular, long-term realignments to be more important than rupture-like changes. The transformation of many social-democratic parties from forces of the working class into representatives of the highly educated and of service sector employees is a case in point. These developments are relevant, because they alter not only the profile of particular parties but also the central conflicts of party politics.

Contemporary partisan structures are shaped by social processes that started after the end of the Cold War: the growing salience of immigration, the politicisation of various cultural issues, the new dilemmas of welfare politics, the rise of populist parties, and the politicisation of European integration. In most accounts, the new political space appears as two dimensional, the first dimension being a version of the classical economic left-right (mainly concerning the degree and type of state redistribution), while the second is dominated by themes such as permissive versus traditional moral positions, and cosmopolitanism versus nationalism or communitarianism (Kriesi et al. 2006; Bornschier 2010; Beramendi et al. 2015).

Even if the space around them is better perceived as two dimensional, the parties themselves may align along one single axis. In Western Europe, for example, left-wing parties tend to be libertarian on cultural issues, and economically right-wing parties are often more authoritarian. In Eastern Europe, in contrast, a culturally conservative orientation is often associated with support for more redistribution (Kitschelt 1994). But the pro-welfare turn of many radical right-wing parties has recently moved the Western patterns closer to the Eastern one (see also Chapter 11).

In the context of issue-dimensions, party system change means not only the changing saliency of particular issues and the changing number of dimensions they are combined into but also the changing relations between the dimensions of the party system. In the latter regard, the most relevant question is whether or not these dimensions are independent of each other (Casal Bértoa 2014). Cleavages that initially cross-cut each other may become cumulative if political entrepreneurs manage to bundle them into a few divides. But the emergence of new issues can reverse the process, disintegrating previously consolidated socio-political blocs. In the Italian case, for example, Silvio Berlusconi was successful in decreasing the importance of minor cleavages within the right, and Italy moved towards a two-bloc pattern, but the subsequent appearance of various populist forces undermined the unidimensional and bipolar logic of the Berlusconi era. These processes are always the outcome of the interaction between deep-seated socio-cultural changes and party strategies aimed at maximising support and access to power.

The sociological approach provides a valuable contribution to the analysis of party systems even if parties are not regarded as the representatives of social groups. Policies cannot be entirely divorced from social preferences and interests, and party strategies cannot avoid reflections on policies. Therefore, the social environment will always constrain and structure party relations, even if the political dynamic is not always predictable from the social conditions.

Size and balance in party politics

The most conventional approach to party system analysis is, in fact, not to bother with the social and attitudinal underpinning of party support but to focus on the number of parties as an indicator of the dispersion of power. The first truly systematic theory of the power of numbers belongs to Duverger (1954), who contrasted one-party and pluralist systems, and, within the second category, two-party systems, associated with stable and consensual democracies, and multi-party systems, associated with unstable and conflictual politics.

Subsequently, the 'two versus many' dichotomy was refined by adding intermediate categories and by complementing the numeric dimension with supplementary criteria. Blondel (1968) introduced the criterion of relative size, distinguishing between two-party systems (in which the two main parties together reach 90 per cent of the vote), and multi-party systems with or without dominant parties. He also introduced the so-called two-and-a-half party system type, an intermediate category containing three parties, two of them much larger than the third one.

The distinction between dominant versus non-dominant parties focuses attention on the likelihood of parties attaining governmental power. The relevance of this perspective was also reflected in Rokkan's (1968) party system typology. This model concentrated on the likelihood of single-party majorities and on the degree to which there was a fragmentation among the minority parties. He contrasted the 'British-German' type, in which the system is dominated by competition between two major parties, complemented by a third, minor party, with the 'Scandinavian'-type in which one big party regularly confronts a more or less formalised alliance between three or four smaller parties, and, finally, an 'even' multi-party system in which competition revolves around three or more parties of equivalent size. This typology took into consideration the distance that separates the largest party from the majority threshold, the second party from the largest, the third party from the second, and so on.

The balance of power approach had a major influence on typologies developed at the end of the twentieth century. Ware (1996), for example, distinguished between predominant party systems, two-party systems, two-and-a-half party systems, and systems with more than two-and-a half parties. The latter category was further divided into systems with one large party, winning 45–50 per cent of legislative seats, and several much smaller ones; systems with two large parties, obtaining more than 65 per cent of seats; and so-called 'even' party systems, in which the largest party obtains less than 45 per cent of seats and the two largest parties obtain less than 65 per cent of the seats.

The phenomenon underlying all these studies is fragmentation. Party systems can be perceived as falling into two large categories: concentrated and fragmented systems. There are many ways to operationalise this dimension in a continuous fashion, and to apply the measurement to the electoral or the parliamentary arena,[4] but this strategy leads to distinct party system types only if one establishes cut-off points within the continuum.

The size of parties and their number play a central role in defining what sort of government coalitions is possible and the competitiveness of elections. The studies focusing on these issues also highlight the role of institutional parameters, as the thresholds needed to be reached for a majority status or for entering the legislature are largely defined by legal-constitutional regulations.

Fragmentation-based approaches often assume that individual parties are the principal actors in politics, and tend to neglect the role of party blocs and alliances. In empirical studies that cover many party systems and large time-spans, this neglect is understandable. But it is important to remember that, in multi-party systems, parties often campaign and compete with each other in teams. Scholars should remain sensitive to such dynamics when they study party systems. Therefore, quantitative analyses need to be accompanied by qualitative assessments of party competition and party autonomy.

Competition: stakes, uncertainty, and style

There exist typologies that place the nature of competition front and centre. At the most abstract level, the degree of competitiveness of a party system equals the degree of uncertainty about the outcome of elections. In competitive systems, the bargaining power of the parties depends on their electoral appeal (Kitschelt 2007, 533).

Many of the classical models of party systems consider the competitive style of parties, that is, their behaviour towards each other. Dahl (1966), for example, distinguished between strictly competitive systems, co-operative-competitive systems, coalescent-competitive systems, and strictly coalescent systems. LaPalombara and Weimer (1966) also considered the style of competition as central, differentiating between systems in which parties behave in an ideological and combative fashion from those in which a more pragmatic orientation prevails. Their model also incorporated the likelihood of one force being more successful than all others, thereby differentiating hegemonic systems, where the incumbents' grip on power is solid, from alternating, that is, competitive systems. The combination of the two dimensions leads to a fourfold typology: (1) systems with ideological alternation; (2) systems with pragmatic alternation; (3) ideologically hegemonic systems; and (4) pragmatically hegemonic systems.

Finally, Kitschelt and his colleagues (2010) differentiated between charismatic, clientelistic, and programmatic party strategies and ranked party systems according to the degree to which party behaviour can be explained by programmatic structures. When this is the case, that is, the appeal of the programmes decides the outcome of the elections, party politics is comparable to the logic of the markets: winning and losing is a function of the distribution of demand and of the ability of parties to offer a matching supply. This is less the case if elections are about the personal appeal of candidates, and even less so if voting is determined by membership in clientelistic networks.

The study of the role of competitive qualities of a system is crucial for determining whether democratic accountability is feasible or not, since only in party systems characterised by programmatic competition can one associate parties and politicians with policy-relevant promises made to the electorate at large.

The Sartorian tradition: ideological competition determined by the number of parties

The fourth type of approach digs deep into the nature of programme-based competition, taking the fragmentation of the party landscape into account. In a flourishing literature, stemming from Schumpeter (1942) and Downs (1957), voters and parties are pictured as rational actors, located within an issue-space, typically identified with the left-right continuum. Since rational voters are expected to support the party closest to them in this space, the ideological profile of the parties reflects the preference-distribution of the electorate, enabling the analyst to foresee the competitive dynamics of the system.

Within the ideological space, parties can converge or diverge, creating more or less polarisation.[5] Polarisation is a constitutive dimension of the most influential typology of the field, developed by Sartori (1976). In this model, centripetal and centrifugal patterns of competition are contrasted, the latter meaning either the movement of the parties towards the extremes or the growth in size of extremist parties due to the movement of the voters away from the centre of the party system.

Sartori's model was, in fact, a synthesis between the fragmentation and the competition-centred approaches. He complemented the focus on numbers with the concern about the ideological distance between the polar opposites of the party system, and differentiated between one-party, hegemonic, predominant, two-party, moderate pluralist, polarised pluralist, and atomised systems.

The two-party and the moderate pluralist configurations exhibit centripetal patterns of competition and low ideological distance between the parties, but in the latter coalitions are needed in order to create majority governments. Therefore, two major alliances of parties compete with each other. Polarised pluralist systems are by definition fragmented. The competition of more than five parties stretches the ideological spectrum, as each party wants to distinguish itself from its neighbours. These systems are characterised by the presence of relevant anti-system parties, that is, parties whose fundamental goal is to undermine the legitimacy of the political regime. Anti-system parties form bilateral opposition to governing parties which occupy the centre-space, offering mutually exclusive and incompatible alternatives to the government. The typical result is the perpetual rule of the centre, political immobilism, multipolarity, a flow of voters from the centrist parties to the extremes, and an irresponsible opposition (Sartori 1976, 132–140). Finally, the 'predominant' configuration reflects not a particular ideological formula or a particular number of the parties, but the ability of one of them to monopolise the executive arena.

While the types described by Sartori acquire some degree of inertia once established, there is room for change. If public opinion in a two-party system becomes more polarised, the degree of fragmentation is also likely to increase. Similarly, in a polarised pluralist system, the radical parties may move towards the centre if they can hope to have some say in governing, thereby limiting the centrifugal nature of the competition. Moreover, as Hazan (1997) has demonstrated, centrist parties may forge alliances with moderate parties constraining the willingness of the latter to embark on a road towards radicalisation.

It is somewhat unclear whether Sartori expected polarised pluralist systems to collapse, as happened in Weimar Germany. On this question, many authors follow the pragmatic approach of von Beyme (1985), who differentiated between those configurations of polarised pluralism where the centre parties are able to stabilise their governmental status and those where the centrifugal tendencies lead to the collapse of the centre.

The Sartori model assumes a close link between fragmentation and polarisation: the higher the number of parties, the higher the ideological distance in the system. Only societies segmented into distinct subcultures are exceptions: they can have many parties without having large degree of polarisation. Electoral volatility is also affected by these factors. More parties allow for more movement among parties, especially if these parties are ideologically close to each other. A larger degree of polarisation, on the other hand, decreases vote switching (Dejaeghere and Dassonneville 2017), because in polarised systems, leaving one party behind and joining another one require a major political and psychological re-positioning.

As mentioned earlier, while fragmentation and polarisation together structure most of Sartori's typology, the essence of the predominant type is the lack of power alternation. The latter aspect plays a larger role in Nwokora and Pelizzo's (2018) typology. They count how often a system shifts among the types identified by Sartori, but also take into consideration whether the switches happen between adjacent types or more distant ones and how many different types of changes occur. The distance between the types is defined by their location on the continuum that begins with one-party systems and ends with atomised systems, with hegemonic, predominant, two-party, moderate pluralist, and polarised pluralist systems in between, in this order.

Sartori's typology, while subjected to many criticisms and refinements (Smith 1990; Siaroff 2000; Mair 2006; Wolinetz 2006; Golosov 2010b; Ignazi 2017), still constitutes the most important point of departure when examining party system change. It has, however, proved to be more useful for the analysis of established democracies than for the interpretation of newly emerging party systems. The latter are nowadays more typically approached through the analytic lens of party system institutionalisation.

Institutionalisation-centred approaches

Originating in the aftermath of the Cold War, the last approach to be discussed in this chapter sidesteps typologies and concentrates on the degree of stability in the structure of inter-party competition instead. The focus on institutionalisation was triggered by the surge of new 'Third Wave' party systems in Eastern Europe, Sub-Saharan Africa, Central America, and South-east Asia characterised by what Sartori would call 'fluid polities' (Mainwaring and Torcal 2006). Using continuous indicators such as Pedersen's electoral volatility index (Pedersen 1979), institutionalisation scholars typically try to capture systemic change in a quantitative, rather than qualitative, manner. While some studies are concerned with the stability of party organisations (Kreuzer and Pettai 2003; Sikk and Köker 2019), or with the stability of the parties' programmatic orientations (Whitefield and Rohrschneider 2009; Rovny and Polk 2017; Borbáth 2021), the bulk of them concentrate on stability at electoral or governmental level.

Instability is typically evaluated negatively, but it can also be perceived as a form of flexibility or adaptability to the changing social, economic, or demographic conditions. Some studies indeed indicate that, for example, high volatility makes parties more responsive (Dassonneville 2018).

The volatility approach and the electoral arena

The concern with the degree of electoral stability has a long history in political science, but in the context of party system institutionalisation, it became central in the 1990s through the pioneering work of Mainwaring and Scully (1995) on Latin America. Mainwaring's initial framework suggested ideological, socio-political, and organisational aspects to distinguish between well institutionalised and weakly institutionalised (or inchoate) party systems. However, in later works, volatility emerged as the principal indicator of stability (Mainwaring 2018). According to this approach, only systems where parties enjoy relatively similar rates of electoral support from one election to the other are to be classified as institutionalised.

Volatility is typically operationalised with the help of Pedersen's index which tries to capture the degree of change in voters' partisan preferences from one election to the next. The index reflects both the movement of voters among parties and the organisational continuity of parties so, in this sense, it is a relatively blunt instrument (Casal Bértoa, Deegan-Krause and Haughton 2017). In order to tackle this problem, scholars like Rose and Munro (2003) proposed a distinction – later elaborated by Powell and Tucker (2014) – between 'supply-side' (or Type A) and 'demand-side' (or Type B) volatility.[6] While the latter looks at electoral change among established parties, the former captures electoral instability due to the exit of old parties and the entry of new ones. Such an approach allows scholars to distinguish intermediate categories between ideal institutionalisation and complete inchoateness: namely, stable but regenerated party systems, typical of polities where old parties conserve a faithful following in spite of the continuous appearance of new political forces, and unstable but not regenerated party systems, where voters continuously change their voting preferences among relatively steady political parties (Chiaramonte and Emanuele 2017, 382–384; Lago and Torcal 2020, 572).

The closure approach and the governmental arena

Building upon Sartori's work, Mair (1997) developed a theory of party system change that focused on the structure of inter-party competition but replaced the electoral with the governmental arena, arguing that the latter is the core of party systems. His ambition was to strike a middle ground between excessively broad approaches that count any minor change in the supply or balance of parties as a change of the party system and the too narrow perspectives that limit the analysis of party system change to the shifts from one configuration to another.

Mair considered both the degree and the format of competition crucial. The degree of competition for votes depends to a large extent on the strength of collective identities. If they are crystallised and politicised, and if they have an adequate expression through a political party, then elections simply record the size of the groups. Multi-party systems can effectively articulate such fragmented identities and demands, but they do not necessarily provide room for actual competition for office. Bipolar systems, on the other hand, tend to evolve around competing governmental alternatives. Floating voters, even if small in numbers, can make the system competitive.

As far as the format of competition is concerned, Mair (1997) introduced three defining aspects: (1) type of *alternation*, (2) the cabinets' organisational makeup (*formula*), and (3) *access* of parties to government. The 'alternation' variable captures the extent to which membership in government is flexible or not. In this regard, there are three possibilities: executive control can change from one party or party coalition to another (wholesale alternation), or it may not change at all (non-alternation), or the newly formed cabinets may contain at least one party from the previous government and one from the opposition (partial alternation). The 'formula' criterion considers the extent to which any governing makeup resembles previously established (familiar formula) patterns (innovative formula). The third criterion, 'access', evaluates each governing party against its own executive record, indicating whether all parties are equally likely to obtain executive power (open access), or certain parties have privileged access to it (closed access). In this context, a party system changes when there is a change in the pattern of competition alternation, when a new governing alternative emerges, and/or when a new party or alliance gains access to office for the first time (Mair 2006, 66).

The initially dichotomic concept of closure was later reconceptualised in a continuous fashion, and party system closure captured in this particular way was shown to be strongly related to the survival of democracies (Casal Bértoa and Enyedi 2021), thereby suggesting that the characteristics of party systems are indeed consequential for the functioning of modern societies.

Conclusions and avenues for further research

The study of stability and change in party politics with the help of party system typologies constitutes one of the most venerable traditions in comparative politics. It is much less certain whether this tradition can serve as the conceptual background for cutting-edge research on the dynamics of contemporary party politics. In order to remain relevant, future works in the field need to provide us with a transparent model of how gradual, evolutionary transformations and qualitative shifts combine and under which conditions different types of changes are more likely. We also need to integrate findings regarding the strategic innovations of political actors (typically opposition parties) aimed at re-aligning the ideological space in their favour (McLean 2002), with the knowledge we have about the changes induced by structural sociological processes.

While we know a reasonable amount about the typical causes of systemic change, we need to explore further their consequences. The analysis of party systems requires a holistic approach to party politics, but one that is, at the same time, well grounded in measurable phenomena. In order to reach these goals, the experience of all world regions needs to be taken into consideration, and the conceptual toolbox needs to be further revised in order to make it applicable to the varying realities across the globe. Fortunately, the theoretical building blocks of the literature, such as fragmentation, polarisation, party alliances, and style of competition, are sufficiently abstract to travel well across cultures, but the manifestation of these general concepts can be highly context- and system-specific, and therefore researchers need to start a new dialogue between operationalisation and concept-formation, with the aim of establishing theoretical frameworks that allow proper comparative analysis.

Finally, further steps are needed to quantify the interactions of parties. We started the chapter by emphasising the role of interactions, but statistically based analyses are rarely able to reflect this emphasis. Instead of leaving the study of interactions to case studies, researchers must find a way to integrate them into comparative and large-N works.

Notes

1 Discussed already by Eckstein (1968).
2 As captured in Sanchez's (2009) notion of 'party non-systems'.
3 Not precluding further developments in the more qualitative, small-N comparative approach (Loomes 2012; Hicken and Kuchonta 2014).
4 See Rae 1967; Molinar 1991; Golosov 2010a; but Laakso and Taagepera's (1979) 'effective' number of parties is the most widely used indicator.
5 Some indices of polarisation simply capture the left-right ideological distance between the two largest (Ware 1996) or leftmost and rightmost (Abedi 2002) parties. Others (Sani and Sartori 1983) take the absolute difference between the mean location divided by the theoretical maximum of the scale. The most frequently used measures weight ideological distances on the basis of the percentage of votes (Dalton 2008) or seats (Hazan 1997) of the respective parties.
6 Names for these phenomena differ: 'cumulative' and 'balancing' volatility (Sikk 2005), 'extra-system' and 'intra-system' volatility (Mainwaring, Gervasoni and España 2017), 'volatility by regeneration' and 'by alteration' (Chiaramonte and Emanuele 2017), 'exogenous' and 'endogenous' volatility (Lago and Torcal 2020).

References

Abedi, A. (2002) 'Challenges to established parties: The effects of party system features on the electoral fortunes of anti-political-establishment parties', *European Journal of Political Research*, 41(4), p551–583.
Beramendi, P., Häusermann, S., Kitschelt, H. and Kriesi, H. (eds.) (2015) *The politics of advanced capitalism*. Cambridge: Cambridge University Press.
Beyme, K. von (1985) *Political parties in western democracies*. Aldershot: Gower.
Blondel, J. (1968) 'Party systems and patterns of government in western democracies', *Canadian Journal of Political Science*, 1(2), p180–203.
Borbáth, E. (2021) 'Two faces of party system stability: Programmatic change and party replacement', *Party Politics*, 27(5), p996–1008.
Bornschier, S. (2010) 'The new cultural divide and the two-dimensional political space in Western Europe', *West European Politics*, 33(3), p419–444.
Broughton, D. and Donovan, M. (1999) *Changing party systems in Western Europe*. London: Pinter.
Burnham, W.D. (1986) 'Periodization schemes and party systems: The 'system of 1896' as a case in point', *Social Science History*, 10(3), p263–314.

Casal Bértoa, F. (2014) 'Party systems and cleavage structures revisited: A sociological explanation of party system institutionalization in East Central Europe', *Party Politics*, 20(1), p16–36.

Casal Bértoa, F., Deegan-Krause, K. and Haughton, T. (2017) 'The volatility of volatility: measuring change in party vote shares', *Electoral Studies*, 50, p142–156.

Casal Bértoa, F. and Enyedi, Z. (2021) *Party system closure: Party alliances, government alternatives, and democracy in Europe*. Oxford: Oxford University Press.

Chiaramonte, A. and Emanuele, V. (2017) 'Party system volatility, regeneration and de-institutionalization in Western Europe (1945–2015)', *Party Politics*, 23(4), p376–388.

Daalder, H. (ed.) (1987) *Party systems in Denmark, Austria, Switzerland, the Netherlands and Belgium*. New York: St. Martin's Press.

Dahl, R.A. (1966) 'Patterns of opposition', in Dahl, R.A. (ed.) *Political oppositions in western democracies*. New Haven: Yale University Press, pp. 332–47.

Dalton, R.J. (2008) 'The quantity and the quality of party systems: Party system polarization, its measurement, and its consequences', *Comparative Political Studies*, 41(7), p899–920.

Dassonneville, R. (2018) 'Electoral volatility and parties' ideological responsiveness', *European Journal of Political Research*, 57(4), p808–828.

Deegan-Krause, K. and Enyedi, Z. (2010) 'Agency and the structure of party competition: alignment, stability and the role of political elites', *West European Politics*, 33(3), p686–710.

Dejaeghere, Y. and Dassonneville, R. (2017) 'A comparative investigation into the effects of party-system variables on party switching using individual-level data', *Party Politics*, 23(2), p110–123.

Downs, A. (1957) *An economic theory of democracy*. New York: Harper and Row.

Duverger, M. (1954) *Political parties: Their organization and activities in the modern state*. London: Methuen.

Eckstein, H. (1968) 'Party systems', in *International encyclopedia of the social sciences*, vol. 11, New York: Crowell, Collier & Macmillan, pp. 436–53.

Enyedi, Z. (2008) 'The social and attitudinal basis of political parties: Cleavage politics revisited', *European Review*, 16(3), p287–304.

Evans, G. and Whitefield, S. (1993) 'Identifying the bases of party competition in Eastern Europe', *British Journal of Political Science*, 23(4), p521–548.

Golosov, G.V. (2010a) 'The effective number of parties: A new approach', *Party Politics*, 16(2), p171–192.

Golosov, G.V. (2010b) 'Party system classification: A methodological inquiry', *Party Politics*, 17(5), p539–560.

Hazan, R.Y. (1997) *Centre parties: Polarization and competition in European parliamentary democracies*. London: Pinter.

Hicken, A. and Kuchonta, E. (2014) *Party system institutionalization in Asia: Democracies, autocracies, and the shadows of the past*. Cambridge: Cambridge University Press.

Hooghe, L. and Marks, G. (2018) 'Cleavage theory meets Europe's crises: Lipset, Rokkan, and the transnational cleavage', *Journal of European Public Policy*, 25(1), p109–135.

Ignazi, P. (2017) 'Sartori's party system typology and the Italian case: The unanticipated outcome of a polarised pluralism without anti-system parties', *Contemporary Italian Politics*, 9(3), p262–276.

Kitschelt, H. (1994) *The transformation of European social democracy*. New York: Cambridge University Press.

Kitschelt, H. (2007) 'Party systems', in Boix, C. and Stokes, S. (eds.) *The Oxford handbook of comparative politics*. Oxford: Oxford University Press, pp. 522–554.

Kitschelt, H., Hawkins, K., Luna, J., Rosas, G. and Zechmeister, E. (2010) *Latin American party systems*. Cambridge: Cambridge University Press.

Knutsen, O. (1988) 'The impact of structural and ideological party cleavages in West European democracies: A comparative empirical analysis', *British Journal of Political Science*, 18(3), p323–352.

Kreuzer, M. and Pettai, V. (2003) 'Patterns of political instability: Affiliation patterns of politicians and voters in post-Communist Estonia, Latvia, and Lithuania', *Studies in Comparative International Development*, 38(2), p76–98.

Kriesi, H., Grande, E., Lachat, R., Dolezal, M., Bornschier, S, and Frey, T. (2006) 'Globalization and the transformation of the national political space: Six European countries compared', *European Journal of Political Research*, 45(6), p921–56.

Laakso, M. and Taagepera, R. (1979) "Effective' number of parties. A measure with application to West Europe', *Comparative Political Studies*, 12(1), p3–27.

Lago, I. and Torcal, M. (2020) 'Electoral coordination and party system institutionalization', *Party Politics*, 26(5), p570–580.

LaPalombara, J. and Weiner, M. (1966) 'The origin and development of political parties', in LaPalombara, J. and Weiner, M. (eds.) *Political parties and political development*. Princeton: Princeton University Press, pp. 3–42.

Lipset, S.M. and Rokkan, S. (1967) 'Cleavage structures, party systems and voter alignments: An introduction', in Lipset, S.M. and Rokkan, S. (eds.) *Party systems and voter alignments*. New York: Free Press, pp. 1–64.

Loomes, G. (2012) *Party strategies in Western Europe: Party competition and electoral outcomes*. London: Routledge.

Mainwaring, S. (2018) 'Party system institutionalization in contemporary Latin America', in Mainwaring, S. (ed.) *Party systems in Latin America: Institutionalization, decay and collapse*. Cambridge: Cambridge University Press.

Mainwaring, S., Gervasoni, C. and España, A. (2017) 'Extra and within-system electoral volatility', *Party Politics*, 23(6), p623–635.

Mainwaring, S. and Scully, T. (1995) *Building democratic institutions: Party systems in Latin America*. Stanford: Stanford University Press.

Mainwaring, S. and Torcal, M. (2006) 'Party system institutionalization and party system theory after the third wave of democratization', in Katz, R.S. and Crotty, W.J. (eds.) *Handbook of party politics*. London: Sage, pp. 204–227.

Mair, P. (2006) 'Party system change', in Katz, R.S. and Crotty, W.J. (eds.) *Handbook of party politics*. London: Sage, pp. 63–73.

Mair, P. (1997) *Party system change. Approaches and interpretations*. Oxford: Clarendon Press.

Mair, P. and Smith, G. (1990) *Understanding party system change in Western Europe*. London: Psychology Press.

McLean, I.C. (2002) 'William H. Riker and the invention of heresthetic(s)', *British Journal of Political Science*, 32(2), p535–558.

Molinar, J. (1991) 'Counting the number of parties: An alternative index', *American Political Science Review*, 85(4), p1383–1391.

Nwokora, Z. and Pelizzo, R. (2018) 'Measuring party system change: A systems perspective', *Political Studies*, 66(1), p100–118.

Powell, E. and Tucker, J. (2014) 'Revisiting electoral volatility in post-communist countries: New data, new results and new approaches', *British Journal of Political Science*, 44(1), p123–147.

Pelizzo, R. and Nwokora, Z. (2018) 'Party system change and the quality of democracy in East Africa', *Politics and Policy*, 46(3), p505–528.

Pedersen, M. (1979) 'The dynamics of European party systems: Changing patterns of electoral volatility', *European Journal of Political Research*, 7(1), p1–26.

Rae, D.W. (1967) *The political consequences of electoral laws*. New Haven, CT: Yale University Press.

Rokkan, S. (1968) 'The growth and structuring of mass politics in smaller European democracies', *Comparative Studies in Society and History*, 10(2), p173–210.

Rose, R. and Munro, N. (2003) *Elections and parties in new European democracies*. Washington, DC: CQ Press.

Rovny, J. and Polk, J. (2017) 'Stepping in the same river twice: Stability amidst change in Eastern European party competition', *European Journal of Political Research*, 56(1), p188–198.

Sanchez, O. (2009) 'Party non-systems: A conceptual innovation', *Party Politics*, 15(4), p487–520.

Sani, G. and Sartori, G. (1983) 'Polarization, fragmentation and competition in western democracies', in Daalder, H. and Mair, P. (eds.) *Western European party systems – Continuity and change*. London: Sage, pp. 307–340.

Sartori, G. (1976) *Parties and party systems. A framework for analysis,* vol. I. Cambridge: Cambridge University Press.

Schumpeter, J. (1942) *Capitalism, socialism and democracy*. New York: Harper and Brothers.

Siaroff, A. (2000) *Comparative European party systems. An analysis of parliamentary elections since 1945*. London: Routledge.

Sikk, A. (2005) 'How unstable? Volatility and the genuinely new parties in Eastern Europe', *European Journal of Political Research*, 44(3), p391–412.

Sikk, A. and Köker, P. (2019) 'Party novelty and congruence: A new approach to measuring party change and volatility', *Party Politics*, 25(6), p759–770.

Smith, G. (1990) 'Core persistence, system change and the 'people's party'', in Mair, P. and Smith, G. (eds.) *Understanding party system change in Western Europe*. London: Frank Cass, pp. 157–68.

Sundquist, J.L. (1983) *Dynamics of the party system*. Washington: Brookings Institution.
Ware, A. (1996) *Political parties and party systems*. Oxford: Oxford University Press.
Whitefield, S. and Rohrschneider, R. (2009) 'Representational consistency: Stability and change in political cleavages in Central and Eastern Europe', *Politics & Policy*, 37(4), p667–690.
Wolinetz, S. (2006) 'Party systems and party system types', in Katz, R.S. and Crotty, W. (eds.) *Handbook of party politics*. London: Sage, pp. 51–62.
Zuckerman, A. (1975) 'Political cleavages: A conceptual and theoretical analysis', *British Journal of Political Science*, 5(2), p231–248.

PART 2

Party as an organisation

4
PARTY ORGANISATION

Anika Gauja

This chapter presents an overview of the research and scholarship on political parties as *organisations*. Tracing the trajectory of more than a century of scholarship in Europe, North America and elsewhere across the globe, it addresses three questions. First, what is distinctive about an organisational lens and how does it contribute to our understanding of parties and their place in democracy and how they have evolved over time? Second, what conceptual tools and models have party scholars developed to analyse the organisation of parties and the functions they perform? Third, what specific challenges – especially around questions of access – does party organisation research pose? While the chapter paints a broad picture of the development of party organisation research, highlights the key questions that have concerned scholars, and those that continue to animate their research, it pays particular attention to new and emerging themes and areas where scholarship is necessary and currently lacking. One such area is the impact of digital technologies on party organisation and participation. I argue that like political party organisations themselves, which are adapting to evolving technologies in the way in which they engage citizens, party organisation research also needs to evolve and adapt to developments in twenty-first-century politics in order to secure its ongoing relevance for both the public and scholarly communities. This includes working across (and with) various social science disciplines, for example, social movement studies, sociology, internet studies and media and communications, to fully capture the impact of changing technologies on modes of participation, shifting social norms and forms of political organisation.

Understanding political parties through the lens of organisation

As one of the oldest strands of research in political science (see e.g. Ostrogorski 1902; Michels 1916), the phrase 'party organisation' has carried multiple uses and meanings. It is often used to denote the part of a political party that exists to support representatives that have been elected to public office and implies an administrative or bureaucratic structure that may or may not be situated within a network of party supporters and/or individual members. However, the phrase 'organisation' can also be used more broadly to describe the way in which a political party is structured, its form and governance arrangements. This is how party organisation is conceptualised in the field of comparative party organisation research (see Gauja and Kosiara-Pedersen 2020), and how it is used here.

As Borz and Janda (2020, 3) argue, the concept of organisation itself is rarely interrogated in party research. Organisation can refer to the structure of a party and the relationships between its constituent actors in a formal sense – what appears in party constitutions or statutes, for example – or it can refer to how a political party operates in practice. Whether data sourced from formal documents or whether informal practices provide a more accurate picture of party organisation is a live debate in the field (Panebianco 1988; Katz and Mair 1993; Scarrow and Webb 2017, 13–14), but both perspectives form an important part of the body of comparative research. Party organisation invokes the concepts of structure and agency and may be either a constraining or enabling force depending on how power is distributed within the association. It is this complex relationship between organisation and control – that is, how power is exercised and distributed within political parties – that is of fundamental interest not only to party organisation scholars – but those concerned with governance more generally (e.g. policy positions, electoral competition and legislative decision-making).

To understand this distribution of power, party organisation researchers often focus on the numerous functions that parties perform, which are seen as central to the workings of representative democracy. Political parties provide policy and leadership/governance alternatives to the electorate; they aggregate and shape public opinion, provide sites for political participation and education, train political elites and select candidates for public office. Scholars who study party organisation ask questions about *how* parties perform these functions and *why they differ* (between parties and across time). Thus, party organisational studies are mostly concerned with intra-party relationships of power. Political parties develop their own internal logic and culture, and these play a crucial role in structuring their dynamics, how they respond to competitive demands and how they change and adapt over time. Nevertheless, there is also an inherent link between internal and external party competition: parties' internal structures and how conflict is avoided or mediated within the party itself will be shaped by how they respond to external pressures of political competition, be they policy-related, ideological, parliamentary or electoral.

Questions concerning party organisation are not exclusively empirical – they are also heavily influenced by normative democratic theory (Katz 2002, 88). For example, since the development of the first social democratic parties in Europe, party scholars have been concerned with questions of intra-party democracy. In this sub-field of inquiry, party scholars ask whether political parties *ought* to structure themselves and function in a particular manner. These normative questions also drive party scholars in searching for forms of party organisation and practices that can better serve modern society.

What do party organisations look like and what do they do?

More than a century of party scholarship has resulted in a proliferation of party types and models (Krouwel 2006, 249). The primary function of these models is to specify a party's relationship with society at a particular point in time or under a specific set of environmental conditions. In doing so, party models seek to describe the organisation of parties, the functions and activities that they perform, and how these have changed over time.

Various scholars have documented a trajectory of development from cadre parties, to mass parties, catch-all parties, to cartel parties and beyond (see also Chapter 1). Each of these party models describes a different type of organisation. Cadre parties – a feature of late nineteenth-century politics that pre-dated mass suffrage – were comprised of local, ad hoc networks of middle- and upper-class supporters that were organised around political elites (Ostrogorski 1902; Duverger 1959). The organisational characteristics of mass parties, which emerged in the early twentieth century in the era of universal suffrage, departed significantly from the cadre model. Described as the 'golden age' of mass party politics (Scarrow 2015, 61–68), the organisational characteristics of this model are now what is typically regarded as the normative standard for political parties and have often been mythologised. Mass party organisations developed to maximise the political participation and extra-parliamentary mobilisation and representation of groups previously excluded from the political process with well-articulated ideological programmes, a centralised bureaucracy and a substantial network of branches and ancillary social and political organisations that popularised participation in the party (e.g. Michels 1916; Kirchheimer 1966). From this 'heyday' of party organisational politics, mass parties then evolved into what are broadly termed 'catch-all' or electoral professional parties, characterised by a more professional party organisation primarily concerned with campaigning and appealing to a broader set of interests through a more 'dilute' ideological and electoral profile. Political participation in the catch-all party was similarly diminished, as these increasingly professionalised parties looked to experts for campaign support and policy advice (Kirchheimer 1966; Panebianco 1988).

Since the 1990s, the cartel party model has been one of the most influential and widely cited in party organisation research. Finding its most succinct expression in the work of Katz and Mair (1995, 2009, 2018), the cartel party model builds on these scholars' important theoretical distinction between the 'three faces' of party organisation: the party on the ground, the party in central office and the party in public office (Katz and Mair 1993). Prior models of party organisation privileged different faces of the party; for example, the party on the ground was instrumental in the mass party and the party in central office important to achieving the coordinated aims of the catch-all party. In contrast, the cartel party is characterised by a rebalancing of these three faces in favour of the party in public office and its organisation is inextricably tied to the state. Direct state support, through, for example, public funding, replaces the resources once provided by party members and supporters. With a focus on governing and maintaining the spoils provided by public office, cartel parties are largely removed from civil society and devoid of anything but a 'hollowed out' party organisation (Mair 2005, 2013). Not only has the cartel party theory prompted party organisation scholars to re-examine the normative role of parties as mechanisms of state–society linkage (Lawson and Merkl 1988; van Biezen 2014), it has also prompted new lines of research and inquiry into state support for political parties (van Biezen 2008; Nassmacher 2009), the relationship between a party's supporters, members and its elected representatives (Hazan and Rahat 2010; Scarrow 2015), and the policy processes of parties as participatory and representative institutions (Gauja 2013).

Theoretical conceptions of political parties, much like the objects they study, are didactic and adaptive. As the trajectory discussed earlier demonstrates, party models have evolved over time in response to the changing nature of political parties and the social, political and technological contexts in which they exist. Thus, as one model no longer serves to adequately explain the reality of party politics and organisation, a new theoretical construct emerges. The cartel party thesis is by no means the latest model in the evolution of party scholarship: in the quarter century since the publication of Katz and Mair's (1995) seminal article in *Party Politics*, several newer party models have been proposed, which aim to capture the impacts of marketisation and digitisation on political party organisation. These models include, for example, business-firm (Hopkin and Paolucci 1999), memberless (Mazzoleni and Voerman 2017), franchise (Carty 2004), entrepreneurial (Krouwel 2006) and digital parties (Margetts 2006; Gerbaudo 2019). The organisational essence of the business-firm party, for example, is the contracting out of essential functions, with only a 'lightweight organisation with the sole basic function of mobilising short-term support at election time' (Hopkin and Paolucci 1999, 315). With a limited membership, 'all party activities and tasks are brought under formal (commercial) contract in terms of labour, services and goods to be delivered to the "party"' (Krouwel 2006, 261). Memberless parties go one step further and have no members at all, 'because the party leader considers members detrimental to party cohesion and the party's main party function, namely, vote maximisation' (Mazzoleni and Voerman 2017, 789). These party models present something of a challenge to party organisation scholars, not only because of the rapidly evolving nature of these entities, because their structure and processes suggest very little organisation at all.

Party organisation and the digitalisation of politics

The internet and social media platforms in particular have radically altered political participation and changed practices of mobilisation and organisation. Political participation mediated by digital technologies and social media is characterised by its immediacy, the expectation that participants are able to see the effects of their actions, and it is driven by an adherence to specific interests or causes rather than movements or ideologies (Zuckerman 2014, 156–157).

Researchers have also highlighted the potential of new communication technologies for political organisations. This includes the emergence of many online groups, often labelled 'digital natives', which include both advocacy organisations such as MoveOn, as well as 'new' political parties such as the Pirate Party and the Five Star Movement (Karpf 2012; Chadwick 2013; Vromen 2017). It also encompasses the extent to which 'traditional' political parties and interest groups have embraced online platforms and digital technologies to perform campaigning, mobilisation and organising functions (Gauja 2017; Gibson, Greffet and Cantijoch 2017; Gerbaudo 2019; Kefford 2021).

What distinguishes this category of political parties and organisations is that the internet is more than an external tool: it is a form of communication that intersects with, and constitutes, organisation. Proposing the model of the 'digital party', Gerbaudo (2019, 4) suggests that these parties

> display evident commonalities in the way in which they promise to deliver a new politics supported by digital technology; a kind of politics that . . . professes to be more democratic, more open to ordinary people, more immediate and direct, more authentic and transparent.

The key defining feature of Margetts' 'cyber party' is that such parties use 'web-based technologies to strengthen the relationship between voters and the party, rather than traditional notions of membership' (2006, 531). Bennett, Segerberg and Knupfer's 'connective party' is distinguished by the fact that 'technologies of engagement are not just grafted onto existing bureaucratic organization, but actually replace core bureaucratic functions' (2018, 1656). These party models have significant implications for the organisational dimensions of political parties as 'technology platforms and affordances are indistinguishable from, and replace, key components of brick and mortar organisation and intra-party functions. These components include affiliation management, policy generation, leader and candidate selection, and public communication' (Bennett, Segerberg and Knupfer 2018, 1677).

Since political parties began creating websites, scholars have, however, taken a rather circumspect position on the overall impact of digital technologies on party organisations and their democratic consequences. On the one hand, it was feared that grassroots participation might be undermined by centralising tendencies of technology, prompting greater elite control of decision-making (see e.g. Lipow and Seyd 1995) and facilitating the process of marketing a 'hollowed out', member-less political party to voters (Gibson and Ward 2009, 88). On the other hand, advances in communication technologies might be seen to strengthen elements of the mass party model by facilitating communication between members, between members and the party, and enhancing its ability to mobilise citizens (Lofgren and Smith 2003). There is also significant debate – more so in the internet and communication literature than within party scholarship – surrounding the 'quality' of online political participation and the legitimacy of acts that are often described as 'clicktivism' or 'low-intensity participation' (see e.g. Halupka 2017; Dennis 2019).

Advances in digital technologies hold promise for the future of political parties and the continued relevance of their organisations. Chadwick and Stromer-Galley (2016, 285) argue that 'it is not at all clear that parties are dying'. Social media and the internet are fertile grounds for organisational experimentation, enabling political parties to harness the personalised forms of online engagement preferred by citizens to effectively aggregate interests and up-scale their mobilisation efforts.

Many opportunities have been identified by scholars linking new technologies to the renovation and rejuvenation of politics and democracy. Others point to the potential of new technologies to develop echo chambers and perpetuate a growing 'digital divide' between citizens. Comparing online political participation among young people in Australia, the UK and the USA, Xenos, Vromen and Loader (2014, 34) found that social media use generated political engagement and reduced political inequalities over time, through a process of generational replacement. A future research agenda for party organisation needs to examine these questions and ask whether or not new modes of organisation and technological advances enable political parties to perform their core functions, and whether the digitalisation of democracy replicates – or ameliorates – hierarchies and relationships of power that have been observed offline. Undertaking one of the first analyses of parties' use of ICTs, Gibson and Ward (1999, 364) reported that the 'organisational context' within which new technologies are harnessed is 'more important than the technology itself' when considering the impact on decision-making and communication: '[w]e need to be careful not to assume that the technology has an inherently democratic or decentralist nature. In respect of political parties, its impact depends partly on existing power structures, the balance of resources and philosophical outlook'. If the organisational context of parties matters, researchers might usefully consider whether certain party types or families are better suited to embracing digital technologies, or in maximising their democratic and participatory potential. This is a question that Ward and Voerman (2000, 213) asked in the context of the green parties more than two decades ago, with the conclusion that 'the greatest gains from adapting new media are more likely to be administrative (saving resources) and campaign based (establishing a profile), rather than participative'. It is a question that should be revisited today.

What do parties do? Subfields of party organisation research

Despite the diversity of models described earlier, each seeks to describe a party's relationship with society and the state and to specify the organisational basis of how political parties perform a series of common functions, including policy development, interest aggregation, political recruitment, campaigning and mobilisation. Many of these subfields are covered in chapters elsewhere in this handbook, so only a brief introduction to party organisation and political recruitment (candidate and leadership selection) is provided here. This discussion is designed to give an example of one area of 'cutting-edge' party organisation research and highlight some of the key questions that scholars have addressed in the last two decades.

As one of the principal activities of political parties, candidate selection is crucial to understanding where power lies within political parties and how it is exercised. It is a high-stakes activity, involving personal, professional and partisan ambitions and factional struggles, but it also offers 'the best opportunity for rank-and-file voters to exercise influence within their party and to have an (indirect) influence on public policy' (Cross 2008, 598). Because of the importance of candidate selection, both for the party as a whole and for the individuals and groups within it, the way in which it is conducted is inextricably linked to the nature of the organisation (see e.g. Katz 2002). However, candidate selection is equally important outside the political party, as it influences the choices before voters, the composition of parliaments, cohesion and discipline within legislative groups, the interests most likely to be heard in policy debates, and legislative outcomes.

Deploying an organisational perspective, studies of candidate selection document and analyse how the process has changed over time – focusing on who participates and the implications this holds for representative democracy. Candidate and leadership selection systems are typically analysed along four dimensions: the requirements of candidacy (who can stand for election?), the selectorate (who selects?), the degree of centralisation in the process and the method of election (voting vs. appointment systems) (Hazan and Rahat 2010). A growing literature considers how leaders are selected, what factors lead to a change in selection processes, and their democratic implications in terms of competition and representation (Cross and Blais 2012; Pilet and Cross 2014; Schumacher and Giger 2017; Cross and Gauja 2021). Empirical studies have taken interest in the movement towards more inclusive selection contests, in particular the increasingly widespread use of both open and closed primaries – a practice copied and adapted from the American mould (see e.g. Sandri, Seddone and Venturino 2015; Cross, Kenig and Rahat 2016). The list of political parties having used open or semi-open primaries for the selection of candidates or party leaders is quite extensive, and includes the French Socialist Party (Faucher 2015, 804), Israeli parties (Hazan and Rahat 2010), the Italian Partito Democratico (Sandri, Seddone and Venturino 2015), the Canadian Liberals, UK Labour and the Conservatives (Gauja 2017). These studies have documented increased numbers of partisan participants as a result of this process, but also question the potential for these large-scale events to accurately reflect the views of party activists. The profound public policy impact of this aspect of a party's organisation and practice has fostered a substantial body of research on political recruitment through parties and who is elected as a result. Numerous studies of political recruitment have highlighted the persistent problem of the under-selection and under-representation of women, younger people and ethnic minorities (see e.g. Caul 1999; Childs 2013; Heidar and Wauters 2019) – suggesting that party organisational processes do not always create diverse representative outcomes. Overall, studies of political recruitment within parties have shifted over time from describing how parties organise to select candidates and leaders, to understanding the consequences of different organisational configurations, to a broader normative concern with the outcomes that party organisations produce, in particular, the representativeness of the political elites they recruit.

What shapes organisation?

As the discussion of party models and political recruitment has illustrated, one of the most important analytic questions that concerns party organisation scholars is that of change. What factors shape political party organisations and the way in which they perform their functions, and how can we account for change over time?

Three main approaches characterise the research on party change, which also serve to highlight a range of different analytical approaches to party organisation more generally. First, approaches that seek to provide a generalisable account of change, applicable across parties and party systems (see e.g. Panebianco 1988; Harmel and Janda 1994; Krouwel 2012). Second, studies seeking to examine change within a particular party or a limited number of parties – rooted in in-depth qualitative case studies (Quinn 2005; Russell 2005; Bale 2012). Third, accounts that concentrate on a specific type of change, typically contained within studies of particular party processes: for example, candidate and leadership selection (Hazan and Rahat 2010; Cross and Blais 2012; and other examples provided earlier) and policy development (Gauja 2013).

Studies of individual party change typically adopt a historically oriented, thick-descriptive account of organisational transformation. Two excellent examples are Bale's (2012) longitudinal study of the drivers of change (both organisational and policy) in the British Conservative Party and Russell's (2005) account of modernisation in the UK Labour Party. This kind of research demonstrates that it is a myriad of complex factors (internal and external to the party) that come together to produce organisational change in particular contexts. It also highlights the crucial importance of thick-descriptive accounts of change for advancing theoretical and empirical scholarship.

For those seeking a more generalisable account of change, the primary concern shifts to identifying the most relevant or salient catalysts and conditions for change. Harmel and Janda's (1994) 'integrated theory' of party goals and party change has perhaps been the most influential example of this approach. In acknowledging that party change 'does not just happen', Harmel and Janda's (1994, 264–266) model incorporates three important explanatory elements: the recognition that change arises from both internal and external drivers; the importance of 'party operatives', or key decision-makers, in advocating for change; and the necessity of building a coalition of support to overcome the organisational resistance that is common within large organisations such as political parties.

A challenge for studies of party organisation is the perennial tension between detailed and more generalisable accounts of political phenomena. Successive contributions to the debate on party change have highlighted the salience of numerous factors, internal and external to the party, in shaping the agenda for change, including factions, party leaders and institutional pressures such as party funding and resources, electoral competition and technological developments. Yet the process by which these pressures are translated into organisational change, and who is responsible for driving this change, remains an area where both theoretical and empirical investigations are dispersed, and consequently, the relationship between these different catalysts is not yet settled. Comparative studies that can balance theoretically grounded explanations for change with nuanced empirical work that accommodates contextual differences are needed to improve our understanding of why – and how – party organisations change. This is especially important if researchers want to *influence* change by engaging with parties in more practical ways in order to achieve the best possible democratic processes and outcomes.

The third approach – studies of specific organisational processes – has become increasingly prominent, as political parties' democratic functions have been carefully scrutinised in the wake of membership decline. A characteristic of these studies, which also marks a relatively recent innovation in empirical party organisation research, is that they are built on a comparative team-based approach whereby a group of country experts collects data on various party functions, which are then brought together in a comparative analysis of various elements of party organisation. Pioneered by Katz and Mair (1992) in their project on comparative party organisation, this approach has been continued by prominent scholars in the field (Poguntke, Scarrow and Webb 2016; Scarrow, Webb and Poguntke 2017) and expanded to various subfields, including party membership (van Haute and Gauja 2015), party leadership (Pilet and Cross 2014) and party-interest group relations (Allern et al. 2021). This approach has transformed comparative studies in the discipline by balancing breadth of coverage with depth of expertise and has provided collaborative opportunities for a diverse range of scholars (Gauja and Kosiara-Pedersen 2021). The collaborative, comparative approach has seen some significant theoretical leaps in understanding the range of different organisational forms and how they impact on the performance of specific functions, with much greater coverage across parties and countries. Gaps still remain, however, with research outside of Europe and North America still not fully incorporated, as well as particular party types – such as far right parties – which are difficult for researchers to access (see later).

The particular challenges of party organisation research

The study of party organisations is inherently challenging because of the difficulty in gaining access to the parties themselves and obtaining reliable data on their internal workings. On the one hand, there is an incentive for party leaders and operatives to paint a rosy picture of their parties – in terms of membership, decision-making, consensus and coherence. Data that points to weaknesses in a political party's operation might damage its reputation with voters and may be concealed. This is a particular concern for researchers gathering data, for example, on party membership, or in the context of qualitative interviews with party elites.

In other cases, a concern for the public image of the party may lead to the wholesale refusal of access to it for the purposes of conducting academic research or cooperation that is contingent on the party's priorities. In one recent research project into party membership, researchers Bale, Webb and Poletti circumvented British parties altogether – working instead with a market research company to field a survey to members. This provided the freedom to ask 'whatever questions we wanted to ask – and without the nagging fear that one or other of the parties would change their mind and veto the project at the last minute' (Bale, Webb and Poletti 2019, 2). Secrecy and access have also been particularly acute challenges for those scholars studying extremist and far right political parties (Art 2018).

Perhaps one of the most interesting debates in party organisation research is 'American exceptionalism' – that is, the extent to which political party organisations in the USA can be compared to those in Canada, Europe and Australia, which are – at least theoretically – built on the premise of memberships and an organisational presence outside the legislature. The *Handbook of Party Politics* (Katz and Crotty 2006) included two entries on American exceptionalism and separate chapters on electoral mobilisation, political financing and party origins in the USA – highlighting some of the difficulties in comparing the rather looser, network-based structures of American parties with their counterparts in Europe and elsewhere. However, many of these parties' organisational adaptations – such as the use of primaries, looser networks of affiliation and digital campaigning – indicate that the dichotomy between European and American political parties may be eroding. Future research may provide more insights if this distinction is removed, and scholars from both regions engage more with their complementary research agendas.

Conclusion and avenues for further research

Despite popular disaffection with political parties, the study of party organisation continues to be crucial into the twenty-first century. Dealing with the transformation and adaptation of parties over time are the key concerns that have animated the research of party scholars, evident in the plethora of theoretical models for understanding existing organisations. However, party organisation scholarship faces important challenges in accommodating developments in digital technologies and new modes of political participation. A way forward in future research is to harness a more interdisciplinary approach, incorporating insights from other disciplines, including media and communications studies, organisational sociology and social movement studies. A further challenge is to recognise that many of the organisational innovations that characterise parties – driven in large part by digital technologies – break down the geographic barriers that form the basis of approaches to party organisation in the European and American traditions. Future research agendas must move beyond European and North American parties in its focus, and take a more open-minded approach to the nature of organisation itself, which appears to be transforming in a new decade marked by more personalised styles of politics, pandemic-induced social isolation and rapidly evolving norms of digital communication.

References

Allern, E.H., Hansen, V., Marshall, D., Rasmussen, A. and Webb, P. (2021) 'Competition and interaction: Party ties to interest groups in a multidimensional policy space', *European Journal of Political Research*, 60(2), p275–294.
Art, D. (2018) 'Party organization and the radical right', in Rydgren, J. (ed.) *The Oxford handbook of the radical right*. Oxford: Oxford University Press, pp. 239–250.
Bale, T. (2012) *The conservatives since 1945: The drivers of party change*. Oxford: Oxford University Press.
Bale, T., Webb, P. and Poletti, M. (2019) *Footsoldiers: Political party membership in the 21st century*. London: Routledge.
Bennett, W.L., Segerberg, A. and Knupfer, C. (2018) 'The democratic interface: Technology, political organization, and diverging patterns of electoral representation', *Information, Communication and Society*, 21(11), p1655–1680.
Borz, G. and Janda, K. (2020) 'Contemporary trends in party organization: Revisiting intra-party democracy', *Party Politics*, 26(1), p3–8.
Carty, K. (2004) 'Parties as franchise systems: The stratarchical organizational imperative', *Party Politics*, 10(1), p5–24.
Caul, M. (1999) 'Women's representation in parliament: The role of political parties', *Party Politics*, 48(1), p72–90.
Chadwick, A. (2013) *The hybrid media system*. Oxford: Oxford University Press.
Chadwick, A. and Stromer-Galley, J. (2016) 'Digital media, power, and democracy in parties and election campaigns: Party decline or party renewal?, *International Journal of Press/Politics*, 21(3), p283–293.
Childs, S. (2013) 'Intra-party democracy: A gendered critique and feminist agenda', in Cross, W. and Katz, R. (eds.) *The challenges of intra-party democracy*. Oxford: Oxford University Press.
Cross, W. (2008) 'Democratic norms and candidate selection: Taking contextual factors into account', *Party Politics*, 14(5), p596–619.
Cross, W. and Blais, A. (2012) *Politics at the centre: The selection and removal of party leaders in the Anglo parliamentary democracies*. Oxford: Oxford University Press.
Cross, W. and Gauja, A. (2021) 'Selecting party leaders, reform processes and methods: Examining the Australian and New Zealand Labour parties', *International Political Science Review*, 42(2), p261–276.
Cross, W., Kenig, O. and Rahat, G. (2016) *The promise and challenge of party primary elections*. Montreal: McGill-Queen's University Press.
Dennis, J. (2019) *Beyond slacktivism: Political participation on social media*. London: Palgrave.
Duverger, M. (1959) *Political parties: Their organization and activity in the modern state*. London: Methuen.
Faucher, F. (2015) 'Leadership elections: What is at stake for parties? A comparison of the British Labour Party and the Parti Socialiste', *Parliamentary Affairs*, 68(4), p794–820.
Gauja, A. (2013) *The politics of party policy: From members to legislators*. Houndmills: Palgrave Macmillan.
Gauja, A. (2017) *Party reform: The causes, challenges and consequences of organizational change*. Oxford: Oxford University Press.
Gauja, A. and Kosiara-Pedersen, K. (2020) 'The comparative study of political party organization: Changing perspectives and prospects', *Ephemera*, 21(2), p19–52.
Gauja, A. and Kosiara-Pedersen, K. (2021) 'Decline, adaptation and relevance: Political parties and their researchers in the 21st Century', *European Political Science*, 20(1), p123–138.
Gerbaudo, P. (2019) *The digital party*. London: Pluto Press.

Gibson, R., Greffet, F. and Cantijoch, M. (2017) 'Friend or foe? Digital technologies and the changing nature of party membership', *Political Communication*, 34(1), p89–111.

Gibson, R. and Ward, S. (1999) 'Party democracy on-line: UK parties and new ICTs', *Information, Communication & Society*, 2(3), p340–367.

Gibson, R. and Ward, S. (2009) 'Parties in the digital age: A review article', *Representation*, 45(1), p87–100.

Halupka, M. (2017) 'The legitimisation of clicktivism', *Australian Journal of Political Science*, 53(1), p130–141.

Harmel, R. and Janda, K. (1994) 'An integrated theory of party goals and party change', *Journal of Theoretical Politics*, 6(3), p259–287.

Hazan, R. and Rahat, G. (2010) *Democracy within parties: Candidate selection methods and their political consequences*. Oxford: Oxford University Press.

Heidar, K. and Wauters, B. (eds.) (2019) *Do parties still represent? An analysis of the representativeness of political parties in western democracies*. London: Routledge.

Hopkin, J. and Paolcci, C. (1999) 'The business firm model of party organisation: Cases from Spain and Italy', *European Journal of Political Research*, 35(3), p307–339.

Karpf, D. (2012) *The MoveOn effect: The unexpected transformation of American political advocacy*. New York: Oxford University Press.

Katz, R. (2002) 'The internal life of parties', in Luther, K.R. and Muller-Rommel, F. (eds.) *Political parties in the new Europe: Political and analytical challenges*. Oxford: Oxford University Press, pp. 87–118.

Katz, R. and Crotty, W. (eds.) (2006) *Handbook of party politics*. London: Sage.

Katz, R. and Mair, P. (1992) *Party organizations: A data handbook*. London: Sage.

Katz, R. and Mair, P. (1993) 'The evolution of party organizations in Europe: The three faces of party organization', *American Review of Politics*, 14, p593–617.

Katz, R. and Mair, P. (1995) 'Changing models of party organisation and party democracy: The emergence of the cartel party', *Party Politics*, 1(1), p5–28.

Katz, R. and Mair, P. (2009) 'The cartel party thesis: A restatement', *Perspectives on Politics*, 7(4), p753–766.

Katz, R. and Mair, P. (2018) *Democracy and the cartelization of political parties*. Oxford: Oxford University Press.

Kefford, G. (2021) *Political parties and campaigning in Australia: Digital, data and field*. London: Palgrave Macmillan.

Kirchheimer, O. (1966) 'The transformation of Western European party systems', in LaPalombara, J. and Weiner, M. (eds.) *Political parties and political development*. Princeton: Princeton University Press, pp. 177–200.

Krouwel, A. (2006) 'Party models', in Katz, R. and Crotty, W. (eds.) *Handbook of party politics*. London: Sage, pp. 249–269.

Krouwel, A. (2012) *Party transformations in European democracies*. Albany: SUNY Press.

Lawson, K. and Merkl, P. (1988) *When parties fail: Emerging alternative organizations*. Princeton: Princeton University Press.

Lipow, A. and Seyd, P. (1995) 'Political parties and the challenge to democracy: From steam-engines to techno-populism', *New Political Science*, 17(1–2), p295–308.

Lofgren, K. and Smith, C. (2003) 'Political parties and democracy in the information age', in Gibson, R., Nixon, P. and Ward, S. (eds.) *Political parties and the internet: Net gain?* London: Routledge, pp. 39–52.

Mair, P. (2005) 'Democracy beyond parties', Discussion paper, Centre for the Study of Democracy, University of California, Irvine.

Mair, P. (2013) *Ruling the void: The hollowing of western democracy*. London: Verso.

Margetts, H. (2006) 'The Cyber Party', in Katz, R. and Crotty, W. (eds.) *Handbook of party politics*. London: Sage, pp. 528–535.

Mazzoleni, O. and Voerman, G. (2017) 'Memberless parties: Beyond the business-firm party model?', *Party Politics*, 23(6), p783–792.

Michels, R. (1916) [1966] *Political parties: A sociological study of the oligarchical tendencies of modern democracy*. New York: Free Press.

Nassmacher, K.H. (2009) *The funding of party competition: Political finance in 25 democracies*. Baden-Baden: Nomos.

Ostrogorski, M. (1902) *Democracy and the organization of political parties*. London: Macmillan.

Panebianco, A. (1988) *Political parties: Organization and power*. Cambridge: Cambridge University Press.

Pilet, J.B. and Cross, W. (2014) *The selection of political party leaders in contemporary parliamentary democracies: A comparative study*. London: Routledge.

Poguntke, T., Scarrow, S. and Webb, P. et al. (2016) 'Party rules, party resources and the politics of parliamentary democracies: How parties organize in the 21st century', *Party Politics*, 22(6), p661–678.

Quinn, T. (2005) *Modernising the labour party: Organisational change since 1983*. Basingstoke: Palgrave Macmillan.

Russell, M. (2005) *Building new labour: The politics of party organisation*. Basingstoke: Palgrave Macmillan.

Sandri, G., Seddone, A. and Venturino, F. (2015) *Party primaries in comparative perspective*. New York: Ashgate.

Scarrow, S. (2015) *Beyond party members: Changing approaches to partisan mobilization*. Oxford: Oxford University Press.

Scarrow, S. and Webb, P. (2017) 'Investigating party organization: Structures, resources and representative strategies', in Scarrow, S., Webb, P. and Poguntke, T. (eds.) *Organizing political parties: Representation, participation and power*. Oxford: Oxford University Press, pp. 1–27.

Scarrow, S., Webb, P. and Poguntke, T. (eds.) (2017) *Organizing political parties: Representation, participation and power*. Oxford: Oxford University Press.

Schumacher, G. and Giger, N. (2017) 'Who leads the party? On membership size, selectorates and party oligarchy', *Political Studies*, 65(1), p162–181.

van Biezen, I. (2008) 'State intervention in party politics: The public funding and regulation of political parties', *European Review*, 16(3), p337–353.

van Biezen, I. (2014) 'The end of party democracy as we know it. A tribute to Peter Mair', *Irish Political Studies*, 29(2), p177–193.

van Haute, E. and Gauja, A. (eds.) (2015) *Party members and activists*. London: Routledge.

Vromen, A. (2017) *Digital citizenship and political engagement*. London: Palgrave.

Ward, S. and Voerman, G. (2000) 'New media and new politics: Green parties, intra-party democracy and the potential of the internet (an Anglo-Dutch comparison)', in Voerman, G. (ed.) *Jaarboek Documentatiecentrum Nederlandse Politeke Partijn 1999*. Groningen: Documentatiecentrum Nederlandse Politieke Partijen, pp. 192–215.

Xenos, M., Vromen, A. Loader, B. (2014) 'The great equalizer? Patterns of social media use and youth political engagement in three advanced democracies', in Loader, B., Vromen, A. and Xenos, M. (eds.) *The networked young citizen: Social media, political participation and civic engagement*. New York: Routledge, pp. 17–38.

Zuckerman, E. (2014) 'New media, new civics?', *Policy and Internet*, 6(2), p151–168.

5
PARTY MEMBERSHIP

Susan E. Scarrow and Paul D. Webb

Most political parties in contemporary democracies are formally constituted as both elite and grassroots organisations. Usually elected officials dominate each party's day-to-day legislative and electoral affairs, and membership organisations help with electoral mobilisation, and sometimes are involved in key party decisions such as selecting party candidates and/or leaders, and with helping set the party's overall policy direction. The idea that parties should be organised as membership-based associations seems firmly rooted around the world, in democracies of all ages and all institutional configurations. Thus, one recent study of 44 democracies on five continents found that 94 per cent of the 232 parties studied provided for dues-paying members in their statutes (Political Party Database [PPDB] Round 2 2022). The continuing and even growing prevalence of membership-based parties seemingly flies in the face of research showing stark membership declines in some of the democracies where party membership has a long history (van Biezen, Mair and Poguntke 2012). This chapter asks how to reconcile these two narratives of party membership. The keys to doing so are:

1) Understanding the different (and possibly changing) definitions of party members.
2) Understanding the ongoing appeal (and liability) of party members from a party point of view.
3) Understanding why individuals would join in the first place (and why they leave).
4) Understanding why some members are more active than others on behalf of their parties.

We engage with each of these themes in the context of a body of research on party members that has grown significantly over the past decade or two not only in the scope of its questions but also in its more expansive conception of different ways in which supporters may 'join' their preferred party. This growth takes in new cases and greater comparative ambition, best exemplified by the birth of the Members and Activists of Political Parties (MAPP) network (www.projectmapp.eu/).

What is party membership?

One of the challenges in studying party membership in a comparative perspective is that 'membership' can mean many different things. Thus, when we compare party membership numbers over time, or across parties or countries, it is seldom an apples-to-apples comparison. These differences are directly due to parties' differing decisions about how to construct party membership; they also reflect contextual forces that shape the perceived meaning and value of party membership.

In political parties, as in other voluntary organisations, membership often brings benefits and – in part for this reason – there generally are costs associated with joining. The benefits may be paid to individual members ('selective benefits'), such as privileged access to government services (for instance, when the party is in charge of local government) or access to services directly provided by the party or its representatives (for instance, party-linked co-ops, or gifts from elected representatives to mark life milestones such as weddings and funerals). The benefits may also take the form of access to political influence, be that more attentive service from elected representatives, or the opportunity to cast a vote in party decision-making. Party members may also benefit if a party pays special attention to the priorities of a particular social segment to which the individual belongs. Such 'collective benefits' may encourage group members to join and maintain their links, to affirm the close relationship between the party and this social group.

Membership costs may be financial, procedural, reputational, or some combination of the three. As seen in the PPDB data mentioned earlier, most parties set a financial requirement to acquiring and maintaining party membership. Such rules make it easier for parties to distinguish who is a member in good standing. On the other hand, for most parties, these fees are quite minimal, at least for low-income supporters. Parties show more variation in terms of the procedural costs of joining. At one end of the spectrum, some parties make it quite easy to join, for instance by allowing supporters to fill out an enrolment form and pay using the national party website. An even more extreme form of this is offered by parties in many U.S. states, which claim all voters eligible to vote in the party's primary election as members. U.S. state parties generally cannot block access to primary voting (equivalent to membership), because these are considered to be public elections (Hine 2003). At the other end of the spectrum are parties that make party membership very difficult to acquire, for instance by imposing long probationary periods or requiring applicants to obtain recommendation letters from existing members. Research suggests that potential party members are attentive to the balance of associated costs and benefits, and that the differences in these balances may shape the number and/or types of supporters who choose to join (Gomez et al. 2019; Achury et al. 2020; Weber 2020).

A third type of membership cost, reputational, is not imposed by the parties themselves. Rather, in some situations, party membership in general, or membership in a particular party, may be viewed negatively. This can deter supporters from taking the step of joining. Parties cannot directly control such costs, but they may try to combat them in other ways, such as offering modes of affiliation or participation that are deliberately constructed to look different to traditional membership. Examples include creating on-line only sections (cyber parties), or by opening some party activities to 'registered supporters' as well as full-fledged members; these activities can even include core party functions such as candidate selection.

Thus, party membership can look quite different depending on the balance parties strike between members' rights and duties and the organisational models they uphold. Parties with the most expansive membership definitions include those which are organised similar to fan clubs, often assembled to support a charismatic leader. Silvio Berlusconi's *Forza Italia* party was an example of this, even taking its name from the chant of fans of the football club which Berlusconi owned (AC Milan). Membership in this organisation was relatively easy to obtain, but members were given little direct (or even indirect) role in policy-making, nor did they obtain many other selective benefits.

Clientelistic parties offer their members higher obvious selective benefits while imposing higher financial or procedural tests in order to monitor that members are living up to their part of the bargain. Turkey's AKP is an example of a clientelistic party which has used its membership network to distribute material benefits, and which uses those benefits to recruit members (Ark-Yildirim 2017). Plebiscitarian parties offer members collective benefits by giving them a say in important party decisions, but they may then impose stiffer membership tests, such as long probationary periods, or have more active expulsion procedures, to deter those who disagree with current leadership. Italy's Five Star Movement offers an example of a party that is ostensibly plebiscitary and open, yet also limits access to more important participation opportunities and is intolerant of dissent (Tronconi 2018).

A particular party's offerings of membership benefits, and the stringency of its membership requirements, are by no means a fixed equation. Thus, the basis of membership may change as a party adopts new organisational strategies, possibly in response to electoral losses. In addition, some parties may decide to offer multiple forms of membership, often intended to accommodate supporters who are interested in a specific campaign or issue, and are not interested in assuming full-fledged membership. So-called multi-speed membership options may include online-only membership, non-voting 'membership-lite' status with reduced dues, registered 'party friends', or financial supporters (Scarrow 2014; Faucher 2015; Gauja 2015).

How many party members are there? A global tour

How many citizens choose to become party members, and how has this varied around the world, and over time? Comparing party enrolments is an imprecise business. One reason is because parties construct their memberships in very different ways, as discussed earlier. For instance, membership numbers are almost inevitably higher in a party that allows all supporters to participate freely in its primaries, and then calls them members, compared to one with a long probationary period and a required annual fee. Other factors also complicate such comparisons. For instance, party records may be poorly kept, and parties vary in the zeal with which they purge their rolls of those who are not current with their dues. Moreover, parties, and party sub-units, often have good reasons to exaggerate their enrolments. Additionally, apparent membership surges or declines are sometimes merely the result of changes in the party's record-keeping practices, rather than changes in the behaviour of their supporters. Some problems with party-reported data can be overcome by looking at trends in self-reported data, for instance, from cross-national surveys that ask respondents if they are party members. Yet such data has its own irregularities, such as over-reporting (e.g. if respondents equate party voting or former party membership with current membership), and over-sampling of the more politically engaged (for more on the challenges of counting party members, see Scarrow 2014).

Despite these caveats about data on comparative party membership, it still proves useful for diagnosing large trends. One of them is that since the 1990s, overall party membership has been declining in both absolute and relative terms in the Western European parliamentary democracies, a region where party membership once flourished. While a few parties in this region have bucked this trend, research has found that overall far fewer citizens are enrolled party members than was true a half century ago (van Biezen, Mair and Poguntke 2012; Webb and Keith 2017). The picture is more mixed in the newer democracies of Central and Eastern Europe. Here many of the former Communist parties lost their members, while some of the newer parties never acquired them. Yet this pattern is far from universal. For example, parties in the countries that once formed Yugoslavia seem to have developed strong membership bases (Čular and Čakar 2020).

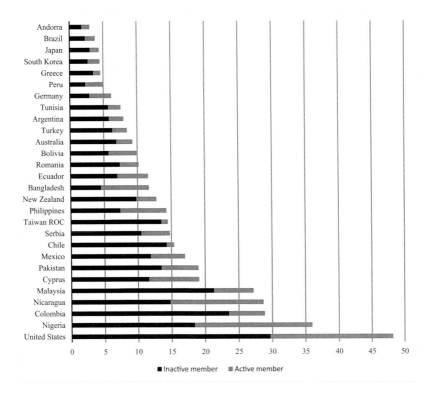

Figure 5.1 Self-identified party members as per cent of respondents of World Values Survey Wave 7 (2017–2020)

On a more global scale, we see wide variation in the proportion of citizens who self-report as party members. In the latest wave of the World Values Survey (conducted between 2017 and 2020), some 4.8 per cent of respondents across 29 countries of varying degrees of democratic consolidation (i.e. those designated 'free' or 'partly free' by Freedom House) declared themselves to be 'active' members of political parties and a further 9.9 per cent to be 'inactive' members (n = 42,069). As Figure 5.1 shows, the proportion of 'active' membership ranges from 1 per cent for Chile, Greece, and Taiwan to 18.5 per cent for the USA, where the definition of party membership is, as we have noted, very broad. In countries where clientelistic practices are widespread, active membership is also reported to be high – for example, 17.6 per cent in Nigeria, 13 per cent in Nicaragua, 12 per cent in Thailand, and 7.2 per cent in Bangladesh (van de Walle 2003; Devine 2006; Gonzalez-Ocantos et al. 2012; Tomsa and Ufen 2013). Countries at the lower end of the spectrum include several of the older established parliamentary democracies in Europe and Australasia.

In order to understand these variations, it is important to take a closer look at what these numbers represent. As argued earlier, some of the differences on display in Figure 5.1 may be more about how parties define and police the boundaries of their membership, and what they offer in return, rather than about differences in popular preferences regarding partisan participation. Thus, we next look more closely at factors that encourage parties to recruit members, and, conversely, at those that encourage supporters to join and be active in parties.

Why do parties want members? The demand-side story

Notwithstanding the evident decline of party memberships across time in most established democracies, political scientists recognise several reasons why modern parties might still be very concerned to maintain and improve membership levels (Scarrow 1994, 1996). In the first place, there are *legitimacy benefits*: a party may hope to enhance its electoral credibility by demonstrating a healthy level of internal activity. Members may also provide *direct electoral benefits*: members constitute a reliable core of loyal voters – so the more a party has, the greater its 'core' vote. Furthermore, members might act as 'ambassadors' for the party in the local community, arguing their case in social situations where talk of politics arises; these are *outreach benefits*. Of particular importance are the obvious *labour benefits* that party members can bring. Despite the changes that communication technology has brought to modern campaigning, parties still rely upon local members to do a great deal of necessary voluntary work during an election campaign, especially the more 'intensive' tasks like canvassing, leafleting, serving on local party campaign committees, and mobilising support on polling day (Bale, Webb and Poletti 2019a). These efforts are not to be underestimated, especially in the context of single-member district elections, as research on the UK has shown (Whiteley and Seyd 1992; Pattie, Johnston and Fieldhouse 1995; Denver and Hands 1997; Karp, Banducci and Bowler 2008; Townsley 2018). There is also evidence that party members, and the local party networks which they staff, produce electoral payoffs even in proportional representation systems where such effects are harder to account for (Tavits 2012; André and Depauw 2016).

Beyond these electoral benefits, there are other attractions. Parties which take internal democracy seriously might regard members as a potentially valuable source of policy ideas. We note, however, that other parties might see this *innovation benefit* as more of a restriction on leadership autonomy, and to that extent a 'cost' rather than a benefit of membership – a point to which we shall shortly return. Relatedly, members can also act as a source of information about public concerns and so provide *linkage benefits*. Critically important is the role that the members play as a source of party candidates for public office: these *personnel benefits* are crucial since the provision of public officials is a vital function of political parties in liberal democratic regimes, and is thus central to the way in which parties infiltrate and control the state. Finally, members can be a source of *financial benefit* to parties. This benefit is especially significant for smaller parties and newer parties that are not able to rely substantially on income emanating from corporations, trade unions, or wealthy donors (although the state has become an increasingly important alternative to any of these sources in many countries [Bolleyer 2013; van Biezen and Kopecky 2017, 86]).

Notwithstanding these benefits to parties, some have questioned just how useful members are in the modern context. In particular, while party leaders might regard the membership as a resource of continuing significance in the battle for votes, this benefit must be set against the potential costs of a membership which may not wholeheartedly endorse the policy package that the leadership wishes to set before the electorate. These costs spring from the widespread perception, shared by many academics, journalists and politicians alike, that grassroots members are inclined to see themselves as keepers of the flame of ideological purity. Of particular note in this respect is John May's well known 'law of curvilinear disparity', which is premised on the notion that different strata within political parties have different incentives and motives. While leaders are driven primarily by vote-maximising imperatives, 'sub-leaders' (a category which includes grassroots activists) are largely motivated by purposive incentives such as the desire for influence over party policy or candidate-selection. Thus, while leaders can be expected to seek out policy positions which approximate those of the median voter as nearly as possible, members may be more concerned to maintain ideologically 'pure' (which is to say radical) positions. A further party stratum of 'non-leaders' includes individuals who do not take out formal membership at all, such as supporters and sympathisers in the wider electorate; these are hypothesised by May to be the most ideologically moderate of the strata (1973, 135–6).

This scenario of systematic ideological disparity between the various party strata suggests that parties with strong membership organisations are likely to experience intra-party tension and difficulties of party management. Yet empirical research suggests that this phenomenon may not be widespread (Kitschelt 1989; Norris 1995; Narud and Skare 1999; Kennedy, Lyons and Fitzgerald 2006; Belchior and Freire 2011; van Holsteyn et al. 2017; Bale et al. 2020; Webb and Bale 2021). Even so, there is little doubt that, in some cases, the membership pulls in a significantly different direction to the leadership (or at least, it seeks to take the leadership further in a certain direction than it is willing to go). When this happens, real problems of intra-party management may arise. This dynamic may lead to factional conflict over questions of policy and party procedures for making decisions and selecting candidates for office.

One way for party leaders to deal with the threat of such conflicts would be to disempower the membership in favour of the supposedly more moderate supporter strata. Some analysts have predicted that parties are likely to do exactly that (most notably, Katz and Mair 1995). And indeed, there are some notable examples of parties doing this, such as the French Socialist Party opening up their 2011 and 2017 presidential primaries to all supporters, or the Canadian Liberal party entirely abolishing dues-paying membership in favour non-paying supporters who register online. Nevertheless, these examples remain relatively rare, and there is still ample evidence that even in the era of the multispeed membership organisations, parties continue to regard full members as the most important supporters, given that they offer a higher level of commitment, especially when it comes to the most intensive forms of activity (Webb, Poletti and Bale 2020).

Why do people join (or leave) parties? The supply-side story

Research into the demographic and attitudinal profiles of party members consistently shows that those who join up tend to be middle class and well educated – that is, they enjoy the personal resource advantages that provide them with the skills and confidence to be politically efficacious. In other words, if they choose to become politically active, they believe that they can make an impact on politics through their chosen parties (van Haute and Gauja 2015; Heidar and Wauters 2019; Bale, Webb and Poletti 2019b). Beyond these demographic correlates of membership, however, there is a well-developed theory of the incentives and costs that influence the decisions of individual to join parties. This is 'the General Incentives Model' (GIM), first developed by Patrick Seyd and Paul Whiteley (1992 – see also Whiteley, Seyd and Richardson 1994; Katz 2015; and van Haute and Gauja 2015). It was inspired by American social scientists, Peter B. Clark and James Q. Wilson (1961), whose research distinguished between three types of incentives – purposive, material, and solidary. *Purposive* incentives are connected with the stated goals of an organisation: people are frequently motivated to join parties by these core organisational purposes. By contrast, *material* incentives reflect the desire to achieve tangible personal material rewards – perhaps in the form of job or career benefits – for participation. *Solidary* incentives relate to the satisfaction derived from the process of participation, including sociability and camaraderie.

Seyd and Whiteley built on Clark and Wilson's work by developing an approach

> grounded in the assumption that participation occurs in response to different kinds of incentives . . . but it goes beyond a narrowly cast economic analysis of incentives to

include emotional attachments to the party, moral concerns, and social norms, variables which lie outside the standard cost-benefit approach to decision-making.

(Whiteley, Seyd and Richardson 1994, 109)

To summarise, the GIM approach incorporates a combination of the following reasons for joining a party:

- The individual's perception of the probability that participation in group activity through the party will achieve a desired collective outcome; in other words, the respondent's sense of *group efficacy*.
- The individual's desired *collective policy outcome*, such as the introduction of a particular policy.
- The individual's assessment of the *selective outcome benefits* of activism; that is, material or career benefits.
- The individual's assessment of the *selective process benefits* of activism; that is, the intrinsic pleasure derived from involvement in political action.
- The individual's *altruistic* motivations for activism.
- The individual's perception of *social norm* incentives for activism; that is, the desire to conform to the behaviour and expectations of personal contacts.
- The individual's *expressive or affective* motivations for activism, such as the strength of commitment to or identification with a given party or leader.
- The individual's perception of the *costs* of activism; properly speaking, this is a *dis*incentive.
- The individual's belief that individual acts can influence and have a real impact upon political decision; that is, the respondent' sense of *personal* efficacy.
- The individual's *ideological* motivations for activism.

Empirical research suggests that ideological, expressive, and policy incentives generally predominate in explaining motivations to join parties in established democracies (e.g. Clarke et al. 2000; Gallagher and Marsh 2002; de Ridder, van Holsteyn and Koole 2015, 142–3; Poletti, Webb and Bale 2019), though some young members in particular may be seeking more selective benefits associated with career advancement inside or outside politics (Bruter and Harrison 2009; Weber 2020). We would not expect that to be the case in more clientelistic parties which are more generous in their use of selective incentives (e.g. Bob-Milliar 2012).

There is rather less research on the reasons why people *leave* parties, once they have joined (van Haute 2015), not least because it is not so easy to identify ex-members in order to survey them about the reasons for quitting. However, this developing field also draws on GIM theory to some extent. It has been established that the same ideological factors that once motivated people to join up, may also play a large part in driving them to leave the same parties. For instance, a left-wing individual attracted to a party which has taken a sharp turn towards socialism may subsequently become disillusioned to the point of departure should the party eventually slide back towards a more moderate position. This example points to the significance of a key factor that interacts with ideological incentives for quitting – (the change of) *leadership* (Wagner 2016; Kölln and Polk 2016; Kosiara Pedersen 2016; Bale, Webb and Poletti 2019a). The British Labour Party offers a salutary example of these types of leadership effect; in the mid-1990s, it is widely recognised that the emergence of Tony Blair at the helm of the party succeeded in attracting many moderate and centrist supporters to the party. By contrast, the surprise victory of veteran left-winger Jeremy Corbyn in the leadership election of 2015 generated an astonishing surge of new members from enthusiastic left-wing followers (some of whom had quit the party in the days of Blair's leadership (Whiteley et al. 2019), but the pattern went into partial reversal when he was succeeded by a new leader widely perceived as being more ideologically moderate (Keir Starmer) in 2020 (Barnfield and Bale 2020). More generally, this points to a need for more research that seeks to assess the extent to which parties experience 'circulation' within their memberships; how far do people leave and re-join the same parties – or, indeed, eventually move to other parties?

Explaining membership activism

Understanding why people join (and leave) parties is one thing, but understanding what they do, and how much they do, for their parties once they have joined is another. Much of the research on this has focused on the UK, following the lead set by Seyd and Whiteley, so this section will largely focus on recent research on British parties. Studies consistently show that only a minority of party members and supporters are truly active. Most members actually do little or nothing for their parties during election campaigns, and even less between elections. For example, Bale, Webb and Poletti (2019a, 98) discovered that, in the UK general election of 2015, 51 per cent of members of six different parties did less than five hours work during the five week campaign, and 61 per cent did less than ten hours; at the next general election two years later, the corresponding figures (for a longer seven week campaign) were 60 per cent and 70 per cent. In general, very few people devote a lot of time to political parties; only ten per cent or so did more than 40 hours campaigning in each of these two elections, pointing to the existence of a small group of highly dedicated people who constitute the core activists. Of course, it is not only registered members who work on behalf of parties during campaigns: sympathisers and partisans who choose not to take up formal membership often contribute as well – and in total the contributions of such individuals may be numerous, although they play little part in the most intensive core activities of any campaign (Fisher, Fieldhouse and Cutts 2014; Webb, Poletti and Bale 2017).

The range of activities that members engage in is numerous, and traditionally includes displaying posters, leafleting households, attending party meetings and election hustings, canvassing potential supporters, mobilising identified support on election day, running party committees, standing for party offices and public office, contributing financially, and engaging in fund-raising activities. It also entails a degree of social and cultural activity from quiz evenings, dances (British Young Conservative dances once being a famous mating agency for the sons and daughters of the middle and upper classes) to large-scale cultural jamborees like the Italian Democrats' *Feste de l'Unità* and the French equivalent *Fêtes de l'Humanité* (the latter being a cross-party event for left-wing activists and supporters). There is some evidence that individuals who become strongly embedded in local party social networks may be somewhat immune to the effects of (short-term) disillusionment with the national party leadership, in so far as they are less likely to disengage from the party (Webb, Poletti and Bale 2020).

Beyond these forms of activity that have been part of the traditional repertoire of the active party membership, we must take account of the impact of modern communication technology, which means that members and supporters can also engage in online activity in support of their parties. Research on the nature and impact of this is in its infancy. We cannot yet say with any certainty whether time spent by members promoting their party online will add to or detract from more traditional activities like canvassing or leafleting. But it is quite possible that the move towards online campaigning will challenge the centralised control model that has generally been the norm offline: parties will have to contend with members creating their own political social media outputs, as well as sharing those which are produced by the party centrally. Moreover, the ease with which people can do this may well further obscure the distinction between formal members and other types of supporter (Dommett and Temple 2018).

Several factors have been found to influence levels of activism among party members. To some extent, the general incentives theory offers a useful framework for researching the question of why some people are more active than others. For instance, it is quite logical to suppose that ideological incentives motivate people not only to join parties but also to be active on their behalf. That said, the most intensely activist core members are more likely to be driven by the desire to pursue political careers themselves (a selective outcome incentive in GIM terms), or to be deeply embedded in the social aspect of local party networks (a selective process incentive) (Webb, Poletti and Bale 2020). In addition, the context of the particular electoral districts in which members operate can have an effect; for instance, levels of membership activity are likely to be highest in closely contested (or 'marginal') single-member districts (Bale, Webb and Poletti 2019b).

Conclusions and avenues for further research

The origins of scholarship on political party members can be traced back to Ostrogorski's extraordinary seminal account of nineteenth-century party development in England and America (Ostrogorski 1902). This notwithstanding, post-war accounts of party politics rarely focused primarily on members, although they were implicit in classic studies of (intra-)party politics such as Duverger (1954) and McKenzie (1955). Modern in-depth studies of party membership became feasible when political scientists were able to exploit the potential of computer technology to start running surveys of party members in Europe in the 1990s, thereby facilitating far more extensive studies of the nature, motivations and behaviour of those citizens who join political parties. Standard theories of membership behaviour such as the General Incentives Model have become orthodox building blocks of our understanding, on which newer work seeks to add further layers of nuance and accretion. While many of the traditional modes of membership participation and action remain relevant today, the impact of modern forms of social and political communication will challenge current and future generations of scholars to investigate their impact on the roles and behaviour of those who join political parties. Recent research has pushed forward our understanding of the varied meanings of party membership, and of the conditions under which party membership can have important political consequences. The tasks for the next generation of party member research include pushing forward the boundaries of our knowledge in two senses. On the one hand, more research is needed to explore the spread and implications of new forms of party affiliation, including social media followers and registered supporters who are not formal party members. On the other hand, more research is needed to explore the construction and consequences of party membership outside the parliamentary democracies where these questions have primarily been studied in the past (see e.g. Meléndez and Umpierrez de Reguero 2021). Scholars who take up these tasks will be able to build on a far broader body of thematic and empirical research than hitherto, taking in questions of numerical trends, motivations for joining, leaving, and even moving parties, the demographic and attitudinal profiles of members, their rights and roles within party organisations, and their value to these key actors in the democratic process.

References

Achury, S., Scarrow, S.E., Kosiara-Pedersen, K. and van Haute, E. (2020) 'The consequences of membership incentives: Do greater political benefits attract different kinds of members?', *Party Politics*, 26(1), p56–68.

André, A. and Depauw, S. (2016) 'The electoral impact of grassroots activity in the 2012 local elections in Flanders', *Acta Politica*, 51, p131–152.

Ark-Yildirim, C. (2017) 'Political parties and grassroots clientelist strategies in urban Turkey: One neighbourhood at a time', *South European Society and Politics*, 22, p473–90.

Bale, T., Cheung, A., Cowley, P., Menon, A. and Wager, A. (2020) *Mind the values gap: The social and economic values of MPs, voters and party members*. London: Kings College London.

Bale, T., Webb, P. and Poletti, M. (2019a) *Footsoldiers: Political party members in the 21st Century*. London: Routledge.

Bale, T., Webb, P. and Poletti, M. (2019b) 'Participating locally and nationally: Explaining the offline and online activism of British party members', *Political Studies*, 67, p658–675.

Barnfield, M. and Bale, T. (2020) 'Leaving the red Tories': Ideology, leaders and why party members quit', *Party Politics*. Available at: https://doi.org/10.1177/1354068820962035 (Accessed 2 October 2021)

Belchior, A. and Freire, A. (2011) 'The law of curvilinear disparity revisited: The case of Portuguese political parties', *Revista de Ciências Sociais e Políticas/Journal of Social and Political Sciences*, 2, p49–67.

Bob-Milliar, G.M. (2012) 'Political party activism in Ghana: Factors influencing the decision of the politically active to join a political party', *Democratization*, 19, p668–689.

Bolleyer, N. (2013) *New parties in old party systems: Persistence and decline in seventeen democracies*. Oxford: Oxford University Press.

Bruter, M. and Harrison, S. (2009) 'Tomorrow's leaders? Understanding the involvement of young party members in six European democracies', *Comparative Political Studies*, 42(10), p1259–1290.

Clark, P.B. and Wilson, J.Q. (1961) 'Incentive systems: A theory of organization', *Administrative Science Quarterly*, 6, p129–166.

Clarke, H.D., Kornberg, A., Ellis, F. and Rapkin, J. (2000) 'Not for fame or fortune: A note on membership and activity in the Canadian Reform Party', *Party Politics*, 6, p75–93.

Čular, G. and Čakar, D.N. (2020) 'Party membership in Central and Eastern Europe: Can we trust the data?', Paper presented at Conference on Comparative Party Organization, Dusseldorf, June.

De Ridder, J., van Holsteyn, J. and Koole, R. (2015) 'Party membership in the Netherlands', in van Haute, E. and Gauja, A. (eds.) *Party members and activists*. Abingdon: Routledge, pp. 134–150.

Denver, D. and Hands, G. (1997) *Modern constituency campaigning: The 1992 general election*. London: Frank Cass.

Devine, J. (2006) 'NGOs, politics and grassroots mobilisation: Evidence from Bangladesh', *Journal of South Asian Development*, 1, p77–99.

Dommett, K. and Temple, L. (2018) 'Digital campaigning: The rise of Facebook and satellite campaigns', *Parliamentary Affairs*, 71(supplement 1), p189–202.

Duverger, M. (1954) *Political parties: Their organisation and activity in the modern state*. London: Methuen.

Faucher, F. (2015) 'New forms of political participation. Changing demands or changing opportunities to participate in political parties?', *Comparative European Politics*, 13, p405–429.

Fisher, J., Fieldhouse, E. and Cutts, D. (2014) 'Members are not the only fruit: Volunteer activity in British political parties in the 2010 general election', *British Journal of Politics and International Relations*, 16, p75–94.

Gallagher, M. and Marsh, M. (2002) *Days of blue loyalty: The politics of membership of the Fine Gael Party*. Dublin: PSAI Press.

Gauja, A. (2015) 'The construction of party membership', *European Journal of Political Research*, 54(2), p232–248.

Gomez, R., Ramiro, L., Morales, L. and Aja, J. (2019) 'Joining the party: Incentives and motivations of members and registered sympathizers in contemporary multi-speed membership parties', *Party Politics*, 27(4), p779–790.

Gonzalez-Ocantos, E., Kiewiet de Jonge, C., Meléndez, C., Osorio, J. and Nickerson, D.W. (2012) 'Vote buying and social desirability bias: Experimental evidence from Nicaragua', *American Journal of Political Science*, 56(1), p202–217.

Heidar, K. and Wauters, B. (2019) *Do parties still represent? An analysis of the representativeness of political parties in western democracies*. London: Routledge.

Hine, D.C. (2003) *Black victory: The rise and fall of the white primary in Texas*. Columbia: University of Missouri Press.

Karp, J., Banducci, S. and Bowler, S. (2008) 'Getting out the vote: Party mobilization in a comparative perspective', *British Journal of Political Science*, 38, p91–112.

Katz, R.S. (2015) 'Should we believe that improved intra-party democracy would arrest party decline?', in Cross, W. and Katz, R.S. (eds.) *The challenges of intra-party democracy*. Oxford: Oxford University Press, pp. 49–64.

Katz, R.S. and Mair, P. (1995) 'Changing models of party organization and party democracy: The emergence of the cartel party', *Party Politics*, 1, p5–28.

Kitschelt, H. (1989) 'The internal politics of parties: The law of curvilinear disparity revisited', *Political Studies*, 37, p400–421.

Kennedy, F., Lyons, P. and Fitzgerald, P. (2006) 'Pragmatists, ideologues and the general law of curvilinear disparity: the case of the Irish Labour Party', *Political Studies*, 54, p786–805.

Kölln, A.K. and Polk, J. (2016) 'Emancipated party members: Examining ideological incongruence within political parties', *Party Politics*, 23, p18–29.

Kosiara-Pedersen, K. (2016) 'Exit: Why party members consider leaving their parties'. Paper presented at European Consortium of Political Research General Conference, Prague, September.

May, J.D. (1973) 'Opinion structure of political parties: The special law of curvilinear disparity', *Political Studies*, 21, p135–151.

McKenzie, R.T. (1955) *Political parties*. London: Heinemann.

Meléndez, C. and Umpierrez de Reguero, S. (2021) 'Party members and activists in Latin America', in *Oxford research encyclopedia of politics*. Oxford: Oxford University Press.

Narud, H.M. and Skara, A. (1999) 'Are party activists the party extremists? The structure of opinion in political parties', *Scandinavian Political Studies*, 22, p45–65.

Norris, P (1995) 'May's law of curvilinear disparity revisited: Leaders, officers, members and voters in British political parties', *Party Politics*, 1, p29–47.

Ostrogorski, M. (1902) *Democracy and the organisation of political parties,* vol. 1. London: Macmillan.

Pattie, C.J., Johnston, R.J. and Fieldhouse, E.A. (1995) 'Winning the local vote: The effectiveness of constituency campaign spending in Great Britain, 1983–1992', *American Political Science Review*, 89, p969–86.

Poletti, M., Webb, P.D. and Bale, T. (2019) 'Why is it that only some people who support parties actually end up joining them? Evidence from Britain', *West European Politics*, 42, p156–172.

Political Party Database Round 2 (2022) Available at: www.politicalpartydb.org.

Scarrow, S.E. (1994) 'The paradox of enrolment: Assessing the costs and benefits of party memberships', *European Journal of Political Research*, 25, p41–60.

Scarrow, S.E. (1996) *Parties and their members*. Oxford: Oxford University Press.

Scarrow, S.E. (2014) *Beyond party members: Changing approaches to partisan mobilization*. Oxford: Oxford University Press.

Seyd, P. and Whiteley, P. (1992) *Labour's grass roots: The politics of party membership*. Oxford: Clarendon.

Tavits, M. (2012) 'Organizing for success: party organizational strength and electoral performance in post-Communist Europe', *The Journal of Politics*, 74, p83–97.

Tomsa, D. and Ufen, A. (2013) *Party politics in Southeast Asia: Clientelism and electoral competition in Thailand, Indonesia and the Philippines*. London: Routledge.

Townsley, J. (2018) 'Is it worth door-knocking? Evidence from a United Kingdom-based Get Out The Vote (GOTV) field experiment on the effect of party leaflets and canvass visits on voter turnout', *Political Science Research and Methods*. 2018, p1–15.

Tronconi, F. (2018) 'The Italian five star movement during the crisis: Towards normalisation?', *South European Society and Politics*, 23, p163–180.

van Biezen, I. and Kopecky, P. (2017) 'The paradox of party funding: The limited impact of state subsidies on party membership', in Scarrow, S.E., Webb, P.D. and Poguntke, T. (eds.) *Organizing political parties: Representation, participation and power*. Oxford: Oxford University Press, pp. 84–105.

van Biezen, I., Mair, P. and Poguntke, T. (2012) **'**Going, going . . . gone? The decline of party membership in contemporary Europe', *European Journal of Political Research*, 51, p24–56.

van de Walle, N. (2003) 'Presidentialism and clientelism in Africa's emerging party systems', *The Journal of Modern African Studies*, 41, p297–321.

van Haute, E. (2015) 'Joining isn't everything: Exit, voice, and loyalty in party organizations' in Johnston, R. and Sharman, C. (eds.) *Parties and party systems: Structure and context*. Vancouver: UBC Press, pp. 184–201.

van Haute, E. and Gauja, A. (2015) *Party members and activists*. Abingdon: Routledge.

van Holsteyn, J., Den Ridder, J.M. and Koole, R.A. (2017) 'From May's laws to May's legacy: On the opinion structure within political parties', *Party Politics*, 23, p471–486.

Wagner, M. (2016) 'Why do party members leave?', *Parliamentary Affairs*, 70, p344–360.

Webb, P.D. and Bale, T. (2021) *The modern British party system*. 2nd edition. Oxford: Oxford University Press.

Webb, P.D. and Keith, D. (2017) 'Assessing the strength of party organizational resources: A survey of the evidence from the political party database' in Scarrow, S., Webb, P.D. and Poguntke, T. (eds.) *Organizing political parties: Representation, participation and power*. Oxford: Oxford University Press, pp. 31–61.

Webb, P.D., Poletti, M. and Bale, T. (2017) 'So, who really does the donkey work in 'multi-speed membership parties'? Comparing the election campaign activity of party members and party supporters', *Electoral Studies*, 46, p64–74.

Webb, P.D., Poletti, M. and Bale, T. (2020) 'Social networkers and careerists: Explaining high-intensity activism among British party members', *International Political Science Review*, 41, p255–270.

Weber, R. (2020) 'Why do young people join parties? The influence of individual resources on motivation', *Party Politics*, 26, p496–509.

Whiteley, P., Poletti, M., Webb, P. and Bale, T. (2019) 'Oh, Jeremy Corbyn! Why did Labour Party membership soar after the 2015 general election?', *British Journal of Politics and International Relations*, 21, p80–98.

Whiteley, P. and Seyd, P. (1992) 'The Labour vote and local activism: The local constituency campaigns', *Parliamentary Affairs*, 45, p582–95.

Whiteley, P., Seyd, P. and Richardson, J. (1994) *True blues: The politics of Conservative Party membership*. Oxford: Oxford University Press.

6
PARTY FINANCE

Daniela R. Piccio

Money and politics have been inseparable from one another, and the way in which money influences the political process has always attracted significant attention from researchers worldwide. Yet there has been a proliferation of studies on party funding over the last few decades. One of the reasons for this has been the greater availability of official data that resulted from the introduction of more stringent transparency requirements and forced political parties to disclose their financial assets in publicly available annual balance sheets (Smulders and Maddens 2016). We now have a far more accurate knowledge of the sources of income and the patterns of spending of political parties as compared to that found in early studies on party funding, which often relied on estimates based on self-reporting and patchy information on party resources and expenses (see Heidenheimer 1963).

Another important factor leading to increased scholarly attention to party funding is the prominence that political corruption has acquired as an issue in international politics (Norris and van Es 2016). The 'anti-corruption crusade' (Walecki 2007, 2) stimulated the publication of reports, guidelines and handbooks by international organisations, often in collaboration with academics.[1] It also encouraged greater monitoring and pressure from international governmental and non-governmental organisations on legislators to adopt more comprehensive legal frameworks on party funding and attempts to expand regulation on party finance. As Ewing and Issacharoff bluntly put it, in modern democracies, 'there is no escape from the regulator's embrace' (2006, 6): despite the rich diversity of regulatory approaches throughout the world, virtually no country has a laissez-faire, self-regulation approach. Thus, party funding regulation has become more complex and more widely documented,[2] which has raised questions about the conditions that have favoured the emergence of different regulatory approaches and their impact.

Not least, the introduction of more comprehensive regulation drew the attention of scholars to new areas of party finance, and analysis moved beyond the income–expenditure inquiries which previously dominated the field, to incorporate a focus on the broader set of rules that relate to party funding, including those on disclosure, transparency obligations and monitoring authorities.

The expansion of research on party funding cannot however be understood without reference to Katz and Mair's (1995) seminal article. The changes they observed in party funding regimes played a central role in the cartel party model. Following their important contribution, which touches upon multiple aspects of political parties and party systems, and which raised fundamental questions about the role of parties in the functioning of representative democracy, scholars have been particularly interested in testing their propositions in different settings, and by placing party-funding-related variables at the centre of analysis (Ignazi 2017; Scarrow, Webb and Poguntke 2017). The field of party funding has also become richer through the growth of single country analyses and regional comparisons (see Norris and van Es 2016, 2–6 for a review).

In the following sections, the key debates about party funding research will be discussed, starting from the core distinction between private and public funding regimes. Next, the specific research questions associated with the two main funding models will be presented. The chapter concludes by presenting gaps and questions for further research and suggests possible paths of convergence in scholarly work in the field.

Discussing funding regimes: private or public?

Universal agreement exists on the fact that access to financial resources is crucial for political actors in order to campaign successfully and that money skews electoral competition in favour of those actors with greater resources. As a response, legislators throughout the world introduced rules oriented at levelling electoral competition. Two main regulatory approaches can be identified. On the one hand, the continental European model, where legislators have introduced significant amounts of public subsidies to political parties; on the other hand, the Anglo-Saxon model, which includes countries such as Canada, the UK, Australia, Malta and the USA, and has been based on the levelling of electoral competition through restrictions on private funding and spending.

According to the International IDEA Political Finance database, currently almost 70 per cent of countries have introduced provisions for direct public funding to political parties, with those countries with the highest levels of public funding being from Europe, confirming the very strong reliance on public funds by political parties in this region (van Biezen and Kopecky 2017). Northern European countries pioneered the idea that political parties should be financed by the state, West Germany being the first country in Europe to introduce state subsidies for political parties.[3] However, despite a growing worldwide trend towards more generous public subsidies (Norris and van Es 2016), the dominant form of funding politics in many democracies is through private sources, money for campaigns coming from private donors, such as individuals and corporations, or from the candidates themselves (Ewing and Issacharoff 2006).

It should be noted that the distinction between public and private funding regimes does not imply that countries sharing the same regulatory approach have identical rules. For example, despite converging to a public funding approach (Nassmacher 2001; Koß 2011), continental European countries differ considerably in terms of party finance regulation (see Piccio 2014). Relevant differences are also found among the Anglo-Saxon countries (Ewing and Issacharoff 2006).

Unsurprisingly therefore, one of the fundamental questions that scholars of party funding have dealt with is: what explains variation in party funding regimes?[4] Institutional factors proved to play a limited role, even though countries with proportional representation seem more likely to use state support to political parties compared to countries that adopt majority voting systems (van Biezen 2010). Scholars have found that variation in funding regimes is not just a reflection of the structural characteristics of political systems. Research has highlighted the role of parties' material or electoral incentives (as in Katz and Mair 1995; Scarrow 2006), normative preferences in society (Clift and Fisher 2004), veto points, individual party goals and societal discourse about corruption (Koß 2011), and more generally, the importance of prevailing ideological approach taken by the state in democratic systems (e.g. whether it is 'libertarian' or 'egalitarian' – the latter being more interventionist) (Koole 2014; Mutch 2014; Norris and van Es 2016). Thus, no single factor but rather a combination of institutional, geographical, historical, ideological and political factors have been seen to shape the development of a countries' regulatory model (Ewing and Issacharoff 2006, 6–7; also Nassmacher 2001 and Scarrow 2011).

As we shall see, however, quoting Ewing and Issacharoff, 'each regulatory regime is unhappy in its own way' (2006, 10), as legislators' attempts to regulate the role of money in politics have been usually seen as incoherent and unsystematic (see Cagé 2020). Additionally, different concerns have been associated with different funding regimes. It is therefore of no surprise that the scholarly literatures on party funding in continental Europe and Anglo-Saxon countries have largely developed separately one from the other and have been raising different questions. The following section discusses the questions surrounding public funding for political parties, before focus turns to private funding regimes.

Public funding to political parties: advantages and disadvantages

As outlined earlier, the benefits of public funding have been emphasised widely, with international organisations becoming increasingly vociferous on the importance of introducing state support to political parties in order to guarantee effective political contestation and to mitigate the risk of corruption in political life. Both objectives stood as fundamental justifications for the introduction of public funding to political parties in Europe and elsewhere (Koß 2011). While recognising the importance of public funding provisions for both parties and democracy, academics have been more nuanced in their assessments.

First, unanimous agreement exists on the fact that the introduction of public funding did not work in curbing corruption in politics and did not decrease parties' reliance on illicit sources of income in either established or new democracies (Alexander and Shiratori 1994; Nassmacher 2001, 2009; Smilov and Toplak 2007; Casal Bértoa et al. 2014). As argued by Casas Zamora, state subsidies 'are not necessarily an antidote to financial dependence on private sources of funding, and, even less, to unsavoury funding practices' (2005, 39).

Second, concerns were raised on the potentially pernicious effects of public funding, which may entrench the electoral position of established groups, petrify the party system and restrict opportunities for new party competitors (Paltiel 1979; Katz and Mair 1995). If proven true, public subsidies would undermine – rather than promote – the fundamental principles of democracy, restrict political pluralism and bias the electoral arena. Empirical research testing the effects of direct public funding on new party entry, however, has mostly contested such claims. With few exceptions (van Biezen and Rashkova 2014), such studies have found that the introduction of public funding to parties does not make it less likely that new parties will emerge (see among others, Detterbeck 2005; Scarrow 2006). Similar results stand out when focusing specifically on the eligibility rules for public funding, as thresholds have been lowered over time to also include parties without parliamentary representation (Bowler, Carter and Farrell 2003; Piccio and van Biezen 2014).

However, public funding also has potential to impact upon the organisations of political parties. Public funding schemes create additional revenue for political parties and have become the most important source of income for parties in virtually all European democracies, including post-Communist ones (Katz and Mair 1995; Nassmacher 2009; van Biezen and Kopecky 2014, 2017). The introduction of state support to political parties and their growing reliance on public sources of income not only constituted 'a fundamental change in the character of the party, furthering its transformation from a private association into a semi-public entity' (Katz

2002, 90), but also affected the internal functioning of party organisations and their interaction with society at large.

The literature on party organisations has long drawn attention to the way in which political parties are financed, for example through associating different organisational models with different patterns of party funding. As a crude synthesis, cadre parties were financed by few influential supporters; mass parties from their members; and catch-all parties by contributions (from interest groups see Krouwel 2006, 261–265). Katz and Mair (1995), however, not only envisaged the cartel party as a new model, stimulated by the introduction of direct public funding to political parties, but also brought attention to the fact that state subventions – mostly disbursed to parliamentary fractions – affected the internal balance of power within party organisations. More specifically, resources and decision-making power were seen to be moving into the hands of the party in public office at the expense of the party in central office and of the party on the ground.

If the tendency towards centralisation of intra-party power was indeed confirmed, scholars have pointed to the remarkably powerful role that the party in central office still holds vis-à-vis the party in public office (Ignazi and Pizzimenti 2014), despite the ascendancy of the party in public office. Moreover, studies observed a weak temporal connection between subsidy introduction and decline in the enrolment of party members (Scarrow 2015), suggesting that state funding does not necessarily undermine party membership (van Biezen and Kopecký 2017).

Yet, while the erosion of party membership may have started independently from the changes in the funding regime, parties that strongly rely on the state may have fewer incentives to recruit and retain new members, particularly for financial reasons (Whiteley 2011). In this sense, the introduction of public funding may have further strengthened the erosion of parties' linkages with society, as stated by Katz and Mair (Ignazi 2017).

In summary, the growing access of political parties to public resources may be beneficial in terms of making electoral competition less unequal, but it presents several risks including increasing levels of anti-party sentiment, a widening gap between the citizenry and political institutions, and the erosion of parties' legitimacy as representative agents.

The role of private funding

Research on party funding in countries with privately funded political competition in Anglo-Saxon countries has tended to focus on different issues than the literature on continental European countries. In private funding systems, a distinction is made between beneficial and pernicious sources of private income, the former being formed by donations by members and supporters, the latter originating from large companies and interest groups. Unsurprisingly, of the two, it is the big donors who provide a highly disproportionate share of campaign funds (Mutch 2014), giving rise to particular concerns regarding the sources of party funding.

The first and most important concern in relation to the private funding of politics has to do with the translation of economic inequality into political inequality and the role of wealth in democratic processes (Hopkin 2004; Cagé 2020). In contexts where state support is limited, candidates heavily rely on private resources if they want to campaign effectively. An extensive literature has shown that candidates with fundraising advantages are more likely to win elections (Barber 2015). A research report issued by the Brennan Center for Justice (Vyas, Lee and Clark 2020) revealed for example that over the past four general elections of the House of Representatives, the average losing candidate raised 640,000 dollars, as compared to the 1.8 million dollars raised on average by the winning candidate. Thus, candidates that have financial means and connections to powerful networks are more likely to run for office and to be elected than those from groups that occupy more marginal positions in society. This has important implications for the reproduction of social inequalities including those relating to gender and minority groups (Muriaas, Wang and Murray 2019).

The influence of moneyed networks on democratic processes is, however, limited to elections and also affects legislative behaviour. Scholars have shown that elected candidates tend to provide donors with preferential treatment in terms of more favourable regulation, in the awarding of government contracts, lower levels of governmental monitoring and more favourable administrative decisions (see Evertsson 2018 for a review). Such developments suggest a clear impact of corporate contributions on policy outcomes (Powell 2012).

Research has also analysed the characteristics of both political donors and the recipients of political funding. It has revealed that whereas individual donors tend to fund candidates based on ideological similarity (Francia et al. 2003), interest groups and large donors tend to give to candidates across the ideological spectrum, suggesting that access to legislators is their primary interest (Barber 2015). Not coincidentally, it is incumbents who have held previous parliamentary or leadership positions that receive the most significant amount of funding. In the eyes of donors, they are more competent, hold a more solid institutional network and have the ability to actually shape those policy sectors they have been working on during their previous term (Fouirnaies and Hall 2014).

As mentioned earlier, Anglo-Saxon countries have found different solutions to these concerns, some introducing greater restrictions on private donations and expenditures than others (Boatright 2015; Mendilow and Phelippeau 2018). Research in this area has also developed a strong focus on the rule of the courts, in particular in the USA and Canada. There constitutional oversight has meant that the courts played an active role in reviewing campaign finance laws. In both countries, the debate revolved around the constitutional protection of freedom of expression and whether this is hindered by restrictive political finance regulations which seek to promote political equality (leading to opposite results, see Boatright 2015).

Limitations of research on party finance

Despite important advances having been made in the field, scholars have highlighted important limitations in party funding research (Scarrow 2007; van Biezen and Kopecky 2017; Mendilow 2018). To be sure, significant improvements have been made in the last two decades in terms of the availability of cross-national data on party finance. In a growing number of countries, party finance data are made publicly available either by official monitoring agencies and/or by political parties, which publish (compulsorily or voluntarily) their annual financial accounts on their websites. However, with the relevant exception of the Political Parties Database Project (PPDB),[5] there have been few systematic efforts to compare such data cross-nationally. According to Mendilow, the scarcity of cross-national empirical analysis is due to relevant 'childhood diseases' in the field, which lacks a shared understanding of some important definitional and operational standards for research, for example on the actual contours of political finance and on how income or spending ought to be measured (2018, 6–7).

Another critical aspect is that party funding research over the latest decade has centred on regulation through focusing on the content of the political finance rules.[6] While extremely useful especially for the investigation of the prevailing ideas about the place of political parties in modern democracies, such an approach is insufficient when it comes to explaining the actual micro-dynamics of party funding, especially in comparative terms. Questions still to be sufficiently addressed include, for example: Into whose pockets does the money from public and private contributions flow? What is the relationship between the party in central office and local branches? What is the party-candidate financial nexus and are funds distributed to candidates?

How do parties spend their money? And what are the answers to these questions across party families and countries? Moving beyond analyses solely centred on party funding rules and official party finance data (see Pinto-Duschinsky 2018, 331) may substantially increase our knowledge in these areas. Medium to large-N investigations on the actual practices of political party funding, through the administration of questionnaires and interviews to party candidates, would therefore constitute an important asset for advancements in the field.[7]

Additionally, some areas of party funding research have received greater attention than others, especially in comparative terms. For example, we know very little of the extent and the way in which political parties spend their money. Noticeably, the comparative index of party spending proposed in one of the very first comparative studies on party funding research (Heidenheimer 1963), which standardised political spending in terms of the number of voters and the average salary of a skilled worker, was never subsequently used (Scarrow 2007; but see Nassmacher 2003, for analysis of spending levels in Anglo-Saxon countries). This is a significant gap in empirical research on party funding, which also has potential implications for (unresolved) debates surrounding the rising cost of politics. Relatively little empirical research exists on this area, which is problematic when it has been common for academics and politicians to justify the expansion of state funding for political parties based on the growing expenses of the latter (Pinto-Duschinsky 2002; also Farrell 2006).

Scholars have highlighted how party funding research remains underdeveloped in theoretical terms (Scarrow 2007). The field has grown significantly following the theoretical contributions of Katz and Mair. However, in studies testing their propositions an over-emphasis of party finance-related factors has emerged, often at the expense of other important institutional factors (Nassmacher 2009; Koß 2011). We may say that the literature on party funding has been suffering from delusions of grandeur which expanded as if it was an autonomous field of research and developed in isolation from the mainstream party literature and research on electoral systems and party systems in particular (see Hopkin 2004). This may also explain why studies that have taken party funding as an independent variable to explain party system characteristics have so often yielded mixed findings. A more consistent dialogue with other relevant strands of the comparative party research, but also with the literature on policy process, may contribute to the development of a more comprehensive and empirically adequate theoretical understanding of the complexity of party funding, both as an independent and as a dependent variable.

Conclusions and avenues for future research

Research on party finance should take notice of important recent developments that have been taking place in contemporary politics. First, there is an urgent need for party funding research to adapt to the changing reality of political campaigning. The movement 'from the fringe to the mainstream' of online campaigning predicted by Gibson and Ward (1998, 33) has important implications. In a recent report, the United Kingdom Electoral Commission showed that 42.8 per cent of the reported spending by parties on advertising for the UK 2017 general elections was digital, almost double than in the 2015 election (Electoral Commission 2021). Political parties have been increasingly relying on the internet as a campaigning tool, but we know very little about the advertising strategies of parties (or candidates) on platforms such as Facebook, Google and Twitter and how their money is spent on such advertising. Building knowledge in this respect is likely to present challenges to established methodologies and also in terms of the availability of the data (Margetts 2017; Dommett and Power 2019). Research must also address the almost non-existent regulation of online political advertising. It is essential that researchers working on party funding develop an understanding of what is going on in this new arena of electoral competition.

The second aspect that needs to be explored relates to the growing use of the conditionality principle in public funding regulations. In what Scarrow (2011) referred to as 'stick and carrot' dynamics, public funding is increasingly accompanied with more stringent regulations that parties are forced to comply with. Under this logic, legislators in a growing number of countries (and at the European Union level) have sought to take advantage of the generous amount of public funding that political parties receive by linking the allocation of money to a number of additional requirements. In particular, public funding schemes have been used as a lever to improve the commitment of political parties to intra-party democracy, gender equality goals and to the respect of broader democratic values (Bale 2007; Kocenov and Morijn 2020; Feo and Piccio 2020). Research may investigate why and in what circumstances such regulations are being adopted, whether they have been effective in reaching their objectives, or if they are rather used as smokescreens with no pretention of being effective.

Finally, the changed role of the state should be considered. Public funding to political parties was introduced in a period in which states were expanding their budgets and functions. In the current conditions of retrenchment, the persistence of high amounts of state support to political parties appears puzzling. As Ewin and Issacharoff put it, 'the state is in retreat but the organisations managing that retreat are themselves seeking support' (2006, 5–6). This situation has become paradoxical following the 2008 Great Recession, and the introduction of austerity measures that entailed a significant reduction of public spending throughout Europe. Legislators seem to have recognised this contradiction. Notably, all European countries that were most affected by the financial crisis (Portugal, Spain, Ireland, Greece and Italy) amended party finance laws in order to reduce – if not repeal, as in the case of Italy[8] – the subsidies available to political parties.

A recent article examining the main parties' balance sheets in France, the UK, Spain, Italy and Germany confirms a connection between the Great Recession and the end of opulent state funding for political parties (Ignazi and Fiorelli 2021). Such developments suggest that countries in Europe may experience diminished state intervention in party finance. If this is the case, it challenges the conventional wisdom that party funding regimes have been moving from private to public subsidisation and not vice versa (Ewing 2007). Therefore, researchers should place greater attention on private sources of funding, including in contexts where state funding to political parties has traditionally been dominant. This is particularly the case for continental Europe, where research on public funding has overshadowed the study of private funding. We now have abundant information on the amounts of state funding that parties receive and how this impacts total party income in European countries, but private funding has remained almost exclusively a field of research in Anglo-Saxon countries (notwithstanding Ponce and Scarrow 2011; Fiorelli 2021). More research is required to analyse the origins of private funding, the incentives of donors and their actual role in democratic politics.

Conversely, greater attention should also be paid to parties' fundraising practices. Research has shown that, in countries where private sources of income are dominant, parties are more actively engaged in fundraising activities (Gibson et al. 2003; see Karlsen 2013 for a continental European perspective). If governments turn off the taps of funding in continental Europe, it is reasonable to expect that parties will adapt. Such developments may have potential benefits if parties do more to reach out to citizens. These changes, in the context of a more general shift from party-centred to candidate-centred campaigning in Europe, may bring the two main approaches to party funding research discussed in this chapter empirically and theoretically closer to one another. In this respect, a degree of 'Americanisation' in party funding research may help scholars to keep up with developments of contemporary politics.

Notes

1. See among others, Venice Commission (2001); van Biezen (2003); International IDEA (2014); OSCE/ODIHR and Venice Commission (2020).
2. The source covering the widest range of countries in the world is the Political Finance Database of the International Institute for Democracy and Electoral Assistance (International IDEA) that provides up-to-date information on the way in which the core areas of party funding are regulated (www.idea.int/data-tools/data/political-finance-database). A second useful source is the database developed within the framework of the 'Party Law in Modern Europe' project by van Biezen, which comprises longitudinal data on the evolution of party funding rules in 33 European democracies, up to 2013 (www.partylaw.leidenuniv.nl/). The Evaluation and Compliance Reports issued by the Group of States against Corruption (GRECO), which provides qualitative information on party funding regulations in all Council of Europe Member States, are a third key source of information on political finance (www.coe.int/en/web/greco/evaluations/round-3).
3. Before Germany, state funding to political parties was introduced in Uruguay (1928) and Costa Rica (1956).
4. By party funding regimes, we mean the institutional norms and decision rules defining party access to resources, party spending and accounting procedures (see Casas-Zamora 2005; Koß 2011).
5. See Scarrow, Webb and Poguntke (2017) and the PPDB project website: www.politicalpartydb.org/.
6. An important impetus in this respect has been provided by the 'Party Law in Modern Europe' project directed by van Biezen (discussed above). See also Norris and van Es 2017.
7. The Comparative Candidate Survey multi-national project is an important step in this direction. See www.comparativecandidates.org/.
8. Italy stands as an exception to Nassmacher's frequently quoted statement 'once introduced, public subsidies are never subsequently abolished' (2003, 33; see Piccio 2020 on Italy's recent reform).

References

Alexander, H.A. and Shiratori, R. (eds.) (1994) *Comparative political finance among the democracies*. Boulder: Westview.
Bale, T. (2007) 'Are bans on political parties bound to turn out badly? A comparative investigation of three 'intolerant' democracies: Turkey, Spain, and Belgium', *Comparative European Politics*, 5, p141–157.
Barber, M.J. (2015) 'Ideological donors, contribution limits, and the polarization of American legislatures', *The Journal of Politics*, 78(1), p296–310.
Boatright, R. (ed.) (2015) *The deregulatory moment? A comparative perspective on changing campaign finance laws*. Ann Arbor: University of Michigan Press.
Bowler, S., Carter, S. and Farrel, D. (2003) 'Changing party access to elections', in Dalton, R.J., Scarrow, S. and Cain, B.E. (eds.) *Democracy transformed? Expanding political opportunities in advanced industrial democracies*. Oxford: Oxford University Press, pp. 81–111.
Cagé, J. (2020) *The Price of democracy*. Cambridge: Harvard University Press.
Casal Bértoa, F., Molenaar, F., Piccio, D.R. and Rashkova, E. (2014) 'The world upside down. Delegitimising political finance regulation', *International Political Science Review*, 35(3), pp. 355–375.
Casas-Zamora, K. (2005) *Paying for democracy: Political finance and state funding for parties*. Colchester: ECPR Press.
Clift, B. and Fisher, J. (2004) 'Comparative party finance reform: The cases of France and Britain', *Party Politics*, 10(6), p677–699.
Detterbeck, K. (2005) 'Cartel parties in Western Europe?', *Party Politics*, 11(2), p173–191.
Dommett, K. and Power, S. (2019) 'The political economy of Facebook advertising: Election spending, regulation and targeting online', *The Political Quarterly*, 90(2), p257–265.
Electoral Commission of the United Kingdom (2021) 'Know who is paying for online political adds'. Available at: www.electoralcommission.org.uk/i-am-a/voter/online-campaigning/know-who-paying-online-political-ads (Accessed 10 June 2021).
Ewing, K.D. (2007) *The cost of democracy: Party funding in modern British politics*. Oxford: Hart Publishing.
Ewing, K.D. and Issacharoff, S. (2006) 'Introduction', in Ewing, D. and Issacharoff, S. (eds.) *Party funding and campaign financing in international perspective*. London: Bloomsbury Publishing, pp. 1–10.

Evertsson, N. (2018) 'Corporate contributions to electoral campaigns. The current state of affairs', in Mendilow, J. and Phelippeau, E. (eds.) *Handbook of political party funding*. Cheltenham: Edward Elgar Publishing, pp. 33–54.

Farrell, D.M. (2006) 'Political parties in a changing campaign environment', in Katz, R.S. and Crotty, W. (eds.) *Handbook of party politics*. London: Sage, pp. 122–133.

Feo, F. and Piccio, D.R. (2020) 'Promoting gender equality through party funding: Symbolic policies at work in Italy', *Politics and Gender*, 16(3), p903–929.

Fiorelli, C. (2021) *Political party funding and private donations in Italy*. London: Palgrave.

Francia, P.L., Herrnson, P.S., Green, J.C., Powell, L.W. and Wilcox, C. (2003) *The financiers of Congressional elections: Investors, ideologues, and intimates*. New York: Columbia University Press.

Fouirnaies, A. and Hall, A.B. (2014) 'The financial incumbency advantage: causes and consequences', *The Journal of Politics*, 76(3), p711–24.

Gibson, R., Margolis, M., Resnick, D. and Ward, S. (2003) 'Election campaigning on the WWW in the US and the UK: A comparative analysis', *Party Politics*, 9(1), p47–76.

Gibson, R. and Ward, S. (1998) 'U.K. political parties and the internet: 'Politics as usual' in the new media?', *Press Politics*, 3, p14–38.

Heidenheimer, A.J. (1963) 'Comparative party finance. Notes on practices and toward a theory', *The Journal of Politics*, 25(4), p790–811.

Hopkin, J. (2004) 'The problem with party finance: Theoretical perspectives on the funding of party politics', *Party Politics*, 10(6), p627–651.

Ignazi, P. (2017) *Party and democracy. The uneven road to party legitimacy*. Oxford: Oxford University Press.

Ignazi, P. and Fiorelli, C. (2021) 'The end of Cornucopia: Party financing after the Great Recession', *Government and Opposition*, p1–24. https://doi.org/10.1017/gov.2021.3.

Ignazi, P. and Pizzimenti, E. (2014) 'The reins of intra-party power in the Italian political parties (1990–2011)', *Rivista Italiana di Scienza Politica*, 44(3), p223–245.

International Institute for Democracy and Electoral Assistance (2014) *Funding of political parties and election campaigns*. Stockholm: International IDEA.

Karlsen, R. (2013) 'Obama's online success and European party organisations: Adoption and adaptation of U.S. online practices in the Norwegian Labor Party', *Journal of Information Technology & Politics*, 10(2), p158–170

Katz, R.S. (2002) 'The internal life of parties', in Luther, K.R. and Müller-Rommel, F. (eds.) *Political challenges in the new Europe: Political and analytical challenges*. Oxford: Oxford University Press, pp. 87–118.

Katz, R.S. and Mair, P. (1995) 'Changing models of party organization and party democracy: The emergence of the cartel party', *Party Politics*, 1(1), p5–28.

Koß, M. (2011) *The politics of party funding: State funding to political parties and party competition in Western Europe*. Oxford: Oxford University Press.

Kochenov, D. and Morijn, J. (2020) 'Augmenting the charter's role in the fight for the rule of law in the European Union: The cases of judicial independence and party financing', RECONNECT Working Paper No. 11.

Koole, R. (2014) 'Dilemmas of regulating political finance', in van Biezen, I. and ten Napel, H.M. (eds.) *Regulating political parties: European democracies in comparative perspective*. Leiden: Leiden University Press, pp. 45–70.

Krouwel, A. (2006) 'Party models', in Katz, R.S. and Crotty, W. (eds.) *Handbook of party politics*. London: Sage, pp. 249–269.

Margetts, H. (2017) 'Why social media may have won the 2017 general election', *The Political Quarterly*, 88(3), p386–390.

Mendilow, J. (2018) 'Introduction: The party funding paradox and attempts at solutions' in Mendilow, J. and Phelippeau, E. (eds.) *Handbook of political party funding*. Cheltenham: Edward Elgar Publishing, pp. 1–14.

Muriaas, R.L., Wang, V. and Murray, R. (eds.) (2019) *Gendered electoral financing: Money, power and representation in comparative perspective*. New York: Routledge.

Mutch, R.E. (2014) *Buying the vote. A history of campaign finance reform*. Oxford: Oxford University Press.

Nassmacher, K.H. (ed.) (2001) *Foundations for democracy: Approaches to comparative political finance*. Baden-Baden: Nomos Verlag.

Nassmacher, K.H. (2003) 'The funding of political parties in the Anglo-Saxon orbit', in Austin, R. and Tjernström, M. (eds.) *Funding of political parties and election campaigns*. Stockholm: International IDEA, pp. 33–54.

Nassmacher, K.H. (2009) *The funding of party competition. Political finance in 25 democracies*. Baden-Baden: Nomos Verlag.

Norris, P. and van Es, A. (2016) *Checkbook elections? Political finance in comparative perspective*. Oxford: Oxford University Press.

OSCE/ODIHR and Venice Commission (2020) *Guidelines on political party regulation*. Strasbourg: OSCE/ODIHR and Venice Commission.

Paltiel, K.Z. (1979) 'The impact of election expenses legislation in Canada, Western Europe and Israel', in Alexander, H.E. (ed.) *Political finance*. London: Sage, pp. 15–39.

Piccio, D.R. (2014) 'Northern, Western and Southern Europe', in Falguera, E., Jones, S. and Ohman, M. (eds.) *Funding of political parties and election campaigns: A Handbook on political finance*. Stockholm: International IDEA, pp. 206–247.

Piccio, D.R. (2020) 'Party funding in Italy: Organizational models, empirical evidence and party self-delegitimation', *Contemporary Italian Politics*, 12(4), p461–475.

Piccio, D.R. and van Biezen, I. (2014) 'More, and more inclusive, regulation: the legal parameters of public funding', in Boatright, R. (ed.) *The deregulatory moment? A comparative perspective on changing campaign finance laws*. Michigan: University of Michigan Press.

Pinto-Duschinsky, M. (2002) 'Financing politics: A global view', *Journal of Democracy*, 13, p69–86.

Pinto-Duschinsky, M. (2018) 'Party funding in Britain', in Mendilow, J. and Phelippeau, E. (eds.) *Handbook of political party funding*. Cheltenham: Edward Elgar Publishing, pp. 310–334.

Ponce, A.F. and Scarrow, S. (2011) 'Who gives? Partisan donations in Europe', *West European Politics*, 34(5), p997–1020.

Powell, L.W. (2012) *The influence of campaign contributions in state legislatures: The effects of institutions and politics*. Ann Arbor: University of Michigan Press.

Scarrow, S.E. (2006) 'Party subsidies and the freezing of party competition: Do cartel mechanisms work?', *West European Politics*, 29(4), p619–639.

Scarrow, S.E. (2007) 'Political finance in comparative perspective', *Annual Review of Political Science*, 10, p193–210.

Scarrow, S.E. (2011) 'Carrot and sticks, chicken and eggs. Understanding variations in party finance regulatory regimes', Paper presented at IPSA/ECPR conference, Sao Paolo, 16–19 February 2011.

Scarrow, S.E. (2015) *Beyond party members. Changing approaches to partisan mobilization*. Oxford: Oxford University Press.

Scarrow, S.E., Webb, P. and Poguntke, T. (eds.) (2017) *Organizing political parties representation, participation, and power*. Oxford: Oxford University Press.

Smilov, D. and Toplak, J. (eds.) (2007) *Political finance and corruption in Eastern Europe: The transition period*. Aldershot: Ashgate Publishing Limited.

Smulders, J. and Maddens, B. (2016) 'Political parties' Annual accounts and the impact of the group of states against corruption in 18 European states: Towards enhanced transparency?', *Election Law Journal: Rules, Politics, and Policy*, 15(2), p175–186.

van Biezen, I. (2003) *Financing of political parties and election campaigns*. Strasbourg: Council of Europe.

van Biezen, I. (2010) 'Campaign and party finance', in Leduc, L., Niemi, R.G. and Norris, P. (eds.) *Comparing democracies 3: Elections and voting in the 21st Century*. London: Sage, pp. 65–97.

van Biezen, I. and Kopecky, P. (2014) 'The cartel party and the state: Party – state linkages in European democracies', *Party Politics*, 20(2), p170–182.

van Biezen, I. and Kopecky, P. (2017) 'The paradox of party funding. The limited impact of state subsidies on party membership', in Scarrow, S.E., Webb, P. and Poguntke, T. (eds.) *Organizing political parties. Representation, participation, and power*. Oxford: Oxford University Press, pp. 84–105.

van Biezen, I. and Rashkova, E. (2014) 'Deterring new party entry? The impact of state regulation on the permeability of party systems', *Party Politics*, 20(6), p890–903.

Venice Commission (2001) *Guidelines and report on the financing of political parties*. Strasbourg: Council of Europe.

Vyas, N., Lee, C. and Clark, G. (2020) *Small donor public financing could advance race and gender equity in congress*. New York: Brennan Centre for Justice.

Walecki, M. (2007) 'The Europeanization of political parties. Influencing the regulations on political finance', EUI Working Papers, MWP No. 2007/29.

Whiteley, P. (2011) 'Is the party over? The decline of party activism and membership across the democratic world', *Party Politics*, 17(1), p21–44.

7
PARTY INSTITUTIONALISATION

Nicole Bolleyer

From its inception, the concept of party institutionalisation – in essence denoting a party's development towards consolidation[1] – was crucially shaped by the mass party model of party organisation initially developed in Western Europe (Panebianco 1988). By now, the concept has successfully travelled to different world regions like Central Eastern Europe or Latin America (e.g. Mainwaring and Scully 1995; Tavits 2012, 2013) and has consequently been refined. Studying party institutionalisation has particular practical relevance in new democracies, since stable parties can be crucial for the viability and functioning of democracy (see, among others, Dix 1992; Randall 2006; Svåsand 2013). Institutionalised parties tend to be more firmly anchored in society, helping parties to overcome collective action problems, and so in turn, allowing for the effective channelling of preferences from citizens to party elites embedded in democratic institutions. Institutionalised parties can help stabilise patterns of party competition, which is relevant to party *system* institutionalisation, a central element in assuring politicians' electoral accountability to citizens at the heart of the democratic process (see also Chapter 3).

While the study of party institutionalisation has without doubt significantly evolved over the last years, the empirical literature on the theme is still dominated either by qualitative studies of a single case or a few cases at the *party level* or, alternatively, by cross-national studies of party *system* institutionalisation at the country level. The latter tend to treat party institutionalisation as one 'building block' of institutionalisation on the system level.[2] One challenge for cross-national empirical research has long been the lack of suitable data preventing research to develop more nuanced frameworks on party organisation (Levitksy 2001a, 106–107). While there is little conceptual disagreement that party institutionalisation *somehow* relates to party organisational features (*how* is an issue I come back to later), cross-national studies on party institutionalisation have (at least in part) used proxies such as age[3] or measures based on electoral participation or party electoral support[4] to capture the phenomenon empirically. As we will see later, these are measures rather removed from the theoretical concept, as they capture consequences assumed to be associated with institutionalisation rather than properties of the phenomenon itself. In this context, large-scale cross-national projects on comparative party organisation across different world regions[5] provide the foundation for a new generation of comparative, cross-national research that has helped to reduce the gap between theoretical and operational concepts in comparative studies of party institutionalisation somewhat (e.g. Kitschelt 2015; Bolleyer and Ruth 2018).

That said, the tendency to measure party institutionalisation through its (assumed) consequences (e.g. age, repeated electoral participation, stable electoral support, adaptability) has roots in ongoing conceptual divides in scholarship dealing with the causes and consequences of institutionalisation of party organisations. Scholars remain divided on how to conceptualise and operationalise party institutionalisation. While agreeing on the complexity and multidimensionality of the phenomenon, rival definitions diverge on what its central dimensions are and how they relate to each other (Randall and Svåsand 2002, 12). Pushing the boundaries of the concept, it is further unclear whether, alongside central dimensions that are – one way or the other – related to the nature of a party organisation, party institutionalisation also ought to have an external dimension: 'Reification' is defined as the extent to which a party's existence is established in the public's imagination (Randall and Svåsand 2002, 14; Harmel, Svåsand and Mjelde 2018), a property that is predominantly defined by the perceptions held by actors *outside* the organisation whose institutionalisation the concept aims at capturing.

What can be said about the evolution of the literature on party institutionalisation more broadly is that the uses of the concept increasingly include not only new democracies but also hybrid regimes, which has led to a growing emphasis on party institutionalisation as a multidimensional concept. This intertwined development reflected the need to consider the growing complexity of institutionalisation patterns that appeared 'partial' or 'incomplete' when being assessed against early notions of the concept originating in Western Europe. Relatedly, it has been increasingly recognised that party institutionalisation should not be equated with a particular organisational form or model (e.g. the presence of formal party branches), as this would effectively prevent 'conceptual travel', de facto maintaining the mass party model as a 'gold standard' and one that the majority of parties in new democracies or transition systems are bound to fail against. Finally, recent studies recognise and explore the variation in institutionalisation patterns *within* party organisations that operate in different arenas simultaneously, which expose the organisation to different demands and pressures and invite intra-organisational differentiation.

To do justice to this growing conceptual differentiation, mirroring the concept's usage in increasingly diverse settings, this chapter is divided into the following sections: I start with the dimensions of party institutionalisation related to the internal life of organisations – what Panebianco (1988) denoted as 'systemness'. This is followed by a discussion of the external dimensions of party institutionalisation concerned with institutionalised organisations' relationships with society – autonomy and reification (Randall and Svåsand 2002, 12). Both sections explore central conceptual debates and highlight how these have shaped existing empirical research. The chapter concludes with a summary of the main arguments and a note on emerging work on the concept's counterpart – party de-institutionalisation.

Internal dimensions of party institutionalisation

Numerous authors have proposed their take on the central properties of institutionalised parties, including Huntington (1968), Janda (1980), Levitksy (1998), Panebianco (1988) and Mainwaring (1999). Overall research on party institutionalisation has approached it as an intra-organisational property with the party as the unit of analysis, while its external dimensions discussed later have played a less central role (Randall and Svåsand 2002, 11–12). Going back to Parsons, institutionalisation can be understood as the extent to which organisations transform into 'institutions' in that organisational actors orient their actions towards a common set of norms and shared value patterns (1951, 39). Parson's reference to norms on the one hand and values on the other hand suitably echoes the current debate which by now widely distinguishes (at least) two dimensions of institutionalisation that align with Panebianco's notion of 'systemness' (1988): *routinisation* and *value infusion*, a distinction initially proposed by Levitsky (1998). It was also usefully characterised by Randall and Svåsand as the structural and an attitudinal dimension of a party's internal institutionalisation (2002, 113).

Routinisation – structural institutionalisation – takes place when processes within an organisation become more rule-guided and regularised. This becomes visible in an increasingly elaborate and stable infrastructure (Panebianco 1988, 49, 53), conducive to organisational rules becoming 'perceived as permanent structures' (Levitsky 1998, 81) and to parties as structures being increasingly dense, regularised and thus able to guide followers' behaviour (Janda 1980).[6] While the structures and practices that party elites decide to invest in can be either conducive or detrimental to institutionalisation (Panebianco 1988, 53–65), the latter is 'not identical with the party's development in purely organisational terms' (Randall and Svåsand 2002, 12). Moreover, party institutionalisation should not be equated with particular rules of decision-making or leader recruitment, as both internally democratic and authoritarian party organisations can be highly institutionalised.

More specifically, routinisation, a process whereby followers are socialised into party rules, is not equivalent to placing constraints on leaders' autonomy through the 'formal institutionalisation of internal participation and contestation at all levels of the party' constituting mechanisms for the rank and file to hold leaders accountable (Samuels 2004, 1010; see on this distinction Wills-Otero 2009, 132–133). The latter presupposes particular types of party rules, while routinisation does *not* require formal, vertical accountability mechanisms between followers and leaders. Routinisation can shape the behaviour of leaders, if leaders themselves are recruited from the party base. The two aspects are assumed to go together in the classical mass party model (e.g. Panebianco 1988). Yet various studies such as those on Latin American parties have indicated that outsider recruitment as well as high leadership autonomy or fluidity can co-exist with a routinised party base (Kitschelt 1994; Levitsky 1998; Wills-Otero 2009), stressing the need to treat leader autonomy or fluidity as separate concepts (e.g. Burgess and Levitsky 2003; Bolleyer and Ruth 2018). These findings further suggest that party institutionalisation including its distinct dimensions can vary across the different faces of party organisation, notably its membership organisation (the party on the ground) and the elite level (be it the party in central or public office), as parties simultaneously operate in different arenas (Katz and Mair 1993; Bolleyer and Ruth 2019).

A related point concerns the concept's application to regions outside Europe, which stresses that the *presence of permanent structures* as a factor conducive to base-level routinisation is not equivalent to the creation of formal party branches in the traditional Western European sense. Instead, such routinisation can equally be assured by networks of local intermediaries (Freidenberg and Levitsky 2006; Kitschelt and Kselman 2010). Permanence does not presuppose one particular 'organisational form' but refers to structures (be those formal *or* informal) which guide followers' behaviour as they interact within them and thereby create continuity between elections. These structures support base-level routinisation, because formal party branches as well as informal networks incorporate members and followers into the party (Freidenberg and Levitsky 2006; Kitschelt and Kselman 2010, 13–14). They provide channels for communication between party and grassroots (Levitsky 2001b, 54–56; Tavits 2012, 85–86), with party officials forming part of these structures, as they 'establish routines and standard operating procedures' (Kitschelt 1994, 222), thereby familiarising followers with rules and procedures that govern the internal life of a party.[7]

In contrast to routinisation, *value infusion* – attitudinal institutionalisation – shows when party actors start caring about the survival of their party as such, rather than seeing it as a mere instrument to achieve a set of goals.[8] This raises the question of possible sources of such attachment which can be usefully approached through the lens of incentive-theoretical approaches. Wilson (1973) and Panebianco (1988) have stressed that most membership organisations will try to combine the provision of different incentives to followers to stabilise voluntary support which parties continuously depend on, since followers are free to leave at any point.

While Panebianco (1988, 10–11) associates value infusion especially with non-material collective incentives such as party identification linked to a particular cause or to social and political goals shared by followers, the provision of such incentives can also be generated by leaders embodying core party values (Pedahzur and Brichta 2002, 40; Rosenblatt 2013). This qualification is important as Panebianco is usually referred to – following Weberian traditions (e.g. Eisenstadt 1968) – as a proponent of the incompatibility between charismatic leadership and institutionalisation (e.g. Pedahzur and Brichta 2002). Yet while he presents party dissolution after a charismatic leader's departure as the likely outcome, he considered *strong* institutionalisation as the *second most likely outcome* (with weak institutionalisation being least likely). While he leaves the question unanswered regarding what conditions might support the latter scenario (Panebianco 1988, 161–162),[9] this suggests that if a 'charismatic party' can outlive a change in leadership, attachments to such past (and especially founding) leaders can help strengthen followers' loyalty and, with this, value infusion (see also Randall and Svåsand 2002, 16–21).

Indeed, research on new parties – that allows us to examine the evolution of parties from fluid movements to fully consolidated organisations or, alternatively, decline and death – stresses the complexity of the relationship between charismatic leadership and the propensity to (un)successfully institutionalise. Cases such as the by now declined Danish Progress Party give credence to classical arguments about charismatic leaders undermining party building (Harmel and Svåsand 1993). However, charismatic leaders can also support party institutionalisation (both value infusion and routinisation) or, alternatively, party institutionalisation can remain restricted to particular arenas – for example, inside parliament to assure parties' functioning within institutions – while movement-like structures prevail in the societal domain as the sphere dominated by a charismatic leader (e.g. Pedahzur and Brichta 2002; de Lange and Art 2011; Bolleyer 2013).

Figure 7.1 depicts the analytical configurations resulting from a two-dimensional conceptualisation of party institutionalisation, distinguishing routinisation from value infusion.

The qualitative difference between value infusion and routinisation is important, as the two party properties do not have to go together,[10] which has been underscored by both qualitative and quantitative research. Levitsky (1998) highlighted cases of 'only' attitudinally institutionalised parties in Latin America, most prominently the Argentinian Justicialist Party (PJ), which has been substantiated by later cross-national work (Bolleyer and Ruth 2018, 294). Purely structural institutionalisation is not only wide-spread in very young democracies (Svåsand 2013, 265), as new parties formed by individual entrepreneurs in old democracies have been found to routinise internal processes to support intra-party coordination with little interest in value infusion (Bolleyer 2013, 215–217). Similarly, Latin American parties have created informal branch structures, without cultivating a committed membership (Freidenberg and Levitsky 2006, 179), a discrepancy also found in Central Eastern Europe (van Biezen 2005, 155–156).

These findings of course raise the question why then treat the two aspects as part of the same the overall concept in the first place? Despite this variation, it is important to note that the two dimensions – especially when approached from the perspective of organisational elites – can and often do function in a complementary fashion. Value infusion makes it less likely that followers defect and more likely that they follow the party line for the 'good of the organisation' (even if this clashes with their own interests or preferences). Routinisation also enhances elite control by strengthening the

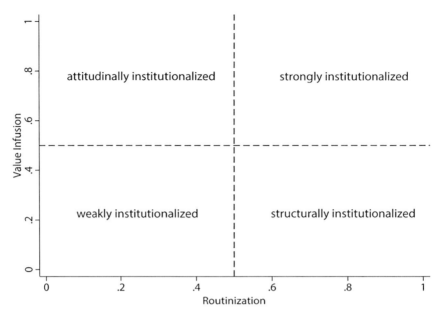

Figure 7.1 Configurations of the internal dimension of party institutionalisation
Source: Bolleyer and Ruth (2018, 290).

predictability of processes. It is an advantage for leaders trying to maintain order over increasingly complex party organisations that become more difficult to oversee, whether they are democratically organised or not (Bolleyer 2013, 55–56). Although incentives for the formation of extra-parliamentary parties institutionalised in the 'traditional sense' (i.e. bringing routinisation and value infusion together) are considered as generally weak in new democracies and increasingly outdated in individualising old democracies, we still find parties operating in different regions that emulate mass party structures (e.g. van Biezen 2003, 2005; Randall 2006; Bolleyer, van Spanje and Wilson 2012; Svåsand 2013; Levitsky, Loxton and Van Dyck 2016).

While this rationalises treating routinisation and value infusion as part of the same overall concept to start with, the distinction is crucial for future research – whether party institutionalisation is considered as a 'dependent variable' or 'independent variable'. Essentially, neither are the two phenomena necessarily supported by the same factors, nor are their consequences necessarily the same. The qualitative difference between the two phenomena understood as distinct dimensions of party-building have informed works theorising and examining founding elites' varying propensity or disinclination to build fully or only partially institutionalised party organisations. The prospect of a party's institutionalisation confronts those in charge of an organisation with a fundamental leadership-structure dilemma: once a party is fully routinised with a support base loyal to the party as such (rather than its leaders), those in charge become replaceable, creating incentives – depending on leaders' time horizon and motivation – towards investing either only structural or in attitudinal institutionalisation (Bolleyer 2013, 21; Rodríguez Teruel and Barrio 2016; Agustín and Briziarelli 2017; Zons and Halstenbach 2019; Farah et al. 2020). Meanwhile, large-N studies have shown that central party system factors have differentiated effects on patterns of institutionalisation: polarisation (indicating the ideological dispersion of parties) is positively associated only with value infusion, fragmentation (shaped by the number and relative size of parties in a party system) only with routinisation. Similar to the latter, state funding and the strength of legislative representation are conducive to routinisation, not value infusion (Bolleyer and Ruth 2018, 296).

Looking at the two dimensions as explanatory variables instead, Levitsky's seminal piece (1998) has shown how value infusion can facilitate party organisational change, while routinisation complicates it.[11] This is fundamental as the ability to adapt is crucial for an organisation's ability to survive which institutionalisation traditionally tends to be associated with (e.g. Huntington 1968; Janda 1980; Panebianco 1988). Similarly fundamental, party institutionalisation is often considered as beneficial for democracy (Huntington 1968; Mainwaring and Scully 1995). Yet it remains unclear whether (too) strongly institutionalised parties might not have negative effects – for example, it might allow parties to acquire a position of dominance thus weakening party competition (e.g. Stockton 2001; Randall 2006; Hicken and Martinez Kuhonta 2011; Casal Bértoa 2016), raising questions about the implications of varying levels of routinisation and value infusion within the same party.

Essentially, research still needs to theorise separately the effects of each dimension on party system institutionalisation and, more broadly, on democracy. If some parties routinise *without* fostering value infusion (i.e. without cultivating an emotional attachment of followers to their party), functional (e.g. clientelistic) linkages underpinned by routinised party structures might support the persistence of parties (Levitsky 2001a; Stokes 2007), which, in turn, might stabilise party competition. Yet such effects are not equivalent to those that can be expected from value infusion in terms of generating citizens' support and attachment to political parties that is not instrumentally driven and might enhance citizens' attachment to democracy more generally.

External dimensions of party institutionalisation

As routinisation and value infusion are qualitatively distinct, so are the properties attributed to party institutionalisation that do not relate to an organisation's internal life but to its relationship with society. Here we can distinguish between two dimensions, one structural and one attitudinal (Randall and Svåsand 2002, 14). Autonomy, the structural external dimension, denotes organisations' ability to define their priorities independently from external actors, hence, organisations are not just an instrument of social groups such as family, clans or class or other societal actors outside the organisation (Huntington 1968, 20; Panebianco 1988; Dix 1992; Stockton 2001). Reification based on Janda (1980) is defined as the extent to which a party's existence is established in the public imagination (Randall and Svåsand 2002, 14).

Autonomy is a criterion which Huntington defined as organisational integrity that finds expression in the organisation's insulation from non-political groups and procedures (1968, 20; Panebianco 1988). Some have questioned whether a party needs autonomy to be institutionalised referring to examples such as social democratic parties' strong ties to unions (Janda 1980, 19; see also Harmel, Svåsand and Mjelde 2018) which taps into questions around the consequences of autonomy on the party organisational level. As further highlighted by Stockton (2001, 109) the concept 'raises a potential contradiction when compared to the necessity for parties to become entrenched in society'. Finally, various studies have shown that ties to pre-existing social organisations, be those unions, environmental or extremist groups, as well as access to state funding can support party institutionalisation (Art 2011; Bolleyer 2013), which seems to clash with the idea of autonomy from external influences – whether located in society or the state – as an expression of enhanced organisational institutionalisation.

Resolving this tension, Randall and Svåsand have offered a useful specification of the concept as 'decisional autonomy' understood as 'freedom from interference in determining its own policies or strategies' (2002, 13–14), thereby allowing for various external dependencies (notably financial ones that [including established] parties are usually subject to) and recognising that such dependencies can but do not necessarily mean that the providers of such resources have any sway over intra-party decisions. Approached in that manner, access to external material and non-material resources for party building during early phases of organisational development might initially reduce decisional autonomy (thereby keeping institutionalisation limited at these early stages), yet at the same time make fully fledged institutionalisation at a later stage more likely.

While debates around the role and consequences of autonomy as a property of party institutionalisation are unresolved, conceptually this feature can be sensibly linked to the two (more widely used) internal dimensions of the overall concept – value infusion and routinisation (both organisational properties) – thereby rationalising its treatment as a component of institutionalisation. Internally stable, routinised processes and a loyal support base can be considered as being complementary to an organisation's ability to define its priorities (relatively) autonomously (Huntington 1968, 20). These elements can thus be considered as jointly contributing to a process through which an organisation transforms into an 'institution' (Parsons 1951; Scott 1995, 75).[12]

In contrast, the second external dimension pushes the boundaries of the concept. Building on Janda's work (1980, 19), 'reification' is defined by Randall and Svåsand as the extent to which a party's existence is established in the public imagination. It denotes when a party's existence 'becomes increasingly a taken-for-granted feature of the political horizon' and when 'individuals and institutions, including other parties . . . more or less consciously adjust their expectations and aspirations accordingly' (2002, 14; Harmel, Svåsand and Mjelde 2018).[13] Unlike the other dimensions, this property is defined by perceptions held by actors (predominantly) *outside* an organisation whose institutionalisation we aim at capturing such as voters and other parties. This contrasts with earlier debates where conceptions of institutions and institutionalisation focused on the orientation and behaviour of the actors within the boundaries of the organisation (Parsons 1951, 39; Selznick 1957, 5; Huntington 1968, 12). Consequently, we can imagine a party organisation that – considering its *own* properties – possesses all other institutionalisation features (routinisation, value infusion and autonomy) but does not meet the threshold for reification. Such a situation would occur if a party is too marginal in terms of institutional access to ever feature in the public imagination or the minds of 'relevant actors' such as established parties (Randall and Svåsand 2002, 14; Harmel, Svåsand and Mjelde 2018).

Furthermore, this 'fourth' dimension brings in a 'relevance threshold', suggesting that parties can only be truly institutionalised if they reach a certain level of importance within their respective systemic context which sits uneasily with the conceptual notions discussed earlier as – methodologically speaking – we move the analysis away from the party level we started out from (and thereby effectively changing our unit of analysis). As relevance thresholds are by definition strongly shaped by institutional barriers defining a political system as well as party system properties (e.g. Pedersen 1982), equally value infused, routinised or autonomous organisations might be 'reified' in one system but not in the other. This is not to say that 'party reification' is not an important phenomenon to study or that the authors discussed presented it as a *necessary* criterion for party institutionalisation to be present (though some do). But the conceptual discrepancies (and the methodological difficulties resulting from them) suggest that factors located outside of the party organisations studied might best be approached as factors benefiting from institutionalisation on the party level or, alternatively, contributing to (or complicating) it, rather than being treated as a defining property of the phenomenon itself.

Conclusions and avenues for further research

Distinguishing internal and external dimensions of party institutionalisation, this chapter discussed central conceptual debates and their repercussions for existing and future research. It showed that this field of research is characterised by disagreement about which qualities define an institutionalised party, how they relate to each other and which properties are – rather than being elements of institutionalisation – likely or at least possible consequences thereof. As such conceptual debates are unlikely to be ever fully resolved, scholars using the concept of party institutionalisation need to strike a balance between analytically exploiting the multidimensionality of the concept while avoiding the tendency to 'over-stretch' its boundaries. One way of doing so is to keep the concept restricted to elements that are clearly located on the party level and refer to party organisational features that can (but do not have to) work in a complementary fashion towards assuring an organisation's persistence as one (possible) outcome closely associated with the concept of 'institution' (Scott 1995, 78). This would suggest that we focus on the properties of routinisation, value infusion and decisional autonomy as *organisation-level* properties.

This has two important consequences, one conceptual and one operational. First, 'reification' defined by external responses and evaluations by actors outside the organisation studied – sometimes included as an external dimension of institutionalisation – should remain outside of the concept's boundaries (see, for a different approach, for instance Harmel, Svåsand and Mjelde 2018), either as a factor potentially impacting on party institutionalisation or as one potentially being impacted upon. Second, rather than using measures of electoral participation, performance or age as institutionalisation proxies – *assuming* that institutionalised parties have more stable support and are more persistent in terms of maintaining core organisational activities (e.g. Arter and Kestilä-Kekkonen 2014; Casal Bértoa 2016) – they would be treated as possible causes or consequences of party institutionalisation and thereby become part of the puzzles that future research on party institutionalisation can explore.

What has not been discussed explicitly in this chapter is the distinction between institutionalisation as a 'process' towards consolidation and as the 'state' of being consolidated. This is because each conceptual dimension associated with party institutionalisation in this chapter – routinisation, value infusion and decisional autonomy – can be approached in both ways. Which one is more appropriate is fundamentally shaped by our substantive interest and whether we approach party institutionalisation as a dependent or independent variable. Studying the conditions for successful or failed institutionalisation suggests a process-orientated approach starting out from an early phase of party development. An interest in how different levels of institutionalisation feed into patterns of party system, institutionalisation treats it as a state varying across the respective party units whose impact on the system level we are interested in. Both perspectives provide valuable perspectives for future research.

This brings me to a final point; while avenues for future research have been mentioned throughout this chapter, one area deserves particular highlighting: with few exceptions, the literature has paid little attention to the 'opposite' to institutionalisation – de-institutionalisation (Randall and Svåsand 2002, 15) despite a considerable body of literature on party decline and failure. Based on Huntington's notion of decay (1965), Harmel, Svåsand and Mjelde define this under-used concept[14] as discrete set-backs during the process of institutionalisation or instances of parties' reversal away from a fully institutionalised state (2018, 6). Much like the literature on party institutionalisation which – for a period – 'trailed behind' research on party system institutionalisation, this theme is bound to gain importance. This seems likely not only because of tendencies of party decline and occasional collapse in consolidated democracies but also due to the de-institutionalisation of party systems which deeply affects the functioning of new democracies (and sometimes old democracies).[15] These developments (yet again) give reasons for scholars to move from the system 'down' to the party level.

Notes

1. According to Huntington, institutionalisation 'is the process by which organisations and procedures acquire value and stability' (1968, 12).
2. Party *system* institutionalisation has been theorised referring to four dimensions: the stability of the rules of competition, the legitimacy of the party system, the stability of parties' roots in society, and the strength of party structures. Roots in society have so far been operationalised through indicators as diverse as party age or ideological party-voter linkage; the strength of party organisation usually is left aside. See on this Mainwaring and Scully (1995), Mainwaring and Torcal (2006), Sanchez (2008), Luna (2014) and Casal Bértoa (2016). Studying party institutionalisation can specifically contribute to the refined measurement of two of the four conceptual dimensions of party system institutionalisation (Luna 2014, 406–407): the rootedness of parties in society suggesting stable ties between parties and followers (echoing the concept of value infusion) and the extent to which party infrastructures are well developed and stabilise relationships with followers (echoing the concept of routinisation).
3. For example Harmel and Janda (1994), Mainwaring (1999), Roberts and Wibbels (1999) and Bolleyer, Ibenskas and Keith (2016). See, for a critical discussion, Luna (2014).
4. For example Janda, 1980; Rose and Mackie, 1988; Pedahzur and Brichta, 2002; Casal Bértoa, 2016.
5. For example https://sites.duke.edu/democracylinkage/data/; www.politicalpartydb.org/, accessed August 20 2020.
6. Similarly, Mainwaring (1999, 27–28) considers party structures as institutionalised if they are firmly established, territorially comprehensive, well organised and equipped with own resources.
7. This is echoed by empirical research in social psychology, management and public administration underlining that the presence of organisational infrastructures (formal offices or informal networks) intensifies and regularises contact between group members, while restricting interaction with others (Borgatti and Foster 2003, 995–996, 1004; Lee and Kim 2011, 206–207). This establishes interconnected relationships that are voluntary but become socially shared, structural facts that constrain behaviour as they support the further assimilation of group members' attitudes and the development of behavioural routines between them through imitation and learning, while decreasing turn-over (Becker 2004, 651; Brass et al. 2004, 796–797). Local units (establishing dense networks and short paths between those operating in them) facilitate the diffusion of practices and norms of reciprocity within and across units, reinforced by officers with formal organisational roles supporting the standardisation of norms and practices and incentivising compliance with them (Brass et al. 2004, 803–807).
8. For example Selznick 1957, 17; Huntingon 1968, 16; Janda 1980, 19; Panebianco 1988, 49, 53; Levitsky 1998, 82.
9. The ability to outlive founding leaders is usually considered a 'critical test' for whether a party is institutionalised (Huntington 1968, 14; Mainwaring 1999; Bolleyer 2013) though it is less clear which dimension it ought to be assigned to. According to Mainwaring, routinisation finds expression in established procedures for selecting and changing party leaders enabling the party to outlive its current leadership (1999, 27–8). Accordingly to Huntington (1968) one of the three internal characteristics of institutionalisation (a fourth one – autonomy – is external) is adaptability (a function of organisations having coped with challenges) finding expression (alongside other things) in the ability to survive a first generation of leaders (1968, 13–14).
10. Also Huntington's conceptualisation has attitudinal and structural elements, both of which, however, deviate from the understanding of value infusion and routinisation. Coherence refers to the degree of consensus within the organisation on the functional boundaries and procedures for dispute resolution within these boundaries, while complexity refers to the number of subunits (1968, 17–18; 22–24).
11. Echoing this, authors such as Randall and Svåsand (2002, 15) have argued in favour of treating 'adaptability' as a possible consequence of institutionalisation rather than as a 'defining' feature of institutionalisation as proposed by Huntington (1968, 13).
12. Note this is not equivalent to self-sufficiency in terms of resources.
13. Going back to Janda's work, while referring to institutionalised parties as those 'reified in the public mind' he ties such external perception back to party-level properties i.e. the party's existence as social organisation apart from its momentary leader that demonstrates recurrent behaviour valued by those belonging to it (1980, 19).

14 As Randall and Svåsand (2002, 15) point out, there is a body of research on individual cases. These include India's Congress Party, the Popular American Revolutionary Alliance in Peru, Democratic Action in Venezuela or the Spanish UCD (see, for instance, Gunther and Hopkin 2009; Nikolenyi 2014).
15 For example Scherlis 2008; Dargent and Muñoz 2011; Emanuele and Chiaramonte 2020. As Mainwaring et al. (2018) point out scholars working on Latin America, Eastern Europe, Africa or Asia often study party system de-institutionalisation because party systems have not developed in a linear way.

References

Agustín, Ó.G. and Briziarelli, M. (eds.) (2017) *Podemos and the new political cycle: Left-wing populism and anti-establishment politics*. London: Palgrave Macmillan.
Art, D. (2011) *Inside the radical right: The development of anti-immigrant parties in Western Europe*. Cambridge: Cambridge University Press.
Arter, D. and Kestilä-Kekkonen, E. (2014) 'Measuring the extent of party institutionalisation: The case of a populist entrepreneur party', *West European Politics*, 37(5), p932–956.
Becker, M.C. (2004) 'Organizational routines: A review of the literature', *Industrial and corporate change*, 13(4), p643–678.
Bolleyer, N. (2013) *New parties in old party systems: Persistence and decline in 17 democracies*. Oxford: Oxford University Press.
Bolleyer, N., Ibenskas, R. and Keith, D. (2016) 'The survival and termination of party mergers in Europe', *European Journal of Political Research*, 55(3), p642–659.
Bolleyer, N. and Ruth, S. (2018) 'Elite investments in party institutionalization in new democracies: A two-dimensional approach', *Journal of Politics*, 80(1), p288–302.
Bolleyer, N. and Ruth, S. (2019) 'Party institutionalization as multilevel concept: Base- versus elite-level routinization', *Zeitschrift für Vergleichende Politikwissenschaft*, 13(2), p175–198.
Bolleyer, N., van Spanje, J. and Wilson, A. (2012) 'New parties in government: The organisational costs of public office', *West European Politics*, 35(5), p971–998.
Borgatti, S.P. and Foster, P.C. (2003) 'The network paradigm in organizational research: A review and typology', *Journal of Management*, 29(6), p991–1013.
Brass, D.J., Galaskiewicz, J., Greve, H.R. and Tsai, W. (2004) 'Taking stock of networks and organizations: A multilevel perspective', *The Academy of Management Journal*, 47(6), p795–817.
Burgess, K. and Levitsky, S. (2003) 'Explaining populist party adaptation in Latin America', *Comparative Political Studies*, 36(8), p881–911.
Casal Bértoa, F. (2016) 'Political parties or party systems? Assessing the 'myth' of institutionalization and democracy', *West European Politics*, 40(2), p402–429.
Dargent, E. and Muñoz, P. (2011) 'Democracy against parties? Party system deinstitutionalization in Colombia', *Journal of Politics in Latin America*, 3(2), p43–71.
De Lange, S.L. and Art, D. (2011) 'Fortuyn versus Wilders: An agency-based approach to radical right party building', *West European Politics*, 34(6), p1229–1249.
Dix, R.H. (1992) 'Democratization and the institutionalization of Latin American political parties', *Comparative Political Studies*, 24(4), p488–511.
Eisenstadt, S.H. (1968) *Max Weber on charisma and institution building*. London: The University of Chicago Press.
Emanuele, V. and Chiaramonte, A. (2020) 'Going out of the ordinary. The de-institutionalization of the Italian party system in comparative perspective', *Contemporary Italian Politics*, 12(1), p4–22.
Farah, B., Elias, R., De Clercy, C. and Rowe, G. (2020) 'Leadership succession in different types of organizations: What business and political successions may learn from each other', *The Leadership Studies Quarterly*, 31(1), p1–21.
Freidenberf, F. and Levitsky, S. (2006) 'Informal institutions and party organization in Latin America', in Helmke, G. and Levitsky, S. (eds.) *Informal institutions and democracy. lessons from Latin America*. Baltimore: The Johns Hopkins University Press, pp. 178–197.
Gunther, R. and Hopkin, J. (2009) 'A crisis of institutionalization: The collapse of the UCD in Spain', in Gunther, R., Montero, J.R. and Linz, J.J. (eds.) *Political parties: Old concepts and new challenges*. Oxford: Oxford University Press, pp. 191–232.
Harmel, R. and Janda, K. (1994) 'An integrated theory of party goals and party change', *Journal of Theoretical Politics*, 6(3), p259–287.

Harmel, R. and Svåsand, L. (1993) 'Party leadership and party institutionalization: Three phases of development', *West European Politics*, 16(2), p67–88.

Harmel, R., Svåsand, L. and Mjelde, H. (2018) *Institutionalisation (and de-institutionalisation) of rightwing protest parties: The progress parties in Denmark and Norway*. Colchester: ECPR Press.

Hicken, A. and Kuhonta, E.M. (2011) 'Shadows from the past: Party system institutionalization in Asia', *Comparative Political Studies*, 44(5), p572–597.

Huntington, S.P. (1968) *Political order in changing societies*. New Haven: Yale University Press.

Janda, K. (1980) *Political parties: A cross-national survey*. New York: The Free Press.

Katz, R.S. and Mair, P. (1993) 'The evolution of party organization in Europe: The three faces of party organization', *American Review of Politics*, 14, p593–617.

Kitschelt, H. (1994) *The transformation of European social democracy*. Cambridge: Cambridge University Press.

Kitschelt, H. (2015) 'Social policy, democratic linkages, and political governance', in *The quality of government and the performance of democracies conference*. Gothenburg: University of Gothenburg.

Kitschelt, H. and Kselman, D.M. (2010) 'The organizational foundations of democratic accountability: Organizational form and the choice of electoral linkage strategy', in *Annual meeting of the APSA*. Washington, DC: APSA.

Lee, J. and Kim, S. (2011) 'Exploring the role of social networks in affective organizational commitment: Network centrality, strength of ties, and structural holes', *The American Review of Public Administration*, 41(2), p205–223.

Levitsky, S. (1998) 'Institutionalization and Peronism: The case, the concept, and the case for unpacking the concept', *Party Politics*, 4(1), p77–92.

Levitsky, S. (2001a) 'Inside the black box: Recent studies of Latin American party organizations', *Studies in Comparative International Development*, 36(2), p92–110.

Levitsky, S. (2001b) 'An 'organised disorganisation': Informal organisation and the persistence of local party structures in Argentine Peronism', *Journal of Latin American Studies*, 33(1), p29–66.

Levitsky, S., Loxton, J. and Van Dyck, B. (2016) 'Introduction: Challenges of party-building in Latin America', in Levitsky, S., Loxton, J., Van Dyck, B. and Domínguez, J.I. (eds.) *Challenges of party-building in Latin America*. Cambridge: Cambridge University Press, pp. 1–48.

Luna, J.P. (2014) 'Party system institutionalization: Do we need a new concept?', *Studies in Comparative International Development*, 49(4), p403–425.

Mainwaring, S. (1999) *Rethinking party systems in the third wave of democratization: The case of Brazil*. Stanford: Stanford University Press.

Mainwaring, S. and Scully, T.R. (1995) *Building democratic institutions. Party systems in Latin America*. Stanford: Stanford University Press.

Mainwaring, S. and Torcal, M. (2006) 'Party system institutionalization and party system theory after the third wave of democratization', in Katz, R.S. and Crotty, B. (eds.) *Handbook of party politics*. London: Sage, pp. 204–227.

Mainwaring, S., Wantanabe, A., Bizzarro, F. and De Negri, M.V. (2018) 'Party system institutionalization in democracies', *Oxford Bibliographies*, Available at: www.oxfordbibliographies.com/view/document/obo-9780199756223/obo-9780199756223-0248.xml (Accessed 19 March 2021)

Nikolenyi, C. (2014) 'Party system institutionalization in India' in Hicken, A. and Martinez Kuhonta, E. (eds.) *Party system institutionalization in Asia*. Cambridge: Cambridge University Press, pp. 189–211.

Panebianco, A. (1988) *Political parties: Organization and power*. Cambridge: Cambridge University Press.

Parsons, T. (1951) *The social system*. New York: Free Press.

Pedahzur, A. and Brichta, A. (2002) 'The institutionalization of extreme right-wing charismatic parties: A paradox?', *Party Politics*, 8(1), p31–49.

Pedersen, M. (1982) 'Towards a new typology of party lifespans and minor parties', *Scandinavian Political Studies*, 5(1), p1–16.

Randall, V. (2006) 'Party institutionalization and its implications for democracy', *IPSA Congress*, Fukuoka, 9–13 July.

Randall, V. and Svåsand, L. (2002) 'Party institutionalization in new democracies', *Party Politics*, 8(1), p5–29.

Roberts, K.M. and Wibbels, E. (1999) 'Party systems and electoral volatility in Latin America: A test of economic, institutional, and structural explanations', *American Political Science Review*, 93(3), p575–590.

Rodríguez Teruel, J. and Barrio, A. (2016) 'Going national: Ciudadanos from Catalonia to Spain', *South European Society and Politics*, 21(4), p587–607.

Rose, R. and Mackie, T.T. (1988) 'Do parties persist or fail? The big trade-off facing organizations', in Lawson, K. and Merkl, P. (eds.) *When parties fail*. Princeton: Princeton University Press, pp. 533–558.

Rosenblatt, F. (2013) *How to party? Static and dynamic party survival in Latin American consolidated democracies*. Santiago de Chile: Pontifica Universidad Catolica de Chile.

Samuels, D. (2004) 'From socialism to social democracy: Party organization and the transformation of the Workers' Party in Brazil', *Comparative Political Studies*, 37(9), p999–1024.

Sanchez, O. (2008) 'Transformation and decay: The de-institutionalisation of party systems in South America', *Third World Quarterly*, 29(2), p315–337.

Scherlis, G. (2008) 'Machine politics and democracy: The deinstitutionalization of the Argentine party system', *Government and Opposition*, 43(4), p579–598.

Scott, W.R. (1995) *Institutions and organizations*. London: Sage.

Selznick, P. (1957) *Leadership in administration: A sociological interpretation*. New York: Harper & Row.

Stockton, H. (2001) 'Political parties, party systems, and democracy in East Asia: Lessons from Latin America', *Comparative Political Studies*, 34(1), p94–119.

Stokes, S.C. (2007) 'Political clientelism', in Boix, C. and Stokes, S.C. (eds.) *The Oxford handbook of comparative politics*. Oxford: Oxford University Press, pp. 604–627.

Svåsand, L. (2013) 'Party development in the old world: And in the new', in Müller, W.C. and Narud, H.M. (eds.) *Party governance and party democracy*. New York: Springer, pp. 253–274.

Tavits, M. (2012) 'Organizing for success: Party organizational strength and electoral performance in post-communist Europe', *The Journal of Politics*, 74(1), p83–97.

Tavits, M. (2013) *Post-Communist democracies and party organization*. Cambridge: Cambridge University Press.

van Biezen, I. (2003) *Political parties in new democracies. Party organization in Southern and East-Central Europe*. New York: Palgrave MacMillian.

van Biezen, I. (2005) 'On the theory and practice of party formation and adaptation in new democracies', *European Journal of Political Research*, 44(1), p147–174.

Wills-Otero, L. (2009) 'From party systems to party organizations: The adaptation of Latin American parties to changing environments', *Journal of Politics in Latin America*, 1(1), p123–141.

Wilson, J.Q. (1973) *Political organisations*. New York: Basic Books.

Zons, G. and Halstenbach, A. (2019) 'The AfD as a, leaderless' right-wing populist party. How the leadership-structure dilemma left an imprint on the party's leadership', *Polish Political Science Review*, 7(1), p41–60.

8
POLITICAL PARTIES AND SOCIAL MOVEMENTS

Myrto Tsakatika

Political parties are understood to operate in an environment of institutionalised politics necessary to the functioning of representative democracy. They are vital in the latter's operation, since they aggregate citizens' preferences and structure democratic politics. Parties are broad organisations that represent diverse interests and seek perpetuation of their influence and resources through participation in competitive democratic elections. They aim to retain their members by socialising them into their ideology and organisational practice and providing them with selective incentives (see also Chapter 5).

Social movements are known to be focused on protest/contentious activity and to aim at bringing forward a more limited and distinct set of claims (Tilly 2003) that are often blind sighted or excluded from the institutional realm of politics. They aim to influence policy 'from the outside'. Social movements are often described as networks, and the activists, groups and organisations that populate them are not tied to an organisational structure or necessarily subscribe to a comprehensive ideology, although they are bound by ties of solidarity and may be considered to be 'on the same side'.

Political parties are meant to last and are likely to seek to root in society and develop their organisation. Even new parties that highlight virtual participation or are built around leaders with weak middle strata share the same aim. In comparison, research highlights the non-linear pattern of protest and the tendency of social movements to wax and wane. That said, the networks that sustain or constitute (Diani 1992) social movements may remain active during their dormant phase (Flesher Fominaya 2014) in non-political spheres such as the cultural sphere (Kriesi et al. 1995).

While scholarship on party relations with movements has a long history, in recent years this area of research has gained increasing attention. There are broadly two ways in which the relationship between political parties and social movements is portrayed in the literature. The two sets of actors are either understood to tread on distinct paths or they are seen to be working in tandem within the bounds of the same social and political environment. Clearly, focusing on the different roles performed by parties and movements points towards the idea that they follow distinct trajectories, whereas putting the spotlight on the similarities between them, such as their role in facilitating political participation, would point us in the direction of mutual influence and co-operation.

In the two sections that follow, the chapter will discuss these competing perspectives. These sections are written with reference mainly to the context of parties and movements at work in western liberal democracies. However, a section on the expansion of the scope of research in this field will follow suit, pointing out the increasing coverage of more political 'families', geographical regions and regime types as diverse contexts within which parties and movements interact and highlighting the emerging empirical advances in the field. The final section turns to recent theoretical challenges arising from new social and technological developments. It proposes that further research is required on the effects that the 'normalisation' of global crisis politics and the digital revolution are having on the links between political parties and social movements.

Separate spheres and separate paths

Keith and Tsakatika (2022) have recently identified four perspectives regarding the relations between political parties and social movements, two of which highlight separation and two that highlight close interaction.

The first of these perspectives is the one that traditionally understands political parties and social movements as operating in 'separate spheres'. If we start from the premise that politics can be neatly divided into an institutionalised and a non-institutionalised arena, political parties and social movements can be seen as actors that occupy different sides of this divide. Alternatively, parties and movements can themselves be seen as separate political arenas in which citizens can engage in different (and sometimes mutually exclusive) types of political participation (Merkl and Lawson 1988). In one of the first volumes that explicitly aimed to explore the relations between institutionalised politics, occurring through 'voting, lobbying, political parties, legislatures, courts and elected leaders' and non-institutionalised politics, to be found among 'protest marches, demonstrations or boycotts', Jack Goldstone argued that, up until the 1980s, social movement actors were understood as external challengers that periodically emerged to confront 'official' party and electoral politics. Social movements were expected either to fade into oblivion if unsuccessful, or to become, as it were, the victims of their own success by becoming recognised and taking their position in institutionalised politics. Naturally, once institutionalised, social movements experience demobilisation (Goldstone 2003, 1–3). This neat conceptual divide between institutionalised and non-institutionalised politics is near-universally questioned by more contemporary scholarship that either qualifies or outright rejects the 'separate spheres' perspective.

The second perspective, which does not indicate separate spheres, but rather separate trajectories for parties and movements, is referred to as the 'co-variation' thesis (Keith and Tsakatika 2022). The assumption here is that both political parties and social movements are affected by significant changes which are instigating differentiation and distance between them, hence the notion of 'co-variation'. This perspective reflects state-of-the-art research conducted primarily by scholars of party change, according to which political parties may have maintained close ties to social movements in the past but are on a trajectory of increasingly weakening their links to these actors. According to the (still) dominant approach in the party change literature, namely, the 'cartel party' thesis, parties not only aim for winning elections and hence need to appeal to broad majorities with an increasingly catch-all appeal (Kircheimer 1966), but also aim for government office and the resources that come with it. This latter aim transforms them into integral components of a 'cartel' that runs the state and sets the rules of the political game in ways that effectively exclude outside challengers (Katz and Mair 1995).

Any links between parties and social movements can therefore be expected to become more pluralistic, since fixed and exclusive party links to a small, well-defined range of social movements carry the risk of alienating other social movements and place excessive constraints on the range of policies parties can pursue (Kirchheimer 1966). Social movements, on their part, can also be expected to refrain from exclusive engagement with particular political parties, as they may be compromising their chances to influence policy when 'their' party is not in government. Party–movement links can also be expected to be becoming weaker, as parties turn their focus towards the state and away from society. A number of scholars have challenged or qualified this view, pointing out that there is no empirical pattern evident to support an overall weakening links argument (e.g. Thomas 2001; Allern and Bale 2012a). Whereas weakening of links can be identified in some cases, particularly where strong social democratic parties have been in government (Thomas 2001), parties have on the whole maintained formal ties to trade unions and affiliated organisations (Aarts 1995; Poguntke 2003). Furthermore, there are a number of reasons for which political parties may still be expected to engage with social movements. First, new parties may follow a 'niche' (Norris 2005, 6–7) rather than a catch-all strategy aiming to represent constituencies that the cartel party has left out in the cold (Yishai 2001). In doing so, they may seek linkages with social movements that emerge to voice the claims of these constituencies. Parties can also be expected to continue to pursue linkage because their electoral stability (Poguntke 2003) and legitimacy (Warner 2000, 164; Allern 2010) continue to depend on it. Likewise, social movements may be expected to continue to pursue 'policy responsive' linkage (Lawson 1980, 13–16) to parties they have closer links to, when the latter are in government.

In summary, both of the trends that may be expected based on the 'co-variation' perspective, that is, pluralisation and weakening of links between parties and movements, are not identified in a conclusive way by current empirical findings and remain open to investigation.

Blurring the boundaries

The third, 'interpenetration' perspective stands in stark contrast to the 'separate spheres' perspective, as it blurs the divide between institutionalised and non-institutionalised politics. Far from the idea that political parties and social movements live separate (or separating) lives, advocates of the 'interpenetration' perspective understand social movements as 'part of the environment and social structures that shape and give rise to parties' (Goldstone 2003, 2). Political party scholars have similarly coined the term 'environmental linkage' when examining the relationship between parties and organised groups in their broader environment (Schwartz 2005, 38–9). Others have argued that both political parties and social movements face similar environmental challenges (Fraussen and Halpin 2016). Consequently, rather than identifying two actors that operate in completely different spheres, it may be best for us to speak of *a 'party–movement nexus'* (March 2017) where several types of interaction are possible.

Recent empirical research has suggested a general picture where the everyday practice and evolution of both parties and movements can be interlinked in a number of ways. A movement might transform into a party (Agustin and Jørgensen 2016), become a 'movement-party' (Kitschelt 2006; Della Porta et al. 2017), infiltrate a party or grow within a party (Zald and Berger 1978). Moreover, movements pursue change from within political parties, as seen for instance with Occupy movements taking place within two major centre-left parties, the Italian Democratic Party (PD) and the Turkish Republican People's Party (CHP) (Bergan Draege, Chironi and Della Porta 2016). Parties may also co-opt (Schwartz 2010) or englobe and suffocate movements (Tarrow 2015). Movements can cause party splits (Ho 2018). They may become active in electoral campaigns in order to proactively or reactively influence the position of political parties participating in the contest (McAdam and Tarrow 2010, 533–4). Movements and parties may join forces in electoral coalitions (Medina, Teruel and Barrio 2016), in the context of networks with a common purpose (Porcaro 2013) or in joint campaigns and protest activities (Della Porta 2007).

Studies have also found that high levels of membership overlap (Allern 2010; Heaney and Rojas 2015), resource dependence or common action on the grounds of ideological affinity, representation of the same interests and long-term goals (Allern and Bale 2012b) may exist among parties and movements, drawing them together in joint action (Zald 2000). Activist networks may operate across parties and movements over time irrespective of the ebbs and flows of protest cycles (Flesher Fominaya 2014). It is thus likely that relations between parties and movements can shape each other's long-term trajectories. Nonetheless, this perspective has been criticised for not taking into account the factors mentioned in the previous section that highlight the different reasons for which parties and movements may increasingly choose to maintain looser ties or keep distance from each other.

The fourth perspective, 'co-evolution' (Keith and Tsakatika 2022), shares the core assumption of the 'interpenetration' perspective that parties and social movements operate in the same social and political environment and influence each other's long-term trajectories. At the same time, unlike the 'interpenetration' thesis, rather than focusing principally on the identification of overt links between parties and social movements, the 'co-evolution' perspective provides greater insight into the subtle ways in which the two actors may be adapting to the long-term changes each other is experiencing. Mutually shifting towards the adoption of more informal and less exclusive linkages, while continuing to select their preferred interlocutor/s on the basis of some degree of ideological kinship, is the key element of this process, according to the 'co-evolution' perspective.

There is enough evidence to suggest that political parties can be shown to have increasingly cultivated informal interactions with social movements through joint committee meetings, common campaigns and invitations for them to engage in drawing up party manifestos and key decision-making (Thomas 2001; Allern 2010). Social movements also seem to prefer more informal interactions with political parties (Poguntke 2003), because they are as much concerned with their legitimacy and public support as parties are and do not necessarily want to be 'tainted' by being seen as long-term allies of parties in the public eye (Allern and Bale 2012b), particularly in times of 'representation crises'. This evidence points towards a process whereby informal links are to some extent replacing, or are being preferred to, formal links. The outcome of this process may not necessarily be *on the whole* weaker linkages between parties and movements (Tsakatika and Lisi 2013), but rather the transformation of these linkages in the direction of greater informality.

Ideological affinity may, to some extent, continue to condition the range of formal and informal linkages that remain possible between parties and social movements, as these are filtered through overlapping networks of activists and members (Allern 2010). While both parties and movements may look beyond their ideological 'comfort zones' when it comes to attracting linkages, for reasons of electoral strategy or external legitimacy, they can only develop closer and substantial links to those movements that share some aspects of their ideology, values and goals. In other words, links between political parties and social movements may be moving towards greater pluralisation, as the 'co-variation' perspective maintains, but such pluralisation remains bounded, or else, delimited by ideological factors.

The story these trends tell could well be one of mutual adaptation or 'co-evolution' of party–movement linkages. As both sets of actors adapt to changes in their environment, their changing relationship to each other is part and parcel of that adaptation. Hence, if we look at the relationship over time, it may be seen as co-evolutionary (Witko 2009) or, put more eloquently, as an *'ongoing conversation'* (Piccio 2015).

A research agenda with an expanding scope

Much research on the linkages between political parties and social movements has, particularly since the 1970s, focused on the left of the political spectrum, the developed world (particularly Western Europe and North America) and the context of established liberal democracies. At the same time, mirroring the sea changes in global politics that have since occurred, involving economic globalisation, the emergence of the new right, de-colonisation and democratisation, the research agenda that concerns itself with the links between the two types of actor is an expanding agenda that points towards increasing variation in the ways these links are configured. In particular, the field has seen the expansion of research from the left to the right, which calls for a systematic comparison across party families and social movement constellations (Allern 2010); a geographical expansion of research to Eastern Europe, South America, Asia and Africa, which calls for identifying regional patterns of relations; and a much broader investigation into social movement and party relations across different regime types or different phases of democratisation, which begs important questions about the role of these actors in sustaining democracy (for regional perspectives on political parties and social movement links, see, in particular, Chapters 32–36).

Earlier political party research highlighted the links between the labour movement and left-wing parties of both the communist and social democratic party families in Europe (Bartolini 2000) finding evidence of close ties and interdependence based on ideological affinity. Research on the anti-nuclear, anti-racist, peace and women's rights movements of the 1960s and 1970s found that the inability that, in some cases, characterised left parties to respond to the claims of 'new social movements' led to the emergence of new parties such as non-communist left parties and Greens (Kitschelt 1988). More recently, research on the global justice movement of the turn of the century as well as research on South European party politics under the 2008 economic crisis has shown that radical left parties have made significant inroads with the new global and local anti-austerity and pro-direct democracy protest movements and bottom-up social solidarity initiatives based on shared values and objectives rather than common 'ideology' (Della Porta 2007; Tsakatika and Lisi 2013). The left's links to social movements seem to endure (Martin, de Lange and van der Brug 2021). On the other hand, the continued relevance of the relationship between social democracy and the Labour movement after the 1970s has been questioned (Howell 2001). In the aftermath of the 'pink tide', high-profile social movements such as the student movement in the Southern Cone of Latin America showed signs of disengagement with party politics, after left-wing governments applied mainstream economic policies (Palacios-Valladares 2016).

On the right, fascism/Nazism (Linz 1976), and Christian democracy (Warner 2000), all had significant links to pre-existing social movements, which acted as social multipliers and buttressed their electoral success. More recently, the new 'globalisation-anti-globalisation' cleavage identified by Kriesi and others has also given rise to a new right (or transformation of more mainstream right) that stresses traditional values and relies on close links to conservative social movements on the right (Williamson, Skocpol and Coggin 2011) or 'counter-movements' (MacKenzie 2005, 129) based on common nativist principles (Pirro 2019). Similar processes have led to the emergence or radical transformation of new Islamic social movements that may or may not decide to take on the mantle of political parties, retaining symbiotic or in some cases antagonistic (as in the Gulenist movement in Turkey) relations (Kirdiş 2019, 167–178) (for discussions about Islamist social movements and party politics, see Chapters 34 and 35).

Regional patterns of relations between parties and movements can be discerned. Post-1989, Western/Southern Europe has witnessed parallel successes for parties and movements on the left, while it would seem on the contrary that where right-wing political parties were electorally successful the far right subculture was weak. In Central and Eastern Europe, where parties are weak, movements are strong (Hutter, Kriesi and Lorenzini 2018). In the USA, a 'mirror' effect has occurred with polarisation between left and right being the outcome of the influence of social movements on the two major parties. Tarrow (2021) argues that both major parties have been 'hollowed' out and the influence of movements has grown in recent years. In Latin America, indigenous movements have been propped up by social movements against austerity. In Asia, social movements have at times substituted for weak party systems, while in Africa, former national liberation movements have in many occasions transformed into dominant political parties which led to the wane of organised independent civil society (Southall 2013) including social movements (for discussions about liberation movements, see Chapters 28 and 34).

Party–movement relations have been shown to differ under different regime types, particularly in democracies, authoritarian and competitive authoritarian regimes (Levitsky and Way 2002). Research has shown that social movements can be vital 'schools' for democracy, sustain social opposition and contribute to building momentum for democratisation under authoritarianism when political parties are unable to operate freely or at all. During democratic transition and the early stages of democratisation, social movements have been known to work alongside political parties by forging alliances against unpopular policies (Almeida 2010) and/or by transforming themselves into political parties (Zollner 2021). Yet once democracy is established, the expectation of many democratic theorists that social movements will flourish and in so doing sustain and strengthen the social fabric necessary to buttress democracy has often been frustrated (Pickvance 1999) and political parties may 'take over' from social movements. Democratic 'backsliding' has been associated with social movements being co-opted (Lorch 2021), divided (Mietzner 2021) or instigated by dominant parties (Greskovits 2017), while distance between social movements and political parties has in some cases acted as a safeguard against democratic backsliding (Rakner 2021). In 'competitive authoritarian' regimes, it has been shown that the role of social movements can be vital both in strengthening and of weakening the regime. Where they are co-opted by the dominant party (Çüngürlü 2021), they strengthen the regime; where they ally with democratic opposition, they may undermine the regime (Giersdorf and Croissant 2011; Dollbaum 2020). This discussion links into the debate that critiques the role of civil society in democracy by arguing that not all social movements within its realm can be expected to bear or support democratic values. Some social movements would even be considered 'bad' or 'uncivil' as such and certainly bad for democracy, as they may focus on the promotion of hate and bigotry, racism, anti-Semitism and aggressive xenophobia (Chambers and Kopstein 2001).

Conclusions and avenues for further research

Focusing principally on the links between political parties and social movements in western liberal democracies, this chapter laid out four perspectives that can be identified in the literature on how those links are configured and how they are developing over time. The 'separate spheres' and 'co-variation' perspectives stress, respectively, constitutive division and weakening links between the two sets of actors. The 'Interpenetration' and 'co-evolution' perspectives portray these links as respectively close and transforming in the direction of greater informalisation and (ideologically circumscribed) pluralisation. The buoyant expansion of the empirical remit of this field of study to cover all party families, regions and regime types, sketched in this chapter, would greatly stand to benefit from testing the relevance of these perspectives from a comparative standpoint. It would be relevant to explore, for instance, whether there are systematic differences in the ways distinct 'party families' (Mair and Mudde 1998) link to distinct 'movement families' (Della Porta and Rucht 1995) across regions and regime types; whether, on the contrary, it is regional differences that determine the types of these links; or indeed, whether it is 'co-variation' or 'co-evolution' that is more likely to follow democratic consolidation.

Beyond the need to examine whether any of these alternative scenarios remain relevant in the context of an expanding agenda of empirical research, the study of the party–movement nexus is confronted with new theoretical challenges emerging from recent social and technological developments that are unfolding in global politics, such as the proliferation of crisis and the digitisation of politics.

First, crisis seems to be increasingly part of 'normal politics'. Crises of political representation, economic crises, health, environmental and migration 'crises' are only some of the 'creeping' global crises (Boin, Ekengren and Rhinard 2021) that define contemporary societies. Some authors have begun to explore the ways in which such crises reshape the possibilities for social movement mobilisation, adoption of new repertoires of action (Gattinara and Zamponi 2020) on their behalf and reconfiguration of their network of potential allies and opponents (Della Porta 2018), including political parties. Others have focused on the complex relationship between populist movement-turn-parties and crises (Moffitt 2015). Hutter, Kriesi and Lorenzini (2018) make the interesting suggestion that during crises of political representation, interactions between parties and movements become 'more frequent, conflictive and complex'. As the boundary between parties and movements becomes blurred, a number of outcomes are possible, such as movements transforming parties, new political parties emerging from movements, or hybrid party–movements.

Such assertions need to become subjected to theoretical reflection. The type of crisis at stake may be important here: health crises such as the COVID-19 crisis gave rise or new impetus to social movements such as those advocating against vaccination. While we have yet to see the emergence of hybrid political movements mobilising along those lines, some authors have argued that these movements contribute to the legitimisation or 'normalisation' of the far right, as they move from the online environment to the streets (Vieten 2020). Some crises may give rise to new social movements and put them on a collision path with political leaderships deemed ineffective in managing crisis. However, such mobilisation, instead of leading to the questioning of existing party-political dynamics, may project a de-politicising, technocratic narrative. De Moor and others find evidence of such effects in the discourse of the new youth movements against climate change who urge world leaders to 'follow the science', such as Fridays for Future and Extinction Rebellion (De Moor et al. 2021). We may need to think about classifying crises and identifying factors more likely to impact the party–movement relationship.

Second, the 2.0 'revolution', is argued to be changing the environment within which political actors organise, articulate and disseminate their message in fundamental ways (see also Chapter 4). Digital platforms make political participation less costly and the capacity for the participation of larger groups more readily available. They also come with risks, such as the concentration of power within political organisations, technopopulism and providing a space from which online abuse and hate speech can proliferate. A key question that must be thought through is what kind of impact, if any, does this new state of affairs have on the relations between movements and parties?

A first indication is that all political parties are to some extent affected by this shift, but there seems to be significant variation in levels and patterns of digitalisation (Correa et al. 2021). Some 'Brick and mortar' organisations (such as established political parties or advocacy groups) may simply use social media platforms as an additional channel to disseminate their message and organise, without this having any meaningful impact on their ideological backbone or organisational structure. There are on the other hand new actors that within this environment operate according to a logic of 'connective action', that is, an individualised and personalised way of articulating political claims through digital platforms that can achieve unprecedented reach and influence among large swathes of the citizenry (Bennett and Segerberg 2012). This logic can be exemplified in the discourses and modes of operation of social movements such as the Indignados as well as in a new genre of political actor, such as the 'digital party', which perceives of itself as a 'movement' (Gerbaudo 2019, 86–88) or the 'digital movement party' (Deseriis 2020). In her recent work, Donatella della Porta critiques the technological determinism she attributes to the scholarship on digital parties, arguing that the participatory ethos in – at least – progressive social movements and movement parties predates the digital medium. She calls for greater attention to the ways in which digital technologies are mediated by agency (of movements and of movement-parties) and specific democratic cultures that political agents carry along with them (Della Porta 2021).

It would seem that certain types of crisis, such as that of political representation, carry the potential to bring parties and social movements closer together, with hybrid forms of party–movement emerging across the political spectrum, at times with astounding electoral success. Other types of crisis, such as the climate change crisis, bear the potential to drive a wedge between political parties and social movements: it is the scientists and not the political parties that are to be trusted to save the world. In other words, whether the proliferation of crisis will likely lead to 'inter-penetration', weakening links or even 'separate spheres' may perhaps be explored by looking at the type of crisis under examination and in particular its potential to politicise or de-politicise key issues. Digital technologies, on the other hand, would prima facie seem to be of lesser importance in determining the configuration of the links between political parties and social movements. They may facilitate an environment where the blurring of the boundaries between the two types of actor and hence new forms of 'interpenetration' and potentially 'co-adaptation' are possible, but the extent to which either is attempted must be examined through the prism of political agency, with all the ideological, organisational and cultural 'baggage' that comes with it.

References

Aarts, K. (1995) 'Intermediate organizations and interest representation' in Klingemann, H.D. and Fuchs, D. (eds.) *Citizens and the state*. Oxford: Oxford University Press, pp. 227–257.

Agustín, O.G. and Jørgensen, M.B. (2016) (eds.) *Solidarity without borders: Gramscian perspectives on migration and civil society alliances*. London: Pluto Press.

Allern, E. (2010) *Political parties and interest groups in Norway*. Colchester: ECPR Press.

Allern, E. and Bale, T. (2012a) 'Conclusion: Qualifying the common wisdom', *Party Politics*, 18(1), p99–106.

Allern, E. and Bale, T. (2012b) 'Political parties and interest groups disentangling complex relationships', *Party Politics*, 18(1), p7–25.

Almeida, P. (2010) 'Social movement partyism: Collective action and oppositional political parties', in Van Dyke, N. and McCammon, H.J. (eds.) *Strategic alliances: Coalition building and social movements*. Minneapolis: University of Minnesota Press, pp. 170–196.

Bartolini, S. (2000) *The Political mobilization of the European left, 1860–1980: The class cleavage*. Cambridge: Cambridge University Press.

Bennett, L. and Segerberg, A. (2012) 'The logic of connective action: The personalization of contentious', *Politics, Information, Communication & Society*, 15(5), p739–768.

Bergan Draege, J., Chironi, D. and Della Porta, D. (2016) 'Social movements within organisations: Occupy parties in Italy and Turkey', *South European Society and Politics*. http://dx.doi.org/10.1080/13608746.2016.1199091.

Boin, A., Ekengren, M. and Rhinard, M. (eds.) (2021) *Understanding the creeping crisis*. Cham: Palgrave Macmillan.

Chambers, S. and Kopstein, J. (2001) 'Bad civil society', *Political Theory*, 29(6), p837–865.

Correa, P., Barberà O., Rodríguez-Teruel, J. and Sandri, G. (2021) 'The digitalisation of political parties in comparative perspective', in Barberà O., Sandri, G., Correa, P. and Rodríguez-Teruel, J. (eds.) *Digital parties. Studies in digital politics and governance*. Cham: Springer.

Çüngürlü, F.M. (2021) 'Autocratic consolidation in competitive authoritarian regimes through party-social movement alliances', MA Thesis, Vienna: Central European University.

De Moor, J., De Vydt, M., Uba, K and Wahlström, M. (2021) 'New kids on the block: Taking stock of the recent cycle of climate activism', *Social Movement Studies*, 20(5), p619–625.

Della Porta, D. (2007) *The global justice movement: Cross-national and transnational perspectives*. Boulder: Paradigm.

Della Porta, D. (2021) 'Communication in progressive movement parties: Against populism and beyond digitalism', *Information, Communication & Society*, 24(10), p1344–1360.

Della Porta, D. (ed.) (2018) *Solidarity mobilizations in the "refugee crisis". Contentious moves*. London: Palgrave Macmillan.

Della Porta, D., Fernández, J., Kouki, H and Mosca, L. (2017) *Movement parties against austerity*. Cambridge: Polity Press.

Della Porta, D. and Rucht, D. (1995) 'Social movement sectors in context: A comparison of Italy and West Germany, 1965–1990', in Jenkins, J.C. and Klandermans, B. (eds.) *The politics of social protest*. Minnesota: University of Minnesota Press, pp. 229–272.

Deseriis, M. (2020) 'Digital movement parties: A comparative analysis of the technopolitical cultures and the participation platforms of the Movimento 5 Stelle and the Piratenpartei', *Information, Communication & Society*, 2(12), p1770–1786.

Diani, M. (1992) 'The concept of social movement', *The Sociological Review*, 40(1), p1–25.

Dollbaum, J. (2020) 'Protest trajectories in electoral authoritarianism: From Russia's 'for fair elections' movement to Alexei Navalny's presidential campaign', *Post-Soviet Affairs*, 36(3), p192–210.

Flesher Fominaya, C. (2014) 'Debunking spontaneity: Spain's 15M/Indignados as autonomous movement', *Social Movement Studies*, 14(2), p142–163.

Fraussen, B. and Halpin, D.R. (2016) 'Political parties and interest organizations at the crossroads: Perspectives on the transformation of political organizations', *Political Studies Review*, 16(1), p25–37.

Gattinara, P.C. and Zamponi, L. (2020) 'Politicizing support and opposition to migration in France: the EU asylum policy crisis and direct social activism', *Journal of European Integration*, 42(5), p625–641.

Gerbaudo, P (2019) *Digital Party: Political organisation and online Democracy*. London: Pluto Press.

Giersdorf, S. and Croissant, A. (2011) 'Civil society and competitive authoritarianism in Malaysia', *Journal of Civil Society*, 7(1), p1–21.

Goldstone, J. (2003) 'Introduction: Bridging institutionalised and noninstitutionalised politics', in Goldstone, J.A. (ed.) *States, parties & social movements*. Cambridge: Cambridge University Press.

Greskovits, B. (2017) 'Rebuilding the Hungarian right through civil organization and contention: The civic circles movement', EUI Working Paper RSCA 2017/37. Florence: Robert Schuman Centre for Advanced Studies. Available from: http://cadmus.eui.eu/handle/1814/47245 (Accessed 7 December 2017)

Heaney, M.T. and Rojas, F. (2015) *Party in the street: The antiwar movement and the Democratic Party after 9/11*. New York: Cambridge University Press.

Ho, M. (2018) 'Taiwan's anti-nuclear movement: The making of a militant citizen movement', *Journal of Contemporary Asia*, 48(3), p445–464.

Howell, C. (2001) 'The end of the relationship between social democratic parties and trade unions?', *Studies in Political Economy*, 65(1), p7–37.

Hutter, S., Kriesi, H. and Lorenzini, J. (2018) 'Social movements in interaction with political parties', in Snow, D.A., Soule, S., Kriesi, H. and McCammon, H. (eds.) *The Wiley Blackwell companion to social movements*. Hoboken: Wiley Blackwell, pp. 322–377.

Katz, R. and Mair, P. (1995) 'Changing models of party organization and party democracy: The emergence of the cartel party', *Party Politics*, 1(1), p5–28.

Keith, D. and Tsakatika, M. (2022) 'Linkages between radical left parties and social movements: mapping co-evolution, explaining variation', in March, L., Escalona, F. and Keith, D. (eds.) *Palgrave handbook of the radical left*. London: Palgrave Macmillan.

Kirchheimer, O. (1966) "The transformation of the Western European party systems' Political parties and political development', in La Palombara, J. and Weiner, M. (eds.) *Political parties and political development*. Princeton: Princeton University Press, pp. 177–200.

Kirdiş, E. (2019) *The rise of Islamic political movements and parties: Morocco, Turkey and Jordan*. Edinburgh: Edinburgh University Press.

Kitschelt, H. (1988) 'Left-libertarian parties: Explaining innovation in competitive party systems', *World Politics*, 40, p194–234.

Kitschelt, H. (2006) 'Movement parties', in Katz, R. and Crotty, W. (eds.) *Handbook of party politics*. London: Sage, pp. 278–290.

Kriesi, H., Koopmans, R., Duyvendak, J.W. and Giugni, M. (1995) *New social movements in Western Europe. A comparative analysis*. Minneapolis: University of Minnesota Press.

Lawson, K. (1980) 'Political parties and linkage', in Lawson, K. (ed.) *Political parties and linkage: A comparative perspective*. New Haven: Yale University Press, pp. 3–24.

Levitsky, S. and Way, L. (2002) 'Elections without democracy: The rise of competitive authoritarianism', *Journal of Democracy*, 13(2), p51–65.

Linz, J. (1976) 'Some notes toward a comparative study of fascism in sociological historical perspective', in Laqueur, W. (ed.) *Fascism: A reader's guide*. Berkeley: University of California Press, pp. 3–121.

Lorch, J. (2021) 'Elite capture, civil society and democratic backsliding in Bangladesh, Thailand and the Philippines', *Democratization*, 28(1), p81–102.

MacKenzie, C. (2005) *Pro-family politics and fringe parties in Canada*. Toronto: UBC Press.

Mair, P. and Mudde, C. (1998) 'The party family and its study', *Annual Review of Political Science*, 1(1), p211–229.

March, L. (2017) 'Radical left parties and movements: Allies, associates or antagonists', in Wennerhag, M., Fröhlich, C. and Piotrowski, G. (eds.) *Radical left movements in Europe*. London: Routledge, pp. 22–42.

Martin, N., de Lange, S.L. and van der Brug, W. (2021) 'Staying connected: explaining parties' enduring connections to civil society', *West European Politics*, 45(2), p1385–1406.

McAdam, D. and Tarrow, S. (2010) 'Ballots and barricades: On the reciprocal relationship between elections and social movements', *Perspectives on Politics*, 8(2), p529–542.

Medina, I., Teruel, J. and Barrio, A. (2016) 'Assessing the identity politics hypothesis: Political parties and interest groups linkages in the case of Catalan Juntos pel Sí', Paper presented at the ECPR General Conference, Charles University, Prague, 10 September.

Merkl, P. and Lawson, K. (1988) *When parties fail: Emerging alternative organisations*. Princeton: Princeton University Press.

Mietzner, M. (2021) 'Sources of resistance to democratic decline: Indonesian civil society and its trials', *Democratization*, 28(1), p161–178.

Moffitt, B. (2015) 'How to perform crisis: A model for understanding the key role of crisis in contemporary populism', *Government and Opposition*, 50(2), p189–217.

Norris, P. (2005) *Radical Right, voters and parties in the electoral market*. Cambridge: Cambridge University Press.

Palacios-Valladares, I. (2016) 'With or without them: Contemporary student movements and parties in the Southern Cone', *The Latin Americanist*, 60(2), p243–268.

Piccio, D.R. (2015) 'How social movements impact political parties', in Giugni, M., Bosi, L. and Uba, K. (eds.) *The consequences of social movements: People, policies, and institutions*. Cambridge: Cambridge University Press.

Pickvance, C. (1999) 'Democratisation and the decline of social movements: The effects of regime change on collective action in Eastern Europe, Southern Europe and Latin America', *Sociology*, 33(2), p353–372.

Pirro, A.L.P. (2019) 'Ballots and barricades enhanced: far-right 'movement parties' and movement-electoral interactions', *Nations and Nationalism*, 25(3), p782–802.

Poguntke, T. (2003) 'Party organizational linkage: parties without firm social roots?' in Luther, K.R. and Müller-Rommel, F. (eds.) *Political parties in the new Europe: Political and analytical challenges*. Oxford: Oxford University Press, pp. 43–62.

Porcaro, M. (2013) 'Occupy Lenin', *Socialist Register*, 49, p84–97.

Rakner, L. (2021) 'Don't touch my constitution! Civil society resistance to democratic backsliding in Africa's pluralist regimes', *Global Policy*, 12(S5), p95–105.

Schwartz, M.A. (2005) 'Linkage processes in party networks', in Farrell, A. and Ignazi, P. (eds.) *Political parties and political systems: The concept of linkage revisited*. Westport: Praeger, pp. 37–60.

Schwartz, M.A. (2010) 'Interactions between social movements and US political parties', *Party Politics*, 16(5), p587–607.

Southall, R. (2013) *Liberation movements in power: Party and state in Southern Africa*. London: James Currey.

Tarrow, S. (2015) 'Contentious politics', in Della Porta, D. and Diani, M. (eds.) *The Oxford handbook of social movements*. Oxford: Oxford University Press, pp. 86–107.

Tarrow, S. (2021) *Movements and parties. Critical connections in American political development*. Cambridge: Cambridge University Press.

Thomas, C. (ed.) (2001) *Political parties and interest groups. Shaping democratic governance*. Boulder, CO: Lynne Rienner.

Tilly, C. (2003) 'Afterword: Agendas for students of social movements', in Goldstone, J.A. (ed.) *States, parties and social movements*. Cambridge: Cambridge University Press, pp. 246–257.

Tsakatika, M. and Lisi, M. (2013) "Zippin' up my boots, goin' back to my roots': Radical left Parties in Southern Europe', *South European Society and Politics*, 18(1), p1–19.

Vieten, U.M. (2020) 'The 'new normal' and 'Pandemic populism': The COVID-19 crisis and anti-hygienic mobilisation of the far-right, *Social Sciences*, 9(9), p165–179.

Warner, C. (2000) *Confessions of an interest group. The Catholic church and political parties in Europe*, Princeton: Princeton University Press.

Witko, C. (2009) 'The ecology of party-organized interest relationships', *Polity*, 41(2), p211–234.

Williamson, V., Skocpol, T. and Coggin, J. (2011) 'The Tea Party and the remaking of Republican conservatism', *Perspectives on Politics*, 9(1), p25–43.

Yishai, Y. (2001) 'Bringing society back in post-cartel parties in Israel', *Party Politics*, 7(6), p667–687.

Zald, M.N. (2000) 'Ideologically structured action: An enlarged agenda for social movement research', *Mobilization*, 5(1), p1–16.

Zald, M.N. and Berger, M.A. (1978) 'Social movements in organizations: Coup d'etat, insurgency, and mass movements', *American Journal of Sociology*, 83, p823–861.

Zollner, B.H.E. (2021) 'The metamorphosis of social movements into political parties. The Egyptian Muslim Brotherhood and the Tunisian al-Nahda as cases for a reflection on party institutionalisation theory', *British Journal of Middle Eastern Studies*, 48(3), p370–387.

9
POLITICAL PARTIES AND GENDER

Tània Verge

Gendering the study of political parties is highly consequential for how scholars theorise, examine empirically and reach conclusions about the central questions of this political science subfield. Such a major re-evaluation has challenged much of the conventional wisdom and opened up new avenues of research that have furthered the understanding of the actors to whom modern democracies accord linkage, representative and governing functions. Despite the numerous contributions made by feminist political scientists in this field since the 1990s, party politics scholars have been rather slow in engaging with gender in their theoretical and analytical constructs. Gender-blindness has left them unprepared to adequately account for the gender gaps observed in intra-party activities or to investigate the gendered dynamics underlying organisational arrangements or candidate selection processes and the resulting gender-biased descriptive (presence) and substantive (policy) representation outcomes.

The chapter reviews these critical omissions and provides a state of the art of the wide range of topics that have been examined through a gender lens, pinpointing how feminist research has advanced our understanding of political parties. In doing so, the remaining sections discuss the following questions: How are gender power relations wielded within political parties? How does gender shape intra-party democracy? Why is candidate selection still strongly gendered despite increasing numbers of women among party members, officials and elected representatives? How can political parties be re-gendered? The final section concludes and pinpoints the gaps to be filled with further research.

Political parties as gendered organisations

Building on new institutionalism, feminist analyses have made important advances to our understanding of party organisations. In particular, they have shown that the procedures and culture in which party decision-making takes place are far from gender-neutral. Where parties were founded by men and historically populated by men, gender has become an organising principle that distributes advantage and disadvantage on a daily basis (see Figure 9.1). As Lovenduski (2005, 56) states, 'if parliament is the warehouse of traditional masculinity, . . . political parties are its major distributors'. To understand how power is wielded in gendered ways within political parties – often intertwining with class, race, age, sexuality or ableness – scholars have paid attention to the inscription of gender in the formal (written) rules, such as party constitutions

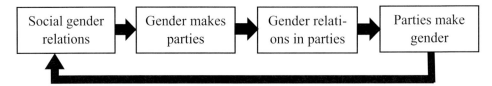

Figure 9.1 Interplay between gender and party
Source: Adapted from Kenny and Verge (2016).

or by-laws, including candidate selection proceedings, and the informal (non-written) rules, such as norms, practices, conventions and rituals (Bjarnegård and Kenny 2016). Research has shown that some of the 'rules of the game' are 'gendered', because they shape different roles, actions or opportunities for women and men, while others are 'apparently gender-neutral' but, nonetheless, produce 'gendered effects' due to their interaction with wider social norms (Lowndes 2020, 545).

Political parties do not operate in a vacuum but are embedded in a specific social context and in the broader political system (Norris and Lovenduski 1995). Gender relations in society play a systematic role in shaping political parties, including the unequal distribution of resources (time, money or political capital) stemming from the sexual division of waged and household labour and deep-seated ideas about what it means to be – and behave – like a 'man' or a 'woman'. Parties' rules, structures and processes are infused by these patterns of inequality and gender socialisation, shaping the experiences of individual and collective actors (Childs 2008, xix). In this vein, as Kenny and Verge (2016, 357) posit, 'gender makes parties', as it is routinely enacted within the organisation, for example, through prevailing types of ideal party member, leader or candidate that are biased towards stereotypically male traits – for example, high levels of competitiveness, forceful assertiveness or adversarial styles of debate (Lovenduski 2005, 53) – or participation modes that reflect the needs of individuals with fewer caring responsibilities – for example, continuation of discussions after party meetings end in informal arenas such as bars and restaurants (Bjarnegård 2013; Verge 2015).

The ways in which gender relations are entrenched in political parties can be illustrated by men's overrepresentation in decision-making bodies (Kittilson 2006), the establishment of gender-appropriate roles – for example, women members commonly perform routine, housekeeping and administrative functions within parties (Bashevkin 1993; Verge and de la Fuente 2014) – or the fact that the global #MeToo campaign has also pointed the finger at political parties and parliaments (Krook 2018). As a result, 'parties make gender' (Kenny and Verge 2016, 359) on a daily basis through the institutionalisation of male-centred norms and practices that discriminate against women in either overt or subtler ways. From this perspective, parties can thus be described as 'institutionally sexist' organisations (Lovenduski 2005, 52–54). As will be discussed throughout the chapter, within political parties, women members, leaders and candidates face segregation, exclusion and gendered hierarchies; their perspectives are substantially neglected in party policy; and organisational arrangements are strongly biased towards certain kinds of masculinity. Furthermore, reforms in formal rules, such as the introduction of gender quotas, tend to be undermined by the 'stickiness' of gendered informal rules, which enables party actors to redeploy 'old ways of doing things' (cf. Bjarnegård and Kenny 2016, 387). Finally, since 'rules inside and outside the political domain interact and co-evolve' (Lowndes 2020, 555), the dynamics of inclusion and exclusion played out in parties reinforce unequal social gender relations. For example, at the symbolic level, the scarcity of women party chairs (Wauters and Pilet 2015) elicits and reinforces the idea that men are better suited to lead.

Intra-party democracy

Can political parties be judged internally democratic if they continue to discriminate against women (Childs 2013a, 93) and fail to adequately represent descriptively (presence) and substantively (policy) the largest social constituency? To answer this question, feminist political scientists have shown that a gender lens must be applied to key issues of intra-party democracy (IPD), such as legal regulations of political parties, party membership, group representation, leadership selection and policy development.

Legal regulations

With the exception of electoral quotas, which have gradually diffused across the globe,[1] very few countries, most prominently from Latin America, have included measures to further gender equality within political parties in national constitutions or party laws (Childs 2013b). Given the linkage, representative and governing functions political parties perform in democratic regimes, such a widespread lack of statutory mandates is, at the very least, paradoxical. The few existing statutory measures can be listed in just a paragraph.

In Costa Rica, party registration is dependent upon commitment to gender equality in the party constitution, and in a few countries, legislated gender quotas also apply to the composition of parties' decision-making bodies – Bolivia, Costa Rica, Ecuador, Honduras, Panama, Paraguay, Peru and Uruguay.[2] A specific share of parties' public funding must be allocated to women's capacity-building and to promoting their political participation in Brazil, Costa Rica, Mexico and Panama, and at least ten per cent of the state-subsidised media time for party propaganda must promote women's political participation in Brazil (Roza, Llanos and Garzón de la Roza 2011, 22–23). Parties must adopt an internal gender action plan in Slovenia, Croatia and Serbia (Verge 2020a, 238), and only in Bolivia must parties have internal anti-harassment policies.

Party membership

Insufficient social representativeness of the rank-and-file may not only taint parties' social legitimacy but also hamper the diversity of the pool of candidates for public and party office. Furthermore, it may have an impact on policy, as women members are generally more progressive, both on gender and on other issues, than their male peers (Childs and Webb 2012, 176; Devroe et al. 2019, 98). Besides being older, more likely to belong to the ethnic majority group and typically having a higher social status than voters, the composition of the party membership is still skewed towards men, particularly in extreme-right parties (Gauja and van Haute 2015, 195), mirroring gendered patterns of voting behaviour (see also Chapter 27). For example, in 2017, in the UK (Audickas, Dempsey and Loft 2017, 19), women made up almost half of Labour (47 per cent) and Green (46 per cent) members but just about a quarter of the Conservative Party's (29 per cent) and UKIP's (25 per cent).

Studies show that women members are less active than men in speaking at local party meetings, applying for a function or mandate or participating in candidate selection procedures (Cross 2019, 21; Devroe et al. 2019, 95). Several mechanisms linking the gendered functioning of parties to women's lower intra-party participation have been identified. Women members and leaders face continuous 'super-surveillance' and receive less recognition for their work (Lovenduski 2005, 148). Simultaneously, gendered rituals, such as repetitive interventions by men and disregard for women' contributions, often turn party meetings into uncomfortable spaces for the latter. Moreover, the prevailing tendency to hold meetings in family-unfriendly hours and male venues (e.g. pubs or clubs) reflects how the uses of time and place help men keep power and pose a double bind for women. Devoting evenings to party work can violate social gender norms about caring or family responsibilities and may result in women finding their capacity to accumulate influence and build networks curtailed (Verge and de la Fuente 2014, 72–76).

Group representation

Party women's organisations initially developed as auxiliary groups aimed at supporting parties' everyday activities, mobilising women voters and recruiting new female members. Contemporarily, despite adopting different forms (e.g. including party sub-organisations or sections, specific party secretariats, networks of female elected representatives, or collateral – external – organisations), most of these organisations seek to promote solidarity among party women, help them build political skills and provide a site for claim-making on behalf of women aimed at gendering party by-laws and policy agendas (Kittilson 2011, 70; Roza, Llanos and Garzón de la Roza 2011, 19–26).

Both party age and ideology explain why some parties have women's organisations. Traditional parties (social democratic and conservative/Christian democratic) are more likely to have these organisations than newer parties (Childs and Kittilson 2016, 604), while they are more commonly found in green parties than in radical left parties (Keith and Verge 2018, 401). Their political weight varies across parties with regard to crucial aspects: descriptive representation rights in decision-making bodies; the degree of integration into party policy-making processes; party bodies or persons to whom they are accountable; and material support (funding, personnel, etc.) accorded by the party (Childs and Kittilson 2016, 606).

Party leadership selection

As Childs (2013a, 93) highlights, women 'have not gained power relative to where power lies'. Since the 1960s, only 11 per cent of the national party leaders selected in Europe, North America and Oceania have been women (Wauters and Pilet 2015, 82). The largest, more electorally competitive parties, from both left and right, are less likely to select women to this position than smaller parties, including radical right parties (O'Brien 2015, 1030). Several gendered dynamics and political opportunities underpin the politics of party leadership selection. Women leaders are more frequently selected in contexts of poor party popularity, when the post is least attractive (Bashevkin 2010, 79). They are rarely acclaimed in party contests (O'Neill and Stewart 2009, 747), serve for shorter periods than their male peers and are more likely to step down when their party experiences unfavourable electoral results (O'Brien 2015, 1033).

Vertical segregation also shapes parties' national executive committees (NECs). The share of women NEC members rose from an average of 15 per cent in 1975 to about 30 per cent in 1997 (Kittilson 2006, 42). No further increases have occurred thereafter. Higher proportions of women in this body are found in left parties, especially when gender quotas are used, when the party structure is centralised, and when party women's organisations exist (Kittilson 2006, 46). Local party committees are particularly masculinised, with several scholars pinpointing that 'male power monopolies' are typically built at this level (Hinojosa 2012, 61; see also Bjarnegård and Kenny 2016). For example, in Canada, in 2016, eight-in-ten local party presidents were male (Cross 2019, 21). Moreover, the distribution of mandates in both the NEC and local party committees follows a gendered horizontal segregation. Women are more likely to be assigned to education and social welfare positions within party secretariats, extending their traditional roles as caregivers to party politics, while men occupy positions with greater influence, such as those related to electoral campaigns and organisational matters (Roza, Llanos and Garzón de la Roza 2011, 30; Verge and de la Fuente 2014, 72). In a similar vein, gender marking informs the distribution of leadership positions, roles and domain areas in both parliamentary party groups and parliamentary committees (Heath, Schwindt-Bayer and Taylor-Robinson 2005; Smrek 2020).

Policy development

Women's agency within parties (women's organisations, share of women in NECs and parliamentary party groups) has been found to instil the adoption of policy agendas that put more emphasis on social justice and gender equality issues such as equal pay, parental leave or childcare policies (Childs 2008; Kittilson 2011). It should also be noted that, while policies for women reflect parties' own ideological stances, the need to attract more women voters or to modernise parties (Lovenduski and Norris 1993; Childs and Webb 2012) also significantly shapes their focus and position on women's issues (see also Chapter 27). By and large, though, there is a critical omission in the literature on how IPD interacts with gender in policy development processes.

One may argue that consultative and direct participation forms may be more advantageous for advancing women's and gender equality claims. Some parties, predominantly from the left, require policy development procedures, including the drafting of electoral manifestoes and legislative or governmental initiatives, to address gender equality concerns (Childs 2013b, 404). To further this aim, formal and informal coordination mechanisms have been established between party women's organisations and the various party committees or secretariats, through either periodical meetings or specific task forces that might eventually include external gender experts (Verge 2020a, 244). By contrast, membership-wide plebiscites seem unlikely to further women's claims, even in parties that define themselves as feminist. For example, when the Spanish left-populist party Podemos (We Can) held its constitutive assembly in 2014, only three out of the almost 100 resolutions submitted by members to define the party's core pledges dealt with gender equality issues.[3]

Candidate selection and representation outcomes

The study of the relationship between candidate gender, recruitment and selection process within parties and representation outcomes owes much to the seminal work of Norris and Lovenduski (1995). Their analytical framework builds on three sets of factors: (1) the supply of available candidates seeking nomination for public office, shaped by their motivation (drive, ambition, interest) and resources (time, money and experience); (2) the demand of party gatekeepers who ultimately select the candidates, especially in strong parliamentary democracies; and (3) the party context (ideology, inclusiveness of the selectorate, degree of centralisation and formalisation of selection processes) and the broader political system (political culture, electoral system, party system). While there has been substantial discussion in the literature on whether gendered outcomes in the vertical ladder of recruitment are due to supply- or demand-side factors, the original framework already pinpointed the underlying interaction between both factors.

Concerning the first interaction illustrated in Figure 9.2, parties' (and parliaments') disregard for reconciliation policies in their inner workings means that having children undermines

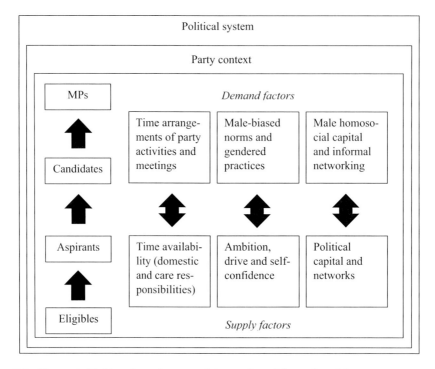

Figure 9.2 The vertical ladder of recruitment and the supply and demand model
Source: Adapted from Lovenduski and Norris (1993), Norris and Lovenduski (1995) and Verge (2015).

women's opportunities – but not men's – to be active party members and elected representatives in both parliamentary (Campbell and Childs 2014) and executive office (Verge and Astudillo 2019). The prevailing 'male politician norm', manifested in family unfriendly organisational arrangements, reinforces the chronic deficit of time availability imposed upon women by the unequal distribution of household labour in wider society. Furthermore, party gatekeepers often build upon social assumptions to assess married women candidates, especially when having young children, as being less politically engaged (Norris and Lovenduski 1995, 116).

As for the second interaction, the supply-side argument that women have less political ambition than men, which predominantly came from American politics (see Fox and Lawless 2010), has been challenged by several studies. The unequal playing field within parties determines candidate emergence. In the face of direct and indirect discrimination by party gatekeepers (Lovenduski 2005), many women aspirants rationally 'opt out of candidacy' (Piscopo and Kenny 2020, 4). Incentivising more women to run or providing leadership training to 'fix' women's (alleged) lower ambition, confidence or skills are, thus, ineffective strategies insofar as 'gatekeepers are more likely to directly recruit and promote people like themselves' (Cheng and Tavits 2011, 461). Indeed, men are seen 'as insiders and as ideal [more likeable and trustworthy] candidates' and women are regarded as 'outsiders' (Bjarnegård and Kenny 2016, 385) and even as a 'liability', although empirical evidence finds no systematic voter bias against women candidates (Lawless and Pearson 2008). It has been argued that these gendered psychological aspects stem from the expressive component of 'male homosocial capital' (Bjarnegård 2013), which leads male selectors to apply not just higher standards but also double standards. When displaying typically male traits like strong assertiveness or adversarial styles of debate, women candidates still fail to pass the screening and, more crucially, they may be informally sanctioned for such a breach of feminine character (Kenny 2013).

Concerning the last interaction shown in Figure 9.2, women aspirants are not just less likely to be sponsored by influential outside groups such as trade unions (Norris and Lovenduski 1995, 153), but party gatekeepers' preference for 'localness' is also far from objective. Participation in local business associations or trade unions, more common among men, is more appreciated by party selectors than community activism, more frequent among women, which reveals a narrow, male-biased consideration of what constitutes political experience (Kenny 2013). Furthermore, women candidates are less likely to be well connected to party networks or political mentors (Crowder-Meyer 2013). However, in both parliamentary or executive office selection processes, holding party office is more valued in men candidates, showcasing how women party officers 'remain outsiders on the inside' (Verge and Claveria 2018, 545). Male homosocial capital thus carries an instrumental dimension, too – that of providing crucial access to informal 'old boy networks' that play a crucial role in selection processes (Bjarnegård 2013).

When it comes to party-context factors, centralised selection processes yield higher levels of women candidates, as the party leadership can coordinate party levels to produce more gender-balanced tickets and is held more directly accountable by voters and members for results on women's representation (Kittilson 2006, 46; Hazan and Rahat 2010, 114). More exclusive selection methods also allow the crafting of 'package deals' that distribute a variety of positions (Wauters and Pilet 2015, 78). By contrast, more inclusive selectorates (e.g. one-member-one-vote systems like primaries) heavily rely on name recognition, financial resources or media coverage, all of these resources that tend to benefit more experienced male candidates (Piscopo and Kenny 2020, 6; see also Bashevkin 2010). Women candidates also face 'more crowded primaries' and they 'endure greater challenges' (Lawless and Pearson 2008, 77–78). Furthermore, while less explicit, detailed or standardised candidate selection criteria and procedures may open the door to greater discretion and bias, rules that are formalised in party documents are not necessarily gender neutral – nor neutral to race/ethnicity (Bjarnegård and Zetterberg 2019). Ideology is also a relevant party-related factor. Left ideology, particularly new left ideology, strongly correlates with both women's presence (and influence) within the organisation and parliamentary party groups and the adoption of voluntary gender quotas (Kittilson 2006).

Among political-system factors, electoral systems and legislated gender quotas are of paramount importance. Women are elected in higher numbers in proportional representation (PR) systems than in plurality systems, since larger district magnitude allows parties to nominate women without deposing male incumbents (McAllister and Studlar 2002). This notwithstanding, each electoral system accords political parties different opportunities to display strategic discrimination, even when legislated or voluntary gender quotas are applied. Under plurality systems, women candidates often run in districts where their parties stand no chance of winning the seat (Murray 2010), while under PR systems, men get the lion's share of top positions in party lists. Legislated gender quotas with placement mandates are more effective at partially containing this discrimination in closed-list systems than in preferential ordered-list systems (Luhiste 2015, 110) or in plurality systems.

Statutory gender quotas are nested in parties' candidate selection processes. They are complementary to party rules when voluntary quotas are already in place, with some parties even competing to overcome the statutory requirements to continue championing women's representation in their party system (Meier 2004). Conversely, they require significant accommodation in parties that reject positive discrimination (Verge and Espírito-Santo 2016, 433). Applying a minimal interpretation of statutory quotas is the most common form of resistance deployed by parties, although in some countries parties have even resorted to more blatant forms such as entering male candidate names under female names or forcing elected women MPs to resign and be substituted by a male alternate (for a review of these practices, see Krook 2016).

Similar gendered patterns are observed for the selection of candidates for executive office. Women candidates frequently run as 'sacrificial lambs' in gubernatorial races wherein an incumbent from the opposing party seeks re-election (Stambough and O'Regan 2007, 356), they benefit less than their male peers from the political resources they possess, such as seniority in party or public office, particularly when having children, and are less likely to be reselected when carrying a vote loss, even when being the incumbent (Verge and Astudillo 2019, 736).

Overall, both formal and informal 'rules of the game' that shape political recruitment and candidate selection processes are fundamentally gendered, despite being cast as objective and meritocratic (Kenny and Verge 2016). Male dominance in party executive bodies and recruitment panels sustains preferential treatment towards men candidates in selection processes, engineering their over-representation in public office. As several studies have shown, more gender-balanced selection committees (Niven 1998; Cheng and Tavits 2011) and recruitment from broader networks of groups and occupations rather than insular party networks (Crowder-Meyer 2013) produce more gender-balanced outcomes. Simultaneously, being the public face of the party secures men's positional power within the organisation (Childs and Murray 2014, 81).

Re-gendering political parties

No party efforts to promote gender equality 'have occurred without an intervention by women making claims' about power redistribution and policy (Lovenduski 1993, 14). Intra-party gender equality strategies are threefold (Lovenduski 1993, 8). First, rhetorical measures include declarations contained in party rules and procedures, party manifestos, parliamentary resolutions or public statements by party leaders aimed at supporting and promoting equal gender participation. For instance, some parties have incorporated feminism in their party constitution in an effort to make it integral to their identity and have included parity democracy or the reconciliation between political activities and family life as organisational principles (Verge 2020a, 244). Such provisions accord women 'statutory legitimacy' when negotiating their demands within their party (Roza, Llanos and Garzón de la Roza 2011, 20).

Second, positive action strategies consist of the training of women aspirants or candidates, the establishment of women's organisations, or the celebration of party women's conventions (Childs 2013b, 405–406). While these measures have been adopted across party families, the third type of strategy, namely the adoption of voluntary gender quotas for the composition of decision-making party bodies and/or electoral tickets, is much more common – albeit nor exclusive – among left parties. This explains why, in the absence of legislated quotas, voluntary quotas can still produce gender-balanced representation, as most Scandinavian parties show (Freidenvall 2013). Yet it should be mentioned that the participation of party women's organisations in the committees that draft candidate tickets or supervise list-building processes and strong commitment of party leaders are pivotal to ensuring an effective implementation of gender quotas (Verge and Espírito-Santo 2016, 434).

A fourth strategy based on gender mainstreaming has been more recently adopted by some left-wing political parties. More specifically, this includes the adoption of internal gender action plans that seek to incorporate a gender equality perspective throughout all party processes, targeting both men and women. In the domain of descriptive representation, actions may encompass, for instance, giving visibility to women public and party officers in election rallies or press conferences and promoting women's (men's) presence in traditionally masculinised (feminised) portfolios. Concerning policy-making, actions include training party members and public officers on gender equality or gathering sex-disaggregated data in all areas of party work. Regarding organisational arrangements, these plans contemplate actions such as providing childcare and playrooms during party meetings and conferences (Verge 2020a).

Regrettably, the adoption of anti-harassment policies and other types of gender-based violence perpetrated by party employees, members or public officers (IPU 2016) is a pending task for most party organisations and parliaments, despite having been repeatedly urged to do so by the United Nations, the Organisation of the American States, the Council of Europe and the European Parliament. Moreover, gender has been reinscribed perniciously in some of these policies, as party whips have been entrusted to find internal solutions and inquiries have been run by committees that lack gender expertise, resulting in victim-blaming. More generally, the informal rules that enable sexist and sexual misconduct to occur, such as the gendered segregation of offices and masculinised adversarial styles of doing politics, have been left intact (Collier and Raney 2018; Verge 2020b).

Conclusions and avenues for further research

As has been reviewed in this chapter, a gender lens enhances the understanding of how political parties work and helps explain why, despite an increasing feminisation of party bodies and candidate tickets, the deep-seated sources of male power within these organisations have not yet been subverted. Male dominance in political parties goes beyond the skewed composition of the rank-and-file, decision-making bodies or candidate tickets. While left parties are more likely to adopt measures to guarantee gender-balanced outcomes in terms of descriptive representation and more gender-friendly policies regarding substantive representation, all party organisations are stratified by gender and productive of power inequalities. Gender-neutral organisations simply do not exist, so participation modes or selection processes cannot be neutral to gender either.

As we seek to deepen the knowledge of the operation of gender within political parties, several gaps remain to be filled and research biases need to be addressed. First, both comparative and single-case studies could expand their regional coverage beyond Western countries. Such an expansion would allow testing the generalisability of existing analytical frameworks and identifying how political parties' gendered 'rules of the game' are played out in socio-political structures like sectarianism (Geha 2019) and caste (Jensenius 2016) or how they operate under electoral authoritarian systems (Bjarnegård and Zetterberg 2016).

Second, building on Norris and Lovenduski's (1995) seminal work, studies should pay more attention to how the intersection of gender with other sources of inequality (e.g. race/ethnicity, class, sexuality, age, ableness) produce specific forms of (dis)empowerment and (under)privilege within parties. For example, party selectorates have been found to be more prejudiced against lesbian than gay candidates (Juvonen 2020). Similarly, parties frequently apply a 'double quota' that renders ethnic minority women candidates as 'the "diversity label" of the party', while the positional power of incumbent senior white men remains intact (Celis, Erzeel and Mügge 2015, 768).

Third, scholars could look more deeply into the ways male homosociality determines access to and survival in party office and how this particular type of capital is (re)produced, including an exploration of whether it is already cultivated in youth party organisations. Simultaneously, while men's informal networking has been vastly documented, works on women's informal networking within and across political parties are scarce (Piscopo 2016), requiring further examination of how the gender composition of networks shapes participation modes and the aims networks pursue.

Last but not least, while studies on the adoption of gender equality strategies provide valuable insights on dynamics of continuity and change within parties, new insights on intra-party democracy can also be gained with analyses of why and when women's parties emerge, how they organise and how they relate to social movements (Evans 2016; Evans and Kenny 2019), such as the feminist movement.

Notes

1 See the online *Gender Quotas Database* created by International IDEA, the Inter-Parliamentary Union and the Stockholm University. Available from: www.idea.int/data-tools/data/gender-quotas (Accessed 5 October 2021).
2 Only Costa Rica and Honduras impose sanctions for non-compliance with quota regulations in the composition of parties' executives.
3 Podemos' members cast 38,000 votes, with the three gender equality resolutions ranking in 16th, 40th and 48th place. Available at: https://podemosbetera.es/resoluciones/(Accessed 5 October 2021).

References

Audickas, L., Dempsey, D. and Loft, P. (2017) *Membership of UK political parties*. Briefing Paper No. SN05125, 9 August 2019. House of Commons Library. Available at: https://commonslibrary.parliament.uk/research-briefings/sn05125/ (Accessed 15 October 2020)

Bashevkin, S. (1993) *Toeing the lines. Women and party politics in English Canada*. Toronto: Oxford University Press.

Bashevkin, S. (2010) 'When do outsiders break in? Institutional circumstances of party leadership victories by women in Canada', *Commonwealth & Comparative Politics*, 48(1), p72–90.

Bjarnegård, E. (2013) *Gender, informal institutions and political recruitment. Explaining male dominance in parliamentary representation*. Basingstoke: Palgrave Macmillan.

Bjarnegård, E. and Kenny, M. (2016) 'Comparing candidate selection: A feminist institutionalist approach', *Government and Opposition*, 51(3), p370–392.

Bjarnegård, E. and Zetterberg, P. (2016) 'Gender equality reforms on an uneven playing field: Candidate selection and quota implementation in electoral authoritarian Tanzania', *Government and Opposition*, 51(3), p464–486.

Bjarnegård, E. and Zetterberg, P. (2019) 'Political parties, formal selection criteria, and gendered parliamentary representation', *Party Politics*, 25(3), p325–335.

Campbell, R. and Childs, S. (2014) 'Parents in parliament: 'Where's mum?'', *Political Quarterly*, 85(4), p487–492.

Celis, K., Erzeel, S. and Mügge, L. (2015) 'Intersectional puzzles: Understanding inclusion and equality in political recruitment', *Politics & Gender*, 11(4), p765–770.

Cheng, C. and Tavits, M. (2011) 'Informal influences in selecting female political candidates', *Political Research Quarterly*, 64(2), p460–471.

Childs, S. (2008) *Women and British party politics*. London: Routledge.

Childs, S. (2013a) 'Intraparty democracy: A gendered critique and a feminist agenda', in Cross, W. and Katz, R. (eds.) *The challenges of intra-party democracy*. Oxford: Oxford University Press, pp. 81–99.

Childs, S. (2013b) 'In the absence of electoral sex quotas: Regulating political parties for women's representation', *Representation*, 49(4): p401–423.

Childs, S. and Kittilson, M.C. (2016) 'Feminizing political parties: Women's party member organizations within European parliamentary parties', *Party Politics*, 22(5), p598–608.

Childs, S. and Murray, R. (2014) 'Feminising political parties', in Campbell, R. and Childs, S. (eds.) *Deeds and words: Gendering politics after Joni Lovenduski*. Colchester: ECPR Press, pp. 73–90.

Childs, S. and Webb, P (2012) *Sex, gender and the conservative party. From iron lady to kitten heels*. Basingstoke: Palgrave.

Collier, C.N. and Raney, T. (2018) 'Canada's member-to-member code of conduct on sexual harassment in the House of Commons: Progress or regress?', *Canadian Journal of Political Science*, 51(4), p795–815.

Cross, W.P. (2019) 'Descriptive representation in local party associations and its implications for representation in parliament: Findings from the Canadian case', in Heidar, K. and Wauters, B. (eds.) *Do parties still represent? An analysis of the representativeness of political parties in western democracies*. New York: Routledge, pp. 15–30.

Crowder-Meyer, M. (2013) 'Gendered recruitment without trying: How local party recruiters affect women's representation', *Politics & Gender*, 9(4), p390–413.

Devroe, R., De Vet, B., Van de Voorde, N. and Wauters, B. (2019) 'Belgium: Parties as distorting mirrors – descriptive and substantive representativeness in Flemish parties under scrutiny', in Heidar, K. and Wauters, B. (eds.) *Do parties still represent? An analysis of the representativeness of political parties in western democracies*. New York: Routledge, pp. 86–104.

Evans, E. (2016) 'Feminist allies and strategic partners: Exploring the relationship between the women's movement and political parties', *Party Politics*, 22(5), p631–640.

Evans, E. and Kenny, M. (2019) 'The women's equality party: Emergence, organisation and challenges', *Political Studies*, 67(4), p855–871.

Freidenvall, L. (2013) 'Sweden: Step by step – women's inroads into parliamentary politics', in Dahlerup, D. and Leyennar, M. (eds.) *Breaking male dominance in old democracies*. Oxford: Oxford University Press, pp. 94–123.

Fox, R. and Lawless, J.L. (2010) 'If only they'd ask: Gender, recruitment, and political ambition', *The Journal of Politics*, 72(2), p310–326.

Gauja, A. and van Haute, E. (2015) 'Conclusion: Members and activists of political parties in comparative perspective', in van Haute, E. and Gauja, A. (eds.) *Party members and activists*, New York: Routledge, pp. 186–201.

Geha, C. (2019) 'The myth of women's political empowerment within Lebanon's sectarian power-sharing system', *Journal of Women, Politics & Policy*, 40(4), p498–521.

Hazan, R.Y. and Rahat, G. (2010) *Democracy within parties: Candidate selection methods and their political consequences*. Oxford: Oxford University Press.

Heath, R.M., Schwindt-Bayer, L.A. and Taylor-Robinson, M.M. (2005) 'Women on the sidelines: Women's representation on committees in Latin American legislatures', *American Journal of Political Science*, p49(2), p420–436.

Hinojosa, M. (2012) *Selecting women, electing women*. Philadelphia: Temple University Press.

IPU (2016) *Sexism, harassment and violence against women parliamentarians*. Geneva: Inter-Parliamentary Union.

Jensenius, F.R. (2016) 'Competing inequalities? On the intersection of gender and ethnicity in candidate nominations in Indian elections', *Government and Opposition*, 51(3), p440–463.

Juvonen, T. (2020) 'Out lesbian and gay politicians in a multiparty system', *Oxford Research Encyclopedia of Politics*. Available at: https://oxfordre.com/politics/view/10.1093/acrefore/9780190228637.001.0001/acrefore-9780190228637-e-1182 (Accessed 8 October 2021)

Keith, D. and Verge, T. (2018) 'Nonmainstream left parties and women's representation in Western Europe', *Party Politics*, 4(4), p397–409.

Kenny, M. (2013) *Gender and political recruitment: Theorizing institutional change*. Basingstoke: Palgrave Macmillan.

Kenny, M. and Verge, T. (2016) 'Opening up the black box: Gender and candidate selection in a new era', *Government and Opposition*, 51(3), p351–369.

Kittilson, M.C. (2006) *Challenging parties, changing parliaments: Women and elected office in contemporary Western Europe*. Columbus: The Ohio State University Press.

Kittilson, M.C. (2011) 'Women, parties and platforms in post-industrial democracies', *Party Politics*, 17(1), p66–92.

Krook, M.L. (2016) 'Contesting gender quotas: Dynamics of resistance', *Politics, Groups, and Identities*, 4(2), p268–283.

Krook, M.L. (2018) 'Westminster too: On sexual harassment in British politics', *Political Quarterly*, 89(1), p65–72.

Lawless, J.L. and Pearson, K. (2008) 'The primary reason for women's underrepresentation? Reevaluating the conventional wisdom', *Journal of Politics*, 70(1), p67–82.

Lovenduski, J. (1993) 'Introduction: The dynamics of gender and party', in Lovenduski, J. and Norris, P. (eds.) *Gender and party politics*. London: Sage, pp. 1–15.

Lovenduski, J. (2005) *Feminizing politics*. Cambridge: Polity.

Lovenduski, J. and Norris, P. (eds.) (1993) *Gender and party politics*. London: Sage.

Lowndes, V. (2020) 'How are political institutions gendered', *Political Studies*, 68(3), p543–564.

Luhiste, M. (2015) 'Party gatekeepers' support for viable female candidacy in PR-list systems', *Politics & Gender*, 11(1), p89–116.

McAllister, I. and Studlar, D.T. (2002), 'Electoral systems and women's representation: A long-term perspective', *Representation*, 39(1), p3–14.

Meier, P. (2004) 'The mutual contagion effect of legal and party quotas: A Belgian perspective', *Party Politics*, 10(5), p583–600.

Murray, R. (2010) *Parties, gender quotas and candidate selection in France*. London: Palgrave Macmillan.

Niven, D. (1998) 'Party elites and women candidates: The shape of bias', *Women and Politics*, 19(2), p57–80.

Norris, P. and Lovenduski, J. (1995) *Political recruitment: Gender, race and class in the British Parliament*. Cambridge: Cambridge University Press.

O'Brien, D.Z. (2015) 'Rising to the top: Gender, political performance, and party leadership in parliamentary democracies', *American Journal of Political Science*, 59(4), p1022–1039.

O'Neill, B. and Stewart, D.K. (2009) 'Gender and political party leadership in Canada', *Party Politics*, 15(6), p737–757.

Piscopo, J.M. (2016) 'When informality advantages women: Quota networks, electoral rules and candidate selection in Mexico', *Government and Opposition*, 51(3), p487–512.

Piscopo, J.M. and Kenny, M. (2020) 'Rethinking the ambition gap: Gender and candidate emergence in comparative perspective', *European Journal of Politics and Gender*, 3(1), p3–10.

Roza, V., Llanos, B. and Garzón de la Roza, G. (2011) *Gender and political parties: Far from parity*. Stockholm: International IDEA and Inter-American Development Bank.

Smrek, M. (2020) 'When is access to political capital gendered? Lessons from the Czech Parliament', *Parliamentary Affairs*. https://doi.org/10.1093/pa/gsaa051.

Stambough, S.J. and O'Regan, V.R. (2007) 'Republican lambs and the Democratic pipeline: Partisan differences in the nomination of female gubernatorial candidates', *Politics & Gender*, 3(3), p349–368.

Verge, T. (2015) 'The gender regime of political parties: Feedback effects between supply and demand', *Politics & Gender*, 11(4), p754–759.

Verge, T. (2020a) 'Political party gender action plans: Pushing gender change forward beyond quotas', *Party Politics*, 26(2), p238–248.

Verge, T. (2020b) 'Too few, too little: Parliaments' response to sexism and sexual harassment conducts', *Parliamentary Affairs*, 75(1), p94–112.

Verge, T. and Astudillo, J. (2019) 'The gender politics of executive candidate selection and reselection', *European Journal of Political Research*, 58(2), p720–740.

Verge, T. and Claveria, S. (2018) 'Gendered political resources: The case of party office', *Party Politics*, 24(5), p536–548.

Verge, T. and de la Fuente, M. (2014) 'Playing with different cards: Party politics, gender quotas and women's empowerment', *International Political Science Review*, 35(1), p67–79.

Verge, T. and Espírito-Santo, A. (2016) 'Interactions between party and legislative quotas: Candidate selection and quota compliance in Portugal and Spain', *Government and Opposition*, 51(3), p416–439.

Wauters, B. and Pilet, J.B. (2015) 'Electing women as party leaders', in Cross, W.P. and Pilet, J.B. (eds.) *The politics of party leadership*. Oxford: Oxford University Press, pp. 73–89.

PART 3

Party ideology and party families

10
CLEAVAGE POLITICS IN THE TWENTY-FIRST CENTURY

James Dennison and Sophia Hunger

Lipset and Rokkan's (1967) 'Party Systems and Voter Alignments' is both the starting point and most influential description of cleavage theory. Although its influence is beyond doubt, its key tenets remain controversial. In this chapter, we review their study and present early evidence supporting their theoretical claims before outlining the growing list of, first, criticisms that it has received and, second, retorts to those critiques. Despite this chapter's focus on advanced industrial societies, we proceed to sketch a brief overview of cleavage politics and related research beyond Europe. We conclude with a discussion of current directions for 'cleavage theory' research – particularly its use to make sense of the marked recent changes to party systems in Europe and beyond – as well as key frontiers going forward.

Lipset and Rokkan's 'cleavage theory' and early supporting evidence

While Lipset and Rokkan had an undeniable impact on social science research, particularly regarding electoral behaviour and political sociology, the core objective of their seminal study – providing insight to the macro-sociological and macro-structural processes of nation-building – is today largely overlooked in favour of their claims regarding the persistence of party systems.

Lipset and Rokkan argue that there are four sets of interchanges between societal subsystems which result in four major divides: centre-periphery, religious-secular, urban-rural, and labour-capital, which pre-date mass suffrage while at the same time also shaping modern democracies through their centrality for state-building. These four fundamental divides became more relevant with democratisation processes and industrialisation and led to the formation of Western European party systems which reflect these cleavages in their set-up. During the national and industrial revolutions, these pre-existing polarisations surfaced. During the national revolutions, the centre-periphery conflict between national elites and regional and ethnic minorities, as well as the conflict between church and state power, grew in importance. The first cleavage represents the conflict between the dominant nation-building culture and ethnical, cultural, linguistic, or religious minorities which are often geographically peripheral. Second, the conflict between the evolving nation-state and the church unfolded, in which the latter sought to defend its entrenched privileges. Additionally, the industrial revolution gave rise to the two other cleavages: between rural, agrarian interests and industrial entrepreneurs and between employers and workers.

While these social divides were to be found in every Western European society, the exact constellation of these conflict lines played out differently in each polity due to historical and institutional conditions during the state-building process, which the authors model according to the sequencing of critical junctures and then empirically test. First, the reformation in which the 'nation-builder' had to either side with the Roman Catholic Church or seize control of the (then national) church. Second, the 'democratic revolution' after 1789 in nation-states and churches competed for control over mass education. Finally, the third dichotomy revolves around a state's commitment to landed or industrial interests. Variation in the shape and timing of these three critical junctures, so the theory goes accounts for differences in European party systems.

This sequential model not only explains the emergence of party systems but also their persistence through voter alignment and institutionalisation. New parties were prevented from emerging by established parties which following the introduction of universal suffrage and their transformation into mass organisations, were able to establish a binding appeal to their core supporters based on these social divides. Commonly referred to as the 'Freezing Hypothesis', Lipset and Rokkan famously posit 'the party systems of the 1960s reflect, with few but significant exceptions, the cleavage structures of the 1920s' (1967, 50).

Several works in the following decades provided early evidence for the freezing hypothesis, underscoring the relevance of cleavages for electoral behaviour and party competition. Rose and Urwin's (1970) systematic assessment of party system stability in Europe from 1945 to 1969 supports the freezing hypothesis, arguing that stability is mostly due to the strength of political parties as social institutions. While Lipset and Rokkan's initial theoretical framework presents parties rather as passive expressions of social conflict, Sartori's (1990) take on cleavages and party system stability also emphasises parties' central role in politicising and thus translating social divides into politics.

Subsequently, the concept of cleavages was refined. Bartolini and Mair's (1990) influential study covers 13 Western European countries from 1885 to 1985. The authors present a threefold concept of cleavages: structural, psychological, and organisational (Bartolini and Mair 1990; see also Knutsen and Scarborough 1995). First, a cleavage requires an opposition between citizens' interests on each side of a social divide. Second, these citizens must be self-aware of this opposition and hence share a stable group identity. Third, the group identities have to be translated into parties, which results in a manifestation of these conflicts into politics. Furthermore, Bartolini and Mair (1990; see also Franklin et al. 1992) presented evidence in favour of stability between ideological clusters of parties. They focused on class cleavages, which further solidified over a 'century of electoral stabilisation' (Bartolini and Mair 1990, 287). The authors trace 'socio-organisational bonds' as the main driver of this stabilisation, while 'institutional incentives', for instance the number of parties in a system, the specificities of the electoral system and voter turnout, cause more volatility (1990, 293).

The refinement of cleavage theory

As summarised by Kriesi (1998, 166), research that tests the claims of cleavage theory has yielded findings that have varied 'depending on the conceptualisation of the fundamental theoretical terms, their operationalisations for the empirical analysis, the types of data used, and the methods applied in the analysis of the data'. The various concepts within the theory have been criticised as unclear (Franklin 2010), with Mair (2001, 27) arguing, with regard to what explains cleavage formation, that there 'remains a marked degree of confusion about what precisely was believed . . . to have settled into place by the 1920s' and Deegan-Krause (2007, 538) arguing that a 'baffling array of inconsistently used terms plagues contemporary scholarship on cleavages'. In particular, advocates of cleavage theory have been casual about the extent to which cleavages are based on structure, with some proposing them as purely the relationship between attitudes and party choice.

Kriesi (1998, 167) attempts to clarify the notion of cleavages by defining them as a division with a structural basis, between 'opposite social groups' that are 'conscious of their collective identity' and which is expressed in organisational terms by political actors. These actors give 'coherence and organised political expression to what otherwise are inchoate and fragmentary beliefs, values and experiences among members of some social group'. However, the question remains as to whether cleavage theory can simply be reduced to the importance of social factors in affecting party choice.

Crucially, some have argued that societal divisions do not define the cleavages on which parties compete but, to the contrary, parties define and thus politicise which societal divisions become salient via increased political contestation on issues (Sartori 1969; Evans 1999), undermining the exogenous explanatory power of social divisions to define cleavages. Lisi (2018, 2–3) states 'new issues, such as European integration, may activate the transformation of party systems through politicisation of specific topics', arguing that it is political elites and parties that reshape political competition by politicising new dimensions. Indeed, as Sartori (1976) pointed out, despite citizens' stable political attitudes structured on multiple dimensions, party competition tends to be over one left-right dimension of economic policies (e.g. van der Eijk and Franklin 1996; Mair 2007), though this notion is increasingly questioned today.

Regarding its explanatory and predictive power, cleavage theory has been criticised in empirical terms by noting its declining – or perhaps always exaggerated – usefulness. As early as 1979, Pedersen concluded that electoral volatility in Europe is too high to support the theory, which relies on slow-moving demographic change or sudden, rare critical junctures. Similarly, Pennings and Lane (1998) argued that 'given the diversity, degree and frequency of gradual and radical party system change we conclude that the cleavage approach, in its *traditional* form, is no longer a fruitful explanatory device'. Making a case for the declining relevance of cleavage theory, Franklin et al. (1992; see also Dalton 2000) argue that the ability of social divisions to predict voting behaviour had declined from an already not overwhelming 30 per cent of variance explained in the 1960s to around 10 per cent in the 1980s for many western countries. They explain this change as the result of the resolution of key conflicts and note that, first, this decline is universal across the west and, second, existing cleavages have *not* been replaced by new social cleavages in this process. More specifically, class voting has been argued to be in long-term decline (Franklin et al. 1992), whereas ethnic and language cleavages have generally remained stable (Elff 2007).

Despite the decline of class voting, scholars have argued that voting still comes down to the left-right spectrum as reflected in party competition. Knutsen (1995) argues that all cleavages express a general left-right orientation. Indeed, attitudes to economics, social liberties, and globalisation issues such as immigration or supranational integration are each recognisable as typically left- or right-wing ideologically. Thus, they are fundamentally psychological rather than representing separate societal, interest-based cleavages.

In Central and Eastern Europe (CEE), cleavages have been argued to be relatively less important than clientelistic and charismatic politics, though are often structured along minority issues, national sovereignty, or democracy versus authoritarianism (Deegan-Krause 2013; for an overview, see Casal

Bértoa 2012). Generally, there are three competing hypotheses to explain this difference: first, that communist regimes have eroded potential divides (Whitefield 2002); second, that various axes of political competition align on one single dimension that resulted from a long-standing tradition of opposition to communist rule (Kitschelt et al. 1999); third, there is a 'structured diversity' perspective. This points out certain commonalities between the region's party systems, while on the other hand stresses that differences may be explained by parties' top-down mobilisation, which can result in a 'new attitudinal correspondence' between parties and voters (Enyedi 2005, 715).

Somewhat similarly, in Western Europe, the waning importance of cleavages has been further supported with findings of declining party identification, forming a part of the broader trend of *dealignment* and ultimately volatility (Pedersen 1979; Dalton et al. 1984; Kriesi 1998). The notion of a decline in sociological effects is compatible with that of an increase in psychological effects on voting, with Knutsen and Scarborough (1995) arguing that value orientations are more important for individual voting than socio-demographics and that, in many European countries, their importance is increasing. These changes have been explained by 'cognitive mobilisation' (Dalton 1984, 2000) resulting from the spread of education and the availability of information through the mass media and, more recently, social media, letting voters choose as individuals rather than groups (for reasons why this is a necessary but not sufficient condition for dealignment, see Elff 2007). They have also been explained by greater societal heterogeneity in terms of experience and life options: in short, economic and social liberalism may have undermined the social conformity necessary for cleavage theory to be effective (Kriesi 2010). These changes are also consequential for research on the issue. With regard to dealignment, von Schoultz (2017, 35) states that 'as a response to this development, the search for new cleavages has involved conceptual stretching and attempts to outline new, and less comprehensive, models of party competition'.

Retorts: realignment and the transformation/restructuration of party systems

The primary retort to the *dealignment* thesis is that of *realignment*, which essentially argues that dealignment is exaggerated (Heath et al. 1991; Evans 1999; Elff 2007), temporary (Crewe 1980), limited primarily to class (Goldthorpe 1999; Manza and Brooks 1999; Van der Waal et al. 2007) as well as illusory owing to out of date and thus mis-measured understandings of social class (Evans 1999; Dalton 2009). Notably, Kriesi (1998) pinpoints the rise of a 'new middle class' or 'service class', which comprises highly skilled professionals who prefer left-libertarian parties, on the one hand, and managers with high levels of delegated authority who vote for conservative parties, on the other hand, as the primary social transformation. He then provides evidence to support this hypothesis, concluding that it brings the structural component back into accounts of the rise of a new value cleavage. Kriesi acknowledges two potential weaknesses of this revised structural cleavage-based account of party system change: first, individuals select into career by pre-existing values and, second, that this approach fails to take into account value change. In order to resolve the latter drawback, Kriesi adds generation to the structural dimension, partially filling the explanatory gap of generation-based value differences.

These differences manifest in the emergence of 'postmaterial' values. Inglehart (1977, 1990; see also Dalton et al. 1984) and others claimed that these values constitute a new, 'value' cleavage, replacing religion and class in importance. However, this would then remove the socio-structural foundation of the theory to more (presumably) proximate cognitive, or value-based differences, formed by both social and non-social factors.

Moreover, it has been questioned whether cleavage theory is a theory at all (Achen 1992). Central to much of this critique is the extent to which it has explanatory power at all or is simply a tautological 'description' of the relationship between societal divisions, attitudes, and voting behaviour. These three components together are in turn argued to comprise cleavages. Similarly, the causal mechanism as to why societal groups vote for certain parties, to varying extents, is often left unclear and is criticised as underdeveloped.

Research building on cleavage theory has expanded in recent years given the dramatic changes to Europe's party systems. These political changes have significant societal bases and are arguably the result of new 'critical junctures', in line with Lipset and Rokkan's theory. Although scholars had already pointed to earlier events such as the expansion of education in the 1970s and 1980s (Bornschier 2009), the acuteness of the multiple crises affecting Europe and what have been dramatic political responses have attracted a great deal of interest from scholars.

Typically, Hooghe and Marks (2018, 2) ask whether 'the euro crisis and the migration crisis congealed a distinctive structure of conflict in Europe?' They name this structure the 'transnational cleavage', with radical right and green parties at the cleavage's antipoles. Theoretically, they (2018, 2) start by 'dropping the presumption that political parties are expressions of already formed, densely organised and socially closed groups'. As such, they remove much of the socio-structural component of the theory, and make no assumptions about any social-based distribution in the effects of such 'exogenous forces' on voting behaviour. Instead, they find evidence of the effect of the economic and migration crises in raising the supply-side salience of European integration and immigration.

If, however, the social component is removed, all that is left is the effect of political attitudes; in particular, the increasingly salient 'transnational divide', which, Hooghe and Marks argue, is determined by (essentially, socio-structural) interests: the 'winners' and 'losers' of globalisation (2018, 7). Moreover, although they argue that 'these crises have raised the salience of Europe and immigration in public debate' (Hooghe and Marks 2018, 8–9); they measure salience according to the emphasis that parties – rather than the public – put on an issue. While Hooghe and Marks argue that divisions between mainstream parties on these issues have intensified, they find that these changes have been in terms of salience rather than parties' positions.

The 'transnational cleavage' that Hooghe and Marks identify has been given numerous other labels in the literature: demarcation-integration (Kriesi et al. 2006, 2012); cosmopolitan-communitarian (Teney et al. 2014); libertarian-universalistic – traditionalist-communitarian (Bornschier 2010); universalism-particularism (Beramendi et al. 2015; Häusermann and Kriesi 2015); and GAL/TAN (Hooghe et al. 2002). In policy terms, this dichotomy sees a preference for free movement of people and supranational government, on the one hand, and national sovereignty and closed borders on the other hand.

The work of Kriesi and his colleagues has extensively examined this divide from a cleavage theoretical perspective as well as using it to explain recent electoral trends. To them, conflicting interests regarding globalisation – 'opposing those who benefit from this process against those who tend to lose' (Kriesi et al. 2006, 921) – have delineated a new cleavage in Europe with an identifiable social base (Grande 2012, 279), which the various crises have brought to the fore as a potential critical juncture in the creation of a European polity. Kriesi et al. (2006, 929) state that 'winners' and 'losers' should also be thought of in terms of values and attitudes, not just material interests, a step away from the purely socio-structural approach of the original theory and towards cognitive concepts such as national identity and national community. Kriesi et al. (2006, 930; see also, Hutter and Kriesi 2019) use party salience, as well as media salience, as a way to measure the political importance of the dimension: 'macro-historical structural change linked to globalisation is articulated by the issue-specific positions taken by the parties during the electoral campaigns and by the salience they attribute to the different issues'. In doing so, they show that, compared to the 1970s, the salience of cultural issues is now typically higher than that of economic issues. Similarly, Grande (2012) concludes that the cleavage structure was consolidated through the globalisation and the transformation in European societies it caused. More recently, Hutter and Kriesi (2019, 4) posit that 'new issues and changes in the dimensions of party competition emerge exogenously, that is, from social conflicts which are products of long-term social change' yet measure these changes via party salience. They, like Hooghe and Marks, simultaneously see salience as a measure of exogenous change and measure salience by how much attention parties give to an issue, arguably risking tautological errors.

Cleavage theory beyond Europe

While European-focused literature on cleavages has less often taken the macro-historical dimensions of cleavage formation and its effect on party systems into account, literature on non-European countries has been more receptive to these parts of Lipset and Rokkan's initial framework. Due to different historical legacies and in many cases the experience of colonialism, non-European research considers the three critical junctures of party system formation to a greater extent. Party system institutionalisation and stability are often seen as crucial for a country's democratisation, as such systems are equipped with routinised sets of rules and benefit from their rootedness and legitimacy in a country's society (Dix 1989; Mainwaring and Scully 1995). Cross-regional research (Birnir 2007) also shows that beyond Europe, religious and linguistic diversity may not be lumped together (see Bartolini and Mair 1990, 228), but rather have opposite effects in new democracies, as linguistic cleavages – unlike other cultural cleavages – tend to stabilise electoral behaviour.

Latin American cleavage research – the most productive strand – often centres around the causes that prevent the formation of stable party systems (Roberts 2015; Mainwaring 2016) and the determinants of widely varying electoral volatility in the region. While early accounts have strongly questioned the applicability of cleavage formation to Latin America (Dix 1989; Coppedge 1998), scholars have associated party system stability with ethnic (Madrid 2005) or class-based cleavages, or related to waves of democratisation (Roberts 2017). The absence of stabilisation is often ascribed to weak party organisation and institutionalisation and the lack of organisational bonds and group identities (Roberts and Wibbels 1999).

Early work on cleavage politics in Sub-Saharan Africa has often stressed the role of ethnicity and ethnic cleavages for African party competition and systems (Horowitz 1985; Mozaffar, Scarritt and Galaich 2003); however, it partly overlooks the diversity of party types, including non-ethnic ones, on the continent (Elischer 2013). While other factors also determine party choice and identification, research on the complex interaction between multiple cleavages is largely underdeveloped (see Bratton et al. 2012).

Research on the Middle East – also rather new and still scarce – typically stresses the paramount importance of the conservative/Islamist versus leftist/secular cleavage which predominantly structures party competition in the region (Eyadat 2015; Dennison and Draege 2020). However, other studies emphasise the increasing importance of reversed left-right divides that shape party systems due to globalisation processes (Wegner and Cavatorta 2019; Aydogan 2021).

Asian- and Southeast Asian-centred research has often borrowed from Latin American research. Hicken and Kuhonta's (2011) findings show little association between cleavages and party system stability. Rather, authoritarianism serves as a significant driver in the origin of institutionalised party systems in Asia. Ufen (2012) argues that cleavage theory has made little impact on Southeast Asian research as many regional party systems are dominated by one single party. His study draws on critical junctures and shows how ethnic cleavage-based party systems evolved in Malaysia and Indonesia, as opposed to clientelist systems in Thailand and the Philippines. The rural-urban cleavage has long shaped Japanese politics, while recently increasing social inequalities have led to a dealignment from that cleavage (Chiavacci 2010). Indian politics are strongly shaped by cleavages, which are structured around religious and caste identity (Chhibber 2001; Banerjee et al. 2019).

Conclusions and avenues for further research

Contemporary applications of 'cleavage theory' offer broad empirical evidence for the political importance of a new dimension based on reactions to globalisation. However, these recent key contributions of cleavage theory are still overshadowed by cleavage theory's long-discussed lack of conceptual and causal clarity, and problems with operationalisation. Moreover, the grandness of the theory, as well as related notions of de- and re-alignment, leaves it as a poor account for the rapidity and vast temporal and spatial variation in recent changes in party systems. The importance of new dimensions on the demand-side (i.e. among electorates) remains unmeasured and the use of dimensions to collapse multiple issues is crude given the vast differences in the political effects between say, immigration and international trade, both of which would exist on a singular globalisation dimension in current research.

Similarly, in Europe, the effects of these cleavages are clearly lopsided: there is far less evidence of pro-transnational political mobilisation than opposition. It is also not clear how the emergence of this new cleavage can explain such events as the rise of an internationalist, radical left in southern Europe. Moreover, these 'cleavages' have seemingly largely been dominated by just two issues – immigration in the north and east of Europe and unemployment in the south. Neither of these are 'new' issues, nor can they be separated from the pre-existing structure of political conflict. Indeed, attitudes to *both* issues have long formed part of the ideological outlooks of conservatives and progressives respectively and both fit neatly into the left-right spectrum, both ideologically and empirically. Furthermore, the assumption that cleavages arise from societal structures is based on an, ultimately, economic instead of a psychological understanding of the forces that determine variation in an individual's political attitudes. This is not supported by most findings and has resulted in socio-structural variation being replaced with political attitudes or values in tests, though remaining theoretically implicit.

Finally, works utilising cleavage theory have been typically supply-side (i.e. party) focused, despite the theory's driving force – particularly central in Lipset and Rokkan's initial framework – being social changes. Consequently, the extent to which actual, largely exogenous macro-social changes such as globalisation, immigration and de-proletarianisation affect party systems is under-considered in a cleavage theory framework. Scholarly attempts to overcome these shortcomings would likely contribute to our understanding of how 'cleavages' affect contemporary politics.

References

Achen, C.H. (1992) 'Social psychology, demographic variables, and linear regression: Breaking the iron triangle in voting research', *Political Behavior*, 14, p195–211.
Aydogan, A. (2021) 'Party systems and ideological cleavages in the Middle East and North Africa', *Party Politics*, 27(4), p814–826.
Banerjee, A., Gethin, A. and Piketty, T. (2019) 'Growing cleavages in India?', *Economic and Political Weekly*, 54(11), p34–44.

Bartolini, S. and Mair, P. (1990) *Identity, competition and electoral availability: The stabilisation of European electorates 1885–1985*. Cambridge: Cambridge University Press.
Beramendi, P., Häusermann, S., Kitschelt, H. and Kriesi, H. (eds.) (2015) *The politics of advanced capitalism*. New York: Cambridge University Press.
Birnir, J.K. (2007) 'Divergence in diversity? The dissimilar effects of cleavages on electoral politics in new democracies', *American Journal of Political Science*, 51(3), p602–619.
Bratton, M., Bhavnani, R. and Chen, T-H. (2012) 'Voting intentions in Africa: Ethnic, economic or partisan?', *Commonwealth & Comparative Politics*. 50(1), p27–52.
Bornschier, S. (2009) 'Cleavage politics in old and new democracies', *Living Reviews in Democracy*. Center for Comparative and International Studies, ETH Zurich and University of Zurich, pp. 1–13.
Bornschier, S. (2010) 'The new cultural divide and the two-dimensional political space in Western Europe', *West European Politics*, 33(3), p419–444.
Casal Bértoa, F. (2012) 'Party systems and cleavage structures revisited: A sociological explanation of party system institutionalization in East Central Europe', *Party Politics*, 20(1), p16–36.
Chhibber, P.K. (2001) *Democracy without associations*. Ann Arbor: University of Michigan Press.
Chiavacci, D. (2010) 'Divided society model and social cleavages in Japanese politics: No alignment by social class, but dealignment of rural-urban division', *Contemporary Japan*, 22(1–2), p47–74.
Crewe, I. (1980) 'Prospects for party realignment: An Anglo-American comparison', *Comparative Politics*, 12, p379–399.
Coppedge, M. (1998) 'The dynamic diversity of Latin American party systems', *Party Politics*, 4(4), p547–568.
Dalton, R.J. (2000) 'The decline of party identifications', in Dalton, R.J. and Wattenberg, M.P. (eds.) *Parties without partisans. Political change in advanced industrial democracies*. Oxford: Oxford University Press, pp. 19–36.
Dalton, R.J. (2009) 'Economics, environmentalism and party alignments: A note on partisan change in advanced industrial democracies', *European Journal of Political Research*, 48, p161–175.
Dalton, R.J., Flanagan, S.C. and Beck, P.A. (eds.) (1984) *Electoral change in advanced industrial democracies. Realignment or dealignment?* Princeton: Princeton University Press.
Deegan-Krause, K. (2007) 'New dimensions of political cleavage', in Dalton, R.J. and Klingemann, H-D. (eds.) *Oxford handbook of political science*. Oxford: Oxford University Press, pp. 538–556.
Deegan-Krause, K. (2013) 'Full and partial cleavages', in Berglund, S., Ekman, J., Deegan-Krause, K. and Knutsen, T. (eds.) *The handbook of political change in eastern Europe*. Cheltenham: Edward Elgar, pp. 35–50.
Dennison, J. and Draege. J. (2020) 'The dynamics of electoral politics after the Arab Spring: Evidence from Tunisia', *Journal of North African Studies*, 4, p756–780.
Dix, R.H. (1989) 'Cleavage structures and party systems in Latin America', *Comparative Politics*, 22(1), p23–37.
Elff, M. (2007) 'Social structure and electoral behavior in comparative perspective: The decline of social cleavages in Western Europe revisited', *Perspectives on Politics*, 5(2), p277–294.
Elischer, S. (2013) *Political parties in Africa: Ethnicity and party formation*. New York: Cambridge University Press.
Enyedi, Z. (2005) 'The role of agency in cleavage formation', *European Journal of Political Research*, 44, p697–720.
Evans, G. (1999) *The end of class politics? Class voting in comparative context*. Oxford: Oxford University Press.
Eyadat, Z. (2015) 'A transition without players: The role of political parties in the Arab revolutions', *Democracy and Security*, 11(2), p160–175.
Franklin, M.N. (1992) 'The decline of cleavage politics', in Franklin, M.N., Mackie, T.T. and Valen, H. (eds.) *Electoral change: Responses to evolving social and attitudinal structures in western countries*. Cambridge: Cambridge University Press, pp. 383–405.
Franklin, M.N. (2010) 'Cleavage research: A critical appraisal', *West European Politics*, 22(3), p648–658.
Goldthorpe, J. (1999) 'Modeling the pattern of class voting in British elections, 1964–1992' in Evans, G. (ed.) *The end of class politics? Class voting in comparative context*, Oxford: Oxford University Press, pp. 59–82.
Grande, E. (2012) 'Conclusion: how much change can we observe and what does it mean?' in Kriesi, H., Grande, E., Dolezal, M., Helbling, M. et al. (eds.) *Political conflict in Western Europe*. Cambridge: Cambridge University Press, pp. 277–301.

Häusermann, S. and Kriesi. H. (2015) 'What do voters want? Dimensions and configurations in individual-level preferences and party choice' in Beramendi, P., Häusermann, S., Kitschelt, H. and Kriesi, H. (eds.) *The politics of advanced capitalism*. New York: Cambridge University Press, pp. 202–230.

Heath, A.F., Jowell, R., Curtice, J., Evans, G., Field, J. and Witherspoon, S. (1991) *Understanding political change: The British voter 1964–1987*, Oxford: Pergamon Press.

Hicken, A. and Martinez Kuhonta, E. (2011) 'Shadows from the past: Party system institutionalization in Asia', *Comparative Political Studies*, 44(5), p572–597.

Hooghe, L. and Marks, G. (2018) 'Cleavage theory meets Europe's crises: Lipset, Rokkan, and the transnational cleavage', *Journal of European Public Policy*, 25(1), p109–13.

Hooghe, L., Marks, G. and Wilson, C.J. (2002) 'Does left/right structure party positions on European integration', *Comparative Political Studies*, 35(8), p965–989.

Horowitz, D.L. (1985) *Ethnic groups in conflict*. Berkeley: University of California Press.

Hutter, S. and Kriesi, H. (eds.) (2019) *European party politics in times of crisis*. Cambridge: Cambridge University Press.

Inglehart, R. (1977) *The silent revolution. Changing values and political styles among western publics*. Princeton: Princeton University Press.

Inglehart, R. (1990) *Culture shift in advanced industrial society*. Princeton: Princeton University Press.

Kitschelt, H., Mansfeldova, Z., Markowski, R. and Toka, G. (1999) *Post-Communist party systems: Competition, representation, and inter-party cooperation*. Cambridge: Cambridge University Press.

Knutsen, O. (1995) 'Value orientations, political conflicts and left-right identification: A comparative study', *European Journal of Political Research*, 28, p63–93.

Knutsen, O. and Scarbrough, E. (1995) 'Cleavage politics', in Deth, J., Van, W. and Scarbrough, E. (eds.) *The impact of values*. Oxford: Oxford University Press, pp. 493–523.

Kriesi, H. (1998) 'The transformation of cleavage politics: The 1997 Stein Rokkan lecture', *European Journal of Political Research*, 33(2), p165–185.

Kriesi, H. (2010) 'Restructuration of partisan politics and the emergence of a new cleavage based on values', *West European Politics*, 33(3), p673–685.

Kriesi, H., Grande, E., Dolezal, M., Helbling, M., Höglinger, D., Hutter, S. and Wüest, B. (2012) *Political conflict in Western Europe*. Cambridge: Cambridge University Press.

Kriesi, H., Grande, E., Lachat, R., Dolezal, M., Bornschier, S. and Frey, T. (2006) 'Globalization and the transformation of the national political space: Six European countries compared', *European Political Science Review*, 45, p921–956.

Lipset, M.S. and Rokkan, S. (1967) *Cleavage structures, party systems, and voter alignments: an introduction*. New York: Free Press.

Lisi, M. (2018) 'Party system change and the European crisis: An introduction', in Lisi, M. (ed.) *Party system change, the European crisis and the state of democracy*. London: Routledge, pp. 1–23.

Madrid, R. (2005) 'Ethnic cleavages and electoral volatility in Latin America', *Comparative Politics*, 38(1), p1–20.

Mainwaring, S. (2016) 'Party system institutionalization, party collapse and party building', *Government and Opposition*, 51(4), p691–716.

Mainwaring, S. and Scully, T. (1995) *Building democratic institutions: Party systems in Latin America*. Stanford: Stanford University Press.

Mair, P. (2001) 'The freezing hypothesis: an evaluation', in Karvonen, L. and Kuhnle, S. (eds.) *Party systems and voter alignments revisited*. London: Routledge, pp. 27–44.

Mair, P. (2007) 'Left-right orientations', in Dalton, R.J. and Klingemann, H-D. (eds.) *Oxford handbook of political science*. Oxford: Oxford University Press, pp. 206–222.

Manza, J. and Brooks, C. (1999) *Social cleavages and political change: Voter alignments and US party coalitions*. New York: Oxford University Press.

Mozaffar, S., Scarritt, J.R. and Galaich, G. (2003) 'Electoral institutions, ethnopolitical cleavages, and party systems in Africa's emerging democracies', *The American Political Science Review*, 97(3), p379–390.

Pedersen, M.N. (1979) 'The dynamics of European party systems: Changing patterns of electoral volatility', *European Journal of Political Research*, 7(1), p1–26.

Pennings, P. and Lane, J-E. (1998) *Comparing party system change*. London: Routledge.

Roberts, K.M. (2015) *Changing course in Latin America: Party systems in the neoliberal era*. Cambridge: Cambridge University Press.

Roberts, K.M. (2017) 'Periodization and party system institutionalization in Latin America: A reply to Mainwaring', *Government and Opposition*, 52(3), p532–548.

Roberts, K.M. and Wibbels, E. (1999) 'Party systems and electoral volatility in Latin America: A test of economic, institutional, and structural explanations', *The American Political Science Review*, 93(3), p575–590.

Rose, R. and Urwin, D.W. (1970) 'Persistence and change in western party systems since 1945', *Political Studies*, 18(3), p287–319.

Sartori, G. (1969) 'From the sociology of politics to political sociology', *Government and Opposition*, 4(2), p195–214.

Sartori, G. (1976) *Parties and party systems*. Cambridge: Cambridge University Press.

Sartori, G. (1990) 'The sociology of parties: A critical review', in Mair, P. (ed.) *The West European party system*. Oxford: Oxford University Press, pp. 150–182.

Teney, C., Lacewell, O.P. and De Wilde, P. (2014) 'Winners and losers of globalization in Europe: Attitudes and ideologies', *European Political Science Review*, 6(4), p575–595.

Ufen, A. (2012) 'Party systems, critical junctures, and cleavages in Southeast Asia', *Asian Survey*, 52(3), p441–464.

van der Eijk, C. and Franklin, M.N. (1996) *Choosing Europe? The European electorate and national politics in the face of union*. Michigan: Michigan University Press.

Van der Waal, J., Achterberg, P. and Houtman, D. (2007) 'Class is not dead – It has been buried alive: Class voting and cultural voting in postwar Western societies (1956–1990)', *Politics and Society*, 35(3), p403–426.

von Schoultz, Å. (2017) 'Party systems and voter alignments' in Arzheimer, K., Evans, J. and Lewis-Beck, M.S. (eds.) *The sage handbook of electoral behaviour*, Thousand Oaks, CA: Sage, pp. 30–55.

Wegner, E. and Cavatorta, F. (2019) 'Revisiting the Islamist – Secular divide: Parties and voters in the Arab world', *International Political Science Review*, 40(4), p558–575.

Whitefield, S. (2002) 'Political cleavages and post-Communist politics', *Annual Review of Political Science*, 5, p181–200.

11
THE FAR RIGHT

Daphne Halikiopoulou

The far right 'momentum' that dominated politics in Europe and elsewhere during the 2010s is characterised by the successful performance of parties pledging to restore national sovereignty and implement policies that consistently prioritise in-groups over out-groups. These parties have become increasingly entrenched in their respective political systems: they have boosted their electoral support, joined government coalitions and/or influenced the policy agenda as main opposition actors. Unsurprisingly, this phenomenon has been accompanied by a proliferation of studies on the topic. Theoretical and empirical challenges notwithstanding, the field has developed substantially. During the past decade, systematic comparative research has addressed various dimensions of the study of the far right through qualitative, quantitative and mixed method approaches. Far right parties have attracted attention not only from political science but also from political sociology, political psychology and more recently political economy (Bonikowski 2017; Gidron and Hall 2017; Mudde 2019; Engler and Weistanner 2021).

The rapid increase in work on the far right is partly associated with the broader twin phenomena of 'populism' and 'democratic discontent' (Mudde and Rovira Kaltwasser 2018; Geurkink et al. 2020). Many recent studies have focused on voting behaviour, often juxtaposing the economic and cultural drivers of (populist) far right party support (Norris and Inglehart 2019). This focus on the demand-side has entailed the advancement of the field through quantitative analyses, perhaps more so compared with the study of other party families. Supply-side accounts seeking to understand the dynamics of party competition that facilitate far right success are also widespread (Meguid 2005). With the evidence inconclusive about the superiority of either demand or supply side accounts in explaining far right success, recent literature emphasises the importance of bridging these explanations (Golder 2016). The field has also developed in the areas of party organisation and membership (Art 2018) as well as the subsequent impact of far right parties on the mainstream (Abou-Chadi and Krause 2020; Spoon and Klüver 2020).

Existing literature is heavily, but not exclusively, focused on Europe. Both comparative as well as single case study research has sought to understand different patterns of support in Western (Rydgren 2008; Lucassen and Lubbers 2012), Eastern (Bustikova 2018) and Southern (Alonso and Rovira Kaltwasser 2015; Halikiopoulou and Vasilopoulou 2018; Rama et al. 2021) European countries. Some recent work focusing on populism has attempted broader comparisons outside Europe (Bonikowski 2017).

This chapter provides an overview of this literature, focusing on the far right party family, its electoral base and the various explanations for its support and political impact. It starts with a brief account of far right party electoral results in Europe in order to map the variation in their electoral success. It then examines the far right's ideological and organisational features, identifying both commonalities and also differences that exist between parties in this broad umbrella category. Next, the chapter examines the far right voter base, focusing on both contextual and attitudinal characteristics of the far right voter profile, which show how the far right electorate has changed over time. The next section assesses explanations of far right party support broadly categorised into demand and supply-side explanations. The chapter then examines the impact of far right parties on mainstream politics, both through government participation and policy influence as opposition. It concludes with a short discussion of this phenomenon outside the European context, and the identification of avenues for future research.

The state of the far right

Far right parties were by and large marginalised and discredited in Europe in the aftermath of the Second World War because of their association with fascism. Those that emerged electorally successful tended to be of the 'new' variety, making systematic attempts to dissociate themselves from racist violence. In the late 1990s and early 2000s, the success of parties such as List Pim Fortuyn in the Netherlands, the Austrian Freedom Party (FPÖ), the French Front National (FN – renamed Rassemblement National) and later the Greek Popular Orthodox Rally (LAOS) marked the beginning of what became the consolidation of a far right trend. Some fluctuations notwithstanding, by the mid-2010s, this had become a Europe-wide phenomenon.

Far right party success can be understood in three ways. First, we can look at electoral performance: many far right parties including the FN, the FPÖ, the Greek Golden Dawn and the Danish People's Party (DF) experienced a dramatic increase in their support during the 2010s in both EP and national elections. Second, far right party success can be evaluated in relation to their access to office: an increasing number of far right parties gained access to government during this period. This has marked a reversal of the cordon sanitaire (see later), suggesting that far right parties are now being treated as legitimate actors both by their voters and by their political competitors. Examples are the Italian Lega, the Danish People's Party (DF), the Latvian National Alliance (NA), the Estonian Conservative People's Party of Estonia (EKRE), the Austrian FPÖ, the Finns Party (PS), the Polish Law and Justice (PiS), the Hungarian Fidesz and the Greek Popular Orthodox Rally (LAOS). Third, far right party success can be assessed through looking at their influence on party systems: the increasing entrenchment of far right parties in mainstream politics has often resulted in the adoption of accommodative strategies, mainly with regard to the immigration issue. Parties such as the RN and UKIP have successfully competed in their domestic systems, influencing the agendas of other parties.

The far right party family: ideology and organisation

Terminology used to describe this party family varies. Frequently used terms include the 'radical right', the 'populist radical right', the 'extreme right', the 'anti-immigrant right' and the 'far right'. While any umbrella term inevitably subsumes a broad range of parties and groups that differ significantly in agenda and policy, scholars increasingly argue that the term 'far right' captures both the overarching similarities that make these parties comparable, and the important differences between parties in this diverse group (Golder 2016; Mudde 2019; Halikiopoulou and Vlandas 2020). Further distinguishing between different variants based, for example, on the ways in which these parties relate to fascism and democracy allows researchers to take into account the idiosyncrasies of specific cases.

The far right umbrella is used to describe parties that are sceptical of immigration and share a focus on sovereignty, nationalist policies and placing 'native' inhabitants first in the provision of welfare and social services. Far right parties compete by emphasising extreme positions on immigration (van Spanje 2010; Wagner and Meyer 2016) and seek to exclude members of the out-group from the national polity on the grounds that they constitute a threat to various dimensions of national cohesion.

Mudde's (2007) three-pronged definition that includes nativism, populism and authoritarianism remains a widely used guide for far right party classification. First, researchers agree that nativism – a narrow form of nationalism – is a core feature of the far right. Broadly understood as an ideological or political movement that pursues the attainment and maintenance of the unity, autonomy and identity of a deemed nation (Breuilly 2005), nationalism draws on a purported distinction between an in-group and out-group, which is key to the far right programmatic agenda. The important point is not simply that far right parties are all, to a degree, nationalist, but rather that they use nationalism to justify their positions on socioeconomic issues (Vasilopoulou and Halikiopoulou 2015). While all far right parties adopt nationalism, however, they do so in different ways, drawing on different configurations of various criteria of national belonging, as will be shown later on in the chapter.

Second, the far right often combines the nationalist axis with a people versus elite axis, claiming to restore national sovereignty on behalf of the people. Not all far right parties, however, are populist. Much recent scholarship focuses on minimum and maximum definitions, suggesting that populism may be a question of degree, for example by defining populism as a communication phenomenon (de Vreese et al. 2018; see also Chapter 23 for a wider discussion of populism).

Third, far right parties differ regarding their authoritarianism. Given the significant variations between these parties, scholars stress that it is important to distinguish between them on the basis of whether they are extreme or radical (Golder 2016). The extreme right includes both vigilante groups and political parties that are often openly racist, have clear ties to fascism and also employ violence and aggressive tactics. These groups may operate either outside or within the realm of electoral politics, or both. They tend to oppose procedural democracy. A good example is the Greek Golden Dawn, an openly fascist party that glorifies violence (Vasilopoulou and Halikiopoulou 2015). Radical right parties, on the other hand, have distanced themselves from fascism. They oppose the far right label and accept procedural democracy. These parties tend to be the most widespread and electorally successful in Europe, for example the French RN, the Dutch PVV, the Sweden Democrats (SD) and the German AfD. While some may employ authoritarian tactics, they also adopt rhetoric that conceals this under a pseudo-liberal democratic façade that focuses on the popular will and emphasises ideological criteria of national belonging. This suggests that the three classification criteria – nationalism, populism and authoritarianism – often overlap.

The significant differences between these parties raise questions about the extent to which the 'far right' is a single party family, and highlight the dangers of describing any democratic challenger as 'far right'. On the one hand, it may be argued that because of their ideological differences, these parties should not be included in a single category. For example, major differences exist between parties such as the Golden Dawn, the PVV and Fidesz. On the other hand, from an empirical perspective, these parties tend to converge in their policy prescriptions, which clearly distinguish them from other party families (Ennser 2012). While it may be more appropriate for qualitative studies comparing a small number of cases to select parties from the same variant (e.g. Halikiopoulou and Vasilopoulou 2018 on extreme right variants) in order to ensure comparability, quantitative studies can, and indeed often do, include far right parties broadly defined in their samples (Rooduijn 2018; Halikiopoulou and Vlandas 2020; Stockemer et al. 2020; Allen and Goodman 2021).

How are far right parties organised? Research has shown that Western European far right parties are characterised by highly centralised organisational structures: hierarchical control mechanisms ensure decisions are made at the top and party organisation tends to revolve around charismatic leaders who rely heavily on media attention. There is some variation in the degree of centralisation and coherence of party organisation across different parties, meaning some are better equipped to withstand internal splits than others, for example the RN and FPÖ in contrast to the German Republikaner (REP) and Belgian National Front (Ellinas 2009). Weak organisational structures suggest that the party is unable to withstand leadership changes and may subsequently implode: for example, the List Pim Fortuyn in the Netherlands (Heinisch and Mazzoleni 2016).

Research challenges in the field of party organisation notwithstanding – for example, the lack of conceptual clarity and absence of reliable data – recent comparative literature seeking to assess what determines organisational strength and how far right parties can endure such changes has made considerable advances (Heinisch and Mazzoleni 2016; Art 2018). This literature emphasises factors such as the existence of a party hierarchy, the establishment of small local branches and party unity as critical in ensuring the party is able to mobilise support and avoid internal splits (Art 2008; Ellinas and Lamprianou 2017). Research suggests that organisational factors are an important determinant of far right electoral performance (Ellinas 2009). For example, charismatic leadership features prominently as a cause of far right party success, yet recently this view has been contested. The charismatic leadership thesis has been criticised as suffering from circular reasoning (Muis and Immerzeel 2017). Overall, evidence suggests that party organisation is more likely to explain why some far right parties survive *after* their initial electoral breakthrough rather than the breakthrough itself (Ellinas 2009).

Who votes for the far right?

An abundance of survey data (e.g. from the European Social Survey and European Election Study) offers scholars insights into the far right voter profile. Research focusing on socio-demographic factors that may prompt support suggests that far right supporters are more likely to be male, lowly educated, older individuals with poor prospects in the labour market (Lucassen and Lubbers 2012; Swank and Betz 2018; Stockemer, Halikiopoulou and Vlandas 2020). Regarding their attitudinal characteristics, these voters are more likely to have stricter views on law and order, support anti-elitist beliefs and have concerns about the impact of out-groups in their societies suggesting these individuals' voter preferences are driven by their authoritarian, populist and nationalist attitudes (Akkerman, Mudde and Zaslove 2014; Lubbers and Coenders 2017; Geurkink et al. 2020). Indeed, one of the strongest predictors of far right voting is immigration scepticism (Ivarsflaten 2008). Far right voters tend to dislike immigrants for a variety of reasons, including perceiving them to be a threat to national cohesion, a source of competition in the labour market and a security threat (Rydgren 2008; Halikiopoulou and Vlandas 2020).

A key characteristic of the recent wave of far right party support has been the gradual broadening of the far right voting base to include more women (Allen and Goodman 2021) as well as younger, more middle-class, educated individuals who may perceive themselves to be experiencing relative economic decline, but are not impoverished (Kurer 2020). Literature that focuses on the far right's widening appeal increasingly distinguishes between ideological and protest voting (see van de Brug, Fennema and Tillie 2000) with recent studies reporting evidence of variation of voter motives. For example, distinguishing between core far right voters who identify fully with the entire far right party platform and peripheral voters who identify only partially with this platform, Halikiopoulou and Vlandas (2020) find that different voter groups vote for the far right for different reasons, forming coalitions of support. An interesting dimension here is the far right appeal to unlikely voter groups that do not conform to the typical voter profile. According to Stockemer, Halikiopoulou and Vlandas (2020), one third of the far right electorate has no strong immigration concerns, pointing to the importance of protest voting by those who do not fully endorse far right parties but vote for them in order to express discontent with the political system (Agerberg 2017). This has important implications for our expectations about the stability of these parties: protest voters are volatile and while they allow far right parties to extend their support beyond their secure voting base, this support is not necessarily stable.

Explaining electoral success

Any discussion of the far right voter profile(s) would be incomplete if not placed within a broader explanatory framework: why and under what circumstances are voters more likely to opt for far right parties, and what do these parties do to maximise their support? The extant literature on the topic spans decades and cuts across disciplines such as political psychology, political sociology and political science. Analyses range from the origins of fascism to contemporary radical right politics in Europe and the USA (see e.g. Adorno 1950; Lipset 1960; Bell 1964; Mudde 2007; Golder 2016). As the field developed, the framework for understanding far right party support has become increasingly systematised in terms of demand and supply. The former includes bottom-up explanations that focus on the underlying societal conditions that trigger far right party support; the latter includes top-down approaches that focus on party competition, the broader political system and party discourse (for a systematic account of the demand and supply framework, see Mudde 2007).

Demand

The literature that approaches the topic from the demand-side has systematically documented a range of grievances that may prompt far right party support (Golder 2016). The overall argument is that rapid societal changes associated with immigration, globalisation, technological advancement, community decline and material deprivation push voters towards the periphery (Kriesi et al. 2006; Hooghe and Marks 2018). These voters express their dissatisfaction by opting for far right parties, which capitalise on a broad range of societal grievances by emphasising policies that prioritise, and protect, in-groups from out-groups. Research has employed both quantitative and qualitative comparative methodologies and used aggregate and individual level data to examine a range of grievances that drive far right party support. While these are complex and often overlap, for the purposes of clarity, this chapter proceeds with a brief overview of the *cultural*, *economic*, *societal* and *institutional* factors that are often highlighted in the literature.

Culture- and value-based grievances

Cultural grievance theories stress the importance of value-based voter concerns within the context of an emerging transnational cleavage (Lucassen and Lubbers 2012; Golder 2016; Hooghe and Marks 2018; Norris and Inglehart 2019). This cleavage essentially creates an additional, or alternative, dimension of societal contestation to that between haves and have-nots by dividing voters with cosmopolitan values from those who are primarily concerned with preserving their national culture and identity. This is why globalisation, immigration and freedom of movement all have become important sources of discontent. Scholars have often based such explanations on the strong predictive power of immigration (Norris and Inglehart 2019).

Economic discontent

Others emphasise the importance of materialist issues, notably actual and relative economic performance (Halikiopoulou and Vlandas 2020; Kurer 2020), wealth inequality (Adler and Ansell 2020) and labour market competition with immigrants (Dancygier and Donnelly 2013). Such approaches suggest that concern with immigration is not by default evidence for the cultural grievance thesis, as many voters have immigration concerns beyond culture (Rydgren 2008; Halikiopoulou and Vlandas 2020), suggesting a story that accounts for a combination of grievances.

Societal grievances

This perspective emphasises drivers such as anxiety and pessimism deriving from a sense of alienation and declining social status (Gidron and Hall 2017; Engler and Weisstanner 2021). Research points out that individuals who perceive themselves to be detached from society, perhaps because of the decline of membership in community organisations such as churches, trade unions and other civic associations, are increasingly likely to vote for far right parties (Gest 2016). This perspective often serves as a bridge between theories that focus on cultural and economic discontent.

Institutional grievances

This perspective highlights 'political trust' as an explanation of protest voting. The key argument is that the populist and authoritarian attitudes of far right voters are triggered by trust-related grievances over elites, institutions and the government. Citizens assess the efficacy and credibility of institutions within the broader context of democratic representation. These assessments shape their voting preferences. Negative assessments, manifested in declining levels of trust, may result in punishment of the mainstream and/or the incumbent and subsequent support for far right parties (Agerberg 2017; Halikiopoulou and Vasilopoulou 2018). Consequently, far right parties could be the main beneficiaries of trust-related grievances, suggesting that the far right vote can be best understood as an anti-establishment vote.

While these factors are much debated – and often juxtaposed against each other in the literature – it is important to emphasise that they are not necessarily mutually exclusive perspectives. As the discussion of the far right voter profile observed, these parties have become increasingly effective in mobilising support beyond their core voting base. What is interesting in this respect is to establish ways in which these different factors prompt different voters, and by extension the conditions under which the interests of diverse groups align, forming potential voter coalitions.

Supply

Supply-side explanations commence from the premise that grievances at the demand level are insufficient in explaining the electoral success of far right parties, because they often fail to explain variation both between and within countries. Supply-side arguments complement this picture, positing that political parties may themselves exert agency, and can shape their own support. Thus, parties not only respond to public opinion but also shape it. There are two distinct, but interrelated, mechanisms behind this: first, the political system may be conducive for far right party success by offering an open, or permissive, political space regarding how parties compete and the system within which they operate. Second, certain strategies far right parties themselves adopt are successful in making their message appealing to broader sectors of the population.

Party competition and political opportunities

The focus here is on the opportunities and constraints offered by the political system within which parties operate. The degree of permissiveness of the system is a product of various factors including the electoral system, party organisation, the policies and agendas of competitor parties and the degree of fragmentation of the right (Meguid 2005; Golder 2016; Halikiopoulou and Vasilopoulou 2018). Regarding electoral rules, majoritarian electoral systems that translate votes into seats disproportionately tend to penalise small parties, excluding them from political representation. Theoretically, therefore, it makes sense to expect far right parties to perform better under PR systems. Empirically, however, this is not always the case. A boost in far right party performance in national level elections can be driven by good results in European Parliament elections. Improved far right party electoral performance can also influence the policies of mainstream parties as the former become more credible competitors, with UKIP and the Brexit referendum being a good example. The ability to influence policy is at the core of party competition arguments, which suggest that the behaviour of mainstream parties can be critical to far right party success, especially regarding particular strategies towards issues that are salient, such as immigration.

Discursive Opportunities and 'winning formulas'

Theories that focus on discursive opportunities examine the evolution of party programmatic agendas. The broad argument is that the de-demonisation, or normalisation, of far right rhetoric has contributed significantly to its electoral success. Perspectives on discursive change often focus on nationalism as a communication tool, putting forward explanations that centre on far right party 'civic' normalisation strategies. This literature notes that more electorally successful far right parties have increasingly adopted a rhetoric that excludes groups not on biological but rather on ideological criteria of national belonging (Koopmans and Statham 1999; Halikiopoulou, Mock and Vasilopoulou 2013), allowing them to appeal to a broad range of social groups with different preferences. These parties present culture as a value issue, refraining from ascriptive criteria of exclusion, and distancing themselves from fascism and right-wing extremism. This approach makes their rhetoric more palatable, especially to peripheral supporters, that is, those groups who vote 'against' the establishment rather than 'for' the far right in ideological terms. Most electorally successful Western European far right parties, including the RN, AfD and the PVV, adopt the 'civic nationalist normalisation' while exceptions include far right parties such as the Greek Golden Dawn, which managed to gain votes while putting forward an openly extremist narrative.

The 'civic nationalist normalisation' rhetoric is often accompanied by a shift from the neoliberal economic 'winning formula' of previous waves (Kitschelt and McGann 1995) towards more economically centrist positions with an increased focus on social welfare (Afonso and Rennwald 2018) that attempt to appeal to the 'left-behind' and/or those who have suffered from economic deprivation (de Lange 2007; Ivaldi 2015). Overall, literature shows that far right parties tend to present 'blurry' economic positions combined with welfare chauvinism (Enggist and Pinggera 2022). For example, the RN's economic policy changed significantly during Marine Le Pen's leadership. This move from free market and support for privatisation in the mid-1980s to late 1980s towards an economic protectionist left-wing stance that places a strong emphasis on social issues constitutes an attempt to appeal to the economically insecure who have been marginalised by societal shifts such as globalisation and technological change (Betz 2013; Ivaldi 2015).

Impact on mainstream politics

What distinguishes the performance of contemporary far right parties to that of previous waves is a shift from the *cordon sanitaire* to far right mainstreaming (Halikiopoulou 2018; Mudde 2019; Wondreys and Mudde 2020). In the past, far right parties tended to be marginalised in their respective political systems, and often stigmatised as fascists and/or extremists. This is still the case in some countries; for example, in Greece, the Golden Dawn remained marginalised during the years it was represented in the Greek parliament (2012–2019) and its leading cadres were sentenced, and subsequently imprisoned, for maintaining a criminal organisation in late 2020. In many other European countries, however, far right parties (especially radical right variants) have become legitimate actors competing for elections, joining coalitions and developing policies; for example the Italian Lega, the Norwegian FrP and the Austrian FPÖ. Moreover, UKIP imploded only after its key policy recommendation, Brexit, was upheld by the UK's mainstream parties and implemented after the 2016 EU referendum. The reversal of the *cordon sanitaire* may be interpreted in two ways: first, more widespread government participation; and second, policy influence in opposition. Far right party success has had an impact on the positions of mainstream parties, many of whom have responded by adopting accommodative strategies, moving to the right on certain policy positions including immigration, multiculturalism and security (Abou-Chadi and Krause 2020; Spoon and Kluver 2020; Wondreys and Mudde 2020). Far right parties have effectively capitalised on the challenges posed by immigration-related issues to mainstream parties, which have tried to compete by tightening their own positions, often leading to the emergence of dormant ideological tensions (for a detailed discussion of the framing of the immigration issue, see Chapter 25). Indeed, the ability to shape the behaviour of other parties suggests a fundamental restructuring of the dynamics of party competition (Abou-Chadi and Krause 2020) centred on emphasising stricter positions on immigration.

This development has broader consequences for the future stability of democratic systems; ultimately, the far right's 'civic normalisation' strategy challenges democracy, because it allows these parties to permeate mainstream ground by appearing legitimate to a broad electorate. However, so far the literature yields mixed results on whether it actually pays off to accommodate the far right, and which far right parties are likely to benefit the most and why.

Conclusions and avenues for further research

The socio-political context of the 2010s presented favourable opportunities for far right parties. First, a series of crises, notably the European economic and migration crises, intensified grievances that may be conducive to far right party support. At the intersection of a persisting materialist, and an emerging value-based cleavage, economic, cultural, societal and institutional discontent have triggered voters with a broad range of socio-demographic and attitudinal characteristics to cast a far right vote. Second, party competition dynamics, including the implosion of the centre-left and the decline of mainstream parties as political alternatives in many countries, have reinforced this phenomenon. Third, the development of a normalisation strategy, at the core of which is a more civic form of nationalism and a conscious attempt to detach from the far right's fascist past, has enabled these parties to step in and occupy the empty space left by other competitors by allowing them to appear legitimate and credible to a broad range of social groups.

There is yet another dimension to this: a domino effect, which has resulted in a broad geographic expansion of far right parties and political actors. Already research sheds light on how the rise of the far right has unfolded within Europe, affecting 'exceptional' cases that had initially resisted this trend such as Sweden and Spain (Alonso and Rovira Kaltwasser 2015; Rydgren and van der Meiden 2019; Rama et al. 2021). Increasingly, the wider trend of the mainstreaming of far right ideas observed outside the European context highlights the possibility that the rise of the far right is a global phenomenon. Jair Bolsonaro in Brazil, Donald Trump in the USA, One Nation in Australia and the Bharatiya Janata Party (BJP) in India are just a few examples of the spread of far right populism in the industrialised world and beyond, revealing the breadth and persistence of this phenomenon.

There are conceptual and methodological reasons why such broad comparisons are not without challenges. Issues such as data availability, ambiguities surrounding which parties/political actors may actually be classified as far right, as well as vastly different political settings, party systems and historical experiences constrain researchers examining the broader manifestations of this phenomenon comparatively. These limitations notwithstanding, new work could complement comparative research on populism outside the European context (see Bonikowski 2017; Moffitt 2017), constituting a good starting point in the development of large-scale accounts of far right populist contagion.

Today, the study of the far right is not only a highly developed field (which is perhaps even overcrowded in some areas) but also one that still presents exciting opportunities for research. Following the 'hype' surrounding populism in the aftermath of the 2014 European Parliament elections, the subsequent election of Donald Trump in 2016 and the Brexit referendum of the same year, new systematic comparative work developed which shed light on many dimensions of the topic, yielding interesting results and adding much to what we already know about who votes for the far right and why. Despite this voluminous literature, however, the far right is still in many ways puzzling. Empirical realities do not always conform to our theoretical expectations; on the contrary, much of the time empirical patterns seem to defy even the most established theories. Many questions remain unresolved either because of data availability constraints, or because of new developments altering political dynamics. This opens up a range of avenues for future research.

First, the issue of party organisation requires greater attention. More comparative research could shed light on local organisational dynamics, the role of women in leadership positions and the overall conditions that allow far right party organisational structures to be more resilient and adaptable. Second, long-standing questions surrounding variation in electoral support, both within and between countries, remain unresolved. While we know a lot about the underlying demand and supply-side forces that drive the far right vote, deviant cases merit further examination. New comparative work could focus on the conditions that facilitate the rise of the far right in some countries but not others, complementing existing work on countries such as Cyprus, Spain and Portugal which did not develop a strong far right in the immediate aftermath of economic crisis despite favourable demand (Alonso and Rovira Kaltwasser 2015; Charalambous and Christoforou 2018; Halikiopoulou and Vasilopoulou 2018).[1] It is also worth examining competition between far right parties in situations where more than one far right party contests elections (e.g. Austria and the Netherlands) and why some parties perform more strongly.

Third, the unlikely far right voters, that is, those that do not conform to the typical far right voter profile remain a puzzle for future research to explore. Why do more women, educated individuals and groups not primarily concerned with immigration also vote for the far right under specific circumstances? Fourth, the issue of party competition and whether it benefits mainstream parties to accommodate far right party strategies warrants further analysis. How can we explain conflicting findings regarding the far right and contagion to other parties in European party systems? Next, there is the issue of emerging opportunities and challenges posed by new developments such as COVID-19. Why are some far right parties proving more resilient despite the unfavourable conditions created by the pandemic? Finally, the question of the breadth of the phenomenon and comparability outside the European context demands greater attention. Are far right populist movements in diverse contexts the symptom of the same malaise despite the fundamental differences that define their political experiences? These puzzles suggest there is considerable scope for future research to investigate variation in the role of demand and supply-side dynamics in shaping far right party success.

Note

1. Note that the rise of Vox and Chega only took place in later elections and not the immediate aftermath of the economic crisis.

References

Abou-Chadi, T. and Krause, W. (2020) 'The causal effect of radical right success on mainstream parties' policy positions: A regression discontinuity approach', *British Journal of Political Science*, 50(3), p829–847.
Adler, D. and Ansell, B. (2020) 'Housing and populism', *West European Politics*, 43(2), p344–365.
Adorno, T.W. (1950) *The authoritarian personality*. New York: Harper.
Afonso, A. and Rennwald, L. (2018) 'Social class and the changing welfare state agenda of Populist Radical Right Parties in Europe', in Manow, P. and Palier, B. (eds.) *Electoral realignments and welfare state transformations in Europe*. Oxford: Oxford University Press, pp. 171–194.
Agerberg, M. (2017) 'Failed expectations: Quality of government and support for populist parties in Europe', *European Journal of Political Research*, 56, p578–600.
Akkerman, A., Mudde, C. and Zaslove, A. (2014) 'How populist are the people? Measuring populist attitudes in voters', *Comparative Political Studies*, 47(9), p1324–1353.
Allen, T. and Goodman, S. (2021) 'Individual- and party-level determinants of far-right support among women in Western Europe', *European Political Science Review*, 13(2), p135–150.
Alonso. S. and Rovira Kaltwasser, C. (2015) 'Spain: No country for the populist radical right?', *South European Society and Politics*, 20(1), p21–45.
Art, D. (2008) 'The organizational origins of the contemporary radical right: The case of Belgium', *Comparative Politics*, 40(4) p421–440.
Art, D. (2018) 'Party organization and the radical right', in Rydgren, J. (ed.) *The Oxford handbook for the radical right*. Oxford: Oxford University Press, pp. 239–250.
Bell, D. (1964) 'The dispossessed', in Bell, D. (ed.) *The radical right*. New York: Anchor, pp. 1–45.
Betz, H.G. (2013) 'The new front national: Still a master case?' Recode Working Paper, Augsberg: European Science Foundation, November 30.
Bonikowski, B. (2017) 'Three lessons of contemporary populism in Europe and the United States', *The Brown Journal of World Affairs*, 23(1), p9–24.
Breuilly, J. (2005) 'Dating the nation: How old is an old nation?' in Ichijo, A. and Uzelac, G. (eds.) *When is the nation? Towards an understanding of theories of nationalism*. London: Routledge, pp. 15–39.
Bustikova, L. (2018) 'The radical right in Eastern Europe', in Rydgren, J. (ed.) *The Oxford handbook for the radical right*. Oxford: Oxford University Press, pp. 565–581.

Charalambous, G. and Christoforou, P. (2018) 'Far-right extremism and populist rhetoric: Greece and Cyprus during an era of crisis', *South European Society and Politics*, 23(4), p451–477.

Dancygier, R.M. and Donnelly, M.J. (2013) 'Sectoral economies, economic contexts, and attitudes toward immigration', *The Journal of Politics*, 75(1), p17–35.

de Lange, S.L. (2007) 'A new winning formula?: The programmatic appeal of the radical right', *Party Politics*, 13(4), p411–435.

de Vreese, C.H., Esser, F., Aalberg, T., Reinemann, C. and Stanyer, J. (2018) 'Populism as an expression of political communication content and style: A new perspective', *The International Journal of Press/Politics*, 23(4), p423–438.

Ellinas, A.A. (2009) 'Chaotic but popular? Extreme-right organisation and performance in the age of media communication', *Journal of Contemporary European Studies*, 17(2), p209–221.

Ellinas, A.A. and Lamprianou, I. (2017) 'How far right local party organizations develop: The organizational buildup of the Greek Golden Dawn', *Party Politics*, 23(6), p804–820.

Enggist, M. and Pinggera, M. (2022) Radical right parties and their welfare state stances – Not so blurry after all?, *West European Politics*, 45(1), p102–128.

Engler, S. and Weisstanner, D. (2021) 'The threat of social decline: Income inequality and radical right support', *Journal of European Public Policy*, 28(2), p153–173.

Ennser, L. (2012) 'The homogeneity of West European party families: The radical right in comparative perspective', *Party Politics*, 18(2), p151–171.

Gest, J. (2016) *The new minority*. Oxford: Oxford University Press.

Geurkink, B., Zaslove, A., Sluiter, R. and Jacobs, K. (2020) 'Populist attitudes, political trust, and external political efficacy: Old wine in new bottles?', *Political Studies*, 68(1), p247–267.

Gidron, N. and Hall, P.A. (2017) 'The politics of social status: Economic and cultural roots of the populist right', *British Journal of Sociology*, 68, p57–84.

Golder, M. (2016) 'Far right parties in Europe', *Annual Review of Political Science*, 19, p477–97.

Halikiopoulou, D. (2018) 'A right-wing populist momentum? A review of 2017 elections across Europe', *Journal of Common Market Studies*, 56, p63–73

Halikiopoulou, D., Mock, S. and Vasilopoulou, S. (2013) 'The civic zeitgeist: nationalism and liberal values in the European radical right', *Nations and Nationalism*, 19(1), p107–127.

Halikiopoulou, D. and Vasilopoulou, S. (2018) 'Breaching the social contract: crises of democratic representation and patterns of extreme right party support', *Government and Opposition*, 53(1), p26–50.

Halikiopoulou, D. and Vlandas, T. (2020) 'When economic and cultural interests align: The anti-immigration voter coalitions driving far right party success in Europe', *European Political Science Review*, 12(4), p427–448.

Heinisch, R. and Mazzoleni, O. (eds.) (2016) *Understanding populist party organisation: The radical right in western Europe*. London: Palgrave Macmillan.

Hooghe, L. and Marks, G. (2018) 'Cleavage theory meets Europe's crises: Lipset, Rokkan, and the transnational cleavage', *Journal of European Public Policy*, 25(1), p109–135.

Ivaldi, G. (2015) 'Towards the median economic crisis voter? The new leftist economic agenda of the Front National in France', *French Politics*, 13, p346–369.

Ivarsflaten, E. (2008) 'What unites right-wing populists in Western Europe? Re-examining grievance mobilization models in seven successful cases', *Comparative Political Studies*, 41, p3–23.

Kitschelt, H. and McGann, A.J. (1995) *The radical right in Western Europe: A comparative analysis*. Ann Arbor: University of Michigan Press.

Kriesi, H., Grande, E., Lachat, R., Dolezal, M., Bornschier, S. and Frey, T. (2006) 'Globalization and the transformation of the national political space: Six European countries compared', *European Journal of Political Research*, 45, p921–956.

Koopmans, R. and Statham, P. (1999) 'Ethnic and civic conceptions of nationhood and the differential success of the extreme right in Germany and Italy', in Giugni, M., McAdam, D. and Tilly, C. (eds.) *How social movements matter*. Minneapolis: University of Minnesota Press, pp. 225–251.

Kurer, T. (2020) 'The declining middle: Occupational change, social status, and the populist right', *Comparative Political Studies*, 53(10–11), p1798–1835.

Lipset, S.M. (1960) *Political man: The social bases of politics*. New York: Doubleday.

Lucassen, G. and Lubbers, M. (2012) 'Who fears what? Explaining far-right-wing preference in Europe by distinguishing perceived cultural and economic ethnic threats', *Comparative Political Studies*, 45(5), p547–574.

Lubbers, M. and Coenders, M. (2017) 'Nationalistic attitudes and voting for the radical right in Europe', *European Union Politics*, 18(1), p98–118.

Meguid, B. (2005) 'Competition between unequals: The role of mainstream party strategy in niche party success', *American Political Science Review*, 99(3), p347–359.

Moffitt, B. (2017) 'Populism in Australia and New Zealand', in Rovira Kaltwasser, C., Taggart, P., Ochoa Espego, P. and Ostiguy, P. (eds.) *The Oxford handbook of populism*. Oxford: Oxford University Press, pp. 121–139.

Mudde, C. (2007) *Populist radical right parties in Europe*. Cambridge: Cambridge University Press.

Mudde, C. (2019) *The far right today*. Cambridge: Polity.

Mudde, C. and Rovira Kaltwasser, C. (2018) 'Studying populism in comparative perspective: Reflections on the contemporary and future research agenda', *Comparative Political Studies*, 51(13), p1667–1693.

Muis, J. and Immerzeel, T. (2017) 'Causes and consequences of the rise of populist radical right parties and movements in Europe', *Current Sociology*, 65(6), p909–930.

Norris, P. and Inglehart, R. (2019) *Cultural backlash: Trump, Brexit, and authoritarian populism*. Cambridge: Cambridge University Press.

Rama, J., Zanotti, L., Turnbull-Dugarte, S. and Santana, A. (2021) *VOX: The rise of the Spanish populist radical right*. New York: Routledge

Rooduijn, M. (2018) 'What unites the voter bases of populist parties? Comparing the electorates of 15 populist parties', *European Political Science Review*, 10(3), p351–368.

Rydgren, J. (2008) 'Immigration sceptics, xenophobes or racists? Radical right-wing voting in six West European countries', *European Journal of Political Research*, 47, p737–765.

Rydgren, J. and van der Meiden, S. (2019) 'The radical right and the end of Swedish exceptionalism', *European Political Science*, 18(3), p439–455.

Spoon, J. and Klüver, H. (2020) 'Responding to far right challengers: Does accommodation pay off?', *Journal of European Public Policy*, 27(2), p273–291.

Stockemer, D., Halikiopoulou, D. and Vlandas, T. (2020) 'Birds of a feather'? Assessing the prevalence of anti-immigration attitudes among the far right electorate', *Journal of Ethnic and Migration Studies*, 47(15), p3409–3436.

Swank, D. and Betz, H.G. (2018) 'Globalization, institutions of social solidarity, and radical right-wing populism in Western Europe', Paper prepared for presentation at the 2018 Annual Meetings of the American Political Science Association, August 30–September 2, Boston, MA.

van der Brug, W., Fennema, M. and Tillie, J. (2000) 'Anti-immigrant parties in Europe: Ideological or protest vote?', *European Journal of Political Research*, 37, p77–102.

van Spanje, J. (2010) 'Contagious parties: Anti-immigrant parties and their impact on other parties' immigration stances in contemporary Western Europe', *Party Politics*, 16(5), p563–586.

Vasilopoulou, S. and Halikiopoulou, D. (2015) *The Golden Dawn's nationalist solution: Explaining the rise of the far right in Greece*. New York: Palgrave Macmillan.

Wagner, M. and Meyer, T. (2016) 'The radical right as niche parties? The ideological landscape of party systems in Western Europe, 1980–2014', *Political Studies*, 65(1), p84–107.

Wondreys, J. and Mudde, C. (2020) 'Victims of the pandemic? European far-right parties and COVID-19', *Nationalities Papers*, 1–18. https://doi.org/10.1017/nps.2020.93.

12

THE CENTRE-RIGHT

Christian Democrats, Conservatives and Liberals

Marija Taflaga

The centre-right is an important party family that encompasses Conservative, Liberal and Christian Democratic parties. It is more heterogeneous than the centre-left. Conservative, Liberal and Christian Democratic parties have been important actors in the development of most party systems since the nineteenth century. Typically, they are office-seeking parties *par excellence*. Scandinavia and Canada are rare examples where the centre-right has not dominated democratic governments since the Second World War, though this trend has declined since the 1990s. Centre-right parties are understudied compared to their centre-left counterparts, which is surprising given their outsized influence on elections, government and public policy in many countries. Indeed, our understanding of the development of centre-right thinking, public policy and government ought to be expanded, particularly as a party family grouping, rather than only understood in the context of specific administrations.

The designated centre-right literature is fragmented when compared with the centre-left and dominated by country-case studies. More general insights drawn from voting behaviour and issue ownership literatures have revealed specific findings about the centre-right, including how these parties have responded to their competitors and what drives their vote. These insights can in turn drive new research to unpack and explain these phenomena. These findings also relate to our relative lack of understanding about how centre-right party organisations renew and adapt and how they are responding to new representational challenges. Overall, there is scope for greater comparative investigation, at both large-N and small-n levels.

What is the centre-right?

Origins

Scholars of the centre-right are less exercised about the content of the centre-right tradition when compared with those studying social democratic parties. Academic discussion demonstrates that the three centre-right traditions – Conservative, Liberal and Christian Democratic – are, broadly, considered to share similar ideological and issue domain preferences. These include an emphasis on law, order and security, and on a unifying vision of national identity, which sometimes translates into a suspicion of immigration and multiculturalism. They diverge on the extent to which private enterprise is favoured over a state-facilitated economy and how far state power is used to preserve existing political institutions and to regulate traditional social institutions. This section considers their origins and development.

Recent investigation has revealed that centre-right parties are less homogeneous than their centre-left opponents, with Liberal parties the most heterogeneous, depending on their emphasis on free markets and/or social freedoms (Ennser 2012). Liberals who emphasise free markets are unambiguously positioned within the centre-right. However, social liberals, who emphasise social freedoms and, often, the state's role in helping individuals meet their full potential, have historically shown a greater propensity to cooperate with centre-left parties. For this reason, social liberals are not a major focus of this chapter (see also Chapter 13). Recognition of the centre-right's heterogeneity has important implications for how we understand the centre-right.

Broadly, all centre-right parties define themselves in opposition to the centre-left and this opposition offers another form of coherence. All three centre-right traditions were shaped by their response to the French Revolution and this underwrites the ongoing debate about whether differences among the sub-groups remain important. Scholars agree that Conservatism is more a philosophy than an ideology, emphasising society's organic hierarchical structure, a preference for incremental change and an overall pessimism about human nature. Modern Conservatism (Oakeshott 1991) credits Edmund Burke and, arguably, seventeenth-century thinkers such as Thomas Hobbes as its founders. As party systems emerged in the nineteenth century, Conservatives represented traditional sources of power, including landed interests, monarchy and church. Their principal opponents were Liberals.

Liberals championed Enlightenment ideals: the potential of the individual; free markets; scientific progress; and anti-clericalism. Broadly, Liberals represented the new commercial interests and (often) democratic reformers. Liberals' faith in individuals' judgement underwrote predictions about how humans and societies would best function. This distinguishes Liberalism from Conservatism as an ideology (Kirchner 1988; van Haute and Close 2019). John Locke's assertion that subjects had a right to their property and to overthrow tyrannical sovereigns forms the core of Liberal thought, with many thinkers contributing to the debate in the centuries since. Liberal parties' vote share has declined since the turn of the twentieth century, unless they were part of hybrid Conservative/Liberal parties.

Christian Democracy emerged as a European Catholic reaction to the anti-clericalism of Liberal forces. Christian Democrats organised into formal political parties in the 1870s, several decades after their Conservative and Liberal opponents. The core of Christian Democratic thinking was encapsulated in Pope Leo XIII's encyclical 'Rights and Duties of Capital and Labour' (see Misner 2003). Christian Democratic thinking positioned itself as a third way between Liberalism and Socialism and had a complex relationship with the church and Conservatives (Kalyvas 1998). Christian Democrats saw Liberalism as their main opponent: not only because of their support for anti-clericalism but also industrialisation and its potential to degrade the human condition. Socialists were also anti-clericalists and opposed to private property, but their lack of political significance during the nineteenth century meant that they were less threatening. However, over the first half of the twentieth century, socialists emerged as their main rival.

Distinctive sub-groups?

The centre-right's heterogeneity presents definitional challenges to scholars, which can explain the fallback position of relying on their anti-left stance. For political scientists, this debate turns on the viability of good comparative work. While specialist scholars tend to view their family sub-group as distinct, more generalist scholars tend to question whether the differences are meaningful. Given that both Christian Democratic (Italy, Germany, the Netherlands, Belgium and Austria) and Conservative/Liberal (the UK, Australia and New Zealand) parties have been disproportionately successful as governing parties since 1945, understanding how the subgroups differ, and under what terms comparisons can be made, is important.

In the Anglosphere, pluralist voting systems saw that Conservative and Liberal forces combine to oppose Labour parties at the beginning of the twentieth century. Conservative parties also formed the main centre-right parties in Scandinavia. By contrast, modern Christian Democratic parties were a European product of the post-war era, where deal-making and coalition formation were facilitated by proportional representation systems. It was a moderate (centrist, rather than right-wing) alternative to pre-war politics that marked the Catholic Church's acceptance of democratic norms (see Mitchell 2012).

What constitutes Christian Democracy is the subject of ongoing debate to a far greater extent than for Conservative/Liberal parties. Is it a distinct set of thought or merely a 'Catholic' form of Conservatism? Is it a distinctive political force, particularly as growing secularism undermines the social and ideological conditions that saw it prosper post-war? While more generalist scholars have often viewed Christian Democracy as a Conservative phenomenon, specialist scholars disagree. A general consensus has emerged arguing that Christian Democratic parties distinguished themselves from Conservative/Liberal parties by their scepticism towards individualism, instead adopting 'personalism', which shares with Conservatism a belief in naturally occurring communities and hierarchies (Accetti 2019). However, personalism rejects the atomisation of individualism, instead holding that individuals achieve their full potential through organic communities whose interest must be balanced. This emphasis on collective identities resulted in corporatist and/or pillarised political models. This collective instinct was also evident in the formation of Europe's supra-national identity, the European Union, drawing on an older idea of 'Christendom'. Anti-communism and support for the U.S. alliance rounded out Christian Democratic principles, driven by the geopolitics of Europe in the post-war era.

Scholars have argued that while notionally pan-Christian, in reality, Christian Democracy was overwhelmingly a Catholic phenomenon (it was made demographically viable in Germany because of post-war partition) (Conway 2003). It played out differently in Protestant countries: it remained a marginal political force in Scandinavia; became associated with Labour in the Anglosphere; and was a product of left-wing politics in South America (Mainwaring and Scully 2003). Increasingly, scholars believe that Western European Christian Democracy was the result of a specific moment, which helps to account for why the Christian Democrats in the Netherlands were stricter than those in Germany, or why it has not emerged in Eastern Europe (Bale and Szczerbiak 2008).

Perhaps the fiercest area of debate – where a consensus has yet to emerge – is whether there is a true continuity between pre-and post-war forms of Christian Democracy and the significance of the Catholic church to its development (Kselman and Buttigieg 2003). While it is clear that there were examples of Christian Democratic thinking, it is less clear that pre-war thinking directly carried over into the post-war era and further research is required. There is ongoing debate about whether the grouping is still meaningfully coherent in the face of party collapse (e.g. Italy's *Democrazia Cristiana*) and the growing secularisation of society (Duncan 2015). Instead, scholars ask whether ideas around 'Christian Europe' have come to signify generic European culture and values?

By contrast, examination of Conservative/Liberal parties in the Anglosphere is more likely to be the work of party specialists. This trend is the result of relatively small political science communities in the Anglo-settler societies and the inherent barriers to close comparative observation that vast distances engender. The British Conservative Party is one of the world's oldest – and arguably the ideal type. In other Anglosphere countries, existing centre-right parties, like their Christian Democratic counterparts, are far younger, formed in the middle twentieth century (New Zealand in 1936, Australia in 1944). They were the products of party fragmentation and reconsolidation. Canada is the exception, where the centre-right party has struggled to maintain organisational stability and coherence and where the party has had minimal impact on national politics outside the recent Harper government (2006–2015). Its current iteration dates from 2003. Politics in the Anglo-settler societies was heavily influenced by the UK – a product of immigration and cultural affinity. However, geographic distance has led to unequal inter-party exchange of ideas and influence. For example, centre-right parties in the Anglo-settler societies have looked to the British Conservatives for inspiration, but the British Conservatives have instead tended to look to the Continent or the USA for inspiration.

Today, Conservative/Liberal parties are typically broad coalitions of both Conservatives and Liberals. These countries do not have traditions of grand coalitions and blocking their centre-left opponents is considered sufficient reason to occupy office. However, these hybrid parties have created tensions which must be navigated. The conflict over the UK's exit from the European Union is perhaps the most acute of the last 30 years. Whether these parties are Conservative or Liberal has occupied scholars, especially during the 1980s, as the post-war consensus broke down. Parties in the Anglosphere embraced the politics of the 'new-right' – de-regulation, neo-conservatism and new public management. While parties in New Zealand and the UK travelled furthest along that path, ironically, Australia's Liberal Party, like the U.S. Republicans, placed a greater emphasis on the rhetoric of smaller government rather than delivering it in reality.

By comparison, the U.S. Republican Party (Gould 2014) is something of an outlier. This is principally a product of the uniqueness of the U.S. party system. Indeed, major shifts in the party's ideological focus can only in part be explained by its longevity (founded in 1854). Unlike its Liberal/Conservative counterparts in the Anglosphere and Europe, the Republican party machine is considerably weaker than any of its counterparts and the frequency of elections has profoundly shaped the way political elites relate to their party and develop policy ideas. Historically, the electoral system has buttressed a true two-party system, which meant building broad coalitions. Today that instinct is countermanded by growing electoral boundary manipulation which sees the party aim to disenfranchise ideological opponents, while narrowcasting to its own ideological base. These features are either unique or extreme by comparison to other centre-right parties discussed here. Given this, it is not surprising that where comparisons between parties have occurred, they have focused on ideological dimensions, policy ideas and the exchange of campaign techniques (see Wineinger and Nugent 2020). A primary driver of comparisons between the USA and other Anglosphere centre-right parties appears to be cultural and language affinities, and if anything, this highlights the relative lack of comparison between centre-right parties in the Anglosphere (such as Australia, the UK, New Zealand, Canada and Ireland) which share greater institutional similarities.

The policy shift to neo-liberalism and neo-conservatism proliferated debate about the significance and meaning of these various right-ward turns and whether Liberal or Conservative forces were dominant. Ideology has remained an important area of debate within the literature, even if it has declined since its peak during the 1980s. Importantly, much of this work is country-case specific, which can provide the basis for future comparative research into the different reactions to the new-right across the Anglosphere, but also to examine the level of cross fertilisation and influence. A similar set of debates and conflicts occurred within Christian Democratic parties, and broadly within European party systems (because of a higher number of effective parties), but there, Liberal forces advocating welfare state retrenchment were met with caution, or where they introduced neo-liberal reforms, they were met with electoral backlash (Duncan 2006).

The messiness of comparing ideal types with the real world has made some scholars cautious in their search for common distinctions, particularly as criteria appear to be temporally and geographically sensitive. Despite the difficulties, a consensus has emerged within the literature that it is worth the attempt (for discussion, see Bale and Krouwel 2013), even if the end goal is elusive. Recent empirical investigations increasingly show that there are different patterns of behaviour between Christian Democrats, Liberal and Conservative parties regarding policy preferences, particularly around the size of the state and the structure of welfare policies (see discussion later). Researchers have noted that centre-right parties look to each other to borrow ideas and techniques, though this too is understudied (Manwaring 2016).

This suggests that while there are differences, there are only a limited number of ways to express centre-right political ideas. All three traditions share more common ground than with the centre-left, which makes comparison a worthwhile strategy. However, it is worth noting distinctions between sub-groups when undertaking large N-studies, because it can prove critical to explaining outcomes (e.g. see O'Brien 2018). This creates both blurred edges and scope for meaningful comparison. What is most important for researchers to consider when designing comparative research is the level of abstraction at which their investigation is taking place.

Explanations for electoral success

The literature is dominated by country-case studies, with Christian Democratic parties coming in for greater comparative treatment than Conservative/Liberal parties (Hanley 1996; Bale and Krouwel 2013). When taken together, it is arguable that an uncontroversial consensus has emerged to account for the success of centre-right parties grounded in these parties' issue ownership of the economy and, broadly, their policy incrementalism.

In line with their office-seeking behaviour, these parties are more likely to have issue ownership over the economy, given their preference for smaller government, emphasis on sound finance and their (relative to left-wing opponents) preferable treatment of capital over labour. Models of economic voting demonstrate that voters reward governments for economic success. Centre-right parties' longevity in government suggests voters have rewarded them for their perceived competence and defence of their economist interests against possible redistributive policies of the left.

Collectively, country case studies observe that centre-right parties in the post-war era emphasised their cross-class electoral appeal in contrast with the 'sectional' or class-conflict-oriented politics of the left. Most were successful in forging coalitions between the aspirational middle class and agricultural interests, which served social as well as political needs through appeals to wealth generation. In continental Europe, Christian Democratic parties were organised along corporatist lines, in effect an analogous microcosm of the corporatist and consociationalist organisation of the societies they governed. Centre-right parties also encountered opportunities to forge cross-class coalitions by speaking to the fear of communism held by the middle and landowning/agricultural classes. Through appealing to different groups centre-right parties were able to present their agenda as being politically neutral. Religion (Conway 2003) and the virtues of the 'moral middle class' (Brett 2003) provided the bridge to unite disparate class interests in societies exhausted by the Great Depression and the Second World War. In the post-war period, both religious identity (Catholic in Europe and Protestant in the Anglosphere) and the un-radical and ameliorating politics of the 'moral middle class' held huge appeal for women (Berthezéne and Gottlieb 2018), which underpinned a favourable and long-running gender voting gap across the western world.

The general findings of the literature point to policy incrementalism, effective government stewardship during economically benign times – or weak opposition – and reinforcement of the status quo as explanations for their longevity in government. To some degree, the success of centre-right parties is the product of the failure of the centre-left either because of perceived radicalism in the past or, more recently, the long-term structural decline of the left's voter base. The collapse of the Bretton Woods system and, later, the Soviet Union placed the post-war iteration of centre-right politics under strain. This happened a decade earlier in the Anglosphere, which embraced neo-liberal economics. Christian Democratic parties' 'third way' approach to governing, which was situated between Socialism and Liberalism, came under strain in the 1990s as the former appeared to be in retreat (Van Hecke and Gerard 2004). In Italy, successive corruption scandals precipitated party collapse, but Catholic political and social thought continued to influence Italian politics (Bailey and Driessen 2016).

A changing electorate?

Since the 1960s, the centre-right's vote share has been in slow decline. Both Conservatives and Christian Democratic parties were successful 'catch-all' interest aggregators. While their hegemonic position has faded, they continue to maintain a large vote-share despite social and demographic changes. Religion remains a key driver of the vote for Christian Democrats, although this group of voters is ageing (Duncan 2015). In the Anglosphere, a plurality-based voting system has insulated their vote-share, though where different voting systems operate, the centre-right's vote share declined.

The wealth of research at the country-case level means that there is significant scope for comparative research, particularly across party sub-families or across the East-West divide (Bale and Szczerbiak 2008; Kosicki and Łukasiewicz 2018). Given both geographical similarity and proximity, there is arguably a greater understanding of how electoral dynamics impact Christian Democratic parties compared with Conservative/Liberal parties in the Anglosphere. Whether there are systematic patterns in electoral outcomes is worthy of further investigation, particularly as party systems are under pressure from both exogenous shocks (such as the Great Recession and the global pandemic) and endogenous social-party system change. So too is the centre-right's – especially Christian Democratic parties' – adaptability, as western democratic societies become post-material and increasingly secularised (Kalyvas and van Kersbergen 2010).

Recent debate has also focused on centre-right parties' capacity to attract and convert votes from traditional 'working class' or authoritarian-left voters, driven by growing concerns about immigration, multiculturalism (Jackman 1998; Bale 2021) and the rise of the far right. No clear consensus has emerged about whether the rise of the far right has been positive or negative for the centre-right, but what is clear (see discussion later) is that the far right has impacted centre-right parties' electoral and governing strategies. Historically, the centre-right could depend upon a higher share of the vote from women voters (Abendschön and Steinmetz 2014; Duncan 2017), but this has also declined and even reversed, though there may be some variation across the centre-right sub-groups which warrants further investigation.

Government participation

In Europe and the Anglosphere, centre-right parties have dominated governing coalitions since 1945. Scandinavia provides a contrasting pattern historically. In the Anglosphere, Canada is the exception. Centre-right parties are often 'office seeking *par excellence*' and are often conceptualised as the 'natural party of government'. They are more likely to be status quo parties, in line with their preference for office-seeking behaviour. Centre-right parties are also more likely to be the senior coalition partner, to supply titular executive leadership and to control budget portfolios. The resilience and enduring quality of these parties' influence on political systems speaks to their championing of political orthodoxy, and in the case of Conservative parties, their ability to transform much of their own radicalism into political orthodoxy.

Given most centre-right parties are broad coalitions of interests, factional politics has been an important dimension of understanding these parties' experience of government (Boucek 2012). Factional disputes have structured accounts of government policy-making, renewal and leadership across polities. In Japan and Italy (prior to the collapse of Democrazia Cristiana in 1994), the centre-right's monopoly on government shifted the discussion to an opposition within government (Bettcher 2005). Conservative/Liberal parties' greater hostility to collective action contrasts with Christian Democratic notions of consociationalism, solidarity and the way their parties are organised around interests. There is some evidence to suggest that these organisational differences can also produce different representational outcomes, particularly for women (Gaunder and Wiliarty 2019). This can further flow into policy differences, with centre-right women typically less conservative than their male colleagues (de Geus and Shorrocks 2020).

In broad policy terms, this has meant a difference of emphasis in policy goals and delivery between Conservative/Liberal parties and Christian Democratic parties. This is most obvious in the sub-groups' different approaches to the size of government, and social/welfare policies. Conservative/Liberal parties readily embraced neo-liberal policy and new public management governance. By contrast, Christian Democratic parties were relatively cautious adopters of neo-liberalism. Christian Democratic parties have faced significant pressure to maintain the principles of 'social market economy', solidarity and subsidiarity or else faced electoral strife (Seeleib-Kaiser, Karls and van Dyk 2008).

While scholars may debate about just how conservative centre-right parties are, the literature reveals that relative to their centre-left counterparts, centre-right parties enjoy a degree of mutability in line with the underlying principle of conservatism – incremental change. In the main, these parties have continuously reinvented themselves and recaptured office. Further comparative investigation of these phenomena will help to uncover which aspects are generalisable to the centre-right, specific party family sub-groups, and which are more dependent on their country contexts.

Challenges facing the centre-right

The centre-right faces several challenges, some of which are systemic to western party systems – such as the rise of niche parties or organisational efficacy and internal party democracy – and others which seem to pose particularly strong challenges to the centre-right, such as the representation of women.

The far right

The rise of the far right is a significant challenge to mainstream political parties across the democratic world, and especially in Europe where proportional voting systems facilitated the far right's rise (see Chapter 11). By comparison, plurality-based voting systems (New Zealand and the Australian Upper House are exceptions) have diluted the far right's capacity to translate votes into parliamentary seats in the Anglosphere.

The far right's success has presented both challenges and opportunities for centre-right parties, principally via increasing the salience of immigration. The far right's advocacy of anti-immigration, anti-multicultural and welfare chauvinist positions was initially considered a challenge for the centre-right because of the potential to steal votes from the centre-right's right flank. Simultaneously, it also reduced the centre-right's scope to form governing coalitions, because of the far right's 'pariah' status. However, as Bale (2003) has argued, many centre-right parties actively adopted such policies and co-operated with the far right, thereby facilitating its political legitimation.

There is an ongoing debate about the precise impact of the far right on European party systems and policy outcomes generally, and the centre-right, specifically. Evidence demonstrates that the far right has provided a pathway for left-authoritarian voters to switch from social democratic parties to the centre-right, either directly or indirectly (Abou-Chadi 2016; Evans and Mellon 2016; Spoon and Klüver 2020). The far right has influenced not only government formation, but also policy positioning across party systems. Some researchers argue that the success of far right parties incentivised centre-right parties to adopt anti-immigration positions (Han 2015; Abou-Chadi and Krause 2020). Conversely, others argue that the influence of the far right is overstated (Akkerman 2015; Meyer and Rosenberger 2015). What is clear is that some centre-right governments have adopted far right policies as a strategy to manage increases in immigration because of critical skills shortages in the economy (Bale 2003). However, as Hadj Abdou, Bale and Geddes (2021) argue, this has resulted in policy incoherence and may have unleashed forces (most obviously the Brexit referendum) that are detrimental to centre-right parties over time. What is comparatively less well understood is how centre-right parties have attempted to respond to the far right institutionally and in policy terms when in government (Bale and Rovira Kaltwasser 2021), or how these trends compare outside of Europe.

Organisational efficacy

Political party organisations continue to remain a relative 'black box' to political scientists. Questions of how parties are attempting (or failing) to reform and renew remain important (see Turner 2013; Convery 2015), as parties struggle with greater pressure to satisfy members, reconcile themselves to calls for greater internal party democracy and adapt to new policy environments (Gidron and Ziblatt 2019).

As Bolleyer (2016) argues, far more research effort has been invested in understanding the democratic linkages between party elites and citizens rather than investigating them as administrative units. Parties are hybrid organisations with administrative and legal responsibilities as well as political functions. Their efficacy is broader than just their capacity to win elections. Our understanding of party organisations among the centre-right is concentrated in single-case studies rather than comparative accounts, especially across the family sub-groupings (however, see Gauja 2016). For example, despite their cross-class appeal, Conservative parties tend to be more hierarchically organised compared with Christian Democratic parties, which were set up to manage interests. How, if at all, do the different institutional arrangements that we find in the organisations of centre-right parties impact upon the capacity of these parties to organise, recruit members and win elections? Can political scientists borrow and adapt tools from the study of public administration to systematically assess the efficacy of their party organisations?

Representing women

In recent decades, centre-right parties have underperformed on women's representation. Historically, the centre-right benefited from a favourable gender-voting gap, which harnessed women's higher levels of religiosity and cross-class appeal. Indeed, in some polities, it was the centre-right that blazed a trail into parliaments (Maguire 1998; Fitzherbert 2009). Today,

Christian Democratic parties outperform Conservative parties on women's representation (Celis and Childs 2014). This trend is in part due to proportional representation voting systems, where party list tickets are common. Comparatively, Christian Democratic parties are more willing to adopt quota models instead of relying on capacity building programmes, which are a key tool of Conservative/Liberal parties (Krook 2009).

Recent research also suggests that parties' institutional design matters for both women's descriptive and substantive representation. Women have needed to act as critical actors and must navigate barriers structured by the ideological constraints of their parties to achieve internal reform. Conservative/Liberal parties' ideological emphasis on merit and aversion to collective claims is a further barrier for women party activists. Centre-right women have appeared to struggle to get their parties to take under-representation seriously. Reforms, when enacted, are often a way for party elites to signal that the party is modernising (Childs and Webb 2012; Wiliarty 2013). Moreover, there appears to be growing evidence that party-level and intra-party institutional constraints also impact the ability of women to successfully achieve reforms (Taflaga and Beauregard 2020).

Centre-right women's ability to gain access to elected office has implications for women's substantive representation, particularly as centre-right parties are often dominant parties of government. Recent research has endeavoured to interrogate the representative claims of right-wing women and take them seriously (Celis and Childs 2012, 2018). This marks a step forward from privileging explicitly feminist positions, while also developing a framework to critically assess centre-right women's claims to represent women's interests (Celis and Childs 2018; Schreiber 2018). As noted, Christian Democratic parties are, broadly, performing better on women's representation than Conservative parties, with recent research pointing to the impact of ideological distinctions on vote choice (O'Brien 2018) and candidate selection (de Geus and Shorrocks 2020). However, the mechanisms that underline these trends and how they interact with party organisations have yet to be fully explained and constitute a rich vein for future research (see Chapters 9 and 27).

Conclusions and avenues for further research

The centre-right is an understudied but important family grouping. The literature on the centre-right remains relatively fragmented, but less so in the case of Christian Democratic parties. As argued earlier, there remains considerable scope for future research at the country-case level where ongoing description remains important. Moreover, even greater potential exists for comparative studies within each party family subgroup and across the broader centre-right. Our current understanding of the centre-right's ideological development is still largely understood through single-case studies.

It is important to understand (both historically and contemporaneously) how parties have engaged, borrowed or reinterpreted ideas (or failed to do so). Given the recent populist turn of centre-right politics, this may also prove to be a fruitful avenue of research to understand the extent to which these movements share factors in common. How these processes impact the centre-right's capacity and approaches to government and public policy are also under-researched, particularly in a comparative context. More research could be undertaken to understand how the centre-right is attempting (or failing) to represent citizens, especially women; to respond to their competitors; and to win citizens' votes as they face new policy and governing challenges.

At the party organisational level, as some of the findings outlined earlier suggest, the mechanisms underpinning intra- and inter-party dynamics of the centre-right have yet to be explicated.

In part, this is due to a lack of understanding about the way parties function as administrative units in general, and among the centre-right, in particular. Tools used to assess efficacy in the public administration and organisational literature may be useful (if adapted) for studying the overall effectiveness of centre-right parties.

References

Abendschön, S. and Steinmetz, S. (2014) 'The gender gap in voting revisited: Women's party preferences in a European context', *Social Politics: International Studies in Gender, State & Society*, 21(2) p315–344.

Abou-Chadi, T. (2016) 'Niche party success and mainstream party policy shifts – How green and radical right parties differ in their impact', *British Journal of Political Science*, 46(2), p417–436.

Abou-Chadi, T. and Krause, W. (2020) 'The causal effect of radical right success on mainstream parties' policy positions: A regression discontinuity approach', *British Journal of Political Science*, 50(3), p829–847.

Accetti, C.I. (2019) *What is Christian democracy?: Politics, religion and ideology*. Cambridge: Cambridge University Press.

Akkerman, T. (2015) 'Immigration policy and electoral competition in Western Europe: A fine-grained analysis of party positions over the past two decades', *Party Politics*, 21(1), p54–67.

Bailey, T. and Driessen, M. (2016) 'Mapping contemporary Catholic politics in Italy', *Journal of Modern Italian Studies*, 21(3), p419–425.

Bale, T. (2003) 'Cinderella and her ugly sisters: The mainstream and extreme right in Europe's bipolarising party systems', *West European Politics*, 26(3), p67–90.

Bale, T. (2021) 'Policy, office, votes – and integrity. The British conservative party, Brexit, and immigration', *Journal of Ethnic and Migration Studies*, p1–20.

Bale, T. and Krouwel, A. (2013) 'Down but not out: A comparison of Germany's CDU/CSU with Christian democratic parties in Austria, Belgium, Italy and the Netherlands', *German Politics*, 22(1–2), p16–45.

Bale, T. and Rovira Kaltwasser, C. (eds.) (2021) *Riding the populist wave: Europe's mainstream right in crisis*. Cambridge: Cambridge University Press.

Bale, T. and Szczerbiak, A. (2008) 'Why is there no Christian democracy in Poland – and why should we care?' *Party Politics*, 14(4), p479–500.

Berthezéne, C. and Gottlieb, J. (eds.) (2018) *Rethinking right-wing women: Gender and the Conservative Party, 1880s to the present*. Manchester: Manchester University Press.

Bettcher, K.E. (2005) 'Factions of interest in Japan and Italy: The organizational and motivational dimensions of factionalism', *Party Politics*, 11(3), p339–358.

Bolleyer, N. (2016) 'Political actors: Parties-interest groups-government', in Keman, H. and Woldendorp, J.J. (eds.) *Handbook of research methods and applications in political science*. Cheltenham: Edward Elgar Publishing, pp. 141–155.

Boucek, F. (2012) *Factional politics: How dominant parties implode or stabilize*. New York: Palgrave Macmillan.

Brett, J. (2003) *The Australian Liberals and the moral middle class: From Alfred Deakin to John Howard*. New York: Cambridge University Press.

Childs, S. and Webb, P. (2012) *Sex, gender and the Conservative Party – from iron lady to kitten heels*. Houndmills: Palgrave Macmillan.

Celis, K. and Childs, S. (2012) 'The substantive representation of women: What to do with Conservative claims?', *Political Studies*, 60(1), p213–225.

Celis, K. and Childs, S. (2014) (eds.) 'Gender, conservatism and political representation', in *Studies in European political science*. Colchester: ECPR Press.

Celis, K. and Childs, S. (2018) 'Conservatism and women's political representation', *Politics & Gender*, 14(1), p5–26.

Convery, A. (2015) *The territorial conservative party: Devolution and party change in Scotland and Wales*. Manchester: Manchester University Press.

Conway, M. (2003) 'The age of Christian democracy: The frontiers of success and failure', Kselman, T. and Buttigieg, J. (eds.) *European Christian democracy: Historical legacies and comparative perspectives*. Notre Dame: University of Notre Dame Press.

Duncan, F. (2006) 'A decade of Christian democratic decline: The dilemmas of the CDU, ÖVP and CDA in the 1990s', *Government and Opposition*, 41(4), p469–490.

Duncan, F. (2015) 'Preaching to the converted? Christian democratic voting in six west European countries', *Party Politics*, 21(4), p577–590.
Duncan, F. (2017) 'Gender, voting and Christian democratic Parties', *European Politics and Society*, 18(2), p218–244.
Ennser, L. (2012) 'The homogeneity of West European party families: The radical right in comparative perspective', *Party Politics*, 18(2), p151–171.
Evans, G. and Mellon, J. (2016) 'Working class votes and Conservative losses: Solving the UKIP puzzle', *Parliamentary Affairs*, 69(2), p464–479.
Fitzherbert, Margaret (2009) *So many firsts: Liberal women from Enid Lyons to the Turnbull Era*. Annandale: Federation Press.
Gauja, A. (2016) *Party reform: The causes, challenges, and consequences of organizational change*. Oxford: Oxford University Press.
Gaunder, A. and Wiliarty, S. (2019) 'Conservative women in Germany and Japan: Chancellors versus Madonnas', *Politics & Gender*, 16(1), p1–24.
de Geus, R.A. de, and Shorrocks, R. (2020) 'Where do female conservatives stand? A cross-national analysis of the issue positions and ideological placement of female right-wing candidates', *Journal of Women, Politics & Policy*, 41(1), p7–35.
Gidron, N. and Ziblatt, D. (2019) 'Center-right political parties in advanced democracies', *Annual Review of Political Science*, 22(1), p17–35.
Gould, L.L. (2014) *The republicans: A history of the grand old party*. New York: Oxford University Press.
Hadj Abdou, L., Bale, T. and Geddes, A. (2021) 'Centre-right parties and immigration in an era of politicisation', *Journal of Ethnic and Migration Studies*, p1–14.
Han, K.J. (2015) 'The impact of radical right-wing parties on the positions of mainstream parties regarding multiculturalism', *West European Politics*, 38(3), p557–76.
Hanley, D.L. (ed.) (1996) *Christian democracy in Europe: A comparative perspective*. London: Pinter.
Jackman, S. (1998) 'Pauline Hanson, the mainstream, and political elites: The place of race in Australian political ideology', *Australian Journal of Political Science*, 33(2), p167–186.
Kalyvas, S.N. (1998) 'From pulpit to party: Party formation and the Christian Democratic phenomenon', *Comparative Politics*, 30(3), p293–312.
Kalyvas, S.N. and van Kersbergen, K. (2010) 'Christian democracy', *Annual Review of Political Science*, 13(1), p183–209.
Kirchner, E.J. (ed.) (1988) *Liberal parties in Western Europe*. Cambridge: Cambridge University Press.
Kosicki, P.H. and Łukasiewicz, S. (2018) *Christian Democracy across the Iron Curtain: Europe redefined*. Cham: Palgrave Macmillan.
Krook, M.L. (2009) *Quotas for women in politics: Gender and candidate selection reform worldwide*. Oxford: Oxford University Press.
Kselman, T. and Buttigieg, J. (eds.) (2003) *European Christian democracy: Historical legacies and comparative perspectives*. Notre Dame: University of Notre Dame Press.
Maguire, G.E. (1998) *Conservative women: A history of women and the conservative party, 1874–1997*. London: Macmillan Press.
Mainwaring, S. and Scully, T.R. (eds.) (2003) *Christian democracy in Latin America: Electoral competition and regime conflicts*. Stanford: Stanford University Press.
Manwaring, R. (2016) 'The big society in Australia: A case of 'non'-policy transfer?' *Australian Journal of Public Administration*, 75(2) p191–201.
Meyer, S. and Rosenberger, S. (2015) 'Just a shadow? The role of radical right parties in the politicization of immigration, 1995–2009', *Politics and Governance*, 3(2), p1–17.
Misner, P. (2003) 'Christian Democratic social policy: Precedents for third way of thinking', in Kselman, T. and Buttigieg, J. (eds.) *European Christian democracy: Historical legacies and comparative perspectives*. Notre Dame: University of Notre Dame Press, pp. 68–92.
Mitchell, M. (2012) *The origins of Christian democracy: Politics and confession in modern Germany*. Michigan: University of Michigan Press.
Oakeshott, M. (1991) *Rationalism in politics and other essays*. Indianapolis: Liberty Press.
O'Brien, D.Z. (2018) 'Righting' conventional wisdom: Women and right parties in established democracies', *Politics & Gender*, 14(1), p27–55.
Schreiber, R. (2018) 'Is there a conservative feminism? An empirical account', *Politics & Gender*, 14(1), p56–79.

Seeleib-Kaiser, M., Eberhard, K. and Dyk, S. van, (eds.) (2008) *Party politics and social welfare: Comparing Christian and social democracy in Austria, Germany and the Netherlands*. London: Edward Elgar Publishing.

Spoon, J. and Klüver, H. (2020) 'Responding to far right challengers: Does accommodation pay off?', *Journal of European Public Policy*, 27(2), p273–91.

Taflaga, M. and Beauregard, K. (2020) 'The merit of party institutions: Women's descriptive representation and conservative parties in Australia and the United Kingdom', *Journal of Women, Politics & Policy*, 41(1), p66–90.

Turner, E. (2013) 'The CDU and party organisational change', *German Politics*, 22(1–2), p114–133.

van Haute, E. and Close, C. (eds.) (2019) *Liberal parties in Europe*. New York: Routledge.

Van Hecke, S. and Gerard, E. (2004) *Christian democratic parties in Europe since the end of the Cold War*. Leuven: University Press.

Wiliarty, S.E. (2013) 'Gender as a modernising force in the German CDU', *German Politics* 22(1–2), p172–90.

Wineinger, C. and Nugent, M.K. (2020) 'Framing identity politics: Right-wing women as strategic party actors in the UK and US', *Journal of Women, Politics & Policy*, 41(1), p91–118.

13
LIBERAL PARTIES

Caroline Close and *Thomas Legein*

The Liberals figure among the oldest of the 'traditional' (European) party families. Liberalism and liberal parties have played a major role in the emergence of many modern Western states, in the building of the European Union, and also in democratisation processes and the promotion of liberal democracy across the globe. Nevertheless, the age and history of these parties only mask the great heterogeneity of this party family whose contours remain complicated to trace. This chapter aims to provide a snapshot of the main points of scholarly discussion about the characteristics and evolutions of liberal parties around the world.

Three general observations can be made about the state of the literature on liberal parties. First, the literature has been dominated by single case studies, except for a couple of comparative examinations. Second, it has focused on cases in advanced democracies – the Liberal Party in Canada for instance has attracted notable attention (Blais 2005; Carty 2015; Jeffrey 2021). Third, comparative endeavours have been usually limited to Europe (Kirchner 1988; De Winter 2000; Close and van Haute 2019a). In Africa, attention has mostly been drawn to the development (and replication) of a western model of *liberal democracy* (Brown and Kaiser 2007), rather than towards liberal parties *per se*. However, there is particular interest in the impact of liberalism on the structuring of the South African party system (van Staden 2019), and on the development of the Democratic Alliance as the major opposition party to the dominant African National Congress (Southern and Southall 2011). In Asia, especially in South-east Asia, the literature points to a limited influence of liberalism (Rodan and Hughes 2014, 6), except in the Philippines (Claudio 2017) and to a certain extent in Thailand (Larsson 2017). The review of the literature provided later is hence inevitably rooted in advanced democracies.

The chapter first assesses the way Mair and Mudde's (1998) four approaches to the concept of party family (name, transnational federation, origins and ideology) have been mobilised to delineate the contours of the liberal party family highlighting the difficulty of defining precisely the boundaries of this family using those criteria. Second, the chapter discusses the reasons for the electoral success (or failure) of liberal parties, among which we discuss their capacity to adapt strategically to party system change. Third, the chapter presents existing knowledge on the sociology of liberal voters, pointing to the sociodemographic diversity of this electorate. Fourth, it discusses liberal parties' unusual ability to gain power, partly explained by their pragmatism and positioning, which is often close to the 'median' legislator. Fifth, the chapter digs into the typical organisational model of liberal parties. Finally, the main challenges of the party family are discussed, before we draw general conclusions.

How has the liberal party family been conceptualised?

Party name

Identifying liberal parties on the basis of their label can be quite misleading. On the one hand, some parties may mobilise the term 'liberal' while, according to other criteria, they can hardly be qualified as such. In advanced democracies, the Japanese Liberal Democratic Party (Crespo 1995) should rather be considered as a conservative force despite its label. The Liberal Party of Australia is another case in point, although the party 'has not been philosophically uniform throughout its history' (Rickard 2007, 29). On the other hand, parties that allegedly develop a liberal ideology and/or adhere to transnational liberal federations do not uniformly refer to 'liberalism' in their labels. Only a minority of the Alliance of Liberals and Democrats for Europe (ALDE) members in the European Parliament makes explicit reference to liberalism in their label (Close and van Haute 2019a). When examining the membership of the Liberal International, a direct reference to liberalism is virtually absent in the labels for parties in Africa, Asia and the Middle East and North Africa (MENA) countries. In these contexts, references to 'democracy', 'democrat', 'democratic', 'freedom', 'renewal' or 'change' are more common. Avoiding referring to 'liberalism' may be strategic, as it may carry negative connotations.[1] By contrast, a 'liberal' label may be used strategically to gain international recognition, as occurred in several post-communist countries as they embraced European integration (Cholova and De Waele 2019, 226).

Transnational affiliation

Because of the ambiguity and value-laden connotations associated with liberalism, affiliation to transnational organisations has been used as a point of departure by comparative studies on liberal parties (Close and van Haute 2019a; Szmolka 2020). These studies have looked both at the parties' membership of the Liberal International (LI) and at their affiliation to regionally based transnational organisations, such as the ALDE or the Arab Liberal Federation (ALF).

However, this approach involves several limitations. First, like labelling, international affiliation has been shown to reflect political strategies rather than identification to common values (Smith 2014; Hloušek and Kopeček 2020). Moreover, transnational organisations can bring together parties with very different political projects and philosophies (Bardi et al. 2014). In that regard, McElroy and Benoit (2012, 163) suggested that the ALDE had 'the widest range of positions among its member parties'. Finally, some parties that allegedly conformed to a 'liberal' ideology may not formally adhere to any transnational federation. For instance, in France, The Republic on the Move! – LaREM, created in 2016 appears neither as a member of LI nor as a member of the ALDE, yet its MEPs sit with the liberal group in the European Parliament (Renew Europe) and it displays a 'liberal' ideological profile. The US Democratic Party, while standing as the 'liberal' opponent to the 'conservative' Republican Party, is not affiliated to any transnational federation.

Origins

The generic approach, which categorises parties according to the structural cleavage(s) from which they originated, has been argued to be better than labels and transnational affiliation for identifying party families (Seiler 1980), yet the liberal party family appears less discernible than other party families on this dimension (Seiler 2002). Indeed, liberal parties appeared 'scattered' over several categories (Steed and Humphreys 1988, 400), depending on national specificities.

In the Benelux countries, liberal parties originated on the secular side of the church versus state cleavage, although they also gradually asserted their liberal (or 'bourgeois') identity on the socio-economic cleavage (Delwit 2016; Voerman 2019). In Germany and Switzerland, liberal parties were primarily entrenched on the 'right' side of the socio-economic cleavage (Bukow 2019). In the UK, in the nineteenth century, the Liberals were committed to promote *reforms* against conservatism, especially favouring free trade (Steed and Humphreys 1988, 399), although the party was divided between different wings, traditions and interests – Whigs, Radicals, moderates, etc. (Cook 2010). In Northern Europe, liberal parties were closely associated with agrarian movements, being positioned on the rural side of the territorial cleavage (Arter 2019; Bolin 2019; Kosiara-Pedersen 2019).

In the second half of the twentieth century, the emergence of 'new' cleavages led to the birth of a second generation of liberal parties (Close and van Haute 2019b). In the Netherlands, Democraten 66 was created by former members of the VVD (Party of Freedom and Freethinking) along 'postmaterialist' values (Voerman 2019). In the 1990s, the 'transnational cleavage' (Hooghe and Marks 2018), also described as demarcation-integration (Kriesi et al. 2006), caused internal tensions among established liberal parties. The Liberal Forum (later merged with NEOS) in Austria and the New Alliance (now Liberal Alliance) in Denmark were formed by dissident liberals in reaction against the ethnocentric and Eurosceptic direction of their parties (Ennser-Jedenastik and Bodlos 2019, 130–131; Kosiara-Pedersen 2019, 46). In Iceland, Bright Future and the Reform Party emerged in the 2010s in a context of polarisation around the European issue (Thorhallsson 2021). In Southern Europe, although marked by the absence of liberal parties (Nuñez 2019), liberal actors also developed, such as *Ciudadanos* (2006) and *Unión, Progreso y Democracia* (2007) in Spain; and liberals also emerged in France *En Marche* (2016). Overall, the liberal party family has gradually come to occupy the 'integration' side of the new cleavage (Kriesi et al. 2006).

In Central and Eastern European countries (CEE) after 1989, liberal actors emerged who positioned themselves as 'anti-communist' through opposing the 'heirs' of communist parties and committing to the transition process (Cholova and De Waele 2019, 226). With the prospect of EU accession, the socio-economic cleavage became blurred, resulting in left- and right-wing parties aligning to promote free-market and privatisation (Tavits and Letki 2009). From the 2010s, the transnational cleavage and the increasing salience of the EU issue reinforced the commitment of liberal parties to 'pro-EU' positions, in relation to both economic and cultural issues.

Elsewhere, the 'cleavage' approach has rarely been applied to examine liberal parties, given the lack of social grounding for political parties. The American continent in the nineteenth and twentieth centuries was marked by a general 'division' between conservatives and liberals (Dix 1989), in the absence of class-based mass parties. The birth of the Canadian Liberal Party was related to the reformist movement in the colonies. Liberals sought greater political autonomy for Canadians and promoted free trade, while the Conservatives emphasised Canada's close relationship to the UK and British Empire and promoted economic protectionism. The linguistic cleavage and regional differences also mattered: the liberals managed to conceal English and French speaking movements, while hostility prevailed between the French Canadians and the Conservatives (Jeffrey 2010; Clarkson 2014). In Latin America, the greater political instability, de-institutionalisation and increased personalisation of party systems (Sanchez 2008) resulted in the virtual disappearance of most traditional conservative and liberal parties (Dix 1989, 25) – except in Paraguay and Honduras, where they remained significant.

Elsewhere, lines of conflict have been diverse. In the MENA countries, liberals have often been associated with the 'secular' or 'anti-Islamist' side of the religious cleavage (Szmolka 2020). South African liberal actors opposed apartheid; then, from the 1990s, they progressively aggregated opposition forces to the dominant African National Congress (van Staden 2019). In Russia, *Yabloko* (Russian United Democratic Party) developed in the 1990s as the principal opposition party (White 2012, 219). However, the party declined at the beginning of the twenty-first century as a result of internal divisions, organisational crisis and lack of financial resources, leading Hale (2004) to conclude that liberalism had failed to establish itself in the Russian party system (see Chapter 30).

Ideology and policy positions

The ideological criterion has been central in the scholarly discussion on the distinctiveness of the liberal party family (Steed and Humphreys 1988; Close 2019; Szmolka 2020). Empirical analyses point to the ambivalence of liberal thought, and highlight the ideological heterogeneity of the liberal party family (Smith 1988, 16; Ennser 2012, 167; Close 2019). First, their position in the left-right space has been described as 'ambivalent' (Smith 1988; De Winter and Marcet 2000), or 'between left and right' (Smith 1988). Indeed, liberals have been perceived to be more *rightist* than the left (socialists, greens, radical left) and more *leftist* than the right (conservatives, Christian democrats, radical right), due to their commitment to two 'types' of freedoms (Smith 1988): economic and cultural. This ambivalence is seen as one of the major distinctive features of the liberal party family (Close 2019): liberals combine a right-wing position on economic issues and a centre-left position on cultural matters. This ambivalent position is also found among non-European liberal parties. For instance, in Latin America, the liberals have advocated free trade and defended commercial interests, federalism and disestablishment of the church (Dix 1989, 24).

Second, liberalism constitutes a complex doctrine or a 'complex of doctrines' (Geuss 2002) that is not easily simplified. Economic liberal positions can range from the commitment to a minimal state to the demand for state intervention in the economy and the promotion of welfare policies. On cultural matters, liberals may defend more or less progressive positions, depending on their origins. Scholars have attempted to look beyond the heterogeneity of the liberal party family by identifying distinct liberal traditions (von Beyme 1985; Ennser 2012; Close 2019). For instance, 'classical liberals' would present a firm economic liberalism and a centre-left position on cultural issues (e.g. the German FDP). In comparison, 'social liberals' would emphasise cultural liberalism, while being more centrist on economic issues (e.g. D66 in the Netherlands, and *Radikale Venstre* in Denmark). Moreover, differences can be observed with 'conservative liberals', which resemble conservative parties given their centre-right placement on both economic and cultural matters (e.g. Centre Party in Finland; the Dutch VVD). Using manifesto data, Close (2019) has shown that the weight of these traditions within the liberal party family has changed over time; but also within each liberal party. Some parties have oscillated between different traditions, reflecting internal divides (e.g. UK Liberal Democrats, Belgian Liberals), while others have remained quite constant (e.g. FDP in Germany, D66 and the Finnish Centre Party). In other contexts, these classifications have proved their usefulness. For instance, in the MENA countries, Szmolka (2020, 77) describes liberal parties as corresponding to a 'liberal-secular' tradition, while Lebanese (Future Movement) and Egyptian (*Wafd* then *New Wafd*; *Free Egyptians Party*) liberal parties as pertaining to classic liberalism; and the Tunisian liberal party *Afek Tounes* adopting social liberalism.

Explanations of electoral success

Liberal parties have been quite 'unequal' regarding their electoral appeal and success. Close and Delwit (2019) provide an overview of the fate of liberal parties in Europe between 1945 and 2017. Their explanations pertain primarily to societal trends and the configuration of the political system. In the Benelux countries, in the absence of strong conservative parties, and given the secularisation process and weakening of Christian Democratic parties, liberal parties have progressively asserted their position as the main right-wing organisations. By contrast, where conservative parties have been strong (e.g. Germany), liberals have struggled to be relevant actors. In the Nordic countries, centrist parties (KESK – Centre Party in Finland and Sweden, *Venstre* in Denmark) have competed with conservative parties to secure the position of major right-wing party, in opposition to the social democrats (Close and Delwit 2019, 287). While KESK and *Venstre* have been relatively successful, in Sweden the Moderate Party (a conservative party) has become the major right-wing political force. Social liberal parties (*Radikale Venstre* in Denmark) or economic liberals (*Liberalna* in Sweden, *Liberal Alliance* in Denmark) are minor parties measured by electoral weight. In CEE, the fate of liberal parties has been marked by high instability and volatility, except in Estonia where the Reform Party and the Centre Party regularly attract 20–30 per cent of the vote.

Other European liberal parties have generally been weak electoral actors, yet some recently formed liberal parties have challenged the existing party systems, notably *Ciudadanos* in Spain and Emmanuel Macron's movement in France. The (ephemeral) success of these new actors seemed rooted in a disaffection and rejection of the traditional left-right two-party systems. Their success can also be attributed to the salience of and polarisation over specific cleavages, on which they came to occupy one pole: in Spain, the territorial cleavage and crisis, since the party was founded against Catalan nationalism (Teruel and Barrio 2016); in France, the cleavage over economic and cultural globalisation issues and more specifically over the EU (Schön-Quinlivan 2017).

Analysing liberals in Canada and in the UK contrasts two different fates in quite a similar, two-party, majoritarian system. The Liberal Party of Canada has been described as one of the 'most successful [liberal] parties in contemporary democracies' (Blais 2005, 821) or as 'the most successful political machine in the Western world' (Jeffrey 2010, 3). By contrast, the Liberals in the UK lost their position of major party when the Labour Party became the main opponent to the Conservative Party in the interwar period.

The dominance of the Canadian Liberal party has been explained by a combination of ideological, sociological, organisational and strategic factors. Ideologically, the party has been able 'to shape and define Liberal values as *Canadian* values, positioning itself as the party of national unity' (Jeffrey 2010, 3), while promoting the country's cultural and regional diversity, and providing 'a combination of nation-building social programs and commitment to strong government' (Jeffrey 2010, 3). The party has attracted the support of key social groups (Blais 2005, 834), mainly Catholics and Canadians of non-European origin. It has appeared less organisationally factionalised than its conservative opponent (Carty 2010; Jeffrey 2010, 3). Finally, the party has adapted to and taken advantage of changing circumstances (electoral defeats, periods of opposition and leadership changes) in order to renew its policies and organisation (Jeffrey 2021).

The electoral fate of the Liberal Democrats in the UK is regularly debated in the literature (Russell and Fieldhouse 2005; Johnson and Middleton 2016). Scholars highlight how the party suffers from the 'wasted vote syndrome' encouraged by a plurality electoral system and that it struggles to breach the 'credibility gap' (Russell and Fieldhouse 2005, 6). In the absence of a stable social base and strong party identification, writers have highlighted the role of 'contest- and context-specific factors' (Cutts 2012, 96), which have helped the party to breach this gap: these include local election successes, incumbent candidates' personal popularity and support and (at times) a high-profile leadership effect.

The electorate

Regarding the profile of liberal voters, again, diversity prevails (van der Brug, Hobolt and Vreese 2009; Close and Delwit 2019). Comparative empirical studies suggest that only a few sociodemographic traits are consistent across Europe: education, socio-economic status and/or occupation (Kirchner 1988; Close and Delwit 2019). Liberal party voters are more educated than the average voter, and more likely to be highly skilled workers, self-employed or employers rather than manual workers or unemployed. Religion and residence come second: liberal party voting is less likely among religious voters, and more likely among urban voters – with some exceptions (e.g. parties closer to 'conservative liberalism' attract religious and rural voters). This profile is also found in non-European contexts. In Russia, in the late 1990s, Yabloko attracted votes from 'the not-so-well-off intelligentsia, those with a higher education and white-collar workers in large and medium cities' (White 2012, 212).

Ethnicity and language are key distinctive features of ethno-regionalist liberal parties, such as the Swedish People's Party of Finland, or the Estonian Centre Party (which appeals to the Russian-speaking minority) (Close and Delwit 2019). In South Africa, the issue of race has been crucially constitutive of party choice and identification. During apartheid, the liberals found support among white English-speaker voters, while the nationalists found support among the white Afrikaners. In the 2000s, the Democratic Alliance was becoming 'the home of the majority of whites, coloureds and Indians' (Southern 2011).

Looking beyond sociodemographic variables, the policy preferences of liberal party voters are also significant (Fieldhouse and Russell 2001). Liberal party voters' general self-placement leans to the centre-right (van der Brug, Hobolt and Vreese 2009; Close and Delwit 2019); and in a two-dimensional space, they would combine a rightist position on socio-economic issues and a centre-left one on cultural issues (De Winter and Marcet 2000; Close and Delwit 2019). However, voters' placement depends on, and reflects, the type of 'liberalism' promoted by the different liberal parties (i.e. classical, social and conservative). Interestingly, following the party system reconfiguration on the new cleavage dimension, support for EU integration stands out as an almost universal determinant of liberal voting in Europe (Close and Delwit 2019). However, liberal party voters seem divided over other issues, such as immigration or the environment.

Government participation

As discussed, the Liberal Party of Canada has been incredibly successful in dominating politics and government (Jeffrey 2021), which has led scholars to talk about the 'natural governing party' (Jeffrey 2010; Clarkson 2014). In Europe too, liberal parties 'have been unusually successful at getting into government' (Hellström and Walther 2019, 310). Despite relatively modest vote and seat shares, liberal parties have been in the majority of governments in many European countries (Hellström and Walther 2019, 310–311) – around 70 per cent of the time or more in Denmark, Germany, Estonia, Finland, Switzerland, Ireland, Slovenia and the Netherlands. Liberal parties have also been quite successful in securing key roles in government (e.g. Prime Minister) despite rarely being the largest parliamentary party.

Explanations for this unusual success are manifold. From a socio-historical perspective, many liberal parties were born among parliamentary elites, and participated in the process of state-building and *liberal* democratisation. They are perceived as central, credible and competent actors, but also as pragmatic decision-makers (Clarkson 2014; Close and van Haute 2019b, 372). From a coalition-theory perspective, liberal parties' ability to join government would be rooted in their ideological closeness to the median legislator (Hellström and Walther 2019, 314–315). Their 'centrist' placement gives them more flexibility to form compromises with government partners, on either side of the spectrum.

Liberals mostly join coalition governments. Single-party liberal governments have, however, been formed in Denmark, Sweden, Ireland and Estonia (Hellström and Walther 2019, 370). In Canada, Liberals have always governed in single-party, majority or minority, administrations. The number and nature of coalition partners that liberal parties work with depends on party system dynamics (some being more or less fragmented), political culture (consensus/consociational) and the liberal 'tradition' of the party. Hence, where large coalitions are common (e.g. Belgium and Finland), liberals ally with partners from different sides of the political spectrum. In Germany, the liberals have more often allied with the conservatives (CDU/CSU) than with the social democrats (SPD) (Bukow 2019). Social-liberals have favoured centre-left partners, while conservative-liberals tended to form centre-right or right coalitions. Finally, the portfolio allocation in coalition governments sees liberals tending to occupy the justice, finance and foreign affairs ministries – in line with their commitment to defend the rule of law, individual rights, free-market and international cooperation – especially in the process of European integration. Overall, the way liberal parties access and exercise power constitutes a key distinctive dimension of the liberal party family, which reflects their pragmatism, adaptability and ideological fluidity (Close and van Haute 2019b, 369–370).

Party organisation

The organisational specificities of party families are rooted in their origins, but also reflect their core ideology and values (Poguntke et al. 2016, 662). On the one hand, the emphasis that liberal parties place on individual freedom is significant. Their aversion to excessive state or political authority can result in a certain reluctance to implement highly institutionalised structures, and a focus on *individuals'* rights and participation rather than that of collective bodies. In their empirical assessment of liberal parties' organisation in Europe, Beyens, van Haute and Verthé (2019) partly confirm this hypothesis. Liberal parties appear reluctant to provide guaranteed representation in the executive bodies to party subgroups. However, they generally allocate less decision-making power to individual members than other parties – although some liberal parties played a pioneering role in the implementation of more intra-party democracy in the 1990s (for instance, in Belgium, see Legein 2021).

On the other hand, the origin of many liberal parties as 'internally created parties' (i.e. parties created by political elites within the parliament) should make their organisation look like the typical 'cadre party' (Panebianco 1988, 51). Beyens, van Haute and Verthé (2019) indeed show that liberal parties in Europe are characterised by a lower (but more stable) membership than other party families. Besides, they present less complex but more expensive membership procedures for members, suggesting a certain degree of 'elitism' in their recruitment. Their parliamentary origins are also reflected in the increasing role of the parliamentary party group that has paradoxically accompanied the shift towards internal membership voting rights. Finally, their origins have led them to experience complex and highly competitive internal power dynamics in the face of decentralised, autonomous leadership with little discipline towards the organisation. Cook (2010, 2) illustrates this in his in-depth study of the UK Liberal Party history: 'It was less a party in the modern sense than a loose alliance of groups of many shades of political opinion and widely differing social background. From the beginning, the Liberal Party was an uneasy coalition'.

Liberal parties outside of Europe do not always fit into this typical organisational model. Their organisations can be shaped by electoral systems which can be highly territorial-based (i.e. single-member district systems), in opposition to the national (proportional) electoral systems of continental European countries (Carty 2010, 8). In Canada, for instance, the Liberal Party has been associated with the *franchise* party model, developed by Carty (2004). This model emphasises the *stratarchical* relations between national and local organisations that characterise political parties in Canada, and which have consequences for other organisational aspects, such as party finance (Coletto, Jansen and Young 2011) and intraparty democracy (Carty and Cross 2006).

Impact on mainstream politics and challenges

A minima, political liberalism involves the defence of individual rights and freedom against any form of tyranny, the promotion of constitutionalism and of the rule of law. Accordingly, 'all modern democratic parties [are] inheritors of nineteenth-century liberalism' (Steed and Humphreys 1988, 399). Liberal parties participated in the building of modern democracies, in consolidating political institutions, in promoting individual freedoms and liberal democracy. Besides, democratisation processes have usually been accompanied by the liberalisation and opening of national economies.

At the end of the twentieth century, most democratic actors accepted and promoted liberal principles at both the political and economic levels, which made it difficult for the liberal party family to assert its distinctiveness. In the meantime, the increasing salience of the demarcation versus integration cleavage resulted in tensions between and within the members of the family (Kriesi et al. 2006). Liberals tending to occupy the right-wing space of the spectrum have asserted themselves as conservative actors (Belgian French-speaking Liberals, Dutch VVD), emphasising market liberalisation but adopting tougher positions on cultural values. Liberals which were 'squeezed' between strong social democrats and conservatives (UK Liberal Democrats, German FDP) have searched for a third way but ran the risk of 'the empty centre phenomenon' (Zur 2021). In post-communist contexts, the 'illiberal' turn of the 2010s has accentuated the perception that liberalism is essentially 'western': European, neoliberal and elitist. Some liberal parties have tended to assert their placement on the 'winning' side of globalisation, hence re-affirming the very essence of liberalism: economic freedom, a globalised economy, open borders, cultural freedom and a cosmopolitan society. In France, this strategy was adopted by Macron against Le Pen in 2017; and to a certain extent by the Liberal Democrats in a post-Brexit context (Sloman 2020).

This 'winning side' strategy comes with costs. Liberals become increasingly associated with a dominant, educated and privileged class. They might appear as unable – or unwilling – to respond to the social consequences of economic, welfare or environmental crises. On the last point, they are challenged by green parties, whose support comes from similar sections of the electorate – educated, urban and cosmopolitan voters (see also Chapter 16). While some Scandinavian liberal parties have sought to position themselves as *green*, most liberals struggle to combine their economic neoliberalism with strong ecologist endeavours. On their right flank, liberals face conservative opponents willing to protect national identity and values. Finally, while they have appeared as credible and competent actors in government, their pragmatism and longevity in power make them an easy target for the anti-establishment arguments of populist parties.

Conclusions and avenues for further research

The literature on liberal parties suffers from an uneven development across different regions of the world. Overall, scholarly appraisal of liberal parties has focused on advanced democracies, notably in Europe. Case studies and comparative examinations have attempted to assess the existence of a liberal party family along Mair and Mudde's (1998) criteria. The Liberals in Canada have also attracted considerable attention, with a focus on its longevity in power, electoral successes (and occasional failures) and its specific organisational structure. In other regions, the study of liberal parties has been closely related to the study of transition and democratisation such as in South Africa, Russia and the MENA countries. Yet, given the scarcity of comparative studies on liberal party organisations in these contexts, it is hard to assess the existence and specificities of their liberal parties.

In advanced democracies, despite extensive analysis, one puzzle remains unresolved: Can we really speak about a single liberal party family? Indeed, this family has been depicted as one of the most heterogeneous, especially in socio-historical perspective. Even when scholars point to ideological commonalities between liberal parties, they recognise the existence of different traditions within the party family, hence questioning its uniformity. Interestingly, the literature points to distinctive elements of the liberals that relate more to what they *do* than to what they *are* (Close and van Haute 2019b): liberal parties are primarily pragmatic actors, using their ambivalent and fluid identity and their flexible organisation to exercise governmental responsibilities, despite modest electoral support. Yet it remains to be seen whether this disproportionate success will accentuate the perception that liberal parties only speak to and for '(liberal) elites', and in the long run, risk eroding their support and credibility

Note

1 In 2011, the former Network of Arab Liberals (NAL) was renamed the Arab Alliance for Freedom and Democracy (AAFD) because of the negative interpretation of the word 'liberal' by the Arab population (see Meinardus 2014).

References

Arter, D. (2019) 'The Norwegian Left and the Finnish Centre: What, no capital "L" liberal parties?' in Close, C. and van Haute, E. (eds.) *Liberal parties in Europe*. Abingdon: Routledge, pp. 23–43.
Bardi, L., Bressanelli, E., Calossi, E., Cicchi, L., Gagatek, W. and Pizzimenti, E. (2014) *Political parties and political foundations at European level. Challenges and opportunities* (No. PE 509.983). European Parliament, Directorate-General for Internal Policies.
Beyens, S., van Haute, E. and Verthé, T. (2019) 'How liberal parties organize', in Close, C. and van Haute, E. (eds.) *Liberal parties in Europe*. Abingdon: Routledge, pp. 348–363.
Blais, A. (2005) 'Accounting for the electoral success of the Liberal Party in Canada Presidential address to the Canadian Political Science Association London, Ontario 3 June 2005', *Canadian Journal of Political Science*, 38(4), p821–840.
Bolin, N. (2019) 'The Centre Party and the Liberals: The Swedish members of the liberal party family?' in Close, C. and van Haute, E. (eds.) *Liberal parties in Europe*. Abingdon: Routledge, pp. 60–76.
Brown, S. and Kaiser, P. (2007) 'Democratisations in Africa: Attempts, hindrances and prospects', *Third World Quarterly*, 28(6), p1131–1149.
Bukow, S.U. (2019) 'It's (not only) the economy, stupid? Past and future of the German Liberal Party', in Close, C. and van Haute, E. (eds.) *Liberal parties in Europe*. Abingdon: Routledge, pp. 146–165.
Carty, R.K. (2004) 'Parties as franchise systems: the stratarchical organizational imperative', *Party Politics*, 10(5), p5–24.
Carty, R.K. (2010) 'Dominance without factions: The liberal party of Canada', in Bogaards, M. and Boucek, F. (eds.) *Dominant political parties and democracy*. Abingdon: Routledge, pp. 158–172.

Carty, R.K. (2015) *Big tent politics: The liberal party's long mastery of Canada's public life.* Vancouver: University of British Columbia Press.

Carty, R.K. and Cross, W. (2006) 'Can stratarchically organized parties be democratic? The Canadian case', *Journal of Elections, Public Opinion and Parties*, 16(2), p93–114.

Cholova, B. and De Waele, J-M. (2019) 'Liberal parties in Central and Eastern Europe', in Close, C. and van Haute, E. (eds.) *Liberal parties in Europe.* Abingdon: Routledge, pp. 225–240.

Clarkson, S. (2014) *The big red machine: How the liberal party dominates Canadian Politics.* Vancouver: University of British Columbia Press.

Claudio, L.E. (2017) *Liberalism and the postcolony: Thinking the state in 20th-century Philippines.* Singapore: National University of Singapore.

Close, C. (2019) 'The liberal party family ideology. Distinct, but diverse', in Close, C. and van Haute, E. (eds.) *Liberal parties in Europe.* Abingdon: Routledge, pp. 326–347.

Close, C. and Delwit, P. (2019) 'Liberal parties and elections. Electoral performances and voters profile', in Close, C. and van Haute, E. (eds.) *Liberal parties in Europe.* Abingdon: Routledge, pp. 281–309.

Close, C. and van Haute, E. (eds.) (2019a) *Liberal parties in Europe.* Abingdon: Routledge.

Close, C. and van Haute, E. (2019b) 'Conclusion', in Close, C. and van Haute, E. (eds.) *Liberal parties in Europe.* Abingdon: Routledge, pp. 364–376.

Coletto, D., Jansen, H.J. and Young, L. (2011) 'Stratarchical party organization and party finance in Canada', *Canadian Journal of Political Science*, 44(1), p111–136.

Cook, C. (2010) *A short history of the Liberal Party: The road back to power.* London: Springer.

Crespo, J.A. (1995) 'The Liberal Democratic Party in Japan: Conservative domination', *International Political Science Review*, 16(2), p199–209.

Cutts, D. (2012) 'Yet another false dawn? An examination of the Liberal Democrats' performance in the 2010 general election', *British Journal of Politics and International Relations*, 14(1), p96–114.

De Winter, L. (ed.) (2000) *Liberalism and liberal parties in the European Union.* Barcelona: Institut de Ciències Polítiques i Socials.

De Winter, L. and Marcet, J. (2000) 'Introduction', in De Winter, L. (ed.), *Liberalism and liberal parties in the European Union.* Barcelona: Institut de Ciències Polítiques i Socials, pp. 13–23.

Delwit, P. (ed.) (2016) *Du parti libéral au MR. 170 ans de libéralisme en Belgique.* Brussels: University of Brussels.

Dix, R. (1989) 'Cleavage structures and party systems in Latin America', *Comparative Politics*, 22(1), p23–37.

Ennser, L. (2012) 'The homogeneity of West European party families: The radical right in comparative perspective', *Party Politics*, 18(2), p151–171.

Ennser-Jedenastik, L. and Bodlos, A. (2019) 'Liberal parties in Austria', in Close, C. and van Haute, E. (eds.) *Liberal parties in Europe.* Abingdon: Routledge, pp. 129–145.

Fieldhouse, E. and Russell, A. (2001) 'Latent liberalism?: Sympathy and support for the Liberal Democrats at the 1997 British general election', *Party Politics*, 7(6), p711–738.

Geuss, R. (2002) 'Liberalism', in Geuss, R. (ed.) *History and illusion in politics.* Cambridge: Cambridge University Press, pp. 69–109.

Hale, H.E. (2004) 'Yabloko and the challenge of building a liberal party in Russia', *Europe-Asia Studies*, 56(7), p993–1020.

Hellström, J. and Walther, D. (2019) 'Government participation and alliances of liberal parties in Europe', in Close, C. and van Haute, E. (eds.) *Liberal parties in Europe.* Abingdon: Routledge, pp. 310–325.

Hloušek, V. and Kopeček, L. (2020) 'Strange bedfellows: A hyper-pragmatic alliance between European liberals and an illiberal Czech technocrat', *East European Politics and Societies and Cultures.* https://doi.org/ 10.1177/0888325420953487.

Hooghe, L. and Marks, G. (2018) 'Cleavage theory meets Europe's crises: Lipset, Rokkan, and the transnational cleavage', *Journal of European Public Policy*, 25(1), p109–135.

Jeffrey, B. (2010) *Divided loyalties: The Liberal Party of Canada, 1984–2008.* Toronto: University of Toronto Press.

Jeffrey, B. (2021) *Road to redemption: The Liberal Party of Canada, 2006–2019.* Toronto: University of Toronto Press.

Johnson, C. and Middleton, A. (2016) 'Junior coalition parties in the British context: Explaining the Liberal Democrat collapse at the 2015 general election', *Electoral Studies*, 43, p63–71.

Kirchner, E.J. (ed.) (1988) *Liberal parties in Western Europe.* Cambridge: Cambridge University Press.

Kosiara-Pedersen, K. (2019) 'The Danish liberal parties', in Close, C. and Van Haute, E. (eds.) *Liberal parties in Europe.* Abingdon: Routledge, pp. 44–59.

Kriesi, H., Grande, E., Lachat, R., Dolezal, M., Bornschier, S. and Frey, T. (2006) 'Globalization and the transformation of the national political space: Six European countries compared', *European Journal of Political Research*, 45(6), p921–956.

Larsson, T. (2017) 'In search of liberalism: Ideological traditions, translations and troubles in Thailand', *Sojourn: Journal of Social Issues in Southeast Asia*, 32(3), p531–561.

Legein, T. (2021) 'Explaining democratic party reforms: A qualitative comparative analysis (QCA) of Belgian mainstream parties'. Paper presented at the ECPR General Conference, online, 2021.

Meinardus, R. (2014) *Liberalism in the Arab World?* Available at: www.theglobalist.com/liberalism-in-the-arab-world/ (Accessed 2 July 2021).

Mair, P. and Mudde, C. (1998) 'The party family and its study', *Annual Review of Political Science*, 1(1), p211–229.

McElroy, G. and Benoit, K. (2012) 'Policy positioning in the European Parliament', *European Union Politics*, 13(1), p150–167.

Nuñez, L. (2019) 'Nuanced liberalism. The weakness of liberal parties in Spain', in Close, C. and van Haute, E. (eds.) *Liberal Parties in Europe*. Abingdon: Routledge, pp. 205–224.

Panebianco, A. (1988) *Political parties: Organization and power*. Cambridge: Cambridge University Press.

Poguntke, T., Scarrow, S.E., Webb, P.D., Allern, E.H. et al. (2016) 'Party rules, party resources and the politics of parliamentary democracies: How parties organize in the 21st century', *Party Politics*, 22(6), p661–678.

Rickard, M. (2007) *Principle and pragmatism. A study of competition between Australia's major parties at the 2004 and other recent Federal Elections*. Canberra: Commonwealth of Australia.

Rodan, G. and Hughes, C. (2014) *The politics of accountability in Southeast Asia: The dominance of moral ideologies*. Oxford: Oxford University Press.

Russell, A.T. and Fieldhouse, E. (2005) *Neither left nor right: The liberal democrats and the electorate*. Manchester: Manchester University Press.

Sanchez, O. (2008) 'Transformation and decay: The de-institutionalisation of party systems in South America', *Third World Quarterly*, 29(2), p315–337.

Schön-Quinlivan, E. (2017) "The elephant in the room' no more: Europe as a structuring line of political cleavage in the 2017 presidential election', *French Politics*, 15(3), p290–302.

Seiler, D-L. (1980) *Partis et familles politiques*. Paris: Presses Universitaires de France.

Seiler, D-L. (2002) 'Le paradoxe libéral: la faiblesse d'une force d'avenir', in Delwit, P. (ed.) *Libéralismes et Partis Libéraux En Europe, Sociologie Politique*. Brussels: University of Brussels, pp. 37–56.

Sloman, P. (2020) 'Squeezed out? The liberal democrats and the 2019 general election. *Political Quarterly*, 91(1), p35–42.

Smith, G. (1988) 'Between left and right: the ambivalence of European liberalism', in Kirchner, E.J. (ed.) *Liberal parties in Western Europe*. Cambridge: Cambridge University Press, pp. 16–28.

Smith, J. (2014) 'Between ideology and pragmatism: Liberal party politics at the European level', *Acta Politica*, 49(1), p105–121.

Southern, N. (2011) 'Political opposition and the challenges of a dominant party system: The Democratic Alliance in South Africa', *Journal of Contemporary African Studies*, 29(3), p281–298.

Southern, N. and Southall, R. (2011) 'Dancing like a monkey: The democratic alliance and opposition politics in South Africa', in Daniel, J., Naidoo, P., Pillay, D. and Southall, R. (eds.) *New South African review 2: New paths, old compromises?* Johannesburg: Wits University Press, pp. 68–82.

Steed, M. and Humphreys, P. (1988) 'Identifying liberal parties', in Kirchner, E.J. (ed.) *Liberal parties in Western Europe*. Cambridge: Cambridge University Press, pp. 396–435.

Szmolka, I. (2020) 'Liberal-secular parties in Arab political systems', in Cavatorta, F., Storm, L. and Resta, V. (eds.) *Routledge handbook on political parties in the Middle East and North Africa*. Abingdon: Routledge, pp. 69–82.

Tavits, M. and Letki, N. (2009) 'When left is right: Party ideology and policy in post-communist Europe', *American Political Science Review*, 103(4), p555–569.

Teruel, J.R. and Barrio, A. (2016) 'Going national: Ciudadanos from Catalonia to Spain', *South European Society and Politics*, 21(4), p587–607.

Thorhallsson, B. (2021) 'Iceland: Hard-line eurosceptics clash with eurosceptics', in Kaeding, M., Pollak, J. and Schmidt, P. (eds.) *Euroscepticism and the future of Europe: Views from the capitals*. London: Palgrave Macmillan, pp. 65–68.

van der Brug, W., Hobolt, S.B. and de Vreese, C.H. (2009) 'Religion and party choice in Europe', *West European Politics*, 32(6), p1266–1283.

van Staden, M. (2019) 'The liberal tradition in South Africa, 1910–2019', *Econ Journal Watch*, 16(2), p258–341.
Voerman, G. (2019) 'Liberalism in the Netherlands', in Close, C. and van Haute, E. (eds.) *Liberal parties in Europe*. Abingdon: Routledge, pp. 77–94.
von Beyme, K. (1985) *Political parties in western democracies*. Aldershot: Gower.
White, D. (2012) 'Re-conceptualising Russian party politics', *East European Politics*, 28(3), p210–224.
Zur, R. (2021) 'Stuck in the middle: Ideology, valence and the electoral failures of centrist parties', *British Journal of Political Science*, 51(2), p706–723.

14
SOCIAL DEMOCRACY

Björn Bremer

Much has been written about social democratic parties (SDPs) in the last few decades. In the second half of the twentieth century, it was largely a success story, as SDPs became one of the dominant party families in Western Europe. Originally born from the labour movement, many SPDs were inspired by radical Marxist ideas. Yet, over time, they established themselves as mainstream political forces (Sassoon 1996; Bartolini 2000). They became mass parties with large membership bases, competed with the centre-right for office, and strongly influenced twentieth-century political and economic institutions.

In recent years, however, accounts of the centre-left have been more pessimistic, as most SDPs lost support (Benedetto, Hix and Mastrorocco 2020): they were decimated in some countries like France, the Netherlands, or Greece, but they also declined significantly in many other countries including Germany, Italy, and Austria. In some countries, the far left benefited from the crisis of SDPs; in others, green parties have flourished; and elsewhere the centre- or far right has been the beneficiary. Consequently, by 2019, the average vote share of the centre-left had dropped to its lowest point since 1945.

This chapter begins by conceptualising the SDP party family. It summarises different explanations for the challenges that SDPs face, highlights different causes of their (varying) electoral success, and discusses their record in government. The chapter argues that the literature provides many insights into SDPs as a party family, but that the ongoing transformation of the left is still not well understood. In particular, the literature too often views individual explanations for this transformation in isolation and would benefit from more systematic comparative analysis. This could also help to reveal where the electoral success of SDPs is shaped by their different programmes and policies and where it is influenced by context-specific variables. Due to the variety of different ideological traditions within the party family, it is often difficult to generalise between cases.

The conceptualisation of social democratic parties

SDPs come under various guises and are associated with various labels, including labour, socialist, and social democratic (see Padgett and Paterson 1991, 2–3; Kitschelt 1994, 1). Collectively SDPs are interchangeably referred to as 'social democratic', 'centre-left', or 'moderate left' parties. Membership is diverse: it includes Anglo-Saxon labour parties (e.g. the British Labour Party), socialist parties (e.g. the *Parti Socialist* in France) as well as Scandinavian and North-Western European SDPs.

Following Mair and Mudde's (1998) conceptualisation of party families, SDPs can be grouped together based on their shared origin as well as their shared policy goals. Historically, SDPs emerged from the labour movement in the late nineteenth and early twentieth century. They were on the left of the class cleavage identified by Lipset and Rokkan (1967) and mostly mobilised their support based on it (Bartolini 2000). Closely allied with trade unions, they primarily represented the interests of the working class. Following the split of working-class parties after the First World War, SDPs chose the electoral route to power. In contrast to communist parties, which remained wedded to revolutionary ideas, SDPs embraced competitive multi-party democracies (Lindemann 1983). They sought to reform capitalism by participating in elections and promoting working class representation in parliament and government (Esping-Andersen 1985; Prezworski and Sprague 1986; Berman 2006).

Beyond accepting the democratic process, SDPs also developed shared goals. As Lipset and Rokkan (1967) noted, the class cleavage existed across all countries, pitting workers against the owners of capital, creating a relatively homogeneous party family, despite different labels. SDPs fought for the introduction of social insurance and a welfare state that would protect the working class from old age, illness, and employment. Yet, in the wake of the Great Depression, ideological differences emerged across countries: whereas many parties initially remained wedded to Marxist ideas of gaining control over the means of production, the Scandinavian left began to champion a regulated and restrained market economy (Berman 1998, 2006). Most importantly, the Swedish Social Democratic Party (SAP) was able to build cross-class coalitions with agrarian parties, which helped it to gain power (Luebbert 1991). After 1945, many SDPs followed the Scandinavian model, pushing for a strong and interventionist state that would create the conditions for full employment and reduce inequalities.

Despite this common blueprint for social democracy, ideological differences between parties continued to exist as individual parties such as the British Labour Party retained distinct intellectual traditions. This resulted in numerous historical and geographical incarnations of social democracy, but the essential goal has always been to 'minimise the costs' of capitalism for the working classes broadly understood (Hirst 1999, 87). Social democracy aims to provide all individuals with the necessary means to actively participate in social, economic, and political life.

Most of the empirical work on SDPs has focused on Western Europe and other advanced economies, but recently much has also been written about the centre-left in Central and Eastern Europe (e.g. Sloam 2005; Holmes and Lightfoot 2011; De Waele and Soare 2008; Benedetto, Hix and Mastrorocco 2020) and Latin America (Levitsky 2003; Weyland, Madrid and Hunter 2010; Levitsky and Roberts 2011; Lupu 2016). In these regions, SDPs were often born out of different historical configurations and operate in different economic and social conditions. For example, in Central and Eastern Europe, many SDPs emerged as post-communist successor parties. In Latin America, they face the constraints of managing developing or emerging economies. Finally, the Democratic Party in the USA is sometimes also considered part of the centre-left and compared to SDPs (e.g. Cronin, Ross and Shoch 2008; Mudge 2018; Piketty 2019), although it has historically different ideological roots. For these reasons, the review later focuses mostly on SDPs in Western Europe and Anglo-Saxon countries.

Challenges facing social democratic parties

Social democracy parties have been one of the most influential party families. However, in the last few decades, SDPs have struggled to maintain their popularity. As Figure 14.1 shows, their average vote share in Western Europe and Anglo-Saxon countries declined from around 35 per cent in the 1970s to 23 per cent in 2019.

Social democracy

Figure 14.1 Average vote share of centre-left and centre-right parties in 22 countries from 1945 to 2020

Note: The figure shows the average vote share of centre-left and centre-right parties in 22 countries from 1945 until 2020. The centre-right includes both conservative and Christian democratic parties, as defined by the ParlGov database. The following countries are included: Australia, Austria, Belgium, Canada, Cyprus, Denmark, Finland France, Germany, Greece, Ireland, Italy, Luxembourg, Malta, the Netherlands, New Zealand, Norway, Portugal, Spain, Sweden, Switzerland, and the UK.

Source: ParlGov database (Döring and Manow 2020), own calculation.

This decline was neither linear across time nor consistent across space. Following the initial decline in the 1970s, SDPs were able to stabilise their vote share in the late 1990s and early 2000s. The decline accelerated again at the beginning of the twenty-first century, as many SDPs further lost support, especially in the wake of the global financial crisis. As a result, some scholars have even spoken of the 'death of social democracy' (Lavelle 2008), but the pattern of decline varied across countries and regions. It was the largest in North-Western Europe, where some parties have been nearly wiped out (e.g. the Netherlands and France). In Anglo-Saxon and Scandinavian countries, centre-left parties also lost support (except in New Zealand) but, in relative terms, their situation is better. Particularly in Scandinavia, social democracy remains strong. Finally, in Southern Europe, the experience of social democracy is varied. The fall of PASOK in Greece was dramatic, as its vote share dropped by more than 35 per cent after it implemented austerity measures (Bojar et al. 2022). In Italy, Spain, and Portugal, the centre-left also lost support but by not nearly as much. Indeed, the Spanish Socialist Workers' Party (PSOE) and the Portuguese Socialist Party (PS) have achieved important electoral victories.

The literature puts forward different explanations for the decline of social democracy. First, the literature explains the decline of SDPs primarily as arising from large, structural transformations. The working class had never become a majority in advanced economies (Przeworksi 1985; Przeworski and Sprague 1986) but de-industrialisation, technological change, and educational expansion reduced the size of the working class further (Fox Piven 1991; Pontusson 1995; Best 2011). Moreover, these secular changes divided the working class into insiders and outsiders (Rueda 2007) and contributed to a decline of traditional class voting (Evans 1999; Knutsen 2004; Rennwald and Evans 2014). In particular, skill-based technological change and educational expansion reduced traditional blue-collar manufacturing employment in many advanced economies. SDPs thus saw their core clientele dwindle, which undermined the 'electoral relevancy' of traditional blue-collar workers for SDPs (Best 2011; Bürgisser and Kurer 2021). According to many, this decline in industrial workers, alongside their lower propensity to vote for SDPs, explains the parties' fall from grace.

Second, other research points to globalisation as a large-scale transformation that undermined social democracy. According to conventional wisdom, globalisation created economic insecurities that hurt the core clientele of SDPs, while also challenging social democracy as a political and social project (e.g. Panitch and Leys 2001; Pierson 2001; Lavelle 2008; Bailey 2009). It limited the ability of governments to regulate domestic markets and implement Keynesian demand management (Scharpf 1991; Boix 1998), reduced the scope of taxation (Beramendi and Rueda 2007), and forced SDPs to address 'new social risks' (Bonoli 2005). Consequently, some argued that globalisation undermined the ability of governments to protect citizens from the vagaries of the markets (e.g. Streeck 2014). Others conceded that globalisation constrains national governments' macroeconomic policies but still saw some scope for social democratic politics (Boix 1998; Garrett 1998; Hirst 1999).

These large-scale transformations clearly had a profound impact on politics in advanced economies, especially in Europe. They increased the salience of non-economic issues, which pitted the winners of globalisation, including related processes such as European integration and immigration, against the losers (Kriesi et al. 2008). This contributed to a realignment of party systems in Western Europe (Flanagan and Dalton 1984; Dalton 2018; Oesch and Rennwald 2018), which presents a third explanation for the decline of social democracy. SDPs increasingly competed with green and liberal parties for the growing educated urban middle classes (Kitschelt 1994; Gingrich and Häusermann 2015; Häusermann 2018). To this end, they adopted progressive policies on 'cultural' issues beyond economic governance, but by doing so, they risked losing support among working-class voters. In recent years, the salience of migration and climate change further exacerbated this tension between working and middle-class voters and made the task of putting a cross-class coalition together even more difficult.

Finally, a fourth explanation focuses on the agency of parties and explains the crisis of social democracy as resulting from the positions that they adopted. In the 1990s, many SDPs shifted towards the centre and embarked on the Third Way (Giddens 1998). Based on economic ideas that became popular among policymakers (Mudge 2018; Bremer and McDaniel 2020), centre-left parties liberalised labour markets, retrenched traditional compensatory social policies, and shifted towards a social investment vision of the welfare state. SDPs believed that these policies were essential for the transition to the knowledge society (Andersson 2010) and, given that they were associated with electoral victories in the late 1990s and early 2000s, they diffused across countries (Schleiter et al. 2021). However, Third Way policies mostly appeal led to the middle classes but were less popular among working-class voters (e.g. Gingrich and Häusermann 2015; Garritzmann, Busemeyer and Neimanns 2018; Häusermann et al. 2021). In particular, research suggests that welfare state retrenchment policies hurt SDPs (Arndt 2013; Karreth, Polk and Allen 2013; Horn 2020; Loxbo et al. 2021). These developments also contributed to a convergence of the centre-left and centre-right on some issues (e.g. Callaghan 2000; Merkel et al. 2008), which further undermined the ties of the working class to social democracy (Evans and Tilley 2017; Berman and Snegovaya 2019).

The literature often presents these explanations as being in competition with each other, but they all contain kernels of truth. Although SDPs always had to appeal to voters beyond the working classes (Przeworksi and Sprague 1986), it became electorally imperative to appeal to the expanded middle classes more directly as large-scale transformations reduced the size of the centre-left's traditional constituency (Kitschelt 1994). The Third Way achieved this, but its success was context-specific. In times of relative economic stability, it allowed the centre-left to implement liberal supply-side policies without abandoning their commitment to the welfare state. In some countries, the Third Way had negative consequences in the long run because it facilitated the creation of new challenger parties, for example, *Die Linke* in Germany (Schwander and Manow 2017). But in many countries, social democrats were able to hold their cross-class coalition together during the 'Great Moderation'.

Yet, following the global financial crisis, the context changed. Economic instability during the Great Recession heightened economic grievances, which were worsened by austerity that became the dominant fiscal policy in advanced economies: it put downward pressures on wages, reduced benefits and pension schemes, and increased economic precarity especially for young people and low-skilled workers. SDPs found it difficult to respond: they rediscovered the need for a regulatory and interventionist state (Bremer 2018; Mainwaring and Holloway 2020) but still supported fiscal orthodoxy (Kraft 2017; Bremer 2018, 2023; Bremer and McDaniel 2020). These inconsistencies diluted the brand of social democracy (Lupu 2016) and undermined the ability of SDPs to manage conflicting preferences among their different constituencies. With limited fiscal resources, SDPs faced difficult trade-offs between policies that appeal to different constituencies, notably the need to invest in human capital versus the need to compensate the losers of globalisation (Beramendi et al. 2015).

Moreover, today, SDPs find themselves squeezed from all sides: libertarian-green parties provide competition for the educated middle classes; leftist parties and, populist radical right parties can vie for working class voters; while competition over swing voters in the centre remains intense with the centre-right. Irrespective of the precise trajectory of individual parties, social democracy thus faces a common challenge, which the literature has not sufficiently explored: the need to manage decline or the fear of such decline. The historic success of SDPs in the twentieth century still ties older voters to them, softening their decline (Bremer and Rennwald 2022). Yet it also comes with some baggage: it means that these parties have numerous stakeholders with expectations that are difficult to meet in fragmenting party systems.

The literature still needs to better conceptualise the resulting organisational challenges. The combination of strong party bureaucracies and large membership bases creates organisational divisions (Kitschelt 1994), which become more salient in a context of decline. As positions of influence (e.g. in government) become fewer, party officials have to split a shrinking pie, while they also have to explain their waning influence to party members. In this context, party leaders often see their authority erode, which undermines their capacity to manage the different lines of conflict within their parties. Electoral defeats led to the frequent turnover of party leaders and repeated policy changes, as parties reacted to one disappointing election result after another. By frequently changing their leadership and their positions, however, social democrats have suffered from brand dilution, and their voters increasingly switched to competing parties. Consequently, SDPs not only adopted policies that can be seen to be in conflict with their ideals (Lupu 2016), but also experienced heightened positional volatility.

The long-term consequences of this brand dilution are not well understood but it represents one of the most important problems facing social democracy today. After three decades of shifting positions, and with SDPs taking different trajectories in different countries, it has become increasingly difficult for voters and party activists to know what SDPs stand for. These processes have eroded the reputation of SDPs and undermined their credibility, even with respect to some issues that are at the heart of social democracy. It is unlikely that short-term policy changes will solve this problem, which makes it increasingly difficult for social democrats to manage their decline.

Social democratic party electoral success and voters

Despite many challenges, the centre-left has been one of the most successful party families since the Second World War. In most countries except in Scandinavia, the centre-right remained the dominant party family in the twentieth century but, as shown in Figure 14.1, the centre-left's vote share often came close to that of the centre-right. On average, they won a vote share of 35 per cent in Western Europe until the late 1970s. Thereafter, their vote share hovered somewhere between 30 and 35 per cent and even in this century, the centre-left remains the dominant party family of the left in most European countries. The radical left has dethroned (e.g. Greece) or eclipsed (e.g. France) SDPs in very few countries. Moreover, in some countries both the centre-left and the radical left do poorly (e.g. the Netherlands and Czech Republic). Everywhere else, the centre-left remains a central pillar of the party system, and the literature highlights several explanations for this continuing success.

Historically, SDPs became the incarnation of the 'mass' and then the 'catch-all' party (Kirchheimer 1966; Sassoon 1996). They successfully mobilised the working class, reaching beyond industrial workers as their core clientele (Rennwald 2020) to develop large membership bases and strong organisational structures. They were closely allied with trade unions and other working-class organisations, which allowed SDPs to mobilise supporters and to create social democratic milieus where their support was strong. After the Second World War, this base enabled SDPs to become the focal point of the labour movement helping them to become the second-largest party family, competing with the centre-right for power. The most successful electoral period for SDPs coincided with the so-called *trente glorieuses*, the three decades after the Second World War. High and stable economic growth paired with full employment created the conditions for SDPs to expand the welfare state and public expenditure when they were in office. Even in countries where SDPs were not the predominant governing party, they were able to use the resources of the labour movement to fight for the interests of their supporters (Stephens 1979; Esping-Andersen 1985). Trade unions and corporatist bargaining secured stable wage increases during the height of Fordism (Cameron 1984; Swenson 1989).

The *trente glorieuses* coincided with the rise of SDPs because it allowed them to build a cross-class coalition by mobilising blue-collar workers and middle-class allies. Since their foundation, SDPs had struggled to reach beyond the working class and attract electoral support from middle-class allies (Prezworski and Sprague 1986). However, the trade-offs during the post-war period were mild, as social democrats were able to appeal to different classes by expanding the welfare state. High economic growth combined with stable wage increases allowed post-war governments to distribute the economic surplus that capitalism generated. The left prioritised full employment as opposed to inflation as the overarching economic policy (Hibbs 1977), but they were still able to appeal to the growing middle class that benefited from rising wages as well as the growth of the welfare state, especially through rapid educational expansion and generous pension systems. In particular, they received high support among public sector employees, whose interests were often aligned to those of the working classes (Benedetto, Hix and Mastrorocco 2020).

Even today, SDPs are successful because their programmes appeal to a wide variety of voters. As the working class shrank in most advanced economies, social democrats successfully appealed to the expanded middle-classes. According to Piketty (2019), SDPs now represent an educational elite, which he calls the 'Brahmin Left'. Others disagree, showing that social democracy still receives support from lower-educated voters (Abou-Chadi and Hix 2021) and remain popular among working-class voters (Rennwald 2020). Still, social democracy's ability to put together cross-coalitions successfully varies by country because different parties operate in different economic contexts.

On the one hand, the size of manufacturing employment varies across countries, as the decline of industrial production has been slower in some countries (e.g. Austria, Germany, Sweden) than in others (e.g. Belgium and the UK). As a result, SDPs find it easier to maintain the support of the working class in the former than the latter. On the other hand, the tools that policymakers have available to respond to contemporary economic problems also differ across countries (Beramendi et al. 2015). For example, generous welfare states give policymakers more tools to address rising economic insecurity and inequality. Historically, social democracy benefited from welfare state expansions at lower levels of generosity (Esping-Andersen 1985), but today welfare state retrenchment particularly hurts the centre-left in the least generous welfare states (Loxbo et al. 2021).

Despite the importance of the political-economic context, past programmatic choices of parties can also help to explain their success. Some SDPs showed flexibility in opening up to movements from the New Left, including environmental, feminist, or civil liberty movements (Kitschelt 1994; Kriesi 1995; Kriesi et al. 2008). This allowed parties to attract younger, more highly educated and professional voters (Abou-Chadi and Wagner 2019), who have progressive second dimension preferences. The assumption, which was also inherent to the Third Way, was that SDPs could do better if they embrace positions on newly salient issues that attract voters beyond the working class. This created tensions with their traditional constituency, but from a party system perspective, adopting progressive positions may have undermined the rise of Green-libertarian parties. The varying success of these 'New Left parties' still influences the fate of social democracy today, as some parties benefit from the salience of climate change while others lose.

Finally, social movements and civil society organisations are a key ingredient for the success of social democracy. Historically, SDPs benefited from their close connection with trade unions and other associations rooted in the working-class movement (Bartolini and Mair 1990; Allern and Bale 2012; Arndt and Rennwald 2016). These institutions are still important because they help to maintain support for SDPs among their traditional clientele in times of realignment (Rennwald and Pontusson 2021). Unions sustain class identities and render their members more loyal to SDPs than non-members (Bremer and Rennwald 2022). Yet these institutions can also be a double-edged sword for parties wanting to adopt progressive policies to attract new constituencies. Abou-Chadi and Wagner (2020), for example, find evidence that SDPs historically benefited from adopting progressive left-libertarian positions paired with economic investment policies but not in the presence of strong labour unions.

Government participation

The electoral success of SDPs enabled them to regularly participate in government in the postwar period. Alongside conservative or Christian democratic parties, they became the most influential party family and often alternated between being in government and opposition. Yet the ability of SDPs to win office varied. In Scandinavia, they became the strongest party governing for much of the second half of the twentieth century, while they shared power with the centre-right more or less equally in Anglo-Saxon countries that predominantly have majoritarian voting systems. Elsewhere, SDPs found it harder to gain power. For example, in Germany, the SDP led governments for only 20 years between first winning federal elections in 1969 and its victory in 2021. In France, François Mitterrand was the first Socialist candidate to win the presidential elections in 1981 (and was re-elected in 1988), a feat repeated only by François Hollande in 2012.

Research highlights that when SDPs managed to win office, they engaged in Keynesian policies and presided over an expansion of the welfare state (Stephens 1979; Esping-Andersen 1985) while targeting full employment (Hibbs 1977), resulting in a decline of economic inequality. However, starting in the 1970s, recurring economic crises made this more difficult: governments increasingly felt unable to use traditional Keynesian policies of demand management (Schapf 1991), which put full employment out of reach. SDPs lost support, and in several countries, including Germany and the UK, they were shut out of office for many years.

Despite lower electoral support, SDPs remained a leading contender for office in many countries. In the early 2000s, at the height of the Third Way, they even controlled 11 out of 15 governments in the European Union (EU). The literature, however, highlights that when in office, SDPs' enacted different policies than in the post-war period. As mentioned earlier, they implemented liberal supply-side policies (Boix 1998; Garret 1998; Merkel et al. 2008), were more likely to adopt conservative reforms to the welfare state (Bonoli and Powell 2004), or recalibrated the welfare state by more strongly emphasising social investment, giving lower priority to traditional social consumption policies (Evans and Tilly 2017). This involved a long-term change in discourse as politicians de-emphasised the interests of the working class (O'Grady 2019). Following the global financial crisis, SDPs also often implemented austerity measures when they were in government, but the literature is divided about whether these centrist policies were caused by economic constraints stemming from globalisation (Streeck 2014), ideological reasons (Mudge 2018, Bremer and McDaniel 2020), and/or strategic political considerations (Bremer 2023).

The change in social democratic policies was also partly caused by the need to make compromises. Due to a loss of support, SDPs more frequently relied on coalition partners to govern. Nonetheless, in some countries electoral institutions have protected SDPs against this trend. Party system fragmentation is more common under proportional representation (e.g. the Netherlands) than in plurality voting systems (e.g. the UK). In the latter, the rise of challenger parties, which can outflank the centre-left, is more difficult. Yet majoritarian electoral institutions do not guarantee protection against decline. In France, where the run-off electoral system traditionally favours large parties, the Socialist Party was replaced as the largest party of the left in 2017 and often struggles to make it into run-off elections since the rise of Emmanuel Macron's *En Marche* party. Restrictive electoral systems can protect SDPs to some extent, but in the context of the Great Recession, electoral and realignment in Europe also occurred in unexpected places (Hutter and Kriesi 2019). Moreover, in Anglo-Saxon countries, fragmentation can take place within parties, as activists try to capture mainstream parties and elect more radical party leaders such as Jeremy Corbyn in the UK (Whiteley, Poletti and Bale 2019).

Conclusion

Historically, SDPs have formed one of the most successful party families. In many countries, social democrats became a powerful political force in the twentieth century and decisively influenced the most important socio-economic institutions that govern our societies today (e.g. the welfare state). However, in this century, the tables have turned: many SDPs have dramatically lost support, especially since the global financial crisis.

This chapter summarised the main findings in the literature regarding the reasons for SDP success as well as the primary challenges that they face. The social democrats are one of the most studied party families and the literature shows how SDPs were most successful when they were able to mobilise cross-class coalitions between the working-class and the expanded middle-class, including socio-cultural professionals and public sector workers. Today, SDPs are struggling to respond to large-scale (economic) transformations and a fragmentation of the political space in advanced economies. However, too often the literature overlooks the way in which SDPs are not only victims of large structural changes but are also agents of their own fate. Past programmatic choices shape the electoral prospects of SDPs and the extent to which they can still assemble cross-class coalitions.

The discussion in this chapter highlights that despite the wealth of research on the left, its transformation is not fully understood and it is possible to identify several important avenues for future research. First, the comparative analysis of the organisational challenges that SDPs face is underdeveloped. This means that we lack insights into the importance of SDP campaigns, leadership, and internal factionalism, and such gaps are problematic given their potential to shape the electoral success of these parties.

Second, discussions about who votes for SDPs today are ongoing, but it is equally important to study the characteristics and attitudes of *potential* SDP voters, and to explore the effectiveness of different cues and strategic appeals on their voting behaviour. If SDPs do not want to become niche parties, they need to reconnect with former supporters or appeal to new ones, and academics and policymakers alike need to better understand the trade-offs between different strategies and their appeal to different (potential) constituencies.

Finally, as a result of past policy choices, internal divisions, and the rapid churning of political leaders and political strategies, the brand of social democracy has become diluted. Neither the process of this brand dilution nor its durability is well understood. It remains to be seen whether SDPs can uncover their shared political goals in the twenty-first century and rejuvenate the party family.

References

Abou-Chadi, T. and Hix, S. (2021) 'Brahmin left versus Merchan right? Education, class, multiparty competition, and redistribution in Western Europe', *British Journal of Sociology*, 72, p79–92.

Abou-Chadi, T. and Wagner, M. (2019) 'The electoral appeal of party strategies in postindustrial societies: When can the mainstream left succeed?', *The Journal of Politics*, 81(4), p1405–1419.

Abou-Chadi, T. and Wagner, M. (2020) 'Electoral fortunes of social democratic parties: do second dimension positions matter?', *Journal of European Public Policy*, 27(2), p246–272.

Allern, E. and Bale, T. (2012) 'Political parties and interest groups: Disentangling complex relationships', *Party Politics*, 18(1), p7–25.

Andersson, J. (2010) *The library and the workshop: Social democracy and capitalism in the knowledge age*. Stanford: Stanford University Press.

Arndt, C. (2013) *The electoral consequences of third way welfare state reforms: Social democracy's transformation and its political costs*. Amsterdam: Amsterdam University Press.

Arndt, C. and Rennwald, L. (2016) 'Union members at the polls in diverse trade union landscapes', *European Journal of Political Research*, 55(4), p702–722.

Bailey, D.J. (2009) 'The transition to 'new' social democracy: The role of capitalism, representation and (hampered) contestation', *The British Journal of Politics and International Relations*, 11(4), p593–612.

Bartolini, S. (2000) *The political mobilization of the European left, 1860–1980: The class cleavage*. Cambridge: Cambridge University Press.

Bartolini, S. and Mair, P. (1990) *Identity, competition and electoral availability: The stabilisation and electoral instability of European electorates 1885–1985*. Cambridge: Cambridge University Press.

Benedetto, G., Hix, S. and Mastrorocco, N. (2020) 'The rise and fall of social democracy, 1918–2017', *American Political Science Review*, 114(3), p928–939.

Beramendi, P., Häusermann, S., Kitschelt, H. and Kriesi, H. (eds.) (2015) *The politics of advanced capitalism*. New York: Cambridge University Press.

Beramendi, P. and Rueda, D. (2007) 'Social democracy constrained: Indirect taxation in industrialized democracies', *British Journal of Political Science*, 37(4), p619–641.

Berman, S. (1998) *The social democratic moment: Ideas and politics in the making of interwar Europe*. Cambridge: Harvard University Press.

Berman, S. (2006) *The primacy of politics: Social democracy and the making of Europe's twentieth century*. New York: Cambridge University Press.

Berman, S. and Snegovaya, M. (2019) 'Populism and the decline of social democracy', *Journal of Democracy*, 30(3), p5–19.

Best, R.E. (2011) 'The declining electoral relevance of traditional cleavage groups', *European Political Science Review*, 3(2), p279–300.

Boix, C. (1998) *Political parties, growth and equality: Conservative and social democratic economic strategies in the world economy*. New York: Cambridge University Press.

Bojar, A., Bremer, B., Kriesi, H. and Wang, C. (2022) 'The effect of austerity packages on government popularity during the Great Recession', *British Journal of Political Science*, 52(1), p181–199.

Bonoli, G. (2005) 'The politics of the new social policies: Providing coverage against new social risks in mature welfare states', *Policy & Politics*, 33(3), p431–449.

Bonoli, G. and Powell, M. (2004) *Social democratic party policies in contemporary Europe*. London: Routledge.

Bremer, B. (2018) 'The missing left? Economic crisis and the programmatic response of social democratic parties in Europe', *Party Politics*, 24(1), p23–38.

Bremer, B. (2023) *Austerity from the Left: Social Democratic Parties in the Shadow of the Great Recession*. Oxford: Oxford University Press.

Bremer, B. and McDaniel, S. (2020) 'The ideational foundations of social democratic austerity in the context of the great recession', *Socio-Economic Review*, 18(2), p439–463.

Bremer, B. and Rennwald, L. (2022). 'Who still likes social democracy? The support base of social democratic parties reconsidered'. *Party Politics*. Online first. Bürgisser, R. and Kurer, T. (2021) 'Insider – outsider representation and social democratic labor market policy', *Socio-Economic Review*, 19(3), p1065–1094.

Callaghan, J. (2000) *The retreat of social democracy*. Manchester: Manchester University Press.

Cameron, D. (1984) 'Social democracy, corporatism, labour quiescence and the representation of economic interest in advanced capitalist society', in Goldthorpe, J.H. (ed.) *Order and conflict in contemporary capitalism*. Oxford: Oxford University Press, pp. 143–187.

Cronin, J., Ross, G. and Shoch, J. (2008) *What's left of the left: Democrats and social democrats in challenging times*. Durham: Duke University Press.

Dalton, R.J. (2018) *Political realignment: Economics, culture, and electoral change*. Oxford: Oxford University Press.

De Waele, J.-M. and Soare, S. (2008) 'The Central European left: A political family under construction', in Cronin, J., George, R. and Shoch, J. (eds.) *What's left of the left: Democrats and social democrats in challenging times*. Durham: Duke University Press, pp. 290–318.

Döring, H. and Manow, P. (2020). ParlGov 2020 Release. *Harvard Dataverse*. https://www.parlgov.org/

Esping-Andersen, G. (1985) *Politics against markets: The social democratic road to power*. Princeton: Princeton University Press.

Evans, G. (ed.) (1999) *The end of class politics? Class voting in comparative context*. New York: Oxford University Press.

Evans, G. and Tilley, J. (2017) *The new politics of class: The political exclusion of the British working class*. Oxford: Oxford University Press.

Flanagan, S.C. and Dalton, R.J. (1984) 'Parties under stress: Realignment and dealignment in advanced industrial societies', *West European Politics*, 7(1), p7–23.

Fox Piven, F. (1991) *Labor parties in postindustrial societies*. New York: Oxford University Press.

Garrett, G. (1998) *Partisan politics in the global economy*. Cambridge: Cambridge University Press.

Garritzmann, J.L., Busemeyer, M.R. and Neimanns, E. (2018) 'Public demand for social investment: new supporting coalitions for welfare state reform in Western Europe?', *Journal of European Public Policy*, 25(6), p844–861.

Giddens, A. (1998) *The third way: The renewal of social democracy*. Malden: Polity Press.

Gingrich, J. and Häusermann, S. (2015) 'The decline of the working-class vote, the reconfiguration of the welfare support coalition and consequences for the welfare state', *Journal of European Social Policy*, 25(1), p50–75.

Häusermann, S. (2018) 'Social democracy and the welfare state in context: the conditioning effect of institutional and party competition', in Manow, P., Palier, B. and Schwander, H. (eds.) *Welfare democracies and party politics: Explaining electoral dynamics in times of changing welfare capitalism*. New York: Oxford University Press.

Häusermann, S., Pingerra, M., Ares, M. and Enggist, M. (2021) 'Class and social policy in the knowledge economy', *European Journal of Political Research*, 61(2), p462–484.

Hibbs, D.A. (1977) 'Political parties and macroeconomic policy', *American Political Science Review*, 71(4), p1467–1487.

Hirst, P. (1999) 'Has globalisation killed social democracy?', *The Political Quarterly*, 70(1), p84–96.

Holmes, M. and Lightfoot, S. (2011) 'Limited influence? The role of the Party of European Socialists in shaping social democracy in Central and Eastern Europe', *Government and Opposition*, 46(1), p32–55.

Horn, A. (2020) 'The asymmetric long-term electoral consequences of unpopular reforms: Why retrenchment really is a losing game for left parties', *Journal of European Public Policy*, 28(9), p1494–1517.

Hutter, S. and Kriesi, H. (eds.) (2019) *European party politics in times of crisis*. Cambridge University Press.

Karreth, J., Polk, J.T. and Allen, C.S. (2013) 'Catchall or catch and release? The electoral consequences of social democratic parties' march to the middle in Western Europe', *Comparative Political Studies*, 46(7), p791–822.

Kirchheimer, O. (1966) 'The transformation of Western European party systems', in Lapalombara, J. and Weiner, M. (eds.) *Political parties and political development*. Princeton: Princeton University Press, pp. 177–200.

Kitschelt, H. (1994) *The transformation of European social democracy*. Cambridge: Cambridge University Press.

Knutsen, O. (2004) *Social structure and party choice in western Europe: A comparative longitudinal study*. Basingstoke: Palgrave Macmillan.

Kraft, J. (2017) 'Social democratic austerity: the conditional role of agenda dynamics and issue ownership', *Journal of European Public Policy*, 24(10), p1430–1449.

Kriesi, H. (1995) *New movements in Western Europe: A comparative analysis*. University of Minnesota Press.

Kriesi, H., Grande, E., Lachat, R., Dolezal, M., Bornschier, S. and Frey, T. (2008) *West European politics in the age of globalization*. Cambridge: Cambridge University Press.

Lavelle, A. (2008) *The death of social democracy: Political consequences in the 21st century*. Aldershot: Ashgate.

Levitsky, S. (2003) *Transforming labor-based parties in Latin America: Argentine Peronism in comparative perspective*. Cambridge: Cambridge University Press.

Levitsky, S. and Roberts, K.M. (2011) *The resurgence of the Latin American left*. Baltimore: JHU Press.

Lindemann, A.S. (1983) *A history of European socialism*. New Haven: Yale University Press.

Lipset, S.M. and Rokkan, S. (1967) *Party systems and voter alignments: Cross national perspectives*. London: The Free Press.

Loxbo, K., Hinnfors, J., Hagevi, M., Blombäck, S. and Demker, M. (2021) 'The decline of Western European social democracy: Exploring the transformed link between welfare state generosity and the electoral strength of social democratic parties, 1975–2014', *Party Politics*, 27(3), p430–441.

Luebbert, G.M. (1991) *Liberalism, fascism, or social democracy: Social classes and the Political origins of regimes in interwar Europe*. Oxford: Oxford University Press.

Lupu, N. (2016) *Party brands in crisis: Partisanship, brand dilution, and the breakdown of political parties in Latin America*. Cambridge: Cambridge University Press.

Mainwaring, R. and Holloway, J. (2020) 'A new wave of social democracy? Policy change across the social democratic party family, 1970s–2010s', *Government and Opposition*, 57(1), p171–191.

Mair, P. and Mudde, C. (1998) 'The party family and its study', *Annual Review of Political Science*, 1(1), p211–229.

Merkel, W., Petring, A., Henkes, C. and Egle, C. (2008) *Social democracy in power: The capacity to reform*. London: Routledge.

Mudge, S.L. (2018) *Leftism reinvented: Western parties from socialism to neoliberalism*. Cambridge: Harvard University Press.

O'Grady, T. (2019) 'Careerists versus coalminers: Welfare reforms and substantive representation of social groups in the British Labour party', *Comparative Political Studies*, 52(4), p544–578.

Oesch, D. and Rennwald, L. (2018) 'Electoral competition in Europe's new tripolar political space: Class voting for the left, centre-right and radical right', *European Journal of Political Research*, 57(4), p783–807.

Padgett, S. and Paterson, W.E. (1991) *A history of social democracy in postwar Europe*. London: Longman Publishing Group.

Panitch, L. and Leys, C. (2001) *The end of parliamentary socialism: From new left to New Labour*. Verso.

Pierson, C. (2001) *Hard choices: Social democracy in the twenty-first century*. Oxford: Polity Press.

Piketty, T. (2019) *Capital and ideology*. Cambridge: Harvard University Press.

Pontusson, J. (1995) 'Explaining the decline of European social democracy: The role of structural economic change', *World Politics*, 47(4), p495–533.

Przeworski, A. (1985) *Capitalism and social democracy*. Cambridge: Cambridge University Press.

Przeworski, A. and Sprague, J.D. (1986) *Paper stones: A history of electoral socialism*. Chicago: University of Chicago Press.

Rennwald, L. (2020) *Social democratic parties and the working class*. London: Palgrave MacMillan.

Rennwald, L. and Evans, G. (2014) 'When supply creates demand: Social democratic party strategies and the evolution of class voting', *West European Politics*, 37(5), p1108–1135.

Rennwald, L. and Pontusson, J. (2021) 'Paper stones revisited: Class voting, unionization and the electoral decline of the mainstream left', *Perspectives on Politics*, 19(1), p36–54.

Rueda, D. (2007) *Social democracy inside out: Partisanship and Labor market policy in industrialized democracies*. Oxford: Oxford University Press.

Sassoon, D. (1996) *One hundred years of socialism: The West European left in the twentieth century*. London: I.B. Tauris.

Scharpf, F.W. (1991) *Crisis and choice in European social democracy*. Ithaca: Cornell University Press.

Schleiter, P., Böhmelt, T., Ezrow, L. and Lehrer, R. (2021) 'Social democratic party exceptionalism and transnational policy linkages', *World Politics*, 73(3), p512–544.

Schwander, H. and Manow, P. (2017) 'Modernize and die'? German social democracy and the electoral consequences of the Agenda 2010', *Socio-Economic Review*, 15(1), p117–134.

Sloam, J. (2005) 'West European social democracy as a model for transfer', *Journal of Communist Studies and Transition Politics*, 21(1), p67–83.

Stephens, J.D. (1979) *The transition from capitalism to socialism*. London: Macmillan.

Streeck, W. (2014) *Buying time: The delayed crisis of democratic capitalism*. London: Verso.

Swenson, P. (1989) *Fair shares: Unions, pay, and politics in Sweden and West Germany*. Cornell University Press.

Weyland, K., Madrid, R.L. and Hunter, W. (eds.) (2010) *Leftist governments in Latin America: Successes and shortcomings*. Cambridge: Cambridge University Press.

Whiteley, P., Poletti, M. and Bale, T. (2019) 'Oh Jeremy Corbyn! Why did Labour Party membership soar after the 2015 general election?', *The British Journal of Politics and International Relations*, 21(1), p80–98.

15
RADICAL LEFT PARTIES

Daniel Keith and Luke March

Some 30 years after the collapse of state socialism in the Soviet Union, it is an exciting time to study RLPs. Although long neglected by political scientists, RLP research is a fast expanding field. RLPs have drawn attention from party scholars for many reasons, several related to the aftermath of the 2008 financial crisis and the electoral successes of RLPs including Syriza, Podemos and La France Insoumise. The 2008 financial crisis brought questions regarding RLP left populism, relations with extra-parliamentary protests, opposition to austerity and organisational innovation to the fore (Calossi 2016). Comparative scholarship on wider political trends including Euroscepticism and the apparent 'populist surge' also encouraged the study of RLPs. It is not overstating matters to say that 'not since the 1970s has the parliamentary road to socialism been so relevant' (Evans 2015).

The chapter begins by analysing the significant progress made in conceptualising the boundaries of this party family. It proceeds by surveying research on RLP electoral success and their impact and in doing so highlights emerging debates in these areas. However, comparative research on RLPs remains relatively underdeveloped (Keith and March 2023). Therefore, the chapter draws attention to (often overlooked) studies which have presented classifications and measures of RLP performance which can facilitate comparative analysis (e.g. on RLP Euroscepticism, organisational strength, intra-party democracy). It ends by identifying considerable empirical gaps on several parties, particularly those beyond Western Europe. It is argued that greater dialogue with the wider comparative literature on political parties can help to advance the relatively weak theorisation in RLP research. The chapter explores how wider party research would also benefit from greater sensitivity to the diversity detailed in research on RLPs.

How have RLPs been conceptualised?

This section outlines the substantial progress made in conceptualising RLPs. It shows how this was complicated by the radical left's pronounced heterogeneity and often ambiguous positions (i.e. promoting anti-capitalism while working through liberal democratic political institutions [Hudson 2012]).

Studies of the disintegration of the communist party family in Western Europe in the late 1980s highlighted their diverse trajectories. Some retained Marxism-Leninism but others repositioned themselves as non-communist left parties, joined other party families or disbanded.

This diversity prompted scholars to question whether research could still find reasons to study its (former) members alongside one another (Bull 1994). Research on east central Europe highlighted how several former ruling communist parties embraced centre-left positions in an attempt to regain power (Grzymala-Busse 2002). Parties to the left of social democracy subsequently received little attention, even though some publications emphasised their relevance and search for renewal through embracing the Global Justice Movement and left-populist leaders including Hugo Chávez (Hudson 2000).

RLPs have been relatively hard to define using conventional criteria for identifying party families (e.g. Mair and Mudde 1998). RLP *names* encompass a variety of terms (e.g. left, workers, labour, socialist, communist, militant, revolutionary) and can be vague (La France Insoumise [France Unbowed] or Podemos [We Can]). RLPs developed *transnational links* through the Left in the European Parliament – GUE/NGL[1] group and the Party of the European Left (EL). However, despite some consolidation, research has shown RLP transnational links are 'nothing like a new International' (March 2012, 22) and play relatively limited roles in shaping RLP campaigns (Dunphy and March 2019). Moreover, at transnational level, RLPs remain divided. Some parties remain outside the EL (e.g. Podemos) and have other affiliations including 'Now the People!' formed in opposition to Syriza's austerity policies. Diversity is also evident in RLP *origins* (e.g. the communist movement, other parties, the new left), and their *ideology and support* (discussed later).

March and Mudde's (2005) attempt to map the landscape of Europe's radical left was a turning point in RLP research. It advanced key definitions, theories and development of a pan-European research agenda. Importantly, this study recognised that RLPs constituted a party family connected by historical ties, ideology and organisational commonalities and reconciled this with the aforementioned heterogeneity through categorising RLPs into subtypes.

March and Mudde (2005) defined RLPs as *left* by their commitment to equality and internationalism; and as *radical* in their aspirations for the fundamental transformation of capitalism. There are advantages in using the term 'radical left'. First, it is also used by many radical left actors (e.g. Syriza [Coalition of the Radical Left]) even if not all RLPs endorse its use. Second, the term 'left' has been associated with several principles, aims and strategies. However, as Bobbio (1996) argued, the core of the left-right distinction is found in their divergent attitudes to equality – for the left inequalities are unnatural, socially produced and eliminable through state action. Accordingly, the radical left identifies economic inequity as the basis for existing arrangements, and espouses collective economic and social rights as its agenda (March 2011, 316).

Third, the term 'radical' has origins in the Latin *radix* ('root'). Its use in this sense by Marx as 'grasping things by the root' (quoted in March 2012, 23) helps to capture the radical left's broad aspiration for 'root-and-branch' systemic transformation (of national political systems, the international system and capitalism). The desire to radically transform and not just reform contemporary capitalism remains the key distinction between RLPs and social democratic parties (SDPs) and Green parties, who partially share aspirations to equality, internationalism and anti-neoliberalism. Consequently, RLPs 'define themselves as *to the left of*, and not merely *on the left of* social democracy, which they see as insufficiently left-wing or even as not left-wing at all' (March 2008, 3). In this way, 'radical' has not just a *substantive* meaning but also a *relational* one.

Most studies now either employ the term 'radical left' (e.g. Bull 2019) or are generally consistent with March and Mudde's definition even if they do not share all of its nuances. There is broad agreement over the core members of the party family, notwithstanding debates over the radical left credentials of some parties (e.g. Sinn Féin). However, the term 'radical' has been criticised (e.g. Calossi 2016). The main objections are that it is pejorative/normative, contested by some RLPs and shared with other parties (e.g. social liberals including the French Parti Radical de Gauche). Yet it remains preferable to use extrinsic heuristic criteria to conceptualise the radical left rather than rely on activists' intrinsic self-descriptions (which risk multiple claims over who are real leftists).

A plethora of alternative terms exist in the literature (e.g. 'far left', 'extreme left', 'anti-capitalist', 'anti-neo-liberal', 'workers parties') but 'radical left' is far less problematic than these alternatives which lack specificity and overlook differences between RLPs (Keith, March and Escalona 2023). For instance, the term 'anti-capitalist' fails to distinguish between the pure anti-capitalists (who utterly reject private property, profit incentives or co-operation with capitalist forces), and anti-neoliberals (who emphasise reforming capitalism in a largely Keynesian fashion). Writers have brought attention to the 'anti-austerity left' (Calossi 2016) and 'movement parties' (della Porta et al. 2017). However, these definitions risk overlooking important differences between RLPs. For example, RLP opposition to austerity has been contingent on context (see later). These definitions also gloss over differences between RLPs and other parties (e.g. those with similar forms of linkage).

Scholars have devised several classifications to account for the considerable diversity of RLPs. The most commonly used typology is derived from the one presented by March and Mudde (2005) subsequently developed in several iterations. Thus Keith and March 2023 identify four RLP subtypes:

- *Conservative communists* which defend the Soviet tradition and define themselves as Marxist-Leninist (e.g. Communist Party of Greece (KKE) and the Portuguese Communist Party). These parties organise themselves according to Leninist democratic centralism (which upheld the principle that the minority was subordinate to the majority).
- *Reform communists* which retain elements of the communist model (e.g. traditional organisational linkages), but differ from Conservative communists in their ideological and strategic positions, particularly in being more open to governmental participation, the market economy and elements of the post-1968 'new left' agenda (e.g. AKEL in Cyprus).
- *Democratic socialists* which adopt a position distinct from both communism (which they often view as authoritarian or obsolete) and social democracy (seen as insufficiently left or 'neoliberal'). They are a broad church with some (e.g. the Dutch Socialist Party [SP]) being arguably little distinct from left-wing social democrats with a greater accent on anti-neoliberalism and extra-parliamentary mobilisation. Others (e.g. the Danish Red-Green Alliance) more fully combine 'old left' emphases on economic equality and redistribution with 'new left' themes (e.g. environmentalism and emphasis on grassroots participation in decision-making).
- *Revolutionary extreme left parties* which are generally inspired by Leninism, Trotskyism or Maoism (e.g. Ireland's People Before Profit). They share the conservative communists' adherence to elements of the Soviet model and highly centralised organisations but generally reject them as bureaucratic and doctrinaire 'Stalinists'. They often promote sectarianism towards other parties and reject parliamentary politics. Instead, their revolutionary views find expression in calls for a 'rupture' with capitalism involving mass insurrection.

Versions of this typology have been applied widely in other studies. Yet it has been contested. Some argue that divisions between traditional and new left issues best capture the fault-lines separating RLPs (Gomez, Morales and Ramiro 2016). However, these categories risk overlooking important ideological differences (e.g. between communist and non-communists). Others find RLPs can combine elements of different subtypes (Chiocchetti 2017). We agree that the typology should not be seen as rigid or unchangeable – sometimes parties do move between categories – it is also important not to reify such categories, which do not always translate exactly into divisions among the radical left. However, the typology provides a heuristic device for illuminating a complex reality. Its usefulness is underscored by its ability to classify most electorally relevant (and extra-parliamentary) RLPs (Keith and March 2023).

Research has detailed a trend towards programmatic de-radicalisation as several RLPs tried to transform themselves into credible electoral competitors (Fagerholm 2017). Few RLPs now emphasise revolution. However, differences between party subtypes remain relevant and have shaped (often in combination with contextual and strategic factors) important policy differences between RLPs, for example, over socio-cultural policy and the environment (Keith and March 2023). Research has also shown how RLP subtypes have developed varied links to social movements (Tsakatika and Lisi 2013).

Electoral performance

Overall, RLPs lost votes following the collapse of the Soviet Union but made a limited recovery after the late 1990s (March 2012). RLPs on average won 8.8 per cent of the vote in parliamentary elections from 2000 to 2019 in 19 European countries (Keith and March 2023). However, since the 2008 financial crisis, different interpretations of RLP electoral trajectory emerged. Some identified a resurgence in radical left support (della Porta 2018); others found increased volatility with initial gains offset by subsequent losses (Chiocchetti 2017) or detected only a marginal overall 'crisis bounce' with cases of expansion (e.g. France, Greece, Moldova) offset by losses elsewhere (e.g. Czechia and Cyprus) (Keith and March 2023).

Emergent research on RLP electoral performance has started to explain such variation through a combination of 'demand-side' factors (socio-economic and electoral variables); 'external supply-side' factors (party-system and institutional factors); and 'internal supply-side' factors (intra-party dynamics) (March and Rommerskirchen 2015).

Research suggests RLP electoral success is rooted in demand-side factors. RLPs are found to succeed in countries where: relatively more voters identify with radical left ideals; there is a strong history of class cleavages; and high levels of Euroscepticism boost protest sentiment (March 2011). RLPs also gain support in poor economic conditions and where elites are seen to have imposed austerity measures (Keith and March 2016). More broadly, the moves to a post-industrial economy and globalisation have been linked with increased insecurity and success for anti-establishment parties (March 2012). When such factors are widespread, demand for RLPs should be the assumption not the puzzle.

Demand might be a necessary condition for RLP success, but research suggests it is not always sufficient (March and Rommerskirchen 2015). For instance, some RLPs lost votes in elections strongly affected by the 2008 financial crisis (Keith and March 2016). Indeed, RLPs often fail to translate support for radical left ideology into votes (March 2016). Thus, the central puzzle in RLP electoral performance and a challenge for research is to explain why demand is rarely met with consistent supply (March 2011).

Supply-side factors have been seen as the main *catalyst* for RLP success (Keith and March 2016). These include external supply side factors, for example, party competition. Social democrats are RLPs' main electoral competitors and tend to dominate the left across Europe (with some exceptions, e.g. Cyprus). When RLPs experience significant electoral gains, it is usually at the cost of centre-left rivals (March 2011).

Therefore, it is problematic that few in-depth comparative studies of RLP-SDP competition exist. Yet the literature offers several diverging perspectives which require further testing.

To some, the neo-liberal trajectory of SDPs created a vacuum of representation to the left of social democracy which RLPs could exploit through: adopting more defensible, welfarist positions (Arter 2002) or by exchanging communist dogma for traditional social democratic appeals (March and Mudde 2005). However, Chiocchetti finds such strategies deliver small or unsustainable electoral gains (2017). Others see RLP programmatic moderation to be more conducive to electoral expansion when SDPs move leftwards thereby legitimising left-wing policies (Krause 2020); or associate electorally successful RLPs with 'challenger' strategies based on differentiation from SDPs (Balampanidis et al. 2021).

RLPs increasingly face competition from other radical parties. Most importantly, competition with the greens and radical right parties may affect RLP vote share (March and Rommerskirchen 2011). Few publications have analysed these processes but initial studies (e.g. Hansen and Olsen 2021) provide a platform for wider comparative analysis.

Small parties are generally weakened by systems with high electoral thresholds and RLPs are no exception (March and Rommerskirchen 2015). Some RLPs also face legal restrictions (e.g. in post-communist countries including Latvia). While RLPs are expected to fare better in proportional electoral systems, studies provide mixed findings (March and Rommerskirchen 2011). Nonetheless, research increasingly shows how judicious exploitation of external conditions is necessary for RLP success.

Several internal supply-side factors have been linked with RLP electoral performance. Party history and origins are relevant: where RLPs were historically weak (e.g. Austria) they remain weak (March 2011). In east central Europe, some RLPs successfully tapped into nostalgia for the Soviet era. However, in countries where communist successor parties took a centrist trajectory RLPs often lack a significant presence (March 2016).

The impact of organisational variables upon RLP electoral performance is relatively unexplored. However, research presents several arguments which require wider analysis. RLPs following democratic centralism have been associated with electoral underperformance and strategic ossification (Keith and March 2016). Conversely, RLPs embracing an organisational model resembling the green belief in *Basisdemokratie* (grassroots democracy and a rejection of hierarchy) have sometimes been hampered by dissent and excessive debate (March 2011). Studies have also stressed the role of professionalisation or centralisation of party organisations in making RLPs more responsive to their environment (March and Rommerskirchen 2015).

RLP electoral performance has also been linked to the skills and attributes of their leaders (March 2011). Some RLPs have had popular, pragmatic and media-savvy leaders. Moreover, leader charisma has been linked to the electoral performance of populist parties (Pappas 2016). Research is therefore needed to systematically investigate such variables despite the challenges in their operationalisation.

Drawing on research on radical right parties, March (2011) established benchmarks for assessing RLP electoral performance based on their vote share in parliamentary elections: *unsuccessful* (<3 per cent), *moderately successful* (3–10 per cent), and *successful* (>10 per cent). Ideological differences have been linked to RLP electoral performance. On average, only the democratic socialist subtype can be classified as *successful* while conservative and reform communists are *moderately successful* and revolutionary extreme left parties are *unsuccessful* (Keith and March 2023).

Party strategies are also relevant. First, following research on party goals (Strom and Müller 1999) some RLPs appear content with predominantly policy-seeking niche positions, but most electorally significant RLPs are office-seekers. Second, research has highlighted how in several countries RLPs formed electoral alliances as they sought to broaden their appeal (Chiocchetti 2017). However, elsewhere RLPs continually fail to unify in common campaigns (e.g. Portugal).

The study of RLP electoral performance *as parties* remains in its relative infancy, but scholars have made many advances in using individual-level data to examine the characteristics of radical left *voters*. Studies suggest RLP voters are more likely to: identify as working class, be trade union members, not follow a religion, feel dissatisfied with democracy and have negative opinions of the EU (Ramiro 2016).

However, this literature highlights multiple exceptions, complexities and features interesting debates on RLP electorates. For instance, research on the relationship between social class and RLP voting presents nuanced findings. Being a manual worker is not a strong predictor of voting RLP (Beaudonnet and Gomez 2017). Several 'new left' parties have also gained disproportionate support from the middle classes (Oesch 2012).

RLPs perform better in poor economic conditions (Gomez and Ramiro 2019), which might be expected given their emphasis on socio-economic issues (March and Rommerskirchen 2015). RLP support has been linked to protest voting when economic conditions worsen and welfare recipients have been seen to be a key constituency (March 2008; Chiocchetti 2017). However, research provides different findings on multiple variables in shaping RLP performance, including unemployment and support from low income groups (and more broadly education and age) (e.g. Visser et al. 2014; Ramiro 2016; Beaudonnet and Gomez 2017). Some also question whether gender affects a voter's chances of voting radical left (Beaudonnet and Gomez 2017); others find this varies between countries (Ramiro 2016).

The degree of overlap between RLP and radical right party electorates is also contested. Scholars have detected commonalities (Visser et al. 2014) but others find RLP voters are more egalitarian and diametrically opposed to radical right party voters on immigration (Rooduijn et al. 2017) and cultural issues (Ramiro 2016). Rooduijn et al. (2017) find that while RLPs and radical right parties fish in the same pool of 'the losers of globalisation', they attract different segments of it.

These debates support Ramiro's (2016) assessment that RLP electorates in Europe are heterogeneous. Indeed, the RLP subtypes have been associated with different electorates. For instance, March (2011) found that communist parties attracted relatively more older, working class, male and less educated voters than democratic socialists. Similarly, Gomez, Morales and Ramiro (2016, 18) find voters of 'new left' RLPs (roughly corresponding to the democratic socialist subtype) were more highly educated and more likely to be secular than those of 'traditional' RLPs. Such findings raise questions as to why some RLPs are more successful in attracting particular constituencies or in building broad coalitions.

Governing and impact on mainstream politics

Following the collapse of the Soviet Union several RLPs moved from being marginal pariahs to being brought 'in from the cold' to gain inclusion in (centre-left) governments (Bale and Dunphy 2011). Most electorally relevant RLPs in Europe have held power through supporting minority governments, participating in coalitions and occasionally leading governments (Keith and March 2023). However, some RLPs have not overcome obstacles that include their own intransigence, the absence of a left parliamentary majority and the ability of their politicians to build a working relationship with SDP counterparts (Olsen, Hough and Koß 2010).

Research finds that governing has been a difficult experience for RLPs. There is almost a consensus that RLPs leave office with limited policy achievements (e.g. Olsen, Hough and Koß 2010; Katsourides 2016), despite some exceptions (De Giorgi and Cancela 2021). Several RLPs participated in centre-left coalitions to 'pull' SDPs to the left. However, Olsen, Hough and Koß (2010) find that differences in RLP and SDP policy positions do not tend to narrow when they cooperate in government. Moreover, inexperienced RLPs have often been out-manoeuvred by coalition partners (Dunphy 2007).

Governing RLPs are often junior coalition partners with too few ministers to enact major changes. However, governments led by RLPs also struggled to enact progressive or lasting structural reforms. Katsourides' (2016, 148) analysis of the AKEL and Syriza governments finds that participation in office amounted to 'one step forward, two steps back' as they encountered the constraints of office and appeared little different from SDPs. Several other governing RLPs also enacted austerity cuts or privatisations (e.g. in Iceland and Moldova). To Chiocchetti (2017), Syriza's experience highlighted that RLPs could do little to challenge neo-liberalism due to constraints imposed by EU institutions.

Different perspectives exist on how to judge RLP performance in office. Some adopt *maximalist* criteria and assess RLPs on their radical credentials and most demanding goals, for example, transforming capitalism. On this basis, governing RLPs are seen to have a record ranging from negative to catastrophic (Chiocchetti 2017). Others adopt less demanding *minimalist* criteria. For example, Olsen, Hough and Koß (2010) argue that entering government has been contingent on weakening the influence of the centre-right, defending against neo-liberal reforms, and demonstrating that RLPs are not a wasted vote. This approach suggests RLP achievements, although limited, are not negligible and have included incremental increases in welfare benefits, dilution of privatisations and progressive social legislation (March 2012).

Most RLPs stayed the course in government (or support roles) despite exceptions (e.g. in Sweden, Portugal, Finland). Nevertheless, scholars have shown that RLPs usually suffer incumbency losses at subsequent elections. Some writers detect substantial losses and so question why RLPs continue to seek office (Chiocchetti 2017). However, others find losses are usually significant, but not disastrous with estimates ranging from 14 to 25 per cent of average RLP vote share (Olsen, Hough and Koß 2010; March 2011).

The radical left has moved from 'Marxism to the mainstream' as it increasingly exploited issues of mainstream concern (e.g. surrounding globalisation) (March 2008). Accordingly, wider comparative studies took greater interest in how RLPs influence politics through opposing European integration and their populism. These areas provide important avenues for research, although there remains a need to account for how these processes (and RLP 'mainstreaming' more broadly) have been shaped by the radical left's considerable diversity (Keith and March 2022).

Research highlights the significant role RLPs played in opposing European integration, that is, the European Constitution and the Transatlantic Trade and Investment Partnership (Keith 2016), and how competition with RLPs has shaped the European policies of mainstream parties (Williams and Ishiyama 2018). However, RLP research has attempted to qualify the tendency in wider comparative studies on Euroscepticism to label RLPs as 'Eurosceptic' while overlooking the wide variation in their approaches to European integration (March 2018). While most (but not all) RLPs accept EU membership, they present diverging calls for an 'alternative Europe' and the restructuring of EU institutions. Some RLPs oppose the EU but favour *greater* transnational integration (Dunphy and March 2019). Several parties also deepened their Euroscepticism following the 2008 financial crisis. Moreover, scholars found some RLPs adopted a new type of Euroscepticism based on *disobedience* of EU policies (Bortun 2022). The sources of RLP Euroscepticism also vary with debate surrounding the role played by nationalism, socialist ideology and strategic motives (see Van Elas, Hakhverdian and Van der Brug 2016).

The populist 'surge' affecting liberal democracies brought attention to those RLPs known to promote populist appeals. This literature has started to examine RLP impact within parliament (Otjes and Louwerse 2015) and democratic systems (Huber and Schimpf 2017). However, foremost have been questions concerning the inherent similarities between left and right-wing populist parties' programmes (and voters). Some detect a significant degree of overlap with populism now defining the radical left's appeal:

> the contemporary radical left in Western Europe is generally populist. Our explanation is that many contemporary radical left parties are not traditionally communist or socialist (anymore). They do not focus on the 'proletariat', but glorify a more general category: the 'good people'. Moreover, they do not reject the system of liberal democracy as such, but only criticise the political and/or economic elites within that system.
> (Rooduijn and Akkerman 2017, 193).

This argument chimes with expert survey data that indicates 'far left' parties promote anti-elitist views more than other parties (Polk et al. 2017). Indeed, scholars have emphasised the apparently transversal nature of populism for the radical left (Gomez, Morales and Ramiro 2016). However, some (including the present authors) have argued that socialism often remains dominant as 'the host ideology' alongside populism (Keith and March 2016). Research is also starting to identify diversity in RLP populism (Dar 2022). Such findings have important implications for those studying its wider impact.

Conclusions and avenues for further research

Since the collapse of the Soviet Union research has highlighted rapid changes within the radical left: RLPs have experienced programmatic deradicalisation, gained in electoral relevance, expanded their presence in government and sometimes pursued organisational innovation. Therefore, RLPs are positioned at the forefront of cutting-edge research on populism, party change, emerging models of party organisation and party–movement linkages (Lourenço 2021). Scholars are increasingly finding reasons to compare RLPs to other party families. This presents researchers working on the radical left with opportunities to contribute to wider party research. However, this chapter also highlighted reasons for comparative party research to pay more attention to the diversity highlighted in RLP research.

Studies of RLPs have prioritised thick contextual description (e.g. Backes and Moreau 2008) and the single case literature has often failed to relate findings to outcomes elsewhere. In this context, those studying the radical left have even more to gain from increased dialogue with the wider discipline. While the literature on RLPs is fast expanding, comparative research is underdeveloped. Therefore, this chapter identified several classifications of RLPs and measures of their performance which provide (unrealised) opportunities for comparative research. It has also been rare for RLP research to build on concepts, categorisations and theories designed to study other parties, although this is demonstrably beneficial (March 2012).

Thus there remains a need to update, deepen and broaden the empirical information available and to test hypotheses already advanced (Keith and March 2016). For instance, several RLPs are under-studied, including some covered in the earlier literature (e.g. in Russia and Finland), those only rarely analysed (e.g. in Iceland, Luxemburg, Slovenia) and newer parties (e.g. in North Macedonia). The scope of research can be broadened through paying greater attention to dependent variables beyond electoral success (and also cases of failure).

The field has taken important steps towards the pan-European study of RLPs. However, most studies still focus largely on EU countries even when incorporating non-EU European RLPs into analysis has been shown to be useful. Comparative research should also pay greater attention to RLPs beyond Europe and emergent literature on them. For example, studies of

RLP electoral performance should assess electorally relevant RLPs elsewhere (Argentina, India, Israel and Japan) and examples of failure (Australia, USA and Canada).

Several reviews have helped to steer the development of research on RLPs through identifying important gaps and research questions (e.g. March 2018; Lourenço 2021). Elsewhere, we have identified the need for relevant research on RLPs that explains their overall limited progress in overcoming longstanding challenges including their electoral underperformance, low policy impact and fragile international cooperation (Keith and March 2023). An alternative approach is to prioritise the weakest areas in RLP research. March (2013) identified these as: 1) RLP organisations; 2) RLPs in the extra-parliamentary realm; 3) the radical left and populism; 4) RLPs and gender politics. The profusion of research in the last decade reflects progress in each area; however, these literatures still require development, particularly the latter.

There are few comparative studies explicitly focused on RLP organisations, that is, attempts to measure their levels of intra-party democracy (Charalambous 2021a) and organisational strength (Chiocchetti 2017). This is problematic when organisational issues are not abstract but have practical relevance. Many communist parties cling to versions of democratic centralism. Although this organisational model was once widely criticised for entrenching dogmatism and bureaucratism, it is surprising its contemporary manifestations are rarely analysed (e.g. Keith and Charalambous 2016).

The organisational models of non-communist RLPs are relatively unexplored. RLPs often claim to promote grassroots participation but research is needed to detail their organisational diversity. The high degree of internal hierarchy found in some parties requires explanation (e.g. the SP). The 'movement parties', including Podemos, that emerged with intimate links with anti-austerity movements and which promoted online direct democracy have attracted substantial attention. However, their attempts to promote participation require long-term analysis – especially as research questions their ability to innovate or to avoid institutionalisation and professionalisation (e.g. Lisi 2019). It is unclear how far such changes have been adopted by RLPs elsewhere. Research is needed at grassroots and elite levels. Relatively little is known about RLP members and activists and few RLP leaders have been studied systematically although research highlights their influence on processes of change within RLPs (Keith and March 2023).

Tsakatika and Lisi's (2013) landmark publication on RLP links with extra-parliamentary groups advanced the study of RLPs' 'environmental' linkages. Wennerhag, Fröhlich and Piotrowski (2018) also bridged the literatures between RLPs and radical left movements and Charalambous (2021b) analysed the history of RLP linkage. However, there is much left to research. Empirically, there are several new cases emerging, particularly new left parties in south east Europe (e.g. Slovenia, North Macedonia, Croatia). Broader questions of the organisational and electoral impact of RLP engagements with social movements require investigation. RLPs which exist in the extra-parliamentary realm have also rarely been studied (e.g. Kelly 2018).

With the rise of Syriza, Podemos and La France Insoumise, interest in left populism has abounded. Unlike longer established RLPs they have adopted a reflexive understanding of left populism which explicitly attempts to develop theory and praxis of populism as a tool for the mobilisation and identity formation of the left (see Chapter 23). The expansion of case studies on high-profile left-populist parties (e.g. Stavrakakis and Katsambekis 2014) enriched the literature. Yet few comparative studies exist on populism and other RLPs (e.g. Katsambekis and Kioupkiolis 2019). This literature may become saturated but it remains underdeveloped compared to with the voluminous output on right populism. Debates are emerging on the conditions under which RLPs promote populism and whether particular parties (e.g. Red-Green Alliance) should be considered populist (Dar 2022). Therefore, it remains necessary to question the often prevailing wisdom that RLPs should be first and foremost understood as populist parties.

There are few studies of gender politics and RLPs. This is problematic when gender equality is a particularly vital issue for the radical left. Formally speaking, as far as positive discrimination goes RLPs appear to be one the most gender-sensitive party families. Many RLPs are committed to formal gender quotas and several identify as feminist. In a rare contribution on RLP (formal) gender representation, Keith and Verge (2018) found some degree of support for this official story but also that RLP subtypes varied in regard to equality promotion (see Chapter 9).

The reality may be quite different. Research identifies a gender gap in RLP support (Spierings and Zaslove 2017). Moreover, studies provide contrasting perspectives on the experience of feminist activists within RLP organisations with some identifying gendered discourses and organisational practices (Kantola and Lombardo 2019; Caravantes 2019). This highlights the need to assess RLP informal organisational practices, culture and attitudes. The paucity of studies on RLPs and gender, ethnicity and LGBTQ+ identities leaves much scope for future research.

Note

1 Named European United Left/Nordic Green Left (GUE/NGL) until January 2021.

References

Arter, D. (2002) "Communists we are no longer, social democrats we can never be": The evolution of the leftist parties in Finland and Sweden', *Journal of Communist Studies and Transition Politics*, 18(3) p1–28.

Backes, U. and Moreau, P. (eds.) (2008) *Communist and post-communist parties in Europe*. Göttingen: Vandenhoeck & Ruprecht.

Balampanidis, I., Vlastaris, I., Xezonakis, G. and Karagkiozoglou, M. (2021) 'Bridges over troubled waters'? The competitive symbiosis of social democracy and radical left in crisis-ridden southern Europe', *Government and Opposition*, 56(1), p59–81.

Bale, T. and Dunphy, R. (2011) 'In from the cold? Left parties and government involvement since 1989', *Comparative European Politics*, 9(3), p269–291.

Beaudonnet, L. and Gomez, R. (2017) 'Red Europe versus no Europe? The impact of attitudes towards the EU and the economic crisis on radical-left voting', *West European Politics*, 40(2), p316–335.

Bobbio, N. (1996) *Left and right: The significance of a political distinction*. Chicago: University of Chicago Press.

Bortun, V. (2022) 'Plan B for Europe: The birth of 'disobedient Euroscepticism'?', *Journal of Common Market Studies*. https://doi.org/10.1111/jcms.13313.

Bull, M.J. (1994) 'The west European communist movement: Past, present and future', in Bull, M.J. and Heywood, P. (eds.) *West European communist parties after the revolutions of 1989*. Basingstoke: Macmillan, pp. 203–222.

Bull, M.J. (2019) 'The radical left since 1989: Decline, transformation, and revival', in Braat, E. and Corduwener, P. (eds.) *1989 and the west: Western Europe since the end of the cold war*. Abingdon: Routledge, pp. 247–265.

Calossi, E. (2016) *Anti-austerity left parties in the European Union. Competition, coordination and integration*. Pisa: Pisa University Press.

Caravantes, P. (2019) 'New versus old politics in Podemos: Feminization and masculinized party discourse', *Men and Masculinities*, 22(3), p465–490.

Charalambous, G. (2021a) '(Il)liberal organisation? Internal party democracy on the European radical left', *Partecipazione e conflitto*, 14(1), p411–434.

Charalambous, G. (2021b) *The European radical left: Movements and parties since the 1960s*. London: Pluto Press.

Chiocchetti, P. (2017) *The radical left party family in Western Europe, 1989–2015*. Abingdon: Routledge.

Dar, O. (2022) 'What is populist about left-wing populism?' Paper presented at PSA Annual Conference, University of York, 13 April.

De Giorgi, E. and Cancela, J. (2021) 'The Portuguese radical left parties supporting government: From policy-takers to policymakers?', *Government and Opposition*, 56(2), p281–300.

Della Porta, D. (2018) 'A resurgence of the radical left? Some notes', in Wennerhag, M., Fröhlich, C. and Piotrowski, G. (eds.) *Radical left movements in Europe*. Abingdon: Routledge, pp. 268–279.

Della Porta, D., Fernández, J., Kouki, H. and Mosca, L. (2017) *Movement parties against austerity*. London: Polity.

Dunphy, R. (2007) 'In search of an identity: Finland's Left Alliance and the experience of coalition government', *Contemporary Politics*, 13(1), p37–55.

Dunphy, R. and March, L. (2019) *The European left party*. Manchester: Manchester University Press.

Evans, B. (2015) 'The rise of Europe's new Left', *Opencanada.org*, 23 February. Available at: www.opencanada.org/features/the-rise-of-europes-new-left/.

Fagerholm, A. (2017) 'What is left for the radical left? A comparative examination of the policies of radical left parties in western Europe before and after 1989', *Journal of Contemporary European Studies*, 25(1), p16–40.

Gomez, R., Morales, L. and Ramiro, L. (2016) 'Varieties of radicalism: Examining the diversity of radical left parties and voters in Western Europe', *West European Politics*, 39(2), p351–379.

Gomez, R. and Ramiro, L. (2019) 'Beyond the 2008 great recession: Economic factors and electoral support for the radical Left in Europe', *Party Politics*, 25(3), p358–368.

Grzymala-Busse, A. (2002) *Redeeming the communist past. The regeneration of communist parties in east central Europe*. Cambridge: CUP.

Hansen, M.A. and Olsen, J. (2021) 'Sibling rivalry: Voters for radical left parties and their competitors in Germany, Sweden, and the Netherlands', *Party Politics*. https://doi.org/13540688211035027.

Huber, R.A. and Schimpf, C.H. (2017) 'On the distinct effects of left-wing and right-wing populism on democratic quality', *Politics and Governance*, 5(4), p146–165.

Hudson, K. (2000) *European communism since 1989: Towards a new European left?* Basingstoke: Palgrave.

Hudson, K. (2012) *The new European left: A socialism for the twenty-first century?* Basingstoke: Palgrave.

Kantola, J. and Lombardo, E. (2019) 'Populism and feminist politics: The cases of Finland and Spain', *European Journal of Political Research*, 58(4), p1108–1128.

Katsambekis, G. and Kioupkiolis, A. (eds.) (2019) *The populist radical left in Europe*. Abingdon: Routledge.

Katsourides, Y. (2016) *Radical left parties in government: The cases of SYRIZA and AKEL*. London: Springer.

Keith, D. (2016) 'Stop TTIP': Towards a transnational Eurosceptic opposing the Transatlantic Trade and Investment Partnership?' in FitzGibbon, J., Leruth, B. and Startin, N. (eds.) *Euroscepticism as a transnational and pan-European phenomenon*. Abingdon: Routledge, pp. 111–126.

Keith, D. and Charalambous, G. (2016) 'On the (non)distinctiveness of Marxism-Leninism: The Portuguese and Greek communist parties compared', *Communist and Post-Communist Studies*, 49(2), p147–161.

Keith, D. and March, L. (2016) 'The European radical left: Past, present, no future?' in March, L. and Keith, D. (eds.) *Europe's Radical Left: From marginality to the mainstream?* London: Rowman and Littlefield, pp. 353–381.

Keith, D. and March, L. (2023) 'Conclusion' in Escalona, F., Keith, D. and March, L. (eds.) *The Palgrave handbook of radical left parties*. London: Palgrave.

Keith, D., March, L. and Escalona, F. (2023) 'Introduction', in Escalona, F., Keith, D. and March, L. (eds.) *The Palgrave handbook of radical left parties*. London: Palgrave.

Keith, D and Verge, T. (2018) 'Nonmainstream left parties and women's representation in western Europe', *Party Politics*, 24(4), p397–409.

Kelly, J. (2018) *Contemporary Trotskyism: Parties, sects and social movements in Britain*. Abingdon: Routledge.

Krause, W. (2020) 'Appearing moderate or radical? Radical left party success and the two-dimensional political space', *West European Politics*, 43(7), p1365–1387.

Lisi, M. (2019) 'Party innovation, hybridization and the crisis: The case of Podemos', *Italian Political Science Review*, 49(3), p245–262.

Lourenço, P. (2021) 'Studying European radical left parties since the fall of the Berlin Wall (1990–2019): A scoping review', *Swiss Political Science Review*, 27(4), p754–777.

Mair, P. and Mudde, C. (1998) 'The party family and its study', *Annual Review of Political Science*, 1(1), p211–229.

March, L. (2008) *Contemporary far left parties in Europe: From Marxism to the mainstream?* Berlin: Friedrich-Ebert-Stiftung.

March, L. (2011) *Radical left parties in Europe*. Abingdon: Routledge.

March, L. (2012) 'Problems and perspectives of contemporary European radical left parties: Chasing a lost world or still a world to win?', *International Critical Thought*, 2(3), p314–339.

March, L. (2013) 'What we know and do not know about the radical left (and what do we want to know?)' paper presented at ECPR General conference, Bordeaux.

March, L. (2016) 'Radical left "success" before and after the Great Recession: Still waiting for the Great Leap Forward?' in March, L. and Keith, D. (eds.) *Europe's radical left: From marginality to the Mainstream?* London: Rowman and Littlefield, pp. 27–50.

March, L. (2018) 'Radical left parties and movements: Allies, associates, or antagonists', in Wennerhag, M., Fröhlich, C. and Piotrowski, G. (eds.) *Radical left movements in Europe*. Abingdon: Routledge, pp. 22–42.

March, L. and Mudde, C. (2005) 'What's left of the radical left? The European radical left after 1989: Decline *and* mutation', *Comparative European Politics*, 3(1), p23–49.

March, L. and Rommerskirchen, C. (2011) 'Explaining electoral success and failure', in March, L. (ed.) *Radical left parties in Europe*. Abingdon: Routledge, pp. 180–200.

March, L. and Rommerskirchen, C. (2015) 'Out of left field? Explaining the variable electoral success of European radical left parties', *Party Politics*, 21(1), p40–53.

Oesch, D. (2012) 'The class basis of the cleavage between the new left and the radical right: An analysis for Austria, Denmark, Norway and Switzerland', in Rydgren, J. (ed.) *Class politics and the radical right*. Abingdon: Routledge, pp. 49–69.

Olsen, J., Hough, D. and Koß, M. (2010) 'Conclusion: Left parties in national governments', in Olsen, J., Koß, M. and Hough, D. (eds.) *Left parties in national governments*. Basingstoke: Palgrave, pp. 173–85.

Otjes, S. and Louwerse, T. (2015) 'Populists in parliament: Comparing left-wing and right-wing populism in the Netherlands', *Political Studies*, 63(1), p60–79.

Pappas, T.S. (2016) 'Are populist leaders 'charismatic"? The evidence from Europe', *Constellations*, 23(3), p378–390.

Polk, J., Rovny, J., Bakker, R., Edwards, E. et al. (2017), 'Explaining the salience of anti-elitism and reducing political corruption for political parties in Europe with the 2014 Chapel Hill Expert Survey Data', *Research & Politics*, 4(1), p1–9.

Ramiro, L. (2016) 'Support for radical left parties in western Europe: Social background, ideology and political orientations', *European Political Science Review*, 8(1), p1–23.

Rooduijn, M., Burgoon, B., van Elsas, E.J. and van de Werfhorst, H.G. (2017) 'Radical distinction: Support for radical left and radical right parties in Europe', *European Union Politics*, 18(4), p536–559.

Rooduijn, M. and Akkerman, T. (2017) 'Flank attacks: Populism and left-right radicalism in western Europe', *Party Politics*, 23(3), p193–204.

Spierings, N. and Zaslove, A. (2017) 'Gender, populist attitudes, and voting: explaining the gender gap in voting for populist radical right and populist radical left parties', *West European Politics*, 40(4), p821–847.

Stavrakakis, Y. and Katsambekis, G. (2014) 'Left-wing populism in the European periphery: the case of SYRIZA', *Journal of Political Ideologies*, 19(2), p119–142.

Strom, K. and Müller, W.C. (1999) 'Political parties and hard choices' in Müller, W.C. and Strom, K. (eds.) *Policy, office or votes? How political parties in western Europe make hard decisions* (Cambridge: CUP), pp. 1–35.

Tsakatika, M. and Lisi, M. (2013) "Zippin' up my boots, goin' back to my roots': Radical left parties in southern Europe', *South European Society and Politics*, 18(1), p1–19.

Van Elsas, E.J., Hakhverdian, A. and Van der Brug, W. (2016) 'United against a common foe? The nature and origins of Euroscepticism among left-wing and right-wing citizens', *West European Politics*, 39(6), p1181–1204.

Visser, M., Lubbers, M., Kraaykamp, G. and Jaspers, E. (2014) 'Support for radical left ideologies in Europe', *European Journal of Political Research*, 53(3), p541–558.

Wennerhag, M., Fröhlich, C. and Piotrowski, G. (eds.) (2018) *Radical left movements in Europe*. Abingdon: Routledge.

Williams, C. and Ishiyama, J. (2018) 'Responding to the left: The effect of far-left parties on mainstream party Euroskepticism', *Journal of Elections, Public Opinion and Parties*, 28(4), p443–466.

16
GREEN PARTIES

Neil Carter

Green parties were first elected to national legislatures in the early 1980s and swiftly established themselves in several West European polities. Today, green parties are represented in around 30 national legislatures, the European Parliament and many more sub-national assemblies, and they have joined national coalition governments in several countries. However, electoral success has been difficult to achieve beyond the industrialised liberal democracies of the global north. With a message about the state of the planet that transcends national borders, the Greens form one of the newest yet probably the most homogeneous of contemporary party families (Ennser 2012, 166–7). Early research on green parties considered the factors explaining their emergence and electoral performance, their commitment to grassroots democracy, factional divisions and tentative first steps into government, with individual country case studies dominating the literature. While these themes persist, there has recently been a growth in comparative quantitative studies and a broadening of themes – examining electoral performance, mainstream party responses, issue ownership, policy impact – although compared to their niche party opponents, the far right, this comparative literature is relatively underdeveloped (see Chapter 11).

This chapter starts by examining key characteristics and defining features of the green party family. It then examines the green party voter base alongside demand and supply side explanations of its electoral performance. Next it assesses the impact of green parties in government before concluding with a discussion of the future prospects for green parties and identifying avenues for future research.

The green party family: ideology and organisation

There is a broad consensus in the literature regarding the categorisation and membership of the green party family, as measured by all four standard approaches to identifying a party family: party name; transnational links; origins and social base; policy and ideology (Mair and Mudde 1998; Ennser 2012). Almost every party that might qualify for membership includes either 'green' or some variation on 'ecologist' in its *name*, while the vast majority belong to *transnational federations* such as the Global Greens or the European Green Party, which share common principles and goals. Indeed, the European Green Party contests elections to the European Parliament on a common manifesto for all green parties across EU member states, and all Green Members of the European Parliament (MEPs) sit in a single parliamentary political group.

Most green parties in Western Europe share common *origins* in the new social movement (NSM) milieu of the late 1960s and 1970s, characterised by a libertarian 'New Left' constituency pursuing cultural innovation and social change. In particular, the broad mix of environmental, peace and leftist groups that formed the anti-nuclear movement was the catalyst for green party formation in Germany, France, Luxembourg and Finland, while the Austrian and Swedish green parties emerged from referendum campaigns against nuclear power (Richardson and Rootes 1995; Frankland, Lucardie and Rihoux 2008). These NSM roots left a distinctive imprint on the organisational structure and the ideology of most green parties (Rüdig and Sajuria 2020). In particular, at their formation, green parties expressed a strong commitment to grassroots democracy, which informed what the prominent German green Petra Kelly called the 'anti-party' party model of organisation.

There is considerable common *ideological* ground regarding green party political principles and policy programmes. Most parties originally modelled their programmes around the four pillars of the German Green Party, which reflected its NSM origins: ecological responsibility, grassroots democracy, social justice and non-violence (Frankland and Schoonmaker 1992, ch. 6). Of course, green parties everywhere emphasise the importance of environmental problems and prioritise ecological sustainability (Talshir 2002; Price-Thomas 2016). Two distinctive ideas underpinning green ideology are the belief that the planet imposes limits to growth and that humans need to re-think the way they treat nature, which together inform a wide-ranging critique of the existing socioeconomic order and the dominant modes of production and consumption. These ideas continue to influence green parties, although they have increasingly adopted more pragmatic policy positions (Blühdorn 2009; van Haute 2016); for example, they have tempered their earlier opposition to economic growth *per se*.

But green parties reject being typecast as single-issue parties. Thus, they embraced grassroots democracy while adopting pacifist foreign policies and liberal positions on issues such as immigration, women's rights and recreational drugs. They like to proclaim that they are 'neither right nor left, but out in front', but in practice, they are widely regarded as left-wing – sometimes earning the (critical) epithet 'water melons' from right-wing opponents, because they are green on the outside but inside they are red (Carter 2013; van Haute 2016). Today, green parties typically present a broad left-wing programme combining radical libertarian positions with more traditional socialist concerns such as expanding the welfare state and education sector, while earlier green priorities such as antimilitarism and decentralisation are somewhat downplayed (Carter 2013; Röth and Schwander 2021). There is some variation within the green party family. Some green parties – as in Finland (Bolin 2016) and Germany (Bürgin and Oppermann 2020) – are located on the centre-left of the left-right scale. Others, as in Belgium (Wavreille and Pilet 2016) and Switzerland (Dolezal 2016), are firmly on the left (Jolly et al. 2022). Green parties in Central and East Europe, such as the Hungarian and Lithuanian Greens, tend to be more centrist on economic issues, although similarly libertarian (Frankland 2016). Expert surveys consistently confirm that green parties are predominantly on the far libertarian end of the GALTAN scale (Carter 2013; Jolly et al. 2022).

Yet, significantly, despite efforts to resist being categorised as a single-issue party, where a green party is well established in the party system research shows that it possesses clear issue ownership over the environment (Walgrave, Lefevere and Tresch 2012; Spoon, Hobolt and de Vries 2014; Christensen, Dahlberg and Martinsson 2015; Abou-Chadi 2016).

Scholars broadly agree that membership of the green party family encompasses parties with a predominantly ecological orientation that are affiliated either to the Global Greens or to the European Greens. This definition includes the Danish Socialist People's Party – a member of the European Greens since 2014 but rooted in a different (socialist) political tradition – and excludes the Latvian Green Party, a socially conservative party associated with nationalist views (Auers 2012), opposition to same-sex marriage and support for former U.S. President Donald Trump, which prompted its expulsion from the European Greens in 2019. It also excludes the Mexican Greens, an opportunistic 'scoundrel' party with little interest in environmental issues (Spoon and Pulido-Gómez 2020).

Explaining green party electoral performance

Green parties have achieved considerable electoral success. In at least 18 countries, mostly in Western Europe, they have contested two or more national elections in succession, secured 3 per cent of the vote and gained representation in the national legislature. Applying these criteria, green parties in ten countries – Austria (excluding a blip in 2017), Belgium, Finland, France, Germany, Luxembourg, the Netherlands, Switzerland, Sweden and New Zealand – have achieved uninterrupted success since the mid-1990s, and some since the 1980s. A second group of parties in Australia, Canada, Colombia, Cyprus, Hungary, Ireland and Norway became established (sometimes precariously) during this century – supplemented by the Danish SSP when it joined the European Greens. Brazil's Green Alliance regularly manages to get Deputies elected, but does not consistently secure 3 per cent of the vote. Significantly, having struggled to break through the 10 per cent barrier in national elections, since 2018 green parties in Australia, Austria, Belgium, Finland, Germany, Luxembourg and Switzerland have done so.

Elsewhere, Green MPs have been elected without the party regularly securing 3 per cent of the vote (e.g. Italy, the UK), have managed success in a single election (e.g. Czechia, Estonia, Rwanda) or as part of wider electoral alliances where it is hard to distinguish a specifically green vote (e.g. Portugal and Spain).

How do we explain the development and electoral performance of green parties, and why are they successful in some countries but not in others? And who votes for the greens? Although the literature on green party electoral performance has tended not to use the terminology of demand and supply side factors (but see Grant and Tilley 2019) – in contrast to scholarship examining far right and radical left parties – in this section, the various explanations are divided into those focusing on voter demands, institutional factors and party competition with a general consensus that some combination of all of these elements is required for a comprehensive understanding of green party electoral performance.

Demand

The emergence of green parties from around 1980 was widely regarded as a manifestation of a broad transformation of industrialised societies that was contributing to the weakening of structural alignments and the emergence of a cluster of issues – the environment, anti-nuclear, peace, feminism, grassroots democracy and alternative lifestyles – associated with a 'new politics' (Poguntke 1993). There are two broad approaches to explaining green voting: the first focuses on value change and the second emphasises structural factors.

The most influential explanation for green party success has been Inglehart's (1977) postmaterialist thesis, which identified a 'silent revolution' involving a fundamental shift in the basic value priorities of young people brought up in the relative prosperity and security of post-war 'Western' industrialised democracies. Inglehart argued that rather than prioritising the material issues of economic growth and redistribution that underpinned traditional class politics, young people reaching adulthood were increasingly engaged by postmaterial quality-of-life issues such as feminism, peace and the environment. This value-shift underpinned the mushrooming of new social movements in the late 1960s/early 1970s, with the environment and anti-nuclear movements later contributing directly to the emergence of green parties (Frankland and Schoonmaker 1992; Poguntke 1993).

Inglehart's thesis has attracted extensive debate, drawing criticism notably for the focus on the pre-adult years, which marginalises the formative independent role of education – especially higher education – and for underestimating the countervailing impact of any adult economic insecurity on values. Indeed, while seven waves of the World Values Survey since the 1980s show increasing levels of postmaterialists in most developed countries, especially in younger generations (Dalton 2020, 94–96), there are few countries where postmaterialists significantly outnumber materialists, and levels of both materialists and postmaterialists often fluctuate significantly between countries and across time (World Values Survey 2022). In short, while values have clearly changed – and continue to do so – it appears that there is no *inexorable* process of inter-generational change leading to the ascendancy of postmaterial values.

Yet if we assume that economic development is a determinant of postmaterialism, then the concentration of successful green parties in richer developed democracies in the global north is consistent with the postmaterialist thesis. A comparative, longitudinal study covering 347 parliamentary elections from 32 countries found strong evidence that as economic development increases so does the green party vote share (Grant and Tilley 2019). A few studies have found a clear correlation between postmaterialism and green voting (Belchior 2010; Miragliotta 2013; Beaudonnet and Vasilopoulos 2014).

Moreover, numerous attitudinal studies show that green voters are located towards the Green-Alternative-Libertarian pole (broadly reflecting postmaterialist values) rather than Traditional-Authoritarian-Nationalism pole of the GALTAN divide (Hooghe, Marks and Wilson 2002). Green voters are much more concerned about environmental issues and support progressive environmental policies more than voters for any other party (e.g. Franklin and Rüdig 1995; Dolezal 2010; Close and Delwit 2016; Marks et al. 2021). They support progressive positions on cultural issues such as immigration, civil unions and legal abortions (Dolezal 2010; Otjes and Krouwel 2015; Close and Delwit 2016; Faas and Klingelhöfer 2019; Satherley et al. 2020). Green voters also generally place themselves on the left of the traditional left-right economic dimension, although usually not on the far left and there is some variation between countries (Dolezal 2010; Close and Delwit 2016; Satherley et al. 2020).

Yet, if green voting is simply a result of value change, how do we explain the distinctive socio-demographic profile of green voters as concentrated among (sections of) the 'new middle class'? European Social Survey (ESS) data from a dozen or more countries consistently reveals that green voters are comparatively younger, more highly educated, urban dwelling, more likely to be female and less attached to the dominant Christian churches (Dolezal 2010; Close and Delwit 2016; Marks et al. 2021). Similar profiles are found in individual country case studies: notably researchers find green voters are disproportionately younger than voters for other parties in Australia (Miragliotta 2013), France (Beaudonnet and Vasilopoulos 2014) and the UK (Dennison 2017), while the strong Green Party performance in the 2021 German federal election saw that it attract more voters aged under 25 and with higher education than any other party (Dw.com 2021).

Thus an alternative structural explanation for green party electoral success suggests that they have achieved stability because of the coalition they have formed with groups of voters who not only share attitudes but a common set of social characteristics (Dolezal 2010). This core green-voting constituency is located among the 'new middle class'; by contrast, farmers, employers, manual workers, unemployed and retired workers are significantly less likely to vote green. However, Dolezal (2010) further distinguishes three groups within the new middle class: managers, technical experts and socio-cultural specialists. He argues that green voting is concentrated among socio-cultural specialists in education, health care and social services who are strongly oriented towards their profession (rather than their organisation) and their clients. Given their emphasis in their work on autonomy and self-actualisation, socio-cultural specialists may be more likely to embrace libertarian values and thus support green parties. A slightly different structural explanation places green voters on the cosmopolitan pole of integration-demarcation cultural cleavage that broadly separates the winners and losers from globalisation, supported by the regular finding that green voters tend to be pro-immigration, although they do not always enthusiastically embrace EU integration (Kriesi et al. 2006).

All these explanations of green party electoral performance see Green political identity as extending beyond a specific concern about the environment; indeed, the environmental programmes of green parties are treated as almost incidental to their electoral performance (Rüdig 2012, 122–3). Yet to bundle up the environment with other postmaterial issues may be misplaced. Many environmental concerns – about the safety of nuclear reactors, or links between air pollution and human health, or between climate change and flooding – might more accurately be defined as material (even existential?) problems associated with personal security and health. Franklin and Rüdig (1995) have speculated about the emergence of a distinctive ecological cleavage and there is some evidence from Germany that it is the salience of the environment, especially opposition to nuclear energy – or proximity to nuclear power stations (Schumacher 2014) – that most sharply distinguishes green voters from supporters of rival parties (Rüdig 2012). However, a study of green voters in New Zealand found very few to be motivated by purely ecological concerns (Cowie, Greaves and Sibley 2015).

Institutional

Postmaterialist and structural theories may be helpful in identifying macro-level factors explaining the performance of green parties across industrialised liberal democracies, but they do not account for differences between countries and across time. Thus the World Values Survey Wave 7 (2017–2020) reported Austria, Canada, Finland, France, Sweden and the USA having virtually identical levels of postmaterialists (between 23.5 and 25.0 per cent), yet green party electoral performance has varied considerably: successful in Austria, Finland and Sweden, mixed success in France, a marginal presence in Canada and markedly unsuccessful in the USA (World Values Survey 2022). To explain such differences, it is helpful to explore how open a political system is to an emerging green party.

The electoral system is critical. Small parties struggle to break into plurality/majoritarian electoral systems that do not translate votes into seats in a broadly proportionate way, which underpins the failure of green parties in Australia, Canada and the UK to secure more than a toehold in their national parliaments. One exception is France, where electoral pacts with the Socialist Party and other leftist parties have secured the election of Europe Ecology/Green (EELV) deputies by giving them a free run against centrist and right-wing opponents. By contrast, successful green parties are all found in proportional electoral systems. New Zealand provides a good example of the impact of the electoral system as its shift from a plurality to proportional representation system in 1996 enabled a dramatic improvement in the electoral performance of the Green Party. Yet a proportional system does not guarantee success, as illustrated by the struggles of green parties across Southern, Central and Eastern Europe (Müller-Rommel 1998; van Haute 2016). On balance, a proportional electoral system maybe a necessary, if not a sufficient, condition for stable green party success (Redding and Viterna 1999).

Green parties have generally performed comparatively better in second order elections for the European Parliament and for sub-national legislatures, which are often characterised by lower turnouts and widespread protest voting that together may benefit small parties. Federal systems seem to have contributed to the development of strong green parties in Austria, Belgium, Germany and Switzerland by providing multiple opportunities to get representatives elected and for those representatives to demonstrate they were credible and competent (Müller-Rommel 1998; see also Grant and Tilley 2019). But federalism is also no guarantee of a successful green party, as evidenced by the USA.

Party competition

Green party performance is shaped by the national context, notably the structure of party competition. Kitschelt (1988) categorised green parties and new left parties as left-libertarian parties that had flourished by mobilising new political demands arising from structural changes in advanced industrialised democracies. Left-libertarian parties criticise the priority given to economic growth, market forces, elitist policy-making and the bureaucratic welfare state. They advocate solutions that combine a leftist concern with equality and solidarity with a libertarian commitment to individual autonomy, popular participation and decentralisation. Kitschelt (1988) argued that established new left parties, such as the Danish and Norwegian Socialist People's Parties (SPP), revamped their programmes in the 1980s to become left-libertarian parties, enabling them to stymie nascent green parties by appealing to a similar voter profile. Elsewhere, notably in Austria, Belgium and Germany, green parties flourished in the absence of competitor left-libertarian parties.

Subsequently, green parties have sometimes found themselves in competition with radical left parties, especially those that emphasise environmental issues (although Wang and Keith (2020) show that radical left parties are very diverse in their commitment to environmentalism). Some RLPs appeal to a similar constituency of young, secular, urban and educated voters (Ramiro 2016). Indeed, two comparative studies find a trade-off between support for radical left and green parties (March and Rommerskirchen 2011; Grant and Tilley 2019). However, despite some similarities radical left parties do not identify with the green party family: they place less emphasis on environmental issues, some adopt socially conservative positions on cultural issues, and low skilled workers still provide their core voters (Ramiro 2016; see also Chapter 15).

Green fortunes are also shaped by the actions of mainstream parties. Kitschelt (1988, 216–8) observed that long periods of government participation by socialist parties in the 1970s were positively associated with the formation of significant green parties in Austria, Belgium and West Germany, because these ruling leftist governments antagonised left-libertarian voters and showed little evidence of responding positively to their new demands (see also Redding and Viterna 1999). Later, Meguid (2008) emphasised the importance of mainstream party responses towards the key issue of a niche party – the environment for a green party – in shaping its electoral success. She identified three types of mainstream party strategy – adversarial, dismissive and accommodative – which can be applied in different combinations in any party system. Meguid found that where both mainstream parties either ignored (dismissive) or adopted (accommodative) the environmental issue the green party vote declined.

A more comprehensive comparative study of green parties over a longer period concluded that the effectiveness of mainstream party accommodative strategies may depend on the age of green parties. They seem to work best early in a green party's development, but as it becomes established over several elections, further accommodative strategies simply raise the salience of environmental issues to the likely benefit of the issue-owning green party (Grant and Tilley 2019).

Green parties are also agents in shaping their own destiny. When green parties first burst onto the political stage, their unconventional 'anti-party' party model probably limited their electoral appeal. This 'amateur-activist' organisational model initially characterised 'practically all Green parties' (Rihoux and Frankland 2008, 266) and led green parties to experiment with various radical initiatives designed to protect the power of the grassroots membership. While some innovations, such as the enforced mid-term rotation of elected MPs, were rapidly discarded, some persist, for example, several green parties bar individuals from holding parliamentary and party offices simultaneously. A process of professionalisation saw party cadres reform some of these 'inefficient' democratic mechanisms. Yet green parties today still *look* different from most other parties – and in ways that may have growing electoral appeal. Thus positive gender discrimination ensures that women play a prominent role in all green parties, typically making up around half the parliamentary group (Keith and Verge 2018). Several green parties also have joint (gender-balanced) leaders, or spokespersons, rather than the traditional single party leader. Moreover, support for grassroots democracy remains strong, especially among members identifying as left-wing, social movement oriented and pacifist (Rüdig and Sajuria 2020).

Green parties have also frequently suffered from very public internal conflicts, such as the Fundi-Realo divide that sometimes threatened to tear the German Greens apart (Frankland and Schoonmaker 1992; Poguntke 1993), while in France, the green party(ies) in the 1990s was almost destroyed by factionalism (Doherty 2002, 101–104). Green parties have become steadily more 'professional' and moderated their programmes, with the aim of broadening their electoral appeal. Of course, divisions still happen. Several resignations and splits contributed to the collapse of the Austrian Green Party vote in 2017 when it failed to get any MPs elected, although just two years later it bounced back to enter government for the first time. Indeed, this growing willingness of green parties to join government coalitions can have a major (negative) electoral impact, as green parties generally perform less well in the next election (Little 2016). Finally, several high-profile green politicians have gained notable national popularity, including Joschka Fischer (Germany) and Alexander Van der Bellen (Austria), which has contributed to the strong electoral performance of their parties.

Government participation and impact on mainstream politics

Green parties long ago dispensed with their principled objection that joining any coalition would require compromises that would betray radical Green principles for short-term political gains. Subsequently, often apprehensively, green parties have joined coalition governments in more than a dozen countries. Despite the widespread perception of green parties as being left-wing, they have entered national coalitions that are not just 'red-green' (Denmark, France, Germany, Italy and Sweden) but also encompass a range of centrist and/or right-wing parties (Austria, Belgium, Czechia, Finland, Germany, Ireland, Luxembourg and Slovakia), and dozens more at sub-national level. There have also been several instances of green parties supporting minority social democratic/labour governments, including Australia, New Zealand and Sweden (Crowley and Moore 2020). Unusually, in 2020, the New Zealand Green Party formed a cooperation agreement with the majority Labour government, securing the party two non-Cabinet ministerial posts. Indeed, as coalition partners green parties are often allocated a handful of middle/low ranking ministerial portfolios, including the environment ministry (Little 2016). However, greater electoral success has brought more substantial rewards: in Sweden, the Green Party held five or six cabinet positions between 2014 and 2021, including Deputy Prime Minister, and in the 17-strong SDP-Green-FDP German cabinet formed in 2021, there were 5 Green Party ministers, including Vice-Chancellor and Foreign Minister.

The study of green parties in office is quite limited, consisting mainly of a few single country case studies (but see Little 2016), although this body of work is sure to expand as more green parties enter government. As junior coalition partners, green parties inevitably struggle to shape the government policy agenda, but there is evidence that they have exerted some *modest* impact on policy (see Chapter 24). Broad cross-national studies provide mixed results: while Jenson and Spoon (2011) show a link between green party participation in government and lower greenhouse gas emissions, Knill, Debus and Heichel (2010, 326) find that green party participation has no significant positive effect on the number of environmental policies adopted by a country. The clearest evidence of green party impact comes from in-depth comparative and single case studies, which are able to identify specific examples of policy interventions (Poguntke 2002; Evrard 2012; van Haute 2016).

The priority issue for green parties first entering coalitions, reflecting its iconic status for them, was to stop nuclear power, but they gained limited success. Green parties secured legislation to phase-out nuclear power over several decades in Belgium and Germany, but the French Greens had little influence over the Jospin government (Evrard 2012) and although EELV later persuaded President Hollande to reduce to 50 per cent the share of French electricity supplied by nuclear power that commitment was later jettisoned by President Macron. The Finnish Greens have twice resigned from office because they could not prevent government legislation approving the construction of new nuclear reactors, while the Swedish Greens reluctantly agreed to the removal of a stringent nuclear tax. Recently, governing green parties have prioritised climate change, generally pushing hard to introduce or increase eco-taxes and feed-in tariffs, expand renewable energy and strengthen emission reduction targets, yet they have often struggled to influence transport, agriculture and food policy.

In government, green parties have been keen to demonstrate that they are not a single issue party. They have worked with social democrat and liberal coalition partners to implement reforms consistent with their left-libertarian platform, such as providing stronger protections to asylum seekers, rights to illegal immigrants and legal status to same-sex couples. A cross-national study of distributive policies found that the inclusion of green parties in government led to higher spending on social investment (childcare, families and education); in addition, it also prevented retrenchment on social consumption spending and decreases in corporate tax or the rates of top marginal income taxes (Röth and Schwander 2021).

Green parties have also tried to show that they can be trusted to hold government office, as competent ministers and reliable coalition partners. But the coalition experience has often been difficult, with Green leaders trying to negotiate the competing challenges of shaping the government agenda as a junior partner while keeping the party membership happy and also sustaining public support. Difficult decisions such as Fischer's support for NATO air strikes on Serbia in 1999 may have earned public respect, but elsewhere the high rate of defection – green parties have resigned prematurely from coalition governments in Belgium, Czechia, Denmark, Finland, France and Ireland – may have reinforced a reputation for unreliability (Little 2016).

Thus successful green parties have become an increasingly important player in political systems by competing for votes and increasingly helping to shape policy by joining governing coalitions or, as Debus and Tosun (2021) demonstrate, playing an active role in legislatures. Where there is a perceived electoral threat from a green party, there is evidence that mainstream parties accommodate the environmental issue, especially mainstream centre-left parties that are ideologically closer to the greens (Carter 2013; Spoon, Hobolt and de Vries 2014). By contrast, Abou-Chadi (2016) finds that mainstream parties may downplay environmental issues in response to green party issue ownership, although that strategy may become harder to sustain if climate change remains high on the global agenda (see Chapter 24 on climate change).

Conclusions and avenues for further research

Green parties are now well established in many industrialised liberal democracies where they are playing an increasingly important agenda-setting and governing role. They have moved a long way since the 1980s when unorthodox, informally dressed politicians propounded radical policies, and tensions between party leaders and their social movement grassroots often spilled out into public divisions. Green parties have become increasingly professional, and internal tensions have less resonance. They have also become more pragmatic, although this shift can be exaggerated: while some radical proposals have been dropped, on many environmental (e.g. support for renewable energy) and social (e.g. same-sex marriage) issues public opinion has actually moved towards Green positions, so they have become mainstream.

To grow further, green parties must reach beyond their youthful new middle-class core constituency. The political runes appear favourable because the environment and climate change – issues owned by green parties everywhere – are likely to remain high on the political agenda. But green parties cannot rely simply on votes from the environmental 'issue public'. In their favour, it appears that even when green parties decrease their emphasis on the environment over successive elections, they continue to benefit from a 'first mover' advantage that seems to entrench that issue ownership (Bischof 2017, 230). But Bergman and Flatt (2020) found no systemic electoral gains for green parties that have broadened their niche focus beyond the environment. And when green parties do reach out to a wider electorate they have to tread carefully. One comparative European study found that, while green parties are congruent with their voters on environmental issues, they were often the party most distant from their voters on some high-profile social issues such as the liberalisation of soft drugs (Costello et al. 2021, 104, 108); the danger is that such libertarian policies may dissuade voters less concerned about environmental issues from switching to the Greens.

If green parties succeed in broadening their electoral appeal, it would raise some interesting research questions. Although issue ownership is clearly very important there is relatively little survey data available on voter attitudes towards green parties and perceptions of their credibility and competence to deliver on the environment and other issues. If green parties move from niche to mainstream parties then how long will they be able to retain first mover issue ownership of the environment (see Chapter 19)? Can they hold on to new middle-class voters at the same time as they reach out to a broader electorate, or will their programmatic appeal become confused? And can they imbue young voters with green party identification sufficient to keep voter loyalty as they age – the greying of the green vote? We also know surprisingly little about green parties in government: how do green ministers operate, what obstacles do they encounter and what is the nature and extent of their influence?

There are still many European democracies where green parties have little or no presence. Some green parties have had brief moments in the sun – joining coalition governments in Czechia and Italy – but have generally struggled to make any electoral impact. Elsewhere, despite some positive electoral results in Brazil and Colombia, green parties have an abject record in the global south, notably in Asia (Jackson 2022). While macro theories such as (the lack of) postmaterialism might explain the failure of green parties in the global south, we need more detailed accounts of who these green activists are and the kinds of challenges they face, as found in Fell's (2021) analysis of Taiwan's green parties.

The green party family is currently the most homogeneous of all the major party families (Ennser 2012), but that might change if green parties do flourish elsewhere. If, say, the ecological imperative becomes the driving force behind burgeoning green parties with voters motivated by environmental concerns rather than a wider left-libertarian agenda, then that homogeneity might be challenged. Perhaps, parties similar to the Swiss Green Liberals will emerge that are progressive on the environment but are economically liberal and reject a left-libertarian social programme.

Finally, even if green parties gain further electoral success, they are likely to still have a long road to travel before they are able to form governments alone, which does not tally with the urgent timelines required to solve the climate crisis and meet ambitious net zero carbon reduction targets. While green party success would increase the pressure for action on climate change, an effective response also requires mainstream parties to embrace the challenge too, which requires them to adopt a positive accommodative strategy towards the environment. How green parties navigate such a shift would be a challenge they would presumably welcome.

References

Abou-Chadi, T. (2016) 'Niche party success and mainstream party policy shifts – How green and radical right parties differ in their impact', *British Journal of Political Science*, 46(2), p417–436.

Auers, D. (2012) 'The curious case of the Latvian Greens', *Environmental Politics*, 21(3), p522–527.

Beaudonnet, L. and Vasilopoulos, P. (2014) 'Green parties in hard times: The case of EELV in the 2012 French presidential election', *Party Politics*, 20(2), p275–85.

Belchior, A.M. (2010) 'Are green political parties more postmaterialist than other parties?', *European Societies*, 12(4), p467–492.

Bergman, M. and Flatt, H. (2020) 'Issue diversification: Which niche parties can succeed electorally by broadening their agenda?', *Political Studies*, 68(3), p710–730.

Bischof, D. (2017) 'Towards a renewal of the niche party concept: Parties, market shares and condensed offers', *Party Politics*, 23(3), p220–235.

Blühdorn, I. (2009) 'Reinventing green politics: On the strategic repositioning of the German Green Party', *German Politics*, 18(1), p36–54.

Bolin, N. (2016) 'Green parties in Finland and Sweden', in Van Haute, E. (ed.) *Green parties in Europe*. London: Routledge, pp. 158–176.

Bürgin, A. and Oppermann, K. (2020) 'The party politics of learning from failure: the German Greens and the lessons drawn from the 2013 general election', *Environmental Politics*, 29(4), p609–627.

Carter, N. (2013) 'Greening the mainstream: Party politics and the environment', *Environmental Politics*, 22(1), p73–94.

Christensen, L., Dahlberg, S. and Martinsson, J. (2015) 'Changes and fluctuations in issue ownership: The case of Sweden, 1979–2010', *Scandinavian Political Studies*, 38(2), p137–157.

Close, C. and Delwit, P. (2016) 'Green parties and elections', in van Haute, E. (ed.), *Green parties in Europe*, London: Routledge, pp. 241–64.

Costello, R., Toshkov, D., Bos, B. and Krouwel, A. (2021) 'Congruence between voters and parties: The role of party-level issue salience', *European Journal of Political Research*, 60(1), p92–113.

Cowie, L., Greaves, L. and Sibley, C. (2015) 'Identifying distinct subgroups of green voters: A latent profile analysis of crux values relating to Green Party support', *New Zealand Journal of Psychology*, 44(1), p45–59.

Crowley, K. and Moore, S. (2020) 'Stepping stone, halfway house or road to nowhere? Green support of minority government in Sweden, New Zealand and Australia', *Government and Opposition*, 55(4), p669–689.

Dalton, R. (2020) *Citizen politics* (7th ed.). Washington, DC: CJ Press.

Debus, M. and Tosun, J. (2021) 'The manifestation of the green agenda: A comparative analysis of parliamentary debates', *Environmental Politics*, 30(6), p918–937.

Dennison, J. (2017) *The Greens in British politics*. Basingstoke: Palgrave Pivot.

Doherty, B. (2002) *Ideas and actions in the green movement*. London: Routledge.

Dolezal, M. (2010) 'Exploring the stabilization of a political force: The social and attitudinal basis of green parties in the age of globalisation, *West European Politics*, 33(3), p534–52.

Dolezal, M. (2016) 'The greens in Austria and Switzerland: Two successful opposition parties', in Van Haute, E. (ed.) *Green parties in Europe*. London: Routledge, pp. 15–41.

Dw.com (2021) 'Germany's election results: facts and figures', 28 September. Available at: www.dw.com/en/germanys-election-results-facts-and-figures/a-59343789.

Ennser, L. (2012) 'The homogeneity of West European party families: The radical right in comparative perspective', *Party Politics*, 18(2), p151–71.

Evrard, A. (2012) 'Political parties and policy change: Explaining the impact of French and German greens on energy policy', *Journal of Comparative Policy Analysis: Research and Practice*, 14(4), p275–291.

Faas, T. and Klingelhöfer, T. (2019) 'The more things change, the more they stay the same? The German federal election of 2017 and its consequences', *West European Politics*, 42(4), p914–926.

Fell, D. (2021) *Taiwan's green parties*, Abingdon: Routledge.

Franklin, M. and Rüdig, W. (1995) 'On the durability of green politics: Evidence from the 1989 European election study', *Comparative Political Studies*, 28(3), p409–439.

Frankland, E.G. (2016) 'Central and Eastern European Green parties: Rise, fall and revival?', in van Haute, E. (ed.), *Green Parties in Europe*. London: Routledge, pp. 59–91.

Frankland, E.G., Lucardie, P. and, Rihoux, B. (eds.) (2008) *Green parties in transition: The end of grass-roots democracy?* Farnham: Ashgate.

Frankland, E.G. and Schoonmaker, D. (1992) *Between protest and power: The Green Party in Germany*. Oxford: Westview.

Grant, Z. and Tilley, J. (2019) 'Fertile soil: Explaining variation in the success of green parties', *West European Politics*, 42(3), p495–516.

Hooghe, L., Marks, G. and Wilson, C. (2002) 'Does left/right structure party positions on European integration?', *Comparative Political Studies*, 35(8), p965–989.

Inglehart, R. (1977) *The silent revolution*. Princeton University Press.

Jackson, S. (2022) 'Going green in Asia? Green parties in a non-western setting', *Asian Journal of Political Science*, doi.org/10.1080/02185377.2022.2048873

Jensen, C. and Spoon, J. (2011) 'Testing the 'party matters' thesis: Explaining progress towards Kyoto protocol targets', *Political Studies*, 59(1), p99–115.

Jolly, S., Bakker, R., Hooghe, L., Marks, G. et al. (2022) 'Chapel Hill expert survey trend file, 1999–2019', *Electoral Studies*, 75, p102420.

Keith, D. and Verge, T. (2018) 'Nonmainstream left parties and women's representation in Western Europe', *Party Politics*, 24(4), p397–409.

Kitschelt, H. (1988)' Left-libertarian parties: Explaining innovation in competitive party systems', *World Politics*, 40(2), p194–234.

Knill, C., Debus, M. and Heichel, S. (2010) 'Do parties matter in internationalised policy areas? The impact of political parties on environmental policy outputs in 18 OECD countries, 1970–2000', *European Journal of Political Research*, 49(3), p301–36.

Kriesi, H., Grande, E., Lachat, R., Dolezak, M., Bornschier, S. and Frey, T. (2006) 'Globalization and the transformation of the national political space: Six European countries compared', *European Journal of Political Research*, 45(6), p921–956.

Little, C. (2016) 'Green parties in government', in Van Haute, E. (ed.) *Green parties in Europe*. London: Routledge, pp. 265–79.

Mair, P. and Mudde, C. (1998) 'The party family and its study', *Annual Review of Political Science*, 1(1), p211–229.

March, L. and Rommerskirchen, C. (2011), 'Explaining electoral success and failure', in March, L. (ed.), *Radical left parties in Europe*. Abingdon: Routledge, pp. 180–200.

Marks, G., Attewell, D., Rovny, J. and Hooghe, L. (2021) 'Cleavage theory', in Riddervold, M., Trondal, J. and Newsome, A. (eds.) *The Palgrave handbook of EU crises*. London: Palgrave Macmillan, pp. 173–194.

Meguid, B. (2008) *Party competition between unequals*. Cambridge: Cambridge University Press.

Miragliotta, N. (2013) 'The Australian Greens: Carving out space in a two-party system', *Environmental Politics*, 22(5), p706–727.

Müller-Rommel, F. (1998) 'Explaining the electoral success of green parties: A cross-national analysis', *Environmental Politics*, 7(4), p145–54.

Otjes, S. and Krouwel, A. (2015) 'Two shades of green? The electorates of GreenLeft and the party for the animals', *Environmental Politics*, 24(6), p991–1013.

Poguntke, T. (1993) *Alternative politics: The German green party*. Edinburgh: Edinburgh University Press.

Poguntke, T. (2002) 'Green parties in national governments: From protest to acquiescence', in Müller-Rommel, F. and Poguntke, T. (eds.), *Green parties in national governments*. London: Frank Cass, pp. 133–45.

Price-Thomas, G. (2016) 'Green Party ideology today: Divergencies and continuities in Germany, France and Britain', in van Haute, E. (ed.) *Green parties in Europe*, London: Routledge, pp. 280–297.

Ramiro, L. (2016) 'Support for radical left parties in Western Europe: Social background, ideology and political orientations', *European Political Science Review*, 8(1), p1–23.

Redding, K. and Viterna, J. (1999) 'Political demands, political opportunities: Explaining the differential success of left-libertarian parties', *Social Forces*, 78(2), p491–510.

Richardson, D. and Rootes, C. (eds.) (1995) *The green challenge*. London: Routledge.

Rihoux, B. and Frankland, E.G. (2008) 'The metamorphosis of amateur-activist newborns into professional-activist centaurs', in Frankland, E.G., Lucardie, P. and Rihoux, B. (eds.) *Green parties in transition: The end of grass-roots democracy?* Farnham: Ashgate, pp. 259–87.

Röth, L. and Schwander, H. (2021) 'Greens in government: The distributive policies of a culturally progressive force', *West European Politics*, 44(3), p661–689.

Rüdig, W. (2012) 'The perennial success of the German Greens', *Environmental Politics*, 21(1), p108–30.

Rüdig, W. and Sajuria, J. (2020) 'Green Party members and grass-roots democracy: A comparative analysis', *Party Politics*, 26(1), p21–31.

Satherley, N., Greaves, L., Osborne, D. and Sibley, C. (2020) 'State of the nation: Trends in New Zealand voters' polarisation from 2009–2018', *Political Science*, 72(1), p1–23.

Schumacher, I. (2014) 'An empirical study of the determinants of Green Party voting', *Ecological Economics*, 105, p306–318.

Spoon, J, Hobolt, S. and de Vries, C. (2014) 'Going green: Explaining issue competition on the environment', *European Journal of Political Research*, 53(2), p363–380.

Spoon, J and Pulido-Gómez, A. (2020) 'Strategic alliances: Red, green, or "watermelon" candidates in Mexican legislative elections', *Party Politics*, 26(6), p760–769.

Talshir, G. (2002) *The political ideology of green parties*. Basingstoke: Palgrave.

van Haute, E. (ed.) (2016) *Green parties in Europe*. London: Routledge.

Walgrave, S., Lefevere, J. and Tresch, A. (2012) 'The associative dimension of issue ownership', *Public Opinion Quarterly*, 76(4), p771–782.

Wang, C. and Keith, D. (2020) 'The greening of European radical left parties: Red and green politics', *Journal of Contemporary European Studies*, 28(4), p494–513.

Wavreille, M-C. and Pilet, J-B. (2016) 'The greens in Belgium's federal landscape: Divergent fates', in Van Haute, E. (ed.) *Green parties in Europe*. London: Routledge, pp. 42–58.

World Values Survey (2022) Online database. Available from: www.worldvaluessurvey.org/WVSOnline.jsp (Accessed 18 March 2022).

PART 4

Party competition and representation

17
PARTY STRATEGIES
Valence versus position

Agnes Magyar, Sarah Wagner and Roi Zur

In this chapter, we provide an overview of the interaction between the spatial theory of party competition (i.e. party competition that involves the strategies with regard to the policy positions of parties) and the valence model of voting (i.e. party competition that involves parties' image of non-positional issues such as competence, integrity and party unity). We claim that while these two models of party strategy have been considered competitive and exogenous to each other, they can also be seen as complementary.

We first look at the foundations of the spatial model of party competition, by examining the assumptions associated with the model. In a unidimensional left-right spatial continuum, the proximity model argues that voters will opt for the party most congruent to their position. Therefore, in a two-party competition, parties are expected to converge towards the median voter of the left-right continuum. Though these two fundamental concepts often hold true, we are interested in understanding which conditions incentivise divergence of party strategies from the median voter in a spatial left-right continuum. In this chapter, we will evaluate and review how this debate has adapted to new challenges posed by multidimensional issues, multilevel party systems, and fluctuations of competency. While we review the theoretical literature, the focus of this chapter is on recent developments in empirical evidence.

Finally, we explore the puzzle of the simultaneous dynamics of valence and spatial models by discussing how a party's valence image affects its positional strategies. We conclude on the question of whether parties strategically emphasise positions or valence, showing how party strategy not only is not made in a vacuum but also evolves around new competition on a spatial and/or valence dimension. This chapter provides an overview of the progress in the spatial versus valence debate, and it shines some light on new and important research pathways. Some questions include: How do parties choose to emphasise their policy or valence positions, and what are the electoral consequences of this choice?

The spatial model of party competition

The spatial model of party competition is based on the economic idea of stability in competition formalised by Hotelling (1929), where entrepreneurs spatially locate their stores to maximise profit. Hotelling noted that parties mimic each other's platforms to ensure electoral success. The spatial model of voting was developed by Black (1948) concerning small group decision-making, and by Downs (1957) concerning voting in elections. Since Downs's (1957) seminal work, ample theoretical and empirical research has utilised the spatial voting (proximity) model in order to explain party strategies. According to this model, voters (consumers) vote (buy) based on the proximity between their policy preference (location of their home) and the parties' policy platforms (location of the store). Put simply, voters opt for the party that announces the policy position closest to their preferred policy. As a result, parties strategically advocate policies that maximise the number of voters who prefer their position over any other party's position in a given party system.

In the simplest spatial model, parties' positional strategies and voters' preferences are modelled across a single policy continuum. In Western democracies, this continuum has been generally associated with a set of economic policies such as government intervention in the economy, redistribution of wealth and the scope of social benefits. Parties on the left end of the continuum advocate the expansion of these policies, while parties on the right support repealing or replacing these policies with neo-liberal or market-based policies. In recent years, the left-right continuum has been increasingly regarded as an overarching dimension of political ideology encompassing economic and non-economic policies.

Researchers are then interested in answering two distinct sets of questions related to this unidimensional model of party competition: theoretical and empirical. In this chapter, we use the terms 'theoretical' and 'formal-model' interchangeably to describe mathematical or game-theoretical models of party competition. Theoretically, scholars seek to understand the positions parties *should take* (defined as '*Nash equilibrium*') under different assumptions about the real world. Drawing upon game theory, the Nash equilibrium in the context of spatial models is a set of policy positions such that no party has the electoral incentive to unilaterally alter its position, given the positions of all other parties. Empirically, research focuses on the positions parties *do take* and the electoral consequences of these positions.

Formal models of party spatial strategies

The spatial model of party strategies originated in the work of Downs (1957) on the unidimensional and two-candidate elections in the USA. The famous game-theoretic Nash equilibrium of the Downsian model refers to the convergence of two parties to the position of the median voter. This outcome lies on a set of assumptions that do not necessarily represent real-world politics. When these assumptions are relaxed, convergence to the position of the median voter is no longer the optimal party strategy. For example, Downs assumes the parties hold complete information about the policy preferences of voters, and voters know parties' positions. Berger, Munger and Potthoff (2000) demonstrate that parties diverge from the position of the median voter when the complete information assumption is relaxed (i.e. voters are uncertain about parties' positions). Downs also assumes that all eligible voters will turn out to vote, but when the complete turnout assumption is relaxed, parties polarise their positions (Adams and Merrill 2003). Another assumption is that parties try to maximise their chance of winning office. Yet, when parties seek to influence policy rather than merely maximise their probability of gaining office, they will diverge from the position of the median voter (Wittman 1973, 1977). Polarisation of parties' platforms also accrues when voters weight, in addition to proximity, the direction of parties' announced policy positions. That is, when voters with left-leaning preferences prefer parties on the left, and right-wing voters are biased towards right-wing parties, even when these parties are further away from them in absolute proximity terms (Rabinowitz and Macdonald 1989). Grofman (2004) reviews the complete set of Downs's assumptions and their relationship to parties' optimal strategies.

While a Nash equilibrium outcome tends to be common in formal models of two-party competition, this is not the case in multi-party competition. To maximise their vote-share, parties must position themselves where the largest number of voters prefer their position over any other party's position. However, such a position is difficult to identify in a multi-party competition setting. This is because parties encounter two opposing forces – a centripetal force that attracts parties towards the centre and a centrifugal force that pushes parties towards the ends of the left-right continuum. On the one hand, the voter distribution tends to be denser around the centre, thus creating a centripetal force. On the other hand, to attract enough voters, parties must distinguish themselves from their counterparts, thus facing a centrifugal force (Cox 1990; Spoon 2011).

To see this logic, think of a party system where voters' preferences are normally distributed and single-peaked around the centre of the (0–10) left-right dimension. As illustrated in Figure 17.1 (panel A), in a two-party competition between party A and party B, both parties will position themselves at (or, given the condition stated earlier, close to) the position of the median voter (5 in the illustrated case). In this situation, party A's vote-share (marked in black) equals party B's vote-share (marked in light grey). When a third party (C) emerges, for example, to the right of the two parties at the centre, it is expected to receive a large share of the votes (marked in dark grey) at the expense of party B. The now middle party (B) is 'squeezed' between A and C and is expected to lose most of its votes. Thus, B has the electoral incentive to leap-frog to the left of party A (shown in panel B). But once B positions itself to the left of A, A has the incentive to take a position to the right of C, because now its vote-share shrank (shown in panel C). Note that with every leap-frog, the vote share of the party in the middle increases incrementally because the parties on the flanks are slightly more polarised with every iteration of this dynamic. Thus, this process of the three parties changing their positions

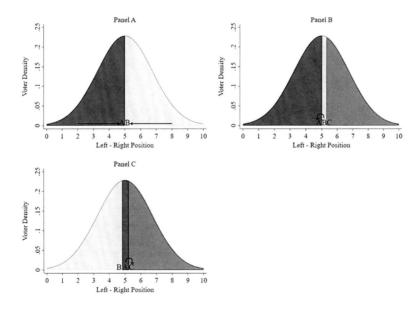

Figure 17.1 Party positions in three-party competition

Note: The figure represents a theoretical example of a three-party competition. In this figure, voter preferences are distributed on a 0–10 left-right continuum with a median of 5 and a standard deviation of 1.75.

continues until the space in the middle exceeds the space on the flanks. At this point, the parties start to converge until the space on the flanks exceeds the space in the middle. The conclusion arising from this process is that under any set of positions, at least one party can increase its vote share by changing its position, and therefore there is no stable equilibrium in a three-party competition.

Similar to the three-party case, in a unidimensional competition between any number of parties, at least one party will have the incentive to move towards the centre of the distribution, or if squeezed between two other parties to leap-frog towards the flanks. Therefore, no Nash equilibrium exists in a multi-party and unidimensional party competition where the voter distribution is single-peaked. Note, however, that a Nash equilibrium can exist when the voter distribution is *not* single-peaked. That is, when the voter distribution has more than one hump and the number of parties is exactly double the number of humps, an equilibrium can exist under a set of specific conditions (see Adams [2018] for a review).

Game theoretical spatial models of multidimensional party strategies are scarce and extremely complicated and do not converge to a clear Nash equilibrium. In the case of two office-seeking parties, based on McKelvey's Global Cycling Theorem, we can expect each party to announce policies that are similar to the announced policies of the other party, and that the two parties will present policies that are similar to the position of the median voter on each dimension. However, for most voter distributions, these announced positions can be defeated by a different set of positions in the multidimensional policy space, and thus motivate parties' strategies to cycle around each other's positions (Adams 2018). Finally, the size of the set of possible winning party strategies in a multidimensional space increases with the number of parties, the number of policy dimensions, the goals of the parties (i.e. office-, vote- or policy-seeking parties) and the electoral rules.

Empirical findings of the electoral consequences of party strategies

The empirical study of party strategies relies, first and foremost, on measures of party positions. Thus, before discussing the empirical studies of parties' strategies, we provide a short overview of major datasets of parties' policy positions across countries and time. Scholars have developed three major approaches to measuring parties' positions. First, party positions are measured through voters' perceptions in surveys, such as the Comparative Study of Electoral Systems (CSES) and the European Election Study (EES); or through a compilation of country-specific election studies, such as the British (BES) or German (GLES) election studies (see data section in Zur 2021a). A second approach to measuring party positions is via expert surveys, in which political experts are asked to place political parties on multiple issue scales. The Chapel Hill Expert Survey (CHES) is the leading example of this approach. In 2020, the Global Party Survey expanded this approach to countries outside Europe (see also Chapter 40). Finally, party positions are measured not through their perceived positions, but via their strategic public communications. The Manifesto Project (see also Chapter 38) codes parties' electoral manifestos and the Comparative Campaign Dynamics Dataset (CCDP) codes parties' pre-election statements in major newspapers. Each of these different approaches has advantages and disadvantages for the study of party strategies, which we do not aim to review here. We do, however, note the finding by Adams et al. (2019) that, while there is a strong correlation between these measures of party positions at any specific point in time, there is no such correlation between the measures of parties' positional *shifts*. Thus, when researching party strategies over time, researchers should be especially conscious of data limitations.

The major expectation from the theoretical literature is that, in a unidimensional competition, parties will balance their strategy between the centripetal force of the moderate electorates (Adams and Somer-Topcu 2009) and the non-centrist policy preferences of their partisans and activists (Adams and Merrill 2005; Adams, Merrill, Grofman 2005; Schofield and Sened 2005, 2006). They will do so while distinguishing their positions from those of their opponents (Spoon 2011; Zur 2019). Thus, parties can be expected to strategically change their positions in response to: (1) changes in public opinion, and mainly the position of the median voter; (2) the position of their core constituency; and (3) the positions of their rivals.

When party competition involves more than a single dimension, party strategy encompasses two distinct, but endogenous, decisions. First, parties need to decide which positions they announce or policies they advocate. Second, parties need to decide which positions to emphasise and which positions to blur. That is, to maximise votes, parties can either alter their positions on one or more issues or they can focus their campaign on emphasising advantageous positions. These two decisions are endogenous because when parties emphasise one issue over another, voters perceive them as moving in the direction of the emphasised issue (Meyer and Wagner 2019) and moving on the overarching left-right dimension (Meyer and Wagner 2020).

The valence model of party competition

Stokes (1963, 373) reviews and criticises the assumptions of the Hotelling-Downs model claiming that, among other failures of the model, it will not work if 'voters are simply reacting to the association of the parties with some goal or state or symbol that is positively or negatively valued'. Thus, Stokes coined the term *'valence issues'* as attributes of parties that all voters approve (or disapprove) of. Therefore, it matters less where parties are positioned on policy issues and instead, other attributes become more central. Such attributes are, but not limited to, competence, the ability to govern, integrity or party unity. Stokes also differentiates between *valence* issues and *positional* issues. That is, issues on which parties advocate and voters prefer alternative government policies. Parties, according to Stokes, are differentiated by the degree to which voters perceive them as possessing desirable attributes, which are not directly related to their policy positions.

To better grasp the difference between valence and positional issues, 'the state of the economy' is a good example: all voters prefer a strong economy over a weak economy, independent of their economic policy preference, thus the state of the economy is a valence issue. If one party is associated with improving the state of the economy (i.e. economic competence) while the other party is associated with an economic collapse (i.e. economic incompetence), the first party can be considered a valence-advantaged party. However, the mechanism to improve the state of the economy (e.g. increase taxes and social benefits vs. decrease taxes and cut social benefits) is a positional issue. Parties advocate and voters prefer different levels of government intervention in the economy.

The concept of valence as described by Stokes has been expanded and refined by scholars of both American and comparative politics. In its broader sense, valence is referred to as *any* electoral advantage a party or a candidate possesses, including the incumbency advantage in American politics, financial resources, in addition to the party attributes discussed earlier (Feld and Grofman 1991; Groseclose 2001). Others argue that valence is an affective heuristic that advantages one party over another. That is, in addition to the party attributes described by Stokes, voters simply like some parties or party leaders while disliking others. Likeable party leaders add a non-spatial advantage to their party (see works by Clarke, Whiteley and their co-authors, e.g. Clarke et al. 2004). Another extension to the original meaning of a valence issue derives from the large body of literature known as 'issue ownership' (see also Chapter 18). Parties enjoy an electoral advantage if voters perceive them as competent proponents of a salient issue (Belanger and Meguid 2008; Stubager 2018), but not necessarily when the party image is merely associated with an issue (Walgrave, Tresch and Lefevere 2015).

The expansion of the term 'valence' motivated scholars of both formal and empirical party competition to distinguish between 'types' of valence. For example, works by Schofield (2004) and Schofield and Sened (2005, 2006) differentiates between valence advantage due to the popularity of the party and specifically its leader, and valence advantage due to the support of party activists. Party activists supply free resources to the campaign in terms of time and money, which enhance parties' electoral support. Relatedly, research by Stone (Stone and Simas 2010; Stone 2017) distinguishes between campaign- and character-valence advantage. Campaign valence advantage refers to parties' ability to attract resources, win prior elections and wage an effective campaign. The concept of character-valence advantage is in line with Stokes's original definition of candidates' or parties' attributes such as competence and integrity.

Lack of comparative measurement of valence

While valence has been an influential concept in the study of party strategies and voting behaviour, to the best of our knowledge, there is no systematic cross-national and cross-time measure of valence. There are, however, numerous attempts to measure parties' valence attributes. The most comprehensive measure of valence has been data collection by Clark (2009, 2014; Clark and Leiter 2014). Clark content-analysed news reports from Keesing's Record of World Events to measure parties' image of competence, integrity and unity in nine West European countries between 1976 and 1998 (Clark 2009). Although not a direct measure of parties' valence image, the Comparative Campaign Dynamics (CCD) dataset is an additional source of valence-related data (in addition to parties' positional and issue emphasis strategies). The CCD dataset codes pre-electoral major newspapers coverage of parties' statements referring to themselves and to their competitors, and the statements the newspapers have made referring to the parties in major newspapers. While this is a comprehensive and meaningful dataset, it is limited to recent elections in ten European countries.

The lack of comprehensive measurement has motivated researchers to estimate parties' valence image using survey data. The works by Clarke and co-authors discussed earlier estimate parties' valence image using a set of available survey questions about party leaders' popularity, parties' ability to handle the most important issue and party identification (e.g. Clarke et al. 2004; Sanders et al. 2011). An even cruder proxy for parties' valence image has been used by Adams and his co-authors (e.g. Adams, Merrill and Grofman 2005; Adams and Merrill 2005; Zur 2021b) and Schofield and his co-authors (e.g. 2004; Schofield and Sened 2005, 2006). These authors capture the non-policy image of parties using statistical approximation (for technical discussion, see appendix 2 in Adams, Merrill and Grofman [2005]). This approach has been criticised as inconsistent and inaccurate (Mauerer 2020).

The relationship between the valence and spatial models of party competition

Traditionally, valence and spatial models have been seen as exogenous to each other, or even as competing explanations of parties' strategies and citizens' vote choice. Recent literature has taken a more holistic approach to the study of party competition through investigating how the valence image of a party influences its positional strategies and vice versa. This research indicates that spatial and valence theories are not necessarily competing theories and complement each other for a deeper understanding of party strategy. Yet many parties do not have the resources to focus on both – positions and valence. Therefore, latest research examines the conditionalities of electoral success for position and valence strategies.

How does parties' valence image affect their positional strategies?

A growing literature studies the effect of parties' *fixed* valence image on their positional strategies (Londregan and Romer 1993; Ansolabehere and Snyder 2000; Serra 2010). These studies demonstrate that *valence-disadvantaged* parties, that is, those perceived by voters as less competent, trustworthy or unified than their counterparts, must differentiate their policy positions from the positions announced by their rivals. This differentiation strategy is crucial for valence-disadvantaged parties, because when citizens vote based on a combination of policy proximity and non-policy considerations, similarities on the policy dimension mean that the non-policy dimension tips the scale of voters' decision rule to the side of the valence-advantaged party. This theoretical conclusion has been supported by a study of the 2006 midterm elections to the U.S. House of Representatives which finds that incumbents' character-based valence advantage draws them closer to the median position in their district and their opponents' disadvantage in character pushes them away from district preferences and the incumbent's positions (Stone and Simas 2010). In comparative studies of European politics, Spoon (2011) shows that green parties, which tend to be valence-disadvantaged relative to mainstream parties, differentiate their positions from those of their immediate social-democratic rivals. Zur (2021a) shows that liberal parties' inability to distinguish their positions from valence-advantaged moderate parties on the left-right dimension obviates any positional strategy.

A second strand of the literature studies the effect of *changes* in parties' image of valence on their positional strategies. Schofield (2004) models vote-seeking parties' positional strategies in reaction to changes in two types of valence. Schofield shows that when parties' popularity-based valence, that is, their leader's charisma or image of competence, deteriorates, parties strategically shift their position towards their (typically) non-centrist activists. Diverging from the centre towards their activists allows parties to 'acquire' activists'-based valence, that is, a valence advantage that derived from the time and financial contribution of party activists. Popular leaders, on the other hand, have the leeway to moderate their parties' position and appeal to centrist and unaffiliated voters, rather than to party activists. That is, in Schofield's model, character-based valence deterioration is a centrifugal force vis-à-vis parties' policy position. This theoretical argument has been supported by empirical evidence shown by Schofield and Sened (2005, 2006).

Adams and Merrill (2009) model valence deterioration as a centripetal force. They demonstrate that when office-seeking parties' valence image deteriorates (e.g. due to scandals, weak leadership, or intra-party divisions), parties have the incentive to moderate their position towards the median voter. Note, however, that Schofield (2004) and Schofield and Sened (2005, 2006) assume that parties aim to maximise their vote-share while Adams and Merrill (2009) assume that parties aim to influence policy. These different assumptions might explain their opposite conclusions about the effect of parties' valence image on their positional strategies. Nonetheless, empirical works show that as parties' valence image deteriorates, parties moderate their left-right positions (Clark 2013).

How do parties' positional strategies affect their image of valence?

To the best of our knowledge, there is no game-theoretical (formal) modelling of the effect of parties' positional strategies on their image of valence. However, from the Schofield's models discussed earlier, it can be inferred that, by moving towards the ends of the political spectrum, parties can increase their activists-based valence. Similarly, works in American politics argued that by taking extreme positions candidates can appeal to donors and then use financial resources to 'buy' valence through political advertisement or name recognition (Erikson and Palfrey 2000; Ashworth and Bueno de Mesquita 2009; Zakharov 2009).

While there is little formal work on the relationship between parties' positional strategies and their valence image, this issue has not been ignored. Zakharova and Warwick's (2014) observational study finds that voters assign higher valence qualities to parties that announce left-right positions closer to their own, especially when their positions are on the same side of the left-right continuum (relative to the midpoint of the scale). Yet most of the work on the effect of parties' positional strategies on their valence image employs experimental designs. For example, Johns and Kölln (2019) show that British respondents assign higher valence attributes, specifically competence, to moderate (but not purely centrist) parties. Moreover, the authors show that voters assign higher competence scores to parties on their side of the left-right continuum. In contrast, an experiment by Fernandez-Vazquez (2019) demonstrates that voters do not take a party's statements at face value, because these messages can be a strategic tool to win elections. Voters doubt the sincerity of popular statements because they may respond to vote-seeking incentives rather than reflect the party's sincere views. Espousing unpopular policies has less instrumental value in obtaining more votes and therefore is more credible. Gooch, Gerber and Huber's (2021) experiment in the context of U.S. elections provides mixed evidence as well. On the one hand, the authors find that when candidates stray from their parties' possible positions they are perceived as less competent overall and less effective legislators compared to mainstream party candidates. On the other hand, extreme candidates tend to be viewed as bold and inventive leaders.

Do parties strategically emphasise positions or valence?

As discussed, both positional and non-positional strategies of political parties are important. Yet, because of their limited campaign resources, parties are often faced with the dilemma of choosing between emphasising policy positions *or* valence issues. Here again, formal models are scarce. Ashworth and Bueno de Mesquita (2009) present a model in which candidates first choose their policy position, then attempt to buy valence through campaign spending. The authors find that when candidates' positions are polarised, they invest more in their valence image.

While the theoretical literature on this question focuses on a competition between two candidates, the empirical literature focuses on multi-party competition. Using the CCD dataset, Bjarnøe, Adams and Boydstun (2022) demonstrate that parties strategically emphasise their issue-positions in their campaign rhetoric and attack their opponents' valence attributes. They argue that both office and policy seeking parties have the incentive to attack their counterparts' valence because, as shown by Clark (2009), negative media coverage of incompetence, dishonesty, and intra-party disagreements causes parties to lose votes.

Adams, Scheiner and Kawasumi (2016) provide similar evidence that candidates to the Japanese House of Representatives running for the long-ruling party (LDP) de-emphasised policy debates compared to candidates of the relatively new opposition party, and that this dynamic flipped once Japan's economy collapsed. Curini (2017) shows that ideological proximity increases parties' incentive to make use of valence appeals (such as corruption) as a competitive strategy. Furthermore, valence considerations are more important to a party when it is spatially squeezed between two competitors and when there is more to gain electorally from engaging in valence campaigning. Related to Curini's theoretical argument, Zur's research (2021a) implies that centrist parties' (predominantly parties from the Liberal and Agrarian families) vote-maximising strategy is to improve their image of valence and avoid investing resources in changing their policy image.

Conclusions and avenues for further research

Understanding party strategies has been a key effort in political science. Researchers have devoted a great deal of attention to discussing the opportunities, incentives and pressures that parties face to attract additional electoral support. At the core of the discussion is the debate about whether political choice is based primarily on congruence between voter preferences and party platforms or on non-ideological considerations. We argued that the strategic use of issues and the strategic use of party image are not competing, but complementary considerations simultaneously shape parties' platforms and campaigns. As such, they present parties with a possibility to ease the dilemma of balancing the centripetal force of tending to the centre and the centrifugal force of appealing to their partisan base and can explain parties' deviation from the median voter's preferences.

Although the two have frequently been portrayed as rivals, we discuss how parties' valence images and positional strategies change synchronously. Valence advantage or improvement can generate further electoral support and permit looser discipline in strategic positioning, while disadvantage may pressure parties into strategically steering their policy positions closer to more popular opinions or to a point that improves their activist-based valence. At the same time, parties' positional strategies can also affect their image of valence in voters' minds and ability to appeal to activist groups. In discussing whether and when parties strategically emphasise positions or valence in their campaigns, we draw attention to the asymmetry in the way parties can utilise spatial strategies to their advantage so that valence considerations become more important to parties that are more restricted in their spatial moves. Our review of the studies identifying conditions that incentivise valence campaigning highlights that much of the conclusions depend on the underlying assumptions about what parties seek to achieve in a competition, and about the resources, opportunities and willingness they have to compromise either on policy or on popularity.

Although we showed that much research has been done on proximity-based versus valence-based party strategies in the past decades, we also emphasise that parts of the discussion call for further attention. Most of the studies addressing how parties' positional strategies affect their valence image rely on experimental designs. Additional formal and observational approaches would add invaluable insights to the debate.

A further crucial avenue of research is a continued inquiry into the nature of valence. Despite a common understanding of what is meant by the notion, researchers have always been open about the complexity of capturing and measuring it. Studies often rely on restricted understandings of valence or make use of proxies or estimates in absence of comprehensive measurement of parties' image. Understanding fully how various forms of valence can be parts of complex campaign strategies requires more systematic research, including the discussion of the distinction between valence image and strategic valence effort, as well as extensive efforts to accurately and consistently measure valence across time and space.

References

Adams, J. (2018) 'Spatial voting models of party competition in two dimensions', in Congleton, R.D., Grofman, B. and Voigt, S. (eds.) *The Oxford handbook of public choice*, vol. 1. Oxford: Oxford University Press. pp. 187–207.

Adams, J., Bernardi, L., Ezrow, L., Oakley, G.B., Liu, T.-P. and Phillips, M.C. (2019) 'A problem with empirical studies of party policy shifts: Alternative measures of party shifts are uncorrelated', *European Journal of Political Research*, 58(4), p1234–1244.

Adams, J. and Merrill, S. (2003) 'Voter turnout and candidate strategies in American elections', *The Journal of Politics*, 65(1), p161–189.

Adams, J. and Merrill, S. (2005) 'Candidates' policy platforms and election outcomes: The three faces of policy representation', *European Journal of Political Research*, 44(6), p899–918.

Adams, J. and Merrill, S. (2009) 'Policy-seeking parties in a parliamentary democracy with proportional representation: A valence-uncertainty model', *British Journal of Political Science*, 39(3), p539–58.

Adams, J., Merrill, S. and Grofman, B. (2005) *A unified theory of party competition: A cross-national analysis integrating spatial and behavioral factors*. Cambridge: Cambridge University Press.

Adams, J. and Somer-Topcu, Z. (2009) 'Moderate now, win votes later: The electoral consequences of parties' policy shifts in 25 postwar democracies', *The Journal of Politics*, 71(2), p678–692.

Adams, J., Scheiner, E. and Kawasumi, J. (2016) 'Running on character? Running on policy? An analysis of Japanese candidates' campaign platforms', *Electoral Studies*, 44, p275–283.

Ansolabehere, S. and Snyder, J.M. (2000) 'Valence politics and equilibrium in spatial election models', *Public Choice*, 103, p327–336.

Ashworth, S. and Bueno de Mesquita, E. (2009) 'Elections with platform and valence competition', *Games and Economic Behavior*, 67(1), p191–216.

Belanger, E. and Meguid, B.M. (2008) 'Issue salience, issue ownership, and issue-based vote choice', *Electoral Studies*, 27(3), p477–491.

Berger, M.M., Munger, M.C. and Potthoff, R.F. (2000) 'The Downsian model predicts divergence', *Journal of Theoretical Politics*, 12(2), p228–240.

Bjarnøe, C., Adams, J. and Boydstun, A. (2022) 'Our issue positions are strong, and our opponents' character is weak: An analysis of parties' campaign strategies in ten West-European democracies', *British Journal of Political Science*, p1–20. doi:10.1017/S0007123421000715.

Black, D. (1948) 'On the rationale of group decision-making', *Journal of Political Economy*, 56(1), p23–34.

Clark, M. (2009) 'Valence and electoral outcomes in Western Europe, 1976–1998', *Electoral Studies*, 28(1), p111–122.

Clark, M. (2013) 'Understanding parties' policy shifts in Western Europe: The role of valence, 1976–2003', *British Journal of Political Science*, 44(2), p261–286.

Clark, M. (2014) 'Does public opinion respond to shifts in party valence? A cross-national analysis of Western Europe, 1976–2002', *West European Politics*, 37(1), p91–112.

Clark, M. and Leiter, D. (2014) 'Does the ideological dispersion of parties mediate the electoral impact of valence? A cross-national study of party support in nine western European democracies', *Comparative Political Studies*, 45(2), p171–202.

Clarke, H.D., Sanders, D., Stewart, M. and Whiteley, P. (2004) *Political choice in Britain*. Oxford: Oxford University Press.

Cox, G. (1990) 'Centripetal and centrifugal incentives in electoral systems', *American Journal of Political Science*, 34(4), p903–935.

Curini, L. (2017) *Corruption, ideology, and populism: The rise of valence political campaigning*. Basingstoke: Palgrave.

Downs, A. (1957) *An economic theory of democracy*. New York: Harper and Row.

Erikson, R.S. and Palfrey, T.R. (2000) 'Equilibria in campaign spending games: Theory and data', *American Political Science Review*, 94(3), p595–609.

Feld, S.L. and Grofman, B. (1991) 'Incumbency advantage, voter loyalty and the benefit of the doubt', *Journal of Theoretical Politics*, 3(2), p115–137.

Fernandez-Vazquez, P. (2019) 'The credibility of party policy rhetoric: Survey experimental evidence', *Journal of Politics*, 81(1), p309–314.

Gooch, A., Gerber, A.S. and Huber, G.A. (2021) 'Evaluations of candidates' non-policy characteristics from issue positions: Evidence of valence spillover', *Electoral Studies*, 69, p102246.

Grofman, B. (2004) 'Downs and two-party convergence', *Annual Review of Political Science*, 7, p25–46.

Groseclose, T. (2001) 'A model of candidate location when one candidate has a valence advantage'. *American Journal of Political Science*, 45(4), p862–886.

Hotelling, H. (1929) 'Stability in competition', *The Economic Journal*, 39(153), p41–57.

Johns, R. and Kölln, A.K. (2019) 'Moderation and competence: How a party's ideological position shapes its valence reputation', *American Journal of Political Science*, 64(3), p649–663.

Klüver, H. and Spoon, J. (2016) 'Who responds? Voters, parties and issue attention', *British Journal of Political Science*, 46(3), p633–654.

Londregan, J. and Romer, T. (1993) 'Polarization, incumbency, and the personal vote', in *Political economy: Institutions, competition, and representation*, Proceedings of the Seventh International Symposium in Economic Theory and Econometrics. Cambridge: Cambridge Univrsity Press, pp. 355–377.

Mauerer, I. (2020) 'The neglected role and variability of party intercepts in the spatial valence approach', *Political Analysis*, 28(3), p303–317.

Meyer, T.M. and Wagner, M. (2019) 'It sounds like they are moving: Understanding and modeling emphasis-based policy change', *Political Science Research and Methods*, 7(4), p757–774.

Meyer, T.M. and Wagner, M. (2020) 'Perceptions of parties' left-right positions: The impact of salience strategies', *Party Politics*, 26(5), p664–674.

Rabinowitz, G. and Macdonald, S.E. (1989) 'A directional theory of issue voting', *American Political Science Review*, 83(1), p93–121.

Rovny, J. (2012) 'Who emphasizes and who blurs? Party strategies in multidimensional competition', *European Union Politics*, 13(2), p269–292.

Sanders, D., Clarke, H.D., Stewart, M.C. and Whiteley, P. (2011) 'Downs, Stokes and the dynamics of electoral choice', *British Journal of Political Science*, 41(2), p287–314.

Schofield, N. (2004) 'Equilibrium in the spatial 'valence' model of politics', *Journal of Theoretical Politics*, 16(4), p447–481.

Schofield, N. and Sened, I. (2005) 'Modeling the interaction of parties, activists and voters: why is the political center so empty?' *European Journal of Political Research*, 44(3), p355–390.

Schofield, N. and Sened, I. (2006) *Multiparty democracy: Elections and legislative politics*. Cambridge: Cambridge University Press.

Serra, G. (2010) 'Polarization of what? A model of elections with endogenous valence', *The Journal of Politics*, 72(2), p426–437.

Spoon, J. (2011) *Political survival of small parties in Europe*. Ann Arbor: University of Michigan Press.

Spoon, J. and Klüver, H. (2014) 'Do parties respond? How electoral context influences party responsiveness', *Electoral Studies*, 35, p48–60.

Stokes, D.E. (1963) 'Spatial models of party competition', *American Political Science Review*, 57(2), p368–377.

Stone, W.J. (2017) *Candidates and voters: Ideology, valence, and representation in US elections*. Cambridge: Cambridge University Press.

Stone, W.J. and Simas, E.N. (2010) 'Candidate valence and ideological positions in US House elections', *American Journal of Political Science*, 54(2), p371–388.

Stubager, R. (2018) 'What is issue ownership and how should we measure it?' *Political Behavior*, 40(2), p345–370.

Wagner, M. (2012) 'Defining and measuring niche parties', *Party Politics*, 18(6), p845–864.

Walgrave, S., Tresch, A. and Lefevere, J. (2015) 'The conceptualisation and measurement of issue ownership', *West European Politics*, 38(4), p778–796.

Wittman, D. (1973) 'Parties as utility maximizers', *American Political Science Review*, 67(2) p490–498.

Wittman, D. (1977) 'Candidates with policy preferences: A dynamic model', *Journal of Economic Theory*, 14, p180–189.

Zakharov, A.V. (2009) 'A model of candidate location with endogenous valence', *Public Choice*, 138, p347–366.

Zakharova, M. and Warwick, P.V. (2014) 'The sources of valence judgments: The role of policy distance and the structure of the left-right spectrum', *Comparative Political Studies*, 47(14), p2000–2025.

Zur, R. (2019) 'Party survival in parliament: Explaining party durability in lower-house parliaments'. *European Journal of Political Research*, 58(3), p960–980.

Zur, R. (2021a) 'Stuck in the middle: Ideology, valence and the electoral failures of centrist parties', *British Journal of Political Science*, 51(2), p706–723.

Zur, R. (2021b) 'The multidimensional disadvantages of centrist parties in Western Europe', *Political Behavior*, 43(4), p1755–1777.

18
ISSUE COMPETITION AND AGENDA SETTING

Christoffer Green-Pedersen

Issue competition – the idea that political parties compete with each other by emphasising certain issues rather than others – is not new in political science. The idea was launched by Robertson (1976) and pushed further by Budge and Farlie (1983). It was born as a criticism of the idea of spatial competition where parties compete by taking different positions on political issues or dimensions. Whereas the idea of issue competition is thus more than 40 years old, the literature on this topic has mainly flourished in the last decade. This chapter first provides the reasons for the growing scholarly interest in issue competition. It will then focus on basic theoretical questions related to the nature of issue competition. The literature can further be divided into two strands: one is focused on the strategic interaction among political parties and the other on how external factors like media attention or real world problems shape issue competition. It is important to stress that this chapter examines issue competition and not party competition in general, especially spatial or positional competition. Thus studies that have party positions on issues as a dependent variable (see Chapter 17) are only included if they also deal with issue attention including the interaction between issue and positional competition.

Why all this attention on issue competition?

It is worth highlighting why the literature on issue competition has boomed in recent decades. The first reason relates to changes to party competition itself and the emergence of new political issues like immigration or the environment. Issue voting has, to some extent, replaced class-based voting. This change within the electorate implies that determining which issues should dominate party competition, that is, issue competition, has become more central for political parties (Green-Pedersen 2007a). This focus on the increased importance of issue competition further dovetails with the literature on the new second or Green/Alternative/Libertarian – Traditional/Authoritarian/Nationalist (GAL-TAN) dimension of party competition in Western Europe linked to a social conflict around globalisation (Kriesi et al. 2012) or transnationalism (Hooghe and Marks 2018). This literature also highlights the increased importance of new issues like immigration or European integration promoted by new niche parties, and the competition with more traditional left-right issues for attention from political parties.

The second reason has more to do with increased availability of data on which issues parties focus on. The Comparative Manifesto Project (CMP) data first became generally available in 2001 (Budge et al. 2001, see also Chapter 38) and are today easily accessible.[1] The CMP data are born out of the idea of 'selective emphasis' (i.e. issue competition) rather than direct confrontation (positional competition) (Robertson 1976), but the main purpose of the data has actually been to measure party positions. Nevertheless, as the dataset offers opportunities to study which issues political parties focus on, it has been widely used (Green-Pedersen 2019a). Still, data sources for studying issue competition go far beyond the CMP dataset. The comparative agendas project (CAP), which is a network of national projects, has generated a wealth of data relevant for studying issue competition (Baumgartner, Breunig and Grossman 2019).[2] In this project, data like parliamentary questions, executive speeches, bills, party manifestos, have been coded according to a common coding scheme with more than 200 subcategories that can then be aggregated into policy issues (Bevan 2019). The Chapel Hill Expert Survey (Bakker et al. 2015; Polk et al. 2017, see also Chapter 40)[3] has also increasingly provided data on issue importance, although the focus of the survey is on party positions, especially on European integration. Beyond these large collaborative projects, technological developments have facilitated data collection of additional sources, such as Tweets (De Sio and Lachat 2020) and press releases (Klüver and Sagarzazu 2016; Seeberg 2020). Developments in automated or computer-based coding (Wilkerson and Casas 2017) have further enabled researchers to code large amounts of data on party behaviour in terms of issue focus.

Issue competition: party preferences and party interaction

The central theoretical starting point for studying issue competition is the idea that political parties have preferred issues. Political parties believe that attention to some issues is better for their electoral support than attention to other issues. This obviously leads to a focus on how to theorise political parties' issue preferences. The original and still prevalent understanding is based on the concept of issue ownership (Budge 2015, see also Chapter 17). Political parties prefer giving attention to issues that they own, that is, where the electorate sees them as more competent. As shown by Seeberg (2017), the issues political parties own are relatively stable across time and countries, which has made issue ownership an attractive concept for theorising issue preferences.

In recent years, new and promising ways of understanding issue preferences have emerged. One prominent example is the idea of 'issue yield' developed by de Sio and Weber (2014). Political parties should focus on issue goals that on the one hand allow them to keep existing voters on board while at the same time attract new voters. How close an issue is to this win–win situation can be measured through an issue yield index that thus generates a prediction about which issues political parties are expected to focus on. Empirical studies of the issues that parties focus on and how they then fare in attracting electoral support provide at least partial support for the theory. Political parties do seem to focus on issues with high issue yield and this does seem an electorally attractive strategy (De Sio and Weber 2014; De Sio and Lachat 2020). Compared to issue ownership, this perspective provided a much more dynamic perspective on political parties' issue preferences. An updated issue yield index may for instance lead to new expectations about which issues parties focus on. It is worth noting that both models (issue ownership and issue yield) share the same theoretical starting point for understanding issue competition, namely individual parties and the electorate. They do not focus as much on the existence and issue focus of other parties. In this sense, these are theoretical models of issue preferences rather than issue competition.

While issue preferences obviously play a key role in issue competition, the need to take the competitive aspect into account has become increasingly clear in the issue competition literature. A political party does not face the electorate in isolation, but in competition with other parties, and this affects their issue strategies. Thus a central finding within many studies of issue competition concerns 'issue-overlap' (Sigelman and Buell 2004). Although parties have divergent issue preferences, they generally end up addressing similar issues. Whereas the original identification of issue overlap related to U.S. presidential elections (Sigelman and Buell 2004), the same tendency can be observed in West-European party systems (e.g. Dolezal et al. 2013; Green-Pedersen and Mortensen 2015; Meyer and Wagner 2015). Issue engagement in the sense that parties pay attention to similar issues is a central element of issue competition.

One reason for this might be that political parties sometimes try to 'steal' each other's issues (Holian 2004). Political parties might try to change a voter's view of which party is most competent at dealing with an issue, that is, winning issue-ownership away from another party. Although issue ownership is typically rather stable over time (Seeberg 2017, see also Chapter 17), this is not an unknown party strategy. However, the issue steal perspective would predict that it would be confined to a few select issues where a party is willing to run the risk of emphasising an issue owned by the opponent with the intention of turning it into an owned issue. The studies of issue overlap suggest that it is a quite widespread phenomenon. Despite parties wanting to stick to their preferred issues, in practice, they may end up focusing on other issues as well. The question is why? For instance, why would radical right-wing parties end up paying attention to climate change?

One type of answer has developed out of what is known as 'policy-agenda setting theory' (Baumgartner and Jones 1993; Green-Pedersen and Walgrave 2014). The relevance of policy agenda-setting theory for issue competition comes from the fact that both theories focus on attention as the key currency of politics. They share the assumptions that attention to political issues is scarce and consequential. Not all issues can receive equal attention; and when some issues receive more attention, the political dynamics around them change. The attitudes of the electorate, for instance, become more important when political attention is high (Mortensen 2010).

What policy agenda-setting theory has to offer is a much more systemic focus on attention dynamics with the concept of an agenda as the focal point. Based on this, Green-Pedersen and Mortensen (2010) have developed the idea of a 'party system agenda'. At any given moment, a hierarchy of attention to issues exists across political parties that shapes their issue attention. Parties perceive certain issues to be important across the entire party system and this makes them pay attention to issues they would rather avoid. At the same time, they try to influence the future content of the party system agenda, so their preferred issues come to rank high on the agenda. A key element of the idea of the party system agenda is the role of political parties' perceptions shaped by their ongoing competition. Thus, the best predictor of which issues dominate the party system agenda at point t are the issues that dominated the party system agenda at point $t-1$. Following the same logic, Seeberg (2022) shows that the closer parties get to an election, the more they engage with the issues other parties focus on. Any party wants to avoid focusing on an issue to which no other parties pay attention. Therefore, the closer it gets to election day, the more parties focus on the issues they perceive will come to dominate the election campaign. From this perspective, the fact that political parties engage with each other and come to focus on similar issues is not surprising, whereas it is if the theoretical focus is only on parties' preferred issues. Instead, the relevant questions to ask are which parties are more influential in shaping the party system agenda and what role forces outside the party system play.

The introduction of a policy agenda-setting perspective into the literature on issue competition has also brought the more descriptive tools of the agenda setting literature into the study of issue competition. The party system agenda has for instance been studied in terms of its capacity and complexity. The capacity of the party system agenda, measured as the average length of party manifestos, has grown; and the agenda has become more complex in the sense that it covers more issues or policy questions (Green-Pedersen 2007a, 2019b). Other studies have also looked at the scope of party agendas in terms of how attention is distributed across policy issues (Greene 2016; Van Heck 2018) and at the stability of party agendas (Bevan and Greene 2018).

Thus, the policy agenda-setting literature has introduced a number of new concepts into the study of issue competition, but also a new theoretical starting point. For the issue competition literature, the starting point has traditionally been individual parties and their issue preferences. The agenda-setting perspective has a more systemic starting point, which leads to a focus on how the interaction of the parties generates and shapes a common agenda. This is not to say that parties do not have issue preferences, but parties do not interact with the electorate in a vacuum. They always have competitors. This raises a further question about how well parties' issue preferences can actually be measured through, for instance, party manifestos, because parties have already taken the preferences of their competitors into account when drafting a manifesto. Political parties are hard to observe in isolation from their competitors because they are in fact never isolated from these competitors.

One other theoretical issue that has received substantial attention in the issue competition literature is the relationship between issue competition and positional competition. Meguid's study (2008) of how the positional strategies of mainstream parties affected the electoral fortune of niche parties was the first attempt at theorising the relationship between issue and positional competition. Depending on which positions mainstream parties take on the core issue of a niche party – the environment for green parties for instance – this issue gets more or less attention, which is crucial for the electoral fortune of niche parties. Other studies have investigated the interconnection between parties' positional strategies and their issue focus (Wagner 2012; Guinaudeau and Persico 2014; Abou-Chadi, Green-Pedersen and Mortensen 2020). It is clear that positional and issue competition are logically related – it is hard for a party to emphasise an issue without taking a position on it, and vice versa. But the exact relationship between the two forms of party competition is still somewhat of an open question. However, it is important to be aware that issue competition is typically the more dynamic aspect of party competition. Changing party positions easily leads to internal conflict and accusations of pandering, so party positions are typically quite stable (Dalton and McAlister 2015). Parties are to some extent expected to change their issue emphasis especially in response to societal problems. All parties are for instance expected to address COVID-19 and its societal implications. Thus, to understand party strategies and party competition, the issue aspect would often be the most promising place to start from because it is more dynamic than the positional aspect.

What have we learned about issue competition?

Moving beyond the general theoretical discussions about how to conceptualise and study issue competition, the literature has produced several more specific insights. These can broadly be grouped into two types of studies: first, studies that focus on the political parties themselves and their interaction; second, literature that examines how issue competition is related to factors external to the party systems.

Which parties prevail in issue competition?

Starting with the first group of studies, an important line of inquiry has been the role of the government versus opposition dynamic in explaining issue emphasis. With government power follows responsibility. Parties in government have to address almost all societal problems regardless of whether or not the government bears any responsibility for them or whether solutions exist. The COVID-19 pandemic is an obvious example in point. In terms of issue competition, this makes it difficult for the parties in government to avoid issues and focus on preferred ones. The media, the opposition and other political actors will ask those in power to come up with solutions. The opposition, on the other hand, has little power, but with this comes the freedom to focus more on preferred issues. Here, the opposition can vehemently attack the government, which cannot avoid the issues. Following this logic, Green-Pedersen and Mortensen (2010) show how opposition parties are more influential in shaping the party system agenda than government parties, and van de Wardt (2015) shows how government parties respond to opposition, mainstream parties. Seeberg (2013) takes this logic one step further and shows how opposition parties are not only sometimes capable of influencing the issues the government pays attention to, but this may further lead governments to implement policies that they did not want to introduce in the first place. These studies show that the 'government versus opposition' party distinction is important for understanding the dynamics of issue competition, at least outside election campaigns. It is thus worth noticing that this literature uses data sources such as executive speeches or parliamentary questions. Studies based on campaign material, especially party manifestos, typically find little difference between government and opposition parties (Green-Pedersen and Mortensen 2015; Green-Pedersen 2019b).

The literature also distinguishes between mainstream parties and niche parties in terms of their incentives for issue emphasis (see Chapter 19). Relatedly, the role of issue entrepreneurs has also become an important theme (Hobolt and de Vries 2015; de Vries and Hobolt 2020). Whether characterised as niche parties or issue entrepreneurs, parties such as green parties or radical right-wing parties are formed around issues like the environment or immigration, which they continue to focus on. One set of questions then relates to when and to what extent these parties expand their issue focus, for instance how economic and other factors may incentivise green parties to address the economy (Spoon and Williams 2020). However, the main focus has been on how the emergence of these parties has affected the other parties. Building on Meguid's work (2008), most studies focus on the positional aspect – whether other parties adjust their positions – but several studies also focus on the issue competition aspect (Spoon, Hobolt and de Vries 2014; Abou-Chadi 2016; Green-Pedersen 2019b). The jury is still out on whether the emergence of these parties affects the issue focus of other parties, and if so whether the effect is positive or negative. Spoon, Hobolt and de Vries (2014) find that the emergence of green parties, under certain conditions, leads to more attention to the environment. Abou-Chadi (2016) finds the opposite and argues that it depends on the characteristics of the issue. A major complication in researching this question is that, as Meguid (2008) showed, the growth or emergence of niche parties is endogenous to the strategies of the mainstream parties. If they start paying attention to issues like immigration or the environment, they may pave the way for niche party success. In a number of countries, including Sweden and the Netherlands, the environment was thus already an important issue before green parties gained electoral momentum (Green-Pedersen 2019b, 114–134).

Another aspect of party interaction that has been studied in relation to issue competition is coalition politics. Which coalition political parties enter into depends mainly on how they position themselves on the general left-right scale. Such coalition incentives or considerations may then cause parties to emphasise or de-emphasise certain issues. For instance, a political opponent may use an issue for 'wedge competition' against a coalition where the partners might be close to each other on a general left-right scale, but disagree on the specific issue. This wedge logic has been used to explain party issue strategies regarding European integration (van der Wardt, de Vries and Hobolt 2014) and morality issues (Green-Pedersen 2007b). Parties may also increase their attention to certain issues in order to foster a coalition with niche parties. Thus, increased attention to immigration has been shown to be important for mainstream right-wing parties that want to gain government power based on the support of radical right-wing parties (Bale 2003; Green-Pedersen and Otjes 2019). The same logic also applies to social democratic parties which start focusing on the environment when green parties emerge or when social liberal parties emphasise the environment (Mair 2001; Green-Pedersen 2019b, 114–134). Thus, an important effect of the emergence of new niche parties is that they may change patterns of coalition building, which implies different incentives for established parties regarding which issues to focus on. The studies focused directly on niche parties mostly take their point of departure in Meguid's (2008) work and focus on the vote-seeking incentives of mainstream parties. However, the electoral breakthrough of niche parties may also substantially change the coalition incentives of mainstream parties.

Issue competition and outside forces

The aforementioned studies focus on the internal party system dynamics related to issue competition. They examine how different political parties (government/opposition, niche/mainstream, etc.) compete on issues and how we may understand this competition. Another trend within the study of issue competition is to focus on how the party system interacts with outside forces. Issue competition clearly does not take place in a vacuum. The party system constantly interacts with, and is influenced by, a number of outside forces such as the media, the public, problem indicators and interest groups. Their role in issue competition has also received growing attention in the literature.

The role of the media in issue competition is an obvious issue to examine and connects the literature on issue competition with the literature on agenda-setting dynamics and media and politics. The classical focus within this literature has been on the question of who sets whose agenda, that is, do the media set the political agenda or is it the other way around? No clear answer to this question has emerged and this has pushed scholarly attention towards the question of conditionality. Under what conditions does media attention to certain issues lead to political attention to the same issues, and when do we see the opposite influence (Walgrave and Van Aaelst 2006)? For the literature on issue competition, this question of when media attention to issues generates party attention to the same issues is the most important one, though parties' ability to attract attention to their issues in the media is also important (Meyer, Haselmayer and Wagner 2020). A number of studies have thus investigated under what circumstances political parties respond to media attention. From a methodological point of view, coupling media attention, which changes on a daily (or even more frequent) basis, with political attention in time is important. Thus, parliamentary questions have been a preferred data source because party attention to issues can be tracked on a daily basis. A general finding here is that of political conditionality (Thesen 2013; Vliegenthart et al. 2016). Political parties do not automatically respond to media attention. They do so when it is politically attractive to respond. In this way, the literature on media and politics provides a potential explanation for why some parties are able to set the party system agenda, that is, force other parties to pay attention to their preferred issues. When the media starts paying more attention to an issue, it puts the parties that would like to see more party system attention to an issue in a stronger position.

Another outside force discussed in relation to issue competition is public opinion or, more precisely, the public agenda, that is, which issues are important to the public. Ansolabehere and Iyengar (1994) presented the classical 'riding the wave' argument, that is, that political parties follow waves of attention from the public agenda. A series of recent studies have shown how public attention to issues seems to drive party attention (e.g. Klüver and Sagarzazu 2016; Klüver and Spoon 2016; Pardos-Prado and Sagarzazu 2019). However, the effect of public opinion is also clearly conditional: for instance, it declines as an election approaches (Pardos-Prado and Sagarzazu 2019) and larger parties seem more responsive than smaller parties (Klüver and Spoon 2016). Furthermore, the effect of public opinion may primarily relate to issues where the public experiences issue developments in their daily life, that is, obtrusive issues (Soroka 2002). This observation points to a broader theoretical question related to the potential role of the public agenda in issue competition. The media and the party system agendas are generated by a relatively limited number of actors, political parties and major media outlets, which monitor each other and compete. By contrast, the public agenda is the sum of the priorities of many individuals who only interact with a small number of the other individuals involved. Thus, on many issues, it is hard to see how the public agenda by itself can change focus, that is, without this being a reflection of changes in media or party system attention. How the public agenda is set by other forces, especially the media, is one of the most classical agenda-setting findings (McCombs and Shaw 1972).

A further 'outside force' receiving more attention is the development of problem indicators such as unemployment figures or crime rate figures. A number of studies have examined how attention to the economy depends on the state of the economy (Pardos-Prado and Sagarzazu 2019; Traber, Schoonvelde and Schumacher 2020). Rising inequality has also been shown to influence party attention (Tavits and Potter 2015). However, surprisingly few studies (though see Kristensen et al. 2022) within the issue competition literature have tried to theorise the role of problem indicators or looked across different issues. It is thus clear that problem indicators or information plays a key role in issue competition, but the exact role is far from clear and deserves more attention.

A few studies have started to investigate the role of interest groups (Otjes and Green-Pedersen 2021; Klüver 2020). These studies show that interest group mobilisation and strength seem to influence issue competition. Thus, having support from strong interest groups may help parties set the party system agenda. However, the role of interest groups in issue competition has only just emerged as a research topic.

Conclusions and avenues for further research

The study of issue competition has been a growth industry in political science. Critical insights like the importance of issue engagement and of the government versus opposition divide have emerged from this work. From a broader perspective, the issue competition literature has also shown that understanding the mechanisms that drive the issue attention of political parties is crucial for understanding not only the development of party competition and party systems but also political systems in a broader sense. The allocation of party attention to different political issues has become a key dynamic to study.

Many important questions about issue competition of course remain unanswered. The exact role of problem indicators deserves more attention as highlighted earlier. Another related question is the role of issue characteristics. The importance of the scope of problems involved is, for instance, a classical argument within the policy agenda-setting literature (Cobb and Elder 1983, 94–109), and other issue characteristics like obtrusiveness (Soroka 2002) or valence (Abou-Chadi 2016) have also been highlighted. Within the literature on issue competition, a sometimes quite extensive literature on issue competition over specific issues like European integration (Hutter, Grande and Kriesi 2016) or immigration (van der Brug et al. 2015; Grande, Schwarzbözl and Fatke 2019) also exists. However, attempts at building typologies have largely failed (Grossmann 2012). Thus, it is clear that the characteristics of the issue in place matters for issue competition, but exactly how to theorise it is still far from settled.

The recent literature implies that our understanding of issue competition dynamics has in many ways caught up with the understanding of spatial or positional competition. A number of studies highlighted earlier also investigate how positional and issue competition strategies interact (e.g. Guinaudeau and Persico 2014). More work on this is needed, while our understanding of how issue competition interacts with party strategies other than positional ones remains limited, notably the understanding of the interaction between framing strategies and issue competition. The importance of issue framing is central within the policy agenda-setting literature (Baumgartner and Jones 1993), but framing strategies have still not become integrated into the study of issue competition. One reason might be that data on framing of a large number of policy issues over considerable time is difficult to obtain.

Thus, despite the recent boom in studies of issue competition, several important questions require further investigation. However, the literature that has emerged within the last ten years has provided a solid theoretical foundation for addressing these questions.

Notes

1 See https://manifestoproject.wzb.eu/
2 See also comparativeagendas.net
3 See also www.chesdata.eu/

References

Abou-Chadi, T. (2016) 'Niche party success & mainstream party policy shifts', *British Journal of Political Science*, 46(2), p417–436.
Abou-Chadi, T., Green-Pedersen., C. and Mortensen, P.B. (2020) 'Parties' policy adjustments in response to changes in issue saliency', *West European Politics*, 43(4), p749–771.
Ansolabehere, S. and Iyengar, S. (1994) 'Riding the wave and claiming ownership over issues: The joint effects of advertising and news coverage in campaigns', *The Public Opinion Quarterly*, 58(3), p335–357.
Bakker, R., de Vries, C., Edwards, E., Hooghe, L., Jolly, S., Marks, G., Polk, J., Rovny, J., Steenbergen, M. and Vachudova, M.A. (2015) 'Measuring party positions in Europe: The Chapel Hill Expert Survey trend file, 1999–2010', *Party Politics*, 21(1), p143–152.
Bale, T. (2003) 'Cinderella and her ugly sisters: The mainstream and extreme right in Europe's bipolarising party systems', *West European Politics*, 26(3), p67–90.
Baumgartner, F.R., Breunig, C. and Grossman, E. (eds.) (2019) *Comparative policy agendas: theory, tools, data*. Oxford: Oxford University Press.
Baumgartner, F.R. and Jones, B.D. (1993) *Agendas and instability in American politics*. Chicago: University of Chicago Press.
Bevan, S. (2019) 'Gone fishing: The creation of the comparative agendas project master codebook', in Baumgartner, F., Breunig, C. and Grossman, E. (eds.) *Comparative policy agendas: Theory, tools, data*. Oxford: Oxford University Press, pp. 17–34.
Bevan, S. and Greene, Z. (2018) 'Cross-national partisan effects on agenda stability', *Journal of European Public Policy*, 25(4), p586–605.
Budge, I. (2015) 'Issue emphases, saliency theory and issue ownership: A historical and conceptual analysis', *West European Politics*, 38(4), p761–777.
Budge, I. and Farlie, D. (1983) 'Party competition – selective emphasis or direct confrontation? An alternative view with data', in Daalder, H. and Mair, P. (eds.) *West European party systems. Continuity & change*. London: Sage Publications, pp. 267–305.
Budge, I., Klingemann, H.-D., Volkens, A., Bara, J. and Tanenbaum, E. (2001) *Mapping policy preferences. Estimates for parties, electors, and governments 1945–1998*. Oxford: Oxford University Press.

Cobb, R.W. and Elder, C.D. (1983) *Participation in American politics*. Baltimore: Johns Hopkins University Press.

Dalton, R.J. and McAllister, I. (2015) 'Random walk or planned excursion? Continuity and change in the left-right positions of political parties', *Comparative Political Studies*, 48(6), p759–787.

De Sio, L. and Lachat, R. (2020) 'Issue competition in Western Europe: An introduction', *West European Politics*, 43(3), p509–517.

De Sio, L. and Webber, T. (2014) 'Issue yield: A model of party strategy in multidimensional space', *American Political Science Review*, 108(4), p870–885.

de Vries, C.E. and Hobolt, S. (2020) *Political entrepreneurs*. Princeton: Princeton University Press.

Dolezal, M., Ennser-Jedenastik, L., Müller, W.C. and Winkler, A.K. (2013) 'How parties compete for votes: A test of saliency theory', *European Journal of Political Research*, 53(1), p57–76.

Grande, E., Schwarzbözl, T. and Fatke, M. (2019) 'Politicizing immigration in Western Europe', *Journal of European Public Policy*, 26(10), p1444–1463.

Greene, Z. (2016) 'Competing on the issues. How experience in government and economic conditions influence the scope of parties' policy messages', *Party Politics*, 22(6), p209–222.

Green-Pedersen, C. (2007a) 'The growing importance of issue competition: The changing nature of party competition in Western Europe', *Political Studies*, 55(3), p607–628.

Green-Pedersen, C. (2007b) 'The conflict of conflicts in comparative perspective. Euthanasia as a political issue in Denmark, Belgium, and the Netherlands', *Comparative Politics*, 39(3), p273–291.

Green-Pedersen, C. (2019a) 'Issue attention in West European party politics: CAP and CMP coding compared', in Baumgartner, F., Breunig, C. and Grossman, E. (eds.) *Comparative policy agendas: Theory, tools, data*. Oxford: Oxford University Press, pp. 373–390.

Green-Pedersen, C. (2019b) *The reshaping of West European party politics*. Oxford: Oxford University Press.

Green-Pedersen, C. and Mortensen, P.B. (2010) 'Who sets the agenda and who responds to it in the Danish Parliament?' *European Journal of Political Research*, 49(2), p257–281.

Green-Pedersen, C. and Mortensen, P.B. (2015) 'Avoidance and engagement: Issue competition in multiparty systems', *Political Studies*, 63(4), p747–764.

Green-Pedersen, C. and Otjes, S. (2019) 'A hot topic? Immigration on the agenda in Western Europe', *Party Politics*, 25(3), p424–434.

Green-Pedersen, C. and Walgrave, S. (eds.) (2014) *Agenda setting, policies, and political systems: A comparative approach*. Chicago: University of Chicago Press.

Grossmann, M. (2012) 'The variable politics of the policy process: Issue-area differences and comparative networks', *The Journal of Politics*, 75(1), p65–79.

Guinaudeau, I. and Persico, S. (2014) 'What is issue competition? Conflict, consensus and issue ownership in party competition', *Journal of Elections, Public Opinion and Parties*, 24(3), p312–333.

Hobolt, S.B. and de Vries, C. (2015) 'Issue entrepreneurship and multiparty competition', *Comparative Political Studies*, 48(9), p1159–1185.

Holian, D. (2004) 'He's stealing my issues! Clinton's crime rhetoric and the dynamics of issue ownership', *Political Behavior*, 26(2), p95–124.

Hooghe, L. and Marks, G. (2018) 'Cleavage theory meets Europe's crises: Lipset, Rokkan, and the transnational cleavage', *Journal of European Public Policy*, 25(1), p109–135.

Hutter, S., Grande, E. and Kriesi, H. (eds.) (2016) *Politicising Europe. Integration and mass politics*. Cambridge: Cambridge University Press.

Klüver, H. (2020) 'Setting the party agenda: Interest groups, voters and issue attention, *British Journal of Political Science,* 50(3), p979–1000.

Klüver, H. and Sagarzazu, I. (2016) 'Setting the agenda or responding to voters? Political parties, voters and issue attention', *West European Politics*, 39(2), p380–398.

Klüver, H. and Spoon, J. (2016) 'Who responds? Voters, parties and issue attention', *British Journal of Political Science*, 46(3), p633–654.

Kriesi, H., Grande, E., Dolezal, M., Helbinger, M., Höglinger, D., Hutter, S. and Wüest, B. (2012) *Political conflict in Western Europe*. Cambridge: Cambridge University Press.

Kristensen, T.A., Green-Pedersen, C., Mortensen, P.B., Seeberg, H.B. (2022) "Avoiding or engaging problems? Issue ownership, problem indicators, and party issue competition", *Journal of European Public Policy,* DOI: 10.1080/13501763.2022.2135754

Mair, P. (2001) 'The green challenge and political competition: How typical is the German experience?', *German Politics*, 10(2), p99–116.

McCombs, M. and Shaw, D. (1972) 'The agenda-setting function of mass media', *Public Opinion Quarterly*, 36(2), p176–187.

Meguid, B. (2008) *Party competition between unequals. Strategies and electoral fortunes in Western Europe.* Cambridge: Cambridge University Press.

Meyer, T.M., Haselmayer, M. and Wagner, M. (2020) 'Who gets into the papers? Party campaign messages and the media', *British Journal of Political Science*, 50(1), p281–302.

Meyer, T.M. and Wagner, M. (2015) 'Issue engagement in election campaigns. The impact of electoral incentives and organizational constraints', *Political Science Research and Methods*, 4(3), p555–571.

Mortensen, P.B. (2010) 'Political attention and public policy: A study of how agenda setting matters', *Scandinavian Political Studies*, 33(4), p356–380.

Otjes, S. and Green-Pedersen, C. (2021) 'When do political parties prioritize labour? Issue attention between party competition and interest group power', *Party Politics*, 27(4), p619–630.

Pardos-Prado, S. and Sagarzazu, I. (2019) 'Economic responsiveness and the political conditioning of the electoral cycle', *The Journal of Politics*, 81(2), p441–455.

Polk, J., Rovny, J., Bakker, R., Edwards, E., Hooghe, L., Jolly, S., Koedam, J., Kostelka, F., Marks, G., Schumacher, G., Steenbergen, M., Vachudova, M.A. and Zilovic, M. (2017) 'Explaining the salience of anti-elitism and reducing political corruption for political parties in Europe with the 2014 Chapel Hill Expert Survey data', *Research & Politics*, p1–9.

Robertson, D.B. (1976) *A theory of party competition.* London: John Wiley & Sons.

Seeberg, H.B. (2013) 'The opposition's policy influence through issue politicisation', *Journal of Public Policy*, 33(1), p89–107.

Seeberg, H.B. (2017) 'How stable is political parties' issue ownership? A cross-time, cross-national analysis', *Political Studies*, 65(2), p475–492.

Seeberg, H.B. (2022) 'First avoidance, then engagement: Political parties' issue competition in the electoral cycle', *Party Politics*, 28(2), p. 284–293.

Sigelman, L. and Buell, E.B. (2004) 'Avoidance or engagement? Issue convergence in US presidential campaigns, 1960–2000', *American Journal of Political Science*, 48(4), p650–661.

Soroka, S. (2002) *Agenda-setting dynamics in Canada.* Vancouver: University of British Columbia Press.

Spoon, J., Hobolt, S.B. and de Vries, C. (2014) 'Going green: Explaining issue competition on the environment', *European Journal of Political Research*, 53(2), p363–380.

Spoon, J. and Williams, C.J. (2020) '"It's the economy, stupid": When new politics parties take on old politics issues', *West European Politics*, 44(4), p802–824.

Tavits, M. and Potter, J. (2015) 'The effect of inequality and social identity on party strategies', *American Journal of Political Science*, 59(3), p744–758.

Thesen, G. (2013) 'When good news is scarce and bad news is good', *European Journal of Political Research*, 52(3), p364–389.

Traber, D., Schoonvelde, M. and Schumacher, G. (2020) 'Errors have been made, others will be blamed: Issue engagement and blame shifting in prime minister speeches during the economic crisis in Europe', *European Journal of Political Research*, 59(1), p45–67.

van der Brug, W., D'Amato, G., Berkhout, J. and Ruedin, D. (2015) *The politicization of migration.* London: Routledge.

van de Wardt, M. (2015) 'Desperate needs, desperate deeds: Why mainstream parties respond to the issues of niche parties', *West European Politics*, 38(1), p93–122.

van de Wardt, M., de Vries, C. and Hobolt, S.B. (2014) 'Exploiting the cracks: Wedge issues in multiparty competition', *The Journal of Politics*, 76(4), p986–999.

Van Heck, S. (2018) 'Appealing broadly or narrowing down? The impact of government experience and party organization on the scope of parties' issue agendas', *Party Politics*, 24(4), p347–357.

Vliegenthart, R., Walgrave, S., Baumgartner, F.R., Bevan, S., Breunig, C., Brouard, S., Bonafont, L.C., Grossman, E., Jennings, W., Mortensen, P.B., Palau, A.M., Sciarini, P. and Tresch, A. (2016) 'Do the media set the parliamentary agenda? A comparative study in seven countries', *European Journal of Political Research*, 55(2), p283–230.

Wagner, M. (2012) 'When do parties emphasize extreme positions? How incentives for policy differentiation influence issue importance', *European Journal of Political Research*, 51(1), p64–88.

Walgrave, S. and Van Aelst, P. (2006) 'The contingency of the mass media's political agenda setting power: Toward a preliminary theory', *Journal of Communication*, 56(1), p88–109.

Wilkerson, J. and Casas, A. (2017) 'Large-scale computerized text analysis in political science: Opportunities and challenges', *Annual Review of Political Science*, 20, p529–544.

19
NICHE PARTIES AND PARTY COMPETITION

Markus Wagner

In many countries, party systems have undergone substantial transformation in recent decades. Contestation based on 'old' issues – the economy and the welfare state – has been complemented by debates on 'new' issues such as immigration, the environment, devolution or European integration. At the same time, new parties have emerged and grown, focusing on precisely these new topics. Many party systems now have radical-right and Green parties, and some party systems also contain parties that focus on regional power or European integration.

This chapter discusses these parties jointly using the term 'niche parties'. As we will see, the precise definition of niche parties is not entirely settled, but there is broad consensus on general points. Thus, typical niche parties are Green parties, radical right parties and regionalist parties; other single-issue parties that focus on issues such as European integration or women's rights may also fit into this category (Mudde 1999). Traditionally, these parties emphasise one topic more than the rest of the party system does, be it the environment, immigration or devolution/independence. These topics also tend to cross-cut existing party system cleavages, which is why these parties present a unique challenge to mainstream party competition (van de Wardt, de Vries and Hobolt 2014).

In this chapter, I will first describe in more detail how 'niche parties' have been defined. Then, I will consider three questions examined by researchers in recent work: What are the strategies of niche parties? How have mainstream parties responded to the threat posed by niche parties? And when are niche parties electorally successful? In the conclusion, I will reflect on whether the niche party label remains a useful way of grouping parties and suggest avenues for further research.

Definitions and characteristics

The label 'niche parties' was coined to find an encompassing term for non-mainstream parties. Mainstream parties are established competitors within party systems and aim to be as large as possible by appealing to centrist voters. Usually, these parties have some form of governing experience (de Vries and Hobolt 2020), but this is not a necessary characteristic. Typical examples of mainstream parties are Labour and the Conservatives in the UK, the Christian Democrats and Social Democrats in Germany or the Socialist Party and the Popular Party in Spain. More broadly, Social Democratic, Christian Democratic and Conservative parties are generally seen as 'mainstream' (see also Chapters 12 and 14).

From the 1980s onwards, party systems were increasingly characterised by competitors that did not fit the mainstream label (de Vries and Hobolt 2020). Green and Radical Right parties started to become consistent competitors in countries such as Austria, Belgium, Germany, the Netherlands, Switzerland and across Nordic countries (Mudde 2014; Spoon, Hobolt and de Vries 2014; Grant and Tilley 2019; see also Chapters 11 and 16). Given this trend, researchers began to study whether these new parties share common strategies and how mainstream parties respond to their emergence; the most influential and path-breaking work is that by Meguid (2005, 2008). The label 'niche parties' signals that these parties share enough characteristics that one umbrella term can be used to describe them. However, there is some disagreement as to what these shared characteristics are (see Table 19.1).

The core meaning of 'niche' is that something is of limited appeal: interests and tastes are 'niche' if they are of interest to only a small section of the population. While, for most people, the product or hobby is too eccentric or otherwise unappealing, some people love it. The equivalent for political parties is a focus on narrow topics that lie outside the core of party competition. This is essentially the approach of Meguid (2005, 2008) who defines niche parties based on three characteristics: they do not focus on traditional topics of party competition, specifically economic debates; they raise topics that do not match established dimensions of party competition; and they pursue a limited range of issue appeals (for issue competition, see also Chapter 18).

Meguid's definition was modified and simplified in later work (Wagner 2012; Meyer and Miller 2015; Zons 2016; Bischof 2017). For instance, Wagner (2012) drops the requirement that the issues niche parties address fail to correlate with established dimensions of party competition as this is difficult to implement empirically, while Meyer and Miller (2015) aim to provide a more general definition of niche parties and therefore additionally drop the requirement that niche parties fail to focus on economic topics. Like Wagner (2012), Bischof (2017) argues that niche parties focus on a narrow range of niche market segments, while Zons (2016) focuses on 'programmatic

Table 19.1 Definitions of niche parties and nicheness

Source	Definition	Measurement
Meguid (2005, 2008)	(1) Niche parties reject the class-based orientation of politics (2) The issues raised by niche parties are novel and do not coincide with existing lines of political division (3) Niche parties limit their issue appeals	Party family (Green, radical-right and ethno-regionalist)
Adams et al. (2006)	Extremist or non-centrist niche ideology	Party family (Communist, Green, radical-right)
Wagner (2012)	Niche parties compete primarily on a small number of non-economic issues	Binary measure based on party manifestos and expert surveys
Meyer/Miller (2015)	Niche parties emphasise policy areas neglected by their competitors	Continuous measure based on party manifestos
Zons (2016)	Niche parties emphasise different issues than their competitors and talk about few issues	Continuous measures based on party manifestos
Bischof (2017)	Niche parties predominantly compete on niche market segments neglected by their competitors, but do not discuss a broad range of these segments	Continuous measure based on party manifestos

concentration'. Related work by Greene (2016), not directly aimed at studying niche parties, uses issue diversity as its key measure. Hence, these later definitions focus in particular on the narrowness of parties' issue appeals, with niche parties essentially defined as emphasising some issues more than competitors. While these later definitions differ in several points, for example in their treatment of economic issues, they all base their definitions around the salience of issue appeals pursued by niche parties rather than on other characteristics such as their issue positions. This later research also tended to move away from using party family membership to decide which parties are niche competitors. Instead, it has classified niche parties based on widely available datasets on party positions and salience (see Chapters 38 and 40).

A second approach to understanding niche parties saw the common feature of the new challenger parties as less about the topics they addressed and more about the positions they took. This second definition, used mainly by Adams et al. (2006), thus sees niche parties as ideologically extreme parties outside of the political mainstream (see also Ezrow 2008; Adams, Ezrow and Leiter 2012). Adams et al. (2006) apply this definition to Green, Communist and Radical Right parties. What unites these parties is therefore their willingness to take positions far from the political centre. Note that the inclusion of Communist parties is the key difference to salience-based definitions of niche parties. As Communist parties emphasise economic topics, almost always a central feature of party competition, this party family is not characterised as niche by Meguid (2005, 2008) and related work.

Use of the second definition has been less widespread, perhaps because the niche-as-extremism definition is less succinct than simply focusing on ideological extremism directly, both theoretically and empirically. Moreover, Green parties are not particularly extreme in most party systems. Finally, researchers may have seen commonalities in terms of issue salience as more characteristic of niche parties than issue positions on a left-right scale. In other words, what unites the newcomers upsetting old patterns of party competition is not that they introduce extreme positions. After all, Communist parties, which took extreme positions on economic issues, had been important competitors in many party systems for several decades. Instead, it is the introduction of new issues that truly captured what was distinctive about this group of parties. In the rest of this chapter, the definition based on Meguid will be used as the main definition of niche parties.

Can parties move in and out of being a niche party? In Meguid's (2005, 2008) and Adams et al.'s (2006) original formulation, niche parties were fixed, at least within the period they studied. However, later work generally allowed for time-specific classification. Most prominently, Meyer and Wagner (2013) show that switching between niche and mainstream profiles is frequent; in their sample, 68 per cent of parties classified as a niche party in one election switch to a mainstream profile in the subsequent one. As discussed later, the narrowness of a party's issue profile is in part a strategic choice.

Finally, niche parties are related to other party types. Most closely related are single-issue parties (e.g. Mudde 1999), a sub-type of niche parties that focus on one specific topic almost exclusively. Another related type of party is the issue entrepreneur (de Vries and Hobolt 2012; Hobolt and de Vries 2015). These parties actively try to mobilise new issues that were hitherto largely ignored by mainstream party competition or where mainstream parties hitherto took centrist positions. Niche parties frequently act as issue entrepreneurs in party competition, especially in their efforts to push party systems to focus on new issues. Niche parties also share features with challenger parties, which are usually defined as parties that have never been in government (de Vries and Hobolt 2012, 2020). Both niche and challenger parties are seen as opposing mainstream parties. The difference is that the niche-mainstream distinction is based on programmatic characteristics, while the challenger-mainstream distinction is based on the simple fact of never having governed. At least until recently, many or even most niche parties had never governed and were thus challenger parties. Challenger parties may also be more likely to choose niche strategies (Allen, Bara and Bartle 2017). However, long-standing niche parties have increasingly entered governments directly or tolerated minority governments in many European countries such as Austria, Germany or the Netherlands (Bischof, Dumont and Strøm 2019; on the radical right, e.g. de Lange 2012; Twist 2019), so the overlap between the categories is declining.

Niche parties also share other characteristics, but these are not essential to their definition. Niche parties tend, on average, to have been founded more recently and to be more ideologically extreme than mainstream parties (Wagner 2012). They are also still less likely to be in government or have governed (Bischof, Dumont and Strøm 2019). Finally, some niche parties may be more likely to be led by activists rather than a narrower cadre of elite politicians. For instance, many radical right parties are often dominated by a small group of leaders. Geert Wilders' party in the Netherlands is an extreme example of this. However, this is not a consistent characteristic of niche parties: the correlation between nicheness and activist influence is positive but very weak (Bischof and Wagner 2020, fn. 49). There is also little evidence that niche parties are particularly policy-seeking rather than office-seeking (Bischof and Wagner 2020, fn. 49). Finally, niche parties in non-European party systems may be different; for instance, in Latin America niche parties often focus on group representation rather than programmatic linkage (Kernecker and Wagner 2019).

Niche party aims and strategies

Niche parties are generally defined by the strong emphasis on their core issues, but they also tend to hold strong policy preferences on these issues. Their ultimate aim is therefore to achieve policy change in the area they focus on. Niche parties may be more single-minded than mainstream parties, which tend to follow a more 'catch-all' strategy, following the preferences of the median voter (Adams et al. 2006; Bischof and Wagner 2020).

There are two ways in which niche parties try to make it more likely that their political goals become reality: politicisation and contagion. Politicisation means that the topic becomes more important across the political system as a whole (Green-Pedersen and Otjes 2019) while also becoming more divisive and polarised (Hutter and Grande 2014). When niche parties manage to turn their main issue into a key debate, polarisation is an inherent consequence, as niche parties tend to have distinctive positions on these issues.

Politicisation is useful to niche parties, because they may be able to attract more voters if an issue becomes more important. Salience determines the weight of issues in citizens' calculus of voting. Given niche parties' distinctive position and frequent ownership of their issue, increased politicisation of their core topic may promise electoral success. Politicisation may also be useful if this means that parties that share their policy goals actually address these topics. This will make it more likely that these issues then become part of government policy. In this way, politicisation is a key step that precedes policy change.

Contagion means that other parties take up the niche party's positions (van Spanje 2010). The aim is to make mainstream parties adopt the niche party's views. For example, one of UKIP's aims was to influence the Conservative Party's position on the EU. Although UKIP never governed, its electoral success was one factor in leading the Conservatives to conduct a referendum on EU membership (Hobolt 2016). Similarly, one goal of green and radical right parties is for mainstream parties to shift towards them.

Through politicisation and contagion, niche parties can achieve their policy aims, even without governing themselves. This does not mean that niche parties do not seek power, even if some green parties were initially reluctant to do so. After all, entering government will be the most straightforward way to implement their desired policies.

Beyond their overarching aim to increase issue politicisation, niche parties differ from mainstream parties in the other issue-based strategies they pursue. Niche parties thus tend to pay less attention to broader attitudes in the general public. Specifically, niche parties do not react to aggregate changes in public opinion, or more specifically to movements in the position of the median voter (Adams et al. 2006). More recent work by Bischof and Wagner (2020) confirms this using a direct measure of niche issue emphasis.

However, niche parties are nevertheless strategic actors. For instance, niche parties are more likely to respond to shifts among their own supporters (Ezrow et al. 2011; Ferland 2020; though see Romeijn 2020). Niche parties (specifically green parties) are responsive to their supporters in the emphasis they give to the environment (Klüver and Spoon 2016). This pattern of response to supporters' preferences may come about because niche parties are more focused on their activists (though see Bischof and Wagner 2020). There is also evidence that niche parties are responsive to external developments such as electoral prospects and competitors' campaigns. Niche parties moderate their positions in order to guarantee survival in parliament (Pereira 2020, though see Maeda 2016). Niche parties also respond to shifts of proximate parties, especially on their core issues (Tromborg 2015). Meyer and Wagner (2013) find that niche parties' decision to broaden their issue focus, thus becoming a more mainstream competitor, is often due to electoral setbacks. Niche parties are no different from other parties in that vote-seeking incentives can inspire changes in party behaviour (Somer-Topcu 2009). Green parties may reflect the variability in nicheness well, as they have recently broadened their profile to encompass other topics such as immigration or pro-European positions.

Mainstream party responses

So far, we have focused on niche parties and how they behave, but how do mainstream parties react to this electoral threat? In her enormously influential article, Meguid (2005) identified three mainstream party responses: dismissive, accommodative and adversarial strategies. First, dismissive strategies are present when mainstream parties try to ignore the niche party in the hope that it will then weaken on its own. For example, mainstream parties may try to reduce the salience of immigration by not addressing the topic. The aim is to reduce or keep the importance of the topic low among voters, while also signalling that the topic does not merit attention (Meguid 2005).

However, dismissive strategies might be quite difficult to pursue in practice. This may be because of the pressure of real-world events and of media attention, while the party system agenda as a whole also exerts pressure on all parties to address an issue. If mainstream parties do decide to take up the issues that niche parties raise, then they face two choices: they can either take positions similar to those of the niche party, or they can take opposing stances. These are the accommodative and adversarial strategies.

Mainstream parties pursue accommodative strategies when they take up similar positions as the niche party on their issue: for example, a mainstream party may become critical of immigration in order to respond to the radical right. van Spanje and de Graaf (2018) term this strategy 'parroting'. The aim of an accommodative strategy is to weaken the niche party's ownership of 'their' issue and steal their (potential) voters by taking up essentially the same position.

Mainstream parties' reputation for competence may be helpful in this goal (Meguid 2005), as may be the low social acceptability of niche parties (van Spanje and de Graaf 2018). Of course, accommodation in the pursuit of electoral success ironically helps niche parties achieve one of their strategic aims, namely contagion. Accommodation thus means that niche parties have managed to influence mainstream party positions, and in a direction they welcome.

Adversarial strategies denote the opposite response: mainstream parties take up a contrasting stance. For instance, a mainstream party may become more supportive of immigration in response to the radical right. The aim of this strategy is complex, as the mainstream party may in fact want to strengthen the niche party and its issue ownership in order to weaken a common rival (Meguid 2005). For example, a centre-right party could aim to strengthen a green party to hurt the appeal of the social democrats. Hence, adversarial strategies make it more difficult for other mainstream parties to successfully pursue a dismissive strategy. In this way, mainstream parties may see politicisation as an opportunity, albeit risky, to weaken a mainstream rival.

Abou-Chadi (2016) finds that green party success does not lead to increased mainstream party emphasis on the environment (though see Spoon, Hobolt and de Vries 2014). Similarly, Carter (2013) shows that there remains a large gap in the programmes of green and mainstream parties in their emphasis on the environment. However, mainstream parties respond much more to radical-right parties by emphasising immigration (Abou-Chadi 2016; Wagner and Meyer 2017), to the extent that it may be hard to speak of immigration as a niche issue in today's context. Emphasis contagion also exists for other types of niche parties, for instance those that focus on feminist issues (Cowell-Meyers 2017).

One reason for the difference between mainstream party responses on environment and immigration may lie in the nature of the debate on these issues. The environment has a clear positive issue owner – green parties – and the topic is largely discussed in so-called valence terms, with all parties largely agreeing on the goal to be achieved (Abou-Chadi 2016; see also Chapter 17). In contrast, immigration lacks a clear issue owner and is characterised by a diversity of party positions. As a result, politicisation of the environment clearly benefits green parties: if the issue is important to voters, then they are likely to turn to the greens as they 'own' the topic in the minds of many. The dynamics on the issue of immigration are quite different, with politicisation less likely to benefit the radical right as parties take diverse positions on the issue and voters disagree on the correct policies to pursue. These patterns could explain why mainstream parties may try to avoid addressing the environment as much as possible, while being quite willing to talk about immigration (Abou-Chadi 2016).

Accommodation is a frequent way that mainstream parties respond to the niche party challenge. Most research here concerns the radical right, with a key finding being that mainstream parties move to the right on immigration issues in response to the rise of the radical right (e.g. Bale et al. 2010; van Spanje 2010; Han 2015; Schumacher and van Kersbergen 2016; Wagner and Meyer 2017; Abou-Chadi and Krause 2020). On the mainstream left, accommodation is more conditional: they will emulate the radical right more if they suffer electoral setbacks or if voter opinion encourages this (Han 2015). In some countries, accommodation was limited by a more effective cordon sanitaire that prevented parties from mainstreaming radical-right positions; in other words, political norms ostracising extreme competitors proved more effective in some countries than in others. For instance, Swedish parties were slow to accommodate the radical-right Sweden Democrats, especially compared to their Nordic neighbours (Heinze 2018). In addition, responses to niche parties are stronger among opposition than among governing parties (van de Wardt 2015). Hence, many mainstream parties tend to pursue an accommodative stance, at least in reaction to radical-right success.

Explaining the electoral success of niche parties

When are niche parties electorally successful? Most centrally, it is essential that the issues these parties address are salient among the public (Lindstam 2019). Green parties benefit during tangible environmental disputes or when many voters have postmaterialist values (Grant and Tilley 2019), while the importance of immigration is associated with radical right success (Dennison 2020). In related work, de Vries and Hobolt (2012) focus on issue entrepreneurs and find that this is an electorally successful strategy, at least for the issue of European integration. This applies in particular to challenger parties, which are parties that have never participated in a national government. It is perhaps this challenger status that helps to explain why niche parties also often attract protest voters, that is, those who care less about the positions of the party they vote for than about punishing mainstream parties (Hong 2015). Further research indicates that niche parties may also benefit from economic crises (Hobolt and Tilley 2016), especially if mainstream parties converge on austerity positions (Hübscher, Sattler and Wagner 2019; but see Grittersova et al. 2016).

Once niche parties emerge on the scene, can mainstream parties effectively respond to the niche threat by taking up their positions? Evidence for this is weak at best. Meguid (2005, 2008) found that mainstream party strategies do affect niche party success. Mainstream party accommodation towards the greens can be successful under certain conditions (Grant and Tilley 2019). However, more recent cross-national analyses fail to identify electoral benefits of accommodation, particularly as concerns the radical right (Krause, Cohen and Abou-Chadi 2022). Mainstream party accommodation on immigration and European integration instead appears often to help the radical right (e.g. Meijers and Williams 2020). This may apply in particular to accommodation by the mainstream left (Abou-Chadi and Wagner 2020; Down and Han 2020; but see Spoon and Klüver 2020). However, some research is more positive on the prospects of accommodation to reduce radical-right support (van Spanje and de Graaf 2018; Hjorth and Vinaes Larsen forthcoming), while Pardos-Prado's (2015) careful, complex analysis highlights that the effectiveness of mainstream right strategies may depend on how immigration is integrated into the core dimensions of party competition.

Importantly, the electoral success of niche party strategies as well as mainstream party strategies to contain them may vary over time. Young niche parties may be combated more effectively than more established niche parties. Thus, Hino's (2012) analysis of challenger parties shows that these are more successful when their core topics are disregarded by mainstream parties, especially just after the emergence of these parties. Similarly, Zons (2016) shows that narrow issue profiles are helpful when these parties have recently entered the electoral arena, but the advantages of these narrow profiles erode as these parties age. Finally, mainstream parties can undermine green parties through accommodative strategies only when these are young (Grant and Tilley 2019). These over-time dynamics may explain why Meguid's (2005, 2008) findings do not hold as strongly anymore.

Niche parties also vary in their strategies, particularly how narrowly they pitch their appeal and how moderately they position themselves. Evidence that these decisions matter is varied. Thus, Bergman and Flatt (2020) show that radical-right parties gain votes by broadening their issue appeal, while green parties do not. Like Abou-Chadi (2016), these findings indicate that the dynamics of niche-mainstream competition is not uniform. Concerning positioning, niche parties do not appear to benefit from moderation, unlike mainstream parties (Adams et al. 2006, Ezrow 2008).

Some work also considers the electoral venues in which niche parties can achieve success most easily. Specifically, contests at the regional level (Farrer 2015) and EU level (Schulte-Cloos 2018) may foster niche party success, allowing them to establish themselves as national competitors.

A distinct question is when niche parties manage to enter government. De Lange (2012) addresses this topic by examining radical-right incorporation in governments. She shows that standard theories of coalition formation can straightforwardly explain why mainstream right parties chose to include radical-right parties in their coalitions. Research on green parties indicates that they are most likely to enter governments if the mainstream left is the formateur (Dumont and Bäck 2006), though there have also been several examples of green coalitions with moderate right parties at the regional or national level in Austria, Finland, Germany and Ireland. Some research also studies regionalist parties (e.g. Tronconi 2015). General research on niche party inclusion in government is so far lacking (but see Bischof, Dumont and Strøm 2019). We also know little about how government participation affects the issue profile of niche parties (though see Greene 2016).

Conclusions and avenues for further research

The term 'niche party' is relatively recent, but in the 15 or so years since its invention, there has been a broad range of research studying their strategies and electoral success. It is undeniable that niche parties have a wide-ranging influence on party competition and party systems. Since Meguid's 2005 publication, a key focus has also been on the systemic effect of niche parties, specifically on how niche parties shape mainstream party programmes and strategies. The political effect of niche parties thus often goes beyond their vote share or their immediate government participation. The best example of this is the effect of the radical right on mainstream parties on the right and, to a lesser extent, on the left. It is perhaps ironic that there is not much evidence that these mainstream party reactions are at all effective in achieving their goal of reducing the niche party threat.

Research on niche and mainstream parties suffers from three shortcomings that are also potential pathways for future innovation. First, the niche/mainstream distinction is just one way in which parties differ. As discussed earlier, parties also differ in their ideological positions, their political goals and their internal organisation (see e.g. Bischof and Wagner 2020). These characteristics also determine party strategies and the reactions of other parties. Future research should do better in examining how being a niche competitor has an impact distinct from being, say, policy-oriented, activist-led and ideologically non-centrist. Bischof and Wagner (2020) made a first attempt, but more needs to be done to isolate the effects of different party characteristics.

Second, the literature on party competition should move towards greater methodological innovation. There are limits to what we can extract from election-level data from European countries and with programmatic data from party manifestos or expert surveys. This is mainly due to the low number of observations this produces, for instance limiting our ability to track over-time changes in rhetoric. On the one hand, we could expand the range of cases we study, so researchers could try harder to examine niche-mainstream competition outside the usual cases, such as in Central and Eastern Europe, Latin America (Kernecker and Wagner 2019) or Asia. In addition, we could expand the range of data we study, for example by examining party press releases (e.g. Klüver and Sagarzazu 2016) and turning towards more fine-grained analyses of how parties engage with each other. We could move towards methods more strongly oriented towards establishing causality, either by using survey experiments (e.g. Hjorth and Vinaes Larsen 2022) or causal inference methods (e.g. Abou-Chadi and Krause 2020).

Finally, it is important to re-evaluate the need and usefulness of the niche-mainstream distinction altogether. Parties once treated as niche are now electorally successful in many European countries, while some of their traditional mainstream parties are in some places close to irrelevance. On the Dutch and French Left, the mainstream social democrats can hardly claim to be significantly stronger than the greens, and such developments are common in many countries. More importantly, the concerns that niche parties address – most prominently immigration and the environment – are by no means 'niche' topics in many countries. It would be interesting to know how time-variant measures of nicheness such as Meyer and Miller (2015) characterise party system changes in the last decade. In any case, it is becoming increasingly hard to treat parties focusing on immigration and the environment as somehow removed from 'normal' party competition.

Instead of the niche-mainstream competition, we have now moved towards a competitive context where multidimensionality is the norm and large mainstream parties are either in decline or under permanent threat (de Vries and Hobolt 2020). Perhaps a more accurate approach to studying contemporary politics would be to abandon programmatic categories in favour of specific measurement of the salience and position of parties on key dimensions. Instead of niche-mainstream, the key distinction is then which dimension a party prioritises. A rallying cry could then be: The era of niche parties is dead, long live the era of multidimensional party competition.

References

Abou-Chadi, T. (2016) 'Niche party success and mainstream party policy shifts – How green and radical right parties differ in their impact', *British Journal of Political Science*, 46(2), p417–436.

Abou-Chadi, T. and Krause, W. (2020) 'The causal effect of radical right success on mainstream parties' policy positions: A regression discontinuity approach', *British Journal of Political Science*. 50(3), 829–847.

Abou-Chadi, T. and Wagner, M. (2020) 'Electoral fortunes of social democratic parties: Do second dimension positions matter?', *Journal of European Public Policy*, 27(2), p246–272.

Adams, J., Clark, M., Ezrow, L. and Glasgow, G. (2006) 'Are niche parties fundamentally different from mainstream parties? The causes and the electoral consequences of Western European parties' policy shifts 1976–1998', *American Journal of Political Science*, 50(3), p513–529.

Adams, J., Ezrow, L. and Leiter, D. (2012) 'Partisan sorting and niche parties in Europe', *West European Politics*, 35(6), p1272–1294.

Allen, N., Bara, J. and Bartle, J. (2017) 'Finding a niche? Challenger parties and issue emphasis in the 2015 televised leaders' debates', *The British Journal of Politics and International Relations*, 19(4), p807–823.

Bale, T., Green-Pedersen, C., Krouwel, A., Luther, K.R. and Sitter, N. (2010) 'If you can't beat them, join them? Explaining social democratic responses to the challenge from the populist radical right in Western Europe', *Political Studies*, 58(3), p410–426.

Bergman, M.E. and Flatt, H. (2020) 'Issue diversification: Which niche parties can succeed electorally by broadening their agenda?', *Political Studies*, 68(3), p710–730.

Bischof, D. (2017) 'Towards a renewal of the niche party concept: Parties, market shares and condensed offers', *Party politics*, 23(3), p220–235.

Bischof, D., Dumont, P. and Strøm, K. (2019) 'How parties of niche origin become junior coalition partners', Working Paper. Available from: https://www.semanticscholar.org/paper/How-Parties-of-Niche-Origin-Become-Junior-Coalition-Bischof-Dumont/568bec55e4bf8826659314b44fab835cfe8bf3d0

Bischof, D. and Wagner, M. (2020) 'What makes parties adapt to voter preferences? The role of party organization, goals and ideology', *British Journal of Political Science*, 50(1), p391–401.

Carter, N. (2013) 'Greening the mainstream: party politics and the environment', *Environmental Politics*, 22(1), p73–94.

Cowell-Meyers, K. (2017) 'The contagion effects of the Feminist Initiative in Sweden: Agenda-setting, niche parties and mainstream parties', *Scandinavian Political Studies*, 40(4), p481–493.

de Lange, S.L. (2012) 'New alliances: why mainstream parties govern with radical right-wing populist parties', *Political Studies*, 60(4), p899–918.

de Vries, C.E. and Hobolt, S.B. (2012) 'When dimensions collide: The electoral success of issue entrepreneurs', *European Union Politics*, 13(2), p246–268.

de Vries, C.E. and Hobolt, S.B. (2020) *Political entrepreneurs*. Princeton: Princeton University Press.

Dennison, J. (2020) 'How issue salience explains the rise of the populist right in Western Europe', *International Journal of Public Opinion Research*, 32(3), p397–420.

Down, I. and Han, K.J. (2020) 'Marginalisation or legitimation? Mainstream party positioning on immigration and support for radical right parties'. *West European Politics*, 43(7), p1388–1414.

Dumont, P. and Bäck, H. (2006) 'Why so few, and why so late? Green parties and the question of governmental participation', *European Journal of Political Research*, 45(1), p35–67.

Ezrow, L. (2008) 'Research note: On the inverse relationship between votes and proximity for niche parties', *European Journal of Political Research*, 47(2), p206–220.

Ezrow, L., De Vries, C., Steenbergen, M. and Edwards, E. (2011) 'Mean voter representation and partisan constituency representation: Do parties respond to the mean voter position or to their supporters?', *Party Politics*, 17(3), p275–301

Farrer, B. (2015) 'Connecting niche party vote change in first-and second-order elections', *Journal of Elections, Public Opinion and Parties*, 25(4), p482–503.

Ferland, B. (2020) 'Party responsiveness to public opinion and party supporters: Revisiting the mechanisms and motivations'. *Party Politics*, 26(4), p366–378.

Grant, Z.P. and Tilley, J. (2019) 'Fertile soil: explaining variation in the success of green parties', *West European Politics*, 42(3), p495–516.

Green-Pedersen, C. and Otjes, S. (2019) 'A hot topic? Immigration on the agenda in Western Europe', *Party Politics*, 25(3), p424–434.

Greene, Z. (2016) 'Competing on the issues: How experience in government and economic conditions influence the scope of parties' policy messages', *Party Politics*, 22(6), p809–822.

Grittersova, J., Indridason, I.H., Gregory, C.C. and Crespo, R. (2016) 'Austerity and niche parties: The electoral consequences of fiscal reforms', *Electoral Studies*, 42, p276–289.

Han, K.J. (2015) 'The impact of radical right-wing parties on the positions of mainstream parties regarding multiculturalism', *West European Politics*, 38(3), p557–576.

Heinze, A.S. (2018) 'Strategies of mainstream parties towards their right-wing populist challengers: Denmark, Norway, Sweden and Finland in comparison', *West European Politics*, 41(2), p287–309.

Hino, A. (2012) *New challenger parties in Western Europe: a comparative analysis*. Abingdon: Routledge.

Hjorth, F. and Vinaes Larsen, M. (2022) 'When Does Accommodation Work? Electoral Effects of Mainstream Left Position-Taking on Immigration', *British Journal of Political Science*, 52(2), p949–957.

Hobolt, S.B. (2016) 'The Brexit vote: a divided nation, a divided continent', *Journal of European Public Policy*, 23(9), p1259–1277.

Hobolt, S.B. and De Vries, C.E. (2015) 'Issue entrepreneurship and multiparty competition', *Comparative Political Studies*, 48(9), p1159–1185.

Hobolt, S.B. and Tilley, J. (2016) 'Fleeing the centre: the rise of challenger parties in the aftermath of the euro crisis', *West European Politics*, 39(5), p971–991.

Hong, G. (2015) 'Explaining vote switching to niche parties in the 2009 European Parliament elections', *European Union Politics*, 16(4), p514–535.

Hübscher, E., Sattler, T. and Wagner, M. (2019) 'Does austerity cause political polarization?', Working Paper. Available from: https://www.semanticscholar.org/paper/Does-Austerity-Cause-Political-Polarization-and-Huebscher-Sattler/3accb29c5dee6c37f915924c32dd04d00a63502a

Hutter, S. and Grande, E. (2014) 'Politicizing Europe in the national electoral arena: A comparative analysis of five West European countries 1970–2010', *JCMS: Journal of Common Market Studies*, 52(5), p1002–1018.

Kernecker, T. and Wagner, M. (2019) 'Niche parties in Latin America', *Journal of Elections, Public Opinion and Parties*, 29(1), p102–124.

Klüver, H. and Sagarzazu, I. (2016) 'Setting the agenda or responding to voters? Political parties, voters and issue attention', *West European Politics*, 39(2), p380–398.

Klüver, H. and Spoon, J. (2016) 'Who responds? Voters, parties and issue attention', *British Journal of Political Science*, 46(3), p633–654.

Krause, W., Cohen, D. and Abou-Chadi, T. (2022) 'Does Accommodation Work? Mainstream Party Strategies and the Success of Radical Right Parties', *Political Science Research and Methods*, p1–8. doi:10.1017/psrm.2022.8

Lindstam, E. (2019) Signalling issue salience: Explaining niche party support in second-order elections. *Electoral Studies*, 60, p1–11.

Maeda, K. (2016) 'What motivates moderation? Policy shifts of ruling parties, opposition parties and niche parties', *Representation*, 52(2–3), p215–226.

Meguid, B.M. (2005) 'Competition between unequals: The role of mainstream party strategy in niche party success', *American Political Science Review*, 99(3), p347–359.

Meguid, B.M. (2008) *Party competition between unequals*. Cambridge: Cambridge University Press.

Meijers, M.J. and Williams, C.J. (2020) 'When shifting backfires: The electoral consequences of responding to niche party EU positions', *Journal of European Public Policy*, 27(10), p1506–1525.

Meyer, T.M. and Miller, B. (2015) 'The niche party concept and its measurement', *Party Politics*, 21(2), p259–271.

Meyer, T.M. and Wagner, M. (2013) 'Mainstream or niche? Vote-seeking incentives and the programmatic strategies of political parties', *Comparative Political Studies*, 46(10), p1246–1272.

Mudde, C. (1999) 'The single-issue party thesis: Extreme right parties and the immigration issue', *West European Politics*, 22(3), p182–197.

Mudde, C. (2014) 'Fighting the system? Populist radical right parties and party system change', *Party Politics*, 20(2), p217–226.

Pardos-Prado, S. (2015) 'How can mainstream parties prevent niche party success? Center-right parties and the immigration issue'. *The Journal of Politics*, 77(2), p352–367.

Pereira, M.M. (2020) 'Responsive Campaigning: Evidence from European Parties'. *The Journal of Politics*, 82(4), p1183–1195.

Romeijn, J. (2020) 'Do political parties listen to the(ir) public? Public opinion – Party linkage on specific policy issues', *Party Politics*, 26(4), p426–436.

Schulte-Cloos, J. (2018) 'Do European Parliament elections foster challenger parties' success on the national level?', *European Union Politics*, 19(3), p408–426.

Schumacher, G. and van Kersbergen, K. (2016) 'Do mainstream parties adapt to the welfare chauvinism of populist parties?', *Party Politics*, 22(3), p300–312.

Somer-Topcu, Z. (2009) 'Timely decision: The effect of past national elections on party policy change', *Journal of Politics*, 71, p238–248.

Spoon, J., Hobolt, S.B. and de Vries, C.E. (2014) 'Going green: Explaining issue competition on the environment', *European Journal of Political Research*, 53(2), p363–380.

Spoon, J. and Klüver, H. (2020) 'Responding to far right challengers: Does accommodation pay off?', *Journal of European Public Policy*, 27(2), p273–291.

Tromborg, M.W. (2015) 'Space jam: Are niche parties strategic or looney?', *Electoral Studies*, 40, p189–199.

Tronconi, F. (2015) 'Ethno-regionalist parties in regional government: Multilevel coalitional strategies in Italy and Spain', *Government and Opposition*, 50(4), p578–606.

Twist, K.A. (2019) *Partnering with extremists: Coalitions between mainstream and far-right parties in Western Europe*. Ann Arbor: University of Michigan Press.

van de Wardt, M. (2015) 'Desperate needs, desperate deeds: Why mainstream parties respond to the issues of niche parties', *West European Politics*, 38(1), p93–122.

van de Wardt, M., de Vries, C.E. and Hobolt, S.B. (2014) 'Exploiting the cracks: Wedge issues in multi-party competition', *The Journal of Politics*, 76(4), p986–999.

van Spanje, J. (2010) 'Contagious parties: Anti-immigration parties and their impact on other parties' immigration stances in contemporary Western Europe', *Party Politics*, 16(5), p563–586.

van Spanje, J. and de Graaf, N.D. (2018) 'How established parties reduce other parties' electoral support: The strategy of parroting the pariah', *West European Politics*, 41(1), p1–27.

Wagner, M. (2012) 'Defining and measuring niche parties', *Party Politics*, 18(6), p845–864.

Wagner, M. and Meyer, T.M. (2017) 'The radical right as niche parties? The ideological landscape of party systems in Western Europe' 1980–2014. *Political Studies*, 65(1_suppl), p84–107.

Zons, G. (2016) 'How programmatic profiles of niche parties affect their electoral performance', *West European Politics*, 39(6), p1205–1229.

20
PARTIES IN GOVERNMENT AND IN COALITIONS

Zachary Greene and Despina Alexiadou

Political parties frequently encounter public derision for their perceived ineffectiveness at governing. Yet parties continue to organise and control government bodies in representative democracies. Moreover, political theorists have not outlined convincing alternatives to representative government that supplant parties' influence. Indeed, all-too-common beliefs that parties fail to fulfil their policy promises may not hold up to detailed scrutiny. For instance, recent criticisms have drawn attention to intra-party disunity as a constraint on their effectiveness while overlooking the extent to which their own decision-making processes can influence their policy positions. In this chapter, we evaluate the roles that parties play in government through consideration of current research on government and coalition behaviour. We propose that parties have substantial impact on policy-making, but also that the challenges of reaching collective action and institutional limits on governance constrain their influence.

Significant research from the European and American continents has led to a wealth of literature on government formation, participation and termination. While the American approach has relied heavily on formal models of coalition formation, initially inspired by studies of the U.S. Congress (Austen-Smith and Banks 1988), the European approach has been inspired primarily by empirical experience and in-depth case analysis of European legislatures (Laver and Hunt 1992). A divergence between formal theoretical models and in-depth case studies is also present in literature investigating the effects of parties on the policy-making process. American approaches rely heavily on models of collective action problems, wars of attrition and veto actors (Tsebelis 2002; Bawn and Rosenbluth 2006), whereas European scholars have tended to explore the influence of history or party ideology (Laver and Shepsle 1996; Bäck and Lindvall 2015). For example, formal/theoretical approaches predict that multi-party coalitions are less suited for reducing public debt than single party governments due to collective action problems (Tsebelis 2002; Bawn and Rosenbluth 2006). This prediction relies on a number of assumptions, such as the absence of prehistory in the coalition formation process and availability of multiple, alternative coalitions. Scholars following the empirical/historical approach have highlighted, instead, the significance of parties' historical joint ability to resolve commitment problems in the coalition formation process. Specifically, Back and Lindvall (2015) argue that coalitions with a history of collaboration are at least as good as single party governments in resolving commitment problems and implementing fiscal adjustments.

This geographic divide lessened in the twenty-first century, however, as European scholars placed greater interest in formal approaches to studying government behaviour (Bergman, Ecker and Müller 2013) and formal modellers sought to test and link model assumptions to historical conditions emphasised by European scholars (Martin and Stevenson 2010). Despite these differences, much of the research studying democratic governance and policy-making has converged on the central question: *Does it matter which parties are in government for policy change?*

More specifically, debates have emerged around a number of important questions (Laver and Shepsle 1996; Tsebelis 2002; Klüver and Bäck 2019): Whom do parties represent once in government? Voters or party members? How constrained are parties by electoral promises? How do parties make policy in coalition cabinets? How do coalition agreements and portfolio allocation affect government policy? Do parties' internal dynamics and policy divisions affect policy priorities in government? We approach these questions by linking the formal/theoretical and empirical/historical perspectives. We consider parties as consisting of strategic and forward-thinking actors as traditional formal models contend (Austen-Smith and Banks 1988), but also as complex organisations operating in highly competitive, and often uncertain, multi-party systems as the more empirically focused tradition shows. Their ability and incentives to propose and negotiate policies is an outcome of multiple factors and processes that we review.

Here, we emphasise longer-term strategic decisions parties and members of parliament (MPs) consider by first addressing rules and conditions that provide parties and – particularly – party leaders with influence over decision-making in parliament. We start from 'party government', that is, a theory on the sources of party influence in parliament and critically evaluate the assumptions made in literatures about the role of parties in American and European legislatures. We then engage with studies on the role of parties in coalition governments and assumptions made by competing schools of thought. We bring these perspectives together in a final section linking this discussion on the role of parties as complex organisations in governments and policy-making. We conclude by highlighting the potential for studies of intra-party politics and cabinet decision-making to better explain policy-making and government behaviour.

Party government, legislative power and policy impact

The party government model refers to the idea that governments represent voters along partisan lines, following competitive elections where voters choose among alternative policy packages. Once in government, voters expect parties, in contrast to an unelected expert cabinet, to deliver on policy promises or be voted out in future elections (Strøm 2000). The individual's position within the party, therefore, marks the primary route to the party's parliamentary leadership and executive positions. An alternative perspective would consider a technocratic government run by prominent experts (Alexiadou 2020; Bertsou and Caramani 2020). Instead, a party government perspective expects the majority party's representatives to systematically fill the executive and implement policies in line with the party's (rather than individual MP's) policy goals.

In a party government, the party leader plays an instrumental role directing the party's policy activities while also acting as the representative selected by the party's own internal decision-making process. These roles become more influential for the largest party, which generally selects the leader to serve as prime minister. Debates over party influence on policy-making lead to differing conclusions dependent on authors' conceptualisation of parties and their goals. Although often implicit, scholars conceive of parties in the legislative arena as a team of parliamentarians or MPs using a common party label with commonly accepted policy goals. Applied in the parliamentary context, this perspective often implies that parties enjoy a high degree of policy agreement with members of the same party generally supporting policies put forward by their leadership. This perspective generally assumes that party leaders provide strong incentives and make use of parliamentary rules for encouraging disciplined behaviour.

As the increase in backbench rebellions in the UK post-2010 exemplifies (Burke et al. 2020), party leader strength is incomplete even in parliaments with historically cohesive or disciplined parties. Conversely, scholars of historically weak parties in the USA emphasise party leaders' influence in a context where parties hold fewer institutional procedures that encourage party discipline (Huber 1996; Dion 1997; Kirkland and Slapin 2017; Burke, Kirkland and Slapin 2020). As the party government perspective illustrates, a theory of policy-making that emphasises the role of parties should consider the parliamentary roots of party leaders' power.

Distinct from a perspective in which MPs use partisan labels solely for electoral purposes, MPs face a trade-off for supporting the party's leadership. Party government approaches conceptualise this trade-off through collective action and delegation models (Müller and Meyer 2010; Sieberer 2011). This perspective centrally assumes that MPs from the same party often hold differing policy goals. Even if distinct policy goals are only instrumental for electoral purposes (Carey and Shugart 1995), MPs compromise on their specific policy- or office-goals to support the leadership in parliament. Ultimately, individual MPs go along with the leader's goals, because they broadly see policy benefits they would not gain if they did not support the government's preferred policies. MP support for this collective action comes at the expense of losing individual influence over the details of policies.

Scholars taking a rational choice perspective question why parliaments can make decisions at all (Shepsle 1989). The party government perspective offers a solution to these concerns. It contends that party influence in parliament derives from an iterative process of delegation of power from MPs to a strong executive. For example, Cox (2005) models the formation of strong parties and Westminster system in the UK. He argues that MPs representing diverse regional consistencies delegated powers to party leaders to draw policy in their desired direction. From Cox's perspective, reforms to the UK electoral and parliamentary system resulted in a strong executive with substantial leeway to shape policy. Thus, party and cabinet leadership selection play central roles in examining parties' parliamentary influence. Indeed, the vote of confidence creates the potential for losing control of government, exemplifying one of the stronger tools at the legislature's disposal (Huber 1996; Döring 2003; Sieberer 2011).

The parliamentary context in many European countries contrasts with presidential systems as the latter provide relatively weak powers for legislative leaders (e.g. those in the U.S. Congress). Scholars have sought to explain parties' persistence and apparent impact in these contexts and substantial Congressional research provides the theoretical foundations for the party government framework. As the vote of confidence provides substantial powers to leaders in parliamentary contexts, absence of this procedure and other legislative incentives in presidential systems limits leaders' ability to create incentives for legislators to vote for contentious policies. Yet parties' influence persists even in contexts such as Congress where appointments to key committees and majority party agenda-setting procedures encourage legislators to support leaders' policies on issues they disagree (Cox and McCubbins 2007). However, as electoral incentives to break from the leader's goals become stronger, such as under single-member districts with open primaries in the USA, elected representatives feel less obliged to support the leadership and deviate from it in legislative votes more often.

In the literature on the U.S. Congress, scholars contrast a party government perspective where legislators compromise on their exact policy goals to support the legislative leadership with other explanations that emphasise information asymmetries legislators gain through the formation of policy expertise and privileged roles such as committee assignments (Shepsle and Wiengast 1994). Disagreements over the source of party influence in Congress led to substantial work on measuring and evaluating legislative voting behaviour (Poole and Rosenthal 2011; Ainsley et al. 2020). These approaches are difficult to apply to comparative cases that experience more uniform legislative discipline (Hug 2010; Rosas et al. 2015; Willumsen and Öhberg 2016; Hix, Noury and Roland 2018). Yet the broader debates over the source of party influence are instructive for parliamentary contexts.

Comparative studies find that a substantial source of party leaders' power derives from control of parliamentary rules (Döring 2003). Yet rules are subject to change by the same majorities that elect the party's leadership (Sieberer 2011). Furthermore, most studies proposing institutional sources of leader influence rely on functionalist perspectives that explain rules' effects not by intended usage, but by immediate results (Gamm and Huber 2002). Party leaders apply the vote of confidence or set the legislative agenda to structure policy outcomes making parties' preferences appear unified (Döring 2003; Strøm 2000), but ultimately, procedural powers are illusory if the leader's prior selection reflects internal compromise.

Scholars' reliance on functionalist approaches to understanding parties' policy influence suffers from a similar criticism. If policy compromises are reached prior to entering government (Kam 2009; Kölln and Polk 2017; Ceron 2019), party influence likely reflects intra-party processes and heterogeneous intra-party positions. The selection of party leader and executive within the party happens before it enters parliament. Stated otherwise, leadership selection is not wholly endogenous to the parliamentary game, but is also a consideration of the future executive selection. Policy goals expressed through electoral platforms also reflect parties' internal compromises later put to the test by those entering parliament (Ceron and Greene 2019). As we ultimately conclude, development of strong party governments in parliamentary contexts further highlights the need to understand decisions made prior and external to the legislative arena for understanding party influence.

In summary, theories of party government emphasise control of the legislative agenda and the executive as a solution to parties' internal collective action problems. The delegation of executive authority in parliament limits individual MP ambition and leads to policy that deviates from an MP's exact policy goals, but allows greater policy change and likelihood of executive influence than if they acted alone. A theory that accounts for parties' organisations and internal decision-making, therefore, raises questions as to how parliamentary structures resolve intra-party divisions at the heart of collective action problems. These structures potentially explain policy change and stability as much as negotiations between parties. Armed with party government theory, we review literature examining party policy influence in the following section.

Empirical determinants of political party policy influence

Though studies debate whether policies reflect the preferences of the median voter or vary by partisan ideology (Korpi and Palme 2003), most scholars who study multi-party governments agree that the partisan composition of governments matters for policy outcomes (Austen-Smith and Banks 1988). The mechanisms through which parties influence policy are less understood. Two competing paradigms take centre stage: coalition compromise (Martin and Vanberg 2014) and ministerial government models (Laver and Shepsle 1996).

According to the coalition compromise model, the proportion of seats parties control in parliament predicts policy influence in multi-party governments – with a higher proportion of seats providing parties greater policy-making influence in government (Korpi and Palme 2003). Empirically, scholars conceptualise policy influence as the weighted sum of voting power and their revealed policy preferences in ideologically coherent parties (Franzese 2002). The specific portfolios that parties control are of no consequence; only the total number of seats they control is important. Similarly, 'power resource theories', adopt this approach, predicting that the more ideologically left a cabinet is, the larger the welfare state. This approach predicts that parties have more policy influence in a single-party than coalition government. Non-cooperative game theory models complement this perspective by predicting the formation of centre-left or centre-right minimum winning coalitions in multi-party systems (Austen-Smith and Banks 1988).

Laver and Shepsle (1996) propose a radically different model, often referred to as the 'portfolio model'. According to ministerial government theory, party size alone cannot predict the policy direction in multi-party governments. Instead, parties dictate policy in their ministries' domains of responsibility, irrespective of coalition partner size and ideology. This is possible because parties have separable preferences across issues. If ministerial autonomy is high, parties set policy independently of coalition partners. Policy complexity, limited ability to monitor policies across government, and tacit rules of non-intervention further contribute to ministers' ability to monopolise the policy agenda within ministerial portfolios. For example, a green party is likely to have more policy influence on environmental policy if they control the ministry in charge of this issue than if they are the largest party in government. Unlike the coalition compromise and power resource theories, a left party need not form a single-party government to maximise policy influence; it needs to control portfolios central to policy priorities such as employment and social welfare portfolios. Mixed evidence supports this argument. For example, Becher (2010) finds support for such ideas in the area of employment policy, but only when multiple veto players are absent, whereas Alexiadou and Hoepfner (2019) find that left parties disproportionately influence social welfare policies (based on their size) when they control the social welfare portfolio, but only when they made an electoral pledge to do so.

This model has motivated substantial empirical research on how coalition partners distribute portfolios, both in the number of cabinet positions each party controls and policy benefits received (Warwick and Druckman 2006; Bäck, Debus and Dumont 2011). According to Warwick and Druckman (2006), portfolio allocation is fundamental to parliamentary governance because cabinet ministers act as gatekeepers, preventing proposals they oppose from cabinet consideration. Parties allocate portfolios on an issue-by-issue basis to build compromises through issue trades or logrolls (Bäck, Debus and Dumont 2011; Greene 2017). A sequential perspective to portfolio allocation leads to similar predictions indicating greatest influence for the largest parties (Ecker, Meyer and Müller 2015). Consequently, substantial empirical literature predicting policy outcomes relies on coalition compromise models (Goodhart 2013; Martin and Vanberg 2014) whereby cabinets make policy collectively with larger parties having the most policy influence.

A weakness of Laver and Shepsle's (1996) model is that it ignores policy disagreement between ministers. For example, how do governments resolve disputes when one minister's proposal directly affects another's department? Veto player theory (Tsebelis 2002) purports that where two disagreeing parties must settle over policy, there will be no policy change. Therefore, the larger the number of coalition partners and larger their ideological distance, the lower the freedom of ministers and subsequently of parties to set policy to their ideal point.

The contradictory predictions between portfolio and veto player models have been the subject of research, which seeks to identify political and institutional conditions that resolve whether individual ministers or collective cabinet decisions decide policy. Empirical evidence suggests that systems with a higher number of institutional veto players reduce the impact of partisan portfolios (Becher 2010), as do legislatures that have the capacity to effectively police ministerial departments through committees (Martin and Vanberg 2014).

Formal agreements offer alternative mechanisms for coalition governments to mitigate policy disputes. Coalition agreements vary in length and detail. Independent of agreement length, specific policy resolutions generally bind cabinets (Moury 2013). Therefore, agreements often include contentious issues to mitigate future conflicts (Eichorst 2014). Klüver and Bäck (2019) provide the first cross-country and over-time empirical analysis of 224 coalition agreements. They find that coalition partners are more likely to extensively describe details of policy compromises on specific issues, in particular when the issue is salient to each partner and when the partners are divided over the issue. Social welfare and economic issues are the most likely to be mentioned. This implies that a social democratic welfare minister, for example, will have substantially less policy influence on social welfare and employment policies in the presence of a detailed coalition agreement than predicted by the ministerial government model. Consequently, they conclude that coalition agreements significantly reduce independent ministerial influence, but highlight the importance of policy negotiations between parties prior to taking office.

Coalition agreements can exert strong influence on coalition governance. But, their proposed impact assumes that government formation and policy-making is a one-period game; governments fix policy goals at each coalition negotiation period and only re-negotiate at the next election. Since agreement determines policy outputs, portfolio allocations, party size and preferences should not independently matter for policy outcomes following a formalised agreement. However, as the authors state, parties negotiate coalition agreements in parallel with allocating portfolios. Questions remain over how parties negotiate and agree on the two and, crucially, how parties resolve disputes left unaddressed by coalition agreements.

One way to create a more collaborative approach to future policy disputes between cabinet ministers is through the allocation of overlapping portfolios between coalition partners. Fernandes, Meinfelder and Moury (2016) show that a number of European countries, such as Germany and Denmark, commonly distribute 'neighbouring' portfolios, whose policy jurisdictions overlap, across coalition partners. This practice encourages collaboration between ministers from different parties in the policy-formation process. Both parties draft policies at an early stage, increasing policies' likelihood of success. Oversight perspectives further highlight the importance of committees and junior ministers to collect information and monitor ministers from other coalition parties (Carroll and Cox 2000; Thies 2001; Greene and Jensen 2016). However, not all governments or countries divide portfolios strategically. Even if governments do, policy disputes still arise between ministers.

An understudied factor in coalition governance is the role of expected electoral loss. The fear of future electoral loss over policy compromise could influence parties' willingness to compromise over policy disputes. Alexiadou and Hoepfner (2019) argue that the fear of future electoral cost due to policy compromise becomes a significant factor for predicting the outcome of policy disagreements in multi-party cabinets. A party is more likely to pull policy away from its partners' or the cabinet's ideal policy if it faces high electoral costs for failing to do so. A party's electoral costs increase if it controls the related portfolio *and* it has made a strong policy pledge on a highly salient issue for core voters. These predictions rest on the assumptions that policy-making is a dynamic process (Baron, Diermeier and Fong 2012) influenced by parties' cost of governing expectations.

To conclude, the discipline produced a significant body of work that outlines the conditions for party policy influence in government, namely party size, electoral pledges, the distribution of portfolios, coalition agreements and, to some extent, expected electoral costs. The next section reviews the recent literature on voters' policy attribution in coalition governments and makes the case for incorporating more explicitly parties' future electoral costs in studies of coalition governments.

The impact of parties' electoral costs and incentives on policy-making

Studies from a party government perspective often assume that voters punish and reward those parties responsible for policies. However, institutional divisions of power in multi-party coalitions are thought to limit voters' ability to hold individual parties to account for unmet policy promises (Powell and Whitten 1993). Yet recent work finds that informed voters and party core voters, alike, are attentive of parties' electoral promises and policy shifts (Thomson et al. 2017; Matthieß 2020).

Empirically, voters in multi-party systems attribute policy responsibility to the prime minister's party, and to the parties that hold agenda-setting power through the control of ministerial portfolios (Duch, Przepiorka and Stevenson 2015; Angelova, König and Proksch 2016). These results hold in both observational and experimental data where respondents attribute responsibility to policymakers holding the power to introduce a policy rather than to the largest decision-makers. Accordingly, when the economy underperforms, voters are more likely to punish the party that controls the finance portfolio (Debus, Stegmaier and Tosun 2014). These findings suggest that not all portfolios are equally powerful as argued by Laver and Sheplse (1996). The ones that have more policy influence also carry greater electoral risks, which should have a direct impact on policy choices.

Policy performance is not the only metric voters use to judge coalition governments. Voters also punish parties for policy compromises (Fortunato 2019). Those who previously supported incumbents are particularly less likely to support parties they see as having compromised on policy while in government. In addition, voters likely discount policy accomplishments which they view as having weakened or failed to uphold promises. There is also evidence that smaller parties disproportionately suffer such misperceptions and pay a higher electoral cost for governing than larger coalition partners (Klüver and Spoon 2020). However, small parties can exhibit a degree of agency. Electoral chances improve when they control ministerial portfolios that are salient to their voters or a larger number of portfolios (Greene, Henceroth and Jensen 2021). This means that party size, portfolio allocation and issue salience interact in more complex ways than coalition compromise and ministerial government models predict (see also Chapter 21).

In summary, governing has costs. These costs vary significantly depending on how much parties can influence policies salient to their voters or at least appear that they do so. The existence of costs questions both short-term payoffs necessary to join coalitions and the future electoral price they are willing to pay to control government.

Conclusions and avenues for further research

Scholars have developed diverse tools to evaluate the impact of parties as they participate in government. In doing so, scholars have drawn on the historically divergent formal/theoretical and empirical/historical approaches for studying their influence. In merging these perspectives, studies increasingly connect the agency of individual actors to policy-making activities, while reflecting the institutional limits of governmental settings. The party government model not only provides a framework for connecting these approaches but also struggles to account for the presence of increased intra-party disunity across advanced democracies. We also require better understanding of why and how rules and institutions for decision-making within parties and parliaments change in line with societal shifts and individual preferences.

The relevance of intra-party divisions presents a need for this research agenda to incorporate perspectives focused on parties' extra-parliamentary characteristics including party members' and leaders' agency and the strategies they employ to maximise their priorities. Although scholars have long hypothesised over the role of intra-party politics (Laver and Shepsle 1996), cross-national tests of these perspectives were limited by data availability. Consequently, studies struggled to evaluate the plausibility of key assumptions and made limited progress in developing mid-level theories capable of linking party government theories to extra-parliamentary organisational perspectives. Promising projects have begun to address these gaps through linking to data on: party rules (Poguntke et al. 2016), members' behaviour in settings such as party conferences (Ceron and Greene 2019; Schumacher et al. 2019; Kaltenegger, Heugl and Müller 2021); and through the expansion of surveys to targeted groups (Kölln and Polk 2017; Webb, Poletti and Bale 2017). These projects enable researchers to test the external validity of hypotheses more directly. Diverse information on party member, leader and MP preferences in contexts outside of the legislative arena also hold substantial promise for better understanding parties' impact, and their decision-making processes on policy-making.

Likewise, extant literature poorly accounts for the impact of bureaucratic organisation of ministerial portfolios and policy-making powers on parties' strategies. Presumably, parties will have greater policy influence when they control a portfolio exclusively than when they control a portfolio whose policy competences overlap with other ministerial portfolios. Since portfolio design and re-allocation of policies are common and results from a strategic process (Dewan and Hortala-Vallve 2011), research that incorporates complex institutional and partisan arrangements will improve explanations of how portfolio allocation and portfolio design interact and shape policy outcomes.

Ministerial policy-making also involves constant negotiation of policy between senior and junior ministers (Thies 2001), ministers across different departments, and the interaction between senior civil servants and ministers. These areas remain mostly unexplored with some important, but rare contributions. Cabinet ministers play a crucial role in policy-making as individuals who bring varying degrees of policy expertise, experience and divergent political and policy ambitions that in themselves likely reflect intra-party divisions over policy and career ambition. A ministerial portfolio is a major prize for politicians because of the prestige of the office and policy-making power. However, governing creates opportunities for intra-party tensions to arise. Although cabinet ministers formally jointly hold agenda-setting power, they differ in the degree to which they use it. Some ministers promote significant policy changes while others maintain the status quo (Alexiadou 2016).

Existing research on cabinet ministers focuses mostly on ministerial selection (Huber and Martinez-Gallardo 2008) and less on the implications of this selection for policy-making. Recent studies suggest a tight connection between the type of minister selected and policy outcomes. Alexiadou (2016) puts forward a typology of ministers on the basis of their background and career objectives: those who prioritise political office (loyalists) are less likely to push forward policy reforms above and beyond the party agenda, whereas those committed to a policy goal (ideologues) are less likely to compromise and more likely to succeed in pushing forward a policy reform.

More generally, policy reforms vary by the interaction of parties' ideological goals and political seniority of cabinet ministers (Alexiadou 2016). Additionally, ministers' career concerns can have concrete policy effects. For example, non-partisan experts, also known as technocrats, bear minimal career costs for adopting unpopular policies and are associated with cuts in government spending (Alexiadou 2020), and also with neoliberal economic reforms in many Latin American countries (Dargent 2015).

References

Ainsley, C., Carrubba, C.J., Crisp, B.F., Demirkaya, B., et al. (2020) 'Roll-call vote selection: Implications for the study of legislative politics', *American Political Science Review*, 114, p691–706.

Alexiadou, D. (2020) 'Technocrats in cabinets and their policy', in Bertsou, E. and Caramani, D. (eds.) *The technocratic challenge to democracy*. Routledge: London, pp. 131–47.

Alexiadou, D. (2016) *Ideologues, partisans, and loyalists: Ministers and policy-making in parliamentary cabinets*. Oxford: Oxford University Press.

Alexiadou, D. and Hoepfner, D. (2019) 'Platforms, portfolios, policy: How audience costs affect social welfare policy in multiparty cabinets', *Political Science Research and Methods*, 7(3), p393–409.

Angelova, M., König, T. and Proksch, S-V. (2016) 'Responsibility attribution in coalition governments: Evidence from Germany', *Electoral Studies*, 43, p133–49.

Austen-Smith, D. and Banks, J. (1988) 'Elections, coalitions and legislative outcomes', *American Political Science Review*, 82(2), p405–22.

Bäck, H., Debus, M. and Dumont, P. (2011) 'Who gets what in coalition governments? Predictors of portfolio allocation in parliamentary democracies', *European Journal of Political Research*, 50(4), p441–78.

Bäck, H. and Lindvall, J. (2015) 'Commitment problems in coalitions: A new look at the fiscal policies of multiparty governments', *Political Science Research and Methods*, 3(1), p53–72.

Baron, D., Diermeier, D. and Fong, P. (2012) 'A dynamic theory of parliamentary democracy', *Economic Theory*, 49(3), p703–38.

Bawn, K. and Rosenbluth, F. (2006) 'Short versus long coalitions: Electoral accountability and the size of the public sector', *American Journal of Political Science*, 50(2), p251–65.

Becher, M. (2010) 'Constraining ministerial power: The impact of veto players on labor market reforms in industrial democracies, 1973–2000', *Comparative Political Studies*, 43(1), p33–60.

Bergman, T., Ecker, A. and Müller, W. (2013) 'How parties govern: Political parties and the internal organization of government', in Müller, W.C. and Narud, H.M. (eds.) *Party Governance and Party Democracy*. Springer: New York, pp. 33–50.

Bertsou, E. and Caramani, D. (2020) 'People haven't had enough of experts: Technocratic attitudes among citizens in nine European democracies', *American Journal of Political Science*, DOI https://doi.org/10.1111/ajps.12554.

Burke, R., Kirkland, J.H. and Slapin, J.H. (2020) 'Party competition, personal votes, and strategic disloyalty in the US states, *Political Research Quarterly*, 74(4), p1024–1036.

Carey, J. and Shugart, M. (1995) 'Incentives to cultivate a personal vote: A rank ordering of electoral formulas', *Electoral Studies*, 14(4), p417–39.

Carroll, R. and Cox, G. (2000) 'Shadowing ministers: Monitoring partners in coalition governments', *Comparative Political Studies*, 45(2), p220–36.

Ceron, A. (2019) *Leaders, factions and the game of intra-party politics*. London: Routledge.

Ceron, A. and Greene, Z. (2019) 'Verba volant, scripta manent? Intra-party politics, party conferences, and issue salience in France', *Party Politics*, 25(5), p701–711.

Cox, G. (2005) *The efficient secret: The Cabinet and the development of political parties in Victorian England*. Cambridge: Cambridge University Press.

Cox, G. and McCubbins, M. (2007) *Legislative leviathan: Party government in the House*. Cambridge: Cambridge University Press.

Dargent, E. (2015) *Technocracy and democracy in Latin America*. New York: Cambridge University Press.

Debus, M., Stegmaier, M. and Tosun, J. (2014) 'Economic voting under coalition governments: Evidence from Germany', *Political Science Research and Methods*, 2(1), p49–67.

Dewan, T. and Hortala-Vallve, R. (2011) 'The three As of government formation: Appointment, allocation, and assignment', *American Journal of Political Science*, 55(3), p610–27.

Dion, D. (1997) *Turning the legislative thumbscrew*. Ann Arbor: University of Michigan Press.

Döring, H. (2003) 'Party discipline and government imposition of restrictive rules', *The Journal of Legislative Studies*, 9(4), p147–63.

Duch, R., Przepiorka, W. and Stevenson, R. (2015) 'Responsibility attribution for collective decision makers', *American Journal of Political Science*, 59(2), p372–89.

Ecker, A., Meyer, T. and Müller, W. (2015) 'The distribution of individual cabinet positions in coalition governments: A sequential approach', *European Journal of Political Research*, 54(4), p802–18.

Eichorst, J. (2014) 'Explaining variation in coalition agreements: The electoral and policy motivations for drafting agreements', *European Journal of Political Research*, 53(1), p98–115.

Fernandes, J., Meinfelder, F. and Moury, C. (2016) 'Wary partners: Strategic portfolio allocation and coalition governance in parliamentary democracies', *Comparative Political Studies*, 49(9), p1270–1300.

Fortunato, D. (2019) 'The electoral implications of coalition policy making', *British Journal of Political Science*, 49(1), p59–80.

Franzese, R. (2002) *Macroeconomic policies of developed democracies*. Cambridge: Cambridge University Press.

Gamm, G. and Huber, J. (2002) 'Legislatures as political institutions: Beyond the contemporary congress', in Katznelson, I. and Milner, H. (eds.) *Political Science: The State of the Discipline*. New York: W. W. Norton, pp. 313–343.

Goodhart, L. (2013) 'Who decides? Coalition governance and ministerial discretion', *Quarterly Journal of Political Science*, 8(3), p205–237.

Greene, Z. (2017) 'Working through the issues: How issue diversity and ideological disagreement influence coalition duration', *European Political Science Review*, 9(4), p561–585.

Greene, Z., Henceroth, N. and Jensen, C. (2021) 'The cost of coalition compromise: The electoral effects of holding salient portfolios', *Party Politics*, 27(4), p827–838.

Greene, Z. and Jensen, C. (2016) 'Manifestos, salience and junior ministerial appointments', *Party Politics*, 22(3), p382–392.

Hix, S., Noury, A. and Roland. G. (2018) 'Is there a selection bias in roll call votes? Evidence from the European Parliament', *Public Choice*, 176(1), p211–28.

Huber, J. (1996) *Rationalizing Parliament: Legislative institutions and party politics in France*. Cambridge: Cambridge University Press.

Huber, J. and Martinez-Gallardo, C. (2008) 'Replacing cabinet ministers: Patterns of ministerial stability in parliamentary democracies', *American Political Science Review*, 102(2), p169–80.

Hug, S. (2010) 'Selection effects in roll call votes', *British Journal of Political Science*, 40(1), p225–35.

Kaltenegger, M., Heugl, K. and Müller, W. (2021) 'Appeasement and rewards: Explaining patterns of party responsiveness towards activist preferences', *Party Politics*, 27(2), p363–375.

Kam, C. (2009) *Party discipline and parliamentary politics*. Cambridge: Cambridge University Press.

Kirkland, J.H. and Slapin, J.B. (2017) 'Ideology and strategic party disloyalty in the US House of Representatives', *Electoral Studies*, 49, p26–37.

Klüver, H. and Bäck, H. (2019) 'Coalition agreements, issue attention, and cabinet governance', *Comparative Political Studies*, 52(13–14), p1995–2031.

Klüver, H. and Spoon, J-J. (2020) 'Helping or hurting? How governing as a junior coalition partner influences electoral outcomes', *The Journal of Politics*, 82(4), p1231–42.

Kölln, A-K. and Polk, J. (2017) 'Emancipated party members', *Party Politics*, 23(1), p18–29.

Korpi, W. and Palme, J. (2003) 'New politics and class politics in the context of austerity and globalization: Welfare state regress in 18 countries, 1975–95', *American Political Science Review*, 97(3), p425–46.

Laver, M. and Hunt, B. (1992) *Policy and party competition*. New York: Routledge.

Laver, M. and Shepsle, K. (1996) *Making and breaking governments: Cabinets and legislatures in parliamentary democracies*. New York: Cambridge University Press.

Martin, L. and Stevenson, R. (2010) 'The conditional impact of incumbency on government formation', *American Political Science Review*, 104(3), p503–18.

Martin, L. and Vanberg, G. (2014) 'Parties and policymaking in multiparty governments: The legislative median, ministerial autonomy, and the coalition compromise', *American Journal of Political Science*, 58(4), p979–96.

Matthieß, T. (2020) 'Retrospective pledge voting: A comparative study of the electoral consequences of government parties' pledge fulfilment', *European Journal of Political Research*, 59(4), p774–96.

Moury, C. (2013) *Coalition government and party mandate: How coalition agreements constrain ministerial action*. Abingdon: Routledge.

Müller, W. and Meyer, T. (2010) 'Meeting the challenges of representation and accountability in multi-party governments', *West European Politics*, 33(5), p1065–92.

Poguntke, T., Scarrow, S.E., Webb, P., Allern, E.H. et al. (2016) 'Party rules, party resources and the politics of parliamentary democracies: How parties organize in the 21st century', *Party Politics*, 22(6), p661–78.

Poole, K.T. and Rosenthal, H. (2011) *Ideology and Congress*. London: Transaction.

Powell, B. and Whitten, G. (1993) 'A cross-national analysis of retrospective voting: Integrating economic and political variables', *American Journal of Political Science*, 37, p391–414.

Rosas, G., Shomer, Y. and Haptonstahl, S. (2015) 'No news is news: Nonignorable nonresponse in roll-call data analysis', *American Journal of Political Science*, 59(2), p511–28.

Schumacher, G., Hansen, D. van der Velden, M. and Kunst, S. (2019) 'A new dataset of Dutch and Danish party congress speeches', *Research & Politics*, 6(2): https://doi.org/205316801983835.

Shepsle, K. (1989) 'Studying institutions: Some lessons from the rational choice approach', *Journal of Theoretical Politics*, 1(2), p131–47.

Shepsle, K. and Weingast, B. (1994) 'Positive theories of congressional institutions', *Legislative Studies Quarterly*, 19(2), p149–179.

Sieberer, U. (2011) 'The institutional power of Western European parliaments: A multidimensional analysis', *West European Politics*, 34(4), p731–54.

Strøm, K. (2000) 'Delegation and accountability in parliamentary democracies', *European Journal of Political Research*, 77, p261–89.

Thies, M. (2001) 'Keeping tabs on one's partners: The logic of delegation in coalition formation', *American Journal of Political Science*, 45(3), p580–98.

Thomson, R., Royed, T., Naurin, E., Artés, J., et al. (2017) 'The fulfillment of parties' election pledges: A comparative study on the impact of power sharing', *American Journal of Political Science*, 61(3), p527–42.

Tsebelis, G. (2002) *Veto players: How political institutions work*. Princeton: Princeton University Press.

Warwick, P. and Druckman, J. (2006) 'The paradox of portfolio allocation: An investigation in the nature of a very strong but puzzling relationship', *European Journal of Political Research*, 45, p635–65.

Webb, P., Poletti, M. and Bale, T. (2017) 'So who really does the donkey work in 'multi-speed membership parties'? Comparing the election campaign activity of party members and party supporters', *Electoral Studies*, 46, p64–74.

Willumsen, D. and Öhberg, P. (2016) 'Toe the line, break the whip: Explaining floor dissent in parliamentary democracies', *West European Politics*, 40(4), p688–716.

21
PARTIES AND REPRESENTATION

Jae-Jae Spoon

Parties at their core are linkage organisations (e.g. Lawson 1980) in that they serve as an important mechanism connecting citizens and their government. Linkage can take many different forms depending on the context – from pork to policy – and can be focused on both descriptive representation – gender, ethnicity and religion among others – and substantive representation – such as issue priorities and policy and partisanship (Pitkin 1967). Kitschelt (2000), for example, describes three kinds of linkage: programmatic (policy-oriented), clientelistic (material benefits-oriented) and charismatic (personality-oriented), thus recognising that linkage can take different forms depending on the context. Moreover, in considering what linkage looks like, Dalton, Farrell and McAllister (2011) posit that there is a 'chain of democratic linkage' which takes on five different forms: campaign, participatory, ideological, representative and policy. These roughly follow Key's (1958) tripartite framework of party functions: the first two are part of the party's role as an organisation; the second, a part of the party in the electorate, and the final two are part of the party's role in government.

This chapter focuses on the representative form of linkage. Representation, importantly, can be both dynamic and static (see Beyer and Hänni 2018). On the dynamic side, representation is an iterative process (Stimson, MacKuen and Erikson 1995) that emphasises responsiveness, which includes both parties listening and responding to voters in their campaign manifestos and in their legislative and governing behaviour, on the one hand, and voters understanding parties' issue priorities and preferences and responding accordingly in their voting decisions, on the other hand. Much of the recent literature on responsiveness has sought to answer two related, yet distinct, questions: Do parties listen to voters and do voters listen to parties? This research has focused on both voters' and parties' issue emphasis or priorities, that is, which issues parties and voters prioritise; and issue preferences or positions, that is, voters' and parties' ideological positions on the right-left scale or their positions on specific issues. On the static side, representation is focused on congruence – or the degree to which the priorities and preferences of elected representatives mirror those of the electorate (see Golder and Ferland 2018 for a review of types of congruence and how electoral rules affect these). Once elected, parties then transform voters' priorities and preferences into policies. Research on congruence typically examines the relationship between voters' opinions and policy outputs in the legislature and executive. According to Golder and Stramski (2010), congruence can be considered as a 'many-to-one' relationship, i.e. how congruent the ideological position of the government is with the ideological preferences of citizens, or a 'many-to-many' relationship, i.e. how congruent the ideological positions of legislators are with the preferences of citizens.

In this chapter, I focus on the dynamic aspect of representation, that is, responsiveness, as research in this area focuses directly on the relationship between parties and voters. In the next section, I examine whether parties respond to voters and how this varies across different types of parties and contexts. Next, I turn to the question of whether voters listen to parties. The following section then examines questions of measurement. I conclude with a discussion of areas for future research.

Do parties respond to voters?

Beginning with Downs's (1957) spatial theory of party competition, we know that, as vote maximisers, parties will move their positions to capture as many voters as possible (see also Chapter 17). As voters shift, so will parties. Ansolabehere and Iyengar (1994) describe this behaviour as 'riding the wave', that is, as voters change their priorities, parties respond by changing their issue emphasis. Adams et al. (2004), for example, demonstrate that parties do respond to shifts in public opinion (although only when public opinion is shifting away from the party). Thus, as voters' issue preferences and positions change, so will parties' positions. Parties do, however, need to be careful about moving and switching positions or priorities too much as they could be accused of 'flip flopping' (Burden 2004). When this happens, voters may have a difficult time both identifying parties' priorities and positions and differentiating among them. Although Downs' spatial model of party competition is a useful starting point, it is important to unpack this relationship between parties and voters. Are certain types of parties more responsive? Does it depend on whether a party is in government or opposition? The size of the party? The goals or internal structure of the party?

Party characteristics

First, party type influences responsiveness. Research has demonstrated that mainstream and niche parties respond differently to voters.[1] Mainstream parties are often big tent catch-all parties (Kirschheimer 1966) which are focused on votes and office (Strøm 1990) and thus seek to be attractive to as many voters as possible. Niche parties are typically more policy-oriented (Wittman 1973; Strøm 1990) and have narrower constituencies, which the parties seek to represent (see also Chapter 19). Adams et al. (2006) and Ezrow et al. (2011), for example, find that mainstream parties respond to left-right shifts in public opinion by shifting their left-right positions, whereas niche parties do not. However, focusing on their own supporters, Ezrow et al. (2011) find that niche parties do respond to shifts in the mean left-right position of their own supporters. Ferland (2020) argues that mainstream and niche party shifts are more nuanced. Whereas mainstream parties adjust their position when the median voter shifts away, niche parties adjust their position when their supporters move towards their position. Klüver and Spoon (2016) furthermore demonstrate that green parties respond to their own supporters on their owned issue of the environment by increasing their issue emphasis (see also Chapters 16 and 18). Similarly, Costello et al. (2021) find that green parties are congruent with their voters on the environment, but are less congruent with their voters on other issues.

Second, whether a party is in government or part of the opposition can influence responsiveness. Although one may assume that governing parties would be more responsive to voters, research has found the opposite to be true. Once in office, parties are more constrained in their behaviour. They are more focused on policy-making and may be less able to compromise on the policy priorities laid out in their manifestos. Moreover, if they did, they may lose credibility among voters, which could hurt them in the next election. Opposition parties, on the other hand, have more flexibility. They, moreover, are more likely to be more responsive to voters, as they would like to (re)gain control of government. In a cross-national analysis of parties' responsiveness to voters' issue priorities, Klüver and Spoon (2016), for example, find that opposition parties are more responsive than governing parties. Furthermore, in their study of whether parties respond to public opinion or to globalisation, Ezrow and Hellwig (2014) find an inverse relationship between national markets' integration in the world economy and the responsiveness of parties with governing experience to shifts in public opinion.

It is important, however, to look further into both how the type of government and the nature of the opposition may influence governing party responsiveness. Klüver and Spoon (2017) show that, when there is a high level of intra-cabinet disagreement in a coalition government on an issue, parties will be less responsive to voters and decrease emphasis on this issue. They will only emphasise the issues on which there is intra-cabinet agreement to present a unified message to voters. Looking at policy- and office-seeking opposition parties on macroeconomic issues, Traber, Giger and Häusermann (2018) find lower levels of congruence between policy-seeking opposition parties and their supporters (compared to government parties and office-seeking opposition parties) during times of economic crisis.

Third, the size of the party can play a role in responsiveness. As vote- and office-seeking parties, larger parties tend to have a broader ideological appeal and seek to attract as many voters as they can. Smaller parties, conversely, are focused on a narrower set of issues and behave differently in elections and in government (e.g. Bolleyer 2007; Spoon 2011). Based on this, researchers have found that larger parties are more responsive to voters (e.g. Klüver and Spoon 2016). Abou-Chadi, Green-Pedersen and Mortensen (2020), moreover, find that large parties adjust their policy positions in response to changes in party system saliency of these issues. Examining parties' responsiveness to voters' Euroscepticism, Williams and Spoon (2015) show that both large parties and opposition parties are more responsive in their position concerning European integration.

Fourth, intra-party dynamics – which can include division over policy, the nature of the selectorate or whether activists or leaders play a role in setting policy – can also influence party responsiveness. Characterising parties by how inclusive or exclusive their selectorate is, Lehrer (2012) finds that inclusive parties respond to shifts in the position of the median supporter; whereas exclusive parties respond to shifts in the median voter, particularly in two-party systems compared to multi-party systems. Schumacher, DeVries and Vis (2013), moreover, demonstrate that party responsiveness to shifts in mean voter position are more likely in leadership-dominated parties compared to activist-dominated parties.

Additional factors

In addition to party characteristics, scholars have identified other variables which influence how responsive parties are to voters. These include polarisation, party competition and economic conditions.

First, the degree of division or polarisation over an issue among the electorate or party supporters can influence how a party responds. Here, the literature has come to different conclusions. On the one hand, van de Wardt (2012) finds that parties respond to divisions among party supporters by decreasing emphasis on an issue, though they find no evidence that niche parties behave differently than mainstream parties. On the other hand, Spoon and Klüver (2015) demonstrate that parties listen when voters are divided. When an issue is highly polarising and the electorate is divided, parties are better able to identify voters' priorities or positions and can respond by offering a clear position or emphasising the issue. They show that, when voters are divided on both the saliency of an issue and policy position, parties are more likely to emphasise the issue.

Second, party competition can play a role in responsiveness. Abou-Chadi (2018) demonstrates that, when electoral competition is greater and when other parties in the party system emphasise the issue, parties are more responsive to voters' issue priorities; however, they are less responsive to their supporters' issue priorities. Abou-Chadi and Orlowski (2016), moreover, find that responsiveness to electoral competition is conditioned by party size and party type when considering party policy shifts. As electoral competition increases, large parties are more likely to moderate their positions. This supports a vote-seeking model of party behaviour. As larger parties want to increase their vote share, they will moderate to attract as many voters as they can (see earlier discussion on party size). Adams and Somer-Topcu (2009a) show that parties shift their policies in the same direction that their opponents had shifted their policies in the previous election and that parties were particularly responsive to shifts by ideologically similar parties.

Third, economic conditions can influence responsiveness. Recognising that there are costs to responding, Ezrow, Hellwig and Fenzl (2020) demonstrate that governments are more likely to respond to shifts in public opinion during periods of economic growth. When growth rates are lower, governments are less responsive. Relatedly, Clements, Nanou and Real-Dato (2018) find that parties are less responsive to public opinion when economic conditions are worse. Moreover, during periods of economic crisis, they find that governing parties will be less responsive compared to opposition parties (following findings on the responsiveness of governing parties discussed earlier). However, turning to how globalisation affects party responsiveness, Ezrow and Hellwig (2014) demonstrate that parties with governing experience respond more to markets than to the median voter as the national economy becomes more integrated with world markets. For parties without governing experience, their policy positions are not affected by the forces of globalisation. Adams, Haupt and Stoll (2009), moreover, examine how party type affects whether parties respond to shifts in public opinion or to global economic conditions. They find that parties of the centre and right respond to both public preferences and the global economy; whereas parties on the left do not respond to the public and are less responsive to the economy. Haupt (2010), however, does find evidence of all parties adjusting their positions in response to changes in economic openness.

Do voters listen?

The other side of the representation puzzle is whether voters listen to parties. In other words, do they make informed decisions based on an understanding of parties' policy positions or preferences? Compared to the research on whether parties respond, the question of whether voters pay attention to parties' shifts in policy positions and issue emphasis has been less studied. Moreover, the research in this area has yielded mixed findings. Adams and Somer-Topcu (2009b) provide some evidence that policy moderation does yield more votes, which implies that voters have paid attention and shifted their votes accordingly. Adams, Ezrow and Somer-Topcu (2011) find that voters do not adjust their perceptions of parties' left-right positions in response to policy statements in their manifestos, but instead, do respond to parties' policy images, defined as voters' placement of parties. Fernandez-Vazquez (2014) and Fernandez-Vazquez and Somer-Topcu (2019), however, find that voters indeed respond to parties' positions, especially when there is a new leader. Examining parties' left-right policy positions through media coverage of election campaigns, Somer-Topcu, Tavits and Baumann (2020), moreover, demonstrate that voters are able to identify parties' messages. Looking at why voters and parties disagree, Walgrave and Lefevre (2013) find that voter–party mismatches are driven by ideology, salience and complexity. They argue that these factors increase or decrease information for voters about parties' positions allowing them to more (less) easily find the best policy match or adapt their own positions to more closely align to their preferred party. Perhaps most interestingly, the more complex the environment, the less likely voters' preferences will match those of their preferred party.

The concept of clarity of responsibility (Powell and Whitten 1993) offers some insight into the circumstances under which voters may be more likely to correctly identify parties' positions. When there is more clarity, voters are able to identify which party to blame or give credit to; when there is less clarity, voters have more trouble doing this. Coalition governments, for example, may make it difficult for voters to differentiate the positions of the coalition partners and especially those of the junior coalition partner (e.g. Fortunato and Stevenson 2013; Spoon and Klüver 2017; Klüver and Spoon 2020). Empirically, Klüver and Spoon (2020) have demonstrated the voters were much more likely to misperceive the ideological position of the party of the junior partner compared to the prime minister's party in the Merkel II cabinet, comprised of the Christian Democrats (CDU) and Free Democrats (FDP).

Voters are furthermore more likely to listen to parties and select a party that is more aligned with their views when there is a distinct choice on offer – what Downs (1957, 141) referred to as 'product differentiation' – as opposed to a more blurry position (on blurring and beclouding as strategies, see Rovny and Polk 2020 and Han 2018, respectively). Studies have found that when there is elite polarisation, parties' positions become clearer and voters are more likely to select a party that more closely matches their preferences (Levendusky 2010). These findings highlight the fact that what may be good from a representation perspective, that is, voters selecting a party that most closely aligns with their policy preferences, may not be as beneficial from a governing perspective. Similarly, a leadership change for an opposition party makes it clearer in voters' minds what the party stands for and they are thus better able to more accurately perceive the left-right position of the party (Fernandez-Vazquez and Somer-Topcu 2019). Finally, Lehrer and Lin (2020) argue that the 'broad appeal strategy' identified by Somer-Topcu (2015) is less effective at attracting voters when voters perceive the party to be divided. This is because, when there is internal conflict, voters can better identify the true positions of the party.

Assuming that voters do pay attention to parties' positions, if parties become too similar in their pursuit of voters (congruence) or if parties move too far from their voters (incongruence), voters may respond by switching to another party. Kitschelt (1988, 1995), for example, demonstrated that, as catch-all parties converged on the middle of the ideological spectrum, both left-libertarian and radical right parties were more likely to form and be successful, as they attracted the voters who felt less represented (see also Chapters 11 and 13). Bartolini and Mair (1990) have shown that as policy distances between the left and right blocs become smaller, electoral volatility increases. Several studies have demonstrated the relationship between ideological incongruence on different issue dimensions and vote switching in European Parliament elections (e.g. Bakker, Jolly and Polk 2018). Spoon and Klüver (2019), moreover, find that voters are more likely to switch from supporting a mainstream party to a nonmainstream party when parties' positions converge on the right-left scale. Following this same assumption, Bakker, Jolly and Polk (2020) demonstrate that, when there is incongruence between a mainstream voter and her party on multiple dimensions, she is more likely to consider voting for an anti-establishment challenger party. When looking at the immigration issue, however, Spoon and Klüver (2020) find that, although mainstream parties may try to accommodate voters who hold more restrictive views on immigration by taking similar positions, this does not have any effect on voters' likelihood either to stay with the party or switch.

Measurement

Measuring voter and party priorities and positions is at the core of the question of responsiveness. Researchers interested in these questions are fortunate that there are several existing time-series cross-sectional datasets covering many countries over long periods which are focused on measuring voter and party issue salience and position.

On the party side, researchers rely primarily on the data from the Manifestos Project (MP-MARPOR) (Volkens et al. 2021) and the Chapel Hill Expert Surveys, CHES (Bakker, Jolly and Polk 2018, 2020; Jolly et al. 2022) to measure issue emphasis and position, although other data are also being collected. For example, the Comparative Campaign Dynamics Dataset (Debus, Somer-Topcu and Tavits 2018) measures party position using media coverage of campaigns. The MP, by conducting a manual content analysis of parties' manifestos, is the most comprehensive dataset on parties' issue emphasis and positions. Human coders have divided the manifesto into 'quasi sentences' corresponding to thematic statements and have classified these quasi-sentences into 56 policy categories based on a coding scheme. For some issues, there are both pro- and anti-categories (such as European integration), and for others, there is only a pro-category (environment). For each category, a percentage is denoted, which represents the percentage of quasi-sentences allocated to that category in the manifesto. A right-left index (RILE) has also been created which assembles 13 categories that have been defined as *left* and 13 as right. The RILE index is commonly used in research on party positions and responsiveness as the left-right scale constitutes the primary dimension of conflict in established democracies (Marks and Steenbergen 2002). To compute emphasis, all of the mentions (both positive and negative) are added up to create a composite percentage of the manifesto that focuses on a given issue. To compute party position, the positive mentions are subtracted from the negative mentions on a given issue. Thus, for European integration, issue attention would be calculated by adding both the pro- and anti-categories and issue position would be calculated by subtracting the percentage of pro-statements from the percentage of anti-statements (see also Chapter 38). The CHES is based on surveys in which experts are asked to place parties on a 0–10 scale on a variety of issues and also includes a general left-right scale. Each party's position on a given issue then reflects the mean of the experts' positions (see also Chapter 40).

On the voter side, survey data is typically used to measure priority and position. Questions which ask voters what the most important problem (MIP) or most important issue (MII) is in the upcoming election are used to assess issue priority. While scholars agree that these are not necessarily the same question, there is general agreement that there is little difference in the questions and responses they produce (see Jennings and Wlezien 2011; Klüver and Spoon 2016). To measure voter position, a question which asks voters to place themselves on a 0–10 left-right scale is typically used. Although less common as fewer cross-national surveys use similar issue position questions, some studies have used these (see e.g. Klüver and Spoon 2016; Spoon and Klüver 2020; Costello et al. 2021; which use Voting Advice Applications, see also Chapter 39). The issues that are often covered are immigration, the environment and European integration. Voter priority and issue position questions can be found in cross-national surveys such as the Comparative Study of Electoral Systems (CSES) and national election studies.

One of the challenges of comparing voter and party salience and position is that the scales are often different.[2] For example, the MP RILE values range from −100 (most left) to 100 (most right), whereas most voter left-right self-placement questions range from 0 to 10. Thus, to calculate responsiveness on left-right, the party values need first be re-scaled. Once this is done, party responsiveness is then calculated by subtracting the voter position in the previous election, $t-1$, from the party position in the current election, $t0$. To examine if voters respond to parties, party position at $t-1$ is compared to voter position at $t0$. Lower scores indicate that there is more congruence in positions and thus more responsiveness; higher scores indicate that there is less congruence as well as responsiveness. Depending on the research question, party issue position/emphasis at $t0$ may be the dependent variable and voter issue position/emphasis at $t-1$ may be the independent variable (or the opposite if voter position/emphasis is the dependent variable).

Conclusions and avenues for future research

This chapter began by asking an important set of questions in the study of linkage and representation: Do parties listen to voters and do voters listen to parties? More specifically, is there empirical evidence of dynamic representation at play? On balance, this review has demonstrated that there is indeed evidence of both relationships, though these relationships are conditioned by both party- and system-level variables. This is good news from the perspective of representation: parties articulate their policy priorities and positions, voters understand these, and then vote accordingly. Although the literature on parties and representation is quite robust, there are some important areas for continued research that remain. These avenues for future research focus on both theoretical and empirical questions.

First, as discussed, the research on responsiveness addresses both issue emphasis or salience and position. However, what has not been addressed is whether we see more responsiveness when looking at salience versus position (or vice versa). Scholars should consider if there is a theoretical reason why we would expect more responsiveness on the part of both voters and parties when considering salience or position. As various articles have noted, the reason we see more (or less) responsiveness may be due to the data or measurements used (see e.g. Fernandez-Vazquez 2014; O'Grady and Abou-Chadi 2019). In addition, future research should build off of extant studies which have explored how parties are responsive to different groups of voters, such as their own supporters (Adams et al. 2006; Klüver and Spoon 2016) or voters who are part of certain demographic groups (and how this may vary across issues). Similarly, there is likely heterogeneity across groups when looking at whether voters listen. It will thus be important to further unpack this relationship as well.

Second, in any research that examines party positions and priorities, the question of how best to measure these arises as well as how best to measure what voters pay attention to. As discussed, the research reviewed earlier uses a variety of data to assess party priorities and positions, including manifestos (Volkens et al. 2021), expert surveys (Bakker, Jolly and Polk 2020) and media coverage (Debus, Somer-Topcu and Tavits 2018). Although the data in these datasets are overall highly correlated, different conclusions are often reached when different data is used. Relatedly, some scholars address questions of responsiveness using the left-right scale, whereas others examine these questions using specific issues (e.g. the environment, immigration or European integration). Results often vary depending on which is used. Dalton (2017), for example, finds that parties are representative of voters on left-right positions and socioeconomic issues, but are less representative on cultural and gender issues. Although decisions on which data to use often rest on availability, scholars have begun to question whether the left-right dimension should be used at all. O'Grady and Abou-Chadi (2019), for example, argue that research on responsiveness based on issue position should not use the left-right dimension, as political conflict is not unidimensional and because voters do not necessarily know which policies are associated with left and right. Instead, they propose a new measure of parties' policy positions using a Bayesian model of survey responses. Thus, there is a continuing need to refine how we both conceptually and empirically measure party positions and priorities.

Third, the extant research into questions of dynamic representation largely focuses either on whether parties are responsive or on whether voters listen, but does not take into account the full relationship. Empirically, panel data is needed to look at both sides of this relationship, which would also allow for determining the endogeneity of the relationship, that is, are voters more likely to listen to parties when the parties have already responded in a previous election; and are parties more likely to be responsive when voters/supporters have already moved closer to the party? With existing panel surveys on issue positions and priorities and more panels with these questions being included in election surveys, these questions can be more easily addressed in future research.

Fourth, the research reviewed earlier largely focuses on the developed democracy context (and Europe and the USA in particular). Research in other contexts would be most welcome. Furthermore, as linkage may take on different forms in less economically developed countries, countries with weaker party systems, a tradition of clientelistic relationships between parties and voters or different institutions (see Kitschelt 2000), research looking at responsiveness in these contexts is an important avenue for future research.

Finally, researchers should continue to explore how exogenous factors – including crises such as the COVID-19 pandemic and climate change – affect responsiveness and how this varies across parties and voters. These external shocks would also enable researchers to apply causal identification strategies to determine the role these factors play in responsiveness by both parties and voters.

Notes

1. Importantly, scholars do not all agree which party families are considered 'niche' (see Meguid 2005; Adams et. al 2006). In addition, some scholars define niche parties more dynamically by issue emphasis (e.g. Wagner 2012; Meyer and Miller 2015).
2. One way around this challenge is to use voter placement of parties instead of parties' or experts' placements, which are scaled similar to the self-placement questions. The CSES, for example, includes a question which asks respondents to place each party on the 0–10 right-left scale. Other scholars have proposed different left-right scaling methods (see e.g. Lowe et al. 2011).

References

Abou-Chadi, T. (2018) 'Electoral competition, political risks, and parties' responsiveness to voters' issue priorities', *Electoral Studies*, 55, p99–108.

Abou-Chadi, T., Green-Pedersen, C. and Mortensen, P.B. (2020) 'Parties' policy adjustments in response to changes in issue saliency,' *West European Politics*, 43(4), p749–771.

Abou-Chadi, T. and Orlowski, M. (2016) 'Moderate as necessary: The role of electoral competitiveness and party size in explaining parties' policy shifts', *Journal of Politics*, 78(3), p868–881.

Adams, J., Clark, M., Ezrow, L. and Glasgow, G. (2004) 'Understanding change and stability in party ideologies: Do parties respond to public opinion or to past election results?', *British Journal of Political Science*, 34(4), p589–610.

Adams, J., Clark, M., Ezrow, L. and Glasgow, G. (2006) 'Are niche parties fundamentally different from mainstream parties? The causes and the electoral consequences of Western European parties' policy shifts, 1976–1998', *American Journal of Political Science*, 50(3), p513–529.

Adams, J., Ezrow, L. and Somer-Topcu, Z. (2011) 'Is anybody listening? Evidence that voters do not respond to European parties' policy statements during elections', *American Journal of Political Science*, 55(2), p370–382.

Adams, J., Haupt, A.B. and Stoll, H. (2009) 'What moves parties? The role of public opinion and global economic conditions in Western Europe', *Comparative Political Studies*, 42(5), p611–639.

Adams, J. and Somer-Topcu, Z. (2009a) 'Do parties adjust their policies in response to rival parties' policy shifts? Spatial theory and the dynamics of party competition in twenty-five democracies', *British Journal of Political Science*, 39(4), p825–846.

Adams, J. and Somer-Topcu, Z. (2009b) 'Moderate now, win votes later: The electoral consequences of parties' policy shifts in 25 postwar democracies', *Journal of Politics*, 71(2), p678–692.

Ansolabehere, S. and Iyangar, S. (1994) 'Riding the wave and claiming ownership over issues: The joint effects of advertising and news coverage in campaigns', *Public Opinion Quarterly*, 58(3), p335–357.

Bakker, R., Jolly, S. and Polk, J. (2018) 'Multidimensional incongruence and vote switching in Europe', *Public Choice*, 176, p267–296.

Bakker, R., Jolly, S. and Polk, J. (2020) 'Multidimensional incongruence, political dissatisfaction, and support for anti-establishment parties', *Journal of European Public Policy*, 27(2), p292–309.

Bartolini, S. and Mair, P. (1990) 'Policy competition, spatial distance and electoral instability', *West European Politics*, 13(4), p1–16.

Beyer, D. and Hänni, M. (2018) 'Two sides of the same coin? Congruence and responsiveness as representative democracy's currencies', *Policy Studies Journal*, 46(S1), pS13–S47.

Bolleyer, N. (2007) 'Small parties: From party pledges to government policy', *West European Politics*, 30(1), p121–147.

Burden, B.C. (2004) 'Candidate positioning in US congressional elections', *British Journal of Political Science*, 34(2), p211–227.

Clements, Ben., Nanou, K. and Real-Dato, J. (2018) 'Economic crisis and party responsiveness on the left-right dimension in the EU', *Party Politics*, 24(1), p52–64.

Costello, R., Toshkov, D., Bos, B. and Krouwel, A. (2021), 'Congruence between voters and parties: The role of party-level issue salience', *European Journal of Political Research*. 60(1), p92–113.

Dalton, R.J. (2017) 'Party representation across multiple issue dimensions', *Party Politics*, 23(6), p609–622.

Dalton, R.J., Farrell, D.M. and McAllister, I. (2011) *Political parties and democratic linkage: How parties organize democracy*. Oxford: Oxford University Press.

Debus, M., Somer-Topcu, Z. and Tavits, M. (2018) *Comparative campaign dynamics dataset*. Mannheim: Mannheim Centre for European Social Research, University of Mannheim.

Downs, A. (1957) *An economic theory of voting*. New York: Harper and Row.

Ezrow, L., De Vries, C., Steenbergen, M. and Edwards, E. (2011) 'Mean voter representation and partisan constituency representation: Do parties respond to the mean voter position or to their supporters?', *Party Politics*, 17(3), p275–301.

Ezrow, L. and Hellwig, T. (2014) 'Responding to voters or responding to markets? Political parties and public opinion in an era of globalization', *International Studies Quarterly*, 58(4), p816–827.

Ezrow, L., Hellwig, T. and Fenzl, M. (2020) 'Responsiveness, if you can afford it: Policy responsiveness in good and bad economic times', *Journal of Politics*, 82(3), p1166–1170.

Ferland, B. (2020) 'Party responsiveness to public opinion and party supporters: Revisiting the mechanisms and motivations', *Party Politics*, 26(4), p366–378.

Fernandez-Vazquez, P. (2014) 'And yet it moves: The effect of election platforms on party policy images', *Comparative Political Studies*, 47(14), p1919–1944.

Fernandez-Vazquez, P. and Somer-Topcu, Z. (2019) 'The informational role of party leader changes on voters' perceptions of party positions', *British Journal of Political Science*, 49(3), p977–996.

Fortunato, D. and Stevenson, R.T. (2013) 'Perceptions of partisan ideologies: The effect of coalition participation', *American Journal of Political Science*, 57(2), p459–477.

Golder, M. and Ferland, B. (2018) 'Electoral rules and citizen-elite ideological congruence', in Herron, E., Pekkanen, R. and Shugart, M. (eds.) *The Oxford handbook of electoral systems*. Oxford: Oxford University Press, pp. 213–246.

Golder, M. and Stramski, J. (2010) 'Ideological Congruence and Electoral Institutions', *American Journal of Political Science*, 54(1), p90–106.

Han, K.J. (2018) 'Beclouding party position as an electoral strategy: Voter polarization, issue priority and position blurring', *British Journal of Political Science*, 50(2), p653–675.

Haupt, A.B. (2010) 'Parties' responses to economic globalization: What is left for the left and right for the right?', *Party Politics*, 16(1), p5–27.

Jennings, W. and Wlezien, C. (2011) 'Distinguishing between most important problems and Issues', *Public Opinion Quarterly*, 75(3), p545–555.

Jolly, S., Bakker, R., Hooghe, L., Marks, G., Polk, J., Rovny, J., Steenbergen, M. and Vachudova, M.A. (2022) 'Chapel Hill Expert Survey Trend File, 1999–2019', *Electoral Studies*, 75, 102420.

Key, V.O. (1958) *Politics, parties, and pressure groups* (4th ed.). New York: Thomas Y. Crowell Company.

Kirschheimer, O. (1966) 'The transformation of the western European party Systems', in LaPalombara, J. and Weiner, M. (eds.) *Political parties and political development*, vol. 6. Princeton: Princeton University Press, p177–200.

Kitschelt, H. (1988) 'Left-libertarian parties: Explaining innovation in competitive party systems', *World Politics*, 40(2), p194–234.

Kitschelt, H. (1995) *The radical right in Western Europe: A comparative analysis*. Ann Arbor, MI: University of Michigan Press.

Kitschelt, H. (2000) 'Linkages between citizens and politicians in democratic polities', *Comparative Political Studies*, 33(6–7), p845–879.

Klüver, H. and Spoon, J. (2016) 'Who responds? Voters, parties, and issue attention', *British Journal of Political Science*, 46(3), p633–654.

Klüver, H. and Spoon, J. (2017) 'Challenges to multi-party governments: How governing in coalitions affects party responsiveness to voters', *Party Politics*, 23(6), p793–803.

Klüver, H. and Spoon, J. (2020) 'Helping or hurting: How governing as a junior coalition partner influences electoral outcomes', *Journal of Politics*, 82(4), p231–1242.

Lawson, K. (1980) 'Political parties and linkage', in Lawson, K. (ed.) *Political parties and linkage: A comparative perspective*. New Haven: Yale University Press, pp. 3–24.

Lehrer, R. (2012) 'Intra-party democracy and party responsiveness', *West European Politics*, 35(6), p1295–1319.

Lehrer, R. and Lin, N. (2020) 'Everything to Everyone? Not When You are Internally Divided', *Party Politics*, 26(6), p783–794.

Levendusky, M.S. (2010) 'Clearer cues, more consistent voters: A benefit of elite polarization', *Political Behavior*, 32(1), p111–131.

Lowe, W., Benoit, K., Mikhaylov, S. and Laver, M. (2011) 'Scaling policy preferences from coded political texts', *Legislative Studies Quarterly*, 36(1), p123–155.

Marks, G. and Steenbergen, M. (2002) 'Understanding political contestation in the European Union', *Comparative Political Studies*, 35(8), p879–892.

Meguid, B.M. (2005) 'Competition between unequals: The role of mainstream party strategy in niche party success', *American Political Science Review*, 99(3), p347–359.

Meyer, T.M. and Miller, B. (2015) 'The niche party concept and its measurement', *Party Politics*, 21(2), p259–271.

O'Grady, T. and Abou-Chadi, T. (2019) 'Not so responsive after all: European parties do not respond to public opinion shifts across multiple issue dimensions', *Research & Politics*, 6(4), p1–7.

Pitkin, H.F. (1967) *The concept of representation*. Berkeley: University of California Press.

Powell Jr., G.B. and Whitten, G.D. (1993) 'A cross-national analysis of economic voting: Taking account of the political context', *American Journal of Political Science*, 37(2), p391–414.

Rovny, J. and Polk, J. (2020) 'Still blurry? Economic salience, position, and voting for radical right parties in western Europe' *European Journal of Political Research*, 59(2), p248–268.

Schumacher, G., de Vries, C. and Vis, B. (2013) 'Why do parties change position? Party organization and environmental incentives', *Journal of Politics*, 75(2) p464–477.

Somer-Topcu, Z. (2015) 'Everything to everyone? The electoral consequences of the broad-appeal strategy in Europe', *American Journal of Political Science*, 59(4), p841–854.

Somer-Topcu, Z., Tavits, M. and Baumann, M. (2020) 'Does party rhetoric affect voter perceptions of party positions', *Electoral Studies*, 65, 102153.

Spoon, J. (2011) *Political survival of small parties*. Ann Arbor: University of Michigan Press.

Spoon, J. and Klüver, H. (2015) 'Voter polarization and party responsiveness: Why parties emphasize divided issues, but remain silent on unified issues', *European Journal of Political Research*, 54(2), p343–362.

Spoon, J. and Klüver, H. (2019) 'Party convergence and vote switching: Explaining mainstream party decline across Europe', *European Journal of Political Research*, 58(4), p1021–1042.

Spoon, J. and Klüver, H. (2020) 'Responding to far right challengers: Does accommodation pay off?' *Journal of European Public Policy*, 27(2), p273–291.

Stimson, J.A., MacKuen, M.B. and Erikson, R.S. (1995) 'Dynamic representation', *American Political Science Review*, 89(3), p543–565.

Strøm, K. (1990) 'A behavioral theory of competitive political parties', *American Journal of Political Science*, 34(2), p565–598.

Traber, D., Giger, N. and Häusermann, S. (2018) 'How economic crises affect political representation: Declining voter-party congruence in times of constrained government', *West European Politics*, 41(5), p1100–1124.

van de Wardt, M. (2012) 'Putting the damper on? Do parties de-emphasize issues in response to internal divisions among their supporters?', *Party Politics*, 20(3), p330–340.

Volkens, A., Burst, T., Krause, W., Lehmann, P., Matthieß, T., Merz, N., Regel, S., Weßels, B. and Zehnter, L. (2021) 'The manifesto data collection', in *Manifesto project (MRG/CMP/MARPOR). Version 2021a.* Berlin: Wissenschaftszentrum Berlin für Sozialforschung (WZB). https://doi.org/10.25522/manifesto.mpds.2021a

Wagner, M. (2012) 'Defining and measuring niche parties', *Party Politics*, 18(6), p845–864.

Walgrave, S. and Lefevere, J. (2013) 'Ideology, salience, and complexity: Determinants of policy issue incongruence between voters and parties', *Journal of Elections, Public Opinion and Parties*, 23(4), p456–483.

Williams, C. and Spoon, J. (2015) 'Differentiated party response: The effect of euroskeptic public opinion on party positions', *European Union Politics*, 16(2), p176–193.

Wittman, D. (1973) 'Parties as utility maximizers', *American Political Science Review*, 67(2), p490–498.

22
PERSONALISATION AND POLITICAL PARTIES

Helene Helboe Pedersen

Personalisation of politics is a process through which political individuals become increasingly important relative to collective political actors such as political parties, cabinets and parliaments (Rahat and Sheafer 2007, 65; Pedersen and Rahat 2021, 1). The extent to which politics is becoming increasingly personalised as a response to intensified mediatisation and cultural individualisation has been the focus of a blossoming research agenda (Karvonen 2010; Kriesi 2012; Lobo and Curtice 2015; Renwick and Pilet 2016; Cross, Katz and Pruysers 2018; Rahat and Kenig 2018). Scholars state that this century 'will be the age of personalisation, just as the previous one was the century of mass collective actors – a trend that political science has a duty to consider with greater attention' (Musella and Webb 2015, 226), and some have concluded that 'political parties are way beyond their peak; personalisation is here to stay' (Rahat and Kenig 2018, 263). Personalisation may thus be one of the most important changes to party democracy as we know it. So there are good reasons to clarify what it entails, to investigate its prevalence and to consider possible causes and consequences.

Focusing primarily on western liberal democracies, this chapter presents the state of the art in the study of personalisation with regard to conceptual clarifications, empirical results, theoretical developments and academic debates regarding the possible democratic implications of increasingly personalised politics.[1] Personalisation has been a key issue in multiple branches of political science, including political communication, legislative studies and political behaviour. While this chapter aims to provide a comprehensive overview of the many insights from the personalisation literature, emphasis is on how personalisation relates to political parties and party democracy. Party democracy is understood as a democratic system in which political parties are the main actors establishing linkages between citizens and the state by organising elections, mobilising voters, influencing and aggregating political opinions and organising legislative behaviour to promote party policy.

This chapter, first, clarifies the concept of personalisation and its sub-dimensions. Second, it reviews empirical results of studies related to different arenas of personalisation: institutional, media and behavioural personalisation. Third, it discusses the theoretical developments in explaining variation in personalised politics. Fourth, it maps academic positions regarding the possible implications of personalisation for political parties and party democracy. Finally, it suggests avenues for further research on personalisation.

Conceptual clarification

Whereas *personalisation* refers to a development over time in which the balance between individuals and collective actors changes, *personalised politics* (Pedersen and Rahat 2021) or *personalism* (Cross, Katz and Pruysers 2018) describes a time-specific situation in which political individuals are relatively more important than collective actors. This fundamental conceptual difference is relevant for empirical research. Studies of personalisation require longitudinal data, while studies of personalism can be based on cross-sectional data comparing levels of personalism across politicians, parties or political systems. For personalisation as well as personalism, the concept describes a political situation, or process towards a situation, different from a non-personalised political situation. Political individuals have always been important – just read any book on political history or look up the history of any political party to notice how significant persons stand out as charismatic leaders or significant decision-makers. Personalisation thus entails more than individuals just being important. It describes changes in what has been called the 'partyness' of a political system (Katz 1987; Pruysers, Cross and Katz 2018, 4; Rahat and Kenig 2018, 1), which involves political parties as the main actors for organising voters, legislators and ministers and their mutual interactions and accountability relations. Personalisation therefore indicates that political individuals become *relatively* more important than political collectives such as political parties for political debates, decision-making and mobilisation.

Even with this general conceptual understanding, the study of personalisation spans multiple literatures and academic realms. To organise this cross-disciplinary research, Pedersen and Rahat (2021) suggest[2] specifying studies of personalisation along three analytical dimensions: arena, level and character. *Arena* refers to where personalisation takes place, *level* relates to which actors (e.g. party leaders or rank-and-file) personalise, and *character* refers to how personalisation manifests, for instance by highlighting the private affairs or individual competences of a given politician.

With regard to arena, personalisation may occur in the institutional, media or behavioural arena of political life (Rahat and Sheafer 2007). Institutional personalisation entails institutional changes that place more importance on the individual, such as introducing primaries for candidate selection or moving from a closed-list to an open-list electoral ballot.

Media personalisation entails a shift in media content towards more emphasis on individuals rather than collective actors. This may appear on media platforms controlled by politicians, who may, on their own social media platforms, self-personalise (McGregor 2018) by providing more stories about themselves and their private lives than they do about their parties. Personalisation may also appear on media platforms uncontrolled by politicians but influenced by journalists and editors prioritising news about individuals over news about collective actors when preparing their news coverage (Holtz-Bacha, Langer and Merkle 2014).

Behavioural personalisation entails changes in voters' and politicians' perceptions of politics and political behaviour. Among voters, political individuals come to be perceived as more important for political participation, opinion formation and vote choice. Among politicians, their own preferences and careers come to be perceived as more important than party programmes and party success for legislative behaviour and campaigning activity (Pedersen and Rahat 2021).

The three arenas have been shown to be causally related, with personalisation in one arena creating pressure for personalisation in other arenas (Rahat and Sheafer 2007). This makes the distinction important for analysing the spread of personalisation.

For each political arena, personalisation may be studied by focusing on different levels. Personalisation can entail increased focus on and power of political leaders (centralised personalisation [Balmas, Rahat and Sheafer 2014]). One type of centralised personalisation is closely linked to the more narrowly defined concept of presidentialisation (Poguntke and Webb 2005, 2018). Personalisation can also entail increased focus on and power of rank-and-file political individuals (decentralised personalisation [Balmas, Rahat and Sheafer 2014]), leading to more candidate-oriented politics (Wattenberg 1991).

Finally, and only relevant for the behavioural and media arenas, personalisation may appear with a different character, namely in the form of privatisation or individualisation (Van Aelst, Shaefer and Stanyer 2012). Personalisation expressed through privatisation increases focus on the private lives of political individuals such as personal relationships, family life, private consumption or hobbies, aimed at describing political individuals as private rather than professional actors (Van Aelst, Shaefer and Stanyer 2012, 207). Personalisation may also appear through individualisation, directing focus towards individual competences, characteristics and policy positions rather than party competences, characteristics and policy positions. Some studies also suggest that personalisation may be reflected in increased focus on the electoral district at the expense of the party, seeing localisation as another expression of personalised politics (Cross and Young 2015; Pedersen and van Heerde-Hudson 2019).

The analytical framework of personalisation based on arena, level and character contributes to the conceptual clarification of personalisation that is needed to evaluate operationalisations and systematically compare empirical studies. It also allows for nuanced debates about the potential consequences of different types of personalisation, as will be elaborated later.

How much personalisation? Results and empirical challenges

There is an ongoing debate regarding how much personalisation modern political systems are witnessing. One of the reasons behind this debate is that studies of personalisation are demanding in terms of data. In order to study the extent to which individuals have become relatively more important than collective actors, we need data from multiple points in time over a long period. This enables us to identify long-term trends rather than sporadic fluctuations. Another reason is that trends of personalisation across different arenas, levels and characters have not been separated, meaning that identified trends of personalisation in one arena may be contrasted with lack of personalisation in another arena. It is therefore important to keep these developments apart, as I will do in the following review of empirical results.

Institutional personalisation

Institutional personalisation includes changes of rules resulting in more emphasis on individual politicians, party members or voters than on the political group. This may relate to various political institutions. A significant political institution is the electoral system, which specifies the rules connecting citizens to their representatives in public office. Renwick and Pilet (2016) have conducted the most comprehensive study of trends towards personalisation in reforms of electoral systems, examining measures that have made them more candidate oriented than party oriented by, for example, increasing the importance of preference votes. Their comprehensive data has been updated by Rahat and Kenig (2018), allowing us to investigate trends in institutional personalisation from the 1940s to 2015. There is some indication of personalisation, for instance in Belgium and the Netherlands, but overall electoral systems are rather stable. There have also been some changes towards strengthening the 'partyness' of the systems, for instance in Japan and New Zealand (Rahat and Kenig 2018, 143; Renwick and Pilet 2016, 26).

Government institutions are crucial in determining the extent to which citizens may hold individuals or political groups accountable. While regime changes are rare, institutional developments increasing the powers of prime ministers relative to the cabinet, for instance by concentrating more resources in the prime minister's office or the prime minister taking a more decisive role in national and supranational political negotiations, have been identified. Based on expert evaluations, Karvonen (2010), Poguntke and Webb (2005) and Rahat and Kenig (2018) document increasing power of prime ministers, although the trend is not uniform. In some cases, such as Greece, Norway and Spain, experts find that prime ministers have become less rather than more powerful.

Institutional personalisation may also take place within political parties. One of the key party political institutions is the rules regarding candidate selection. If selection processes become more inclusive by including all party members or even all party supporters, the party loses some control over the process, and individual candidates may succeed by mobilising loosely organised supporters rather than building support within the party's executive organs.[3] A comprehensive literature has documented that political parties have democratised their candidate selection procedures (e.g. Scarrow, Webb and Farrell 2000; Bille 2001), serving as an indicator of personalisation of party institutions (Rahat and Kenig 2018, 153). Similarly, the literature has documented trends towards more inclusive processes of party leader selection (LeDuc 2001). Besides this more common use of plebiscitary modes of intra-party decision-making, contacts with party members have become more individualised by inviting them to engage in ad hoc campaigns for specific issues to accommodate more modern forms of political engagement (Gauja 2018). It is notable that more uniform trends of institutional personalisation are identified with regard to rules that are most directly under the control of political parties, namely their own procedures for selecting candidates and leaders and for engaging voters.

Media personalisation

Media personalisation describes a process in which the media system produces relatively more news about political individuals than about political groups. While media and political communication scholars are among those producing the most research related to personalisation of politics (Pedersen and Rahat 2021), surprisingly few comparative and longitudinal studies exist (some exceptions are Karvonen 2010; Kriesi 2012; Gattermann 2018). These studies have been summarised and related to country-specific longitudinal studies by Rahat and Kenig (2018, 156), who conclude that trends of personalisation are limited in most countries, and strong (e.g. Israel and Italy) or non-existent (Belgium and Canada) in a few. Most studies identify variation – across countries and time – rather than a general and evident trend towards greater personalisation.

These studies, however, are based on press coverage, that is, media content not controlled by politicians alone. This is almost the only existing indicator when the ambition is to describe developments over long time spans. Social media platforms only arrived in the twenty-first century, which makes these sources less valuable for investigating long-term trends. Press releases, editorial letters or newsletters from individual politicians or parties are hard to collect systematically over time and often also subject to editorial decisions. Innovative scholars have turned to campaign material to investigate media personalisation more directly under the control of politicians. They find evidence for personalisation in media campaigns in Israel (Balmas, Rahat and Shaefer 2014) and the Netherlands (Vliegenthart 2012), but country comparative analyses are missing.

A rich literature has emerged about personalised political communication on social media (Facebook, Twitter and websites). The mere adoption of social media as a communication channel by individual politicians has been interpreted as one indicator of personalised politics (Enli and Skogerbø 2013; Rahat and Kenig 2018). Others have focused on online strategies such as the usage of interactive tools to promote personal dialogue between politicians and voters (Kruikemeier et al. 2013), or on how individualised campaign strategies correlate with the usage of social media (Karlsen and Enjolras 2016). Very few studies have explored the content of social media coverage to investigate the extent to which these personal online platforms are dominated by stories about political individuals or political groups. McGregor, Lawrence and Cardona (2017) find only limited privatised communication on social media platforms among U.S. candidates. Metz, Kruikemeier and Lecheler (2020) find substantial self-personalisation on the Facebook pages of German 'spitzenkandidaten' but do not measure this against the prevalence of party-oriented stories. Pedersen and van Heerde-Hudson (2019) find that British MPs provide almost equal amounts of information about themselves and their parties on their personal websites, while Danish MPs on average provide more information about their parties.

Behavioural personalisation

Behavioural personalisation may occur among voters as well as politicians. Among voters, personalisation entails changes of perceptions or preferences regarding representation; if voters increasingly find who their MP is to be more important than which party he/she represents, it is an indication of personalisation. Such perceptions may result in personalised political participation, most often studied as voting behaviour motivated by preferences for party leaders or specific candidates (Bittner 2011; Ferreira da Silva, Garzia and De Angelis 2021). The evidence for personalisation of political participation is still mixed. Based on national election surveys from 13 countries from 1974 to 2016, Ferreira da Silva, Garzia and De Angelis (2021) find that party leader evaluations have become more important for electoral turnout. Wauters et al. (2018) illuminate a complex mix of decreasing decentralised personalisation and increased centralised personalisation when it comes to Belgian voters' use of preference votes: 'Candidates other than party leaders appear to have growing difficulties in attracting [preference] votes' (Wauters et al. 2018, 511). Garzia (2014) finds evidence for the increasing importance of leadership evaluation on vote choice, while others (Karvonen 2010; Bittner 2011) find the impact to vary across elections but with no general trend of personalisation. Experimental studies (Lee and Oh 2012) and survey-based analyses (Costa Lobo 2008) suggest that voters differ in their sensitivity towards personalised political communication and party leader evaluations depending on their party identification. In summary, evidence for personalisation is mixed, and voters vary in their propensity for personalised political participation.

Among politicians, the study of personalised political behaviour is still limited. The comparative candidate survey gave rise to studies of personalised electoral campaigns showing substantial variation across countries (Zittel 2015), although they were not able to trace changes over time given the non-longitudinal data. For the Netherlands, Vliegenthart (2012) documents not only increasing prominence of party leaders on election posters but also increased use of party logos, suggesting a change towards professionalisation rather than personalisation. The consequences of personalised campaigning for legislative behaviour are still uncertain. Chiru (2018) as well as Zittel and Nyhuis (2021) find that those candidates running a personalised electoral campaign are more likely to ask parliamentary questions regarding their constituency as a legislative strategy of personalised representation. However, only in Germany are Zittel and Nyhuis (2021) able to show that personalised campaigning also decreases party discipline in roll-call votes, which is not the case in Hungary and Romania (Chiru 2018). Longitudinal studies of parliamentary behaviour are rare, but Wauters, Bouteca and de Vet's (2021) study of the Belgian case shows no personalisation trend in the period from 1995 to 2015 regarding individualised activities (questions) relative to collective activities (bill proposals), single- relative to co-sponsored bills or the number of party switches. Again, comparative studies are missing in this regard.

Across arenas, the evidence for personalisation is mixed. Trends vary across countries and parties, suggesting that personalisation is no simple response to general societal developments but constrained or incentivised by the existing political context. Researchers have made great efforts to disentangle these variations and develop increasingly advanced theoretical models to understand the causes behind political personalisation.

Personalisation when, where and why? Theoretical developments

Theoretical developments explaining the process of personalisation or variation in levels of personalism can be summarised into three steps: (1) the structural explanation, (2) the (neo-) institutional explanation and (3) the political explanation. The underlying theoretical model is sketched in Figure 22.1.

The first line of theoretical explanation was concerned with how broad societal changes such as political mediatisation, cultural individualisation and developments in media technologies translate into personalisation of politics (Strömbäck 2008; Adam and Maier 2010; Karvonen 2010). As voters become increasingly volatile, party dealignment increases, and political information primarily provided by commercial or at least party-independent (televised) media seeks to maximise profit or viewers, politicians need to respond in order to succeed in the competition for votes, office and political influence. Personalisation was in that sense *done* to politics and theorised as an almost automatic adaptation by political actors to broad societal changes.

However, the difficulties in detecting these general trends of political personalisation indicate that structural changes, which have been similar across most modern democracies, are not sufficient to catalyse political personalisation. The next theoretical step looked towards factors making personalisation a more or less attractive strategy for politicians to use – hence,

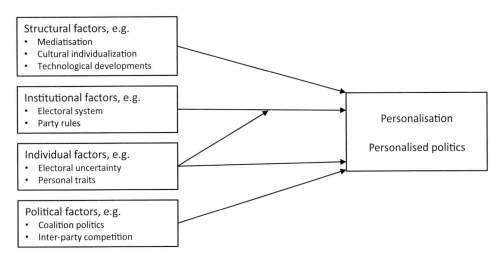

Figure 22.1 Illustration of theoretical model explaining personalisation or personalised politics

personalisation is seen as something politicians choose to do under the right circumstances. This theoretical development also moved more towards understanding variation in personalised politics across countries, parties and politicians.

Among the important factors influencing incentives to personalise is the electoral system. Inspired by the personal vote literature, which is concerned with explaining how electoral systems influence representative behaviour (Cain, Ferejohn and Fiorina 1987; Carey and Shugart 1995), scholars have argued that personalisation is more likely when politicians can benefit personally from mobilising dealigned voters able to cast their vote for a specific candidate rather than the party list. As such, scholars have hypothesised that candidates elected in preferential systems are more likely to personalise (Andre, Freire and Papp 2014; Zittel 2015). Others propose that the electoral system may influence the *character* of personalised politics. They argue that since politicians elected in single-member districts are more visible and directly accountable to district voters, single-member district systems will induce a localised expression of personalised politics, making politicians more attentive to district concerns and constituency service (Cross and Young 2015; Pedersen and van Heerde-Hudson 2019).

Party institutions are another important factor for creating or limiting incentives to personalise. The argument goes that the more central party offices control the political careers of individual politicians through nomination, selection, campaign funding or political promotion, the less likely that politicians will personalise, because party leaders prefer loyal party soldiers who invest their time and energy in promoting party policy. Under strict party control, personalisation comes with the risk of sanctions and fewer opportunities to realise political goals, which should decrease personalisation among legislators (Önnudottir 2014; Bøggild and Pedersen 2018). According to this perspective, party organisations constitute an important hurdle for personalisation – at least in the behavioural arena – among politicians.

Within this institutional framework, a second theoretical layer focuses on how the institutional incentives may be moderated by individual-level factors. In particular, marginality has been introduced as a factor important for politicians' incentives to personalise (Andre, Depauw and Martin 2015). Politicians in marginal seats are expected to be more likely to personalise because they are willing to risk the potential party sanctions associated with running personalised campaigns or behaving more independently in parliament. However, empirical results supporting this argument are mixed (Pedersen 2022). Less commonly, personal traits of the politicians have been taken into account. For instance, female and male politicians are hypothesised to face different opportunities and constraints with regard to utilising personalisation as a vote-maximising strategy due to cultural stereotypes (McGregor, Lawrence and Cardona 2017). Others have hypothesised that extroverted politicians are more likely to attract media attention and win from personalised representative behaviour (Amsalem et al. 2018; Bøggild et al. 2021).

The last and most recent theoretical step is scholars' attempts to theorise about the importance of political circumstances – or more specifically, the importance of party competition – for levels of personalised politics (Langer and Sagarzazu 2018). One part of the argument is somewhat similar to the party institutional argument that, when parties intensify control of intra-party politics, personalism will decrease. In this political line of reasoning, however, party control is not strong due to party institutions but because of the political necessity, for instance, to coordinate inter-party cooperation and maintain a coalition government. The second part of the argument is more path-breaking, as it suggests that, when party competition is intense, it produces more newsworthy stories for the media to cover, and consequently the relative balance between news coverage of political parties versus political individuals results in lower levels of personalism. This line of thinking constitutes an innovative way to integrate the literature on party systems, party competition and personalisation, although this is still in its early phases theoretically as well as empirically.

In summary, these theoretical developments help to clarify when, where and how personalised politics is more likely. The full model provides plausible explanations for variation across time, countries, parties, media platforms, voters and politicians. It is, however, also very demanding in terms of data, which makes comparative studies challenging and longitudinal studies covering the relevant time period sometimes impossible. However, specifying the model is helpful for designing empirical studies focusing on testing one or more of the relevant factors.

Consequences of personalisation

The main reason why scholars are concerned with describing indications of personalisation and understanding its causes is that personalisation of politics has raised many concerns regarding its potential consequences for political parties, party governance and representative democracy as such. However, some of these concerns have been questioned, and a promising way forward for the study of personalisation is to theorise about and empirically investigate the possible challenges and potentials associated with increasingly personalised politics.

With regard to representative democracy, many concerns have been raised from the media arena, where an increased focus on politicians' private lifestyles may crowd out substantial coverage of policy issues and political processes. As a result, the electorate may become less knowledgeable and capable of holding representatives to account. Democratic deliberation could be devalued or at least escape public attention. However, the challenge media personalisation poses to representative democracy depends on the character it takes. Privatisation is held to be more damaging for political news coverage than individualisation. In contrast to privatisation, individualisation provides relevant political information about politicians' competences, preferences and behaviour. Moreover, personalised media coverage is also argued to hold potential for increasing political knowledge and participation among voters. Political information 'piggybacked' in talk shows as 'infotainment' or 'soft news' may induce more citizens – and especially those with low political interest – to opt in to political news and receive relevant political information almost by accident (Baum and Jamison 2006). Similarly, personalised media interactions between voters and politicians via social media are also held to offer valuable possibilities for representative linkage (Jackson 2003; Kruikemeier et al. 2013). Media personalisation may thus have negative as well as positive implications for representative democracy. The balance between good and bad is still open to further empirical investigation.

With regard to party government, the verdict seems almost given, as personalisation is defined as a process in which individuals become more important at the expense of political parties. However, exactly how personalisation challenges political parties and thus party government is debatable. Given the mixed evidence of personalisation, a democracy with fully independent politicians is not in sight. The question, rather, is how and under what conditions personalisation changes party government. In order to discuss this, Katz (2018) argues, we need to clarify what is meant by party government. According to Katz (1987, 2018, 217), the ideal party government consists of five elements: (1) decisions are made by elected party officials, (2) policy is decided within parties, (3) which act cohesively to enact it, (4) officials are recruited through parties and (5) are held accountable through parties. The more a system adheres to these requirements, the stronger the 'partyness' of the government.

Party cohesion is the key to all elements of this understanding of party government. As such, personalisation only erodes party government if parties are unable to work as unitary actors, for instance when personalisation is expressed through rebellion or party switching. But the elements entail nothing about *how* parties should bring about this cohesion. Therefore, party government can be realised in many ways, even in a personalised way. For instance, the personalised party is defined as a party dominated by a strong leader held accountable only by a weak organisation (Kostadinova and Levitt 2014). It is organised to promote the ambitions and political ideas of the leader rather than a deep-seated group-based ideology (Ignazi 1996). But it is not necessarily less cohesive, and therefore even a personalised party can adhere to the elements defining party government. It follows that personalisation may not happen at the expense of party government. Many examples testify to the fact that personalised politics indeed do not challenge all parties. Macron's En Marche, Berlusconi's Forza Italia or Gert Wilders' Partij voor de Vrijheid are extreme cases of political parties depending on their leaders' ability to deliver electoral and political results. But even in less extreme cases, parties might benefit from promoting their popular leaders or celebrity candidates.

In this sense, personalisation does not happen at the expense of the individual party, but it might still influence the 'partyness' of party government. For a personalised party, the five elements of party government would translate into a situation where: (1) decisions are made by the party leader, (2) policy is decided by the party leader, (3) legislators act cohesively to enact the party leader's programme, (4) candidates or officials are recruited by the party leader and (5) legislators are held accountable by the party leader. Even if this does not influence the degree of party cohesion, it changes the very nature of party government. With no or limited organisational capacity, parties are more likely to supply less comprehensive and stable policy programmes (Jones 2003, 401; Schumacher and Giger 2018). The interest-aggregating and structuring function of parties is likely to vanish, and if this is the case, voters will face a more difficult time delegating political power to parties and holding them accountable. Personalised parties may not undermine party government, but they might undermine the qualities therein.

Conclusions and avenues for further research

Even though the study of personalisation has developed significantly in terms of conceptualisation, empirical description and theory building, many questions are still open and relevant for further research. First, descriptive country comparative studies mapping trends in personalisation across arenas, level and character are still rare, and we therefore remain uncertain as to how prevalent personalisation really is. To find answers, we depend not only on significant data collection but also on innovative measurement. Text analysis tapping into personalised language may be one way forward (McGregor, Lawrence and Cardona 2017).

Second, the complex mix of structures, institutions and individual traits making personalisation more or less likely remains under-theorised, and there are very few empirical tests disentangling the direct and moderated impact of the different factors. There are thus significant contributions to be made with regard to explaining variation in personalised politics. Here, we may look towards literature on legislative and voter behaviour that does not directly refer to or conduct its studies primarily to understand personalisation. Relatedly, integrating political circumstances into the study of personalisation is promising. The fluctuations of the relative importance of parties and politicians identified over time within countries and parties suggest that personalisation may be something that voters, politicians and the media turn to under specific political circumstances of low party competition. In particular, charismatic populist leaders may be able to fuel such a situation and benefit from personalised voter behaviour and media coverage.

Third, the study of personalisation would benefit from moving beyond speculation with regard to its potential democratic consequences. Scholars of media personalisation have already moved some way towards understanding how personalised political communication influences citizens' perceptions of and engagement in politics, but, with regard to institutional and behavioural personalisation, we are still uncertain about implications. For instance, are personalised parties less capable of offering comprehensive and consistent political programmes to voters? Are voters less likely to vote and mobilise in accordance with their political values and attitudes when focusing on political leaders rather than parties?

With personalisation identified by some observers as the most salient change to politics this century (Musella and Webb 2015), there is good reason to substantiate the claim and investigate its causes and consequences. While the research agenda has blossomed over the last two decades, many important questions remain open for new research projects.

Notes

1 For more information on personalisation trends outside this region, please see Chapter 30 on Russia, Chapter 32 on Southeast Asia and Chapter 34 on Sub-Saharan Africa.
2 Their suggestion is based on a literature review that identifies these different dimensions. Pedersen and Rahat's (2019) main contribution is to synthesise these insights from the growing literature in the field.
3 Selection processes may also personalise in a centralised fashion, leaving all selection power with the party leader (Rahat and Kenig 2018, 151).

References

Adam, S. and Maier, M. (2010) 'Personalization of politics: A critical review and agenda for research', *Annals of the International Communication Association*, 34(1), p213–257.

Amsalem, E., Zoizner, A., Sheafer, T., Walgrave, S. and Loewen, P.J. (2018) 'The effect of politicians' personality on their media visibility', *Communication Research*, 47(7), p1079–1102.

Andre, A., Depauw, S. and Martin, S. (2015) 'Electoral systems and legislators' constituency effort: The mediating effect of electoral vulnerability', *Comparative Political Studies*, 48(4), p464–496.

Andre, A., Freire, A. and Papp, Z. (2014) 'Electoral rules and legislators' personal vote-seeking', in Deschouwer, K. and Depauw, S. (eds.) *Representing the people: A survey among members of statewide and substate parliament*. Oxford: Oxford University Press, p87–109.

Balmas, M., Rahat, G. and Sheafer, T. (2014) 'Two routes to personalized politics: Centralized and decentralized personalization', *Party Politics*, 20(1), p37–51.

Baum, M.A. and Jamison, A.S. (2006) 'The Oprah effect: How soft news helps inattentive citizens vote consistently', *The Journal of Politics*, 68(4), p946–959.

Bille, L. (2001) 'Democratizing a democratic procedure: myth or reality? Candidate selection in Western European parties, 1960–1990', *Party Politics*, 7(3), p363–380.

Bittner, A. (2011) *Platform or personality?: The role of party leaders in elections*. Oxford: Oxford University Press.

Bøggild, T., Campbell, R., Nielsen, M.K., Pedersen, H.H. and van Heerde-Hudson, J.A. (2021) 'Which personality fits personalized representation?' *Party Politics*, 27(2), p269–281.

Bøggild, T. and Pedersen, H.H. (2018) 'Campaigning on behalf of the party? Party constraints on candidate campaign personalisation', *European Journal of Political Research*, 57(4), p883–899.

Cain, B., Ferejohn, J. and Fiorina, M. (1987) *The personal vote: Constituency service and electoral independence*. Cambridge: Harvard University Press.

Carey, J.M. and Shugart, M.S. (1995) 'Incentives to cultivate a personal vote: A rank ordering of electoral formulas', *Electoral Studies*, 14(4), p417–439.

Chiru, M. (2018) 'Exploring the role of decentralized personalization for legislative behaviour and constituency service', in Cross, W.P., Katz, R.S. and Pruysers, S. (eds.) *The personalization of democratic politics and the challenge for political parties*. London: ECPR Press, p143–161.

Costa Lobo, M. (2008) 'Parties and leader effects: Impact of leaders in the vote for different types of parties', *Party Politics*, 14(3), p281–298.

Cross, W.P., Katz, R.S. and Pruysers, S. (eds.) (2018) *The personalization of democratic politics and the challenge for political parties*. London: ECPR Press.

Cross, W.P. and Young, L. (2015) 'Personalization of campaigns in an SMP system: The Canadian case', *Electoral Studies*, 39, p306–315.

Enli, G.S. and Skogerbø, E. (2013) 'Personalized campaigns in party-centred politics: Twitter and Facebook as arenas for political communication', *Information, Communication & Society*, 16(5), p757–774.

Ferreira da Silva, F., Garzia, D. and De Angelis, A. (2021) 'From party to leader mobilization? The personalization of voter turnout', *Party Politics*, 27(2), p220–233.

Gattermann, K. (2018) 'Mediated personalization of executive European Union politics: Examining patterns in the broadsheet coverage of the European Commission, 1992–2016', *The International Journal of Press/Politics*, 23(3), p345–366.

Garzia, D. (2014) *Personalization of politics and electoral change*. New York: Springer.

Gauja, A. (2018) 'Party organization and personalization', in Cross, W.P., Katz, R.S. and Pruysers, S. (eds.) *The personalization of democratic politics and the challenge for political parties*. London: ECPR Press, p125–142.

Holtz-Bacha, C., Langer, A.I. and Merkle, S. (2014) 'The personalization of politics in comparative perspective: Campaign coverage in Germany and the United Kingdom', *European Journal of Communication*, 29(2), p153–170.

Ignazi, P. (1996) 'The crisis of parties and the rise of new political parties', *Party Politics*, 2(4), p549–566.

Jackson, N. (2003) 'MPs and web technologies: An untapped opportunity?' *Journal of Public Affairs: An International Journal*, 3(2), p124–137.

Jones, B.D. (2003) 'Bounded rationality and political science: Lessons from public administration and public policy', *Journal of Public Administration Research and Theory*, 13(4), p395–412.

Karlsen, R. and Enjolras, B. (2016) 'Styles of social media campaigning and influence in a hybrid political communication system: Linking candidate survey data with Twitter data', *The International Journal of Press/Politics*, 21(3), p338–357.

Karvonen, L. (2010) *The personalization of politics: A study of parliamentary democracies*. Colchester: ECPR Press.

Katz, R.S. (1987) 'Party government and its alternatives', in Katz, R.S. (ed.) *Party governments: European and American experiences*. Berlin: de Gruyter, p215–232.

Katz, R.S. (2018) 'Personalization, party government and democracy', in Cross, W.P., Katz, R.S. and Pruysers, S. (eds.) *The personalization of democratic politics and the challenge for political parties*. London: ECPR Press, p1–18.

Kostadinova, T. and Levitt, B. (2014) 'Toward a theory of personalist parties: Concept formation and theory building', *Politics & Policy*, 42(4), p490–512.

Kriesi, H.P. (2012) 'Personalization of national election campaigns', *Party Politics*, 18(6), p825–844.

Kruikemeier, S., van Noort, G., Vliegenthart, R. and De Vreese, C.H. (2013) 'Getting closer: The effects of personalized and interactive online political communication', *European Journal of Communication*, 28(1), p53–66.

Langer, A.I. and Sagarzazu, I. (2018) 'Bring back the party: Personalisation, the media and coalition politics', *West European Politics*, 41(2), p472–495.

LeDuc, L. (2001) 'Democratizing party leadership selection', *Party Politics*, 7(3), p323–341.

Lee, E.J. and Oh, S.Y. (2012) 'To personalize or depersonalize? When and how politicians' personalized tweets affect the public's reactions', *Journal of Communication*, 62(6), p932–949.

Lobo, M.C. and Curtice, J. (eds.) (2015) *Personality politics? The role of leader evaluations in democratic elections*. Oxford: Oxford University Press.

McGregor, S.C. (2018) 'Personalization, social media, and voting: Effects of candidate self-personalization on vote intention', *New Media & Society*, 20(3), p1139–1160.

McGregor, S.C., Lawrence, R.G. and Cardona, A. (2017) 'Personalization, gender, and social media: Gubernatorial candidates' social media strategies', *Information, Communication & Society*, 20(2), p264–283.

Metz, M., Kruikemeier, S. and Lecheler, S. (2020) 'Personalization of politics on Facebook: Examining the content and effects of professional, emotional and private self-personalization', *Information, Communication & Society*, 23(10), p1481–1498.

Musella, F. and Webb, P. (2015) 'The revolution of personal leaders', *Rivista Italiana di Scienza Politica*, 45(3), p223–226.

Onnudottir, E.H. (2014) 'Political parties and styles of representation', *Party Politics*, 22(6), p732–745.

Pedersen, H.H. (2022) 'Party soldiers on personal platforms? Politicians' personlized use of social media', *Party Politics*, doi: 1354688221140252

Pedersen, H.H. and Rahat, G. (2021) 'Introduction: Political personalization and personalized politics within and beyond the behavioural arena', *Party Politics*, 27(2), p211–219.

Pedersen, H.H. and van Heerde-Hudson, J. (2019) 'Two strategies for building a personal vote: Personalized representation in the UK and Denmark', *Electoral Studies*, 59, p17–26.

Poguntke, T. and Webb, P.D. (2005) *The presidentialization of politics: A comparative study of modern democracies*. Oxford: Oxford University Press.

Poguntke, T. and Webb, P.D. (2018) 'Presidentialization, personalization and populism: The hollowing out of party government', in Cross, W.P., Katz, R.S. and Pruysers, S. (eds.) *The personalization of democratic politics and the challenge for political parties*. London: ECPR Press, p181–196.

Pruysers, S., Cross, W.P. and Katz, R.S. (2018) 'Personalism, personalization and party politics', in Cross, W.P., Katz, R.S. and Pruysers, S. (eds.) *The personalization of democratic politics and the challenge for political parties*. London: ECPR Press, p1–18.

Rahat, G. and Kenig, O. (2018) *From party politics to personalized politics? Party change and political personalization in democracies*. Oxford: Oxford University Press.

Rahat, G. and Sheafer, T. (2007) 'The personalization(s) of politics: Israel 1949–2003', *Political Communication*, 24(1), p65–80.

Renwick, A. and Pilet, J. (2016) *Faces on the ballot: The personalization of electoral systems in Europe*. Oxford: Oxford University Press.

Scarrow, S.E., Webb, P. and Farrell, D.M. (2000) 'From social integration to electoral contestation: The changing distribution of power within political parties', in Dalton, R.J. and Wattenberg, M.P. (eds.) *Parties without partisans: Political change in advanced industrial democracies*, Oxford: Oxford University Press, p129–156.

Schumacher, G. and Giger, N. (2018) 'Do leadership-dominated parties change more?' *Journal of Elections, Public Opinion and Parties*, 28(3), p349–360.

Strömbäck, J. (2008) 'Four phases of mediatization: An analysis of the mediatization of politics', *The International Journal of Press/Politics*, 13(3), p228–246.

Van Aelst, P., Sheafer, T. and Stanyer, J. (2012) 'The personalization of mediated political communication: A review of concepts, operationalizations and key findings', *Journalism*, 13(2), p203–220.

Vliegenthart, R. (2012) 'The professionalization of political communication? A longitudinal analysis of Dutch election campaign posters', *American Behavioral Scientist*, 56(2), p135–150.

Wattenberg, M.P. (1991) *The rise of candidate-centered politics*. Cambridge: Harvard University Press.

Wauters, B., Bouteca, N. and de Vet, B. (2021) Personalization of parliamentary behaviour: Conceptualization and empirical evidence from Belgium (1995–2014)', *Party Politics*, 27(2), p246–257.

Wauters, B., Thijssen, P., Van Aelst, P. and Pilet, J.B. (2018) 'Centralized personalization at the expense of decentralized personalization: The decline of preferential voting in Belgium (2003–2014)', *Party Politics*, 24(5), p511–523.

Zittel, T. (2015) 'Constituency candidates in comparative perspective: How personalized are constituency campaigns, why, and does it matter?' *Electoral Studies*, 39, p286–294.

Zittel, T. and Nyhuis, D. (2021) 'The legislative effects of campaign personalization: An analysis on the legislative behavior of successful German constituency candidates', *Comparative Political Studies*, 54(2), p312–338.

PART 5

Contemporary issues and challenges

23
POPULISM AND PARTIES

Stijn van Kessel

The phenomenon of populism has attracted a vast amount of attention in recent years, and has been associated with a wide variety of other concepts and themes. The link between populism and political parties is an almost natural one; Kenneth Roberts (2017, 287) goes so far as to state that populist politics 'can hardly be understood in isolation from party politics'. That is not to say populism only comes in the shape of political parties; scholars have for instance studied populism as a feature of (transnational) social movements (e.g. Aslanidis 2017). Yet populist mobilisation is usually aided by some form of party-political organisation. The extent to which parties and populism are intertwined has varied across time and context. Furthermore, even though there is considerable consensus about the concept's core traits, continuing disagreements about how populism should be understood as a phenomenon have influenced analyses of populist party mobilisation.

This chapter will therefore begin by outlining the most common approaches to conceptualising populism, and their implications for applying the concept to political parties. It continues by discussing populist parties in practice, touching on certain notable historical cases, but primarily on contemporary populist parties. The subsequent sections discuss the reasons for the supposed surge of populist parties, and its implications for party competition and (liberal) democracy. The final section concludes and identifies several avenues for future study. Despite ongoing conceptual and methodological disagreements, the academic use and empirical application of the concept of populism have become more sophisticated and precise. Among the areas that remain relevant for future studies are the relationship between populism and democracy (both at the individual and macro-level), and the potential connection between populist mobilisation, social media and the spread of misinformation.

Approaches to populism (and parties)

Both in the scholarly literature and in the vernacular, populism is a term that is widely used (and abused) to refer to a range of phenomena, actors and (adjacent) concepts such as demagoguery, opportunism or xenophobia (Mudde 2004; Bale, van Kessel and Taggart 2011). The academic debate on the concept is nevertheless well developed and there appears to be a broad consensus that populism denotes a normative distinction between the 'people' and the out-of-touch or corrupt 'elites'. Political elites should, according to the populist worldview, respect popular sovereignty and respond to citizens' concerns. There are still quite important distinctions between key approaches to populism, which also have consequences for studying populism empirically. Moffitt (2020), for instance, distinguishes between 'ideational', 'discursive-performative' and 'strategic' approaches to populism – a typology that will also broadly be followed in the following discussion.

The 'ideational' approach is currently dominant among political scientists, who note its usefulness for empirical application (see Hawkins et al. 2019). These scholars tend to follow Cas Mudde's (2004, 543) definition of populism as

> an ideology that considers society to be ultimately separated into two homogeneous and antagonistic groups, 'the pure people' versus 'the corrupt elite', and which argues that politics should be an expression of the *volonté générale* (general will) of the people.

Mudde thus defines populism as an ideology, albeit a 'thin-centred' one.[1] Accordingly, populism makes claims about the (real and desired) relationship between elites and the people, but lacks a concrete policy agenda. When mobilised, populism is usually attached to more established 'host ideologies' of various kinds. Mudde's 'minimal definition' also implies that populism is in essence a set of ideas; features such as party organisation and leadership are not essential to determine whether a phenomenon is populist. A final point worth emphasising is that, according to Mudde, populism is not only anti-elitist but also anti-pluralistic. Populists express the idea that a 'general will' exists and downplay the multitude of socio-economic and socio-cultural divisions among 'the people' in society.

The assertion that populism is anti-pluralistic remains contested, not least by scholars following the 'discursive' approach inspired by the social constructivist work of Ernesto Laclau (2005). For them, populism is essentially a logic of political mobilisation centred on a dichotomy between the people and (those in) power. It is not the case that the inherent differences between the people are cast aside in this process. Populists are argued to bring together a variety of societal demands and identities through the construction of a so-called 'chain of equivalence', which links together diverse constituencies that share a grievance with power holders.

The question of whether populism is anti-pluralist or not has implications for the range of political actors that can be associated with the term. If Mudde's definition is strictly followed, it is questionable whether parties with a liberal profile that celebrate cultural diversity can genuinely be populist.[2] Scholars including Abts and Rummens (2007) and Müller (2016) indeed place great emphasis on the supposed anti-pluralist nature of populism, and their approach would logically lead to excluding such cases. The idea of the 'chain of equivalence', conversely, allows for a more inclusive conception of 'the people', and scholars following the 'Laclauian' approach often consider populism to be a potential emancipatory force when it is employed by the 'left' (e.g. Stavrakakis and Katsambekis 2014; Mouffe 2018) (see also Chapter 15).

Scholars in the 'ideational' and 'discursive' traditions also have different views about how we can understand populism as a *phenomenon*, which has implications for applying the term to real-world (party) politics. The former often apply the term to describe or classify political actors as 'populist' (i.e. those that adhere to the ideas central to populism), or to refer to an element of a certain party family, such as the populist radical right (Mudde 2007). Scholars inspired by Laclau instead tend to see populism as a logic of political mobilisation, and not a characteristic of individual political actors as such. In more recent work, Laclau (2005) himself went so far as to argue that populism is the central logic to *all* political agency. If taken this far, the approach can be criticised for reducing the concept's usefulness for empirical application, in particular if the aim is to discriminate between political actors or types of behaviour.

Beyond 'Laclauians', there are also other scholars who prefer to see populism more as a particular style or strategy that refers less to the attributes of political actors, and more to the particular way in which politics is *practiced* (Moffitt 2020, 25). Political communication scholars often refer to populism as a 'political communication style', focusing primarily on the messages voiced by politicians, and assessing whether or not these display 'proximity to the people', anti-establishment rhetoric or other identified traits of populism (e.g. Jagers and Walgrave 2007; de Vreese et al. 2018). Moffitt (2016, 29) also treats populism as a *style* but looks beyond the contents of messages as such. In his view, populism is characterised not only by an appeal to 'the people' versus 'the elite' but also by its more performative features: namely, the display of 'bad manners' and a reference to 'crisis, breakdown or threat'.

One key proponent of treating populism as a 'strategy' simultaneously associates the concept with a form of organisation. According to Weyland (2001, 14), who applied the concept to individual political leaders in Latin America, 'populism is best defined as a political strategy through which a personalistic leader seeks or exercises government power based on direct, unmediated, uninstitutionalised support from large numbers of mostly unorganized followers'. When this definition is followed, populism becomes a much less useful concept for the study of political parties, given that populist mobilisation is then essentially at odds with institutionalised party politics. Taking a rather unconventional position, Weyland (2017) has indeed asserted that some of the radical right parties that have recently witnessed electoral success in Europe should not be seen as instances of populism (see Chapter 11).

As became clear from the previous discussion, the way in which populism is conceptualised has consequences for its application to the study of party politics. Yet even when scholars agree on a certain approach, there are still various ways to operationalise populism in practice. While, for instance, Jagers and Walgrave (2007, 322) consider 'merely making reference to the people' as 'thin' populism, other scholars argue that populism should be operationalised as a multidimensional concept with jointly necessary properties (e.g. people-centrism *and* anti-elitism) (March 2017; Wuttke, Schimpf and Schoen 2020). There also exist methodological debates about how best to measure populism and regarding the most appropriate sources for doing so. The possible options include content analysis of manifestos or speeches (e.g. Hawkins 2009; Rooduijn, de Lange and van der Brug 2014) and expert surveys (e.g. Norris 2020; Meijers and Zaslove 2021).

For the purpose of this contribution, populism will be treated as a set of jointly necessary ideas or claims that revolve around the normative distinction between 'people' and 'elite'. This is in line with the ideational approach, although it is still a matter of debate whether populism constitutes a genuine 'ideology' (thin-centred or not) or whether it is perhaps more useful to consider it as a 'discursive frame' that provides a certain interpretation of reality (Aslanidis 2017). Given that certain political parties express populism frequently and more or less consistently (while others do not), it also makes sense to identify a group of so-called 'populist parties' (see van Kessel 2014). This does not preclude the possibility that populist claims can be made (whether for strategic reasons or not) by 'non-populists' as well. By means of this approach, it is possible to make some key observations about the (ideological) characteristics of populist parties, the conditions underlying their success or failure, as well as the impact they have in contemporary liberal democracies.

Populist parties in practice

Several contributions have appeared that discussed populist actors from a historical and global perspective (e.g. Ionescu and Gellner 1969; Canovan 1981; Taggart 2000). Not all of these cases necessarily took the form of political parties. The *Narodniki* in nineteenth-century Russia, for instance, constituted a revolutionary anti-Tsarist movement led by young intelligentsia. Operating within an authoritarian regime, the movement had no real opportunity to mobilise as a legitimate political party. This was different in the case of the People's Party (dubbed the 'Populists') in the USA, which was established towards the end of the nineteenth century in a more democratic context. The party emerged out of an agrarian grassroots movement and its existence as more institutionalised political party was short-lived. Considerable scholarly attention has also gone out to the various 'waves of populism' that landed upon Latin American countries (Mudde and Rovira Kaltwasser 2017). In each of these waves, populism could be associated with personalistic leaders and presidents (including Juan Perón in Argentina, Alberto Fujimori in Peru, and Hugo Chávez in Venezuela) more than party organisations.

These cases illustrate that the organisational form in which populism appears is to a considerable degree conditioned by institutional context. In non-democratic settings, political parties of opposition are not allowed to mobilise freely; in presidential systems, politics tends to revolve more around individuals than parties. Indeed, also various twentieth-century U.S. presidents or presidential candidates – and not so much the parties they represented – have been associated with populist politics (Canovan 1981; Taggart 2000). The election of President Donald Trump in 2016 has given new impetus to this practice: Trump has widely been labelled as a populist politician in academic as well as public debates, while this description has much less frequently been used for the Republican Party as a whole.

Be that as it may, in presidential systems populist candidates also typically have to use political parties as vehicles in their quest for power (see Roberts 2017). The precise development, function and shape of these parties differ across cases. The Justicialist Party of Perón, founded at the start of his reign in 1947, survives up until today – albeit divided in several factions – and has delivered numerous other presidents following the 'Perónist tradition' since. The Movement of the Fifth Republic (MVR) that was established to support the presidential candidacy of Chávez in 1998 eventually merged into the regime-supporting United Socialist Party of Venezuela (PSUV) in 2007. Trump, on the other hand, clearly benefited from running on the ticket of the long-established Republican Party (or 'Grand Old Party'). It would have been very difficult for him to have gained office as an independent candidate.

Attesting to the increased 'popularity' of the concept, populism has recently been used to characterise leaders and their parties, in opposition as well as in power, in more parts of the world. Examples include cases in Africa such as Michael Sata and his Zambia's Patriotic Front (PF), Julius Malema's Economic Freedom Fighters (EFF) in South Africa, and Kenya's Orange Democratic Movement (ODM) and its leader Raila Odinga (Resnick 2015). Several heads of government and/or state in various parts of Asia have also been credibly associated with populism. Examples include Recep Tayyip Erdoğan in Turkey, Narendra Modi in India, Thaksin Shinawatra in Thailand and Rodrigo Duterte in the Philippines (e.g. Curato 2016; Gürsoy 2021). The latter's authoritarianism and extreme law and order policies led to habitual comparisons with Donald Trump and Jair Bolsonaro, who won the Brazilian presidential elections of 2018.

All of the aforementioned leaders mobilised by means of more or less institutionalised party organisations. However, the continent where populism is most strongly associated with political parties (as opposed to individuals) is Europe. This is partly a result of political institutions: parliamentary regimes are the norm in Europe, which means citizens do not directly elect a head of government. Especially in countries in the Western part of the continent with a longer history of liberal democracy, political parties tend to be well organised and institutionalised. Even though populist parties are often associated with personalistic leadership in Europe as well, many have outlived their erstwhile leaders, and prospered afterwards. Examples include the French *Front National* (now *Rassemblement National*), the *Lega* in Italy (previously *Lega Nord*) and the Austrian Freedom Party (FPÖ). The resignations of their supposed 'charismatic' former leaders (respectively, Jean-Marie Le Pen, Umberto Bossi and Jörg Haider) did clearly not eliminate the demand for these parties' political agendas. What is more, irrespective of the existence of highly personalised parties like Geert Wilders' Freedom Party (PVV) in the Netherlands, some populist parties have actively developed 'rootedness on the ground', making a real effort to attract activist members and to build extensive party organisations (Heinisch and Mazzoleni 2016; van Kessel and Albertazzi 2021).

The examples listed earlier present us with a heterogeneous collection of politicians and parties. Beyond their shared populist 'common denominator', instances of populism across time and space vary significantly, not only in terms of electoral strength and organisation but also in terms of their broader ideology. Mudde and Rovira Kaltwasser (2013), for instance, have distinguished between 'inclusionary' and 'exclusionary' populism in their analysis of dominant types of populism in contemporary Latin America and Europe. The 'Third wave' populist leaders in Latin America, they argue, combined populism with socialist policies and promised to 'include' underprivileged parts of society in the political process and safeguard their material interests. Conversely, the 'populist radical right' parties that are dominant in Western Europe focus predominantly on socio-cultural issues such as immigration and ethnic diversity (Mudde 2007). Their appeal is mainly centred on excluding 'non-natives' from political participation and social welfare. The proposed dichotomous typology may not always work neatly for populist parties outside of Europe and Latin America, which often seem to combine specific inclusionary (socio-economic) and exclusionary (socio-cultural) elements (e.g. Gürsoy 2021). What is more, inside the two continents, we also find several examples that clearly do not fit the general regional pattern. Cases in point are Bolsonaro in Brazil, who has taken economically liberal and culturally exclusivist stances, and several left-wing populist parties in Southern Europe, such as SYRIZA and Podemos, which have voiced culturally and economically inclusionary messages.

What is clear, in any case, is that populist parties come in various ideological guises, and that the meaning they give to the abstract concepts of 'people' and 'elite' is also largely informed by their so-called host ideology. Populist radical right parties, for example, define the people in socio-cultural and/or ethnic terms – though they are still often clearer about whom they *exclude*: typically, immigrants or ethnic minorities (Mudde 2007). The elites they oppose are typically out-of-touch liberals who do little to halt the supposed cultural decay of the nation. Socio-economically left-wing populists usually appeal the underprivileged and downtrodden 'people', and oppose corporate 'elites' and established politicians who are portrayed as lackeys of neo-liberalism. The ideological diversity among populist parties also means that we cannot genuinely speak about a populist 'party family'. Moreover, given that different types of populists address different issues and context-specific grievances, any theories explaining the emergence of populism need to be 'abstract' enough to capture the wide variety of populist mobilisations.

Populist party success and failure

There are no one-size-fits-all explanations for the emergence of populism in all of its different guises. Arguments that explain populism in general with reference to either socio-economic or socio-cultural grievances should be met with caution, because different types of populist parties focus on different kinds of issues and public concerns. This observation is hardly new. In her seminal study on populism, Canovan (1981) was pessimistic about a single, globally applicable, approach to populism. After having described a broad range of historical and more contemporary populist movements and politicians across the world, Canovan (1981, 133) argued that it is not possible 'to unite all these movements into a single political phenomenon with a single ideology, program or socioeconomic base', and instead distinguished seven general categories of populism.

Recent scholarly literature has been less reluctant to provide and follow clear definitions and categorisations of populism, such as the ones introduced earlier in this chapter. Yet context-specific explanations are still required to account for individual instances of populism. This point can be illustrated when we consider the European context, where populist parties of various kinds have broken through (van Kessel 2015; Zulianello 2020). In long-established democracies in Western Europe, the rise of populism needs to be understood by considering long-term processes of partisan dealignment, as well as realignment along new lines of political conflict (e.g. Kriesi et al. 2008). Citizens have gradually become more 'available' to parties that challenge the traditional establishment and address salient issues such as immigration and multiculturalism. The populist radical right in Western Europe has been successful in mobilising on the basis of these 'new' cultural issues. Meanwhile, socio-economic issues and grievances remained more salient in several Southern European countries which were severely hit by the Global Recession in 2008, spurring the demand for left-wing populist parties (e.g. Stavrakakis and Katsambekis 2014). In former communist countries in Central and Eastern Europe, processes of partisan dealignment and realignment did not genuinely take place. Yet in the years after the fall of the Berlin Wall, economic crises, corruption scandals and more general disillusionment with the transition to liberal democracy and free-market capitalism created a favourable context for populism. Here 'centrist' populist parties often focused primarily on the supposed flaws of the political system as such, rather than on specific socio-economic or socio-cultural issues (e.g. Stanley 2017).

Explaining why (a certain type of) populism emerges thus requires consideration of the political, economic and socio-cultural context. Furthermore, in order to explain why some populist parties succeed and others fail in relatively similar contexts, or why the electoral results of individual populist parties can fluctuate rather heavily in a short span of time, the political 'supply side' also needs to be considered. Particularly important in this regard is the competition between populist parties and mainstream rivals. Populists need to present themselves as credible alternatives to more 'established' parties (van Kessel 2015). They need capable and visible leadership in order to put their agenda across to the electorate, and should frame their grievances with the current state of affairs in a non-extremist way to remain palatable to sufficient voters. After their parliamentary breakthrough, furthermore, they need to remain organisationally cohesive enough in order to survive. Indeed, various contributions, especially on the radical right, have stressed the importance of party organisation and (ideological) cohesiveness as conditions underlying party survival or demise (Carter 2005; Art 2011). Once in government, populist parties furthermore need to preserve their credibility as populist anti-establishment forces, which is a challenging yet not impossible balancing act (Albertazzi and McDonnell 2015).

Besides macro-level explanations, an increasing amount of scholarly attention has recently been paid to the role of 'populist attitudes' at the individual level, which are measured by means of a battery of survey questions that revolve around the normative distinction between 'people' and 'elite' (see Wuttke, Schimpf and Schoen 2020). Several scholars in the 'ideational' tradition have theorised that such attitudes are quite widespread yet often 'latent', waiting to be activated by successful populist political entrepreneurs (Hawkins et al. 2019). This idea is in line with the notion that populists may not only benefit from 'genuine' crises, but that they may also be able to fuel a *sense* of crisis, and successfully attribute blame to elites who are supposedly responsible for adverse circumstances, or unable to deal with them (e.g. Taggart 2000; Moffitt 2016).

Others have found that populist attitudes are particularly strong among populist party supporters and also contribute to the success of those parties (Akkerman, Mudde and Zaslove 2014; Van Hauwaert and van Kessel 2018). On the basis of a comparative analysis of populist party support in nine European countries, Van Hauwaert and van Kessel (2018) nevertheless find that there are also important differences between supporters of (culturally conservative) right-wing populist parties and (socio-economically) left-wing populist parties (see also Rooduijn 2018). Irrespective of their shared populist attitudes, the electorates of both types of party differ very much in terms of their policy preferences, which tend to be broadly in line with the ideas espoused by the parties they support.

Implications: party competition and democracy

While the rise of populism (or absence thereof) is worthwhile studying in its own right, understanding its implications is arguably even more important. In this regard, it is important to bear in mind that populists not only have an impact when in government but may also influence politics from opposition. If we consider populism in the form of parties, what effects does the success of those parties have on political competition and, ultimately, democracy? Starting with the former, Mudde (2004) has argued that, since the 1990s, Western democracies have been marked by a populist *Zeitgeist*, which implies that mainstream politicians have increasingly adopted populist language, often in reaction to the electoral challenge of populist parties on the ideological fringes. This *Zeitgeist* thesis, however, remains an area of debate. On the basis of an analysis of election manifestos, Rooduijn, de Lange and Van der Brug (2014) found little evidence of increased populism in mainstream parties. March (2017) came to a similar conclusion upon analysing British election manifestos, and warned that populism ought not to be confused with 'demoticism': an expression of *closeness* to ordinary people without an anti-establishment element. It can be debated, however, whether political parties mainly express populism through written manifestos, or whether other sources, such as speeches, are more suitable for testing the *Zeitgeist* theory (see e.g. Hawkins 2009).

There is more definitive evidence that populist parties are able to affect the more concrete policy positions of political rivals. Western Europe provides the most suitable context in which this can be demonstrated, given that a distinction can (still) be drawn between traditional mainstream parties and populist parties challenging them. The focus of research has primarily been on mainstream party responses to populist radical right success. There is ample evidence by now that many mainstream parties across Europe have strategically shifted towards more culturally protectionist and anti-immigration positions (e.g. Wolinetz and Zaslove 2018; Abou-Chadi and Krause 2020). It is important to note, however, that such strategic responses are not so much related to the *populism* of electoral challengers, but rather to the perceived electoral appeal of their radical right host ideology, and their nativism in particular.

In debates about how the rise of populism affects liberal democracy, it is also important to make an analytical distinction between populism and the attached host ideology. Some scholars, particularly in the Laclauian tradition, have shown distaste for the xenophobia and illiberalism of radical-right forms of populism but portrayed inclusionary left-wing populism as a potential emancipatory force, or even a much-needed means to revitalise democracy (Stavrakakis and Katsambekis 2014, Mouffe 2018). The perceived relationship between populism and democracy is also very much dependent on the conception of populism *as such*. Some who emphasise its anti-pluralist character, and thus depart from a Laclauian interpretation, even argue that populism is also inherently anti-democratic. Abts and Rummens (2007, 414), for example, argue that populism 'generates a logic which disregards the idea of otherness at the heart of democracy and aims at the suppression of diversity within society'. For similar reasons, Jan-Werner Müller (2016, 103) argues that '[p]opulists should be criticized for what they are – a real danger to democracy (and not just to "liberalism")'.

Others adopt positions somewhere in between, arguing that populism can act as a disruptive yet frank 'drunken guest at a dinner party' (Arditi 2005, 90); a 'warning signal about the defects, limits and weaknesses of representative systems' (Mény and Surel 2002, 17); or as a phenomenon that emerges when democratic regimes are not seen to live up to their 'redemptive' promises (Canovan 1999). Mudde and Rovira Kaltwasser (2017, 116) argue that populism is part of democracy and forms the '(bad) conscience of liberal democracy'; populism can essentially be seen as 'an illiberal democratic response to undemocratic liberalism'.

Mudde and Rovira Kaltwasser (2013) put this idea to the test in their edited volume comprising case studies in Europe and the Americas. The general findings indicate that populism, especially when in opposition, can have modest 'positive' effects, such as placing previously ignored issues on the political agenda, forcing mainstream parties to be responsive, and giving voice to previously excluded segments of society. In government, on the other hand, populism can prove a threat to liberal democratic checks and balances. Certainly in non-consolidated democracies, populism can breed authoritarianism. With the rise to power of supposed populist parties and leaders, such as Bolsonaro in Brazil, Trump in the USA, Law and Justice in Poland and FIDESZ in Hungary, debates about populism's role in observed democratic 'backsliding' have become ever more salient (e.g. Weyland 2020).

Conclusions and avenues for further research

Although there is considerable consensus about the general attributes of populism, different approaches to the concept still feed into different ways of studying populism in practice, and reaching different conclusions about its implications. If populism is seen as a set of ideas or a frame that juxtaposes the (good) people and the (bad) elites, and defends the idea of popular sovereignty, it can in principle be applied by a wide range of political (and non-political) actors. In practice, however, populism is often expressed by political parties, or at least by leaders who build some form of party organisation around them. It is also fair to say that some of these parties express populism frequently and reasonably consistently, and that they can therefore be classified as 'populist parties'.

The ideological diversity of these parties, as well as the vastly different contexts in which they operate, necessitate a theory about their emergence (or failure) that is relatively abstract. Although it is clear that populists invariably appeal to a segment of the population that is dissatisfied with the current political regime (and whose populist attitudes have arguably been 'activated'), we need to consider context-specific conditions as well as the host ideology of given populist parties in order to explain their individual performance. Their impact on liberal democratic institutions also varies from case to case, and future studies should investigate in more detail the conditions that moderate this effect (see e.g. Weyland 2020). It is also important to bear in mind that normative evaluations about populism's impact often hinge on contested theoretical conceptions of democracy as well as populism itself (Urbinati 2019).

While there are various ways in which 'populism scholars' disagree, academic debates about populism have become much more informed and focused over the past few decades. Scholars are continuing to address new and pertinent questions. These include how to measure populism on both the 'demand' and 'supply' side of politics and the relationship between populist attitudes or support for populist parties and perceptions of democracy (e.g. Zaslove et al. 2021). Clearly, the presumed 'elective affinity' between populism and social media is also a potent field for future research (Gerbaudo 2018). And what precisely is the relationship between populism and the spread of, or inclination towards, conspiracy theories or misinformation (e.g. Eberl, Huber, and Greussing 2021; van Kessel, Sajuria and Van Hauwaert 2021)? Finally, now that populist parties have become established actors in West European democracies in particular, we need to question the notion they can still all be treated as 'newcomers' and investigate the consequences of their longevity (e.g. Krause and Wagner 2021). While the current wave of studies on populism may recede at some point, the continuing electoral success of populist politicians and parties is very likely to keep the topic high on the academic agenda for the foreseeable future.

Notes

1 The concept of a thin-centred ideology was developed by Michael Freeden, who has more recently expressed his view that populism was too 'thin' to be an ideology at all (Freeden 2017).
2 Notably, however, many scholars in the ideational tradition still consider socially liberal parties such as Podemos in Spain and SYRIZA in Greece as instances of 'left-wing' populism. Furthermore, Mudde and Rovira Kaltwasser (2013) claim it is possible to identify an 'inclusionary' form of populism based on Mudde's definition.

References

Abou-Chadi, T. and Krause, W. (2020) 'The causal effect of radical right success on mainstream parties' policy positions: A regression discontinuity approach', *British Journal of Political Science*, 50(3), p829–847.
Abts, K. and Rummens, S. (2007) 'Populism versus democracy', *Political Studies*, 55(2), p405–424.
Akkerman, A., Mudde, C. and Zaslove, A. (2014) 'How populist are the people? Measuring populist attitudes in voters', *Comparative Political Studies*, 47(9), p1324–1353.
Albertazzi, D. and McDonnell, D. (2015) *Populists in power*. Oxon: Routledge.
Arditi, B. (2005) 'Populism as an internal periphery of democratic politics', in Panizza, F. (ed.) *Populism and the mirror of democracy*. London: Verso, pp. 72–98.
Art, D. (2011) *Inside the Radical Right: The development of anti-immigrant parties in Western Europe*. Cambridge: Cambridge University Press.
Aslanidis, P. (2017) 'Populism and social movements', in Rovira Kaltwasser, C., Taggart, P. Ochoa Espejo, P. and Ostiguy, P. (eds.) *The Oxford handbook of populism*. Oxford: Oxford University Press, pp. 305–325.
Bale, T., van Kessel, S. and Taggart, P. (2011) 'Thrown around with abandon? Popular understandings of populism as conveyed by the print media: A UK case study', *Acta Politica*, 46(2), p111–131.
Canovan, M. (1981) *Populism*. Oxford and London: Harcourt Brace Jovanovich.
Canovan, M. (1999) 'Trust the People! Populism and the two faces of democracy', *Political Studies*, 47(1), p2–16.
Carter, E. (2005) *The extreme right in Western Europe*. Manchester: Manchester University Press.
Curato, N. (2016) 'Politics of anxiety, politics of hope: Penal populism and Duterte's rise to power', *Journal of Contemporary Southeast Asian Affairs*, 35(3), p91–109.
de Vreese, C., Esser, F., Aalberg, T., Reinemann, C. and Stanyer, J. (2018) 'Populism as an expression of political communication content and style: A new perspective', *International Journal of Press/Politics*, 23(4), p423–438.
Eberl, J., Huber, R. and Greussing, E. (2021) 'From populism to the "plandemic": why populists believe in COVID-19 conspiracies', *Journal of Elections, Public Opinion and Parties*, 31(sup. 1), p272–284.
Freeden, M. (2017) 'After the Brexit referendum: revisiting populism as an ideology', *Journal of Political Ideologies*, 22(1), p1–11.
Gerbaudo, P. (2018) 'Social Media and Populism: An elective affinity?', *Media Culture & Society*, 40(5), p745–753.
Gürsoy, Y. (2021) 'Moving beyond European and Latin American typologies: The peculiarities of AKP's populism in Turkey', *Journal of Contemporary Asia*, 51(1), p157–178.
Hawkins, K. (2009) 'Is Chávez Populist?: Measuring populist discourse in comparative perspective', *Comparative Political Studies*, 42(8), p1040–1067.

Hawkins, K., Carlin, R., Littvay, L. and Rovira Kaltwasser, C. (eds.) (2019) *The ideational approach to populism. Concept, theory, and analysis*. Oxon: Routledge.
Heinisch, R. and Mazzoleni, O. (eds.) (2016) *Understanding populist party organisation. The radical right in Western Europe*. Basingstoke: Palgrave Macmillan.
Ionescu, G. and Gellner, E. (eds.) (1969) *Populism, its meanings and national characteristics*. London: Weidenfeld and Nicolson.
Jagers, J. and Walgrave, S. (2007) 'Populism as political communication style: An empirical study of political parties' discourse in Belgium', *European Journal of Political Research*, 46(3), p319–345.
Krause, W. and Wagner, A. (2021) 'Becoming part of the gang? Established and nonestablished populist parties and the role of external efficacy', *Party Politics*, 27(1), p161–173.
Kriesi, H., Grande, E., Lachat, R., Dolezal, M., Bornschier, S. and Frey, T. (2008) *West European politics in the age of globalization*. Cambridge: Cambridge University Press.
Laclau, E. (2005) 'Populism: what's in a name?', in Panizza, F. (ed.) *Populism and the mirror of democracy*. London: Verso, pp. 32–49.
March, L. (2017) 'Left and right populism compared: The British case', *The British Journal of Politics and International Relations*, 19(2), p282–303.
Meijers, M. and Zaslove, A. (2021) 'Measuring populism in political parties: Appraisal of a new approach', *Comparative Political Studies*, 54(2), p372–407.
Mény, Y. and Surel, Y. (2002) 'The constitutive ambiguity of populism', in Mény, Y. and Surel, Y. (eds.) *Democracies and the populist challenge*. Basingstoke: Palgrave, pp. 1–21.
Moffitt, B. (2016) *The global rise of populism: Performance, political style, and representation*. Stanford: Stanford University Press.
Moffitt, B. (2020) *Populism*. Cambridge: Polity Press.
Mouffe, C. (2018) *For a left populism*. London: Verso.
Mudde, C. (2004) 'The Populist Zeitgeist', *Government and Opposition*, 39(4), p542–63.
Mudde, C. (2007) *Populist radical right parties in Europe*. Cambridge: Cambridge University Press.
Mudde, C. and Rovira Kaltwasser, C. (2013) 'Exclusionary vs. inclusionary populism: Comparing contemporary Europe and Latin America', *Government and Opposition*, 48(2), p147–174.
Mudde, C. and Rovira Kaltwasser, C. (2017) *Populism: A very short introduction*. Oxford: Oxford University Press.
Müller, J-W. (2016) *What is populism?*. London: Penguin.
Norris, P. (2020) 'Measuring populism worldwide', *Party Politics*, 26(6), p697–717
Resnick, D. (2015) 'Varieties of African populism in comparative perspective', in De la Torre, C. (ed.) *The promise and perils of populism: Global perspectives*. Lexington: University of Kentucky Press, pp. 317–348.
Roberts, K. (2017) 'Populism and political parties', in Rovira Kaltwasser, C., Taggart, P., Ochoa Espejo, P. and Ostiguy, P. (eds.) *The Oxford handbook of populism*. Oxford: Oxford University Press, pp. 287–304.
Rooduijn, M. (2018) 'What unites the voter bases of populist parties? Comparing the electorates of 15 populist parties', *European Political Science Review*, 10(3), p351–368.
Rooduijn, M., de Lange, S. and van der Brug, W. (2014) 'A populist Zeitgeist? Programmatic contagion by populist parties in Western Europe', *Party Politics*, 20(4), p563–575.
Stanley, B. (2017) 'Populism in Central and Eastern Europe', in Rovira Kaltwasser, C., Taggart, P., Ochoa Espejo, P. and Ostiguy, P. (eds.) *The Oxford handbook of populism*. Oxford: Oxford University Press, pp. 140–160.
Stavrakakis, Y. and Katsambekis, G. (2014) 'Left-wing populism in the European periphery: The case of SYRIZA', *Journal of Political Ideologies*, 19(2), p119–142.
Taggart, P. (2000) *Populism*. Buckingham: Open University Press.
Urbinati, N. (2019) 'Political Theory of Populism', *Annual Review of Political Science*, 22(1), p111–127.
Van Hauwaert, S. and van Kessel, S. (2018) 'Beyond protest and discontent: A cross-national analysis of the effect of populist attitudes and issue positions on populist party support', *European Journal of Political Research*, 57(1), p68–92.
van Kessel, S. (2014) 'The populist cat-dog. Applying the concept of populism to contemporary European party systems', *Journal of Political Ideologies*, 19(1), p99–118.
van Kessel, S. (2015) *Populist parties in Europe: Agents of discontent?*. Basingstoke: Palgrave Macmillan.
van Kessel, S. and Albertazzi, D. (2021) 'Right-wing populist party organisation across Europe: The survival of the mass-party?', *Politics and Governance*, 9(4).
van Kessel, S., Sajuria, J. and Van Hauwaert, S. (2021) 'Informed, uninformed or misinformed? A cross-national analysis of populist party supporters across European democracies', *West European Politics*, 44(3), p585–610.

Weyland, K. (2001) 'Clarifying a contested concept – Populism in the study of Latin American politics', *Comparative Politics*, 34(1), p1–22.

Weyland, K. (2017) 'Populism: A political-strategic approach', in Rovira Kaltwasser, C., Taggart, P., Ochoa Espejo, P. and Ostiguy, P. (eds.) *The Oxford handbook of populism*. Oxford: Oxford University Press, pp. 48–72.

Weyland, K. (2020) 'Populism's threat to democracy: Comparative lessons for the United States', *Perspectives on Politics*, 18(2), p389–406.

Wolinetz, S. and Zaslove, A. (eds.) (2018) *Absorbing the blow. Populist parties and their impact on parties and party systems*. Colchester: ECPR Press.

Wuttke, A., Schimpf, C. and Schoen, H. (2020) 'When the whole is greater than the sum of its parts: On the conceptualization and measurement of populist attitudes and other multidimensional constructs', *American Political Science Review*, 114(2), p356–374.

Zaslove, A., Geurkink, B., Jacobs, K. and Akkerman, A. (2021) 'Power to the people? Populism, democracy, and political participation: a citizen's perspective', *West European Politics*, 44(4), p727–751.

Zulianello, M. (2020) 'Varieties of Populist Parties and Party Systems in Europe: From State-of-the-Art to the Application of a Novel Classification Scheme to 66 Parties in 33 Countries', *Government and Opposition,* 55(2), p327–347.

24
PARTIES AND CLIMATE CHANGE

Conor Little

As the world heads towards an average temperature increase of 2.8°C above pre-industrial levels by 2100 under existing policies (UNEP 2022), climate change is becoming an ever more pressing global crisis. It presents complex technological, economic, and social challenges, and it presents significant political challenges. The 'bottom-up' architecture of the current global framework for confronting climate change – the 2015 Paris Agreement – puts the onus on domestic political actors to respond to those challenges, and this has significant implications for political parties due to their centrality to domestic politics.

In the first instance, political parties' significance relates to their role in shaping governments' climate policies, and in effecting the rapid and far-reaching policy changes required to address climate change. Yet their roles extend beyond policy-making. Parties are expected to represent the public's policy preferences and they also shape the attitudes of the public, who have a pivotal role in addressing climate change. As governors, representatives, and societal leaders, parties are therefore subject to strong political tensions that characterise climate politics: typically, they are caught between an immense policy problem and a public that has rarely prioritised it; they can foresee some of the medium-term consequences of climate change while domestic institutional incentives compel them to prioritise short-term policy outcomes; and they are expected to lead far-reaching policy and behavioural change affecting every part of society.

This chapter reviews research on the party politics of climate change in established democracies. Most of this research has been published recently, building upon decades of research on parties and environmental policy and broader literatures in party politics on party preferences and representation, party government, and the relationship between elites and public attitudes. Due to the close conceptual and scientific links between the study of climate politics and the study of environmental politics (conceptually, the climate is one aspect of the environment), the chapter makes reference to research on the party politics of environmental policy where it can shed light on the party politics of climate change. Its focus on established democracies is justified by broad similarities in the significance and nature of representative politics in those countries. Democracies also tend to be the countries with greatest responsibility for cumulative greenhouse gas (GHG) emissions (Ritchie 2019) and they continue to have substantially higher GHG emissions per capita than other countries, partly due to their greater wealth and in spite of their democratic institutions (Povitkina 2018).

The chapter highlights the importance of party politics in addressing the problem of climate change. While documenting substantial scholarly attention devoted to the party politics of climate change in recent years, it also finds that there is further work to be done in developing a comprehensive understanding of how parties have responded to the challenge of climate change, particularly in the form of broad cross-national comparative studies.

It proceeds as follows. First, it describes research on parties' climate policy preferences: how they have been conceptualised and measured and how differences in parties' climate policy preferences have been explained. Second, focusing on parties' governing and policy-making roles, it examines the evidence for their influence on governments' climate policies. Third, it reviews the evidence for parties as societal leaders, examining their effects on public attitudes to climate change and climate policy. In the final section, the chapter focuses on opportunities for research on the three topics that it has reviewed, as well as highlighting research opportunities that cut across these topics, including the party politics of climate change adaptation.

Parties' preferences on climate policy

Conceptualising and measuring parties' climate policy preferences

Climate change's parent issue – the environment – is often described as an archetypal valence issue on which parties broadly agree. Consistent with a 'valence competition' perspective on climate politics, parties' preferences on climate policy are most commonly conceptualised in cross-national studies as the *salience* (priority) of climate change to those parties. Climate and environmental preferences are closely related conceptually and therefore studies that require data on parties' climate policy preferences have tended to draw on existing manifesto or expert survey data sets which offer measures of the salience to political parties of *environmental* policy (e.g. Bakker et al. 2015, 2020; Bevan 2019; Volkens et al. 2020,17). Climate change-specific measures have been developed by Farstad (2018), who codes a subset of climate-specific manifesto sentences previously coded as 'environmental protection' (*per* 501) in the Comparative Manifestos Project, and Carter et al. (2018), who code manifesto text with a binary variable that identifies sentences favouring climate protection across policy sectors and throughout the manifesto. The Comparative Agendas Project framework also includes a subtopic on 'Air pollution, Global Warming, and Noise Pollution' (Bevan 2019). Empirically, these data on climate policy preferences are positively but only moderately correlated with data on environmental policy preferences (Carter et al. 2018, 737).

The assumption that climate change is a valence issue is borne out in some places and at some times. In Europe, party preferences on climate change have tended to remain within certain boundaries; European conservative parties, for example, tend not to deny climate science (Båtstrand 2015; Hess and Renner 2019). When the salience of climate change has increased in these contexts, competition on climate policy has sometimes taken the form of a 'competitive consensus', wherein parties compete to be perceived as the most competent or credible, rather than offering significantly different policy positions (Carter and Jacobs 2014).

But there are also several challenges to the valence politics assumption as it is applied to climate policy, not least that parties' preferences on climate politics are obviously not only a matter of variation in salience: parties hold different *positions* on specific climate policies and on climate policy writ large. This is more evident in some countries (e.g. the USA and Australia; see Fielding et al. 2012; Tranter 2013; Dunlap, McCright and Yarosh 2016) and at particular times (Carter and Clements 2015). Within countries, positional politics on climate change is often most evident when comparing green and far right parties: while green parties are among the strongest proponents of climate and environmental action (Carter 2013; CAN 2019), parties on the far right oppose climate action and are often sceptical of climate science (Gemenis, Katsanidou and Vasilopoulou 2012; Lockwood 2018; Forchtner 2019; Hess and Renner 2019; Schaller and Carius 2019).

Parties' positions on climate policy have been inferred from expert surveys on environmental policy (e.g. Bakker et al. 2015, 2020; Polk et al. 2017); parliamentary votes on climate or environmental policy issues (Dunlap, McCright and Yarosh 2016, 7; CAN 2019; Schaller and Carius 2019, 25); and quasi-positional manifesto-coding schemes that subtract 'anti-green' from 'green' content on the climate or the environment (Carter et al. 2018). Single-country studies have used a wider variety of approaches, including surveys of party representatives (e.g. Fielding et al. 2012) and automated text analysis of parliamentary speeches (Marcinkiewicz and Tosun 2015). Some of these positional measures specify the position of political parties on climate policy or the environment *versus* economic goods, thus assuming that environmental policy takes a particular, and narrow, form (Jensen and Spoon 2011, 124). Overall, the observation that parties hold different positions on climate policy challenges the 'valence' assumption.

So too does climate politics' failure to fulfil other assumptions associated with valence politics. In some contexts, there is both agreement between parties and competition, but that competition is not oriented towards climate protection (see e.g. Little 2020 on agriculture and climate policy in Ireland). In others, there is agreement, but the competition that exists is of such low salience that it makes little sense to describe it as 'valence' politics (see e.g. Marcinkiewicz and Tosun 2015 on Poland).

Ultimately, it matters both whether a party is for or against more ambitious climate policies *and* the extent to which it prioritises its positions, so the 'valence versus position' discussion is perhaps less one to be resolved than to be accommodated. Carter and Little (2021) have proposed a framework for conceptualising the structure of party competition on climate policy as both a matter of salience and (positional) polarisation. While this framework lacks the parsimony of one-dimensional salience-based or positional measures, the pay-off is a fuller description of party preferences on climate policy.

Explaining parties' climate policy preferences

When it comes to explaining differences between parties' climate policy preferences, it is often the case that these preferences are moulded by other political imperatives (Compston and Bailey 2008), all the more so because climate change has usually been a second-(if not third-)order issue. The main factors shaping parties' climate policy preferences relate to vote-seeking, office-seeking, and existing party ideologies, as well as party-interest group relations.

The vote-seeking incentives associated with public attitudes are noted in case studies as powerful influences on parties' climate policy preferences (Carter and Jacobs 2014; Carter and Clements 2015; Ladrech and Little 2019). But notwithstanding the developing literature on the public opinion-climate policy link (e.g. Bromley-Trujillo and Poe 2020), there has been little by way of broad comparative studies of how *parties*' climate policy preferences are shaped by public attitudes (Marcinkiewicz and Tosun 2015, 201; see Spoon, Hobolt and de Vries 2014 on the environment).

Parties also adapt their climate policy preferences in response to electoral competition. There are conflicting findings on whether parties accommodate environmental issues in response to green parties' success (Spoon, Hobolt and de Vries 2014) or de-emphasise them because of green parties' issue-ownership (Abou-Chadi 2016). Evidence from case studies tends to support the 'accommodation' perspective, with parties driven not only by electoral competition but also by public opinion and by the goal of maximising their compatibility with green parties for coalition formation (Ladrech and Little 2019). Parties have responded even more strongly to mainstream competition on climate policy, especially when it has come from the main party of the centre-right. The cases of the UK and Denmark in the late 2000s illustrate this competitive dynamic (Carter and Jacobs 2014; Ladrech and Little 2019), while Marcinkiewicz and Tosun's (2015) study of Poland suggests that where competition on climate policy is absent the salience of climate change remains low. The case of the UK in the mid-2010s further shows that the success of climate sceptics caused their 'anti-climate' preferences to be accommodated by the UK Conservative Party (Carter and Little 2021). Overall, the strong influence of short-term, tactical vote- and office-seeking considerations means that parties' climate policy preferences can change rapidly (Carter and Clements 2015).

Another important and quite consistent influence on parties' climate policy preferences has deeper roots in party identity: political ideology, and thus parties' non-climate policy preferences. The influence of ideological commitments is hinted at by comparative studies that suggest that parties of the left are better-placed to accommodate climate policy than parties of the right (Carter et al. 2018, 736; Farstad 2018), while case study research has documented these issue-relationships in more granular detail (Båtstrand 2014; Forchtner and Kølvraa 2015; Ladrech and Little 2019; Carter and Little 2021; Huber et al. 2021). These issue-relationships can work in various ways: a low-tax agenda may foreclose the option of supporting taxes on GHG emissions, for example. Supporting deregulation may lead a party to oppose regulatory climate policies. Lockwood (2018) has also argued that explanations of right-wing populist hostility to climate policy need to refer to their anti-elite, anti-cosmopolitan ideology, and not only to their interests and their electorate.

Ideology is not the only intra-party factor that can shape parties' climate policy preferences: individual politicians also play a role, albeit studies suggest that they are usually strongly constrained by their party's vote-seeking, office-seeking, and ideological imperatives. Carter and Jacob's (2014) study of the UK shows the importance of individual party representatives (including party leaders) in driving changes in party preferences and government policy, in conjunction with contextual factors. A study of 'intra-party policy entrepreneurs' in Ireland suggests that, in that context, they have failed more often than they have succeeded, with their efforts coming to fruition only when they benefited from the tailwind of alignment with the party's vote- and office-seeking interests (Little 2017).

Finally, a wide variety of interest groups – workers' representatives and business interests, green and 'brown' sectoral interests, and environmental non-governmental organisations (ENGOs) – influence parties' climate policy preferences (Carter and Jacobs 2014; Leiren, Inderberg and Rayner 2020; Carter and Little 2021). The relationships between interest groups and parties are moderated by the institutions through which interest group relations with the state are coordinated (Farstad 2019; Mildenberger 2020). Mildenberger (2020) argues that, due to the cross-cutting nature of climate politics and their status quo advantage, economic interests benefit from 'double representation' in existing political conflict structures, which is conditioned by institutions of interest group coordination and interest groups' ties with parties. The activities of interest groups and associated think tanks have been particularly well studied in the USA, where parties have been important sites of influence for interest groups, including by funding candidates in party primaries (Stokes 2020).

The influence of parties on climate change mitigation policy

The preferences and capacities of political parties are, in turn, among the determinants of governments' climate policies. Knill, Debus and Heichel (2010) argued that the highly internationalised nature of environmental policy makes it a difficult or 'least likely' case for the party government hypothesis (partisan influence on government policy). There are further reasons to expect partisan influence to be at its most marginal: climate policy cuts across traditional partisan divides, parties may be crowded out by significant economic interests, and national interests may subsume party politics. As a 'least-likely' case of partisan influence on environmental and climate policy, positive findings of partisan influence arguably have implications for the study of party government more generally.

Studies of partisan influence on climate policy have used diverse dependent variables: specific and general measures of policy outputs, as well as policy outcomes, primarily GHG emissions. The attributes of incumbent parties that have received most attention are left-right ideology, environmental and climate policy preferences, and whether they are green parties or not. Left-right ideology has been examined most often, but is associated with mixed results: some studies find that left-of-centre ideology is associated with climate policy ambition or performance (or right-of-centre ideology with the opposite outcomes) (Aklin and Urpelainen 2013; Garmann 2014; Tobin 2017; Jahn 2021; Schulze 2021), while others do not (Jensen and Spoon 2011; Fankhauser et al. 2015; Bayer and Urpelainen 2016).[1]

Surprisingly, the effects of parties' climate and environmental policy preferences on climate policies have received much less attention. The link between these preferences and climate policy performance has found some support (Jensen and Spoon 2011) and it is corroborated by a slew of findings in comparative research on environmental policy (Knill et al. 2010; Ward and Cao 2012; Schulze 2014; Jahn 2016; Leinaweaver and Thomson 2016). Case studies of individual countries and climate policy initiatives are suggestive in a more general sense of a link between incumbent parties' policy preferences and climate policy outputs (Smith 2008; Crowley 2017).

Likewise, the effect of green parties' participation in government is little-tested: Jensen and Spoon (2011) found that it was associated with lower GHG emissions; Wurster and Hagemann (2018) find little evidence of any effect on renewable energy deployment in the German *Länder*; and Schulze (2021) did not find support for the expectation that green parties' participation would be associated with more climate policy outputs. Evrard's (2012) comparative case study, focusing on energy policy in France and Germany, shows how national and sectoral institutions, party organisation, and coalitional politics moderate the policy influence of green parties in government.

Membership of government is not the only way in which parties can influence climate policy, but other avenues of partisan influence have yet to be explored comprehensively. Studies have shown that the opposition can influence environmental and climate policy (Seeberg 2016), even in Westminster systems (Carter and Jacobs 2014), while Bromely-Trujillo and Poe (2020) find that Republican majorities in state legislatures in the USA impede the adoption of climate policies. Parties – especially the representation of green parties – also play a central role in mechanisms linking proportional electoral systems to more ambitious climate policies (e.g. Harrison 2010; Andersen 2019).

In summary, the study of partisan influence on climate policy remains incomplete. Its lacunae and outstanding questions range from the paucity of studies on the influence on climate policies of parties' climate policy preferences and of green parties in government, to the mixed findings on the influence of left-right ideology, and the very few studies of partisan influence from outside government. Across this literature, the wide variety in data and methods used, and especially in the dependent variable, means that there is now a wealth of findings, but these key questions have not been answered conclusively.

The influence of parties on public attitudes on climate change

Government policy is not the only important object of partisan influence; parties also influence public attitudes, including climate change beliefs, concern, and support for specific policies. Public attitudes feed back into the political system and they also feed outwards, shaping public behaviour. Climate change is arguably a 'more-likely' case of partisan influence on attitudes because of its complexity (Egan and Mullin 2017; Linde 2020).

There is plentiful evidence that public attitudes to climate change and climate policy align with partisanship and ideology. This has especially been a focus of studies of the USA (e.g. McCright and Dunlap 2011; Guber 2013; Dunlap McCright and Yarosh 2016; Carmichael and Brulle 2017) and there is a growing body of evidence from studies of other countries and from cross-national studies (e.g. Poortinga et al. 2011; Tranter 2011, 2013; Drews and van den Bergh 2016; Hornsey et al. 2016; McCright, Dunlap and Marquart-Pyatt 2016; Smith and Mayer 2019; Chen et al. 2020). There is also some evidence that party polarisation *per se* is associated with climate change attitudes, leading to reduced risk perceptions (Linde 2020).

The relationship between parties and public attitudes is often explained by the top-down influence of parties on public attitudes (party sorting), which is accentuated by the increased dependence on party cues present in polarised contexts. Overall, party politics is a strong — even 'dominant' – influence on public attitudes to climate change and climate policy (Egan and Mullin 2017, fn. 216), which moderates the effects of information and education (Malka, Krosnick and Langer 2009; McCright and Dunlap 2011; Guber 2013; Hornsey et al. 2016; McCright et al. 2016).

Testing the party sorting explanation involves examining specific partisan cues and how the public responds to them. Researchers have used a variety of indicators of political cues on climate policy or the environment, including congressional attention (Carmichael and Brulle 2017) and subjective perceptions of parties' positions (Linde 2020). Overall, however, there is further work to be done on investigating the mechanisms by which parties lead public attitudes on climate change through studies incorporating measures of party cues (Linde 2020).

Conclusions and avenues for further research

Party politics is often noted for its ubiquity and resilience. In this, it shares something with the problem of climate change: both political parties and climate change will be central to society and policymaking for the foreseeable future. This chapter has outlined outputs from the vibrant research activity that has developed at the intersection of party politics and climate change. Notwithstanding the rapid growth of research on the party politics of climate change, there remains considerable work to be done on the three themes covered by this chapter – parties' climate policy preferences, party government and climate policy, and parties' role in shaping public attitudes on climate change – as well as on the party politics of climate change adaptation.

In the measurement of parties' climate policy preferences, there remains significant scope for developing comparative, cross-nationally applicable and climate-specific measures of parties' climate policy preferences, rather than general indicators of environmental policy preferences, which could employ a wider range of methods (e.g. automated text analysis) and focus on a wider range of political texts and activities (speeches, legislative activity, media content, etc.). In particular, there is scope for developing positional data on climate policy preferences; existing research relies heavily on salience-based indicators, which do not always reflect the pronounced positional politics of climate change that has emerged in some contexts. Partly as a result of the paucity of positional climate-specific measures, the literature is lacking broad, cross-national studies of party preferences and the structure of party competition on climate policy that incorporate both salience and position (see Carter and Little 2021).

One promising avenue for furthering the measurement and explanation of parties' climate policy preferences is to distinguish between preferences over 'soft' and 'hard' climate policy measures (or 'carrots' and 'sticks'), mirroring the distinction that has been made among policy outputs in some studies (e.g. Mildenberger 2020; Schulze 2021). Explanations focusing on interest group influence on party preferences are another important frontier that is being developed both within the climate politics literature and in the broader literature on interest group influence on party preferences (e.g. Klüver 2020). The less proximate influence of historical cleavage structures on climate politics has yet to be explored.

The two-way relationship between parties and public attitudes appears to be central to how parties and the public respond to climate change. The bottom-up influence of public opinion on parties' climate policy preferences is under-studied in cross-national perspective (Marcinkiewicz and Tosun 2015, 201). While this chapter has referred to the role of parties as representatives only indirectly, there is also potential for studies of the congruence of parties' climate policy preferences with public preferences. The top-down influence of parties on public attitudes can also be developed further: while the overall association between partisanship and public climate attitudes is relatively well documented, far fewer studies include party cues that allow them to investigate *how* parties influence those attitudes.

Considering the variety in dependent and independent variables used in studies of parties' influence on government climate policy, conflicting findings (on left-right effects and on green party effects), and a surprising lack of attention to the influence of parties' climate policy preferences in government, coverage of this question could not yet be described as exhaustive. Outside of government, there has been relatively little attention paid to the policy influence of 'support parties' or opposition parties. Nor have the influence of system-level structures been explored in cross-national comparative analyses: the overall salience of climate policy among parties, the overall mean position of the party system on climate policy, and polarisation (consensus) on climate policy.

Developing our knowledge of parties' preferences and their influence on government policy is not only important in its own terms; it is arguably a pre-requisite for the systematic study of individual ministers' influence on policy (Alexiadou 2016). This in turn would contribute to the study of intra-party politics and climate policy, which to date have been limited to case studies within a narrow range of countries (Tranter 2013; Carter and Jacobs 2014; Little 2017).

Transcending the topics that have been the focus of this chapter, climate change adaptation – dubbed by Javeline (2014) as 'The Most Important Topic That Political Scientists Are Not Studying'– remains an important topic that scholars of political parties are not studying. We lack theories and empirical analyses on parties' roles in reducing societies' vulnerability to the effects of climate change. It is possible that the politics of climate change adaptation will be close to distributional and spending stances (Javeline 2014, 424–428). The politics of climate change adaptation is also likely to be more 'multi-level' than climate change mitigation, with an even more significant role for subnational government and, thus, representative politics at subnational level. Adaptation is an area in which research on the party politics of climate change can benefit most from engaging with climate politics in countries and regions that have experienced severe climate change impacts (e.g. Struthers 2020).

There are other lacunae in our knowledge, of which I flag three empirical gaps here: the party politics of specific emissions sectors, especially those outside of electricity generation (e.g.

transport, land use and agriculture, buildings); the party politics of climate change in lesser-studied cases and beyond established democracies; and, finally the party politics of climate policy at EU level, justified not only by the importance of the EU for many democratic states' climate policies but also by the significance of representative politics in the EU, in the context of what is likely to remain among its most pressing policy problems.

The chapter has assumed that the substantive importance of climate change justifies attention in political science. Yet we can also think of climate policy as a useful case that can shed light on other, cross-cutting questions. It is a case with particular characteristics – a typically low-salience issue, a set of policies associated with diffuse benefits, an issue associated with enormous policy change implications, a complex cross-sectoral issue – which can allow us to gain insights into important questions in party politics and comparative politics more generally. The development of climate change-specific measures of party preferences, for example, may hold lessons for how the study of representative politics and (specifically for how general-purpose time series data sets of party preferences) can accommodate the emergence of significant new cross-sectoral issues.

The study of how political parties and climate change relate to one another is an important research frontier. Pushing out that frontier is all the more urgent given the apparent difficulties that political leaders and organisations have had in responding adequately to the challenge of climate change; in short, we need to know how the party politics of climate change works in order to make representative politics work (or work better) to address climate change, and for representative politics to continue functioning in an era of climate change.

Note

1 Garmann (2014) finds that governments of the centre and left achieve better climate policy outcomes compared to governments of the right. There is further support in the environmental policy literature for a left-right effect (Ward and Cao 2012; Jahn 2016). Jahn (2021) finds that right-wing populism is associated with increased emissions (see also Ćetković and Hagemann 2020).

References

Abou-Chadi, T. (2016) 'Niche party success and mainstream party policy shifts – How green and radical right parties differ in their impact', *British Journal of Political Science*, 46(2), p417–436.

Aklin, M. and Urpelainen, J. (2013) 'Political competition, path dependence, and the strategy of sustainable energy transitions', *American Journal of Political Science*, 57(3), p643–658.

Alexiadou, D. (2016) *Ideologues, partisans, and loyalists: Ministers and policymaking in parliamentary cabinets*. Oxford: OUP.

Andersen, M.S. (2019) 'The politics of carbon taxation: How varieties of policy style matter', *Environmental Politics*, 28(6), p1084–1104.

Bakker, R. et al. (2015) 'Measuring party positions in Europe: The Chapel Hill expert survey trend file, 1999–2010', *Party Politics*, 21(1), p143–152.

Bakker, R. et al. (2020) '2019 Chapel Hill Expert Survey. Version 2019.1.', Available from: www.chesdata.eu/2019-chapel-hill-expert-survey (Accessed 22 October 2021)

Båtstrand, S. (2014) 'Giving content to new politics. From broad hypothesis to empirical analysis using Norwegian manifesto data on climate change', *Party Politics*, 20(6), p930–939.

Båtstrand, S. (2015) 'More than markets: A comparative study of nine conservative parties on climate change', *Politics & Policy*, 43(4), p538–561.

Bayer, P. and Urpelainen, J. (2016) 'It is all about political incentives: Democracy and the renewable feed-in tariff', *The Journal of Politics*, 78(2), p603–619.

Bevan, S. (2019) 'Gone fishing. The creation of the comparative agendas project master codebook', in Baumgartner, F.R., Breunig, C. and Grossman, E. (eds.) *Comparative policy agendas: Theory, tools, data*. Oxford: OUP, p17–34.

Bromley-Trujillo, R. and Poe, J. (2020) 'The importance of salience: Public opinion and state policy action on climate change', *Journal of Public Policy*, 40(2), p280–304.

CAN (2019) 'Defenders, delayers, dinosaurs. Ranking of EU political groups and national parties on climate change', *Brussels: Climate Action Network*. Available from: www.caneurope.org/publications/reports-and-briefings/1757-defenders-delayers-dinosaurs-ranking-of-eu-political-groups-and-national-parties-on-climate-change (Accessed 22 October 2021)

Carmichael, J.T. and Brulle, R.J. (2017) 'Elite cues, media coverage, and public concern: An integrated path analysis of public opinion on climate change, 2001–2013', *Environmental Politics*, 26(2), p232–252.

Carter, N. (2013) 'Greening the mainstream: Party politics and the environment', *Environmental Politics*, 22(1), p73–94.

Carter, N. and Clements, B. (2015) 'From "greenest government ever" to "get rid of all the green crap": David Cameron, the Conservatives and the environment', *British Politics*, 10(2), p204–225.

Carter, N. and Jacobs, M. (2014) 'Explaining radical policy change: The case of climate change and energy policy under the British Labour Government 2006–10', *Public Administration*, 92(1), p125–141.

Carter, N., Ladrech, R., Little, C. and Tsagkroni, V. (2018) 'Political parties and climate policy: A new approach to measuring parties' climate policy preferences', *Party Politics*, 24(6), p731–742.

Carter, N. and Little, C. (2021) 'Party competition on climate policy: The roles of interest groups, ideology and challenger parties in the UK and Ireland', *International Political Science Review*, 42(1), p16–32.

Ćetković, S. and Hagemann, C. (2020) 'Changing climate for populists? Examining the influence of radical-right political parties on low-carbon energy transitions in Western Europe', *Energy Research & Social Science*, 66, p101571.

Chen, T., Yun, H., Salloum, A., Antti Gronow, A. Ylä-Anttila, T. and Kivelä, M. (2020) 'Polarization of climate politics results from partisan sorting: Evidence from Finnish Twittersphere', *Global Environmental Change*, 71, p102348.

Compston, H.W. and Bailey, I. (eds.) (2008) *Turning down the heat: The politics of climate policy in affluent democracies*. Basingstoke: Palgrave Macmillan.

Crowley, K. (2017) 'Up and down with climate politics 2013–2016: The repeal of carbon pricing in Australia', *Wiley Interdisciplinary Reviews: Climate Change*, 8(3), p1–13, e458.

Drews, S. and van den Bergh, J.C.J.M. (2016) 'What explains public support for climate policies? A review of empirical and experimental studies', *Climate Policy*, 16(7), p855–876.

Dunlap, R.E., McCright, A.M. and Yarosh, J.H. (2016) 'The political divide on climate change: Partisan polarization widens in the U.S.', *Environment: Science and policy for sustainable development*, 58(5), p4–23.

Egan, P.J. and Mullin, M. (2017) 'Climate change: US public opinion', *Annual Review of Political Science*, 20(1), p209–227.

Evrard, A. (2012) 'Political parties and policy change: Explaining the impact of French and German Greens on energy policy', *Journal of Comparative Policy Analysis: Research and Practice*, 14(4), p275–291.

Fankhauser, S., Gennaioli, C. and Collins, M. (2015) 'The political economy of passing climate change legislation: Evidence from a survey', *Global Environmental Change*, 35, p52–61.

Farstad, F.M. (2018) 'What explains variation in parties' climate change salience?', *Party Politics*, 24(6), p698–707.

Farstad, F.M. (2019) 'Does size matter? Comparing the party politics of climate change in Australia and Norway', *Environmental Politics*, 28(6), p997–1016.

Fielding, K.S., Head, B.W., Laffan, W., Western, M. and Hoegh-Guldberg, O. (2012) 'Australian politicians' beliefs about climate change: political partisanship and political ideology', *Environmental Politics*, 21(5), p712–733.

Forchtner, B. (2019) 'Climate change and the far right', *WIREs Climate Change*, 10(5), e604.

Forchtner, B. and Kølvraa, C. (2015) 'The nature of nationalism: Populist radical right parties on countryside and climate', *Nature & Culture*, 10(2), p199–224.

Garmann, S. (2014) 'Do government ideology and fragmentation matter for reducing CO2-emissions? Empirical evidence from OECD countries', *Ecological Economics*, 105, p1–10.

Gemenis, K., Katsanidou, A. and Vasilopoulou, S. (2012) 'The politics of anti-environmentalism: positional issue framing by the European radical right', Paper prepared for the MPSA Annual Conference, 12–15 April, Chicago.

Guber, D.L. (2013) 'A cooling climate for change? Party polarization and the politics of global warming', *American Behavioral Scientist*, 57(1), p93–115.

Harrison, K. (2010) 'The comparative politics of carbon taxation', *Annual Review of Law and Social Science*, 6(1), p507–529.

Hess, D.J. and Renner, M. (2019) 'Conservative political parties and energy transitions in Europe: Opposition to climate mitigation policies', *Renewable & Sustainable Energy Reviews*, 104, p419–428.

Hornsey, M.J., Harris, E.A., Bain, P.G. and Fielding, K.S. (2016) 'Meta-analyses of the determinants and outcomes of belief in climate change', *Nature Climate Change*, 6(6), p622–626.

Huber, R.A., Maltby, T., Szulecki, K. and Ćetković S. (2021) 'Is populism a challenge to European energy and climate policy? Empirical evidence across varieties of populism', *Journal of European Public Policy*, 28(7), p998–1017.

Jahn, D. (2016) *The politics of environmental performance, institutions and preferences in industrialized democracies*. Cambridge: CUP.

Jahn, D. (2021) 'Quick and dirty: how populist parties in government affect greenhouse gas emissions in EU member states', *Journal of European Public Policy*, 28(7), p980–997.

Javeline, D. (2014) 'The most important topic political scientists are not studying: Adapting to climate change', *Perspectives on Politics*, 12(2), p420–434.

Jensen, C.B. and Spoon, J-J. (2011) 'Testing the "party matters" thesis: Explaining progress towards Kyoto Protocol targets', *Political Studies*, 59(1), p99–115.

Klüver, H. (2020) 'Setting the party agenda: Interest groups, voters and issue attention', *British Journal of Political Science*, 50(3), p979–1000.

Knill, C., Debus, M. and Heichel, S. (2010) 'Do parties matter in internationalised policy areas? The impact of political parties on environmental policy outputs in 18 OECD countries, 1970–2000', *European Journal of Political Research*, 49(3), p301–336.

Ladrech, R. and Little, C. (2019) 'Drivers of political parties' climate policy preferences: Lessons from Denmark and Ireland', *Environmental Politics*, 28(6), p1017–1038.

Leinaweaver, J. and Thomson, R. (2016) 'Greener governments: partisan ideologies, executive institutions, and environmental policies', *Environmental Politics*, 25(4), p633–660.

Leiren, M.D., Inderberg, T.H.J. and Rayner, T. (2020) 'Policy styles, opportunity structures and proportionality: Comparing renewable electricity policies in the UK', *International Political Science Review*, 42(1), p33–47.

Linde, S. (2020) 'The politicization of risk: Party cues, polarization, and public perceptions of climate change risk', *Risk Analysis*, 40(10), p2002–2018.

Little, C. (2017) 'Intra-party policy entrepreneurship and party goals: the case of political parties' climate policy preferences in Ireland', *Irish Political Studies*, 32(2), p199–223.

Little, C. (2020) 'The party politics of climate change in Ireland', in Robbins, D., Torney, D. and Brereton, P. (eds.) *Ireland and the Climate Crisis*. Cham: Springer International Publishing, pp. 91–107.

Lockwood, M. (2018) 'Right-wing populism and the climate change agenda: Exploring the linkages', *Environmental Politics*, 27(4), p712–732.

Malka, A., Krosnick, J.A. and Langer, G. (2009) 'The association of knowledge with concern about global warming: Trusted information sources shape public thinking', *Risk Analysis*, 29(5), p633–647.

Marcinkiewicz, K. and Tosun, J. (2015) 'Contesting climate change: Mapping the political debate in Poland', *East European Politics*, 31(2), p187–207.

McCright, A.M. and Dunlap, R.E. (2011) 'The politicization of climate change and polarization in the American public's views of global warming, 2001–2010', *Sociological Quarterly*, 52(2), p155–194.

McCright, A.M., Dunlap, R.E. and Marquart-Pyatt, S.T. (2016) 'Political ideology and views about climate change in the European Union', *Environmental Politics*, 25(2), p338–358.

Mildenberger, M. (2020) *Carbon captured: How business and labor control climate politics*. Cambridge: MIT Press.

Polk, J., et al. (2017) 'Explaining the salience of anti-elitism and reducing political corruption for political parties in Europe with the 2014 Chapel Hill Expert Survey data', *Research & Politics*, 4(1), p1–9.

Poortinga, W., Spence, A., Whitmarsh, L., Capstick, S. and Pidgeon, N.F. (2011) 'Uncertain climate: An investigation into public scepticism about anthropogenic climate change', *Global Environmental Change*, 21(3), p1015–1024.

Povitkina, M. (2018) 'The limits of democracy in tackling climate change', *Environmental Politics*, 27(3), p411–432.

Ritchie, H. (2019, October 1). 'Who has contributed most to global CO2 emissions?' *Our World in Data*. https://ourworldindata.org/contributed-most-global-co2. Accessed 15 December 2022.

Schaller, S. and Carius, A. (2019) *Convenient truths. Mapping climate agendas of right-wing populist parties in Europe*. Berlin: Adelphi consult GmbH. Available from: www.adelphi.de/en/publication/convenient-truths (Accessed 22 October 2021)

Schulze, K. (2014) 'Do parties matter for international environmental cooperation? An analysis of environmental treaty participation by advanced industrialised democracies', *Environmental Politics*, 23(1), p115–139.

Schulze, K. (2021) 'Policy characteristics, electoral cycles, and the partisan politics of climate change', *Global Environmental Politics*, 21(2), p44–72.

Seeberg, H.B. (2016) 'Opposition policy influence through agenda-setting: The environment in Denmark, 1993–2009', *Scandinavian Political Studies*, 39(2), p185–206.

Smith, E.K. and Mayer, A. (2019) 'Anomalous Anglophones? Contours of free market ideology, political polarization, and climate change attitudes in English-speaking countries, Western European and post-Communist states', *Climatic Change*, 152(1), p17–34.

Smith, H.A. (2008) 'Political parties and Canadian climate change policy political parties & foreign policy', *International Journal*, 64(1), p47–66.

Spoon, J-J., Hobolt, S.B. and de Vries, C.E. (2014) 'Going green: Explaining issue competition on the environment', *European Journal of Political Research*, 53(2), p363–380.

Stokes, L.C. (2020) *Short circuiting policy: interest groups and the battle over clean energy and climate policy in the American states*. New York: OUP.

Struthers, C.L. (2020) 'The political in the technical: Understanding the influence of national political institutions on climate adaptation', *Climate and Development*, 12(8), p756–768.

Tobin, P. (2017) 'Leaders and laggards: Climate policy ambition in developed states', *Global Environmental Politics*, 17(4), p28–47.

Tranter, B. (2011) 'Political divisions over climate change and environmental issues in Australia', *Environmental Politics*, 20(1), p78–96.

Tranter, B. (2013) 'The great divide: Political candidate and voter polarisation over global warming in Australia', *Australian Journal of Politics & History*, 59(3), p397–413.

UNEP (2022) 'Emissions Gap Report 2022: The Closing Window—Climate crisis calls for rapid transformation of societies.' *UN Environment Programme*. https://www.unep.org/emissions-gap-report-2022 (Accessed 15 December 2022).

Volkens, A. et al. (2020) 'The Manifesto data collection', *Manifesto project (MRG/CMP/MARPOR). Version 2020a*. Wissenschaftszentrum Berlin fur Sozialforschung (WZB). Available at: https://doi.org/10.25522/manifesto.mpds.2020a (Accessed 22 October 2021)

Ward, H. and Cao, X. (2012) 'Domestic and international influences on green taxation', *Comparative Political Studies*, 45(9), p1075–1103.

Wurster, S. and Hagemann, C. (2018) 'Two ways to success expansion of renewable energies in comparison between Germany's federal states', *Energy Policy*, 119, p610–619.

25
PARTIES AND IMMIGRATION

Pontus Odmalm

This chapter addresses the contradictory and often strained relationships mainstream political parties have with immigration and integration (see e.g. Schinkel 2017; Wahlbeck 2019; Vrânceanu and Lachat 2021). It focuses particularly on the challenging issue of dimensional fit, which affects parties across the ideological spectrum. Unlike most of the post-war areas of disagreement, immigration and integration were amorphous questions which tended to move between different cleavages over time. The result was a series of ideological tensions, which developed within – as well as between – parties (Odmalm 2014). Their policy responses were often perceived as inconsistent therefore and mainstream parties were accused of not taking voters' concerns into consideration, which subsequently provided fertile ground for the populist radical right (PRR) (see also Chapter 23). This chapter shows how political parties *as well as* researchers have often struggled to conceptualise and understand immigration and integration and to determine which type of 'issue' they represent.

Moreover, it connects these developments to contemporary research in the fields of parties and elections. As immigration and integration moved away from questions of demography and the labour market, and developed into sources of electoral and party-political conflict, they also caught the attention of political scientists. One consequently observes a higher frequency of publications, especially since the early 2000s, which sought to explain (mainstream) parties' engagement with immigration and integration (e.g. van Spanje 2010; Pardos-Prado 2015); why these 'new' policy areas were more challenging compared to 'old' ones (e.g. van der Brug and van Spanje 2009; Odmalm and Bale 2015), and, more importantly, the reasons for immigration and integration moving up on the electoral agendas of the centre-right *as well as* the centre-left (e.g. Akkerman 2018; Green-Pedersen and Otjes 2019).

The chapter is structured accordingly. It first surveys the changing patterns of immigration, the different reasons for migration to Western Europe and how these developments presented particular challenges to the political mainstream. It shows how the elusive nature of both immigration and integration made their incorporation into existing dimensions of party competition a complex process. This also posed challenges for scholars seeking to categorise and understand the positions of mainstream parties on these issues. As a concluding reflection, the chapter suggests that future research could benefit from a twofold shift in attention regarding the relationship between mainstream and PRR parties – first, through focusing on the *intensity* of their policy positions on immigration and integration, and, second, by adopting a nuanced definition of 'immigration' which accounts for the full variety of migrant categories.

Immigration and integration: a challenge to the political mainstream

The twinned areas of regulating entry for non-citizens (that is, immigration control) and how to incorporate the new population in the economic, social and political spheres of the host society (that is, modes of integration) have become increasingly important on the political agendas in Western European countries (Hammar 1985; Dennison and Geddes 2018; Green-Pedersen and Otjes 2019). The increase in salience was due to a combination of factors. On the one hand, political upheaval in the Middle East and parts of Africa and Asia meant that asylum applications went from manageable to unprecedented levels in a relatively short period of time (Bernhard and Kaufmann 2018). Tied to these developments were the diversification of migratory flows, and the popular and elite conflation of the categories 'asylum' and 'undocumented' migration (Gattinara and Morales 2017; Menjívar and Perreira 2019). On the other hand, the PRR went from minor irritant to a serious challenger to mainstream parties. The latter had to engage with a question with no obvious fit along established lines of conflict as well as with a party family who redefined immigration and integration along a new fault line (Gedddes and Scholten 2016). That said, questions concerning immigration had bubbled beneath the surface since (at least) the formal stop to organised overseas recruitment in the aftermath of the oil crisis in 1973 (Pries 2016). The subsequent broadening of categories of migration – from labour to asylum to family reunification to unaccompanied minors and student migration – meant that the politics of migration became increasingly multi-dimensional and increasingly difficult to pin down to any one cleavage (see Fekete 2007; Kanics, Senovilla and Touzenis 2010; Raghuram 2013; Parusel 2017; Grande, Schwarzbözl and Fatke 2019; Menjivar and Perrerira 2019). These different reasons for migrating generated a series of strategic dilemmas for the political mainstream yet the impact of these changes varied across different party families.

Immigration

In the post-war era of labour migration, the movement of people served a specific and often time-limited purpose, and integration was said to follow organically from social interactions in the workplace (Caviedes 2010). Since immigration and integration were closely associated with the labour market, political conflict (when present) was aligned with the pre-existing left-right divide, namely, between a restrictive and social-democratic axis versus a lenient and liberal-conservative one. The former worried about the effects that labour migration would have on the balance of power between the suppliers of labour and the owners of capital (Laubenthal 2017). A particular fear was that the influx of an overseas and, especially, a non-national, labour force could undermine the collectively bargained wage agreements and potentially split the working class into indigenous and migrant factions. Liberal and conservative parties, on the other hand, were typically more favourable to increasing the pool of labour as it meant low levels of wage inflation and that employers had plenty of choice in order to fill vacant positions (Balch 2010; Bucken-Knapp et al. 2014). Although immigration was a 'new' type of question, it nevertheless played out according to old cleavages and long-established views parties held on the state-market relationship.

However, following enlargement of the EU in 2004, the political conversation began to shift. The crux for mainstream parties was how to balance views on EU mobility with their established positions on labour migration from third countries. Although these stances would once again map onto the old left-right cleavage, the presence (and success) of green and PRR parties impacted on the framing of the migration debates. For 'new' left parties, EU mobility rights and the freedom to migrate were very much fundamental human rights, and green parties across Europe tended to side with their liberal and conservative counterparts regarding labour migration.

The 'new' right parties, conversely, championed the restrictive alternative. As such, their positions echoed those of the old centre-left, but the PRR had a different rationale. Further labour migration not only had negative economic consequences but also socio-cultural ones (Helbling 2014). The PRR advocated a type of labour market chauvinism, which juxtaposed the deserving indigenous work force with the undeserving foreign one. The electoral relevance of the PRR is, and has been, a particular challenge to social democratic parties (Hjort and Vinæs Larsen 2019). The way it debates and frames labour migration tapped into long-standing centre-left quarrels of how to maintain labour market stability as well as the hesitation many social democratic and reformed left parties felt towards recruiting foreign workers.

Although labour migration was eventually incorporated into existing cleavages, the categories of asylum and family reunification proved more challenging (Berneri 2017; Watson 2018). In part, the challenges are explained not only by the human rights framework the two categories derive from but also by path-dependence. The 1951 Refugee Convention offered little room for interpretation, and the key statement – 'the right of persons to seek asylum from persecution in other countries' – meant that questions of asylum became challenging to incorporate and frame according to prevailing cleavages. The issue consensus, which characterised most West European states, would also discourage mainstream parties from going against the official line on asylum and family reunification (König 2017). Elections were thus characterised by struggles over issue ownership between social-democratic and liberal-conservative party families in particular rather than by opposing stances that parties offered the electorate. However, convergence between mainstream parties meant that there was a lack of a restrictive alternative, and this was a gap which the PRR was well placed to fill. It offered a hard-line and assimilationist option to voters who were dissatisfied with the status quo and also reframed the debate on immigration according to the GAL/TAN-dimension (that is, the green/alternative/libertarian – traditional/authoritarian/nationalist axis).

These developments presented a number of challenges to the political mainstream. The economic case for admitting asylum-seekers and family reunification-type migrants was increasingly difficult to make due to their prolonged entry into the labour market. The human rights angle proved equally difficult, as the PRR reiterated the incompatibility of non-Western – and particularly Muslim – asylum-seekers and refugees with host society values, gender norms and ways of life (Korteweg and Yurdakul 2009; Brubaker 2013; Hercowitz-Amir and Raijman 2020). The outcome was that the centre-left found itself stranded on the same territory as the PRR regarding labour migration, whereas the TAN-type framing of asylum and family reunification meant that the centre-right and the PRR were positioned closer together. This situation forced liberal-conservative parties, and also Christian democratic ones, to engage with a cleavage, which had for a long time remained second order on their respective party agendas.

For voters, then, the PRR could be seen to offer an alternative, as it stressed a reduction in the number of migrants, regardless of category and reasons for migrating. Moreover, the issue of immigration was as multi-dimensional for the electorate, as it was for parties, and largely followed the trajectory of attention witnessed in the party system at large. That is, further immigration was initially associated with socio-economic effects and implications, which later on were replaced by socio-cultural ones. Brady, Ferejohn and Paparo (2020) point to increased anxieties over migration as the key development in recent years. They argue that 'the representation gap' between the (liberal) mainstream and the (restrictive) electorate left a large space for the PRR to fill. This gap was particularly pronounced among voters who identified as culturally conservative and economically vulnerable (see van der Brug and van Spanje 2009). Elsewhere, these identities have been understood in terms of 'immigration scepticism' (Rydgren 2008). The primary driver for these voters was to reduce the existing level of migration rather than to express xenophobic or racist sentiments. Immigration sceptics tended therefore to gravitate towards the PRR, since it not only offered a reductionist position but also was significantly more *intense* in its stance than the political mainstream (Rabinowitz and MacDonald 1989).

Integration

Mainstream parties' engagement with integration has also been characterised by ideological tensions (Joppke 2007; Vliegenhart and Roggeband 2007). For starters, what is commonly referred to as 'integration policy' spans laws and initiatives, which cut across several different policy domains, ranging from basic legal and social protection to anti-discrimination laws, naturalisation policies and funding of ethnic and religious organisations. Moreover, it includes hands-on procedures relating to as public housing, law and order, security, access to services as well as to education (Favell 2001). Taken together, integration can be even more challenging to accommodate into existing cleavages than immigration. The question of integration also gave rise to a divide of its own, namely, between assimilationist and multicultural understandings of inclusion. A particular challenge concerned the type of relationship the state should have with its citizens and residents who identified (or were identified) as 'different' from the imagined community (Anderson 1983), and, perhaps more crucially, whether these differences also should be recognised in the public sphere.

The rationale behind assimilation, for example, could result in either an extensive or a limited role for the state. Regarding the latter, issues of cultural and linguistic preservation were understood as private matters, whereas the public spheres of, say, education, labour and health care would be characterised by a common language, understanding of history and national identity. In other words, the cohesive and uniform society was considered more important than acknowledging and preserving individual and/or group differences. In the long run, assimilation is the inevitable outcome, the argument goes and any measures to maintain or preserve cultural identities merely postpone this trajectory.

While inter-generational assimilation is commonplace, especially in socio-economic terms, it has been more challenging to achieve socio-cultural assimilation, especially for visibly different migrants and ethnic minorities (Drouhot and Nee 2019). However, processes of assimilation can also be accompanied by a more interventionist state, and policies have often been based on previous attempts at (forcefully) incorporating indigenous minorities into the nation-state. The result typically is the legal enforcement of neutrality in the public sphere alongside the absence of any formal procedures to promote or maintain cultural diversity (Bertaux 2016).

That said, multicultural forms of integration have been equally challenging for the political mainstream (Mitchell 2004; Koopmans 2010). The literature distinguishes between *de facto* and *official* forms of multiculturalism (Joppke and Morawska 2002; Mitchell 2004). De facto approaches denote an understanding of the nation-state as ethnically, culturally and religiously diverse but do not follow through with any further group rights or exemptions from the legal framework. The state remains non-interventionist and the recognition of difference – but not its promotion – is a natural outcome of the logic of the liberal-democratic state. Official multiculturalism, conversely, means a more involved state, since these types of policies create, set and maintain boundaries between the majority population and different ethnic and migrant groups.

In practice, however, multicultural-type policies show ample variation and have ranged from the provision of information in multiple languages to public funding for migrant media and the offering of targeted support to ethnic civil society (Igarashi 2019). But in contrast to North American, and especially Canadian, forms of multiculturalism, European states have typically placed the emphasis on *facilitating* socio-economic integration and *acknowledging* their status as countries of immigration rather than through providing rights to self-rule or group specific representation.

However, a notable shift took place at the turn of the millennium. The so-called multicultural consensus was challenged by parties across the ideological spectrum. Critics pointed to the 'failure' of multiculturalism and how said policies, in fact, had not resulted in a more cohesive society but rather cemented a form of ethnic exclusion with parallel societies. In tandem with this rerouting, the PRR gained in electoral strength and developed a semi-permanent presence in several national parliaments. Questions were raised therefore as to whether a more aggressive form of integration was justified. Triadafilopoulos (2011) refers to this shift as involving illiberal means to liberal ends, and migrants and ethnic minorities consequently were 'forced' to become liberal-democratic citizens. In practical terms, then, the political conversation moved away from issues of rights and how to access the (welfare) state towards evidencing conformity and fulfilment of various duties and responsibilities. Although most mainstream parties shied away from labelling this as a return to 'assimilation', the change in emphasis nevertheless contained elements which echoed the approaches pursued in the past.

Questions surrounding the acquisition of citizenship have, for example, increased in salience and, in particular, the issue of how to turn it into something more than merely holding a new passport. The introduction of a variety of citizenship and integration tests is indicative of what has been coined as the 'civic turn' (Wallace Goodman 2010) in the politics of integration. As a middle way between cultural assimilation and official multiculturalism, civic integration sought to foster attachment to the democratic, legal and political institutions of the host society (Cochran Bech, Borevi and Mourtisen 2017). Early incarnations of citizenship tests asked potential citizens about key social and political institutions, yet recent versions emphasised questions of culture, history and national ways-of-life. These changes also mapped onto previous debates about the appropriate role of the state – namely, as a facilitator or gate-keeper in the integration process. The former, often championed by the centre-left and green party families, understood citizenship and integration tests as a means to an end. In other words, they were there to inform applicants about how the state 'works' and how to access those rights associated with formal membership of the polity. The latter type, often favoured by conservative and Christian democratic parties, conversely stressed the achievement aspect of naturalisation. Citizenship and integration tests consequently would ensure that the right type of migrant (eventually) was granted full admission to the nation-state (see Kiwan 2008; van Oers 2008, 2014; Vink and de Groot 2010; Michalowski 2011; Paquet 2012).

The (late) awakening of party scholars to the relevance of immigration and integration

As mainstream parties struggled to make sense of immigration and integration, scholarly attention was placed elsewhere. As Bale (2008, 316) noted, 'the political science communities working on asylum and immigration, on the one hand, and parties, on the other hand, have traditionally sat at separate tables'. The politics of migration primarily involved the study of voters' attitudes (O'Rourke and Sinnott 2006), the growth of the (populist) radical right (van Spanje and van der Brug 2009) and governmental policies (Somerville 2007). Consequently, the political mainstream was often overlooked despite the role it played in setting the agenda and voting on immigration and integration policies. However, as the PRR solidified its presence across Western Europe, the mid-2000s saw that party scholars become increasingly interested in the dynamics of competition between mainstream and PRR parties.

Pardos-Prado (2015), for example, considered the type of conditions that allowed mainstream parties, especially on the centre-right, to limit the success of the PRR. Multi-dimensional competition has challenged the mainstream in particular and the study draws attention to how the issue of immigration was framed and the relative electoral successes that followed from this choice. Van Spanje (2010), on the other hand, is indicative of the growing body of work seeking to assess the 'contagion' effect the PRR has on the positions of the mainstream. The comparative findings suggest that the anti-immigration agenda of the PRR has had an impact on *entire* party systems rather than on discrete party families.

Elsewhere, studies labelled this shift as the 'accommodation' (Meguid 2005) and 'mainstreaming' (Mondon and Winter 2020) of the PRR and its signature solutions. Others suggest that the challenge mainstream parties have with immigration and integration are connected to the nature of these policy areas. Scholars have thus highlighted how multi-dimensional competition on these complex issues has impacted upon the dynamics of party systems. On the one hand, it has forced mainstream parties to address the issue of immigration according to the specific terms set out by the PRR. That is, the effects of immigration are not only socio-economic but also socio-cultural (van der Brug and van Spanje 2009). On the other hand, it has allowed latent ideological tensions to (re)emerge, which, in turn have led to intra-party turmoil and the potential for further splintering (Odmalm and Bale 2015).

Moving beyond the field of parties and elections, a third strand assessed the post-election environment and how questions of immigration and integration have interacted with policy-making and agenda-setting. Akkerman (2018) suggests that mainstream parties face numerous challenges when they try to turn hard-line campaign messages into implementable options that can be voted on in parliament. Mainstream parties find themselves stuck therefore in an endless cycle of addressing the issue of immigration while the number of migrants and support for the PRR increases (Green-Pedersen and Otjes 2019).

Conclusions and avenues for further research

The politics of migration continues to present mainstream parties with ideological as well as electoral challenges. The policy areas of immigration and integration have been difficult to slot into prevailing fault lines and have often refused to stay settled, which meant ample disruption and deviation from the 'politics as usual'. An important explanation to this puzzle is the shifting ground with regard to how mainstream parties frame immigration and integration. The combination of diversifying migration streams – from labour to asylum; family reunification; clandestine; unaccompanied minors; and student migration – and the increasingly multi-dimensional nature of the 'issue' have presented novel dilemmas for mainstream parties across the ideological spectrum.

Consequently, the question of whether to admit individuals and families is no longer a simple matter of calculating the costs and benefits to the economy, but has rather become intertwined with a number of disparate policy areas. Although economic integration remains a top priority for most mainstream parties, further immigration has also prompted parties to address issues which connect to the very core of what the nation-state should be, who is included, and what the criteria are for belonging. Such queries proved difficult to translate into concrete policy proposals due to their nebulous nature and reliance on emotions and feelings rather than on rational responses. As such, questions of immigration and integration have tended to function as empty containers, which can be filled with a variety of grievances, victims and societal ills, but not necessarily with any tangible solutions. On top of these developments, the PRR has established itself as a serious contender to the political mainstream. The result has been a further fragmentation of party systems across Europe, and old coalitions have given way to new, and often unstable, groupings between different party families with little in common except their desire to hold office.

Having surveyed the literature, which tied research on parties and elections to migration studies, it is possible to identify three avenues that future research can pursue. First, to what extent have immigration and integration been (successfully) incorporated into existing cleavages? On the whole, mainstream parties find it challenging to come up with consistent narratives, especially regarding how to justify their entry policies and how they intend to achieve a cohesive society. Despite some signs that the immigration and integration debates are framed according to the GAL/TAN-dimension, the shift from uni- to multi-dimensional competition is also ongoing and haphazard. As such, mainstream parties tend to alternate between socio-economic and socio-cultural remedies when they address different types of immigration and integration 'failures'. The PRR, on the other hand, has remained unaffected by any similar ideological tensions since immigration and integration, quite clearly, are about 'the nation' and 'the people' and not about economics. What can perhaps be established (at least before the COVID-19 pandemic and the war in Ukraine) is that immigration control and muscular approaches to integration have received an increased amount of attention. Accordingly, the way that mainstream parties frame and discuss the issue of immigration has also changed. With regard to immigration control, they have increasingly called for the state to assume a more active role in the vetting of migrants, particularly for the categories of labour and family reunification, but also for overseas students and asylum seekers. In terms of integration, migrants and refugees are less likely to be 'encouraged' to acquire the necessary cultural skills they need to evidence sufficient levels of adaptation. Instead, these skills are now 'required' and states have put out additional hurdles, which migrants must overcome before they are officially admitted into the host society.

Second, will the accommodative strategies by mainstream parties neutralise or normalise the PRR? Across Western Europe, mainstream responses appear to be aimed at outdoing the PRR through harsher immigration policies and more demanding forms of integration. The rationale being that a hard-line approach will entice back votes lost to the PRR. The empirical evidence for this tactic is mixed, however, since moving towards the PRR, while adopting similar types of discourses, might not only legitimise this party family but also normalise its descriptions of reality and its proposed policy solutions. Moreover, if accommodative shifts take place across the party system, then it is likely to result in a converging mainstream. A new normal will thus develop as the centre-ground becomes defined along strict and *even* stricter stances on immigration and integration. However, if mainstream parties continue to accommodate the PRR, it, more often than not, leads to a game of catch-up with the latter always being one step ahead of the former. Such a development might not necessarily address the democratic deficit and the lack of choice that voters associate with mainstream parties and the issue of immigration. The political mainstream is also constrained by the liberal-democratic institutions and 'plays by the rules' to a greater extent than the PRR. The ever-growing disconnect between mainstream parties and the electorate is likely to remain therefore even though mainstream positions on immigration and integration have become stricter.

Third, will these processes of mainstreaming further complicate the traditional classifications and understandings of different party families? The issue of immigration has so far been a clear divider between the parties understood to be 'mainstream' and those considered 'radical' or 'extreme'. The cordon sanitaire that the former applied has also served to reinforce this distinction. The electoral choice has thus ranged from degrees of regulated immigration to halting flows completely and to encourage repatriation. But as the traditionally defined mainstream – of both the centre-left and centre-right variety – has appropriated the discourses and policies of the PRR, the boundaries between mainstream and non-mainstream parties have started to blur. Or as van Klingeren, Zaslove and Verbeek (2017, 127) suggest, it might not involve substantial policy differences anymore but rather that the PRR has become 'a radicalised version of a mainstream party'.

The aforementioned developments and associated questions open up two possibilities for future research to focus on. First, the ways that immigration and integration play out between mainstream parties might be better understood as different degrees of intensity rather than as different policy stances. As it also seems likely that most mainstream parties will occupy the same policy space as the PRR, a potential distinction between 'mainstream' and 'PRR' parties could therefore be the relative strengths of their reductionist positions. Second, it is worth appreciating the full range of migrant categories and whether or not party competition also becomes characterised by equally intense positions *across the board*. One anticipates that the PRR will not discriminate between the different reasons for migration, but it remains an open question if the political mainstream (eventually) will follow its lead in the future and also adopt an overall restrictive position. If this is the case, however, then it most certainly will challenge existing conceptualisations and definitions of what constitutes the mainstream party politics of migration.

References

Akkerman, T. (2018) *The impact of populist radical-right parties on immigration policy agendas: A look at the Netherlands*. Washington, DC: Migration Policy Institute.
Anderson, B. (1983) *Imagined communities: Reflections on the origin and spread of nationalism*. London: Verso.
Balch, A. (2010) *Managing labour migration in Europe: Ideas, knowledge and policy change*. Manchester: Manchester University Press.
Bale, T. (2008) 'Turning round the telescope. Centre-right parties and immigration and integration policy in Europe', *Journal of European Public Policy*, 15(3), p315–330.
Berneri, C. (2017) *Family reunification in the EU: The movement and residence of third country national family members of EU citizens*. Oxford: Hart.
Bernhard, L. and Kaufmann, D. (2018) 'Coping with the asylum challenge: Tightening and streamlining policies in Western Europe', *Journal of Ethnic and Migration Studies*, 44(15), p2506–2523.
Bertaux, S. (2016) 'Towards the unmaking of the French mainstream: the empirical turn in immigrant assimilation and the making of Frenchness', *Journal of Ethnic and Migration Studies*, 42(9), p1496–1512.
Brady, D.W., Ferejohn, J.A. and Paparo, A. (2020) '"Are we losing touch?" Mainstream parties' failure to represent their voters on immigration and its electoral consequences', *Italian Political Science Review*, 50(3), p398–421.
Brubaker, R. (2013) 'Categories of analysis and categories of practice: A note on the study of Muslims in European countries of immigration', *Ethnic and Racial Studies*, 36(1), p1–8.
Bucken-Knapp, G., Hinnfors, J., Spehar, A. and Levin, P. (2014) 'No Nordic model: Understanding differences in the labour migration policy preferences of mainstream Finnish and Swedish political parties', *Comparative European Politics*, 12(6), p584–602.
Caviedes, A. (2010) 'The sectoral turn in labour migration policy', in Menz, G. and Caviedes, A. (eds.) *Labour migration in Europe*. Basingstoke: Palgrave, pp. 54–75.
Cochran Bech, E., Borevi, K. and Mourtisen, P. (2017) 'A 'civic turn', in Scandinavian family migration policies? Comparing Denmark, Norway and Sweden', *Comparative Migration Studies*, 5(7), p1–24.
Dennison, J. and Geddes, A. (2018) 'A rising tide? The salience of immigration and the rise of anti-immigration political parties in Western Europe', *The Political Quarterly*, 90(1), p107–116.

Drouhot, L.G. and Nee, V. (2019) 'Assimilation and the second generation in Europe and America: blending and segregating social dynamics between immigrants and natives', *Annual Review of Sociology*, 45, p177–199.

Favell, Adrian (2001) 'Integration policy and integration research in Europe: A review and critique' in Aleinikoff, T.A. and Klusmeyer, D. (eds.) *Citizenship today: Global perspectives and practices*. Washington, DC: Brookings Institution Press, pp. 349–401.

Fekete, L. (2007) 'Detained: Foreign children in Europe', *Race & Class*, 49(1), p93–104.

Gattinara Castelli, P. and Morales, L. (2017) 'The politicization and securitization of migration in Western Europe: Public opinion, political parties and the immigration issue', in Bourbeau, P. (ed.) *Handbook on migration and security*. Cheltenham: Edward Elgar, pp. 273–295.

Geddes, A. and Scholten, P. (2016) *The politics of migration and immigration in Europe*. London: Sage.

Grande, E., Schwarzbözl, T. and Fatke, M. (2019) 'Politicizing immigration in Western Europe', *Journal of European Public Policy*, 26(10), p1444–1463.

Green-Pedersen, C. and Otjes, S. (2019) 'A hot topic? Immigration on the agenda in Western Europe', *Party Politics*, 25(3), p424–434.

Hammar, T. (1985) 'Introduction', in Hammar, T. (ed.) *European immigration policy. A comparative study*. Cambridge: Cambridge University Press, pp. 1–14.

Helbling, M. (2014) 'Framing immigration in Western Europe', *Journal of Ethnic and Migration Studies*, 20(1), p21–41.

Hercowitz-Amir, A. and Raijman, R. (2020) 'Restrictive borders and rights: attitudes of the Danish public to asylum seekers', *Ethnic and Racial Studies*, 43(4), p787–806.

Hjort, F. and Vinæs Larsen, M. (2019) 'When does accommodation work? Electoral effects of mainstream left position taking on immigration', *British Journal of Political Science*, https://doi.org/10.1017/S0007123420000563.

Igarashi, A. (2019) 'Till multiculturalism do us apart: Multicultural polices and the national identification of immigrants in European countries', *Social Science Research*, 77, p88–100.

Joppke, C. (2007) 'Beyond national models: Civic integration policies for immigrants in Western Europe', *West European Politics*, 30(1), p1–22.

Joppke, C. and Morawska, E. (2002) *Toward assimilation and citizenship: Immigrants in liberal nation-states*. Basingstoke: Palgrave.

Kanics, J., Hernandez Senovilla, D. and Touzenis, K. (eds.) (2010) *Migrating alone: Unaccompanied and Separated Children's Migration to Europe*. Paris: UNESCO Publishing.

Kiwan, D. (2008) 'A journey to citizenship in the United Kingdom', *International Journal on Multicultural Societies*, 10(1), p60–75.

Koopmans, R. (2010) 'Trade-offs between equality and difference: Immigrant integration, multiculturalism and the welfare state in cross-national perspective', *Journal of Ethnic and Migration Studies*, 36(1), p1–26.

Korteweg, A. and Yurdakul, G. (2009) 'Islam, gender, and immigrant integration: Boundary drawing in discourses on honour killing in the Netherlands and Germany', *Journal of Ethnic and Migration Studies*, 32(2), p218–238.

König, P.D. (2017) 'Intra-party dissent as a constraint in policy competition: Mapping and analysing the positioning of political parties in the German refugee debate from August to November 2015', *German Politics*, 26(3), p337–359.

Laubenthal, B. (2017) 'Labour migration in Europe: changing policies – Changing organizations – changing people', *International Migration*, 55(51), p3–10.

Meguid, B. (2005) 'Competition between unequals: The role of mainstream party strategy in niche party success', *American Political Science Review*, 90(3), p347–359.

Menjívar, C. and Perreira, K.M. (2019) 'Undocumented and unaccompanied: Children of migration in the European Union and the United States', *Journal of Ethnic and Migration Studies*, 45(2), p197–217.

Michalowski, I. (2011) 'Required to assimilate? The content of citizenship tests in five countries', *Citizenship Studies*, 15(6–7), p749–768.

Mitchell, K. (2004) 'Geographies of identity: multiculturalism unplugged', *Progress in Human Geography*, 25(5), p641–651.

Mondon, A. and Winter, A. (2020) 'Racist movements, the far right and mainstreaming', in Solomos, J. (ed.) *Routledge international handbook of contemporary racisms*. Abingdon: Routledge, pp. 147–159.

Odmalm, P. (2014) *The party politics of the EU and immigration*. Basingstoke: Palgrave.

Odmalm, P. and Bale, T. (2015) 'Immigration into the mainstream: Conflicting ideological streams, strategic reasoning and party competition', *Acta Politica*, 50(4), p365–378.

O'Rourke, K.H. and Sinnott, R. (2006) 'The determinants of individual attitudes towards immigration', *European Journal of Political Economy*, 22(4), p838–861.

Paquet, M. (2012) 'Beyond appearances: Citizenship tests in Canada and the UK', *Journal of International Migration and Integration*, 13(2), p243–20.

Pardos-Prado, S. (2015) 'How can mainstream parties prevent niche party success? Center-right parties and the immigration issue', *The Journal of Politics*, 77(2), p352–367.

Parusel, B. (2017) 'Unaccompanied minors in the European Union – Definitions, trends and policy overview', *Social Work and Society*, 18(1), p1–15.

Pries, L. (2016) 'Circular migration as (new) strategy in migration policy? Lessons from historical and sociological migration research', in Nadler, R., Kovács, Z., Glorius, B. and Lang, T. (eds.) *Return migration and regional development in Europe: Mobility against the stream*. Basingstoke: Palgrave Macmillan, pp. 25–54.

Raghuram, P. (2013) 'Theorising the spaces for student migration', *Population, Space and Place*, 19(2), p138–154.

Rabinowitz, G. and Macdonald, S.E. (1989) 'A directional theory of issue voting', *The American Political Science Review*, 83(1), p93–121.

Rydgren, J. (2008) 'Immigration sceptics, xenophobes or racists? Radical right-wing voting in six West European countries', *European Journal of Political Research*, 47(6), p737–765.

Schinkel, W. (2017) *Imagined societies: A critique if immigrant integration in Western Europe*. Cambridge: Cambridge University Press.

Somerville, W. (2007) *Immigration under New Labour*. Bristol: Policy Press.

Triadafilopoulos, T. (2011) 'Illiberal means to liberal ends? Understanding recent immigrant integration policies in Europe', *Journal of Ethnic and Migration Studies*, 37(6), p861–880.

van der Brug, W. and van Spanje, J. (2009) 'Immigration, Europe and the 'new' cultural dimension', *European Journal of Political Research*, 48(3), p309–334.

van Klingeren, M., Zaslove, A. and Verbeek, B. (2017) 'Accommodating the Dutch populist radical right in a multi-party system: success of failure?' in Odmalm, P. and Hepburn, E. (eds.) *The European mainstream and populist radical right*. Abingdon: Routledge, pp. 108–130.

van Oers, R. (2008) 'From liberal to restrictive citizenship: The case of the Netherlands', *International Journal of Multicultural Societies*, 10(1), p40–59.

van Oers, R. (2014) *Deserving citizenship: Citizenship tests in Germany, the Netherlands and the United Kingdom*. Leiden: Martinus Nijhoff Publishers.

van Spanje, J. (2010) Contagious parties: Anti-immigration parties and their impact on other parties' immigration stances in contemporary Western Europe', *Party Politics*, 16(5), p563–586.

van Spanje, J. and van der Brug, W. (2009) 'Being intolerant of the intolerant. The exclusion of Western European anti-immigration parties and its consequences for party choice', *Acta Politica*, 44(4), p353–384.

Vink, M.P. and de Groot, G-R. (2010) 'Citizenship attribution in Western Europe: international framework and domestic trends', *Journal of Ethnic and Migration Studies*, 36(5), p713–734.

Vrânceanu, A. and Lachat, R. (2021) 'Do parties influence public opinion on immigration? Evidence from Europe', *Journal of Elections, Public Opinion and Parties*, 31(1), p1–21.

Vliegenhart, R. and Roggeband, C. (2007) 'Framing immigration and integration: Relationships between press and parliament in the Netherlands, *International Communication Gazette*, 69(3), p295–319.

Wahlbeck, Ö. (2019) 'To share or not to share responsibility? Finnish refugee policy and the hesitant support for a common European asylum system', *Journal of Immigrant & Refugee Studies*, 17(3), p299–316.

Wallace Goodman, S. (2010) 'Integration requirements for integration's sake? Identifying, categorising and comparing civic integration policies', *Journal of Ethnic and Migration Studies*, 36(5), p753–772.

Watson, J. (2018) 'Family ideation, immigration, and the racial state: Explaining divergent family reunification policies in Britain and the US', *Ethnic and Racial Studies*, 41(2), p324–342.

26
PARTIES AND EUROPEAN INTEGRATION

Sofia Vasilopoulou

International cooperation through the European Union (EU) has been one of the key features of European politics since the end of the Second World War. Over the decades, EU member states have agreed to share their sovereignty in exchange for peace, stability and prosperity. Shifts in authority from the national to the supranational level have, however, brought radical change to domestic politics and decision-making. The Maastricht treaty has been considered a turning point in the history of European integration. It marked a transformation from an intergovernmental project to a multi-level polity, and gave rise to elite and popular divisions on the nature, scope and direction of European integration.

Although political opposition to the EU is not necessarily a new phenomenon (Vasilopoulou 2013), the literature on the party politics of European integration has mushroomed since the late 1990s. Reflecting the novelty of the issue, scholarly work started by debating concepts and typologies in order to understand the nature of party-based Euroscepticism. The definitions of Euroscepticism developed over time in order to account for differences between and within party families and in response to the changing dynamics of European integration. A second core debate focused on whether long-standing political cleavages embedded in European societies or party/national strategic considerations were better at explaining party responses to European integration. Both lines of research had a common starting point: the EU issue was 'new'. Yet, while the literature focusing on ideology prioritised long-term patterns and trends across party families, research on party strategies centred on within party family heterogeneity and change over time. As the EU became more politicised, however, scholarly work shifted its focus on how the EU issue is increasingly shaping – and is not just shaped by – political division in European domestic politics. The EU issue informs and shapes domestic patterns of competition with some parties viewing it an opportunity and others as a threat. Party mobilisation has also contributed to the heightened importance of the EU issue in national and European elections.

The chapter identifies several opportunities for future research. Specifically, it calls for new theories and methods to analyse parties' ambiguity on the EU. A pathway for innovation could also be more research on the tone of political debates, and questions of representation and responsiveness. Finally, interdisciplinary synergies and collaborations could theorise and empirically connect party responses to different aspects of globalisation – of which European integration is just one.

Defining party responses to European integration

Opposition to and support for the EU are 'rarely either binary or absolute' (Taggart 1998, 365). This is reflected in scholarly debates on how to define it. Taggart (1998, 366) was the first to describe Euroscepticism as 'the idea of contingent or qualified opposition, as well as incorporating outright and unqualified opposition to the process of European integration'. Taggart and Szczerbiak (2001, 10) further distinguished between hard and soft Euroscepticism. Hard Euroscepticism implies 'outright rejection of the entire project of European political and economic integration and opposition to their country joining or remaining members of the EU', whereas soft Euroscepticism refers to 'contingent or qualified opposition to European integration' rather than to a principled objection to EU membership or integration.

Although the hard-soft distinction is perhaps the most frequently used, it has also been criticised for being too broad. Kopecky and Mudde (2002) draw upon Easton's concepts of diffuse versus specific support for political regimes. They differentiate between party support for the general ideas underpinning European integration and support for the practice of European integration, that is, how the EU is and how it is developing. On this basis, they construct a two-by-two framework that differentiates between Euroenthusiasts, Europragmatists, Eurosceptics and Eurorejects.

To further specify party positions on the EU, Vasilopoulou (2011) differentiates between party positions on the principle, practice and future of European integration. This leads to the rejectionist, conditional and compromising categories of Euroscepticism. Rejectionist Eurosceptics oppose any aspect of current and future EU cooperation. Conditional Eurosceptics broadly accept the principle of European cooperation, but are critical of the EU's policy practice and thus oppose any future extension of EU competence. Compromising Eurosceptics presents a lukewarm support of both the principle and practice of European cooperation, but fully oppose further integration (see also Vasilopoulou 2018). Although this typology was designed to analyse the far right, its comparative framework has also been applied to the far left party family. Keith (2017) replaces the compromising category of Euroscepticism with a new one, that is, expansionist/integrationist, to describe those parties that accept the principle of European cooperation, are critical of EU decision-making processes, but want a federalist socialist Europe.

Another distinction relates to the 'polity-versus-policy' dimension of EU politics (see also Mair 2007). Braun, Hutter and Kerscher (2019) have emphasised that Europe is a compound political issue. They argue that we need to distinguish between party positions on constitutive issues, which relate to membership, competencies and decision-making rules; and polity-day-to-day policy-making and policy proposals. This can help us further explore the trade-offs parties face. On the one hand, during electoral campaigns, parties choose whether to prioritise European over national issues. On the other hand, they also need to balance their focus between constitutive or policy-related aspects of European integration.

Parties problematise European integration differently. They can use cultural, economic and other utilitarian frames (i.e. arguments to justify their positions) (Helbling, Hoeglinger and Wüerst 2010). Parties' use of frames depends on the interests they traditionally defend. Eurosceptic fringe parties use a much more consistent discourse whereas mainstream pro-EU forces tend to apply different frames in different situations. Scholars often juxtapose the economically protectionist, anti-liberal Euroscepticism of the left with the nationalist Euroscepticism of the right (e.g. van Elsas and van der Brug 2015). Left-wing Eurosceptics view the EU as enabling international competition and thus posing a threat to national welfare states (Charalambous 2013). Right-wing parties tend to oppose European integration from a predominantly sovereignty-based perspective justified on ethno-cultural grounds (Vasilopoulou 2018). Drawing upon the distinction between ethnic and civic nationalism, Halikiopoulou, Nanou and Vasilopoulou (2012) show that in fact nationalism is the common denominator of far right and far left Euroscepticism. Far right Euroscepticism is grounded on ethnic conceptions of the nation and identity, which go against European diversity. Far left Euroscepticism draws upon the civic tenets of nationalism. The EU is seen as an imperialist project serving capitalist interests and posing a threat to the economic and territorial integrity of the nation-state.

The definitions of Euroscepticism have developed a great deal over time becoming more specific to account for the ideological differences between party families and in response to the changing dynamics of European integration. As EU politics has become increasingly complex, parties have also tended to espouse somewhat contradictory views. Far right parties often articulate an ambivalent stance towards the EU combining both hard and soft Euroscepticism, or what Heinisch, McDonnell and Werner (2021) label 'equivocal' Euroscepticism (see also Lorimer 2021). Far left parties have been characterised as 'disobedient' Eurosceptics (Bortun 2022). They challenge the 'reform versus exit' dichotomy, that is, they advocate EU reform while, at the same time, they seek preparations for a potential EU exit and disobey EU rules.

Explaining party responses to European integration

Adjusting to a new issue

During its early years, European integration was treated as an international phenomenon. New structures put in place at Maastricht, however, set the EU apart from other international organisations. This development sparked greater interest among scholars of comparative politics and multi-level governance. This early work treated Europe as a new issue in party competition, and attempted to understand how existing political divisions were related to new conflicts arising from European integration. For example, Hix and Lord (1997) and Hix (1999) argued that the left-right and EU dimensions of political contestation are orthogonal to each other. This suggests that knowing where a party stands on the left-right dimension does not necessarily allow us to predict how it would respond to pressures posed by European integration. This is because, the authors argue, whereas the left-right dimension relates to long-standing class conflicts, the EU dimension reflects different national and territorial group interests.

Subsequent work, which zoomed in on the role of political cleavages in understanding party responses to integration, questioned this model (Marks and Wilson 2000; Hooghe, Marks and Wilson 2002; Marks, Wilson and Ray 2002; see also Chapter 10). Drawing upon Lipset and Rokkan's (1967) seminal work on cleavages, this line of research argues that parties accommodate new issues, including European integration, within existing deep-seated ideologies, summarised by long-standing social cleavages that are deeply embedded in European societies (Marks and Wilson 2000). Drawing evidence on party positions on European integration from four expert surveys carried out in the 1980s and 1990s (1984, 1988, 1992, 1996), Marks, Wilson and Ray (2002) emphasised the powerful role of cleavages in structuring party responses to European integration. They showed how party family is a stronger predictor of parties' EU positions compared to alternative frameworks that focus on strategic competition, national location, participation in government, or the position of a party's supporters. Their analyses indicate party families' positions on European integration as follows: Extreme left/communists are strongly opposed; greens are moderately opposed; social democrats are moderately to strongly favourable; liberals are strongly in favour; agrarian parties are moderately opposed; Christian democrats are strongly favourable; protestant parties are moderately opposed; conservative parties are moderately in favour; the extreme right is strongly opposed; and regionalist parties are moderately to strongly in favour.

However, the relationship between deep-seated ideologies and the issue of European integration was more complex. Hooghe, Marks and Wilson (2002) showed that the European political space was characterised by a left-right dimension, which represents conflict over government intervention and regulation; and by the 'new politics' axis of contestation summarising issues related to culture. The left-right dimension was found to shape party positions on redistribution and state regulation. This suggested that centre-left parties supported European integration to the extent that it regulated capitalism (note that socialist parties' response to European integration in the 1980s was mixed, see Featherstone 1998). Centre-right conservative and Christian Democratic parties were found to support market integration through the EU, but to oppose EU policies that regulated capitalism. Radical/far left parties, on the other hand, were found to be strongly Eurosceptic, which accounted for the inverted U-shape of this relationship. For these parties, the EU represented the very tenets of capitalism and as such threatened far left goals and ideals. Hooghe, Marks and Wilson (2002) also introduced a second dimension, that is, the 'new politics' dimension relating to new issues, such as lifestyle, ecology, immigration and nationalism. The authors labelled this dimension Green/alternative/libertarian (GAL) – traditional/authoritarian/nationalist (TAN) and argued that it was the most powerful predictor of party positions on European integration. Parties close to the GAL end of the dimension were seen to support the EU, because it advanced 'GAL' issues such as asylum or the environment. Parties close to the TAN end of the spectrum were seen to view the EU as a threat because it weakened national authority.

Indeed, a two-dimensional conception of political competition, that is, one that includes both the economic left–right and a social liberal–conservative dimension, is found to have more power at explaining parties' positions on European integration compared to a 'unidimensional left-right' model. As integration progressed, this relationship also changed 'shifting from a situation in which party positions are largely determined by attitudes towards economic issues to one in which positions are more strongly influenced by stances on social issues' (Prosser 2016, 731). Zooming further in on this finding, Schäfer et al. (2021) differentiate between member states and specific critical junctures. They find that pre-Maastricht economic concerns primarily drove party positions on European integration in Western Europe. In the post-Maastricht era, the cultural dimension has played a more important role in structuring positions on European integration. In Southern Europe, however, economics has seemed to explain party positions on the EU while culture played a less significant role.

To recap, the literature that draws upon cleavage theory tends to emphasise long-term patterns and trends. Yet such an approach is less able to account for change and diversity. For example, as EU environmental policy developed and greens entered government coalitions, they became increasingly supportive of EU (Bomberg 2002). Regionalist parties' support of the EU, on the other hand, has gradually decreased over time (Massetti and Schakel 2021). In addition, many party families, including the far right, communists and socialists have not been homogenous in their EU responses over time (e.g. Featherstone 1998; Benedetto and Quaglia 2007; Vasilopoulou 2018; Heinisch, McDonnell and Werner 2021).

Going beyond cleavage theory, therefore, a second line of research has examined party responses to European integration through the prism of national-level explanations, including party strategies and party competition. Taggart (1998) coined the term Euroscepticism as a 'touchstone of dissent'. He argued that ideology alone is not enough to predict Euroscepticism. Different ideologies can lead to opposition, often for different reasons; and therefore, parties belonging to the same party family may adopt different positions in different national contexts.

His analysis showed that Euroscepticism may be observed among single-issue parties, protest-based parties, established parties and parties with Eurosceptic factions. However, protest-based party Euroscepticism was shown to be the most prominent type of opposition to European integration. Euroscepticism was used as an additional mobilising issue among those parties which voice a critique of the functioning of political systems.

As party strategies change and evolve, parties also change their attitudes towards the EU. Euroscepticism is driven by government-opposition dynamics, with parties participating in governing coalitions or aspiring to do so being much more likely to avoid Euroscepticism (Sitter 2001). Parties' long-term policy goals, their positions in their party systems and their competitors' strategies are core to understanding their behaviour vis-à-vis Europe (e.g. Batory and Sitter 2004; Szczerbiak and Taggart 2008a; 2008b). This is true even within communist or far right parties, that is, party families that based on the cleavage theory are ideologically predisposed towards Euroscepticism. For example, domestic vote- and coalition-seeking opportunities have informed communist parties' varying response towards Europe as much as international and geopolitical factors (Benedetto and Quaglia 2007). Far right parties have not been uniform in their response to European integration (Vasilopoulou 2018). Their approach has been shaped by their relationship with democracy, their attitude towards the polity, their target electorate and their behaviour towards competitors. Their attempts to balance often competing interests across these dimensions have impacted upon their divergent stances on European integration.

Europe as a threat or an opportunity?

With the expansion of EU competences, the nature of the EU as a political issue has also changed over time. Although there is cross-time and cross-country variation, European integration has become politicised: that is, it is more salient in domestic politics, more actors are involved in EU-related debates and there is polarisation of partisan and public opinion over the EU issue (Hooghe and Marks 2009; de Wilde et al. 2016; Hutter and Kriesi 2019). Economic, cultural and political competition in Europe has also resulted in the emergence of a new transnational cleavage between the so-called losers and winners from globalisation (Kriesi et al. 2006; Hutter, Grande and Kriesi 2016; Hooghe and Marks 2018). These new lines of division do not align with previous dimensions of contestation. Equally, the EU is increasingly shaping – and is not just shaped by – political division in European politics. In light of such changes in European politics, the 'ideology versus strategy' debate has lost some of its relevance. Besides, parties' ideological and strategic considerations both are integral to party behaviour (Vasilopoulou 2018).

Theories of issue competition are instructive here (see also Chapters 17 and 18). From a spatial perspective, parties change their issue positions in response to the stances of their voters in order to maximise their electoral returns (Downs 1957). Issue salience theories, on the other hand, assume that parties compete over issue attention. They focus their campaigns on issues on which they have a comparative advantage over their competitors while they ignore others. Over time this allows them to claim ownership of a given issue. This is either because voters persistently identify them with this issue or because voters view them as the most competent party to address this issue (Walgrave et al. 2015). Parties therefore not only strive to offer alternatives on policies. They also compete on policy priorities by trying to make the election about those issues on which they have a comparative advantage.

Drawing upon theories of issue competition, van de Wardt, de Vries and Hobolt (2014) conceptualise the EU as a wedge issue. This has two key characteristics. First, it cuts across the traditional left-right axis of political competition; and second, it can be a source of significant division within party systems and can destabilise a governing party or coalition. Multi-faceted issues, such as European integration, cannot be easily integrated into the traditional left-right dimension, which represents conflict over wealth redistribution and state intervention. European integration, therefore, can pose a threat to parties that compete on the left-right dimension. These tend to be major centre-left and centre-right parties that are regularly part of a government coalition, and 'compete in the wake of past and in the shadow of future coalition negotiations' (van de Wardt, de Vries and Hobolt 2014, 987). These mainstream parties do not want wedge-issue competition to threaten their coalition opportunities. They have therefore strong incentives to downplay the EU issue.

Mainstream parties are faced with competing pressures (Rohrschneider and Whitefield 2016). One the one hand, as voters become more Eurosceptic over time (Ejrnæs and Dagnis Jensen 2019) and consider the EU issue more salient, these major parties would also be expected to match their views in order to be competitive in the electoral market. On the other hand, they may face reputational costs if they respond to growing public Euroscepticism. This is because the EU and its policies are fundamentally a product of those centrist parties with extensive records of government experience. These are the parties that have attended EU summits, have been part of EU decision-making and have implemented EU policies domestically. The expansion of EU decision-making also limits the range of mainstream parties' options and tends to result in policy convergence (Nanou and Dorussen 2013). At the same time, however, these parties are prone to internal dissent over the EU issue (Hooghe and Marks 2018). Therefore, they have strong incentives to downplay the issue and collude on a pro-EU stance in order to avoid reputational costs (Rohrschneider and Whitefield 2016; Hooghe and Marks 2018).

In contrast to mainstream parties that routinely alternate in government, the EU issue creates opportunities for those parties without significant government experience. Often conceptualised as 'niche' or 'challenger' (see Chapter 19), these parties are the electoral 'losers' on the dominant left-right dimension of political contestation. Their lack of government participation means that they have limited reputational constraints imposed by prior policy positions. Their comparative advantage lies in innovation rather than competence (de Vries and Hobolt 2020). By politicising a new or previously ignored issue that fits poorly into the main lines of cleavage, these actors can create a political niche or a comparative advantage for themselves (de Vries and Hobolt 2012; Hobolt and de Vries 2015). This strategy of issue entrepreneurship allows them to disrupt the status quo and discredit the dominant actors in the system. Position and salience can become complementary strategies in this respect. Emphasising extreme positions achieves ideological distinctiveness and product differentiation (Wagner 2012). These parties, therefore, have strong incentives to compete on the EU issue, which cuts across the dominant left-right dimension on which mainstream party success is built. Emphasising their extreme positions on Europe allows them to mobilise against the pro-EU consensus and to 'exploit the cracks' in European party systems (van de Wardt, de Vries and Hobolt 2014).

Comparing party stances before and after the European financial crisis, Rohrschneider and Whitefield (2016) empirically tested these arguments. They started from the premise that addressing the crisis involved both economic measures and political integration at the EU level, both of which took place against a background of rising popular Euroscepticism. Responsive mainstream parties would be expected to also change their EU stance. On the one hand, centre-left social democratic parties have incentives to become sceptical towards EU-imposed austerity whereas centre-right parties may become critical of further political integration. In contrast to expectations deriving from a spatial perspective, their expert surveys showed that parties belonging to mainstream party families, including socialists, greens, social democrats, liberals, Christian democrats and Conservatives, did not change their position significantly between 2008 and 2013. Communists and nationalists, on the other hand, became more critical of the

EU in terms of both the principle of integration and EU democracy performance. Communist and nationalist parties also increased the salience of European integration between these two time points in both Western and Eastern European countries. Salience remained similar across other party families, especially in Western Europe (Whitefield and Rohrschneider 2015).

Yet research has also shown that support for Eurosceptic challenger parties has a contagion effect on mainstream party positions in Western Europe. Specifically, mainstream parties have shifted their EU positions when Eurosceptic challengers have been electorally successful and emphasised the EU issue. Whereas centre-left parties tend to be influenced by both far right and far left success, centre-right parties are more susceptible to far right success (Meijers 2015). Van de Wardt (2015) has shown further that mainstream opposition parties, which are more risk-acceptant, tend to increase the salience of the EU issue in response to greater emphasis by Eurosceptic challengers. More risk-averse mainstream governing parties, however, do not respond to such shifts. It has also been shown that when far left parties increase the salience of the issue of state control of the economy, that is, the issue they 'own', then mainstream parties, including the social democrats, liberals, Christian democrats and conservatives, tend to take anti-neoliberal and anti-globalisation positions, thus tilting towards higher levels of Euroscepticism (Williams and Ishiyama 2018).

Studies focusing on the analysis of manifestos (rather than expert surveys) show that political parties devote a significant proportion of their euromanifestos to European issues (Spoon 2012). The precise amount of attention varies as a function of national party system polarisation on European issues, parties' internal dissent and party type. Interestingly as niche parties improve their electoral fortunes, they talk more about Europe in their euromanifestos. This finding is particularly prominent among regional parties.

There are in fact differences in the type of EU issue parties emphasise (Braun, Hutter and Kerscher 2016). Eurosceptic parties tend to focus on constitutive issues of the EU polity, that is, issues related to EU membership, competencies and decision-making rules. These tend to be more divisive and thus more likely to drive a wedge between parties. Europhile parties, on the other hand, prefer to emphasise day-to-day policy. This is because policy issues tend to be embedded in the general left-right dimension of political contestation and thus do not pose a substantive threat to their internal unity. This suggests that pro-European [mainstream] parties do not necessarily avoid debating Europe altogether. They prefer instead to shift the attention towards day-to-day policy. Comparing position and salience across national and EP electoral arenas, Braun and Schmitt (2020) show that although party positions on the EU do not change depending on election type, the salience of European integration is higher in EP elections compared to national elections.

Voters, party cues and the issue of Europe

The early years of European integration were characterised by a 'permissive consensus' with the public giving indirect consent to elite-level bargaining. Yet, as a political union became part of the agenda from Maastricht onwards, EU integration entered the contentious world of politics; or what Hooghe and Marks (2009, 5) call a period of 'constraining dissensus'. Van der Eijk and Franklin (2004) warned that there were identifiable differences in citizens' attitudes towards the EU; yet in the eyes of the voters, parties offered limited choice regarding their EU orientations. The EU dimension was ripe for politicisation, but parties had not caught up. In other words, public opinion constituted a 'sleeping giant' that, if awoken, would shake up European politics.

Tillman's (2004) analysis shows that European integration was an electoral issue in national elections as early as the mid-1990s in Austria, Finland and Sweden, which were then new member states. de Vries (2007) further tested the 'sleeping giant' proposition comparing the UK, Danish, Dutch and German elections between 1992 and 2002. EU issue voting, that is, the 'process in which attitudes towards European integration translate into national vote choice' varies across national contexts (de Vries 2007, 384). It depends on a combination of high issue salience and perceived partisan conflict over European integration. Indeed, EU issue voting takes place in both national and European elections with greater distance between a voter and a party decreasing the likelihood of that citizen opting for that party (de Vries and Hobolt 2016).

Mass-elite linkages on the EU issue consist of a dual-process, whereby elites both respond to and shape voters' views on European integration (Steenbergen, Edwards and De Vries 2007). Yet political agency is important as EU issue voting is moderated by the extent to which Eurosceptic political entrepreneurs mobilise the EU issue (de Vries 2007). Far right and far left parties have provided the strongest cues in this respect. For example, Gómez-Reino and Llamazares (2013) show that far right parties have established programmatic links with their voters on the EU issue. Yet most far right party supporters tend to be less Eurosceptic than the far right party in their domestic party system; and they tend to attach less importance to the EU issue (McDonnell and Werner 2019). At the same time, far left parties that take Eurosceptic positions are more likely to be electorally successful (Wagner 2021).

Conclusion and avenues for further research

The literature on party-based Euroscepticism has developed considerably over time reflecting both different academic approaches and the evolution of European integration. Arguably it already constitutes a very rich field. Yet political parties change and evolve, as does the EU project. This presents exciting opportunities for future research, especially around three key areas.

First, we need new theories and methods to capture the fact that political parties do not put forward internally consistent views on European integration (Heinisch, McDonnell and Werner 2021; Lorimer 2021). The economic, refugee and health crises have shown that party responses to European integration can vary depending on contingency. In addition, parties – as well as voters – do not take the same position on all EU-related topics and policies. Political parties need to carefully balance between interest representation, policy promotion and electoral politics, which provides them with different strategic incentives at different time points. Position 'blurring', that is, obscuring party preferences on a given issue, is becoming a popular strategy in a multidimensional political environment (see Koedam 2021). Future research should focus on how parties blur their EU positions and the conditions under which they engage in such a strategy.

Second, while there has been extensive research on parties' EU issue positions and their salience, we know less about the political psychology of party strategies and communication. Future research could examine the precise ways in which parties choose to make appeals to voters on the EU issue. A focus on the tone of parties' EU debates could examine whether parties and politicians use positive or negative emotions when they talk about European integration, including what type of discrete emotions they evoke (fear, anger, disgust, enthusiasm, pride, hope, etc.). It would also be interesting to know how such appeals may vary across parties and over time. This is an important line of research in an era of rising affective polarisation across Europe, especially because emotions can influence citizens' opinion and behaviour. Empirically, such a study would require a systematic, comparative and longitudinal data collection.

Third, researchers should continue to systematically study party responses to European integration from longitudinal and comparative perspectives. How stable are parties' stances and voters' opinions over time? We need to know more about specific patterns of fluctuation and change; and whether these also vary depending on EU policy. There is great potential for this line of research to also closely consider questions of representation and responsiveness on the EU issue, for example: How far are parties from voters on the EU issue? To what extent do parties respond to their voters' concerns on the EU issue? Have these dynamics changed over time? (see Williams and Spoon 2015; Vasilopoulou and Gattermann 2021).

This field has been primarily influenced by political scientists and political sociologists. Yet there is great scope for fruitful collaboration with political economists and international relations scholars working on international collaboration, and globalisation more broadly, including trade and environmental politics. Such interdisciplinary synergies would theorise and empirically connect party responses to different aspects of globalisation – of which European integration is just one.

References

Batory, A. and Sitter, N. (2004) 'Cleavages, competition and coalition-building: Agrarian parties and the European question in Western and East Central Europe', *European Journal of Political Research*, 43, p523–546.

Benedetto, G. and Quaglia, L. (2007) 'The comparative politics of Communist Euroscepticism in France, Italy and Spain', *Party Politics*, 13(4), p478–499.

Bomberg, E. (2002) 'The Europeanisation of Green Parties: Exploring the EU's Impact', *West European Politics*, 25(3), p29–50.

Bortun, V. (2022) Plan B for Europe: The Birth of 'Disobedient Euroscepticism'? *JCMS: Journal of Common Market Studies*. https://doi.org/10.1111/jcms.13313.

Braun, D., Hutter, S. and Kerscher, A. (2016) 'What type of Europe? The salience of polity and policy issues in European Parliament elections', *European Union Politics*, 17(4), p570–592.

Braun, D. and Schmitt, H. (2020) 'Different emphases, same positions? The election manifestos of political parties in the EU multilevel electoral system compared', *Party Politics*, 26(5), p640–650.

Charalambous, G. (2013) *European integration and the Communist dilemma: Communist Party responses to Europe in Greece, Cyprus and Italy*. Oxon: Routledge.

de Vries, C. (2007) 'Sleeping giant: Fact or fairytale? How European integration affects national elections', *European Union Politics*, 8(3), p363–385.

de Vries, C. and Hobolt, S. (2012) 'When dimensions collide: The electoral success of issue entrepreneurs', *European Union Politics*, 13(2), p246–268.

de Vries, C. and Hobolt, S. (2016) 'EU issue voting in national and European parliamentary elections, in van der Brug, W. and de Vreese, C. (eds.) *(Un)intended consequences of European parliamentary elections*. Oxford: Oxford University Press, pp. 101–124.

de Vries, C. and Hobolt, S. (2020) *Political Entrepreneurs: The Rise of Challenger Parties in Europe*. New Jersey: Princeton University Press.

De Wilde, P., Laupold, A. and Schmidtke, H. (2016) 'Introduction: The differentiated politicisation of European governance', *West European Politics*, 39(1), p3–22.

Downs, A. (1957) *An economic theory of democracy*. New York: Harper & Row.

Ejrnæs, A. and Dagnis Jensen, M. (2019) 'Divided but united: Explaining nested public support for European integration', *West European Politics*, 42(7), p1390–1419.

Featherstone, K. (1998) *Socialist parties and European integration: A comparative history*. Manchester: Manchester University Press.

Gómez-Reino, M. and Llamazares, I. (2013) 'The populist radical right and European integration: A comparative analysis of party – voter links, *West European Politics*, 36(4), p789–816.

Halikiopoulou, D., Nanou, K. and Vasilopoulou, S. (2012) 'The paradox of nationalism: The common denominator of radical right and radical left Euroscepticism', *European Journal of Political Research*, 51(4), p504–39.

Heinisch, R., McDonnell, D. and Werner, A. (2021) 'Equivocal Euroscepticism: How populist radical right parties can have their EU cake and eat it', *JCMS: Journal of Common Market Studies*, 59(2), p189–205.

Helbling, M., Hoeglinger, D. and Wüest, B. (2010) 'How political parties frame European integration', *European Journal of Political Research*, 49(4), p496–521.

Hix, S. (1999) 'Dimensions and alignments in European Union politics: Cognitive constraints and partisan responses', *European Journal of Political Research*, 35, p69–125.

Hix, S. and Lord, C. (1997) *Political parties in the European Union*. London: Macmillan Press Ltd.

Hobolt, S. and de Vries, C. (2015) 'Issue entrepreneurship and multiparty competition', *Comparative Political Studies*, 48(9), p1159–1185.

Hooghe, L. and Marks, G. (2009) 'A postfunctionalist theory of European integration: From permissive consensus to constraining dissensus', *British Journal of Political Science*, 39(1), p1–23.

Hooghe, L. and Marks, G. (2018) 'Cleavage theory meets Europe's crises: Lipset, Rokkan, and the transnational cleavage', *Journal of European Public Policy*, 25(1), p109–135.

Hooghe, L., Marks, G. and Wilson, C. (2002) 'Does left/right structure party positions on European integration?', *Comparative Political Studies*, 35(8), p965–989.

Hutter, S. and Kriesi, H. (2019) 'Politicizing Europe in times of crisis', *Journal of European Public Policy*, 26(7), p996–1017.

Hutter, S., Grande, E. and Kriesi, H. (2016) *Politicising Europe: Integration and mass politics*. Cambridge: Cambridge University Press.

Keith, D. (2017) 'Opposing Europe, opposing austerity: Radical left parties and the Eurosceptic debate', in Leruth, B., Startin, N. and Usherwood, S. (eds.) *The Routledge handbook of Euroscepticism*. London: Routledge, pp. 86–99.

Koedam, J. (2021) 'Avoidance, ambiguity, alternation: Position blurring strategies in multidimensional party competition', *European Union Politics*, 22(4), p655–675.

Kopecky, P. and Mudde, C. (2002) 'The two sides of Euroscepticism: Party positions on Euroscepticism in East Central Europe', *European Union Politics*, 3(3), p297–326.

Kriesi, H., Grande, E., Lachat, R. et al. (2006) 'Globalization and the transformation of the national political space: Six European countries compared', *European Journal of Political Research*, 45(6), p921–956.

Lipset, S.M. and Rokkan, S. (1967) 'Cleavage Structures, party systems and voter alignments: An introduction', in Lipset, S.M. and Rokkan, S. (eds.) *Party systems and voter alignments: crossnational perspectives*. New York: Free Press, pp. 1–64.

Lorimer, M. (2021) 'What do they talk about when they talk about Europe? Euro-ambivalence in far right ideology', *Ethnic and Racial Studies*, 44(11), p2016–2033.

Mair, P. (2007) 'Political opposition and the European Union', *Government and Opposition*, 42(1), p1–17.

Marks, G. and Wilson, C. (2000) 'The past in the present: A cleavage theory of party positions on European integration', *British Journal of Political Science*, 30, p433–459.

Marks, G., Wilson, C. and Ray, L. (2002) 'National political parties and European integration', *American Journal of Political Science*, 46(3), p585–94.

Masseti, E. and Schakel, A.H. (2021) 'From staunch supporters to critical observers: Explaining the turn towards Euroscepticism among regionalist parties', *European Union Politics*, 22(3), p424–445.

McDonnell, D. and Werner, A. (2019) 'Differently Eurosceptic: Radical right populist parties and their supporters', *Journal of European Public Policy*, 26(12), p1761–1778.

Meijers, M. (2015) 'Contagious Euroscepticism: The impact of Eurosceptic support on mainstream party positions on European integration', *Party Politics*, 23(4), p413–423.

Nanou, K. and Dorussen, H. (2013) 'European integration and electoral democracy: How the European Union constrains party competition in the Member States', *European Journal of Political Research*, 52(1), p71–93.

Prosser, C. (2016) 'Dimensionality, ideology and party positions towards European integration', *West European Politics*, 39(4), p731–754.

Rohrschneider, R. and Whitefield, S. (2016) 'Responding to growing European Union-skepticism? The stances of political parties toward European integration in Western and Eastern Europe following the financial crisis', *European Union Politics*, 17(1), p138–161.

Schäfer, C., Popa, S.A., Braun, D. and Schmitt, H. (2021) 'The reshaping of political conflict over Europe: from pre-Maastricht to post-'Euro crisis'', *West European Politics*, 44(3), p531–557.

Sitter, N. (2001) 'The politics of opposition and European integration in Scandinavia: Is Euro-scepticism a government – opposition dynamic?', *West European Politics*, 24(4), p22–39.

Spoon, J. (2012) 'How salient is Europe? An analysis of European election manifestos, 1979–2004', *European Union Politics*, 13(4), p558–579.

Steenbergen, M., Edwards, E. and de Vries, C. (2007) 'Who's cueing whom? Mass-elite linkages and the future of European integration', *European Union Politics*, 8(1), p13–35.

Szczerbiak, A. and Taggart, P. (eds.) (2008a) *Opposing Europe? The comparative party politics of Euroscepticism, volume 1, case studies and country surveys*. Oxford: Oxford University Press.

Szczerbiak, A. and Taggart, P. (eds.) (2008b) *Opposing Europe? The comparative party politics of Euroscepticism, volume 2, comparative and theoretical perspectives*. Oxford: Oxford University Press.

Taggart, P. (1998) 'A touchstone of dissent: Euroscepticism in contemporary western European party systems', *European Journal of Political Research*, 33(3), p363–388.

Taggart, P. and Szczerbiak, A. (2001) 'Parties, positions and Europe: Euroscepticism in the EU candidate states of Central and Eastern Europe', Opposing Europe, Sussex European Institute Working Paper 46, Brighton.

Tillman, E.R. (2004) 'The European Union at the ballot box? European integration and voting behavior in the new member states', *Comparative Political Studies*, 37(5), p590–610.

van de Wardt, M. (2015) 'Desperate needs, desperate deeds: Why mainstream parties respond to the issues of niche parties', *West European Politics*, 38(1), p93–122.

van de Wardt, M. de Vries, C. and Hobolt, S. (2014) 'Exploiting the cracks: Wedge issues in multiparty competition', *The Journal of Politics*, 76(4), p986–999.

Van der Eijk, C. and Franklin, M. (2004) 'Potential for contestation on European matters at national elections in Europe', in Marks, G. and Steenbergen, M. (eds.) *European integration and political conflict*. Cambridge: Cambridge University Press, pp. 32–50.

van Elsas, E. and van der Brug, W. (2015) The changing relationship between left–right ideology and Euroscepticism, 1973–2010, *European Union Politics*, 16(2), p194–215.

Vasilopoulou, S. (2011) 'European integration and the radical right: Three patterns of opposition', *Government and Opposition*, 46(2), p223–44.

Vasilopoulou, S. (2013) Continuity and change in the study of Euroscepticism: Plus ça change?, *JCMS: Journal of Common Market Studies*, 51(1), p153–168.

Vasilopoulou, S. (2018) *Far right parties and Euroscepticism: Patterns of opposition*. London: ECPR press/Rowman & Littlefield.

Vasilopoulou, S. and Gattermann, K. (2021) 'Does politicization matter for EU representation? A comparison of four European Parliament elections', *Journal of Common Market Studies*, 59(3), p661–678.

Wagner, M. (2012) 'When do parties emphasise extreme positions? How strategic incentives for policy differentiation influence issue importance', *European Journal of Political Research*, 51, p64–88.

Wagner, S. (2021) 'Euroscepticism as a radical left party strategy for success', *Party Politics*, https://doi.org/10.1177/13540688211038917.

Walgrave, S., Tresch, A. and Lefevere, J. (2015) The conceptualisation and measurement of issue ownership, *West European Politics*, 38(4), p778–796.

Williams, C. and Ishiyama, J. (2018) 'Responding to the left: the effect of far-left parties on mainstream party Euroskepticism', *Journal of Elections, Public Opinion and Parties*, 28(4), p443–466.

Williams, C. and Spoon, J. (2015) 'Differentiated party response: The effect of Euroskeptic public opinion on party positions', *European Union Politics*, 16(2), p176–193.

Whitefield, S. and Rohrschneider, R. (2015) 'The salience of European integration to party competition: Western and Eastern Europe compared', *East European Politics and Societies and Cultures*, 29(1), p12–39.

27
PARTIES, ISSUES AND GENDER

*Hilde Coffé, Miki Caul Kittilson, Bonnie M. Meguid
and Ana Catalano Weeks*

Historically, women's experience in the political arena has been characterised by exclusion in most democracies. Women only won the right to vote in the first half of the twentieth century in many Western democracies, and as late as 1971 in Switzerland. Much has, however, changed since then. For example, women have increasingly achieved higher levels of education and entered the paid workforce. As a consequence of these changes, since the 1950s, women have moved towards the left and now disproportionately support leftist parties. And, in certain contexts, women have been found to be more likely to prioritise certain issues and policy positions such as support for gender equality, women's rights and expanded welfare states, relative to men.

This chapter focuses on the dynamics of gender differences in the electorate and the implications for political parties. Drawing on our unique and extensive dataset of male/female voter ratios by party family across Europe from 1985 to 2018, we show that there are indeed important gender gaps in party support, which vary by party family and across this time period. Past explanations for these gender differences are often structural, overlooking the strategic role of parties in shaping or addressing these gaps. After reviewing these common explanations, we turn our attention to how parties respond to the challenge of gender differences in party support, especially parties facing a deficit in women's support. Parties can employ a variety of tactics to improve their electoral support among women: they may introduce programmatic changes, initiate institutional changes and/or increase the descriptive representation of women to target women voters. We highlight the crucial role of strategic incentives: parties will shift party programmes and women's representation when they perceive feasible gains from doing so.

Gender differences in party support

Since women gained suffrage, gender differences in support for political parties have fluctuated across democracies. Some of the earliest studies found that women disproportionately supported conservative parties (Duverger 1955; Lipset 1960).[1]

Attention to gender-based differences waned during the 1970s and 1980s, emerging again in the 1990s, when longitudinal studies unearthed important differences in the voting behaviour of men and women in the post-Second World War era (e.g. Listhaug 1985; Oskarson 1995; Manza and Brooks 1998; Knutsen 2001; Giger 2009). For instance, this work shows that, by the 1980s, women were increasingly supporting left-wing parties, a trend that has continued since.

Women's disproportionate support for left-wing parties is considered a pervasive feature of the contemporary political landscape in many post-industrialised democracies (Inglehart and Norris 2000; Box-Steffensmeier et al. 2004; Iversen and Rosenbluth 2006). Yet research has also highlighted regional differences. For example, Abendschön and Steinmetz (2014) draw a contrast between Western and Eastern Europe, with women in the former increasingly supporting leftist parties, and Eastern European women favouring rightist parties. Looking at Latin America, Morgan (2015) finds narrow ideological gender gaps for most countries, with women favouring the right slightly more than men.

Focusing on Europe, Figure 27.1 shows gender differences among voters by party families between 1985 and 2018, based on national parliamentary voting behaviour data from the Comparative Study of Electoral Systems (CSES), and when not available, the European Election Study (EES) and the European Social Study (ESS). Gender differences in party choice are measured as the ratio of the percentage of men respondents who report voting for a party to the percentage of women respondents who report voting for the same party. A score of 1 thus indicates an equal proportion of men compared with women as voters, a score higher than 1 reveals a higher proportion of men compared with women as voters, and a score lower than 1 suggests a lower proportion of men compared with women as voters.

Figure 27.1 reveals important variation in gender differences in voting across party families and time. For instance, we see a greater tendency of women to support Social Democratic parties compared with men; the male–female voter ratio values have hovered at or below the unity line of equal male–female support since the beginning of the 2000s. Green and New Left parties were once men-dominated, but since 2010, they attract more women than men. Over the period under study (1985–2018), women are – despite some ebb and flow over time – also more likely than men to support Christian Democratic parties. Figure 27.1 also reveals a tendency of men being overrepresented among the Conservative party electorate.

The radical right populist (RRP) party family stands out with the largest overrepresentation of men among voters of all parties. This finding is consistent with cross-national data, showing that women are significantly less likely to support RRP parties than men (e.g. Givens 2004; Rippeyoung 2007; Harteveld et al. 2015; Immerzeel et al. 2015; Spierings and Zaslove 2015; Coffé 2018; Harteveld and Ivarsflaten 2018). Over time, this gender gap has narrowed and

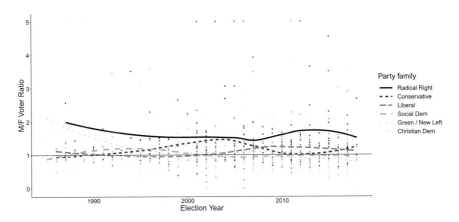

Figure 27.1 Gender differences (male/female voter ratio) in voting behaviour for different party families, Europe 1985–2018 (Loess Smoothing)

Note: M/F voter ratio data compiled from CSES, EES and ESS surveys (Weeks et al. 2022).

plateaued, but increased in the late 2000s, ending at close to 2.0: double the percentage of men voters supporting the RRP parties as women voters.

Explaining gender differences in party support

Researchers have identified a host of individual and contextual factors explaining gender differences in party support. These studies have particularly accounted for women's greater likelihood of voting for left-leaning parties. Many studies have highlighted changes in women's structural socioeconomic characteristics and related changes in policy interests and positions. Women's greater participation in the paid labour force exposes women to pay inequities and provides them with life experiences that women are less likely to experience as homemakers (Manza and Brooks 1998; Box-Steffensmeier et al. 2004; Morgan 2015). Working women are expected to be more likely to support public spending on child and elderly care, work that was traditionally unpaid and done by women (Iversen and Rosenbluth 2006). Furthermore, women's greater likelihood of working in the public sector makes them more dependent on the expansion of the welfare state and thus more likely to be supportive of left-wing parties (Knutsen 2001). Additional structural explanations include the growth of women's educational opportunities, more women heading households given the increase in divorce and rise of non-marriage, and associated increasing levels of poverty among women (e.g. Manza and Brooks 1998; Inglehart and Norris 2000).

Women's support for left-leaning parties has also been attributed to women's greater emphasis on particular issues and their issue positions, including support for gender equality, women's rights and expanded welfare states (Jelen et al. 1994; Studlar et al. 1998; Gidengil et al. 2003; Alexander et al. 2020); topics often referred to as 'women's issues'. Scholars have defined such 'women's issues' in different ways, including based on gender differences (both among the public and politicians) in policy preferences or the distinction between private spheres ('women's space') and public spheres ('men's domain'). Using the former approach and examining gender differences among citizens in policy positions, Weeks (2022) finds that, across democracies and over time, women prefer greater governmental spending on health, retirement and unemployment, and are more likely to say it is the government's responsibility to keep prices under control, provide a job for everyone and reduce income inequality. Even larger gender gaps are found over issues related to gender roles in the family and work, with women on average nine points less likely than men to say that a preschool child will suffer when mothers work outside the home (Weeks 2022).

Women's issue positions related to redistribution and government intervention align with left-wing parties' greater attention to social policies and positional support for policies aimed at improving gender equality (such as gender quotas) (Caul 1999; Wängnerud 2009; Kittilson 2011; Lilliefeldt 2012). However, gender differences on issues related to gender roles in society do not fall neatly along the left-right dimension. Indeed, left-wing parties have been criticised for their failure to support measures to promote women's employment, for fear that gender equality might compete with the importance of class-based concerns (Gelb 1989; Huber and Stephens 2001). Parties often frame the issue of women's employment differently, the left highlighting gender equality and the right, fertility or productivity ('business case') arguments. Gender gaps on both redistributive and social issues also exist *within* parties' electorate. For example, analysis from the USA finds that Republican women tend to be significantly more moderate than Republican men (Barnes and Cassese 2017). As such, parties on both the left and the right can and have shifted positions on these issues to gain women's votes, as we discuss later in the chapter.

Explaining men's overrepresentation in support for RRP parties has proved more challenging than explaining women's overrepresentation among left-leaning parties. Common explanations for gender differences in RRP voting include men's larger share of manual jobs in blue-collar sectors, which are seen to be threatened by modernisation and globalisation (Kitschelt 1995). Men are more likely to lose their jobs or to be forced into lower-paying jobs in the new global economy, raising the salience of these issues for men as voters (Givens 2004). Consequently, men may develop a sense of economic insecurity and resentment that leads to support for nativist policies (Studlar et al. 1998). This insecurity and resentment are especially likely to affect men without a college education. Research finds that this group's relative social status has declined in recent decades, due in no small part to the *rise* of women's social status (given rising levels of women's employment) – and that low subjective social status predicts voting for radical right populists (Gidron and Hall 2017).

Other common explanations of the gender gap in RRP voting are men's greater prioritisation of law and order and focus on individual responsibility compared with women (Gilligan 1982) – attitudes that fit well with RRP parties' authoritarian discourse. It has also been argued that RRP parties' traditional views of a woman's role in society are more strongly supported by men than women (Inglehart and Norris 2003). Finally, some studies suggest that the male-dominated leadership of RRP parties may explain this gender gap. Mayer (2013) demonstrates that gender differences in support for the Front National narrowed as Marine Le Pen took a leading role within the party and gave it a more modern image.

Yet recent research shows that some of these explanations offer less leverage over time. For example, Mayer (2013) points out that service sector jobs, dominated by women, are increasingly uncertain (the COVID-19 pandemic only confirms this). Scholars have also argued that women do not necessarily hold less strict attitudes towards law and order or immigration than men (Mudde 2007; Mayer 2015). Harteveld and Ivarsflaten (2018) found few gender differences in policy preferences over migration, showing instead that women are more motivated to control prejudice. Furthermore, some Northern European RRP parties have embraced femonationalism, which refers to the trend of exploiting gender equality issues in campaigns against Muslims, on the grounds that Islam is unsupportive of women's rights (Farris 2017, see also, e.g. Mayer 2013; Akkerman 2015; de Lange and Mügge 2015; Mudde et al. 2015). Hence, the explanation about the RRP parties' positions towards women's role in society becomes less convincing.

Implications of the gender gap for party strategies

The structural explanations dominant in past research on gender differences in party support suggest a passive role for parties. However, studies of party politics demonstrate that parties actively target groups of voters during elections. Bringing together these two streams of the literature suggests that parties may play a strategic role in shaping gender differences. Extant work on party competition in general posits that parties act strategically to increase their vote share. Applying this logic, political parties may make concerted efforts to gain women voters in particular. In this review, we focus on three sets of tactics identified in previous research: shifting programmatic appeals, making institutional reforms and increasing women's presence among party candidates, MPs and leaders.

Changes in issue emphases and positions

Political parties diversify their issue offerings or alter their policy stances to appeal to untapped voters (Downs 1957). Recent work (Meguid 2005, 2008; Bale et al. 2010; Han 2015; Abou-Chadi 2016) extending this argument to single-issue parties has shown that mainstream parties approximate the position of threatening niche parties to win over their voters. There are ample examples of political parties shifting their policy stance and heightening the salience of gender-related issues to attract women voters. For example, Morgan (2013) presents the cases of conservative parties in the Netherlands, the UK and Germany, promising more progressive social programmes including childcare, parental leave and working time flexibility, to appeal to previously alienated women voters on the basis of work-family policies. Weeks (2019) shows that gender quota laws cue party leaders to increase competition over gender equality issues to target or retain women voters.

Another example is the strategy of femonationalism discussed earlier, which shows how RRP parties are diversifying their policy stance to attract women nominally on the basis of feminist issues. This tactic goes beyond the simple addition of a new issue, however. It is rather the linking of the party's existing anti-Islam stance to a central 'women's issue' of women's control over their bodies and rejection of subjugation to men.

In these cases, parties feel the need to alter their policy stances because of the differential preferences of women and men voters. As discussed previously, these preferences may include differences in prioritisation of issues and policy positions such as support for gender equality, women's rights and expanded welfare states, relative to men. Of course, the strategy to change issue emphases and positions will only be pursued by rational parties if their electoral costs are outweighed by the benefits. If the policy shifts or issue diversification necessary to attract women voters will alienate more existing voters or if the party is already successful under the existing programmatic stances, such tactics will not be pursued (Meguid 2022).

Institutional reform

Parties may also press for institutional reforms to target specific groups of voters. Specific to women's party support, two examples of institutional reforms initiated by political parties are nationwide reforms allowing women to vote and nationwide and intraparty gender quotas for political candidates.

When women received the right to vote – in the first half of the twentieth century in many Western countries – they were expected to be more likely to support conservative parties than men. This expectation was based on women's higher levels of religiosity, their roles as housewives and their generally conservative attitudes at the time. Many parties, both left- and right-leaning, were split on the issue of women's suffrage (e.g. Maguire 2007). Within the British Conservative party, some members realised that giving the vote to women on the same basis as men (a property franchise) would give the vote to middle- and upper-class women, who would be more likely to vote for them. In other words, suffrage extension could be a strategy to increase and broaden the Conservative's electorate. By contrast, despite full adult suffrage being the Labour Party's policy as of 1912, some Labour members initially opposed votes for all women. They argued that the Labour Party was set up to represent the working class and believed that campaigning for women's votes, in addition to those of working class men, would weaken their cause and hurt their electoral appeal. Thus, the extension of female suffrage was viewed through a strategic lens by parties of the left and right.

In modern eras, suffrage extension has been replaced with other institutional strategies such as gender quota laws. Quota adoption can be used strategically to attain different goals depending on the national and international context. One such goal is increasing support among women voters. For example, when presented with polling data revealing a deficit in women's votes in the 1990s, the British Labour Party adopted women-only shortlists in some constituencies to quickly raise women's descriptive representation in parliament (Eagle and Lovenduski

1998; Childs and Webb 2012; Campbell 2016). Previous research in wealthy democracies demonstrates that parties are more likely to adopt quota laws in times of high electoral uncertainty as an attempt to increase their support among women voters (Baldez 2004; Murray et al. 2012; Weeks 2018). Parties will also adopt a quota law as a way of exerting control over their candidate lists when decentralised candidate selection procedures give party leaders little control otherwise (Weeks 2018). In countries where women have low status, quotas can be adopted as a way to demonstrate the country's commitment to democracy, and thus to secure foreign aid (Bush 2011). (For a wider discussion of institutional reforms, see Chapter 9.)

Changes in women's representation

A third tool for targeting women's support is to increase the number of women faces in the party when it is politically expedient, without the use of a quota. Concerted efforts have been made by party elites across Europe and the USA to boost the number of women candidates, MPs and party leaders within their parties. Figure 27.2 shows the share of women in the parliamentary party across party families in Europe from 1980 to 2018. The figure reveals that not only has the average share of women elected increased, but this rise is also found in every party family since 2000. Research has shown that women's descriptive representation tends to be higher in left-wing parties, which is related to their greater likelihood of introducing party-level gender quotas (e.g. Reynolds 1999; Kittilson 2011).

Several factors may explain this positive trend in women's representation. Beyond the idea that good democratic government requires representation of all citizens, more tactical explanations emerge for closing the gender gap in political representation (Teele 2018; Weeks 2018). Valdini (2019) theorises that men party gatekeepers strategically calculate that running more women for office will improve a party's less-than-positive image, thereby increasing women's electoral support for the party. Women's presence serves as a visible symbol of the party's support for the issue of equality, without the party necessarily needing to implement more fundamental gender-based reforms. Evidence of this tactic can be seen across a wide variety of world regions and political organisations, from party actions following corruption scandals in Spain, Portugal

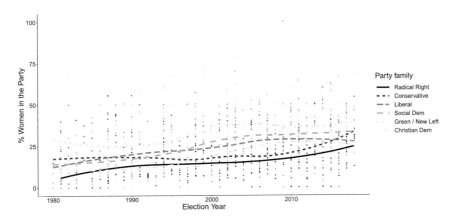

Figure 27.2 Share of women in parliamentary party by party family, Europe 1980–2018 (Loess Smoothing)

Note: Data from own data collection (Weeks et al. 2022).

and Ireland (Valdini 2019), to Jordanian tribes reacting to gender quotas (Bush and Gao 2017), to patriarchal social movements (Nielsen 2020). O'Brien (2015: 1022) finds similar evidence of the tactical use of women in her study of party leaders, concluding that parties are more likely to consider women leaders when their electoral performance is declining.

Even if the presence of more women does not signal policy or reputational changes, parties may increase women's representation because women voters are more likely to vote for women as candidates. Indeed, in the USA, voters are more likely to support representatives who share their race or gender, even after controlling for party affiliation (Box-Steffensmeier et al. 2003), and women in the electorate are more likely to support women candidates and parties that run and elect more women (Plutzer and Zipp 1996; Banducci and Karp 2000).

In recent work (Weeks et al. 2022), we propose a new theory of *strategic descriptive representation* to describe this tactic of descriptive representation (increasing the number of women MPs) as a tool to appeal to a broader set of voters. The theory has the factors of electoral loss and the oft-overlooked variable of gender differences in voter support at its core. We argue that electorally struggling parties with large gender gaps in voter support will increase their proportion of women MPs to attract previously untapped women voters.

Having the largest gender gaps in support across Europe, RRP parties emerge as key employers of strategic descriptive representation. Unlike green parties who view gender equality as central to their electoral programme and *raison d'être* (Keith and Verge 2018) and have decentralised party organisations with a wealth of women representatives already, RRP parties seem to be bolstering their representation of women as a strategic tool to gain women's votes. In time-series cross-sectional analyses relying on survey data and data on women's representation in 30 European countries from 1985 to 2018, we find that RRP parties across Europe increase their percentage of women MPs when they have both men-dominated electorates and experienced vote loss (Weeks et al. 2022). We argue that this vote-seeking strategy may be less costly than programmatic changes, as increasing the number of women does not require shifting the position of core issues or diversifying policy stances. Our analyses further demonstrate that strategic descriptive representation has a more significant effect on shaping the number of women MPs in RRP parties than other institutional tactics, such as national gender quotas.

One illustration of this mechanism of strategic descriptive representation can be seen in the behaviour of the Dutch RRP party, the Party of Freedom (PVV), in 2017. The PVV had lost votes in the previous 2012 parliamentary elections (10.1 per cent in 2012 compared with 15.5 per cent in the 2010 elections) and they faced an underrepresentation of women in their electorate. In line with our argument, in 2017, the PVV presented a party list top-heavy with women MP candidates: the second and third spots on the list were both occupied by women. Party leader Wilders acknowledged that the placement of the women was part of a tactic to draw a broader electorate to the PVV. While the PVV did not increase the share of women candidates on the list (28 per cent in 2012 compared with 26 per cent in 2017), more women were placed higher on the list – in winnable positions – in 2017. As a result, the share of elected women MPs increased from 20 per cent in 2012 to 30 per cent in 2017.

Conclusions and avenues for future research

The study of gender, parties and issues has evolved over time from describing trends in women's support for parties to considering the causes and consequences of gender differences in party support. However, existing work has downplayed the role that parties can play in building and exploiting gender gaps. Our review highlights the tools with which parties appeal to women voters and explores the strategic considerations behind party decision-making related to the representation of women and their interests.

Numerous questions remain about how gender affects voter preferences and behaviour and, in turn, party strategy. However, our exploration of these questions is hindered by data availability and measurement. For instance, women have entered the labour force rapidly over recent decades, but we have seen a much smaller shift in the gender gap in household labour or in top leadership roles. Yet we lack cross-national time series data on support for specific policies that women in particular would benefit from like child care, shared parental leave, gender quotas and also policies related to violence against women. When the rare survey does ask questions about these topics, large gender gaps are often revealed. We cannot fully understand women's preferences, or how parties do or do not address them, without expanding data collection to a broader scope of issues. Similarly, to date, most work has focused on gender as a binary identity. Only recently has path-breaking research begun to measure gender as a continuum, offering new opportunities for understanding gendered lived experiences, attitudes and political behaviour using finer-grained measures of gender identification (e.g. Hatemi et al. 2012; McDermott 2016; Coffé 2019; Wängnerud, Solevid and Djerf-Pierre 2019; Solevid et al. 2021; Coffé and Bolzendahl 2021; Gidengil and Stolle 2021).

Future research should also explore intersections of gender and other forms of marginalisation such as race and ethnicity, class, religion, age and sexual orientation. Women are not a monolithic category, and differently situated groups of women have different issue priorities, policy positions and vote choices (Crenshaw 1991; Bejarano 2013; Bird et al. 2016; Junn and Masuoka 2019; Wolbrecht and Corder 2020). Consequently, parties may adapt certain strategies to attract specific groups of women. Following the idea of strategic descriptive representation, parties facing an underrepresentation of ethnic minority women in their electorate may increase the proportion of ethnic minority women. Focusing on changes in programmatic appeals, parties might choose to highlight a specific set of policy stances to attract underrepresented groups of women voters. For example, RRP parties could highlight conservative stances on ethical issues to attract conservative women voters often supporting Christian Democratic parties.

Finally, in line with most research on gender, our chapter has mostly focused on women. We introduced the theory of strategic descriptive representation arguing that electorally struggling parties with an underrepresentation of women among their voters will increase their proportion of women MPs to attract previously untapped women voters. An interesting avenue for future research would be to explore to what extent and how the argument of strategic descriptive representation holds for men. In other words, do parties that have an underrepresentation of men as voters and that are facing electoral decline increase their descriptive representation of men, with the hope of gaining men voters? In addition, many emerging issues that women are said to prefer also affect *men's* lives in important ways. For example, more countries are passing paid paternity leave and shared parental leave policies with dedicated fathers' quotas. More research is needed that considers men's attitudes towards these policies and the social pressures that prevent them from taking a more hands-on role in caring (e.g. Tanquerel and Grau Grau 2020), in order to make real progress towards gender equality in the future.

Note

1 Using historical data on voter turnout, Morgan-Collins and Teele's 2018 study, however, challenges this wisdom, concluding that women's suffrage generally favoured left-leaning parties, and this was driven by lower and middle-class women.

References

Abendschön, S. and Steinmetz, S. (2014) 'The gender gap in voting revisited: Women's party preferences in a European context', *Social Politics: International Studies in Gender, State and Society*, 21(2), p315–344.

Abou-Chadi, T. (2016) 'Niche party success and mainstream party policy shifts – How green and radical right parties differ in their impact', *British Journal of Political Science*, 46(2), p417–436.

Akkerman, T. (2015) 'Gender and the radical right in Western Europe: A comparative analysis of policy agendas', *Patterns of Prejudice*, 49(1–2), p37–60.

Alexander, A.C., Bågenholm, A. and Charron, N. (2020) 'Are women more likely to throw the rascals out? The mobilizing effect of social service spending on female voters', *Public Choice*, 184(3), p235–61.

Barnes, T.D. and Cassese, E.C. (2017) 'American party women: A look at the gender gap within parties', *Political Research Quarterly*, 70(1), p127–141.

Baldez, L. (2004) 'Elected bodies: The gender quota law for legislative candidates in Mexico', *Legislative Studies Quarterly*, 29(2), p231–258.

Bale, T., Green-Pedersen, C. and Krouwel, A. (2010) 'If you can't beat them, join them? Explaining social democratic responses to the challenge from the populist radical right in Western Europe', *Political Studies*, 58(3), p410–426.

Banducci, S. and Karp, J. (2000) 'Gender, leadership and choice in multiparty systems', *Political Research Quarterly*, 53(4), p815–848.

Bejarano, C.E. (2013) *The Latino gender gap in U.S. politics*. New York: Routledge.

Bird, K., Jackson, S., McGregor, M.R., Moore, A. and Stephenson, L. (2016) 'Sex (and ethnicity) in the city: Affinity voting in the 2014 Toronto Mayoral Election', *Canadian Journal of Political Science/Revue Canadienne de science politique*, 49(2), p359–383.

Box-Steffensmeier, J.M., de Boef, S. and Lin, T. (2004) 'The dynamics of the partisan gender gap', *American Political Science Review*, 98(3), p515–528.

Box-Steffensmeier, J.M., Kimball, D., Meinke, S. and Tate, K. (2003) 'The effects of political representation on the electoral advantages of house incumbents', *Political Research Quarterly*, 56(3), p259–70.

Bush, S. (2011) 'International politics and the spread of quotas for women in legislatures', *International Organization*, 65(1), p103–137.

Bush, S. and Gao, E. (2017) 'Small tribes, big gains: The strategic uses of gender quotas in the Middle East', *Comparative Politics*, 49(2), p149–167.

Campbell, R. (2016) 'Representing women voters: The role of the gender gap and the response of political parties', *Party Politics*, 22(5), p587–97.

Caul, M. (1999) 'Women's representation in parliament. The role of political parties', *Party Politics*, 5(1), p79–98.

Childs, S. and Webb, P. (2012) *Sex, gender and the conservative party: From iron lady to kitten heels*. Basingstoke: Palgrave.

Coffé, H. (2018) 'Gender and the radical right', in Rydgren, J. (ed.) *The Oxford handbook of the radical right*. Oxford: Oxford University Press, pp. 200–211.

Coffé, H. (2019) 'Gender, gendered personality traits and radical right populist voting', *Politics*, 39(2) p170–185.

Coffé, H. and Bolzendahl, C. (2021) 'Are all politics masculine? Gender socialized personality traits and diversity in political engagement', *European Journal of Politics and Gender*, 4(1), p113–133.

Crenshaw, K. (1991) 'Mapping the margins: Intersectionality, identity politics, and violence against women of color', *Stanford Law Review*, 43(6), p1241–1299.

de Lange, S.L. and Mügge, L. (2015) 'Gender and right-wing populism in the low countries: Ideological variations across parties and time', *Patterns of Prejudice*, 49(1–2), p61–80.

Downs, A. (1957) *An Economic theory of democracy*. New York: Harper Collins.

Duverger, M. (1955) *The political role of women*. Unesco.

Eagle, M. and Lovenduski, J. (1998) *High time or high tide for labour women* (No. 585). London: Fabian Society.

Farris, S. (2017) *In the name of women's rights: The rise of femonationalism*. Durham: Duke University Press.

Gelb, J. (1989) *Feminism and politics: A comparative perspective*. Ann Anbor: University of California Press.

Gidengil, E., Blais, A., Nadeau, R. and Nevitte, N. (2003) 'Women to the left? Gender differences in political beliefs and policy preferences', in Tremblay, M. and Trimble, J. (eds.) *Women and electoral politics in Canada*. Don Mills: Oxford University Press, pp. 140–159.

Gidengil, E. and Stolle, D. (2021) 'Comparing self-categorisation approaches to measuring gender identity', *European Journal of Politics and Gender*, 4(1), p31–50.

Gidron, N. and Hall, P.A. (2017) 'The politics of social status: Economic and cultural roots of the populist right', *British Journal of Sociology*, 68, pS57–S84.

Giger, N. (2009) 'Towards a modern gender gap in Europe? A comparative analysis of voting behavior in 12 countries', *Social Science Journal*, 46, p474–492;

Gilligan, C. (1982) *In a different voice*. Cambridge: Harvard University Press.

Givens, T. (2004) 'The radical right gender gap', *Comparative Political Studies*, 37, p30–54.

Han, K. (2015) 'The impact of radical right-wing parties on the positions of mainstream parties regarding multiculturalism', *West European Politics*, 38(3), p557–576.

Harteveld, E. and Ivarsflaten, E. (2018) 'Why women avoid the radical right: Internalized norms and policy reputations', *British Journal of Political Science*, 48(2), p369–384.

Harteveld, E., van der Brug, W., Dahlberg, S. and Kokkonen, A. (2015) 'The gender gap in radical-right voting: examining the demand side in Western and Eastern Europe', *Patterns of Prejudice*, 49(1–2), p103–134.

Hatemi, P.K., McDermott, R., Bailey, J.M. and Martin, N.G. (2012) 'The different effects of gender and sex on vote choice', *Political Research Quarterly*, 65(1), p76–92.

Huber, E. and Stephens, J.D. (2001) *Development and crisis of the welfare state: Parties and policies in global markets*. Chicago: University of Chicago Press.

Immerzeel, T., Coffé, H. and van der Lippe, T. (2015) 'Explaining the gender gap in radical right voting: A cross-national investigation in 12 Western-European countries', *Comparative European Politics*, 13(2), p263 286.

Inglehart, R. and Norris, P. (2000) 'The developmental theory of the gender gap: Women's and men's voting behavior in global perspective', *International Political Science Review*, 21(4), p441–463.

Inglehart, R. and Norris, P. (2003) *Rising tide: Gender equality and cultural change around the world*. Cambridge: Cambridge University Press.

Iversen, T. and Rosenbluth, F. (2006) 'The political economy of gender: Explaining cross-national variation in the gender division of labor and the gender voting gap', *American Journal of Political Science*, 50(1), p1–19.

Jelen, T.G., Thomas, S. and Wilcox, C. (1994) 'The gender gap in comparative perspective: Gender differences in abstract ideology in Western Europe', *European Journal of Political Research*, 25(2), p171–186.

Junn, J. and Masuoka, N. (2019) 'The gender gap is a race gap: Women voters in U.S. Presidential Elections', *Perspectives on Politics*, 18(4), p1135–45.

Keith, D. and Verge, T. (2018) 'Nonmainstream left parties and women's representation in Western Europe', *Party Politics*, 24(4), p397–409.

Kitschelt, H. (1995) *The radical right in Western Europe. A comparative analysis*. Ann Arbor: The University of Michigan Press.

Kittilson, M.C. (2011) 'Women, parties and platforms in post-industrial democracies', *Party Politics*, 17(1), p66–92.

Knutsen, O. (2001) 'Social class, sector employment, and gender as party cleavages in the Scandinavian countries: A comparative longitudinal study, 1970–95', *Scandinavian Political Studies*, 24(4), p311–350.

Lilliefeldt, E. (2012) 'Party and gender in Western Europe revisited: A fuzzy-set qualitative comparative analysis of gender-balanced parliamentary parties', *Party Politics*, 18(2), p193–214.

Lipset, S.M. (1960) *Political man: The social bases of politics*. New York: Doubleday.

Listhaug, O. (1985) 'The gender gap in Norwegian voting behaviour', *Scandinavian Political Studies*, 8(3), p187–206.

Maguire, L. (2007) 'The conservative party and women's suffrage. Suffrage outside suffragism', in Boussahba-Bravard, M. (ed.) *Women's vote in Britain, 1880–1914*. London: Palgrave McMillan, pp. 52–76.

Manza, J. and Brooks, C. (1998) 'The gender gap in U.S. presidential elections: When? Why? Implications?' *American Journal of Sociology*, 103(5), p1235–1266.

Mayer, N. (2013) 'From Jean-Marie to Marine Le Pen: Electoral change on the far right', *Parliamentary Affairs*, 66, p160–178.

Mayer, N. (2015) 'The closing gap of the radical right gender gap in France?' *French Politics*, 13(4), p391–414.

McDermott, M. (2016) *Masculinity, femininity, and American political behavior*. Oxford: Oxford University Press.

Meguid, B.M. (2005) 'Competition between unequals: The role of mainstream party strategy in Niche Party Success', *American Political Science Review*, 99(3), p347–359.

Meguid, B.M. (2008) *Party competition between unequals*. New York: Cambridge University Press.

Meguid, B.M. (2022). 'Adaptation or inflexibility? Niche party responsiveness to policy competition, with evidence from regionalist parties', *European Journal of Political Research*. doi.org/10.1111/1475-6765.12540

Morgan, J. (2015) 'Gender and the Latin American voter', in Carlin, R.E., Singer, M.M. and Zechmeister, E.J. (eds.) *The Latin American voter: Pursuing representation and accountability in challenging contexts*. Ann Arbor: University of Michigan Press, pp. 143–168.

Morgan, K. (2013) 'Path shifting of the welfare state: Electoral competition and the expansion of work-family policies in Western Europe', *World Politics*, 65(1), p73–115.

Morgan-Collins, M. and Teele, D. (2018) 'Revisiting the gender voting gap in the era of women's suffrage', Working Paper. Available from: http://dawnteele.weebly.com/uploads/2/4/9/3/24931233/mmc_and_teele_10.17.pdf

Mudde, C. (2007) *Populist radical right parties in Europe*. Cambridge: Cambridge University Press.

Mudde, C. and Kaltwasser, C. (2015) 'Vox populi or vox masculini? Populism and gender in Northern Europe and South America', *Patterns of Prejudice*, 49(1–2), p16–36.

Murray, R., Krook, M. and Opello, K. (2012) 'Why are gender quotas adopted? Party pragmatism and parity in France', *Political Research Quarterly*, 65(3), p529–543.

Nielsen, B. (2020) 'Women's authority in patriarchal social movements: The case of female Salafi preachers', *American Journal of Political Science*, 64(1), p52–66.

O'Brien, D. (2015) 'Rising to the top: Gender, political performance, and party leadership in parliamentary democracies', *American Journal of Political Science*, 59(4), p1022–1039.

Oskarson, M. (1995) 'Gender gaps in Nordic voting behavior', in Karvonen, L. and Selle, P. (eds.) *Women in Nordic politics: Closing the gap*. Hanover: Dartmouth, pp. 59–81

Plutzer, E. and Zipp, J. (1996) Identity politics, partisanship and voting for women candidates, *Public Opinion Quarterly*, 60(1), p30–57.

Reynolds, A. (1999) 'Women in the legislatures and executives of the world: Knocking at the highest glass ceiling', *World Politics*, 51(4), p547–572.

Rippeyoung, P. (2007) 'When women are right: The influence of gender, work and values on European far-right party support', *International Feminist Journal of Politics*, 9(3), p379–397.

Solevid, M., Wängnerud, L., Djerf-Pierre, M. and Markstedt, E. (2021) 'Gender gaps in political attitudes revisited', *European Journal of Politics and Gender*, 4(1), p93–112

Spierings, N. and Zaslove, A. (2015) 'Gendering the vote for populist radical-right parties', *Patterns of Prejudice*, 49(1–2), p135–162.

Studlar, D., McAllister, I. and Hayes, B. (1998) Explaining the gender gap in voting', *Social Science Quarterly*, 79(4), p779–798.

Tanquerel, S. and Grau-Grau, M. (2020) 'Unmasking work-family balance barriers and strategies among working fathers in the workplace', *Organization*, 27(5), p680–700.

Teele, D. (2018) *Forging the franchise: The political origins of the women's vote*. Princeton: Princeton University Press.

Valdini, M. (2019) *The inclusion calculation*. Oxford: Oxford University Press.

Wängnerud, L. (2009) 'Women in parliaments: Descriptive and substantive representation', *Annual Review of Political Science*, 12, p51–69.

Wängnerud, L., Solevid, M. and Djerf-Pierre, M. (2019) 'Moving beyond categorical gender in studies of risk aversion and anxiety', *Politics and Gender*, 15(4), p826–50.

Weeks, A.C. (2018) 'Why are gender quota laws adopted by men? The role of inter-and intraparty competition', *Comparative Political Studies*, 51(14), p1935–1973.

Weeks, A.C. (2019) 'Quotas and party priorities: Direct and indirect effects of quota laws', *Political Research Quarterly*, 72(4), p849–862.

Weeks, A.C. (2022) *Making gender salient: From gender quota laws to policy*. Cambridge: Cambridge University Press.

Weeks, A.C., Meguid, B.M., Kittilson, M.C. and Coffé, H. (2022) 'When do Männerparteien elect women? Radical right populist parties and strategic descriptive representation'. *American Political Science Review*, p1–18. doi.org/10.1017/S000305542200010

Wolbrecht, C. and Corder, J.K. (2020) *A century of votes for women: American Elections since suffrage*. Cambridge: Cambridge University Press.

28
POST-CONFLICT POLITICAL PARTIES

Carrie Manning and Gyda M. Sindre

The study of political party formation and party change by former armed opposition groups was sparked in large part by the onset of the liberal peacebuilding era, in which international actors, notably the United Nations, embraced the view that lasting peace could successfully be built on multi-party politics. Since the end of the Cold War, civil war endings have more often than not been accompanied by the introduction or expansion of party-based electoral politics and the provisions for armed groups to transform into political parties. This shift from bullets to ballots theoretically allows for wartime divisions to be reflected and integrated into formal institution-level politics and party systems.

In this chapter, we focus on these *post-rebel parties*, defined as political parties that are formed out of rebel groups after civil wars, usually as part of an externally led or sanctioned peace process built on the establishment or expansion of party based electoral politics. Across the globe, political parties such as Sinn Fein in Northern Ireland, the African National Congress (ANC) in South Africa, the Democratic Party of Kosovo (PDK), the Farabundo Martí National Liberation Front (FMLN) and the Communist Party of Nepal Maoists (CPN-M) have emerged as mainstream political parties and stable electoral contenders. Indeed, more than 50 per cent of rebel groups that signed agreements after 1990 have transformed into political parties and as many as 60 per cent of these 'post-rebel parties' have competed in all subsequent post-war elections (Manning and Smith 2019). These are surprising outcomes, given limited experience with democracy in many of these countries, not to mention the bellicose backgrounds of actors who would become significant peacetime political actors. We include only those post-rebel parties that compete in elections, thus excluding rebel groups that formed one-party regimes immediately after the war.[1]

Drawing on a growing research body on post-rebel political parties (e.g. Manning 2008; Ishiyama 2016; Manning and Smith 2016, 2019; Curtis and Sindre 2019), we discuss the varying dynamics of post-conflict party politics. Until recently, research on political parties in conflict-prone and divided societies or conflict-affected countries has tended to focus on institutional reform and party regulation (e.g. Reilly and Nordlund 2008), overlooking how these parties originated, developed, and governed in the aftermath of civil war. A growing research body on post-rebel parties suggests that electoral participation can provide a durable basis for shifting conflict from the battlefield into formal institutional-level politics, irrespective of whether this translates into fully fledged democracy or not (e.g. Ishiyama and Marshall 2015; Manning and Smith 2016). Importantly, the notion that if rebel groups can channel their interests into party politics, this will forge more peaceful relations across wartime divides, has also become increasingly prevalent as a starting point for peacebuilding practices. Not only are provisions for political party formation a central aspect of peace negotiations, but a plethora of international NGOs and the United Nations have expanded their programmes to include attention to party building and party support in post-war societies.

We argue that the study of party formation and development after civil wars also brings new perspectives to the field of party research. In the study of historical development of European party systems, Caramani (2004) notes that well-structured party systems require well-structured or at least coherent parties – parties whose leaders see electoral competition as an important route to securing and consolidating power. This competition is in turn structured by macro-historical processes, like industrialisation, that put a premium on and make the state a prize worth competing over. Arguably, sustained armed mobilisation and subsequent post-conflict peacebuilding, including the resources brought to this endeavour by powerful outside actors, can create conditions that have similar effects on the behaviour of ambitious politicians.

A focus on post-rebel parties bring attention to large number of contemporary democracies emerging out of civil wars, which have often been overlooked in contemporary party research. Arguably, the prevalence of rebel party formation as a global phenomenon challenges the notion that these political parties should be treated as exceptions or as niche. A focus on post-rebel parties provides a unique opportunity to test the general applicability of established theories of party formation and party system institutionalisation that have been developed primarily on the basis of political parties in advanced democracies, and only secondarily on parties in new and emerging democracies.

This chapter is organised as follows. First, we explore the challenges of transforming from armed groups to political parties including their organisational adaptation to electoral participation. Second, we address the questions related to what types of political parties former armed groups become and the effects of electoral participation on parties. Third, we engage with the debates about whether these parties have 'moderated' and adapted to peacetime politics, specifically linked to the tradition the inclusion-moderation thesis, that is, the notion that electoral participation triggers radical parties to moderate and adjust their agendas to broaden the range of supporters (e.g. Przeworski 1980; Kalyvas 1998; Tezcur 2010). The conclusion identifies questions for future research and identifies relevant datasets on post-war party politics.

Organisational dimensions: from armed group to political party

One of the main strands of research on post-conflict political parties seeks to understand the process of organisational transformation from armed military organisation to political party, as a means to achieve political change via peaceful means (e.g. Manning 2007; de Zeeuw 2008; Ishiyama and Batta 2011). While, traditionally, rebel groups are often seen as xenophobic, secretive and introverted, as they have evolved in the war environment to maximise their military capacity through a combination of intimidation, compliance, and popular mobilisation (e.g. Weinstein 2007; de Zeeuw 2008), the fast-growing scholarship on rebel group successor parties has paid close attention to the non-militaristic, or civilian/political aspects of rebel behaviour during war to explain their relative success as post-war political parties (e.g. Sindre and Söderstrom 2016). Clearly, the organisational demands that come with running military operations are very different from those required for campaigning for elections and accumulating governance, yet it is useful to highlight the many similarities between rebel groups and political parties as particularly important for explaining rebel to party transitions. Berti (2013, 11–12), for instance, notes that both are (1) non-state actors that serve as intermediary institutions between individuals and the state; (2) political and social organisations with leaders and members that adhere to an organisational hierarchy; (3) formed with the goals of seeking specific political, economic, and social change – and sometimes radical change; and (4) political organisations that have invested resources in political survival. Yet scholars have warned against seeing the evolution from armed group to political party as a foregone conclusion. Not all rebel groups opt for the party route, and even when they do their electoral survival cannot be guaranteed by peacebuilding interventions.

Organisational legacies and party building

Insights from the parties-as-organisations literature have been important for identifying convertible 'organisational capital', whether in the form of ideational appeals or organisational capacities for rebel group successor parties (e.g. Manning 2008; Ishiyama and Batta 2011; Speight and Wittig 2017). Manning and Smith (2019) find that a stronger electoral performance by post-rebel parties is positively correlated with prior political experience. Some rebel groups, such as the Revolutionary United Front for an Independent East Timor (Fretilin), the Communist Party of Nepal-Maoists (CPN-M) and the Serb Democratic Party (SDS) in Bosnia Herzegovina (BiH) originated as political parties only to develop military wings later during the conflict (Sindre and Söderström 2016). Other groups such as the FMLN in El Salvador and the African National Congress (ANC) in South Africa originated as anti-regime protest movements prior to taking up arms.

Other rebel groups have developed well-functioning 'political wings' during war that resemble autonomous political parties and, as Dresden (2017) notes, rebel organisations that have developed a political wing in wartime do better in post-conflict politics than political parties without such legacies. Some rebel groups have institutionalised a hybrid model in which political wings operate as formal political parties that are invited to participate in national-level elections. Prominent examples of such hybrid movements include Hezbollah in Lebanon, Hamas in Palestine, and Sinn Feín, the political wing of the Provisional Irish Republican Army (IRA) in Northern Ireland (Berti 2013; Whiting 2017). In these instances, organisational strength combined with strong links to their constituencies have translated into electoral support and thus awarded these groups significant legitimacy and formal powers to govern and shape policy even without a peace settlement. While these cases are anomalies, when it comes to their formal inclusion into electoral politics without the demobilisation of their armed wings, other rebel groups also strategise to develop their civilian capacities that otherwise correlate positively with their post-war electoral success. However, as Ishiyama and Widmeier (2020, 42–43) show, 'bureaucratisation' in itself does not sufficiently explain post-war electoral success. Rather, where the rebel group relied on civilian support during the civil war, such as taxation, rather than more extractive forms of interaction, they were more likely to do well electorally as political parties after the war ended (Ishiyama and Widmeier 2020).

Rebel groups often have sustained transnational ties and sponsorship that can set their successor parties apart from conventional political parties. As Marshall (2019) finds, rebel groups with foreign sponsorship are more likely to participate in post-war elections and do well in these elections than those without such forms of sponsorship. Effects of transnational ties are also reflected in activism among exiled leaders and diaspora networks. For instance, secessionist movements, such as the Kosovo Liberation Army (KLA), the Free Aceh Movement (GAM) in Indonesia, and Fretilin in East Timor, set up diplomatic missions abroad that functioned as political offices, as the main contact point for international mediators, and as a base for the development of civilian political capacities. Leaders of these offices often take on prominent leadership positions after the war ends (Sindre 2018; Marshall 2019). Similarly, rebel organisations that originated from pre-war political parties have a civilian support base as well as the organisational know-how to (re)-build the political party after the war. As noted by Manning and Smith (2016), the leaders of these parties are more likely to feel confident in their ability to compete in post-war elections. The idea that rebel groups' organisational endowments affect their electoral success later on also finds support in the political parties literature (e.g. Ishiyama 2001; Grzymala-Busse 2002; van Biezen 2003).

As is clear from the previous discussion, wartime organisational structures have lasting implications for how well parties do in post-war elections. Scholars have increasingly focused attention on analysing the enduring consequences of rebel group political inclusion, pointing to the difficulties involved in turning former armed groups into peaceful democratic political parties (Sindre and Söderström 2016; Wittig 2016). This raises a set of new questions also relevant to the wider field of party scholarship: are rebel group successor parties different from other 'new' or 'established' political parties that mobilise within the same context? Some indications point to important differences and similarities.

Importantly, political parties formed by rebel groups after a civil war come into post-war politics with certain organisational advantages vis-à-vis other political parties, thus challenging many of the common assumptions, such as parties being weakly founded or lacking in administrative capital, raised by the literature about new parties in new democracies (e.g. Randall and Svåsand 2002). In many countries in which multi-party politics form the foundation of the peace settlement, there is little prior experience with democracy and thus few experienced competitors. Opposition parties are generally weak and under-resourced, and they often have little reach beyond major urban areas. Rebel groups, by contrast, tend to have geographically extensive organisational networks beyond urban centres and name recognition. The strength of such vertical ties linking the rebel organisation with their social base, and the horizontal ties that bind the group's leadership, have implications for their performance in wartime (e.g. Manning 2007; Staniland 2014; Lyons 2016b; Sindre 2016b). These parties also enjoy the benefits of strong and durable partisan identity and 'hardened' partisan boundaries leading to stronger elite cohesion that make it possible to impose unity (Levitsky and Way 2013; Muriaas, Rakner and Skage 2016).

The context of negotiated settlements where there are no clear victors also differentiates rebel group successor parties from other 'new' political parties as well as from social movements that evolve into political parties (see Chapter 8). Importantly, the inclusion of armed actors in peace talks gives them an opportunity to shape electoral rules and other institutions in their favour (e.g. Manning 2007, 2008). Following the Good Friday Agreement in Northern Ireland, republican leaders retained considerable leverage over the power sharing arrangements and electoral rules (Whiting 2017). Settlements often include explicit provisions for rebels to form political parties (Söderberg Kovacs and Hatz 2016). Even where the political settlements do not explicitly guarantee pre-eminence to a post-rebel party, in many post-war settings, the former rebels emerge as the most well known and cohesive of the opposition groups. In some cases, post-rebel parties also received a major boost from international actors whose active participation in the peace process was essential to the success of that process. Often such support served to bolster party leaders facing internal challenges from rivals who might seek to spoil the peace settlement by, for example, opting out of elections (Manning 2008; Matanock 2017). In some cases, peace settlements rested on political arrangements that 'froze' the balance of power between incumbents and the armed opposition group it fought against (Manning 2008). This was particularly true in cases like Kosovo and Northern Ireland, where claims for self-determination by armed opposition groups were supported and enshrined in peace settlements brokered by powerful international actors. It was also true in cases where the peace process counted on heavy and sustained support from such actors, as in Mozambique and El Salvador (e.g. Manning 2008; Matanock 2017). Thus, many rebel groups have clear incentives to transform into political parties merely to secure the means of survival.

However, advantages created by the political settlement, or even organisational legacies that give post-rebel parties a leg up on the competitions, are not immutable. They tend to dissipate over time forcing parties to accommodate and adapt their organisation in order to remain politically relevant. Ultimately, drawing on insights from the literature on party change, scholars of former rebel parties have sought to explain the conditions under which these parties adapt, the extent of adaptation, and the relative costs to their survival. Moreover, bridging with insights into the field of peace research, scholars and practitioners are also concerned with when parties do not undergo significant change: What are the costs to long-term peace, stability, and democracy if parties continue to mobilise around wartime cleavages and divisions (Curtis and Sindre 2019; Manning, Smith and Tuncel 2022)?

Rebel group inclusion and party system development after civil war

While there is some early work suggesting that civil wars have a potential 'freezing' effect on the shape of party systems in historical cases such as Finland, Spain or Ireland (Gallagher 1985; Alapuro 1988), the link between civil wars and party system development in more contemporary cases has not received substantial scholarly attention. In one exception, Ishiyama (2014) finds that the bloodier the civil war, the more likely the emergence of dominant party systems. Research on how post-rebel parties adapt to electoral politics – and that identifies factors that explain their institutionalisation – provides some insights into party system development. However, this is an emerging field that requires more in-depth data generation and theorisation before causal links can be established. Furthermore, an understanding of how parties encapsulate existing cleavages, such as ethnic divisions, forged or hardened during war, is therefore critical. What is more, the extent to which parties adapt or change their ideological profiles also becomes important both in how they impact on peace (e.g. dampening divisions) and by the way in which they might push for specific outcomes. The next section discusses the impact of electoral participation on post-rebel parties, followed by a discussion about party identity and ideologies.

Effects of electoral participation on post-rebel parties

Competing in elections presents parties with challenges to their organisational competencies. Specifically, elections require parties to perform a specific set of tasks, develop routines, find people to run as candidates, and ensure that those candidates remain loyal and consistent with the party's values. As elections impose new challenges on parties, post-rebel parties must often re-examine, and sometimes reformulate, their links to voters. They must also retain competent and loyal cadres. During the first post-war elections, many post-rebel parties do well – compared to other parties – at the polls, riding on a wave of popularity anchored in name recognition and symbolism of being liberation fighters and of securing a peace deal. However, as post-rebel parties face growing competition from other parties, this wave of popularity often dwindles over time, forcing parties to adapt their organisation and strategies. This was the case for the Kosovo Democratic Party (PDK), the successor party of the Kosovo Liberation Army (KLA), which was the largest party when the armed conflict ended. It secured around 34 per cent of the votes in the 2007 elections but its vote share dropped to around 20 per cent within a decade (Beha 2017). Similarly, FRETILIN in Timor Leste and the Aceh Party in Indonesia's Aceh province were on route to becoming dominant parties after their first and second post-war elections, only to see the vote share decrease dramatically forcing the parties to significantly restructure their organisation and redefine their links to voters (see Sindre 2016a; Aspinall et al. 2018).

Strategic adaptation can take place along many fronts. Some of these are specific to the post-war scenario and concern integration with broader peacebuilding agendas. One important factor shaping post-war party governance that is different from other political parties pertains to how the groups relate to their former rank and file (Sindre 2016b). While relying on veterans and ex-combatants may be useful as a rallying point around election time, continued dependence on this group may also alienate other support bases that are important for electoral support. In Kosovo, veterans provide a stable support base to the leaders of the two main post-rebel parties, the PDK and the AAK (the Alliance for the Future of Kosovo), but these parties' popularity also declined following allegations of corruption where ties to illegal veterans' networks were at the forefront (Tadić and Elbasani 2018).

Adapting electoral appeals in response to electoral competition often poses a threat to the party's leadership. It is quite common for post-rebel parties to split following heightened intra-party competition, often taking the form of internal challenges to incumbent leaders (the party hierarchy) by those who have found a new power base through their elected position (the 'party-in-office'). As armed groups transform into political parties, there are always tensions dividing the leadership and the rank-and-file fighters involving leaders who often seek a way to gain power and the rank and file who fought the war for ideological or 'ideational' reasons (Ishiyama 2015). One example is the split within the Communist Party of Nepal (Maoists), the largest party in the Nepalese national assembly that led to the resumption of irregular warfare in 2012, which did not come to an end until 2021. In this case, the breakaway faction rejected the 2006 peace settlement accusing the signatories of selling out on the revolution.[2]

While splits and factionalism within major political parties are generally considered minor threats to democratic stability, when post-rebel parties split, it may destabilise the entire peace process. Even when factionalism does not lead to resurgence of war, it can affect a group's stock of ideational and organisational capital. For example, as post-rebel parties split or merge with other groups, retain or alternate leaders, or win elected office, they may dilute the credibility of their appeals and devise new internal decision-making rules, and so on. For instance, in Kosovo the PDK has experienced multiple splits along the lines of regional military commanders, including the formation of the AAK under the leadership of the KLA commander of eastern Kosovo, Ramush Haradinaj. However, a decline in electoral support to all post-rebel parties in Kosovo vis-à-vis other newcomers pressured the post-rebel parties to run as a wartime alliance, reverting to the wartime legacies as a primary mobilising tool. In many instances, parties may rely overly on high-profile personalities, which in the case of post-rebel parties will usually be wartime military commanders.

Like many other political parties, post-rebel parties have frequently turned to clientelism in response to the demands of electoral politics (e.g. Duverger 1963; Janda 1980), One example, cited earlier, was Fretilin's relationship with veterans in Timor Leste. The FMLN in El Salvador also gradually replaced their ideological commitment with clientelism, particularly after it won executive power following the 2009 election, which it held until 2014. The implications for the party's electoral appeal have not been positive (Sprenkels 2018). While research into these organisational dynamics of post-rebel parties remains nascent, evidence suggests that many post-rebel parties remain personalistic and/or clientelist, while a minority have developed some form of organisational thickness and/or intra-party democracy (Sindre 2016a; Manning and Smith 2019; Ishiyama and Basnet 2020).

Moderation and adaptation: structuring political cleavages

Like other parties, post-rebel parties' leaders aim to achieve electoral gains while minimising the need to make risky organisational changes. Post-rebel parties often seek to preserve cleavages that helped them mobilise support during wartime. This may end up entrenching stable cleavage structures that set a predictable agenda for competition and stabilise post-war politics into predictable patterns. And this in turn may offer useful signals to potential new contenders about the kinds of appeals that are likely to succeed – thus emboldening them to invest in electoral politics.

Recent research on post-war party politics has addressed the issue of cleavage structures by focusing attention on the ideological dimensions of party politics and specifically the continued relevance of wartime ideologies. A central question concerns whether former armed groups that enter politics moderate and adapt their ideology and programmatic profiles to peacetime politics – and ultimately the relative impact of such processes of adaptation on the quality of peace and democracy. It is expected that the extent to which parties moderate will have implications for post-war political stability and the quality of democracy. At the same time, as Ishiyama (2019) points out, there is a risk that if parties move too far beyond their original base, they become less relevant to their constituencies, which may further reinforce notions of exclusion that underpinned the war in the first place. Conversely, if parties do not moderate but continue to mobilise around deeply divisive issues such as ethnic supremacy or secession, this might derail and destabilise the peace process in the long run (Sindre 2019).

Research has also identified a number of external and internal factors that interact to help explain why some post-rebel parties opt to moderate while others do not. First, some groups are strategically well positioned from the outset to shape their environments – through a combination of circumstances of the peace settlement and their own 'convertible capacities'. Thus equipped, these parties then act as dynamic and strategic shapers of their political environments, actively exploiting and reproducing the conditions that initially played to their advantage. A critical resource for these parties is the wartime cleavage. This cleavage is what enabled them to mobilise support during the war, helped shape the organisation's competencies and ideational capital, and thus determines the party's dependence on external actors. When wartime cleavages remain politically salient, it reduces the extent to which parties must adapt their organisational structures and routines, devise new voter appeals, and seek to broaden their appeal to new groups of voters. Given these challenges, the initial expectation of parties in general is that their leaders will seek to maintain the mobilising appeals they have relied on for as long as possible, thus minimising the costs of adaptation (Harmel and Janda 1994). However, political parties in countries coming out of civil war are often subject to strict, externally imposed regulations that challenge this presumption (e.g. Reilly and Nordlund 2008). For instance, the premises set out in peace agreements often place specific constraints on the autonomy of political parties including their ideological and programmatic profiles. For instance, several countries prohibit parties from mobilising for secession. This was one of the conditions set out in the peace settlement between the Free Aceh Movement (GAM) and the Government of Indonesia, that is, that the rebel group successor party had to formally abandon their original goal of secession. Consequently, as they joined competitive party politics, the former rebels were forced to significantly reframe their mobilising appeal including their programmatic profile (e.g. endorsing regionalism over secession) and party symbols such as flags and emblems (see Sindre 2019). In contrast, in other contexts, post-war political parties are able to continue mobilising around the main wartime cleavage. This has been the case in Northern Ireland where, following the signing of the Good Friday Agreement, after the demobilisation of its armed wing, Sinn Fein was not required to abandon its goal of republicanism and unification with the consequence that the end of armed conflict did not mean an automatic restructuring of the main wartime cleavage (Whiting 2018).

Certainly, the circumstances that prevail at the onset of post-war politics do not remain static, and post-war parties, as with any other party, might opt to redefine their ideological premise later on. This shift can go either way, that is, it can instigate further *moderation* or even promote *re-radicalisation*. In Bosnia Herzegovina, the Dayton Agreement had awarded the Office of the High Representative, the international body set up to oversee the implementation of the peace agreement, unprecedented powers to intervene in the internal affairs of political parties. The successor party of the Serb army, the Serb Democratic Party (SDS), thus underwent a significant de-radicalisation on issues concerning ethnic identity. However, as Sindre (2019) finds, the process of de-radicalisation on the core conflict cleavage corresponded to a fall in vote share that forced the post-rebel party into opposition in 2006. This corresponded with the rise of a new Serb party, the Alliance for Independent Social Democrats (SNSD) and its leader Milorad Dodik, described by most observers as a hard-line ultra-nationalist, which has intensified debates over the identity of the Bosnian state and in particular the future direction of the Serb entity (Republika Srpska). Thus, while post-rebel parties in Bosnia Herzegovina underwent initial de-radicalisation on ethnic issues, the party system remained fragmented along ethnic lines. With sufficient numbers of voters retaining radical views, more than two decades after the end of the civil war in Bosnia Herzegovina, political parties have yet again become drivers of ethnic outbidding and divisive cleavage structures of the war have become revitalised (Sindre 2019).

Set against this backdrop, over time electoral competition may lead to a shift in the central cleavages of the political system, requiring all parties to adapt. When this happens, the leaders of the more consistent parties, as exemplified by the SDS in Bosnia, strategically work to restore the wartime cleavage to primacy. One of the tools post-rebel parties use to reproduce the wartime cleavage is precisely to remind voters and political rivals of the party's capacity to deploy violence. Indeed, in Mozambique, RENAMO returned to arms after nearly two decades of peace in an attempt to do just that. However, both RENAMO and the government have taken pains to ensure that violence did not prevent the country's fifth consecutive national elections in 2014 (Manning 2022). Other external factors might also lead wartime cleavages to resurface. For instance, in Northern Ireland, Brexit and the Northern Ireland Protocol have revived debates about the Good Friday Agreement.

Conclusion and avenues for future research

This chapter has focused on the emerging field of post-war party politics, which bridges fields of party research, peace and conflict studies and comparative politics more broadly. Since the end of the Cold War, the end of armed conflict has more often than not been accompanied by the introduction or expansion of party-based electoral politics and the provisions for armed groups to transform into political parties. As we have discussed throughout this chapter, this shift from bullets to ballots theoretically allows for wartime divisions to be reflected and integrated into formal institution-level politics and party systems. The study of rebel group to political party transformation thus has the potential implications for the study of party politics and associated processes of political mobilisation, governance, and democratisation after war and beyond. Chief among these is the question of whether parties that are only instrumentally committed to democracy can promote democratisation. Electoral politics can prompt tactical and strategic changes in parties without bringing substantive change. As has been highlighted in our discussion, post-rebel parties have often become effective electoral actors, committed to electoral democracy, without discarding appeals to voters that may be considered divisive or radical. Moreover, these parties often anchor party systems that are quite stable and even institutionalised, even if, as organisations, these parties are often weak and fragmented.

There is much future promise attached to this research agenda. Specifically, a number of new datasets promise to enable further discoveries into post-rebel parties as political actors that can aid future studies in this field. Daly's *Civil War Successor Party (CWSP) dataset* tracks decisions by post-rebel parties to remilitarise or demilitarise after participating in transitional elections (Daly 2020). Manning, Tuncel and Smith's (2022) *Post-Rebel Electoral Parties (PESP) dataset* promises insight into the long-term dynamics of rebel to party transformation. It provides longitudinal data, for all post-war legislative elections, on the electoral participation and performance of every rebel group that formed a political party after a civil war that ended in the post-Cold War era (1990 or later). Braithewaite and Cunningham (2020) explore the organisational roots of rebel groups while Matanock (2017) tracks the use of elections by militarised groups as either an alternative or a complement to violence. Huang's (2016) *Rebel Governance* dataset further links post-rebel parties to their wartime governance capacities. These datasets hold promise for the testing of a number of theoretical propositions from the mainstream party literature, for instance on the links between civil wars and party – and party system institutionalisation, democracy, and stability.

With up to three decades of experience in some countries with former armed opposition groups participating in electoral politics, we are in a position to advance our understanding of the slow-moving, dynamic processes that constitute lasting political change. In this context, it is interesting to consider how different these parties are from 'ordinary' electoral parties in contexts without a history of conflict. How well do our theories about party system stability and change hold up in these contexts? How does voting behaviour differ in these contexts? Do post-rebel parties have deeper, or more stable, links to their voting base than do parties in other new democracies? How do they maintain these links? How do the changes that these parties make affect their viability? Is that different from what we might expect from the broader comparative literature on parties? For instance, studies on the impact of party name and identity changes (e.g. Ishiyama and Marshall 2017; Curtis and Sindre 2019); the public disavowal of violence (Ishiyama 2019); the inclusion of outsider candidates for president or head of list (Ishiyama and Marshall 2015); the governance behaviour of these parties once elected to different offices (Whiting and Bauchowitz 2022); the impact of civil wars on party system development (Ishiyama 2014; Manning, Smith and Tuncel 2022); and the role that post-rebel parties play in shaping democracy, peace and stability (Ishiyama and Sindre 2023), can inform the wider field of party research. Furthermore, insights into party politics in post-civil war countries bring to the table new perspectives on party politics in regions that have generally been considered peaceful, but that have seen increasing trends of instability and political volatility in recent years.

Notes

1 The discussion thus excludes such one-party regimes as the EPRDF in Ethiopia, the RPF in Rwanda, the NRA in Uganda and earlier regimes founded by anti-colonial liberation movements. For discussions of these post-war regimes see for instance Lyons (2016a, 2016b).
2 'Government, rebels formally sign peace agreement in Nepal' *AP News* 5 March 2021 https://apnews.com/article/khadga-prasad-oli-bombings-nepal-43a5d771a3dba4bd05086d11384f765e. Accessed 2 December 2021.

References

Alapuro, R. (1988) *State and revolution in Finland*. Berkeley and Los Angeles: University of California University Press.

Aspinall, E., Hicken, A., Scambary, J. and Weiss, M.L. (2018) 'Timor-Leste votes: Parties and Patronage', *Journal of Democracy*, 29(1), p153–167.

Beha, A. (2017) *Between stabilisation and democratisation. Elections, political parties and intra-party democracy in Kosovo*. Prishtina: CPC/Friedrich Ebert Stiftung.

Berti, B. (2013) *Armed political organizations: From conflict to integration*. Baltimore: Johns Hopkins University Press

Braithewaite, J.M. and Cunningham, K.G. (2020) 'When organizations rebel: Introducing the Foundations of Rebel Group Emergence (FORGE) Dataset', *International Studies Quarterly*, 64(1), p183–193.

Caramani, D. (2004) *The nationalization of politics: The formation of national electorates and party systems in Western Europe*, Cambridge: Cambridge University Press.

Curtis, D. and Sindre, G. (2019) 'Transforming state visions: Ideology and ideas in armed groups turned political parties', *Government and Opposition*, 54(3), p387–414.

Daly, S.Z. (2020) 'Political life after civil wars: Introducing the civil war successor party dataset', *Journal of Peace Research*, 58(4), p839–848.

De Zeeuw, J. (2008) *From soldiers to politicians: Transforming rebel movements after civil war*. Boulder Colo: Lynne Rienner

Dresden, J.R. (2017) 'From combatants to candidates: Electoral competition and the legacy of armed conflict', *Conflict Management and Peace Science*, 34(3), p240–263.

Duverger, M. (1963) *Political parties: Their organization and activity in the modern state*. Hoboken, NJ: Wiley

Gallagher, M. (1985) *Political parties in the Republic of Ireland*. Manchester: Manchester University Press.

Grzymala-Busse, A. (2002) *Redeeming the communist past*. New York: Cambridge University Press.

Harmel, R. and Janda, K. (1994) 'An integrated theory of party goals and party change', *Journal of Theoretical Politics*, 6(3), p259–287.

Huang, R. (2016) *The wartime origins of democratization: Civil war, rebel governance, and political regimes*. Cambridge: Cambridge University Press.

Ishiyama, J. (2001) 'Ethnopolitical parties and democratic consolidation in post-community Eastern Europe' *Nationalism and Ethnic Politics*, 7, p25–45.

Ishiyama, J. (2014) 'Civil wars and party systems', *Social Science Quarterly*, 95(2), p425–447.

Ishiyama, J. (2016) 'Introduction to the special issue: "From bullets to ballots: the transformation of rebel groups into political parties"', *Democratization*, 23(6), p969–971.

Ishiyama, J. (2019) 'Identity change and rebel party success', *Government and Opposition*, 54(3), p454–484.

Ishiyama, J. and Basnet, P. (2020) 'What kind of political parties do former rebel parties become?' Paper presented at the Midwest Political Science Association (MPSA), 14–17 April.

Ishiyama, J. and Batta, A. (2011) 'Swords into plowshares: The organizational transformation of rebel groups into political parties', *Communist and Post-Communist Studies*, 44(4), p369–379.

Ishiyama, J. and Marshall, M. (2015) 'Candidate recruitment and former rebel parties' *Party Politics*, 21(4), p591–602.

Ishiyama, J. and Marshall, M. (2017) 'What explains former rebel party name changes after a civil conflict ends? External and internal factors and the transition to political competition' *Party Politics*, 23(4), p364–375.

Ishiyama, J. and Sindre, G.M. (eds.) (2023) *The effects of rebel parties on governance, democracy and stability after civil wars: From guns to governing*. London: Routledge.

Ishiyama, J. and Widmeier, M. (2020) 'From "bush bureaucracies" to electoral competitors: what explains the political success of rebel parties after civil wars?', *Journal of Elections, Public Opinions and Parties*, 30(1), p42–63.

Janda, K. (1980) *Political parties: A cross-national survey*. New York: MacMillan (The Free Press).

Kalyvas, S. (1998) 'Democracy and religious politics: Evidence from Belgium', *Comparative Political Studies*, 32, p379–398.

Levitsky, S. and Way, L.A. (2013) 'The durability of revolutionary regimes', *Journal of Democracy*, 24(3), p5–17.

Lyons, T. (2016a) 'The importance of winning: Victorious insurgent groups and authoritarian politics', *Comparative Politics*, 48(2), p167–184.

Lyons, T. (2016b) 'From victorious rebels to strong authoritarian parties: prospects for post-war democratization', *Democratization*, 23(6), p1026–1041.
Manning, C. (2007) 'Party-building on the heels of war: El Salvador, Bosnia, Kosovo and Mozambique', *Democratization*, 14(2), p253–272.
Manning, C. (2008) *The making of democrats: Elections and party development in postwar Bosnia, El Salvador, and Mozambique*, New York: Palgrave Macmillan.
Manning, C. and Smith, I. (2016) 'Political party formation by former armed opposition groups after civil war', *Democratization*, 23(6), p972–989.
Manning, C. and Smith, I. (2019) 'Electoral performance by post-rebel parties', *Government and Opposition*, 54(3), p415–453.
Manning, C., Smith, I. and Tuncel, O. (2022) 'Rebels with a cause: Introducing the post-rebel electoral parties dataset', *Journal of Peace Research*, Forthcoming.
Marshall, M. (2019) 'Foreign rebel sponsorship: A patron – client analysis of party viability in elections following negotiated settlements', *The Journal of Conflict Resolution*, 63(2), p555–584.
Matanock, A. (2017) *Electing peace: From civil conflict to political participation*. Cambridge: Cambridge University Press.
Muriaas, R., Rakner, L. and Skage, I. (2016) 'Political capital of ruling parties after regime change: Contrasting successful insurgencies to peaceful pro-democracy movements', *Civil Wars*, 18(2), 175–191.
Przeworkski, A. (1980) 'Social democracy as a historical phenomenon', *New Left Review*, 1, p27–58.
Randall, V. and Svåsand, L. (2002) 'Party institutionalization in new democracies', *Party Politics*, 8(1), p5–29.
Reilly, B. and Nordlund, P. (eds.) (2008) *Political parties in conflict-prone societies: Regulation, engineering and democratic development*. Tokyo: United Nations University Press.
Sindre, G.M. (2016a) 'Internal party democracy in former rebel parties', *Party Politics*, 22(4), p501–5011.
Sindre, G. (2016b) 'In whose interests: Former rebel parties and ex-combatant interest organization in Aceh and East Timor', *Civil Wars*, 18(2), p192–213.
Sindre, G. (2018) 'From secessionism to regionalism: Intra-organizational change and ideological moderation within armed secessionist movements', *Political Geography*, 64, p23–32.
Sindre, G. (2019) 'Adapting to peacetime politics? Rebranding and ideological change in former rebel parties', *Government and Opposition*, 54(3), p485–512.
Sindre, G. and Söderström, J. (2016) 'Introduction to special issue: Understanding armed groups and party politics', *Civil Wars*, 18(2), p109–117.
Speight, J. and Wittig, K. (2017) 'Pathways from rebellion: Rebel-party configurations in Côte d'Ivoire and Burundi', *African Affairs*, 177/466, p21–43.
Sprenkels, R. (2018) *After insurgency: Revolution and electoral politics in El Salvador*. Notre Dame: Notre Dame University Press.
Staniland, P. (2014) *Networks of rebellion: Explaining insurgent cohesion and collapse*. Ithaca: Cornell University Press.
Söderberg Kovacs, M. and Hatz, S. (2016) 'Rebel-to-party transformation in civil war peace processes, 1975–2011', *Democratization*, 23(6), p990–1008.
Tadić, K. and Elbasani, A. (2018) 'State-building and patronage networks: How political parties embezzled the bureaucracy in post-war Kosovo', *Southeast European and Black Sea Studies*, 18(2), p185–202.
Tezcur, G.M. (2010) 'The moderation theory revisited: The case of Islamic political actors', *Party Politics*, 16(1), p69–88.
van Biezen, I. (2003) *Political parties in new democracies: Party organization in Southern and East-Central Europe*. New York: Palgrave.
Weinstein, J. (2007) *Inside rebellion: The politics of insurgent violence*. Cambridge: Cambridge University Press.
Whiting, M. (2017) *Sinn Féin and the IRA: From revolution to moderation*. Edinburgh: Edinburgh University Press.
Whiting, M. (2018) 'Moderation without change: The strategic transformation of Sinn Fein and the IRA in Northern Ireland', *Government and Opposition*, 52(2), p288–311.
Whiting, M. and Bauchowitz, S. (2022) The myth of power sharing and polarization: Evidence from Northern Ireland, *Political Studies*, 70(1), p81–109.
Wittig, K. (2016) 'Politics in the shadow of the gun: Revisiting the literature on 'Rebel-to-Party Transformations' through the case of Burundi', *Civil Wars*, 18(2), p137–159.

29
CLIENTELISM AND POLITICAL PARTIES

Sergiu Gherghina and *Clara Volintiru*

Clientelism is an informal exchange system through which political parties use privileged access to state resources to enhance their support within society (Kitschelt and Wilkinson 2007; Kopecký, Mair and Spirova 2012; Stokes et al. 2013). It is 'a strategy of partial mobilisation that differs from more universal patterns, such as programmatic appeals or mobilisation motivated by parties' achievement records' (Roniger 2004, 354). Beyond its characteristics as an instrument that mobilises political support (Chubb 1981), clientelism can also be considered a way to maintain access to political power (Piattoni 2001), a method of electoral mobilisation (Medina and Stokes 2007) or a mechanism of accountability (Kitschelt and Wilkinson 2007). Clientelism leverages public resources to maximise the electoral appeal of political patrons, but requires discretionary control of public resources. Depending on the goals pursued by political patrons, clientelistic exchanges can address the voters directly, the party members and elites, or even third-party key supporters such as party donors (Gherghina and Volintiru 2017). As such, it is difficult to associate clientelism with a single approach or a particular context (Medina and Stokes 2002). Evidence from earlier research shows that clientelism occurs across countries with different degrees of democracy (see e.g. Chapters 32 and 34). Although the examples provided in this chapter come mainly from transition countries and new democracies due to its higher incidence, such practices are common also in established democracies (Denmark 2021; Gherghina and Nemčok 2021; Howlett and Rayner 2021).

Clientelism is often a black box that includes a series of practices. The confusion about its meaning has three sources: in some political settings it exists in parallel with nepotism, favouritism, or forms of bribery; it is a multi-faceted process with overlapping causes and consequences; and it includes several types of patrons, brokers and clients that complicate the bigger picture. This chapter has a threefold goal: to provide a conceptual clarification of the term, to explain the ways in which political parties use clientelism and to outline the most common consequences encountered at party and society level. Our discussion focuses on clientelism and party politics in competitive democracies or transition countries rather than competitive autocracies or single party regimes.

The chapter's structure mirrors these goals, with each of the following three substantive sections being devoted to one. Section two conceptualises clientelism with the help of a typology that accounts for the context and targeted participants, level of deployment and methods used. The next section provides an overview of the main elements that facilitate the use of clientelism by political parties. These elements range from the strength of states to propensity of territorial party organisations. The fourth section covers the consequences of clientelism for political parties both internally and externally, for political representation and democratic accountability, and for the broad functioning of public institutions. The final section concludes and identifies several avenues for future research.

Types of clientelism

Clientelistic exchanges involve a political patron who distributes benefits, and clients who receive goods and services in exchange for their political support. Political patrons can be either party leaders or the political party organisation. Different political patrons might prefer different clientelistic tactics (e.g. targeting strongholds or swing votes) and instruments (e.g. public goods, public services, cash payments), as they differ among themselves and react to different circumstances in their electoral career. Clients are primarily voters, but they can also be party members or supporters. There are different types of clientelism, based on the context of the exchange and targeted group of beneficiaries, on the level of deployment and on the methods employed (see Figure 29.1).

Electoral and organisational clientelism

The context of exchange and the targeted beneficiaries allow us to differentiate between electoral and organisational clientelism. Electoral clientelism is geared outward, being exerted by political parties in their efforts to harness electoral support from voters and win elections. The immediacy of many exchanges (e.g. vote buying) makes electoral clientelism more likely to occur during political campaigns. Most empirical case studies on clientelism in the literature reflect upon these iterative or non-iterative informal transactions during electoral periods. Exchanges usually involve easily transactional goods such as money, food, products (ranging from clothes, cigarettes or TV sets to ad-hoc items such as medicines, tyres or birthday cakes), free access to private services such as plastic surgery, teeth cleaning or funerals, the promise of jobs, the promise of access to public services or goods, and conveyance (Schaffer 2007; Brun and Diamond 2014; Kuo 2018).

Clientelism can also be used for organisational goals such as developing territorial presence, mobilising financial support or controlling public institutions. Organisational clientelism is geared inwards, targets primarily the party members and entails somewhat more complex exchanges such as public employment or long-term preferential access to public goods and services. In this sense, the organisational clientelism can be seen as the continuation of electoral clientelism: what is promised during election campaigns is delivered outside the campaigns. Party patronage is the most common form of organisational clientelism and means the preferential

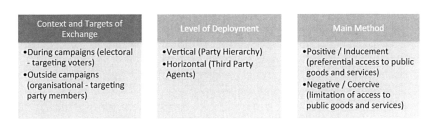

Figure 29.1 Types of clientelism

appointment of a supporter in a public sector job (Piattoni 2001). Loyal appointees make sure public resources are distributed to party strongholds through budgetary allocations and discretionary public programmes, or directly to clients themselves through conditional cash transfers or social programmes. It is not just public administration employment but also public sector jobs that fall under political influence. Consequently, organisational clientelism consolidates the direct dependency of clients on their political patron, and it involves a much more asymmetrical relationship of power than in the case of electoral clientelism. Through iterations and personal relationships, organisational clientelism also involves bonds of trust, solidarity and respect between clients and patrons. It could be even regarded as a foundational aspect of cohesion and coordinated action within party organisations, when deployed systematically and at a large scale.

Political patrons and brokers do not always target individuals. Sometimes politicians may reward a whole village with social programmes or funds meant to provide electricity connection, access to water, building a school, repairing a cultural building or a road (Berenschot and Aspinall 2020). Party members are the primary beneficiaries of this type of clientelism, because they are loyal to the party and subject to multiple interactions. Nevertheless, organisational clientelism can go beyond the relationship with party members and targets external supporters that can contribute to the political goals of the party or the party leader. In brief, although the electoral and organisational clientelism are two different types of clientelistic transactions, they should be regarded as mutually enforcing and complementary.

Horizontal and vertical clientelism

Another dimension of differentiation of the concept clientelism concerns the vertical or horizontal coordination involved in the process. As the clientelistic relationship between patrons and clients is usually asymmetrical, with patrons exerting discretionary and conditional control over resources, it can be characterised as a vertical coordination mechanism. Vertical clientelism can be both electoral and organisational. There is an evolutionary path that begins with the dyadic bond between patrons and clients in hierarchical societies (Scott 1969). It developed into broader networks characterised by a pyramidal structure of clientelism (Chubb 1983; Auyero 2000; Hopkin 2001). The literature referred to it with the generic name of 'clientelistic machine', which is in essence an efficient system of electoral mobilisation and informal benefits distribution (Chubb 1983; Nichter 2008). It stands in contrast to the previously social, personalised relationship between the parties involved that was closer to a code of conduct based on reciprocity and deference (Weingrod 1968). This personalised relationship can still be found in the case of clientelistic linkages active in smaller, local communities, but party organisations today usually engage in much more complex forms of resource distribution.

For example, local bosses could engage in direct, personal relationships that cannot be maintained by leaders of a nationwide political party. Strong local leaders can sometimes use the clientelistic system to develop a national level platform, as it is sometimes the case of larger and richer regions and cities. However, because of this potential, national patrons tend to be very careful in terms of how they condition the resource distribution in the territory to prevent potential rivals from emerging. The local interaction between patrons and clients also has an integrative function, linking citizens to their representatives in a direct relationship, personalising the communication and facilitating the articulation of needs from clients to patrons (Auyero 2000; Hopkin 2006). Local bosses can even have a stronger electoral support in their constituency than national party leaders. This can be observed, for example, in the national legislative elections when the notoriety of local bosses can help them win parliamentary seats for their parties in their constituency. Nevertheless, for most political parties, the position of these bosses within the party organisation is still subordinated to that of the party leader and national party leadership structures. The local bosses are aware that they rarely have sufficient strength to maintain their popularity on their own in the territory.

The extent to which a party member can exert discretionary control over public resources thus dictates the vertical distance from power in the clientelistic hierarchy. If local party bosses have weak control over clientelistic resources – either due to the administrative structure in a country or due to internal power dynamics – then their position is often constrained to that of an intermediary in the clientelistic machine. While clientelistic practices are more frequent in transition countries and new democracies, the development of electoral mobilisation strategies is accompanied by complex clientelistic relationships also in democracies. These relationships integrate systems of monitoring and enforcement to make efficient use of the distributional channels it exerts (Kitschelt 2000; Stokes et al. 2013; Gherghina and Volintiru 2021). They usually involve a dense network of intermediaries, called brokers, who effectively transform a reciprocal support relationship into an economy of scale in electoral mobilisation. Many contemporary parties engaging in clientelism use their territorial organisations to fill these brokerage roles, but the latter can be played by external actors such as private companies.

Horizontal clientelism refers to specific actions in which organisations from outside the political party (e.g. private companies) mobilise the electorate. These third-party organisations can be involved directly or indirectly in the mobilisation strategy of the political party. Political parties have discretionary access to public resources only when they are in government. If the party is in opposition or their resource base is depleted by specific circumstances such as austerity measures or a poor state (Trantidis and Tsagkroni 2017), it is only the promise of future gains that can be transacted. Even such a promise is important, since, in democracies, the alternation in power is common and credible; thus, opposition parties stand a good chance of joining the government after contesting elections. Nevertheless, the promise of future gains does not help with most electoral clientelistic incentives such as vote buying, which require cash and material resources during the election campaign. Consequently, political parties sometimes involve external actors to get the necessary resources to fuel the clientelistic relationship. Private sector contractors can offer political parties or politicians both formal party donations and informal access to resources (e.g. cash, goods) in exchange for future economic gains, usually through public procurement, once the patron wins elections. Private sector actors can also act as brokers themselves, since companies sometimes play an important role in the electoral mobilisation of their employees (Mares, Muntean and Petrova 2018). Evidence from Romania, India, the Philippines and Indonesia illustrates the horizontal model of clientelism (Doroftei 2016; Gherghina and Volintiru 2017; Das and Maiorano 2019; Aspinall and Hicken 2020). For example, in Romania, several companies that donate large sums during the electoral campaigns to the main three political parties are the main beneficiaries of public procurement. They make profit and continue to donate, thus completing a vicious circle that is not interrupted by any of the large political parties, even when any of them is in opposition (Mares, Muntean and Petrova 2018).

This link with business actors in clientelism is a largely overlooked area that is very important in explaining economic policies and contracting in certain sectors of activity in different transition countries or new democracies such as Ghana, Morocco, Romania or Ukraine (Hirvi and Whitfield 2015; Corduneanu-Huci 2016; Doroftei 2016; Mazepus *et al.* 2021). In contrast, private sector actors can also be targeted for resource extraction through corruption, by publicly employed party brokers who cannot extract benefits from the state, but through the state functions they control, as is the case in Greece (Trantidis and Tsagkroni 2017). This narrow resource extraction component can be a form of organisational clientelism in which party supporters (not just party members) are rewarded, but it is not a mechanism of electoral clientelism given the short loop of the clientelistic transaction.

Horizontal clientelism is therefore a relationship of less asymmetrical power as political patrons depend on the resources provided by economic actors to the same extent as the latter depends on this political connection to ensure its business gains. Horizontal clientelism can be summed up as such: private actors receive preferential access to public contracts in exchange for their direct (e.g. employment mobilisation) or indirect (i.e. party donations) mobilisation services (Gherghina and Volintiru 2017, 116).

Positive and negative clientelism

Positive inducements include both material and non-material benefits. Material benefits concern money in the form of cash payments for all types of electoral behaviour (turnout, vote buying and abstention buying) and all goods outlined earlier in the section on electoral clientelism. This is called spot market clientelism and involves short and underdeveloped relationships between citizens and candidates/parties. For voters, food and drinks are seen as remuneration, tokens of appreciation and a one-time interaction with the candidate broker. Non-material benefits include jobs, access to public services and access to public goods. The distribution of such favours is meant to convince voters that the candidates pay attention to their needs and will continue to have the same attention after they get elected (Yıldırım and Kitschelt 2020). For example, property ownership records can be altered, building permits can be issued more swiftly or not at all for competitors, functions of public spaces can be changed or parking places allocated preferentially. All these make it relational clientelism, which is characterised by a more solid and long-time interaction in which politicians use their influence, make promises for clientelistic exchanges and keep them once they get into office.

Negative clientelism conveys the idea of a punishment for voting the wrong way. It is based on explicit threats in which the voters assess the value of the particular utility they have and which they are under threat of losing (Gherghina, Saikkonen and Bankov 2021). Negative clientelism uses a combination of coercion and threats of benefits removal. Negative clientelism was defined almost three decades ago as 'a relationship marked by asymmetrical power, in which the subordination of clients is maintained through coercion, either threatened or real' (Fox 1994, 153) or when patrons try to ensure voters' compliance by threatening benefit removal (Fox 1994, 157–158). Initially, negative clientelism was limited to coercion associated with physical violence (Chubb 1981), but this has diversified greatly over time. Today, negative clientelism includes threats to cut voters off from benefits on which they depend, removal from their land or residences, or the use of violence, including assault and death (Mares and Young 2019).

The most effective threats or punishments will rarely be implemented because the voters will act based on fear of reprisal rather than under direct coercion. In most situations, the coercion or reprisal is conducted by brokers (Stokes et al. 2013). They are equally effective. For example, in the 2016 Ugandan elections, a party was re-elected after state security forces and various militias used coercion and intimidation to persuade voters of the risk of not voting for them (Vokes and Wilkins 2016). In rural areas in Romania, mayors or brokers known as 'mayor's men' made effective threats to cut voters off from welfare benefits based on how they voted (Mares and Muntean 2015).

Political parties and clientelism

Many contemporary political parties have faced similar challenges over recent decades: declining party membership, lower trust from the citizens and higher availability of voters even in countries once characterised by high partisan loyalties. Clientelism can be a powerful strategy for many political parties to appeal to the electorate especially in a context where the poor system of checks and balances allows the use of state resources for party electoral gains. Comparative studies on clientelism illustrate the existence of electoral and organisational clientelism also in affluent Western Europe societies with long administrative traditions (Piattoni 2001; Kopecký, Mair and Spirova 2012). For example, comparative evidence from many West and South European countries indicates that political parties have different mechanisms through which they ensure strong political control of public office. Although there is some degree of variation in this control, the bottom line is that there is a certain degree of politicisation in the appointment of high-profile administrative elites (Gherghina and Kopecký 2016). The explanation for this broad presence of clientelism is straightforward: while clientelism can occur more frequently in a weak state or a poor institutional context (see Part 6, this volume), clientelism is 'not a sufficiently powerful brake on it [i.e. economic development] to slow the rate of expansion of high-growth economies' (Stokes 2021, 2). When possible, political parties are likely to engage in clientelistic transactions due to its effectiveness in achieving voter mobilisation.

Clientelism, weak states and poverty

A weak state allows for a much more powerful political patron as it offers the possibility of discretionary control of public resources. Clientelism in general is prevalent when there is a poor institutionalisation of the social contract (i.e. what citizens give and expect in return from their state). When the democratic accountability mechanisms are distorted, no one is directly held accountable for failing to deliver public goods. In a context of poor accountability, the discretionary power over resource allocation is growing higher and political patrons have a much larger space to manoeuvre and determine who gets what from the state. In such a context, positive incentives (i.e. offering access to public goods and services in exchange for political support) or negative conditionalities (i.e. refusing somebody access to public goods or resources) can be deployed more easily than in a more consolidated institutional system. The weak enforcement of regulatory provisions favours clientelism, whether it is electoral clientelism through such practices as vote buying – in a context of poor enforcement of electoral legislation, or organisational clientelism through such practices as political appointments – in a context of politicisation of the civil service.

As party leaders use public resources for political gains, there is often a depreciation of the service quality provision by the state, at least from the perspective of accessibility – as access to public goods and services becomes conditional upon political support. It also involves a path dependency, as informal networks become more entrenched pathways to public goods and service provision than formal administrative mechanisms. If a voter is discontented or disillusioned with the performance of her elected representative, she will still be likely to vote and support her the second time around, because of the conditionality of the networks of resource distribution (Volintiru 2012). It is precisely clientelistic exchanges that enhance the credibility of patron political candidates (Keefer and Vlaicu 2008; Stokes et al. 2013). A strengthening of checks and balances in a society leads to a less developed clientelistic machine. Democratic accountability mechanisms constrain discretionary control over public resources, which results in lower clientelistic resources (Kitschelt and Wilkinson 2007; Kitschelt and Kselman 2013).

The clientelistic system in a country thrives due to limited economic opportunities, so the preferential access to public employment and other benefits can serve as a powerful leverage for political patrons' vis-à-vis their clients (Stokes 2021). Clientelism is more likely to be present in poorer countries (Keefer 2007; Bustikova and Corduneanu-Huci 2011), while high level of poverty may lead voters to be more responsive to money or other clientelistic incentives (Brusco, Nazareno and Stokes 2004; Remmer 2007; Stokes et al. 2013). Electoral clientelism is more cost-effective in a context of poverty as lower value goods must be disbursed. Clients can eventually break away from the dependency on political patrons induced by poverty through the formal or informal redistributive systems. Since 'permanent reductions in poverty can break the voter's dependence on clientelism' (Frey 2019, 2), the clientelistic system can be to a limited extent a long-lasting 'poverty trap' (Stokes 2021).

How parties control and distribute clientelism

Empirical studies cover diverse objects of clientelistic transactions, but all of them are directly or indirectly linked to political control of public goods, services and decisions. Clientelism leverages public resources to maximise the electoral appeal of political patrons, and in order to do so, it requires discretionary control of public resources.

Depending on the specific balance of power, the power of local governments and their functions, the necessary resources may be controlled either by local patrons or by national party leaders. National political patrons have a much larger variety of resources at their disposal to deploy in clientelistic exchanges, but they also have less capacity to target voters directly and to monitor their compliance following such transactions. National leaders can deploy large amounts of public resources not only through public expenditures in direct cash transfer programmes and other social programmes but also through the available public employment positions at their disposal. Local political leaders have access to a much narrower resource base for informal exchanges, but they have the advantage of being in direct contact with targeted clients. Therefore, local party elites have a much greater awareness of what clients' need (Auyero 1999), and much better control over clients' political stances – both during and between elections.

Beyond budgetary allocations, local political leaders, such as mayors and city councillors, have control over many important decisions that can be valuable objects of clientelistic transactions: the issuing of permits and commercial licences, allocation of parking spaces, leasing of public spaces, or the granting of various favourable administrative decisions. For many clients, the direct, preferential access to both local and national political patrons and their decision-making power can be as important as directly receiving public goods or services. This is why the literature refers to clientelistic exchanges not only as instances of informal resources allocation but also as mechanisms of transmission of people's grievances and needs (Auyero 1999; Brun and Diamond 2014).

Resource availability contributes greatly to both electoral and organisational clientelism, but monitoring and enforcement is nevertheless a key element of clientelistic systems (Medina and Stokes 2007). Monitoring ensures that electoral support or loyalty is received by political patrons in exchange for the resources that are conditionally distributed. Having strong local political organisations and a large territorial presence are both conducive to clientelism (Gherghina and Volintiru 2021) and important outcomes of clientelistic distribution of public goods and services in local communities. The more the local communities are flooded with preferential access to public resources, the stronger the local political organisation gets. In this context, it is relevant to note that political parties use electoral clientelism both in their electoral strongholds and in the constituencies where they wish to increase their share of votes. This shows that the distribution of clientelism has a dual function depending on the context: to increase voters' loyalty and to persuade new voters.

Consequences of clientelism on democracy and representation

The use of clientelism has several important consequences. This section focuses on those effects observable for political parties, representation and democratic accountability, and the functioning of public institutions. Looking at political parties specifically, clientelism produces both internal and external effects. The internal effects refer to the role of the party leader and the intra-party cohesion. Party leaders who use organisational clientelism are likely to strengthen their position in the party and diminish internal competition and contestation. They can acquire the loyalty of party members and supporters through the provision of jobs and access to services and goods in the medium and long run. In addition to the solid relationships established with party members, such practices allow them to amplify their mobilisation capacity and maximise their ability to boost or stabilise parties' electoral performance. Under these circumstances, it is difficult for challengers to contest their positions and to provide alternatives to the use of clientelism. This mechanism is in line with earlier research suggesting that higher internal party leadership competition is associated with lower incidence of patronage jobs distributed along party hierarchical lines (Kemahlioğlu 2012).

Intra-party cohesion can also be increased by the use of electoral and organisational clientelism. In their role as key brokers for their parties during election campaigns, party members use the same means to achieve electoral goals and thus the sense of belonging to political parties is enhanced beyond the ideological or programmatic lines (Gherghina, Saikkonen and Bankov 2021). The rewarding of members with patronage builds loyalty and reduces defections. However, there are particular instances in which the use of clientelism decreases intra-party cohesion. For example, if the central party office decides to use electoral clientelism and some party factions or territorial branches are against such practices, it is likely to have a greater divide between them in the aftermath of elections.

The external party consequences of clientelism relate mainly to electoral mobilisation and inter-party competition. The provision of goods and services through electoral clientelism complements parties' ideological offer and can distinguish them from their competitors. Previous studies identify it as one of the few viable electoral strategies to increase turnout (González-Ocantos, Kiewiet de Jonge and Nickerson 2015). The offer of small rewards during election campaigns can take various forms depending on the expected behaviour. Citizens can be asked to go and vote for a certain candidate, stay at home, or change their vote. Such 'turnout-buying' rewards demobilised supporters for showing up to the polls, while 'abstention-buying' is a demobilisation strategy that rewards individuals for not voting (Gans-Morse, Mazzuca and Nichter 2014; Hagene 2015). Organisational clientelism provides roots in society and builds relationships of trust with the electorate (Weingrod 1968; Eisenstadt and Roniger 1984). As part of an ongoing relationship between politicians and citizens, particularistic benefits can also go to supporters who would vote anyway (Gans-Morse, Mazzuca and Nichter 2014). Party supporters who get access to public employment can mobilise voters in their social networks, pick voters up and bring them to polls, or even facilitate party interests as official delegates in the electoral process (Mares and Young 2019).

Inter-party competition can also be influenced by the use of electoral or organisational clientelism. Political parties target voters with incentives both in their electoral strongholds to reward loyal supporters and in the constituencies where they are weak to determine vote swings. Such behaviour triggers two types of reactions. On the one hand, other parties may engage in clientelism themselves to counter-attack and diminish the potential loss in the electorate. In this case, programmatic promises and ideological stances are secondary and the competition revolves around the idea of the highest bidder. On the other hand, the use of clientelism by some political parties may produce demands for more clientelism among voters. As such, citizens may expect all parties to use clientelism, and this results in a similar type of competition as described earlier, that is, revolving around the use of resources.

The consequences of clientelism for representation are related mainly to the alteration of the nature of choices. The voters may not express their genuine preferences when supporting parties that provide incentives. As a result, interest representation and political competition are biased. Political parties and politicians invest resources in such practices rather than performing well in office or promoting policies for broader segments of the electorate. This diminishes the importance of competition over ideas for both political actors and voters. When the competition is limited, citizens make decisions according to other criteria. Recent evidence indicates that some voters who are disappointed with the classic way of doing politics support clientelistic politicians hoping to get something in return for their vote (Gherghina, Saikkonen and Bankov 2021). The use of clientelism also reduces the importance of democratic accountability for voters. For example, when the relatives of current office-holders are more likely to be employed in better paying jobs (Fafchamps and Labonne 2017), citizens' priorities shift from holding politicians accountable to establishing relationships with them. In this context, priority is given to patron-client relationships and democratic accountability is difficult to achieve. Clientelism generates an alternative type of accountability in which politicians and their voters are accountable to each other relative to their direct transaction (Kitschelt and Wilkinson 2007).

The functioning of public institutions is negatively affected when their resources are used for electoral clientelism. The most common problems occur when voters are promised preferential access to public goods or services and when financial means are used to buy and distribute products to a particular group of voters. Local councils in many countries, for example, collect taxes to address the most salient community issues. When electoral clientelism is used by the incumbents, financial resources are steered towards positive inducements for voters and the institution performs weakly in solving community problems. Similarly, there are instances in which public institutions are used by politicians and political parties to make credible threats to voters, for instance police or labour force institutions. Organisational clientelism can be deployed in a strategic manner to control public institutions through appointments that can ensure loyalty and continuous access to public resources (Kopecký, Mair and Spirova 2012). Party patronage can thus lead to state capture (Innes 2014), which is often used to ensure the necessary resources for electoral clientelism. All these factors indicate how public institutions can be caught in a vicious circle that involves both electoral and organisational clientelism.

Conclusions and avenues for further research

This chapter has clarified the conceptual meaning of clientelism, explained the ways in which political parties use clientelism across competitive democracies and transition countries and outlined its consequences for democracy. The various forms of electoral clientelism are traceable in different political settings and they are rarely context specific. As such, it is insufficient and over-simplifying for research to refer to clientelism as being present or not. The content of this chapter illustrates how clientelism can be a flaw of representative democracy and one of the most important challenges faced by contemporary party systems and political regimes. This challenge increases proportionally to the number of political parties using clientelism to maintain or gain access to positions of power within a given system.

The developments outlined in this chapter indicate the necessity for a research agenda more practically oriented in the direction of reducing clientelism. So far, we know much about practices of clientelism, who uses clientelism and when, and what are the main effects on the functioning of democracy. However, we know little about how they can be stopped and prevented from reoccurring. In this sense, one avenue for further research could develop conceptual discussions about how practices of clientelism resemble each other according to the types of used resources or the target groups. While Figure 29.1 may be a useful point of departure, this line of research could dig deeper to understand the ways in which such practices can be limited. Future empirical studies may refer to the emergence of institutions, legal provisions and specific policies aimed at curbing the clientelistic phenomenon and thereby also assess their impact. Such a direction for research has beneficial trans-disciplinary features, because it can address issues ranging from brokers and agents to the legality or control of resources.

References

Aspinall, E. and Hicken, A. (2020) 'Guns for hire and enduring machines: Clientelism beyond parties in Indonesia and the Philippines', *Democratization*, 27(1), p137–156.
Auyero, J. (1999) '"From the client's point(s) of view": How poor people perceive and evaluate political clientelism', *Theory and Society*, 28(2), p297–334.
Auyero, J. (2000) 'The logic of clientelism in Argentina: An ethnographic account', *Latin American Research Review*, 35(3), p55–81.
Berenschot, W. and Aspinall, E. (2020) 'How clientelism varies: Comparing patronage democracies', *Democratization*, 27(1), p1–19.
Brun, D.A. and Diamond, L. (2014) *Clientelism, social policy, and the quality of democracy*. Baltimore: Johns Hopkins University Press.
Brusco, V., Nazareno, M. and Stokes, S. (2004) 'Vote buying in Argentina', *Latin American Research Review*, 39(2), p66–88.
Bustikova, L. and Corduneanu-Huci, C. (2011) *Clientelism, state capacity and economic development: A crossnational study*. Toronto: APSA 2009 Toronto Meeting Paper.
Chubb, J. (1981) 'The social bases of an urban political machine: The case of Palermo', *Political Science Quarterly*, 96(1), p107–125.
Chubb, J. (1983) *Patronage, power and poverty in Southern Italy: A tale of two cities*. Cambridge: Cambridge University Press.
Corduneanu-Huci, C. (2016) 'Taming corruption: Rent potential, collective action, and taxability in Morocco', *Business and Politics*, 18(3), p297–335.
Das, U. and Maiorano, D. (2019) 'Post-clientelistic initiatives in a patronage democracy: The distributive politics of India's MGNREGA', *World Development*, 117, p239–252.
Denemark, D. (2021) 'Clientelism and distributive politics in Australia: Comparing partisan pork barrel with contingency-based vote-buying', *Acta Politica*, 56(4), 600–621.
Doroftei, I.M. (2016) 'Measuring government favouritism objectively: The case of Romanian public construction sector', *European Journal on Criminal Policy and Research*, 22(3), p399–413.
Eisenstadt, S.N. and Roniger, L. (1984) *Patrons, clients and friends: Interpersonal relations and the structure of trust in society*. Cambridge: Cambridge University Press.
Fafchamps, M. and Labonne, J. (2017) 'Do politicians' relatives get better jobs? Evidence from municipal elections', *Journal of Law, Economics, and Organization*, 33(2), p268–300.
Fox, J. (1994) 'The difficult transition from clientelism to citizenship: Lessons from Mexico', *World Politics*, 46(2), p151–184.
Frey, A. (2019) 'Cash transfers, clientelism, and political enfranchisement: Evidence from Brazil', *Journal of Public Economics*, 176, p1–17.
Gans-Morse, J., Mazzuca, S. and Nichter, S. (2014) 'Varieties of clientelism: Machine politics during elections', *American Journal of Political Science*, 58(2), p415–432.
Gherghina, S. and Kopecký, P. (2016) 'Politicization of administrative elites in Western Europe: An introduction', *Acta Politica*, 51(4), p407–412.
Gherghina, S. and Nemčok, M. (2021) 'Political parties, state resources and electoral clientelism', *Acta Politica*, 56(4), p591–599.
Gherghina, S., Saikkonen, I. and Bankov, P. (2021) 'Dissatisfied, uninformed or both? Democratic satisfaction, political knowledge and the acceptance of clientelism in a new democracy', *Democratization*. https://doi.org/ 10.1080/13510347.2021.1947250.
Gherghina, S. and Volintiru, C. (2017) 'A new model of clientelism: Political parties, public resources, and private contributors', *European Political Science Review*, 9(1), p115–137.
Gherghina, S. and Volintiru, C. (2021) 'Political parties and clientelism in transition countries: Evidence from Georgia, Moldova and Ukraine', *Acta Politica*, 56(4), p677–693.
González-Ocantos, E., Kiewiet de Jonge, C. and Nickerson, D.W. (2015) 'Legitimacy buying: The dynamics of clientelism in the face of legitimacy challenges', *Comparative Political Studies*, 48(9), p1127–1158.

Hagene, T. (2015) 'Political clientelism in Mexico: Bridging the gap between citizens and the state', *Latin American Politics and Society*, 57(1), p139–162.

Hirvi, M. and Whitfield, L. (2015) 'Public-service provision in clientelist political settlements: Lessons from Ghana's urban water sector', *Development Policy Review*, 33(2), p135–158.

Hopkin, J. (2001) 'A "southern model" of electoral mobilisation?: Clientelism and electoral politics in post-Franco Spain', *West European Politics*, 24(1), p115–136.

Hopkin, J. (2006) 'Clientelism and party politics', in Katz, R.S. and Crotty, W. (eds.) *Handbook of party politics*. London: Sage Publications Ltd., pp. 406–412.

Howlett, M. and Rayner, J. (2021) 'Administrative clientelism and policy reform failure: the Western Canada Integrated Land Management experience 1990–2015', *Acta Politica*, 56(4), 622–638.

Innes, A. (2014) 'The political economy of state capture in Central Europe', *JCMS: Journal of Common Market Studies*, 52(1), p88–104.

Keefer, P. (2007) 'Clientelism, credibility, and the policy choices of young democracies', *American Journal of Political Science*, 51(4), p804–821.

Keefer, P. and Vlaicu, R. (2008) 'Democracy, credibility, and clientelism', *Journal of Law, Economics, and Organization*, 24(2), p371–406.

Kemahlioğlu, Ö. (2012) *Agents or bosses? Patronage and intra-party politics in Argentina and Turkey*. Colchester: ECPR Press.

Kitschelt, H. (2000) 'Linkages between citizens and politicians in democratic polities', *Comparative Political Studies*, 33(6–7), p845–879.

Kitschelt, H. and Kselman, D.M. (2013) 'Economic development, democratic experience, and political parties' linkage strategies', *Comparative Political Studies*, 46(11), p1453–1484.

Kitschelt, H. and Wilkinson, S.I. (eds.) (2007) *Patrons, clients, and policies: Patterns of democratic accountability and political competition*. Cambridge: Cambridge University Press.

Kopecký, P., Mair, P. and Spirova, M. (eds.) (2012) *Party patronage and party government in European democracies*. Oxford: Oxford University Press.

Kuo, D. (2018) *Clientelism, capitalism, and democracy, clientelism, capitalism, and democracy*. Cambridge: Cambridge University Press.

Mares, I. and Muntean, A. (2015) 'Mayors, ethnic intermediaries and party brokers: examining variation in clientelistic strategies in rural settings', Paper presented at the European Political Science Association.

Mares, I., Muntean, A. and Petrova, T. (2018) 'Economic intimidation in contemporary elections: Evidence from Romania and Bulgaria', *Government and Opposition*, 53(3), p486–517.

Mares, I. and Young, L.E. (2019) *Conditionality and coercion: Electoral clientelism in Eastern Europe*. Oxford: Oxford University Press.

Mazepus, H., Dimitrova, A., Frear, M., Toshkov, D. and Onopriychuk, N. (2021) 'When business and politics mix: Local networks and socio-political transformations in Ukraine', *East European Politics and Societies*, 35(2), 437–459.

Medina, L.F. and Stokes, S. (2002) *Clientelism as political monopoly*. Chicago: University of Chicago Press.

Medina, L.F. and Stokes, S. (2007) 'Monopoly and monitoring: An approach to political clientelism', in Kitschelt, H. and Wilkinson, S.I. (eds.) *Patrons, clients, and policies: Patterns of democratic accountability and political competition*. Cambridge: Cambridge University Press, pp. 68–82.

Nichter, S. (2008) 'Vote buying or turnout buying? Machine politics and the secret ballot', *American Political Science Review*, 102(1), p19–31.

Piattoni, S. (ed.) (2001) *Clientelism, interests, and democratic representation: The European experience in historical and comparative perspective*. Cambridge: Cambridge University Press.

Remmer, K.L. (2007) 'The political economy of patronage: Expenditure patterns in the Argentine provinces, 1983–2003', *The Journal of Politics*, 69(2), p363–377.

Roniger, L. (2004) 'Political clientelism, democracy, and market economy', *Comparative Politics*, 36(3), p353–375.

Schaffer, F.C. (ed.) (2007) *Elections for sale: The causes and consequences of vote buying*. Boulder: Lynne Rienner Publishers.

Scott, J.C. (1969) 'Corruption, machine politics, and political change', *American Political Science Review*, 63(4), p1142–1158.

Stokes, S. (2021) 'Clientelism and development: Is there a poverty trap?', *WIDER Working Paper*, 91, p1–16.

Stokes, S., Dunning, T., Nazareno, M. and Brusco, V. (2013) *Brokers, voters, and clientelism: The puzzle of distributive politics*. Cambridge: Cambridge University Press.

Trantidis, A. and Tsagkroni, V. (2017) 'Clientelism and corruption: Institutional adaptation of state capture strategies in view of resource scarcity in Greece', *British Journal of Politics and International Relations*, 19(2), p263–281.

Vokes, R. and Wilkins, S. (2016) 'Party, patronage and coercion in the NRM'S 2016 re-election in Uganda: imposed or embedded?', *Journal of Eastern African Studies*, 10(4), p581–600.

Volintiru, C. (2012) 'Institutional distorsions, clientelism and corruption: Evidence from Romania', CREI Working Papers Series 1(2012 June), Bucuresti: Department of International Economies and Business Buchurest University of Economic Studies.

Weingrod, A. (1968) 'Patrons, patronage, and political parties', *Comparative Studies in Society and History*, 10(4), p377–400.

Yıldırım, K. and Kitschelt, H. (2020) 'Analytical perspectives on varieties of clientelism', *Democratization*, 27(1), p20–43.

PART 6

Regional comparisons

30
POLITICAL PARTIES IN RUSSIA AND POST-SOVIET STATES

Neil Robinson

Authoritarianism in Russia and other post-Soviet states has developed through democratic erosion rather than through the rapid displacement of democracy via events like coup d'états. Since authoritarianism develops from within democratic institutions, political parties can play a larger role than in traditional authoritarian polities. Constitutions drafted in more democratic times are kept for the most part and so are the institutions that they establish: elections still occur and parties compete in them in national, regional and local elections. Consequently, these regimes have been labelled 'hybrids' and classified as forms of 'competitive' or 'electoral' authoritarianism (Levitsky and Way 2010; Schedler 2013). Political parties play contradictory roles in such regimes. On the one hand, they can stabilise non-democratic politics by providing a façade of democracy and by helping rulers control elite members, or by constraining leaders so that they rule in tandem with elite factions (Brownlee 2007, 10–13; Magaloni 2008). On the other hand, parties are part of the opposition that resists authoritarian consolidation in some post-Soviet states.

This chapter will examine how parties have developed to play out these different functions in post-Soviet states. We will concentrate on those post-Soviet states that have never developed as weak democracies (so not Georgia, Kyrgyzstan and Moldova), or which have reverted to non-democratic rule after a period of weak democratic government. These are the countries where party behaviour is most different from that of parties in established democracies. The differences between parties in the post-Soviet region and parties in established democracies have influenced the study of parties in the region. The difficulties of accessing information and party cadres have meant that the focus of research has been on the roles that parties play in regime development and stability rather than on party organisation, composition and internal politics.

The emergence of political parties

Political parties began to develop in the late 1980s when Mikhail Gorbachev's *perestroika* (restructuring) reforms enabled free association and political organisation. The initial waves of political mobilisation that took place in the 1980s generally took the form of popular fronts in support of *perestroika* (Tolz 1990, 16–22). These popular fronts were formed in most of the Soviet republics (soon to be states), as well as in major cities like Moscow and Leningrad, and initially supported Gorbachev's reforms. They took on more critical stances to the USSR and

Gorbachev when the official reform process failed to meet popular expectations. The strength of these movements varied from republic to republic. Ethnic mobilisation made them strong in the Baltic states and parts of the Caucasus. They were weaker, however, in Russia, Ukraine and Central Asia where the costs of political participation were higher than in the Baltic states, which had more social consensus over the need for radical change, and less fear of reprisals from local communist party elites. Popular fronts in the Baltic states, Ukraine and the Caucasus became the main proponents of state sovereignty and then independence for the republics. Elites maintained high degrees of control in Central Asia, eastern Ukraine and outside of the largest cities in Russia. Ukraine was divided on the issue of independence along ethnic and linguistic lines, which limited support for the popular front. An all-Russian movement for democratic change, Democratic Russia, was only created in the spring of 1990.

Political parties were formed in addition to the popular fronts across the USSR, especially after 1990. These parties were generally very small. People were uncertain what might befall them if they joined a party. Parties were also subject to fragmentation. Only the most committed activists were prepared to join parties. These were people with strong views and clashes over points of principle frequently led to the fragmentation of what were already very small organisations (Fish 1995). As a result, parties did not replace the popular fronts as the focal point of opposition activity. The popular fronts and Democratic Russia were successful in accelerating the pace of change, breaking down the monopoly power of the CPSU, and getting pro-independence deputies into republican parliaments. However, this meant that the new states had no effective political parties when they achieved independence at the end of 1991.

Independence did not stimulate the development of more effective parties. One reason was that new states did not hold fresh parliamentary elections. Russia held its first post-communist elections at the end of 1993, the first parliamentary elections in Kazakhstan and Ukraine were in 1994, and in Belarus in 1995. Some parties developed from within the parliaments that had been elected in 1990, but these parties often did not put down any organisational roots, or delineate constituencies for themselves. In short, they were parliamentary factions rather than parties. Many of the new parties that emerged in Russia and Ukraine were jokingly called 'taxi' or 'sofa' parties, that is, they were so small that you could 'fit' their membership in the back of one cab or on a sofa. Parties in Belarus hardly developed in the 1990s. Most parliamentary deputies are independents and support President Alexander Lukashenko, as do those few deputies elected to parliament from political parties. Over time opposition parties in Belarus have been suppressed and have either failed to win seats or been denied the right to participate in elections (Frear 2018).

The second reason for weak party development was that post-Soviet constitutional development favoured presidentialism (Easter 1997). Many of these presidents – in Ukraine and most of Central Asia, for example, and in Azerbaijan from 1993 – were communist party leaders who moved from their party posts to presidencies as the USSR began to collapse. They had little interest in facilitating the development of political parties that might challenge them. The only parties developed as mass organisations were successors to the CPSU led by strongmen presidents who had been the first secretary of the republican branches of the CPSU and who in essence transformed these communist party branches into new presidential parties by decree. The ways that this happened can be seen in Table 30.1, which shows where former first secretaries of republican branches of the CPSU took over as presidents when their republics became independent states, where they were supported by a successor party to the CPSU republican branch, whether that party was subsequently replaced by a new presidential party, and whether the successor party to the CPSU or the new presidential party achieved political dominance alongside the president. This was the case in Kazakhstan, Tajikistan, Turkmenistan

Table 30.1 CPSU successor parties and presidential parties

	Former communist party leader takes over	Supported by successor party (new name in brackets)	New pro-presidential party created	Pro-presidential party achieves political dominance
Azerbaijan	Yes – after an interregnum	No	New Azerbaijan Party (2003)	Yes
Kazakhstan	Yes	Yes (Socialist Party)	Nur Otan (1999)	Yes
Russia	No	No	United Russia (2001)	Yes
Tajikistan	Yes	Yes (People's Democratic Party of Tajikistan)	No	Yes
Turkmenistan	Yes	Yes (Democratic Party of Turkmenistan)	No	Yes
Ukraine	Yes	No	Party of Regions (1997)	No
Uzbekistan	Yes	Yes (People's Democratic Party of Uzbekistan)	Liberal Democratic Party of Uzbekistan (2003)	Yes

and Uzbekistan (Olimova and Bowyer 2002; Ishiyama 2008; Isaacs 2010). Azerbaijan is a variant of this model. The CPSU was banned in 1991, but Heydar Aliyev, who had been the first secretary of the Azerbaijan communist party between 1969 and 1982, came to power in 1993. Aliyev formed a new party, the New Azerbaijan Party, which supported him and his son Ilham after his death, as president (Ergun 2010). These parties all became electorally dominant and allowed their leaders to monopolise political power, but it is debatable if these parties act independently of their leaders, as we will discuss later.

Party development in Russia and Ukraine in the 1990s

The only real variations to the basic pattern of post-Soviet party development were Russia and Ukraine. Leonid Kravchuk, the first president of Ukraine, had been a leader of the Ukrainian republican communist party, but was an 'independent' president and only joined the Social Democratic Party of Ukraine after leaving office. His successor, Leonid Kuchma, had been a CPSU member but never joined a party after the demise of the USSR. In Russia, Boris Yeltsin broke with the CPSU in 1990 and had been a part of Democratic Russia, but he never engaged in party building after being elected President of Russia in 1991.

There were grounds for the consolidation of parties in Russia and Ukraine, because there was some social and ideological structure to voting in these countries. There was a basic left-right division among people on economic issues that reflected voters' class positions, age and education, and differences over attitudes towards the communist past and over moral and political attitudes that overlay these social interests (Whitefield 2002; Hale 2006). However, social and attitudinal cleavages around class, ideology and region were not translated into support for a few parties that could represent these cleavages, because there was an oversupply of political parties and the development of highly fragmented and polarised party systems in which multiple parties competed for votes.

The basis of fragmented and polarised party systems was primarily institutional: fragmentation and polarisation were products of electoral rules and constitutional orders – presidentialism – and their interaction with what was already a weakly structured party political space, rather than social and ideological. Electoral rules did not encourage politicians to coalesce in a few parties that could consolidate a social or ideological bloc of support. In Ukraine, the 1994 elections required successful candidates to get over 50 per cent of the valid vote to secure election, with run-offs between the top two candidates, where this was not achieved in a first round vote. This encouraged local elites to run as independents and try to use name recognition and so-called 'administrative resources' to secure election, rather than make them seek office through parties. It also encouraged oversupply of parties. Parties were not well established brand-names for the most part so there were low barriers to entry for anyone who wanted to try their hand and run a new party in elections. Sixteen parties won seats in the 1994 Ukrainian Verkhovna Rada elections, but deputies from these parties made up only half of the elected deputies, the others being independents. The weakness of parties and the large number of independently elected deputies meant that party stability and discipline in the Verkhovna Rada were weak, and this ensured that parties remained poorly thought of in general. Many that competed in 1994 did not survive to compete in the next elections. Ukraine changed its electoral system to try to encourage party development, but the mixed system introduced for the next elections in 1998, with half the Verkhovna Rada elected through single mandate district plurality elections and half through a proportional representation (PR) list vote (with a 4 per cent threshold), did not fully resolve the problem. There was still an oversupply of parties, as 30 parties and electoral blocs competed in the election. Independents took over half the single mandate district seats, the rest being divided between 17 parties. Only eight parties exceeded the 4 per cent threshold, but the victory of independents and nine other parties in the single mandate seats meant that there was only a weak incentive to amalgamate parties to secure representation through the PR vote.

The failure of the Ukrainian 1998 election to strengthen parties should not have been a surprise since the Ukrainian system was the same as that adopted in Russia in 1993. The mixed electoral system sent out contradictory signals as to what was best for politicians and undermined 'the ability of candidates or parties to learn over time and begin to make decisions that yield issue-based partisan competition' (Smyth 2006: 195). Politicians did not have to be loyal to a party or work to consolidate party development to have a chance of winning a seat in the parliament (Duma). Politicians were as incentivised to build up their personal following and compete for a seat as an individual as they were to support party development. The Russian system produced large numbers of independent deputies in the 1993, 1995 and 1999 Duma elections. Parties, with a few exceptions, that were formed in a hurry to compete in the first elections in 1993 failed to lay down roots and develop organisational structures and so either collapsed entirely before the next elections or performed badly at them and then disbanded. This was the fate of pro-government parties that were formed from within the administration, like the Party of Russian Unity and Accord, which competed in the 1993 election and then faded away, and Our Home is Russia, which competed in 1995. As in Ukraine, parties were not well established brand-names and barriers to entry were low for anyone who wanted to try their hand and run a new party in elections. The 1993 election was contested by 13 parties. Since most of these parties failed to cross the 5 per cent threshold of the PR list vote or died away after the election, incentives to create new parties were higher than incentives to amalgamate existing parties: in 1995 over 40 parties and electoral blocs ran.

The huge oversupply of parties meant that many voters cast their ballot for parties that could not get over the PR threshold. In Russia in 1995 and Ukraine in 1998, half and a third of voters, respectively, did not see the party they voted for secure a seat through PR. This should have incentivised politicians to flock to the more successful parties or to amalgamate their parties to capture these voters. Parties that were successful like the CPRF, Yabloko (the only Russian liberal party successful in all elections between 1993 and 2003) or the Communist Party of Ukraine (CPU), should have developed their platforms to attract some of these unrepresented voters. Electoral rules, because they gave politicians other options for securing office through running as independents, worked against this process, and oversupply itself encouraged fragmentation and polarisation. Fragmentation meant that the party system in the 1990s was a series of 'sub-systems' within a fragmented whole, with competition within these sub-systems helping to prevent party consolidation. Relations and interactions between parties took place within these sub-systems, as much as between the major parties (Robinson 1998). These sub-systems can be classified, roughly, as a communist/'left' sub-system, a 'nationalist' sub-system, and a 'pro-liberal reform, centrist' sub-system. Within each of these sub-systems a large party, like the CPRF in the communist/'left' sub-system in Russia and the CPU in Ukraine, or the (ironically titled) Liberal Democratic Party of Russia (LDPR), which represented nationalist and authoritarian voters, in the 'nationalist' sub-system, was surrounded by a host of smaller radical groups, rival claimants to the title of successor to the CPSU, such as the Socialist Party of Ukraine (SPU). This competition stopped them from shifting towards the centre ground to pick up more votes since they would have lost votes to the more radical parties on the left and right. Keeping their vote share – and the parliamentary privileges, most notably the resources that came from securing seats in parliament – meant that the CPRF, CPU and LDPR were stuck ideologically and programmatically.

The 'pro-liberal reform, centrist' sub-system was split between government and non-government parties. These parties divided the vote between them so that the broad centrist, pro-liberal reform vote was always split. Part of the pro-liberal reform vote in Russia went to government parties as a vote for stability, which limited the electoral success of opposition liberal centrist parties like Yabloko in the 1990s, and Yabloko and parties like the Union of Right Forces in the early 2000s. Opposition liberal parties' ability to break out of their electoral ghetto was further weakened by their failure to unite and provide a single focus for liberal voters in the 1990s and anti-Putin liberals in the 2000s. Yabloko was hostile to parties like Russia's Democratic Choice in the 1990s and the Union of Right Forces in the early 2000s that were 'compromised', because they were founded by politicians who had been in government, and has rejected alliances, because other parties refused to support Yabloko leader Grigorii Yavlinskii's presidential ambitions (White 2005).

Convergence on authoritarianism: party development since 2000

The existence of multiple parties in Russia and Ukraine in the 1990s created a rough form of democracy. This democracy was inherently unstable, however, as both countries lurched between economic and political crises over the course of the decade. The tenures of the two countries' presidents, Yeltsin in Russia, Kravchuk and Kuchma in Ukraine, were not guaranteed, as Kravchuk's failure to secure a second term in 1994 showed, and they faced serious opposition in the legislatures from the CPRF, the CPU and the SPU.

Achieving regime stability and protecting presidential power had to involve greater governmental success in elections and a diminution of the threat to weak post-communist capitalism from the left so that elite assets could be protected. The dangers of not controlling the political system were graphically illustrated by the 'colour revolutions' (non-violent protests often over electoral corruption) that saw the defeat of presidential incumbents, or their hand-picked successors, in Georgia (2003), Ukraine (2004–2005) and Kyrgyzstan (2005 and 2010). These showed that avoiding overthrow through loss of control over political competition meant not just securing control over political competition but *over*-securing such control, as had been achieved in countries like Azerbaijan and Uzbekistan. Elections should be controlled to achieve not just victory but acclamation of the regime and of its 'right' to hold power. This meant securing control over the media and weakening the autonomy of powerful groups like business and regional elites. It meant electoral fraud to ensure large electoral majorities that 'showed' the legitimacy of the regime and the futility of challenging it. Controlling party development meant that elite factions could not create parties and use them to weaken presidential power. Voters would be forced to choose between officially licensed political parties at elections. These parties would not protest electoral fraud – such protests were a factor in all the 'colour revolutions' – and would be compliant in parliament. Control over parliament meant that elite factions that might be tempted to break with the regime would be denied allies and easier to censure (Robinson 2012).

The possibility of over-securing control of politics varied very greatly in Russia and Ukraine, and the outcome of trying to manage the political system had very different ends: fluctuation between management and revolt in Ukraine versus increased authoritarian political closure in Russia.

In Ukraine, there were multiple attempts at creating parties that could represent elite interests to leverage their interests in the legislative processes and capture the presidency. The most successful of these was the Party of Regions, formed with the support of business and political elites in Eastern Ukraine (Kudelia and Kuzio 2015). It secured seats in the Verkhovna Rada and its leader, Viktor Yanukovych served as Prime Minister between 2002 and 2005. Its electoral success was based on its combining – cynically – a left wing platform to capture votes from the CPU and the SPU, with support from business and political elites in Eastern Ukraine whose interests it protected. Yanukovych lost the 2004 presidential election due to the electoral protests of the 'Orange Revolution', but the Party of Regions, along with the SPU and CPU, was able to create a majority coalition and influence government formation after the 2006 Vekhovna Rada election, even getting Yanukovych re-appointed as Prime Minister between August 2006 and December 2007.

In 2010, Yanukovych was elected President of Ukraine, but the Party of Regions was unable to stabilise its rule. Yanukovych could not force a majority of Ukraine's economic and political elites to join the Party of Regions, co-opt all media and a substantial part of civil society. The Party of Regions made only limited headway electorally and among elites in the west and centre of Ukraine. This meant that there were possibilities for mobilisation against Yanukovych, which materialised in opposition to plans for closer economic integration with Russia in 2013 and led to the ousting of Yanukovych and his exile after the Euromaidan revolution in 2014. The removal of Yanukovych meant the end of the Party of Regions, particularly as its electoral strongholds in the east declared independence from Ukraine. Ukraine returned to the fragmented pluralism of the 1990s, a form of rough and ready democracy in which the party system was split between parties representing economic blocs (such as former President Petr Poroshenko's European Solidarity party), nationalist parties from western Ukraine (including neo-fascist parties, like Svoboda, Freedom), and a smattering of liberal, social and Christian democratic parties. Dissatisfaction with this state of affairs led to the growth in popularity of a party named after a TV programme, Sluha narodu (Servant of the People). In the programme, a teacher becomes president after a clip of him raging against corruption goes viral. Life imitated bad art when the programme's star, Volodymyr Zelensky, became Sluha narodu's presidential candidate in 2019 and won. The party then won a majority in the Verkhovna Rada elections in December 2019.

The Russian invasion in 2022 had two immediate effects on party politics in Ukraine. First, Zelensky's popularity and that of his party, which had declined as the difficulties of governing Ukraine made themselves felt after the 2019 elections, rose. Second, 11 left-wing and/or pro-Russian parties were banned. Most of these parties were small, but one, the Opposition Party for Life, had 44 deputies in the Rada and was a main opposition party. The long-term impact that this has on Ukrainian party politics, particularly on the fortunes of nationalist parties, will be something to watch.

Authoritarian political closure was achieved in Russia, because Vladimir Putin was able to co-opt or repress Russian elites. Co-option came through the creation of a presidential party, United Russia, from the merger of Unity, established to support the government in the 1999 Duma elections, and Fatherland-All Russia, the electoral wing of regional leaders who had tried to manoeuvre themselves into a position to control Yeltsin's presidential succession in 1999. Putin's popularity and media support gave Unity a greater share of the vote than had been expected. Between them, Unity and Fatherland-All Russia had 31 per cent of Duma seats, more than the CPRF, which had topped the poll. Unity's association with Putin led many independents and Fatherland-All Russia deputies to join it. As Putin consolidated his power Fatherland-All Russia joined Unity in July 2001 to form a new party, the Union of Unity and Fatherland, renamed United Russia in 2003 (Hale 2004). The merger of Fatherland-All Russian and Unity into United Russia gave the party a Duma majority. Unlike previous parties formed from within the government, United Russia bound together central and regional political elites. Its electoral dominance was ensured by changes to electoral laws for the 2003 and 2007 Duma elections: SMD seats were abolished, removing the chance for regional elite members to run as independents. United Russia expanded rapidly, opening branches in all of Russia's regions, developing youth and supporter's associations, forging links with a wide variety of civic organisations (some of which were set up to liaise with it). Consequently, it became the largest party in Russia with over two million members, 2,595 local branches, and 82,631 grassroots organisers at the end of 2016.

The rise to dominance of United Russia was assisted by limiting the number of effective parties, the management of voting through the creation of so-called 'project parties' and through fraud, and the emasculation of the opposition. Changes to electoral laws in 2005 (the raising of the threshold for securing seats through the PR vote from 5 to 7 per cent, and the abolition of SMD district seats) reduced the number of parties competing and securing seats in parliament, although the SMD seats were reintroduced to help United Russia gain a Duma majority after its vote share shrank in 2011. New laws on parties introduced tighter rules on the standards that parties had to meet to be registered and on party financing. These registration requirements set a high bar for parties to meet and provided grounds for preventing registration, or for banning parties. The number of registered parties has fallen overtime: in 2016, there were 76, which had been winnowed down to 34 by 2021, and most of these parties play no role in elections. 'Project parties' were set up as 'independent' parties by the Presidential Administration to manage voting. Parties like Rodina (Motherland) and A Just Russia were formed to take votes from the left and nationalists in order to weaken support for the CPRF, which had been the most successful party electorally in the 1990s, so that it could not challenge United Russia. In 2021, a party called Noviye Lyudi (New People) was allowed to run in the Duma elections as a pro-Putin liberal party to try to get younger people to ignore opposition calls for a boycott of elections. There has always been some electoral fraud in Russian elections but in the 1990s it was difficult to direct because of elite disagreements over which party to support; most of the beneficiaries of fraud were probably independent candidates supported by local political machines. The establishment of United Russia and the tightened control over regional administration by Putin gave regional elites an incentive to commit electoral fraud: votes for Putin and United Russia proved their loyalty to the regime (Moser and White 2017).

Finally, opposition was emasculated (Gel'man 2005). There were two sides to this development. In the Duma opposition is made up of the CPRF, the LDPR and project parties like A Just Russia and Noviye lyudi. These parties have been labelled the 'systemic opposition'. They are a part of the formal political system since they have parliamentary seats and positions but are in 'opposition' because they are not in government. Their opposition is tokenistic, however, since they are *of* the system, either directly created by it in the case of the project parties, or reliant upon it. The CPRF and the LDPR depend on winning Duma seats for access to the state resources that they use to organise and support party organisation. Consequently, the CPRF and LDPR collaborate with the Putin regime in order to survive. They provide support for the regime (e.g. over foreign policy), and have not contested Putin's political reforms seriously. The demise of the CPRF as an anti-systemic party, the political quiescence of the LDPR and both parties' reliance on state resources point to Russia having a 'cartelized' party system (Hutcheson 2013). In such a system party members play little role in the life of the party and parties conspire with one another to try to raise barriers of entry to new electoral forces. In Russia's case, this conspiracy is driven from the regime, rather than achieved through co-operation between parties. However, the systemic opposition has colluded with it and an electoral status quo has been created in which only United Russia, the CPRF, the LDPR and one or more project parties can be successful.

Cartelisation leaves the so-called 'non-systemic opposition', the parties that want to see Putin removed, little space to compete in. At best, non-systemic opposition politicians have been able to take a few local council seats. Divisions within the non-systemic opposition have helped to keep it weak. There has been a failure to build alliances among opposition parties to create an actual 'non-systemic opposition' rather than a series of 'non-systemic oppositions', which are easier for the regime to isolate and repress. Non-systemic opposition parties have failed to agree on tactics – should they run candidates against Putin in presidential elections, for example, or boycott elections? – and have failed to merge parties or create larger umbrella movements. There have been several attempts to build a larger opposition movement. For example, opposition politicians tried to form a Co-ordinating Council of the Russian Opposition to capitalise on the mass demonstrations against electoral fraud in 2011 and 2012. However, the Council was riven by disputes and dissolved after a year. The small size of opposition parties has meant that they have not attracted mass support and are very dependent on their leaders, who have far higher public profiles than the parties they lead, like Aleksei Navalny of the 'Russia of the Future' Party. The ability of opposition parties to actually oppose is thus relatively small and declining. In this respect, Russia is not unlike other post-Soviet states where opposition groups have been marginalised and made politically irrelevant (LaPorte 2015). The closure of Russia's last independent media following Putin's invasion of Ukraine in 2022 will limit the impact of the anti-systemic opposition even further, although they hope that their opposition to Putin's war will be a watershed in the regime's fortunes.

These developments brought Russia into line with what had been achieved in most of Central Asia in the 1990s and led to speculation that post-Soviet states might be developing a form of party-based authoritarianism in which 'hegemonic' parties become the organisational centre of dictatorship and create mechanisms for sustaining authoritarianism over time (Roberts 2015; Reuter 2017). Hegemonic parties globally have been a powerful force for political stabilisation and a reason why non-democratic regimes based on a political party last longer than other forms of non-democracy (Geddes, Wright and Frantz 2014). Elite division and competition can be contained within the party and is less likely to spill out into the wider political arena and destabilise the regime.

There are some similarities between 'hegemonic' parties elsewhere in the world and parties like United Russia, the New Azerbaijan Party and Nur Otan in Kazakhstan. They have been able to secure electoral victories over time and force other parties to work with them. They are vehicles for ruling elites to show their legitimacy when parties secure electoral victories (albeit with limited electoral competition), and overwhelming parliamentary majorities. However, elsewhere, hegemonic parties organise patronage, are a part of the machinery of government and arbitrate between different elite demands. Parties often decide on leadership succession and access to office. In performing these functions, hegemonic parties can play a powerful stabilising role adjudicating between elite factions. They are not simply emanations of the president and his power, and at the service of the presidential clique. Post-Soviet ruling parties, however, were formed at the instigation of the president and elites are loyal to the president rather than to 'their' ruling party. Advancement is achieved primarily through relationships with the president rather than through the party. United Russia might be seen as a slight variation on this theme since it was formed from a merger between the presidential party, Unity, and the party of regional leaders, Fatherland-All Russia, and was thus a coalition at its foundation. However, Putin controlled access to executive power independently of United Russia, used patronage and financial incentives to make coalition members loyal to him, and consolidated his power over regional elites so as a coalition United Russia was short-lived (Chaisty, Cheeseman and Power 2018, 160–162, 180–181). At best, it is a coalition of Putin's dependents. Moreover, the role of so-called hegemonic parties in succession in post-Soviet states has been slight. United Russia approved Putin's replacement in 2008 by Dmitry Medvedev, but Medvedev was Putin's choice. It was also Putin, not the party, who decided on his own return to the presidency in 2012. In Azerbaijan presidential power passed from father to son. Kazakhstan's Nur Otan and the Liberal Democratic Party of Uzbekistan do not seem to have played any formal role in determining who would succeed to power when the first post-communist presidents, Nursultan Nazarbayev and Islam Karimov, respectively, stepped down and died. For these reasons, the move to party-based authoritarianism seems to be incomplete, and parties in the region are more personalist than hegemonic (Bader 2011; Isaacs and Whitmore 2014). They dominate electoral politics but do so at the behest of, and to the benefit of, the president, and may have limited life expectancy if the president decides that another vehicle might serve his interests better, or if a successor decides that the party needs to be replaced with a machine loyal to them, rather than their predecessor. As White (2012, 217) put it (describing United Russia), post-Soviet ruling parties do not possess power in their own right but are more 'agent[s] of power' that do not have the same levels of autonomy as hegemonic parties elsewhere in the world.

Conclusion and avenues for further research

Party development in the post-Soviet states has confirmed the importance of parties in both democratic consolidation and authoritarian development. The weakness of parties and their inability to challenge presidents has been a key factor in the drift to authoritarianism. Most of the post-Soviet states we have discussed saw democracy diminish rapidly as former Communist

Party leaders became presidents, presidential parties supported them, and other parties were either suppressed or forced into alliance with the regime. In Russia and Ukraine in the 1990s, the fragmentation of party systems and conflict between parties and presidents supported the argument that the existence of a large number of parties in a democratising polity increases the risk of conflict between legislatures and presidents, and weakens democracy (Mainwaring 1993). Efforts at constructing coalitions between presidents and parties, which might have stabilised democracy by aligning executive and legislative agendas (Chaisty, Cheeseman and Power 2018), failed. Coalitions either did not become dominant, as in Ukraine where the Party of Regions did not manage to co-opt enough of civil society or other parties to stabilise the political system, or coalition was a step towards personalist authoritarianism as in Russia where United Russia moved from its being a coalition to becoming a political machine to support Putin.

The role that parties play in regime development will continue to be the primary focus of future research into parties in the post-Soviet space. Parties may be weak and lack autonomy from rulers but they are the only organisations that can use the main formal institutions of democracy that still exist in post-Soviet states, elections and parliaments. Elections will remain points of contestation between opposition and regime, parties will try to organise to compete in those elections in the hope that they can effect regime change (if they are part of non-systemic oppositions), or gain votes and increase the resources they earn from the regime if they are part of the systemic opposition. Ruling parties' relations with rulers and the extent to which these parties can move away from personalism will continue to be a major research focus, especially where there is leadership turnover. One possible democratisation route is a slow change first from personalist parties to elite coalition parties, where new leaders fail to personalise a ruling party, and then to competition between rival elite coalition parties that seek advantage through developing social representation instead of relying on personalistic politics. A route to democratisation like this may be slow or reversed, and how it might be travelled will depend on how ruling parties are currently constructed. This is an under-researched topic, but a vital one since the composition of parties during succession or leadership crises will influence how they behave. If parties are dominated by state functionaries, for example, we might expect them to react differently to a leadership crisis than if the party is comprised of business elites or strong regional networks: might state functionaries rally around a regime but businessmen or regional cliques seek relief from political rent seeking or decentralisation through using the party to constrain rulers? Understanding the roles that parties might play over the longer term in the post-Soviet region requires that we look into parties as well as at how they facilitate general regime legitimacy and stability.

References

Bader, M. (2011) 'Hegemonic political parties in post-Soviet Eurasia: towards party-based authoritarianism?', *Communist and Post-Communist Studies*, 44(3), p189–197.
Brownlee, J. (2007) *Authoritarianism in an age of democratization*. Cambridge: Cambridge University Press.
Chaisty, P., Cheeseman, N. and Power, T. (2018) *Coalitional presidentialism in comparative perspective*. Oxford: Oxford University Press.
Easter, G. (1997) 'Preference for presidentialism: Post-communist regime change in Russia and the NIS', *World Politics*, 49(2), p184–211.
Ergun, A. (2010) 'Post-Soviet political transformation in Azerbaijan', *Uluslararası İlişkiler Dergisi*, 7(26), p67–85.
Fish, M. (1995) *Democracy from scratch. Opposition and regime in the new Russian revolution*. Princeton: Princeton University Press.
Frear, M. (2018) *Belarus under Lukashenka. Adaptive authoritarianism*. London: Routledge.

Geddes, B., Wright, J. and Frantz, E. (2014) 'Autocratic breakdown and regime transitions: A new data set', *Perspectives on Politics*, 12(2), p313–331.

Gel'man, V. (2005) 'Political opposition in Russia: A dying species?' *Post-Soviet Affairs*, 21(3), p226–46.

Hale, H. (2004) 'The origins of United Russia and the Putin presidency: The role of contingency in party-system development', *Demokratizatsiya*, 12(2), p169–194.

Hale, H. (2006) *Why not parties in Russia? Democracy, federalism, and the state*. Cambridge: Cambridge University Press.

Hutcheson, D. (2013) 'Party cartels beyond Western Europe: evidence from Russia', *Party Politics*, 19(6), p907–924.

Isaacs, R. (2010) *Party system formation in Kazakhstan*. London: Routledge.

Isaacs, R. and Whitmore, S. (2014) 'The limited agency and life-cycles of personalized dominant parties in the post-Soviet space: The cases of United Russia and Nur Otan', *Democratization*, 21(4), p699–721.

Ishiyama, J. (2008) 'Political party development and party "gravity" in semi-authoritarian states', *Taiwan Journal of Democracy*, 4(1), p33–53.

Kudelia, S and Kuzio, T. (2015) 'Nothing personal: Explaining the rise and decline of political machines in Ukraine, *Post-Soviet Affairs*, 31(3), p250–278.

LaPorte, J. (2015) 'Hidden in plain sight: Political opposition and hegemonic authoritarianism in Azerbaijan', *Post-Soviet Affairs*, 31(4), p339–366.

Levitsky, S. and Way, L. (2010) *Competitive authoritarianism: Hybrid regimes after the Cold War*. Cambridge: Cambridge University Press.

Magaloni, B. (2008) 'Credible power-sharing and the longevity of authoritarian rule' *Comparative Political Studies*, 41(4/5), p715–741.

Mainwaring, S. (1993) 'Presidentialism, multipartism, and democracy: The difficult combination', *Comparative Political Studies*, 26(2), p198–228.

Moser, R. and White, A. (2017) 'Does electoral fraud spread? The expansion of electoral manipulation in Russia?', *Post-Soviet Affairs*, 33(2), p85–99.

Olimova, S. and Bowyer, A. (2002) *Political parties in Tajikistan*. Dushanbe: International Foundation for Electoral Systems.

Reuter, O. (2017) *The origins of dominant parties: Building authoritarian institutions in post-Soviet Russia*. Cambridge: Cambridge University Press.

Roberts, S. (2015) 'Converging party systems in Russia and Central Asia: A case of authoritarian norm diffusion?' *Communist and Post-Communist Studies*, 48(2–3), p147–157

Robinson, N. (1998) 'Classifying Russia's party system', *Journal of Communist Studies and Transition Politics*, 14(1), p159–177.

Robinson, N. (2012) 'Institutional factors and Russian political parties', *East European Politics*, 28(3), p298–309.

Schedler, A. (2013) *The politics of uncertainty: sustaining and subverting electoral authoritarianism*. Oxford: Oxford University Press.

Smyth, R. (2006) *Candidate strategies and electoral competition in the Russian Federation*. New York: Cambridge University Press.

Tolz, V. (1990) *The USSR's emerging multiparty system*. New York: Praeger.

White, D. (2005) 'Going their own way: The Yabloko Party's opposition to unification', *Journal of Communist Studies and Transition Politics*, 21(4), p462–486.

White, D. (2012) 'Re-conceptualising Russian party politics', *East European Politics*, 28(3), p210–224

Whitefield, S. (2002) 'Political cleavages and post-communist politics', *Annual Review of Political Science*, 5, p181–200.

31
POLITICAL PARTIES IN EAST ASIA

Ko Maeda

This chapter discusses political parties and party systems in three East Asian democracies: Taiwan, South Korea, and Japan. Japan has had democratic party politics since the end of the Second World War, whereas South Korea and Taiwan democratised in the 1980s and 1990s, respectively. These three East Asian states were important U.S. allies in East Asia during the Cold War and pro-U.S. political forces stayed in power for a long time in all three countries: the Liberal Democratic Party (LDP) in Japan, Kuomintang (KMT) in Taiwan, and conservative parties under various labels in South Korea.[1]

This chapter is organised as follows. The next section provides an overview of the political parties and party systems in the three countries, while the remainder of the chapter is organised into three thematic discussions: issue evolution and opposition party development, regionalism and nationalisation of political parties, and recent challenges by anti-establishment parties. The three East Asian democracies have had different experiences with how opposition parties grew to compete against dominant parties. Two-party systems have taken root in Taiwan and South Korea while Japan still has a dominant party system. There are also important similarities across the three democracies in that regional parties and anti-establishment parties have not grown large.

Party politics in Japan, South Korea, and Taiwan

Japan's case is unique in this region in that it has a much longer history of party politics than other states in the region, dating back to the 1890s. All political parties were disbanded during the Second World War, but electoral politics restarted in 1946 – a year after the end of the war. The current constitution came into effect in 1947. The bicameral legislature, the Diet, consists of the lower house whose members serve for a maximum of four years and the upper house where half of its members are renewed every three years. The prime minister is selected from the legislature and heads the cabinet.

The early post-war years saw tumultuous party politics, but pro-U.S. conservative political forces were in power most of the time. The LDP was established by a merger of two major conservative parties in 1955. In the same year, the Japan Socialist Party (JPS) was also founded by two socialist parties' merger. Subsequently, the LDP kept winning elections, and the JSP remained as the largest opposition party for decades (the so-called 1955 system). Komeito and the Democratic Socialist Party were other opposition parties located between the LDP and the JSP. The Japanese Communist Party was the far left party.

The LDP has been in opposition twice. It briefly lost power in 1993–1994 when a non-LDP coalition took over, which fell apart shortly after enacting an electoral law reform of the lower house. Between 2009 and 2012, the centre-left Democratic Party of Japan (DPJ) was in power, but its popularity plummeted while the party was in office (see Kushida and Lipscy 2013). Since returning to power in 2012, the LDP has held on to its dominant position with its smaller coalition partner Komeito.[2] The DPJ incorporated another party in 2016 and changed its name. It then split into two before the 2017 election. Since 2017, the largest opposition has been the Constitutional Democratic Party of Japan (CDP).

South Korea has had a series of authoritarian rulers since its foundation in 1948. Conceding to a pro-democracy movement, the government announced a plan to transition to democracy on 29 June 1987. A presidential election was held in December of that year, and regular elections have been taking place since then. The president is elected in a one-round, direct election for a non-renewable five-year term. The unicameral legislature, the National Assembly, currently has 300 members who serve a four-year term.

Party politics in South Korea since democratisation, especially in the twenty-first century, features a system with two major parties, one on the 'conservative' camp and the other on the 'progressive' camp. The two largest parties have won at least 75 per cent and often more than 90 per cent of the seats in every legislative election since 2000. The names of the parties have been changing frequently. Table 31.1 shows the names of the major parties at each presidential election.

Table 31.1 Major parties of South Korea and Taiwan in presidential elections

	Year	Main 'Conservative' Party	Main 'Progressive' Party
South Korea	1987	Democratic Justice Party (36.6%)	(a)
	1992	Democratic Liberal Party (42.0%)	Democratic Party (33.8%)
	1997	Grand National Party (38.7%)	*National Congress for New Politics (40.3%)*
	2002	Grand National Party (46.6%)	*Millennium Democratic Party (48.9%)*
	2007	*Grand National Party (48.7%)*	Unified New Democratic Party (26.1%)
	2012	*Saenuri Party (51.6%)*	Democratic United Party (48.0%)
	2017	Liberty Korea Party (24.0%)	*Minjoo Party of Korea (41.1%)*
	2022	People Power Party (48.6%)	Democratic Party (47.8%)
	Year	Main 'Pan-Blue' Party	Main 'Pan-Green' Party
Taiwan	1996	*Kuomintang (54.0%)*	Democratic Progressive Party (21.1%)
	2000	Kuomintang (23.1%)[(b)]	*Democratic Progressive Party (39.3%)*
	2004	Kuomintang (49.9%)	*Democratic Progressive Party (50.1%)*
	2008	*Kuomintang (58.4%)*	Democratic Progressive Party (41.6%)
	2012	*Kuomintang (51.6%)*	Democratic Progressive Party (45.6%)
	2016	Kuomintang (31.0%)	*Democratic Progressive Party (56.1%)*
	2020	Kuomintang (38.6%)	*Democratic Progressive Party (57.1%)*

Note: Numbers in parentheses are vote shares in presidential elections. Italic fonts indicate the winner of the presidency.

(a) In the 1987 Korean presidential election, there were mainly three parties that ran campaigns against the ruling Democratic Justice Party. The parties and their vote shares are: the Reunification Democratic Party (28.0 per cent), the Peaceful Democratic Party (27.0 per cent), and the New Democratic Republican Party (8.1 per cent).
(b) In the 2000 presidential election in Taiwan, an independent candidate James Soong, who later created the People First Party, won 36.8 per cent of votes.

Source: www.nec.go.kr/site/eng/main.do; www.cec.gov.tw/english/cms/pe.

At the time of South Korea's transition to democracy in 1987, the former authoritarian ruling party, the Democratic Justice Party (DJP) was able to win the presidency and stay in power. In 1990, two opposition parties joined the DJP and formed the Democratic Liberal Party (DLP), the main party of the 'conservative' camp. Since then, it has gone through many name changes, splits, and mergers. The conservatives won the presidential elections in 1987, 1992, 2007, 2012 and 2022.

On the other side of the political spectrum, in the founding 1987 presidential election, three opposition parties challenged the ruling DJP. After two of them joined the ruling party, the Peace Democratic Party remained in opposition and became the main party on the 'progressive' side. Just like the conservatives, the progressives also have experienced many changes. The progressives won the presidency in 1997, 2002, and 2017.

Taiwan was under the KMT's one-party dictatorship for several decades after the KMT was defeated in the Chinese Civil War and fled to the island where it established the Republic of China of which it became the ruling party. The people who emigrated from the mainland to Taiwan about the time of the KMT's arrival are often referred to as 'mainlanders' in contrast to the 'Taiwanese' people who are native to the island (their different political attitudes will be discussed in the next section), a division which is also reflected in the party system. President Lee Teng-hui (in office, 1988–2000) initiated a movement for democracy. A democratic legislative election was held for the first time in 1992, and in 1996, he conducted the first-ever direct presidential election, in which he was elected. Since then, democratic elections have regularly been held. The president is elected in a one-round, direct election for a four-year term, limited to two terms. The unicameral legislature, the Legislative Yuan, currently has 113 members who serve a four-year term.

The long-time ruling party KMT continues to be a major party to this day. The Democratic Progressive Party (DPP), founded in 1986, increased its popularity in the 1990s, and won the presidency for the first time in 2000. Since then, the KMT and the DPP have dominated Taiwanese party politics as the two major parties. The DPP won the presidential elections in 2000, 2004, 2016, and 2020, and the KMT won the 2008 and 2012 elections.

The party system of Taiwan since democratisation has been stable with no major changes in the line-up of the two major parties to this day (see Table 31.1). Wong (2014) explains that Taiwan's two major parties became gradually institutionalised and professionalised during the authoritarian era, which helps the current stability of the party system. Other parties in competition include the New Party (NP), the People First Party (PFP), and the Taiwan Solidarity Union (TSU), all of which were created by politicians who split off from the KMT.

Issue evolution and opposition party development

As noted, a common feature of the party politics in Taiwan, South Korea, and Japan is that all had a dominant, pro-U.S. political force during the Cold War. Japan's LDP is still in a dominant position – 68 years after its foundation. In contrast, South Korea and Taiwan have competitive party systems. In both countries, the ruling party from the authoritarian era won the first democratic presidential election (the victories of South Korea's DJP in 1987 and Taiwan's KMT in 1996). Yet the main opposition party became stronger afterwards and defeated the formerly dominant party or its successor party (the victories of South Korea's National Congress for New Politics [NCNP] in 1997 and Taiwan's DPP in 2000). Since then, both South Korea and Taiwan have had competitive electoral politics between two major parties. Clearly, there is a contrast between a dominant party system in Japan and competitive party systems in South Korea and Taiwan, which raises the pertinent question of what made them different.

Political parties in mature Western democracies have traditionally been divided by social cleavages (Lipset and Rokkan 1967). If one party is in a dominant position and the cleavages are firm and enduring, the one-party dominance is likely to be sustained. If opposition parties want to challenge the dominant party and end the dominance, they need to destabilise the structure. One way in which an existing cleavage structure may be altered is by 'issue evolution', a situation where a new salient issue emerges and divides voters (Carmines and Stimson 1986).

This view is in line with Greene's (2002) theory, where he argues that in a country with a dominant party, public resources are monopolised by the dominant party, and opposition parties lack access to patronage goods. Thus, if opposition parties try to gain popular support, they cannot employ a clientelistic strategy but need to make a programmatic appeal. If they are successful in creating a new issue dimension and attract supporters with it, the country's mode of party competition is transformed. As I will discuss later, Taiwan, South Korea, and Japan had different experiences with respect to the ways in which opposition parties have been able to create a new issue dimension.

Before moving on, let us consider a matter related to Greene's (2002) argument. A dominant party monopolises public resources and thus has an advantage in clientelistic practices over opposition parties. Indeed, clientelism and patronage have been used by the dominant parties in the three East Asian democracies discussed in this chapter. Yet it has been demonstrated in the literature that economic development is inversely related to the prevalence of clientelism (Hicken 2011). Since Japan, South Korea, and Taiwan have all become economically developed, the basis of political clientelism must have become less strong than in the past. It has been argued that a clientelistic political style has become less effective in South Korea (Hellmann 2014), Taiwan (Mobrand 2020), and Japan (Krauss and Pekkanen 2010).

Now let us examine how issue evolutions and party system changes happened in the three democracies. Taiwan is the case where a new issue dimension transformed the party system most clearly. The contrasting opinions of 'unification with China' and 'Taiwan independence' constitute the most salient policy dimension in Taiwan. As Taiwan was becoming increasingly democratic, the main opposition DPP mobilised support from the ethnic Taiwanese population (as opposed to the 'mainlanders'; see the previous section) who lean towards independence. By doing so, the DPP was able to differentiate itself from the ruling KMT that was strongly supported by the 'mainlanders' who otherwise favoured the 'unification' policy with the People's Republic of China.

As the two major parties took different positions on the most salient policy issue, Taiwanese party politics has come to be characterised by competition on one single dimension, that is, independence versus reunification. The KMT and two smaller parties, the NP and the PFP, often referred to as the Pan-Blue Camp, are on the 'unification' side and advocate a deeper economic integration with China. In contrast, the DPP and a few smaller parties are known as the 'Pan-Green' camp. They are on the 'independence' side and are opposed to a deepening of cross-strait economic exchange with mainland China.

The China question that defines the Blue-Green division is so prominent in Taiwanese politics that it overshadows all other issue dimensions. In fact, people – even politicians, journalists, and scholars – do not use the words 'left' and 'right' in describing political ideologies or positions (Hsiao, Cheng and Achen 2017, 199). It is even said that the two major parties are 'flexible, low intensity, and opportunistic on social welfare policies' (Hsiao, Cheng and Achen 2017, 201).

In 2001, a new party, the TSU, that took a more extreme position than the DPP on Taiwan independence, was formed. Fearing that pro-independence voters may switch their support to the TSU, the DPP shifted to a slightly more pro-independence position after the 2001 legislative election (Sheng and Kiao 2017). This event underscores the importance of the unification/independence issue and the unidimensional nature of the Taiwanese party politics.

As shown in Table 31.1, the KMT and the DPP have been alternating in power in regular intervals. Close competition between the Pan-Blue camp and the Pan-Green camp has been the basic structure of Taiwanese party politics in the twenty-first century. Yet the two presidential elections in 2016 and 2020 were won by the DPP's Tsai Ing-wen in a landslide fashion, which may be a sign of a changing power balance between the two camps.

In South Korea, in contrast to Taiwan where an issue-based competition between two major parties almost instantly started after democratisation, the differences among political parties were not based on policies or ideologies during the first decade of democratic politics. Yet, after that, Korean politics has been characterised by a deep divide between the 'conservatives' and the 'progressives'.

During the early years after democratisation, there were no significant programmatic differences between government and opposition, and the parties' electoral campaigns were based on the leaders' personal popularity and regional sentiments (Wong 2014). Wong (2014) explains that the conservative ruling party pre-emptively adopted progressive policies, such as an introduction of universal medical insurance, and eliminated potential opposition agendas that could have developed into an ideological cleavage. Also, the experience of the Korean War and the subsequent confrontation with the communist neighbour prevented the development of the left-right ideology (see e.g. Kim, Choi and Cho 2008). Thus, the opposition was not able to show a clear programmatic difference between them and the government and was instead forced to resort to non-programmatic appeals.

In the 1997 election, the opposition won the presidency for the first time. The winner Kim Dae-jung of the NCPN was well known as a fighter for democratisation and had extremely enthusiastic supporters in his home region of Jeolla (the southwestern part of the country). Kim's election was helped by several factors. First, the election was held during a massive economic crisis for which the ruling party was blamed. Second, votes for the ruling party were split because of a candidate who defected from the ruling party and ran for a new party. Third, Kim was endorsed by Kim Jong-pil, a veteran conservative politician who had a strong local support base in his home province (Kang and Jaung 1999). The fact that Kim Jung-pil crossed the aisle from the conservative side to form a successful alliance with the progressive NCPN clearly indicates that an ideology-based cleavage was underdeveloped, and politics was still largely personalistic.

However, after Kim Dae-jung's election in 1997, the nature of South Korean party competition transformed. It became less personalistic and region-based, and the differences between the two sides – conservative and progressive – over policy issues became increasingly clear. This transformation was caused by two key factors. First, Kim's 'Sunshine Policy', which aimed to engage North Korea, was highly controversial. This policy debate happened while the George W. Bush administration of the USA took a tough stance towards North Korea and massive anti-U.S. demonstrations took place in South Korea after two schoolgirls were struck and killed by a U.S. military vehicle in 2002 (the Yangju highway incident). As a result, foreign policy in regard to North Korea and the USA emerged as a contentious issue. Generally, older people who remember the Korean War were more sceptical and thus critical of Kim's Sunshine Policy (Kim, Choi and Cho 2008).

Second, five years rule by the first progressive administration by Kim Dae-jung expanded the width of the ideological spectrum. According to Hahm (2008), since Kim took office during a major economic crisis, the public was accepting of Kim's progressive welfare policies that might have been rejected as communist-like in normal time. Having realised that Kim's progressive economic policies did not turn their country socialist or communist, people came to accept such policies as legitimate. The range of acceptable policies thus became wider.

Empirically, Kim, Choi and Cho (2008) analyse survey data from the 2000 and 2004 legislative elections and demonstrate that ideology became more important in determining citizens' voting behaviour and the intensity of regionalism declined between the two elections. In addition, a new party, the Democratic Labor Party, was formed that was located left of the mainstream progressive party and became the third-largest party in the 2004 legislative election despite lacking any regional strongholds. Those who voted for this party appeared to be ideological voters (Kim, Choi and Cho 2008).

In fact, ideological polarisation is becoming an increasingly serious issue in South Korean politics. The impeachment of Roh Moo-hyun in 2004, after which he was reinstated by the court, and the subsequent impeachment of Park Geun-hye in 2016 were both highly contentious and partisan events. Shin (2020, 101) argues that the country now has 'a politics of confrontation, resentment, and even hatred' where political opponents demonise each other. Lee and Han (2018, 197) show that the ideological distance between the two major parties has 'drastically' increased since 2004. Even though the parties' names often change, a structure of a two-party competition between the progressive side and the conservative side has become highly stable in South Korea.

Japan is different from Taiwan and South Korea in that it still has a dominant party system. One possible explanation for this difference is that long-lasting party control is more common in parliamentary systems than in presidential systems (Maeda and Nishikawa 2006). Presidential elections in South Korea and Taiwan are so important that small parties that cannot viably compete for the presidency are either abandoned by supporters or compelled to join an electoral alliance with other parties. Presidential elections thus become competitive, making a long-lasting one-party control less likely. In Japan, in contrast, opposition parties have not been able to pose a serious challenge to the dominant party, except for a short period in the twenty-first century.

The JSP was the largest opposition from 1955 to 1993. It was a union-backed left-wing party, and it criticised the LDP's capitalist, pro-U.S. policies. As the country's economy rapidly modernised, blue-collar workers decreased, and the JSP's support base shrunk. Furthermore, as other opposition parties emerged and started offering alternative choices to anti-LDP voters, the JSP's status as the main contender to the dominant LDP eroded (Rosenbluth and Thies 2010). It has been argued that the single non-transferable vote (SNTV) electoral system (used until 1993) fragmented the opposition by allowing small opposition parties to survive (Reed 1990) and hindering the largest opposition party from taking moderate policy positions (Maeda 2012).

The LDP, on the contrary, was able to claim credits for the country's economic success. It skilfully gathered votes while mobilising its extensive clientelistic networks and providing favourable policies to its supporting groups and industries. Even though the LDP is generally a right-wing, pro-business party, it did not pursue – at least most of the time – neoliberal, free-market economic policies. Rather, its policies were characterised by large public spending and active intervention into the market (Krauss and Pekkanen 2010; Rosenbluth and Thies 2010). The LDP was also ideologically flexible enough to pre-emptively adopt policies that could have become the opposition's agenda.

As noted earlier, the LDP was out of power between 1993 and 1994. Interestingly, when the LDP suffered an electoral loss in 1993, the JSP performed even worse in the same election, nearly halving its lower house seats. The winners of the election were the new parties. This shows that the JSP could not act as an alternative governing party to the dominant LDP. The first rival of the LDP thus fell (the JSP now exists as the Social Democratic Party with a handful of seats in the Diet).

The next rival of the LDP was the DPJ. A de facto two-party system of the LDP and the DPJ was established in 2003 when the second-largest opposition party coalesced into the DPJ. Compared with the JSP, the DPJ took a more moderate policy position, and the electorate came to accept it as an alternative ruling party. The DPJ won a landslide victory in 2009 when the LDP's popularity dropped due to some scandals, some unpopular policies, and the government's mishandling of some administrative issues (Maeda 2010). The DPJ's victory was not necessarily a result of an ideology-based or policy-based appeal, but it was largely a result of the LDP's failure. Japan's two-party system ended in 2012 when the DPJ suffered a crushing defeat (its seat share became less than one-fifth of what it won in the previous election) and other opposition parties emerged and grew.

The LDP's renewed dominance since 2012 has been helped by the weak and fragmented opposition. As Rosenbluth and Thies (2010) argue, the post-reform electoral system creates an environment within which political parties have incentives to appeal to voters with programmatic policy positions. Yet opposition parties have not been able to attract enough support to make politics competitive again.

Regionalism and nationalisation of political parties

The world's democracies vary greatly in the degree of party system nationalisation. In a nationalised party system, political parties receive similar shares of votes throughout the country, but a country with a low level of party system nationalisation has regional parties and/or parties that receive highly uneven levels of support across the regions of the country. The literature shows that levels of party system nationalisation influence various factors such as survival of democracy, legislative behaviour, and the types of issues over which political parties compete (Jones and Mainwaring 2003). Let us examine the three East Asian countries' party systems in this regard.

In South Korea, regionalism has been a well-known feature of its party system. Since the 1961 military coup until the election of Kim Dae-jung in 1997, all presidents were from the Gyeongsang area (the south-eastern part of the country), and the area developed due to government support (Heo and Stockton 2005). Naturally, this created tension between Gyeongsang and the rest of the country. In particular, a rivalry between Gyeongsang and Jeolla (southwest) grew, because Jeolla is where Kim Dae-jung, a fierce critic of the military government who later became president, was from and was a local hero, and a popular uprising against the military government in the city of Gwangju in Jeolla in 1980 was violently quelled.

Due to this background, political parties in post-democratisation South Korea had uneven support levels across regions. Regionalism became 'the most dominant cleavage line since the democratic transition' (Kang and Jaung 1999, 601). In the 1997 presidential election, Kim Dae-jung's vote share was well above 90 per cent in Jeolla but was below 15 per cent in Gyeongsang. On the contrary, his main rival Lee Hoi-chang performed well in Gyeongsang but not in Jeolla (Kang and Jaung 1999). For an ethnically homogeneous country, this level of regional disparity is quite remarkable.

However, there are signs of weakening regionalism in South Korean politics. As cited earlier, Kim, Choi and Cho's (2008) research reveals that the intensity of regionalism declined between 2000 and 2004. Kim Dae-jung's progressive successor, Roh Moo-hyun, who won the 2002 presidential election, was from Gyeongsang, which was a deviation from the traditional correspondence of regions and parties up to that point. Roh's election was made possible by energetic young supporters who were driven by ideology rather than region-based sentiments

(Hahm 2008). Unlike the Kim administration that was filled with Jeolla people, the core of the Roh administration consisted of younger people, regardless of home regions, who belonged to the so-called '386 generation' (Hahm 2008). Lee and Han (2018) also argue that the increasing polarisation between parties is weakening the regional cleavage.

In Taiwan, there is a north-south divide that separates the northern part where the KMT is stronger and the southern part where the DPP is stronger. Lay, Chen and Yap's (2006) spatial analysis reveals that the advancement of the DPP between the 1996 and 2000 presidential elections was made possible by mobilising Hohlo (a sub-ethnic group within the Taiwanese people) voters in southern Taiwan, and 'a remarkably high degree of clustering' of DPP supporters was created there (Lay, Chen and Yap 2006, 19). After 2000, the DPP expanded its strongholds from there, and the widely accepted image of 'north Blue, south Green' was thus created. According to Tsai (2017), the north-south divide in the economic sense emerged because the government traditionally invested more on the northern region, which includes the capital city Taipei, than the rest of the country. Also, as the economic relationship with China deepened, the support for the China-friendly KMT grew in the north where industries that benefit from the cross-Strait trade are concentrated. The 'north Blue, south Green' pattern continues to this day.

In Japan, unlike South Korea and Taiwan that have noticeable regional disparities in party strength, major regional divides do not exist in politics even though the urban-rural difference is significant. However, since 2010, several regional political parties have been formed by prefectural governors and city mayors. The first instance of this movement happened in Osaka, a major city in the western part of the country. Toru Hashimoto, a lawyer who regularly appeared in popular TV shows, won the gubernatorial election in 2008 as an independent candidate and founded his party in 2010. The party's name is Osaka Ishin No Kai (there is no official English name, but it roughly means Osaka Renewal Association), and its main policy issue is to restructure and unify the two levels of local governments: the Osaka Prefecture and the City of Osaka (Reed 2013). This party has been dominating the political scene of Osaka, even after Hashimoto's retirement from politics in 2015. The party also launched a national-level political party, which is currently called the Japan Innovation Party. Its supporters are concentrated in Osaka and surrounding areas.[3] Regional parties initiated by governors and mayors have been formed in other places, namely, Tokyo and Nagoya. But they have been less successful than the one in Osaka.

In summary, the three countries do have regionalism in politics with varying degrees. But their party competition is fairly nationalised, and there are no major parties that receive votes solely from a specific region as Bloc Québécois in Canada does. This may be because of the relative homogeneity of the ethnic composition of the population (especially in South Korea and Japan) and the importance of foreign policy issues in the electoral competition (especially in Taiwan and South Korea). Another possible factor is that the three countries are all politically and fiscally centralised. Decentralisation is known to hinder party system nationalisation (see e.g. Harbers 2010).

Recent challenges by anti-establishment parties

An important recent trend in many liberal democracies is the rise of populist and/or anti-establishment new parties (see Chapter 23). These parties criticise mainstream parties as corrupt and detached from ordinary citizens, and their growth has destabilised party systems in several countries, but in this section, I argue that in East Asia anti-establishment parties have not become strong enough to fundamentally alter the party systems.

In Taiwan, a controversial trade deal proposal with China, initiated by a KMT government, triggered a student-led occupation of the floor of the Legislative Yuan for three weeks in 2014. This activism came to be called the Sunflower Student Movement, and as a result of the protest, the trade deal was not ratified. Some of the leaders of the movement went on to establish a new political party, the New Power Party (NPP). Initially, the NPP based its appeal on a call to create a 'third force', distinguished from the Blue-Green rivalry, but it eventually formed an electoral alliance with the DPP before the 2016 legislative election (Templeman 2020). The NPP won five seats in 2016 and three seats in 2020, and it is now part of the Pan-Green camp and takes a more pro-independence position than the DPP. Templeman (2020) argues that the fact that the NPP could not establish a third force but became incorporated into the Pan-Green camp is evidence of the unidimensional and institutionalised nature of the party politics in Taiwan.

In South Korea, a system of two major parties' dominance is firmly established as in Taiwan, which makes it difficult for any other parties to grow as a viable political contender. Ahn Cheol-soo, a medical doctor and successful software entrepreneur, emerged as a fresh political face before the 2012 presidential election. Ahn 'played a "politics of anti-politics", exploiting widespread sentiment against established politics' and gained popular support especially from young voters (Sohn and Kang 2013). He withdrew his candidacy before the presidential election so as not to split votes with the leading progressive candidate Moon Jae-in. Ahn ran for the 2017 presidential election, but finished third – after the two major parties' candidates. According to Lee and Repkine (2020, 434), Ahn's failure was due to 'his lax political course in the wake of the presidential impeachment in 2016 and a corruption scandal in his party'. While he initially created a boom that was even called the 'Ahn Syndrome' (Sohn and Kang 2013), his movement could not become strong enough to destabilise the dominance of the established two parties.

In Japan, new parties are frequently formed, but anti-establishment ones are rare. Perhaps the most successful one so far is Reiwa Shinsengumi (this party has no official English name), founded in 2019 by Taro Yamamoto. Yamamoto was an actor who turned into an anti-nuclear energy activist after the 2011 Fukushima disaster. He won a seat in the 2013 upper house election as an independent candidate. He later joined a small party but left it in 2019 to run for the upcoming upper house election with his new party, Reiwa Shinsengumi. The party advocates the abolition of the consumption tax, an immediate ban on nuclear energy, among other things. The party's unorthodox electoral campaigns attracted voters' attention, and it ran a successful fundraising drive (Jain 2020). Although Reiwa Shinsengumi won two seats in the 2019 election out of the 124 contested seats, it subsequently struggled to increase its popularity.

In summary, anti-establishment political movements and parties in East Asia have had limited success. The three countries' mainstream parties have been able to defend themselves from recent challengers. Why is East Asia different from other parts of the world that have seen a rapid rise of new parties? One reason may be the majoritarian electoral systems currently used in all three countries. Compared to the proportional representation systems used in most European countries, it is difficult for new parties to secure electoral success in majoritarian systems. Another reason may be the economic conditions. Hobolt and Tilly (2016) argue that the eurozone crisis created a situation where voters enduring economic hardship were attracted by challenger parties that criticised the mainstream parties' consensus on austerity and European integration. East Asian countries were hit by the 2008 Great Recession, but the damage was much less than what European countries experienced. Challenger parties succeed electorally when they can introduce a new issue dimension on which mainstream parties differ little among themselves. In Japan, South Korea and Taiwan, no such issue dimensions have been created in their arenas of electoral competition. Perhaps relatedly, in his study on the dearth of populism in East Asia, Hellmann (2017) explains that because post-material values are not strong in East Asia, potential populist challengers have not been able to advertise themselves as the embodiment of traditional values.

Conclusion and avenues for future research

The word 'stable' can be used to describe the party politics of the three countries analysed in this chapter – but in somewhat different ways. In Taiwan, the KMT-DPP two-party system has been stable since the democratisation. In South Korea, the line-up of parties has been extremely unstable, but the structure of party competition has stabilised into a conservative-progressive duality. In Japan, the LDP's one-party dominance ended once but has returned and is stable again. As this chapter has argued, the opposition parties in Taiwan and South Korea have been able to mobilise support by contrasting themselves from the former dominant parties along the major policy/ideological dimensions. Japan's opposition has not been able to do so. The difference in the institutional arrangement (presidential and parliamentary systems) may partly explain this contrast, but further comparative investigations are necessary.

While regionalism in politics and regional parties are becoming stronger in many countries around the world, the politics in Japan, South Korea, and Taiwan are highly nationalised without significant regional parties. Regionalism was strong in South Korean politics but has become weaker as ideology-based party competition has taken root. These East Asian cases may inspire further theoretical and/or cross-national research on political regionalism and nationalisation.

A curious commonality among the three countries is that anti-establishment parties have not been successful in becoming a major player in politics. There have been such attempts, but mainstream parties have contained them. As established parties in many democracies around the world are losing supporters to challenger parties, the resilience of the East Asian major parties is an intriguing puzzle for future research.

Notes

1 Namely, the Liberal Party, the Democratic Republican Party, and the Democratic Justice Party.
2 Following the 2021 election, the LDP secured 261 lower house seats.
3 In the 2021 lower house election, the Japan Innovation Party won 41 seats out of the total 465 seats, an increase from 11 seats in the 2017 election.

References

Carmines, E.G. and Stimson, J.A. (1986) 'On the structure and sequence of issue evolution', *American Political Science Review*, 80(3), p901–920.
Greene, K.F. (2002) 'Opposition party strategy and spatial competition in dominant party regimes: A theory and the case of Mexico', *Comparative Political Studies*, 35(7), p755–783.
Hahm, C. (2008) 'South Korea's miraculous democracy', *Journal of Democracy*, 19(3), p128–142.
Harbers, I. (2010) 'Decentralization and the development of nationalized party systems in new democracies: Evidence from Latin America', *Comparative Political Studies*, 43(5), p606–627.
Hellmann, O. (2014) 'Party system institutionalization without parties: Evidence from Korea', *Journal of East Asian Studies*, 14(1), p53–84.
Hellmann, O. (2017) 'Populism in East Asia', in Kastwasser, C.R., Taggart, P., Espejo, P.O. and Ostiguy, P. (eds.) *The Oxford handbook of populism*. Oxford: Oxford University Press, pp. 161–178.
Heo, U. and Stockton, H. (2005) 'The impact of democratic transition on elections and parties in South Korea', *Party Politics*, 11(6), p674–688.
Hicken, A. (2011) 'Clientelism', *Annual Review of Political Science*, 14, p289–310.

Hobolt, S.B. and Tilly, J. (2016) 'Fleeing the centre: The rise of challenger parties in the aftermath of the Euro crisis', *West European Politics*, 39(5), p971–991.

Hsiao, Y., Cheng, S. and Achen, C.H. (2017) 'Political left and right in Taiwan', in Achen, C.H. and Wang, T.Y. (eds.) *The Taiwan voter*. Ann Arbor: University of Michigan Press, pp. 198–222.

Jain, P. (2020) 'Japan's 2019 upper house election: Solidifying Abe, the LDP, and return to a one-party dominant political system', *Asian Journal of Comparative Politics*, 5(1), p23–37.

Jones, M.P. and Mainwaring, S. (2003) 'The nationalization of parties and party systems: An empirical measure and an application to the Americas', *Party Politics*, 9(2), p139–166.

Kang, W. and Jaung, H. (1999) 'The 1997 presidential election in South Korea', *Electoral Studies*, 18, p599–608.

Kim, H., Choi, J.Y. and Cho, J. (2008) 'Changing cleavage structure in new democracies: An empirical analysis of political cleavages in Korea', *Electoral Studies*, 27, p136–150.

Krauss, E.S. and Pekkanen, R.J. (2010) *The rise and fall of Japan's LDP: Political party organizations as historical institutions*. Ithaca: Cornell UP.

Kushida, K.E. and Lipscy, P.Y., Ed. (2013) *Japan under the DPJ: The politics of transition and governance*. Stanford: Shorenstein Asia-Pacific Research Center.

Lay, J., Chen, Y. and Yap, K. (2006) 'Spatial variation of the DPP's expansion between Taiwan's presidential elections', *Issues & Studies*, 42(4), p1–22.

Lee, H. and Repkine, A. (2020) 'Changes in and continuity of regionalism in South Korea', *Asian Survey*, 60(3), p417–440.

Lee, N.L. and Han, S.M. (2018) 'Politics of party polarization in East Asia', in Cheng, T. and Chu, Y. (eds.) *The Routledge handbook of democratization in East Asia*. London: Routledge, pp. 193–208.

Lipset, S.M. and Rokkan, S. (1967) 'Cleavage structures, party systems, and voter alignments: An introduction', in Lipset, S.M. and Rokkan, S. (eds.) *Party systems and voter alignments: Cross-national perspectives*. Toronto: The Free Press, pp. 1–64.

Maeda, K. (2010) 'Factors behind the historic defeat of Japan's liberal democratic party in 2009', *Asian Survey*. 50(5), p888–907.

Maeda, K. (2012) 'An irrational party of rational members: The collision of legislators' reelection quest with party success in the Japan socialist party', *Comparative Political Studies*, 45(3), p341–365.

Maeda, K. and Nishikawa, M. (2006) 'Duration of party control in parliamentary and presidential governments: A study of 65 democracies, 1950–1998', *Comparative Political Studies*, 39(3), p352–374.

Mobrand, E. (2020) 'Corruption, democracy, and the business of politics in Taiwan', *Taiwan Insight*. Available from: https://taiwaninsight.org/2020/11/02/corruption-democracy-and-the-business-of-politics-in-taiwan/ (Accessed on 29 May 2021).

Reed, S.R. (1990) 'Structure and behaviour: Extending Duverger's law to the Japanese case', *British Journal of Political Science*, 20(3), p335–356.

Reed, S.R. (2013) 'Challenging the two-party system: Third force parties in the 2012 election', in Pekkanen, R., Reed, S.R. and Scheiner, E. (eds.) *Japan decides 2012: The Japanese general election*. Basingstoke: Palgrave Macmillan, pp. 72–83.

Rosenbluth, F.M. and Thies, M.F. (2010) *Japan transformed: Political change and economic restructuring*. Princeton: Princeton University Press.

Sheng, S. and Kiao, H.M. (2017) 'Issues, political cleavages, and party competition in Taiwan', in Achen, C. and Wang, T.Y. (eds.) *The Taiwan vote*. Ann Arbor: University of Michigan Press, pp. 98–138.

Shin, G. (2020) 'South Korea's democratic decay', *Journal of Democracy*, 31(3), p100–114.

Sohn, Y. and Kang, W. (2013) 'South Korea in 2012: An election year under rebalancing challenges', *Asian Survey*, 53(1), p198–205.

Templeman, K. (2020) 'The party system before and after the 2016 elections', in Templeman, K., Chu, Y. and Diamond, L. (eds.) *Dynamics of democracy in Taiwan: The Ma Ying-jeou years*. Boulder: Lynne Rienner, pp. 105–129.

Tsai, C. (2017) 'Who is the Taiwan voter?', in Achen, C.H. and Wang, T.Y. (eds.) *The Taiwan voter*. Ann Arbor: University of Michigan Press, pp. 26–43.

Wong, J. (2014) 'South Korea's weakly institutionalized party system', in Hicken, A. and Kuhonta, E.M. (eds.) *Party system institutionalization in Asia: Democracies, autocracies, and the shadows of the past*. New York: Cambridge University Press, pp. 260–279.

32
POLITICAL PARTIES IN SOUTHEAST ASIA

Andreas Ufen

The focus of this chapter is on regimes with democratic breakthroughs (though not always successful in the long run) during the third wave of democratisation. In Southeast Asia, the cases are the Philippines (1986), Thailand (1992), Indonesia (1998), East Timor (2002) and Malaysia (2018). Myanmar, Cambodia and Singapore and closed authoritarian regimes such as Vietnam, Laos and Brunei are excluded. Myanmar is still essentially military-controlled, although the National League for Democracy (NLD) has won in elections against the Union Solidarity and Development Party (USDP) that is close to the military leaders. In Cambodia and Singapore, the hegemony of single parties (the Cambodian People's Party or CPP and the People's Action Party or PAP in Singapore) is so marked that party competition is weak. This is all the more true of nominally socialist countries like Vietnam and Laos ruled by the Communist Party of Vietnam (CPV) and the Lao People's Revolutionary Party (LPRP), respectively. Brunei is still an absolute monarchy without parliament.

It is common knowledge that political parties in Southeast Asia are usually weak, ridden by 'money politics' and clientelism, do not have meaningful platforms, are factionalised and dominated by rich men (Sachsenroeder and Frings 1998; Manikas and Thornton 2003; Dalton, Shin and Chu 2008; Blondel, Inoguchi and Marsh 2012; Tomsa and Ufen 2013; Hicken and Kuhonta 2014). Nevertheless, there are still evident differences between parties and party systems.

This chapter starts with an analysis of party systems with relatively well-rooted parties and then of those with a strong impact of clientelism, factions and clans. In the second part, common features of party systems as well as gaps and emergent research areas are identified. The chapter shows that in general political parties rooted in social milieus and formed by social movements or by leaders with strong connections to such movements are better institutionalised than those with poor links to voters and supporters and with a low programmatic profile.

The significance of cleavages and rooted parties

There are three examples of party systems that have been characterised by parties that are quite well rooted in socio-cultural milieus and/or are programmatically quite strong: Indonesia, Malaysia and East Timor. In Indonesia, the party system was already shaped by strong cleavages in the 1950s. The four biggest parties, the PNI (Partai Nasional Indonesia, Indonesian

National Party), the PKI (Partai Komunis Indonesia, Communist Party of Indonesia), Masyumi (Majelis Syuro Muslimin Indonesia, Consultative Council of Indonesian Muslims) and Nahdatul Ulama (Renaissance of Islamic scholars) represented so-called *aliran* or 'streams' (Geertz 1963). The four parties had their own affiliated mass organisations and their supporters were mostly secular (PNI and the PKI) or Islamic (NU and Masyumi), concentrated in Java (PNI, NU and PKI) or the Outer Islands (Masyumi), rural-based (NU) or centred in urban areas (especially Masyumi). Moreover, a class cleavage separated the PKI from the other parties. The PKI and the PNI existed previously for decades under the Dutch colonial regime, NU emerged at the beginning of the century as a traditionalist Muslim organisation and Masyumi was created by the Japanese during their occupation of the Indonesian archipelago. These political parties in the 1950s were rooted in social milieus, but with the exception of the PKI not very well organised.

Under President Suharto during the authoritarian New Order regime (1966–1998), party politics was strongly tamed with two semi-opposition parties representing secular and/or non-Muslim (PDI) or orthodox Islamic (PPP) voters, but with a new regime party, Golkar (Golongan Karya or Functional Groups). Golkar was a hegemon always winning over 60 per cent of the votes in manipulated elections. With re-democratisation in 1998/99, the party system of the 1950s re-emerged to an extent (Ufen 2008a; King 2003a), but this time without the banned PKI (many of whose members and supporters fell victim to systematic slaughtering in the mid-1960s), with Golkar as a kind of catch-all party, but with successors of the PNI (now: Golkar (Golongan Karya), of NU (now: PKB, National Awakening Party) and a few other Islamic parties, partly as successors of NU, Masyumi and/or the PPP.

The 1999 elections were the first since 1955 held freely and fairly. The proportional system without threshold resulted in a proliferation of parties. Moreover, the parliamentary system with a special assembly electing the president was so inappropriate that it caused a deep rift between the president and members of parliament. Subsequently, lawmakers introduced a full presidential system with direct presidential elections since 2004 (see Horowitz 2013). This was complemented by direct local elections at different levels since 2004/2005, a parliamentary threshold (currently at 4 per cent) and open candidate lists (fully established since 2009). The number of parties has been reduced via a regulation demanding parties to have branches nationwide. Therefore, with the exception of Aceh regional parties are disallowed. These institutional reforms have somehow not only stabilised the relationship between president and parliament but also propelled a focus on candidates rather than parties and on presidential elections. An individual wishing to be elected as mayor, governor or president needs large financial resources or has to be backed by very wealthy businessmen seeking direct access to the executive in order to facilitate their commercial operations (Aspinall and Berenschot 2019). These weaknesses still exist and have been compounded in recent years by dealignment, the fragmentation of the party system and the emergence of a few programmatically hollow political parties used as mere vehicles for would-be presidential candidates (Ufen 2018).

Parties are less rooted since 1998, and they are increasingly dependent on rich people at the top. The lack of leftist parties and the detachment of parties from most social mass organisations such as trade unions or peasant associations have left an ideological vacuum that is mostly filled by a politicised Islam (Fossati 2019), by technocratic ideas or by populist sentiments. Even the religious cleavage is not strongly represented in the party system. This is primarily because radical groups organise opposition outside of the parliament (Mietzner and Muhtadi 2018, 490). Moreover, due to the introduction of a full presidential system, there are now several parties in parliament that function as mere vehicles for presidential candidates (Ufen 2018). In addition, political parties tend to build grand coalitions or cartels (Slater 2018). Consequently, party identification is currently low and fell from almost 90 per cent in 1999 to about 20 per cent in 2014. Party membership decreased to around 5 per cent (Kenny 2018, 39).

In Malaysia, the nationalist movement was weaker than in the Netherlands–Indies, political parties and mass organisations were established late, and the transfer of power from the British colonial government to the indigenous elites was relatively smooth. During a period of 'emergency', the British had worn down the Malayan Communist Party and in parallel had prepared the country for independence by supporting rather conservative, ethnically based parties such as UMNO (United Malays National Organisation), the MCA (Malaysian Chinese Association) and the MIC (Malaysian Indian Congress).

Because of deep ethnic and religious cleavages as well as a divide between status quo and reformist forces, the electoral system has produced multiple political parties. Since 1957, most parties have represented predominantly one of the three major ethnic groups (Saravanamuttu 2016). Because Malays were at the time often poor peasants led by aristocrats within UMNO, whereas the ethnic Chinese were economically usually better off, ethnicity has always been connected to class differences. Moreover, because Malays are always Muslims (this according to a definition in the Constitution), a religious cleavage sustains the ethnic one. The competition between UMNO and the PAS (Parti Islam SeMalaysia – Pan-Malaysian Islamic Party) has deepened this cleavage over the years. Moreover, the electoral authoritarian system has produced an overarching cleavage separating pro-regime parties from those who want major reforms.

Malaysia took over major elements of the British majoritarian plurality system, with 222 MPs are now elected in single-member districts (SMDs). There is a tendency, especially since the late 1990s, to coordinate the nomination of candidates among parties so that in many cases one candidate from the ruling coalition has competed with one from the opposition coalition. In addition, in the two East Malaysian states of Sarawak and Sabah, regional parties play an important role. The ruling coalition (until 2018 the National Front or Barisan Nasional) has been able to manipulate national and state elections and to systematically restrict political rights and civil liberties. Opposition parties were weak until the late 1990s and did not have a realistic chance of winning elections. But splits in the hegemonic UMNO in 1999 and 2015 and the rise of a civil society *Reformasi* movement with links to the opposition parties resulted in a surprising defeat of the governing coalition in 2018 (Ufen 2020). Afterwards, intensive debates about reforming the electoral system were initiated. The new government (2018–2020) tried to fundamentally reform the electoral system, but failed due to strong civil society and parliamentary opposition and legal hindrances.

Whereas Indonesia is a case of growing dealignment, and Malaysia's party system is now highly fragmented and characterised by factionalism, party-switching and shifting coalitions, but still with some relatively well-institutionalised parties, in East Timor a multi-party system has evolved within a political environment shaped by its liberation struggle and guerrilla heritage. East Timor has conducted free and fair elections in 2002, 2007, 2012, 2017 and 2018. Formally, the president in the semi-presidential system is weak, but every president since Xanana Gusmão (2002–2007), has been able to wield enormous informal power. Political parties were established at the end of Portuguese colonialism in 1974/75. After the invasion by Indonesian military, the Revolutionary Front for an Independent Timor-Leste or FRETILIN led a guerrilla war against an oppressive regime. During the occupation, FRETILIN changed from a Marxist organisation to one accepting multi-partyism and democracy (Sindre 2016), and the independence movement was increasingly split into factions dominated by guerrilla fighters, civilians and diplomats, respectively. When East Timor finally reached independence in 2002 under an UN administration, the FRETILIN party won 55 out of 88 seats, whereas the opposition consisting of 11 parties was fragmented (King 2003b). This predominant party system with FRETILIN acting as the sole legitimate voice of the Timorese people underwent fundamental change with the emergence of the National Congress for Timorese Reconstruction (*Conselho Nacional de Reconstrução de Timor*, CNRT) under Xanana Gusmão. In 2007, after the country had experienced months of bitter intra-elite fights leading to unrest in different parts of the island, Gusmão assembled a governing coalition (with 39 out of 65 seats), but it was seen as illegitimate by the FRETILIN party; it was only after the 2012 parliamentary election that FRETILIN accepted defeat. In 2015, surprisingly, Gusmão initiated single-handedly the formation of a government of 'national unity' and Rui Maria de Araújo from FRETILIN became prime minister. All four parties represented in the national parliament took part in the new government. Yet the 2017 elections resulted in a FRETILIN minority government that was soon challenged by the opposition coalition, the Change for Progress Alliance (AMP) led by CNRT. Early elections in 2018 were won by the AMP and the old polarisation between forces around FRETILIN (including the new President Francisco Guterres) and the AMP with Prime Minister Taur Matan Ruak re-emerged. Polarisation between the two sides then palpably increased in 2020 when the CNRT-led coalition collapsed.

East Timor's politics is strongly personalised. This is enhanced by party leaders deciding on the ranking of candidates on the party list (Shoesmith 2020). It is difficult to identify cleavages in the party system. At least in the 2007 elections, a divide between Easterners, *Lorosa'e* (or *Firaku*), the 'true resistance fighters', and Westerners, *Loromonu* (or *Kaladi*), was reflected in divergent geographical support. But otherwise, the two biggest parties are little different programmatically. They are relatively strong in terms of party identification because of the past as a guerrilla movement (FRETILIN and CNRT), but FRETILIN is less dependent on a single charismatic leader and better organised than CNRT (Berlie 2018).

In summary, many political parties in Indonesia, Malaysia and East Timor have been relatively well rooted since independence, although with decreasing intensity in Indonesia and with a high degree of personalisation in East Timor.

The predominance of clientelism, clans and factions

Parties in the Philippines and Thailand have historically been clientelistic networks (Ufen 2008b), although in Thailand since the late 1990s, a few parties have started to develop stronger links to supporters and voters.

In the Philippines, parties were founded during American colonial rule. When the first national elections were conducted in 1907, some of the patterns of clientelism and elitism were already put in place. In the following years, the NP, a party dominated by rich landowners, controlled party politics. After national independence in 1946, two parties, the NP (Nacionalista Party) and the LP (Liberal Party), competed with each other within a presidential system modelled after the U.S. model (Hutchcroft and Rocamora 2003). The electoral democracy was dominated by wealthy families who usurped the two political parties and whose members from time-to-time switched parties. These two parties were programmatically almost identical, organisationally very weak and consisted of patron-client networks reaching down to the local level. The still dominant patron-client model was at that time popularised by Landé (1965), later refined and altered by Machado (1974), Kimura (1998) and Sidel (1999).

When under President Ferdinand Marcos, martial law was introduced in 1972, and party politics came to a standstill for a few years. Yet a range of (rigged) elections in the final years of the authoritarian Marcos regime allowed for the formation of opposition alliances. A legacy of the Marcos era was the establishment of new parties and coalitions that contributed to the formation of a multi-party system after 1986. Other reasons for the fragmentation of the party system until today are the one-term limit of the presidency that discourages the building of solid party structures and motivates the formation of often short-term presidential vehicles.

The presidential system has contributed to weakening political parties. Senators are elected nationwide with the whole country as one electoral district. The 1987 constitution prescribes a first-past-the-post system for all elective officials: president, vice president, senators, MPs, local chief executives, and local legislators. Members of the House of Representatives are elected in SMDs. In addition, up to 20 per cent of the seats in the House of Representatives are reserved for party list candidates who run for parties or organisations each of which can win up to three seats. The party-list system allows civil society organisations and social movements representing the marginalised sector according to the Party-list System Act. Yet often they are front organisations for elite politicians. In the 2019 midterm elections, 134 groups took part and 51 of them won at least one seat.

Yet the parties of the presidents are able to attract most MPs of the other parties because he/she disposes of major patronage resources. Accordingly, some 'dominant presidential parties' (Teehankee 2020, 110) have emerged over time, such as the *Labanng Demokratikong Pilipino* under the administration of Corason Aquino; the Lakas NUCD-UMDP under Fidel Ramos; the *Lapian ng Masang Pilipino* (LAMP) under Joseph Estrada; the Lakas-Kampi-CMD under Gloria Macapagal Arroyo; the LP under Benigno Aquino III; and the *Partido Demokratiko Pilipino-Lakas ng Bayan* (PDP-Laban) under Rodrigo Duterte.

But a consolidation 'into two major coalitions representing the administration and opposition forces' took place only until 2010 (Teehankee 2020, 114). There are, for example, regional (Landé 1996, 148) or centre-periphery cleavages (McAllister 2008, 83), but these hardly structure the party system as such (Manacsa and Tan 2005). All in all, Philippine political parties are 'candidate-centred coalitions of provincial bosses, political machines, and local clans' (Teehankee 2012, 188), factionalised, programmatically weak, and subject to frequent dissolutions and to party-switching. Coalitions are so ephemeral and diverse that most voters elect candidates regardless of their party allegiances. In between elections, party organisation is usually shallow.

In Thailand, parties were from the beginning elitist and programmatically weak and were largely unable to translate social cleavages into the party system (Kuhonta 2014). Vote-canvasser networks developed prior to the formation of political parties. During the 1930s, political parties (aside from the then ruling People's Party) were banned. Party activities started in 1946 with frequent interventions by the armed forces (in total, there were 22 military coups in Thai history) that dominated politics until 1992, and then again during 2006–2008 and 2014–2019 (Chambers and Waitoolkiat 2020, 147). Sometimes, the army created their own parties. Furthermore, the monarch has directly interfered politically from time to time at critical junctures. The 20 constitutions and 7 laws governing political parties that were implemented in the period from 1955 to 2018 included all kinds of legal loopholes and are also testimony to this erratic development.

For a long time, officers and bureaucrats stood at the centre of a 'bureaucratic polity' (Riggs 1966), but there were intermezzi with a high degree of popular mobilisation between 1973 and 1976 when leftist parties took part in elections. Generally, elitist parties shallowly represented conservative royalists, Bangkok centralists, and their respective opponents. Between 1980 and 1988, Thailand morphed into a military-controlled hybrid regime with competitive elections for the national parliament and a second chamber with appointed senators. In this period local politicians and businesspeople as 'godfathers' or *chao pho* formed regional vote – canvasser networks. In the early 1990s, Thailand was an electoral democracy with unstable governments. The new Constitution in 1997 established a mixed-member system with 400 SMDs and 100 seats determined through proportional elections with national party list seats substituting the

MMD plurality elections formerly used to elect the House of Representatives. Members of the Senate who were not allowed to be party members were for the first time directly elected. The comprehensive 1997 reforms contributed to decreasing the effective number of parties in the parliament from 6.2 to 3.1 in 2001 and 1.6 in 2005 (Sawasdee 2012, 151), but they also ironically paved the way for the dominance of the Thai Rak Thai (TRT, 'Thais Love Thais'), the first party able to survive the full legislative period in Thai politics. Its leader Thaksin Shinawatra employed managers from his own corporation to serve the TRT, paid MPs extra salaries, and made other parties or factions of them join his party (McCargo and Pathmanand 2005; Pasuk and Baker 2009). Thaksin's rise was also due to the political party act of 1998 that brought finances more under the control of party executives. TRT was innovative not only because of new organisational structures but also because of a platform based on policy innovations such as basic health care schemes. It forced other parties to follow suit in sharpening their programmatic profiles.

The TRT hegemony caused resistance by the military and the monarchy as well as their supporters and prompted a strong polarisation within Thai society with fierce protests by so-called 'Yellow Shirts' and 'Red Shirts' (Sinpeng 2014). After two military coups in 2006 and 2014, a new constitution was promulgated in 2017: 350 constituency seats are won in plurality elections, another 150 party list seats give each party a total number of seats ('overhang seats') proportional to the nationwide number of votes they received. The prime minister is selected by the combined National Assembly including the 250 members of the Senate whose members are appointed by the military leaders. Parties now again seem to be weakened: since the July 2019 election, 'party leaders remain constitutionally unable to control MP behaviour and MP factions can easily migrate from one party to another' (Chambers and Waitoolkiat 2020, 162).

Until today, there are cleavages between the Bangkok Metropolitan Region and the periphery as well as between urban and rural voters. Yet, in general, political parties in Thailand are still organisationally and programmatically weak, remain dependent upon rich financiers and only represent these cleavages shallowly (Ockey 2005). Party switching by whole factions is not uncommon. In summary, Thailand and the Philippines are examples of predominance of clientelism and of parties with shallow social roots.

Common features of Southeast Asian party politics

Despite the differences outlined earlier, Southeast Asian parties and party systems share some characteristics: Weak party organisations, a marginalised political left, flawed candidate – and party financing, and shifting institutional landscapes. This section discusses these in closer detail.

Weak party organisation

The European-type mass organisation party is absent in the region. Many parties are rather vehicles for presidential candidates or for wealthy clans or factions led by rich businesspeople. Programmatic profiles are usually shallow and membership figures as well as party identification are low. Nevertheless, there are exceptions. There are new reform-oriented parties trying to represent younger voters such as KHUNTO in East Timor, Future Forward in Thailand (McCargo and Chattharakul 2020) or the Indonesian Solidarity Party (Partai Solidaritas Indonesia, PSI).

In East Timor, the FRETILIN party as a former rebel party is still deeply rooted at least in some parts of the country. Some parties are still able to mobilise supporters on the grounds of religion and/or ethnicity or they offer regime change such as those parties in Malaysia belonging to the opposition against the governing coalition around UMNO until 2018. Other parties such as Gerindra and Partai Demokrat in Indonesia or CNRT in East Timor have become popular due to charismatic leaders.

A marginalised political left

The predominance of *clientelistic* over programmatic linkages is also a result of the systematic enervation, repression or even eradication of the political left. In Indonesia, the Communist Party (PKI) and its supporters were killed or imprisoned in 1965–1968, parts of the Communist Party in the Philippines have become marginalised with only a few seats won via the party-list system as some factions opted to take up arms, the Malayan Communist Party was almost fully defeated during the emergency period (1948–1960) by the British and socialist parties were further marginalised in the 1950s and 1960s. Leftist parties that emerged in Thailand from 1973 to 1976 have been equally marginalised. FRETILIN in East Timor has a Marxist past, but has evolved into a mainstream political party. Across Southeast Asia even moderate social-democratic parties are very weak or non-existent. Thus, the usual left-right spectrum is not helpful in describing Southeast Asian party systems. Moreover, liberal or green parties exist only as rudiments in the region.

Flawed candidate and party financing

Southeast Asian parties in most cases depend on rich financiers, and candidates often finance their campaigns themselves. Membership dues are unimportant, and state subsidies, if they exist such as in Indonesia, Thailand, and East Timor, contribute only a minor share of party incomes. Disclosure requirements are often vague causing under-reporting, and weak oversight bodies are unable to scrutinise violations of regulations or enforce legislation (Ufen 2014). At the same time, expenses are rising. This trend is not yet that glaring in East Timor (Scambary 2019), but even here, major parties allegedly frequently misused the government machinery during recent election campaigns. Political financing is opaque, but the campaigning is not as sophisticated and expensive as in other Southeast Asian countries. In the Philippines, campaigning has always been very expensive. The continuous dominance of the leading clans after the fall of Ferdinand Marcos in 1986 also signifies a persistence of patronage and pork barrel politics at all political levels (Hicken, Aspinall and Weiss 2019). Costs of campaigning and costs associated with maintaining patronage networks soared in Malaysia beginning in the 1970s (Gomez 2012), but this was mostly confined to the ruling National Front coalition, especially to UMNO. While in the 1950s, UMNO was dominated by aristocrats at the top and by teachers and bureaucrats at lower levels, with economic development and globalisation, MPs became themselves businesspeople or intermediaries for entrepreneurs seeking links to the regime (Weiss 2020). In Indonesia, campaign costs surged after 1998, and in particular since the 2004 elections. Around that time, surveys, TV advertising and the employment of 'spin doctors' signified a remarkable commercialisation of politics and a growing impact of media oligarchs (Mietzner 2013; Aspinall and Sukmajati 2016; Tapsell 2017).

In recent years, patronage and vote buying have risen (Muhtadi 2019). Political parties are paid *mahar politik* or 'political dowry' for the nomination of candidates and legislators build clientelistic linkages, either via mass organisations or via brokers (Aspinall and Berenschot 2019). In Thailand, expenditures by candidates and parties rose in the 1980s and 1990s with 'rural network politicians' (Sawasdee 2006) building clientelistic links and forming factions at the national level. A new dimension was the establishment of a 'business firm party', the TRT, by billionaire Thaksin (Pasuk and Baker 2009).

Shifting institutional landscapes

Institutional frameworks in many Southeast Asian countries have been changed frequently. East Timor switched from a mixed system in 2002 to pure proportional representation in 2007 with the whole country as one constituency. Yet, elsewhere, Reilly (2015, 229) noticed a tendency to move towards electoral majoritarianism across Southeast Asia with 'distinctively majoritarian mixed-member models' in Thailand and the Philippines similar to Northeast Asia (Japan, Korea, Taiwan and Mongolia) that combine both plurality and proportional voting. In Indonesia, the open list proportional representation system uses a relatively small district magnitude resulting in a plurality system rather than a proportional one (Reilly 2015, 226).

In these young democracies, institutional engineering has been a constant preoccupation of politicians. Reformers in these countries still try to strengthen political parties by boosting party organisation or introducing state subsidies. In Indonesia, numerous reforms were the result of a protracted transition since 1998 involving substantial sections of the old New Order elites and at times vigorous civil society actors demanding fundamental changes. A legacy of institutions not well designed for a democratic polity has contributed to necessitating numerous institutional reforms (Horowitz 2013). In Thailand, the introduction of new constitutions every few years, frequent military coups, and relatively short democratic intermezzi have prevented the development of strong parties and stable, reliable rules of the game (Waitoolkiat and Chambers 2015). In Malaysia, in addition to the legal restraints on political rights and civil liberties, the design of electoral laws favoured the ruling coalition by means of gerrymandering, malapportionment and political financing (Ostwald 2017). For this reason, the main priority of opposition parties and civil society organisations in Malaysia such as the electoral reform movement *Bersih* is to alter election and party laws.

Conclusions and avenues for further research

The literature on political developments in Southeast Asia are single-country studies that mostly focus on elections and on the visible political altercations at the national level. Moreover, there is little research comparing different parties or party systems based on political science approaches, for example regarding party types, party structure/organisation and party institutionalisation.[1] This is also due to a scarcity of reliable data. The extreme instability of party systems in Thailand and the Philippines, that is, the frequency of party-switching by single MPs and whole factions, of party dissolutions, of regime and constitutional changes (in Thailand) render it almost impossible to identify enduring patterns. Many of the indicators measuring, for example, electoral volatility or party and party system institutionalisation are difficult to apply, because patron-client networks as well as factions are often more important entities than political parties. To date, methodologically most scholars are oriented towards qualitative designs, but the use of surveys and the examination of voter behaviour with quantitative data is on the rise (e.g. Mujani, Liddle and Ambardi 2018).

Surprisingly, there are also few monographs on single political parties,[2] on party systems (Sawasdee 2006; Mietzner 2013), or on sub-national party systems. There is, however, a diverse corpus of literature on local elections, especially in Indonesia and Malaysia.

Emerging areas of research are the role of social media in political campaigns, for example, the impact of fake news and trolls (Tapsell 2017; Sinpeng, Gueorguiev and Arugay 2020; Tan 2020), the often-flawed participation of women in legislatures and parties,[3] the complex relationship between candidates/parties and social movements (Sinpeng 2014; Tomsa and Setijadi 2018), and populism.

The fight over general political questions sometimes takes place outside of the usual channels of parties and parliaments. Examples are the polarisation between pro-Thaksin 'Red Shirts' and anti-Thaksin 'Yellow Shirts' in Thailand and the politicisation of Islam and ethnicity within the Indonesian and the Malaysian civil societies. The trend of polarisation and politicisation also partly explains the growing populist mobilisation in many Southeast Asian countries. In Indonesia, this led to the controversial downfall of the governor of Jakarta in 2017 and to presidential elections in 2014 and 2019 marked by a heated competition between Joko Widodo (Mietzner 2015), who eventually won both elections, and his challenger, former General Prabowo Subianto. Even Islamists are, according to some analysts, part of this populist wave (Hadiz and Robison 2017). Whereas in the Philippines, populists (if we accept a wide definition) frequently emerged ahead of presidential elections with politicians such as Fernando Poe, Joseph Estrada and Rodrigo Duterte (Curato 2017; Thompson 2022), in Thailand, Thaksin Shinawatra started to use populist styles and strategies rather late in his career when he increasingly came under pressure as Prime Minister (2001–2006) and was finally toppled by a military coup (Hewison 2017). In all these cases, weak parties and the personalisation of politics have played a part.

Notes

1 See on institutionalisation: Croissant and Völkel 2012; Hicken and Kuhonta 2014; on factions: Chambers and Ufen 2020; on clientelism: Tomsa and Ufen 2013.
2 For exceptions, see McCargo and Pathmanand 2005; Askew 2008; Tomsa 2008; Noor 2014; Welsh 2016; McCargo and Chattharakul 2020.
3 See Bjarnegård 2013; Prihatini 2019; Perdana and Hillman 2020; White and Aspinall 2021; Journal of Current Southeast Asian Affairs 2021.

References

Askew, M. (2008) *Performing political identity: The Democrat Party in Thailand*. Chiang Mai: Silkworm.
Aspinall, E. and Berenschot, W. (2019) *Democracy for sale: Elections, clientelism, and the state in Indonesia*. Ithaca: Cornell University Press.
Aspinall, E. and Sukmajati, M. (eds.) (2016) *Electoral dynamics in Indonesia: Money, politics and clientelism at the grassroots*. Singapore: Singapore University Press.
Berlie, J.A. (2018) 'Fretilin and CNRT: A short comparative study of the two main political parties of East Timor', in Berlie, J.A. (ed.) *East Timor's independence, Indonesia and ASEAN*. Cham: Palgrave Macmillan, pp. 113–138.
Bjarnegård, E. (2013) *Gender, informal institutions and political recruitment. Explaining male dominance in parliamentary representation*. Hampshire: Palgrave Macmillan.
Blondel, J., Inoguchi, T. and Marsh, I. (eds.) (2012) *Political parties and democracy: Western Europe, East and Southeast Asia 1990–2010*. Hampshire: Palgrave Macmillan.
Chambers, P. and Ufen, A. (eds.) (2020) 'Special issue: Intra-party factionalism in Southeast Asia', *Journal of Current Southeast Asian Affairs*, 39(1).
Chambers, P. and Waitoolkiat, N. (2020) 'Faction politics in an interrupted democracy: The case of Thailand', *Journal of Current Southeast Asian Affairs*, 39(1), p144–166.
Croissant, A. and Völkel, P. (2012) 'Party system types and party system institutionalization. Comparing new democracies in East and Southeast Asia', *Party Politics*, 18(2), p235–262.
Curato, N. (2017) 'Flirting with authoritarian fantasies? Rodrigo Duterte and the new terms of Philippine populism', *Journal of Contemporary Asia*, 47(1), p142–153.
Dalton, R.J., Shin, D.C. and Chu, Y. (eds.) (2008) *Party politics in East Asia: Citizens, elections, and democratic development*. London: Lynne Rienner.
Fossati, D. (2019) 'The resurgence of ideology in Indonesia: Political Islam, aliran and political behaviour', *Journal of Current Southeast Asian Affairs*, 38(2), p119–148.
Geertz, C. (1963) *Peddlers and Princes*. Chicago: University of Chicago Press.
Gomez, E.T. (2012) 'Monetizing politics: Financing parties and elections in Malaysia', *Modern Asian Studies*, 46(5), p1370–1397.
Hadiz, V.R. and Robison, R. (2017) 'Competing populisms in post-authoritarian Indonesia', *International Political Science Review*, 38(4), p488–502.

Hewison, K. (2017) 'Reluctant populists: Learning populism in Thailand', *International Political Science Review*, 38(4), p426–440.

Hicken, A., Aspinall, E. and Weiss, M. (eds.) (2019) *Electoral dynamics in the Philippines: Money politics, patronage, and clientelism at the grassroots*. Singapore: NUS Press.

Hicken, A. and Kuhonta, E. (2014) *Party and party system institutionalization in Asia*. Cambridge: Cambridge University Press.

Horowitz, D.L. (2013) *Constitutional change and democracy in Indonesia*. Cambridge: Cambridge University Press.

Hutchcroft, P. and Rocamora, J. (2003) 'Strong demands and weak institutions: The origins and evolution of the democratic deficit in the Philippines', *Journal of East Asian Studies*, 3(2), p259–292.

Kenny, P.D. (2018) *Populism in Southeast Asia*. Cambridge, Cambridge University Press.

Kimura, M. (1998) 'Changing patterns of leadership recruitment and the emergence of the professional politician in Philippine local politics re-examined: An aspect of political development and decay', *Southeast Asian Studies*, 36(2), p206–229.

King, D.Y. (2003a) *Half-hearted reform. Electoral institutions and the struggle for democracy in Indonesia*. Connecticut: Praeger.

King, D.Y. (2003b) 'East Timor's founding elections and emerging party system', *Asian Survey*, 43(5), p745–757.

Kuhonta, E. (2014) 'Thailand's feckless parties and party system: a path-dependent Analysis', in Hicken, A. and Kuhonta, E. (eds.) *Party system institutionalization in Asia: Democracies, autocracies, and the shadows of the past*. Cambridge: Cambridge University Press, pp. 280–306.

Landé, C.H. (1965) *Leaders, factions and parties: The structure of Philippine politics*. New Haven: Yale University.

Landé, C.H. (1996) *Post-Marcos politics: A geographical and statistical analysis of the 1992 presidential elections*. Singapore: Institute of Southeast Asian Studies.

Machado, K.G. (1974) 'From traditional faction to machine: Changing patterns of political leadership and organization in the rural Philippines', *Journal of Asian Studies*, 33(4), p523–547.

Manacsa, R. C. and Tan, A. C. (2005) 'Manufacturing parties: Re-examining the transient nature of the Philippine political parties', *Party Politics*, 11(6), p748–765.

Manikas, P.M. and Thornton, L.L. (eds.) (2003) *Political parties in Asia: Promoting reform and combating corruption in eight countries*. Washington, DC: National Democratic Institute for International Affairs.

McAllister, I. (2008) 'Social structure and party support', in Dalton, R.J., Shin, D.C. and Chu, Y. (eds.) *Party politics in Asia: citizens, elections, and, democratic development*. Colorado: Lynne Rienner, pp. 69–93.

McCargo, D. and Chattharakul, A. (2020) *Future forward: The rise and fall of a Thai political party*. Copenhagen: NIAS.

McCargo, D. and Pathmanand, U. (2005) *The Thaksinization of Thailand*. Copenhagen: Nordic Institute of Asian Studies.

Mietzner, M. (2013) *Money, power, and ideology: Political parties in post-authoritarian Indonesia*. Singapore: National University Press.

Mietzner, M. (2015) *Reinventing Asian populism: Jokowi's rise, democracy, and political contestation in Indonesia*. Honolulu: East-West Center.

Mietzner, M. and Muhtadi, B. (2018) 'Explaining the 2016 Islamist mobilisation in Indonesia: Religious intolerance, militant groups and the politics of accommodation', *Asian Studies Review*, 42(3), p479–497.

Muhtadi, B. (2019) *Vote buying in Indonesia. The mechanics of electoral bribery*. Hampshire: Palgrave Macmillan.

Mujani, S., Liddle, R.W. and Ambardi, K. (2018) *Voting behavior in Indonesia since democratization: Critical democrats*. New York: Cambridge University Press.

Noor, F.A. (2014) *The Malaysian Islamic Party PAS 1951–2013: Islamism in a mottled nation*. Amsterdam: Amsterdam University Press.

Ockey, J. (2005) 'Variations on a theme: Societal cleavages and party orientations through multiple transitions in Thailand', *Party Politics*, 11(6), p728–747.

Ostwald, K. (2017) *Malaysia's electoral process: The methods and costs of perpetuating UMNO Rule*. Singapore: ISEAS – Yusof Ishak Institute.

Pasuk, P. and Baker, C. (2009) *Thaksin*. Chiang Mai: Silkworm Books.

Perdana, A. and Hillman, B. (2020) 'Quotas and ballots: The impact of positive action policies on women's representation in Indonesia', *Asia Pacific Policy Studies*, 7(2), p158–170.

Prihatini, E. (2019) 'Islam, parties, and women's political nomination in Indonesia', *Politics & Gender*, 16(3), p637–659.

Reilly, B. (2015) 'Electoral systems', in Case, W. (ed.) *Routledge Handbook of Southeast Asian Democratization*. London: Routledge, pp. 225–236.

Riggs, F.W. (1966) *Thailand: The modernization of a bureaucratic polity*. Honolulu: East-West Centre Press.

Sachsenroeder, W. and Frings, U. (eds.) (1998) *Political party systems and democratic development in East and Southeast Asia*. Brookfield: Ashgate.

Saravanamuttu, J. (2016) *Power sharing in a divided nation: Mediated communalism and new politics in six decades of Malaysia's elections*. Singapore: ISEAS – Yusof Ishak Institute.

Sawasdee, S.N. (2006) *Thai political parties in the age of reform*. Bangkok: Institute of Public Policy Studies.

Sawasdee, S.N. (2012) 'Thailand', in Inoguchi, T. and Blondel, J. (eds.) *Political parties and democracy: Contemporary Western Europe and Asia*. New York: Palgrave Macmillan, pp. 143–164.

Scambary, J. (2019) 'Robbing Peter to pay Paul: Changing clientelist patterns in East Timor's 2017 parliamentary elections', *Democratization*, 26(7), p1114–1131.

Shoesmith, D. (2020) 'Party systems and factionalism in Timor-Leste', *Journal of Current Southeast Asian Affairs*, 39(1), p167–186.

Sidel, J.T. (1999) *Capital, coercion and crime: Bossism in the Philippines*. Stanford: Stanford University Press.

Sindre, G.M. (2016) 'Internal party democracy in former rebel parties', *Party Politics*, 22(4), p501–511.

Sinpeng, A. (2014) 'Party-social movement coalition in Thailand's political conflict (2005–2011)', in Liamputtong, P. (ed.) *Contemporary socio-cultural and political perspectives in Thailand*. New York: Springer Netherlands, pp. 157–168.

Sinpeng, A., Gueorguiev, D. and Arugay, A. (2020) 'Strong fans, weak campaigns: Social media and Duterte in the 2016 Philippine elections', *Journal of East Asian Studies*, p1–22.

Slater, D. (2018) 'Party cartelization, Indonesian style: Presidential power-sharing and the contingency of democratic opposition', *Journal of East Asian Studies*, 18(1), p23–46.

Tan, N. (2020) 'Electoral management of digital campaigns and disinformation in East and Southeast Asia', *Election Law Journal*, 19(2), p1–26.

Tapsell, R. (2017) *Media power in Indonesia: Oligarchs, citizens and the digital revolution*. London: Rowman & Littlefield.

Teehankee, J. (2012) 'The Philippines' in Blondel, J., Inoguchi, T. and Marsh, I. (eds.) *Political parties and democracy: Western Europe, East and Southeast Asia 1990–2010*. Hampshire: Palgrave Macmillan, pp. 187–205.

Teehankee, J. (2020) 'Factional dynamics in Philippine party politics, 1900–2019', *Journal of Current Southeast Asian Affairs*, 39(1), p98–123.

Thompson, M.R. (2022) 'Duterte's violent populism: Mass murder, political legitimacy and the "death of development" in the Philippines', *Journal of Contemporary Asia*, 52(3), p403–428.

Tomsa, D. (2008) *Party politics and democratization in Indonesia: Golkar in the Post-Suharto Era*. Abingdon: Routledge.

Tomsa, D. and Setijadi, C. (2018) 'New forms of political activism in Indonesia. Redefining the nexus between electoral and movement Politics', *Asian Survey*, 58(3), p557–581.

Tomsa, D. and Ufen, A. (eds.) (2013) *Party politics in Southeast Asia. Clientelism and electoral competition in Indonesia, Thailand and the Philippines*. Abingdon: Routledge.

Ufen, A. (2008a), 'From aliran to dealignment. Political parties in post-Suharto Indonesia', *South East Asia Research*, 16(1), p5–41.

Ufen, A. (2008b) 'Political party and party system institutionalisation in Southeast Asia: Lessons for democratic consolidation in Indonesia, the Philippines and Thailand', *Pacific Review*, 21(3), p327–355.

Ufen, A. (2014) 'Political finance in Asia', in Falguera, E., Johns, S. and Öhman, M. (eds.) *Political Finance: An International IDEA Handbook*. Stockholm: International IDEA, pp. 82–127.

Ufen, A. (2018) 'Party presidentialization in post-Suharto Indonesia', *Contemporary Politics*, 24(3), p306–324.

Ufen, A. (2020) 'Opposition in transition: Pre-electoral coalitions and the 2018 electoral breakthrough in Malaysia', *Democratization*, 27(2), p167–184.

Waitoolkiat, N. and Chambers, P. (2015) 'Political party finance in Thailand today: Evolution, reform and control', *Critical Asian Studies*, 47(4), p611–640.

Weiss, M.L. (2020) *The roots of resilience: Party machines and grassroots politics in Southeast Asia*. Ithaca: Cornell University Press.

Welsh, B. (ed.) (2016) *The end of UMNO?: Essays on Malaysia's dominant party*. Petaling Jaya: Strategic Information and Research Development Centre (SIRD).

White, S., Savirani, A. and Aspinall, E. (eds.) (2021) 'Special Issue: Women and elections in Indonesia', *Journal of Current Southeast Asian Affairs*, 40(1), p3–27.

33
POLITICAL PARTIES IN LATIN AMERICA

Saskia P. Ruth-Lovell

Political parties in Latin America have had a rocky history for quite some time now. A few traditional parties survived the autocratic episodes in the twentieth century and democratic party system breakdowns at the beginning of the twenty-first century (Levitsky, Loxton and Van Dyck 2016, 849; Mainwaring 2018a). Both old and new parties in the region have long competed in difficult settings, marked by high levels of electoral volatility, low levels of citizen trust and dwindling partisan attachments (Diamond and Gunther 2001; Mainwaring and Zoco 2007; Lupu 2015; Baker and Dorr 2019). Moreover, although they are still seen as important agents within Latin America's democratic systems, their role in making democracy work is ambiguous at best and many describe them as weak, flawed, or diminished subtypes unable to fulfil the most basic democratic functions (Levitsky, Loxton, Van Dyck, et al. 2016; Luna et al. 2021). Recognising these dynamics, the main focus of this chapter is on the two most basic functions parties need to fulfil, namely *recruitment* and *representation*.

Despite (or maybe because of) their misgivings, political parties, their interactions within party systems and their relationship to democracy spurred a lot of innovative research on them since the 1980s. Some key concepts derived from research on Latin American political parties and party systems, such as 'party system institutionalisation' (Mainwaring and Scully 1995), have travelled beyond the region, most importantly to Africa and Asia (Hicken and Kuhonta 2011; Weghorst and Bernhard 2014), but recently also to the traditional party politics literature on Western democracies (Bolleyer and Ruth-Lovell 2019). Much of the debate on political parties in Latin America circulates around the themes of stability and change. Moreover, recent additions to the literature also study stories of successful party-building and vibrant party organisations (Van Dyck 2016; Rosenblatt 2018).

In this chapter, I highlight some of the major contributions to the field made by scholars of Latin American party politics since the Third Wave of democratisation and shine a spotlight on recent additions to the literature. Therefore, this chapter mainly focuses on the party level and parties as political agents within electoral politics and democratic representation, highlighting parties' electoral trajectories, party development in hard times as well as their linkages with society. The concluding section reflects on future avenues of research and on how theoretical, conceptual and empirical innovations in research on Latin American party politics can travel and inform research in other regions of the world.

Latin American political parties, elections and representation

Due to the difficult, and sometimes hostile, environments within which Latin American political parties must operate, their electoral trajectories are often unstable or short-lived (with only a few exceptions). The electoral fates of traditional political parties in the region have gained a lot of attention, and researchers set out to explain why some of them faced decay and breakdown, while others managed to survive and thrive even under the most challenging conditions (Lupu 2016b; Wills-Otero 2016; Cyr 2017; Rosenblatt 2018). Examples of successful traditional parties are the (Peronist) Justicialista Party (PJ) in Argentina and the Institutional Revolutionary Party (PRI) in Mexico (see Burgess and Levitsky 2003), which were able to survive and thrive even in the context of regime change and severe economic crises. Other traditional parties, like the Venezuelan Independent Electoral Political Organization Committee (COPEI) or the Bolivian Revolutionary Nationalist Movement (MNR), however, struggled to survive after national electoral defeats contributing to the breakdown of long-established party systems in the region (see Cyr 2016, 2017).

In some places, the decay and breakdown of traditional parties as well as the availability of large numbers of non-partisan voters offered fertile ground for new party formations. However, as Mustillo (2009) and more recently, Levitsky, Loxton and Van Dyck (2016) highlight, only a minor fraction of new party formations – approximately 3–4 per cent – were able to win a considerable number of votes in more than one election. Most ventures of new party formation managed to win only a small fraction of less than 0.1 per cent of the vote share in one election before disappearing again in the next electoral race (so called 'flop' parties, Mustillo [2009]). Nevertheless, the region has also seen a few exceptions of very successful party-building throughout the last decades, for example, the Workers Party (PT) in Brazil, which has emerged the largest left-wing party in Latin America (see Hunter 2010; Lupu 2016a) or the Movement towards Socialism (MAS) in Bolivia, which under the leadership of Evo Morales has become a leading left-wing and indigenous political party (see Anria 2018).

What allows some older parties to thrive over time and even the odds against party breakdown and decay? What allows new party formations to take hold in challenging contexts? To answer these questions, researchers have recently shifted their attention towards the internal spheres of political parties. Irrespective of the age of political parties, scholars highlight the importance of elite investments in party building – organisational and ideational – to weather the storm (Levitsky, Loxton, Van Dyck, et al. 2016; Wills-Otero 2016). To survive over time, political parties in general need to fulfil a dual role within contemporary democracies: on the one hand, political parties are vehicles that band together ambitious politicians to stand together in elections (*elite coordination*). In a more demanding light, political parties are also expected to link elected representatives to their voters in a meaningful way, that is, make them responsive to their supporters' needs and preferences. For both tasks, organisational and ideational resources are highly relevant.

Party organisations

Even though contextual conditions weaken incentives of political elites to invest in party building (Mainwaring and Zoco 2007), and hence, a lot of political parties in Latin America remain weakly institutionalised, many successful parties (both old and new) managed to invest in the routinisation of their organisations (Bolleyer and Ruth 2018; Davila Gordillo and Wylie 2021).[1] Although structured in different ways, both the Broad Front (FA) in Uruguay and the

Independent Democratic Union (UDI) in Chile serve as examples of routinised political parties, a quality which incentivises their stability and success across time (Rosenblatt 2018).

Historically, political parties in the region were heavily dominated by central party elites who held the power over intra-party decision-making processes, like candidate selection or party strategy (Burgess and Levitsky 2003; Wills-Otero 2016). In the extreme, such parties were mere electoral vehicles of powerful party leaders, who shied away from investments in party building to avoid limiting their leverage and flexibility with regard to their party's behaviour (Weyland 1999; Kitschelt 2000; Roberts 2002). This is why party leaders have often been seen as detrimental to party building, as exemplified by the paradigmatic case of Alberto Fujimori in Peru and his ever-changing electoral vehicles (Levitsky and Cameron 2003).[2]

Recent research on new party formations, party survival and revival, partially challenges this view, indicating that party leaders can play an important role in party building if they are willing and capable to invest in organisational resources (Cyr 2017; Rosenblatt 2018; Van Dyck 2018). Moreover, beyond the types of elite dominated party organisations or personalised electoral vehicles, many new types of political parties arose and with them new models of intra-party decision-making and candidate selection (Barragán and Bohigues 2018). On the one hand, this led to an increased involvement of the citizenry in the process of candidate selection through primaries (Carey and Polga-Hecimovich 2006). On the other hand, new forms of candidate selection also impacted the types of candidates selected to stand in election, namely an increase in the number of women and ethnic candidates in politics. For instance, the MAS in Bolivia substantially increased the representation of marginalised, indigenous groups through inclusive, grassroots candidate selection procedures, while the Chilean UDI ensures a high level of female representatives among their ranks through exclusive-centralised candidate selection procedures (Hinojosa 2012; Funk et al. 2021).

Apart from the selection of candidates, to fulfil their representative function within contemporary democracies, political parties also need to build extra-parliamentary organisations to structure their interactions with activists (*elite-base coordination*), in particular, as well as contribute to the rootedness of the party within society (Levitsky 2001; Alcántara Sáez 2004; Levitsky, Loxton, Van Dyck et al. 2016; Rosenblatt 2018). Political parties that are organisationally linked with society can, for example, better counter anti-party sentiments and alienation from politics that are widespread among citizens in Latin American democracies as well as weather difficult circumstances, like being in opposition or surviving authoritarian regimes (Van Dyck 2016). For example, party elites of Mexico's Party of the Democratic Revolution (PRD), which was born in opposition to and under the hegemonic, authoritarian rule of the PRI in the late 1980s, invested in the institutionalisation of their party organisation by building a strong territorial organisation and a committed activist base (Van Dyck 2016, 144–150).

While party membership is one of the most established measures of party organisational consolidation in developed democracies (Mair and van Biezen 2001; van Haute and Gauja 2015), parties in Latin America – or other developing democracies across the globe – rely less on the formal encapsulation of individual party supporters into rule guided, regularised structures (Roberts 2002; Levitsky and Freidenberg 2007; Kitschelt and Kselman 2013). Instead, they may rely more on informal links through patron–broker networks or on the incorporation of societal groups – such as religious-, ethnic- or class-based organisations – whose local infrastructure can be highly beneficial for routinisation and at the same time provide additional ideational resources as well (Holland and Palmer-Rubin 2015; Bolleyer and Ruth 2018; Anria and Chambers-Ju 2019). Irrespective of the formalisation of organisational links between a party and its members or activists, several successful political parties in Latin America do manage to invest in the routinisation of vertical connections between party elites, the party base and society in general (Bolleyer and Ruth 2018; Meléndez and Umpierrez de Reguero 2021). Relatedly, studying parties in Chile, Costa Rica and Uruguay, Rosenblatt (2018) coined the term party vibrancy, which refers to the ability of parties to engage activists and supporters beyond election campaigns through regular in-between election activities which bind supporters to the party long term. The simultaneous presence of a shared vision or worldview, a collective experience of trauma, the satisfaction of career interests and the power to bind rank-and-file members to the party organisation explains the organisational vibrancy of both the Chilean UDI and the FA in Uruguay (Rosenblatt 2018).

Programmatic and non-programmatic linkages

However, organisational resources of political parties are only one side of party development and party institutionalisation. To fulfil their representative function within democratic systems, political parties are expected to provide substantive *links* between society and the state as well. In the party politics literature on developed democracies, political parties are assumed to be 'agents of interest mediation' (Kitschelt et al. 1999, 5) and therefore linked to their supporters and voters based on policy programmes. Research on political parties in Latin America, however, acknowledges the variety of mechanisms that establish the representative link between parties and voters beyond policy programmes. Therefore, scholars frequently build on the linkage concept as a tool to analyse different (electoral) party strategies to build short or long-term linkages (Kitschelt 2000; Kitschelt et al. 2010; Luna 2014). These different linkages which political parties can pursue to connect themselves with the electorate 'set the tone' for democratic representation on the system level (Moreno et al. 2003; Roberts 2016).

Ideational resources

Ideational resources play an important role in both studies focused on the supply side of party politics, for example, linked to the label of 'value infusion' as a feature of party institutionalisation (Levitsky 1998; Bolleyer and Ruth 2018), as well as in studies with a demand side focus on 'partisanship' or 'partisan attachments' (Carreras et al. 2015; Lupu 2015). There are different ways as to how party elites establish links with society and infuse their organisation with value for elites, activists and supporters alike. The most common ideational resource a *party brand* can build on is a programmatic party platform (Roberts 2002; Lupu 2016b).[3] Strong party brands provide incentives for elites, activists and voters to develop long-lasting loyalties and attachments to their party. Latin American parties with a strong programmatic brand are, for example, the Workers Party (PT) in Brazil, or the Broad Front (FA) in Uruguay on the left (Hunter 2010; Lupu 2016a; Rosenblatt 2018) as well as the Independent Democratic Union (UDI) in Chile and the National Republican Alliance (ARENA) in El Salvador on the right (Loxton 2016; Rosenblatt 2018).

Researchers highlight that these programmatic parties play an important role in shaping systemic trends of voter dealignment and realignment since the 2000s in the region (Carreras et al. 2015), with both parties on the right and the left of the ideological spectrum, showing signs of resilience to the often propagated crisis of representation (Levitsky and Roberts 2011; Luna and Rovira Kaltwasser 2014; Kapiszewski et al. 2021). The resilience of programmatic parties and their capacity to counter the crisis of representation in the region does, however, depend not only on the consistency with which party elites deploy party labels but also on the systemic context in which they cooperate and compete with each other. For example, studies show that ideological conflict and polarisation between parties within a party system increase the incentives of party elites to invest in programmatic linkages (Kitschelt et al. 2010; Roberts 2016) and at the same time reinforce ideological voting as well as voter attachments to their parties (Lupu 2015; Singer 2016). Hence, it is these types of parties that, in theory, enable substantive representation on the system level, since it is more likely in contexts where 'politicians employ party labels and develop coherent policy alternatives in their public appeals. These alternatives define the competitive space of democratic electoral contests' (Kitschelt et al. 2010, 3).

Recently, researchers have also shown that despite the potential of strong programmatic profiles to make parties more resilient to volatile electoral contexts and economic crisis, they also restrict the room to manoeuver for political elites in the political arena. In line with the trade-offs between policy-seeking and office-seeking incentives of party elites (Strom 1990), programmatic linkage decay and party brand dilution may result from political elites prioritising government participation, coalitional unity or crisis management over programmatic differentiation and consistency, with severe consequences for their electoral trajectories (Stokes 2001; Lupu 2016b). The Argentinean Radical Civic Union (UCR) serves as an example of party breakdown following a process of brand dilution (Lupu 2016b). Morgan and Meléndez (2016) highlight how coalitional dynamics and emphasis on valence issue representation contributed to the ideological convergence of the two major Chilean coalitions, Nueva Mazoría and Alianza, and an ensuing decay of programmatic linkages in Chile.

Non-programmatic linkages

The study of political parties in Latin America, however, has also shown that many political parties do not dispose of a strong and consistent programmatic platform to begin with and instead have to resort to different ways to link with their supporters, for example, clientelism and personalism (Kitschelt and Wilkinson 2007; Kostadinova and Levitt 2014; Rhodes-Purdy and Madrid 2020).

Although the decline of clientelism in democratic contexts has often been predicted, this party strategy has proven to be highly adaptive (Nichter 2018; Ruth-Lovell and Spirova 2019). It is usually understood as a political strategy deployed by so-called patrons, which builds on the mobilisation of clients through the distribution of selective benefits, like consumer goods, selective access to policy programmes, or jobs to citizens conditional on their political support (Kitschelt 2000; Stokes 2007). Research on Latin America has shown that parties engaging in clientelism form dense problem-solving networks linking patrons, brokers and clients in a pyramidal structure (Auyero 2000; Szwarcberg 2012). Apart from sporadic, one-shot electoral practices, like vote or turnout buying (Stokes 2005; Nichter 2008), research on Latin American parties has shown that these practices can foster long-term bonds between party elites, activists and supporters, resulting in relational clientelism, extending exchanges between the actors involved beyond elections (Kitschelt and Wilkinson 2007; Nichter 2018). The loyalties that bind patrons, brokers and clients together are based on the norm of reciprocity and reinforced both through the behaviour of patrons and brokers on the supply side as well as through clients on the demand side (Finan and Schechter 2012; Lawson and Greene 2014). These party links resemble the resilience of political identities formed by programmatic parties in many ways. For one, they provide a means for clients to address the uncertainty in the political arena, most importantly, with respect to the insufficient coverage of welfare states against poverty and vulnerability (Nichter 2018). Moreover, non-state actors have also been identified as potential partners in upholding clientelistic linkages, through party-interest group collaboration (Holland and Palmer-Rubin 2015). Paradigmatic examples of political parties in Latin America, who successfully rely on clientelistic linkages with their supporters, are the (Peronist) Justicialist

Party (PJ) in Argentina (Auyero 2000), as well as the Institutional Revolutionary Party (PRI) in Mexico (Magaloni et al. 2007).

More recently, researchers have turned their attention towards the possibility of mixing programmatic and clientelistic linkages to mobilise support, as a consequence of either risk-aversion of political elites (Magaloni et al. 2007) or the parallel appeal to diverse constituencies which according to Gibson (1997) are then combined into one 'electoral coalition' (see also Luna 2014). However, the feasibility of linkage mixing may differ depending on where on the ideological spectrum political actors are located and pursuing a clientelistic linkage strategy may entail trade-offs (Kitschelt 2000). More specifically, right-wing parties, which prefer a conservative welfare regime, have a comparative advantage in complementing their mobilisation repertoire with clientelistic practices compared to left-wing parties, since paying off the poor in return for their vote provides these parties with greater leverage to pursue an elitist welfare agenda (Pribble 2013). Recent research on the party level, for example, revealed that clientelism indeed goes together with a more conservative policy advocacy on several social policy dimensions, likely contributing to more residual welfare states in the region (Berens and Ruth-Lovell 2021).

Finally, due to beneficial institutional contexts of presidential systems in the region, political parties in Latin America can also rely on a personalistic linkage strategy (Kostadinova and Levitt 2014; Rhodes-Purdy and Madrid 2020). Political parties that maintain such bonds with their voters base their strategy on the personal skills of one or a few (charismatic) leaders. Often these parties are referred to as mere electoral vehicles (Diamond and Gunther 2001). As mentioned before, the organisational structure of these parties tends to be weakly institutionalised, since party leaders do not want to limit their leverage on the intraparty decision-making process (Weyland 1999; Samuels 2002). In analogy to this, the pledges personalistic parties make to their voters remain opaque. Party leaders 'tend to promise all things to all people to maintain maximum personal discretion over the strategy of their party vehicle' (Kitschelt 2000, 849). Examples of a personalist parties in Latin America abound, like Hugo Chávez' Fifth Republic Movement (MVR), later renamed into the United Socialist Party of Venezuela (PSUV) (Hawkins 2009; Corrales and Penfold 2015), or the various electoral vehicles of the Alberto Fujimori, for example, Cambio 90, Vamos Vecinos or Sí Cumple (Levitsky and Cameron 2003; Loxton and Levitsky 2018).

Conclusion and avenues for future research

Latin American party politics marks a vibrant field of study with a rich tradition, with respect to both theoretical and empirical innovation (Levitsky, Loxton, Van Dyck, et al. 2016; Mainwaring 2018b). The region provides for a broad variety of party types, with respect to both their organisational development and their linkage with society. Shifting their attention away from the party system level and towards political parties as agents of democratic representation, researchers were able to show that it is the investments of party elites in organisational and ideational resources to build and develop their parties which ultimately set the tone for the institutionalisation as well as the programmatic structuration of party systems in the region (Kitschelt et al. 2010; Mainwaring 2018b). Future research will have to continue on this journey and add to this promising line of research by further testing newly developed typologies and theoretical arguments, beyond paradigmatic cases. For example, does the concept of party vibrancy travel to political parties in countries that are less shaped by programmatic party competition than Chile, Costa Rica and Uruguay?

Moreover, new lines of research in the field take a more critical perspective towards political parties as pillars of democracy, by highlighting their diminished capacity to fulfil basic democratic functions of coordinating interactions between citizens and the state (Luna et. al. 2021). Future research needs to further investigate the links and trade-offs between organisational and ideational resources and how these enable political parties to fulfil their basic democratic representative function. For example, which organisational structures are more likely conducive to maintain programmatic, clientelistic or personalistic linkages and which trade-offs arise for party elites when they aim to maximise their electoral fortune by diversifying and mixing linkages to society (see also Magaloni et al. 2007), and thereby, potentially compromising substantive democratic representation.

Finally, while theory building and in-depth analysis of political parties are a forte of Latin American party politics, more large-N comparative analyses have the potential to complement and add to the field, by testing theories within and ideally also beyond the region, adding to their generalisability and explanatory power. Luckily, in recent years, several comparative data sources have become available which centre on capturing different features and profiles of political parties on the party level. For example, expert survey data from the Democratic Accountability and Linkages Project (DALP, Kitschelt 2013), the Political Representation, Executives, and Political Parties Survey (PREPPS) (Wiesehomeier, Singer and Ruth-Lovell 2021), as well as the Varieties of Party Identity and Organization Survey (V-Party, Lührmann et al. 2020) allow researchers to delve into both the organisational and ideational outlooks of political parties both within and beyond Latin America. These data sources also hold the potential to bridge the regionally segmented party politics literature in the future.

Notes

1. Note that routinisation may vary depending on whose behaviour within a party organisation we focus on: the party elite or the party base (see Bolleyer and Ruth-Lovell 2019).
2. Alberto Fujimori was affiliated with a number of different political parties throughout his political career that served as his electoral vehicles, like Cambio 90 (Change 90) or Sí Cumple (Let's Go Neighbor), which he founded in 1998 to run in municipal elections, and other alliances such as Alliance for the Future and Change 21.
3. Researchers, however, also highlight other ideational resources that can strengthen a party's brand like a formational myth (e.g. surrounding a founding leader) or the shared experience of trauma (e.g. crisis, discrimination, or repression) (see Levitsky et al. 2016; Rosenblatt 2018).

References

Alcántara Sáez, M. (2004) ¿Instituciones o máquinas ideológicas? Origen, programa y organización de los partidos latinoamericanos. Barcelona: Institut de Ciénces Politiques i Socials.

Anria, S. (2018) When Movements Become Parties: The Bolivian MAS in Comparative Perspective. Cambridge: Cambridge University Press.

Anria, S. and Chambers-Ju, C. (2019) Parties and Non-State actors in Latin America. Oxford: Oxford University Press.

Auyero, J. (2000)'The logic of clientelism in Argentina: An ethnographic account', Latin American Research Review, 35(3), p55–81.

Baker, A. and Dorr, D. (2019) 'Mass partisanship in three Latin American democracies', in Lupu, N., Oliveros, V. and Schiumerini, L. (eds.) Campaigns and voters in developing democracies: Argentina in comparative perspective. Ann Arbor: University of Michigan Press, pp. 89–113

Barragán, M. and Bohigues, A. (2018) 'New political parties in Latin America: A new way of selection and new elite profiles', in Coller, X., Cordero, G. and Jaime-Castillo, A.M. (eds.) The selection of politicians in times of crisis. London: Routledge, pp. 165–188.

Berens, S. and Ruth-Lovell, S.P. (2021) 'Does clientelism hinder progressive social policy in Latin America?', Acta Politica, 56(4), p694–718.

Bolleyer, N. and Ruth, S.P. (2018) 'Elite investments in party institutionalization in new democracies: A two-dimensional approach', *The Journal of Politics*, 80(1), p288–302.

Bolleyer, N. and Ruth-Lovell, S.P. (2019) 'Party institutionalization as multilevel concept: Base- versus elite-level routinization', *Zeitschrift für Vergleichende Politikwissenschaft*, 13(2), p175–198.

Burgess, K. and Levitsky, S. (2003) 'Explaining populist party adaptation in Latin America: Environmental and organizational determinants of party change in Argentina, Mexico, Peru, and Venezuela. *Comparative Political Studies*, 36(8), p881–911.

Carey, J.M. and Polga-Hecimovich, J. (2006) 'Primary elections and candidate strength in Latin America', *Journal of Politics*, 68(3), p530–543.

Carreras, M., Morgenstern, S. and Su, Y.P. (2015) 'Refining the theory of partisan alignments: Evidence from Latin America', *Party Politics*, 21(5), p671–685.

Corrales, J. and Penfold, M. (2015) *Dragon in the tropics: Venezuela and the legacy of Hugo Chávez*. Washington, DC: The Brookings Institution Press.

Cyr, J. (2016) 'Between adaptation and breakdown: Conceptualizing party survival', *Comparative Politics*, 49(1), p125–145.

Cyr, J. (2017) *The fates of political parties: Institutional crisis, continuity, and change in Latin America*. Cambridge: Cambridge University Press.

Davila Gordillo, D. and Wylie, K.N. (2021) *Party leadership and institutionalization in Latin America*. Oxford: Oxford University Press.

Diamond, L.J. and Gunther, R. (2001) *Political parties and democracy*. Baltimore: Johns Hopkins University Press.

Finan, F. and Schechter, L. (2012) 'Vote-Buying and reciprocity', *Econometrica*, 80(2), p863–881.

Funk, K.D., Hinojosa, M. and Piscopo, J.M. (2021) 'Women to the rescue: The gendered effects of public discontent on legislative nominations in Latin America', *Party Politics*, 27(3), p465–477.

Gibson, E.L. (1997) 'The populist road to market reform: Policy and electoral coalitions in Mexico and Argentina', *World Politics*, 49(3), p339–370.

Hawkins, K.A. (2009) 'Is Chávez populist?: Measuring populist discourse in comparative perspective', *Comparative Political Studies*, 42(8), p1040–1067.

Hicken, A. and Kuhonta, E.M. (2011) 'Shadows from the past: Party system institutionalization in Asia', *Comparative Political Studies*, 44(5), p572–597.

Hinojosa, M. (2012) *Selecting women, electing women political representation and candidate selection in Latin America*. Philadelphia: Temple University Press.

Holland, A.C. and Palmer-Rubin, B. (2015) 'Beyond the machine: Clientelist brokers and interest organizations in Latin America', *Comparative political studies*, 48(9), p1186–1223.

Hunter, W. (2010) *The transformation of the Workers Party in Brazil, 1989–2009*. Cambridge: Cambridge University Press.

Kapiszewski, D., Levitsky, S. and Yashar, D.J. (2021) *The Inclusionary Turn in Latin American Democracies*. Cambridge: Cambridge University Press.

Kitschelt, H. (2000) 'Linkages between citizens and politicians in democratic Polities', *Comparative Political Studies*, 33(6–7), p845–879.

Kitschelt, H. (2013) *Democratic accountability and linkages project* Durham: Duke University.

Kitschelt, H., Hawkins, K.A., Luna, J.P., Rosas, G. and Zechmeister, E.J. (2010) *Latin American party systems*. Cambridge: Cambridge University Press.

Kitschelt, H. and Kselman, D.M. (2013) 'Economic Development, Democratic Experience, and Political Parties' Linkage Strategies. *Comparative Political Studies*, 46(11), p1453–1484.

Kitschelt, H., Mansfeldova, Z., Markowski, R. and Tóka, G. (1999) *Post-communist party systems. Competition, representation, and inter-party cooperation*. Cambridge: Cambridge University Press.

Kitschelt, H. and Wilkinson, S. (Eds.). (2007) *Patrons, clients, and policies: Patterns of democratic accountability and political competition*. Cambridge: Cambridge University Press.

Kostadinova, T. and Levitt, B. (2014) 'Toward a theory of personalist parties: Concept formation and theory building', *Politics and Policy*, 42(4), p490–512.

Lawson, C. and Greene, K.F. (2014) 'Making clientelism work: How norms of reciprocity increase voter compliance', *Comparative Politics*, 47(1), p61–85.

Levitsky, S. (1998) 'Institutionalization and Peronism: The concept, the case and the case for unpacking the concept', *Party Politics*, 4(1), p77–92.

Levitsky, S. (2001) Inside the black box: Recent studies of Latin American party organizations. *Studies in Comparative International Development*, 36(2), p92–110.

Levitsky, S. and Cameron, M.A. (2003) 'Democracy without parties? Political parties and regime change in Fujimori's Peru', *Latin American Politics and Society*, 45(3), p1–33.

Levitsky, S. and Freidenberg, F. (2007) 'Organizacion informal de los partidos en America Latina', *Desarrollo Economico*, 46(184), p539–568.

Levitsky, S., Loxton, J. and Van Dyck, B. (2016) 'Introduction. Challenges of party-building in Latin America', in Levitsky, S., Loxton, J., Van Dyck, B. and Domínguez, J.I. (eds.) *Challenges of party-building in Latin America*. Cambridge: Cambridge University Press, pp. 1–48.

Levitsky, S., Loxton, J., Van Dyck, B. and Domínguez, J.I. (2016) *Challenges of party-building in Latin America*. Cambridge: Cambridge University Press.

Levitsky, S. and Roberts, K.M. (2011) *The resurgence of the Latin American left*. Baltimore: Johns Hopkins University Press.

Loxton, J. (2016) 'Authoritarian successor parties and the new right in Latin America', in Van Dyck, B., Loxton, J.J., Domínguez, J.I. and Levitsky, S. (eds.) *Challenges of party-building in Latin America*. Cambridge: Cambridge University Press, pp. 245–272.

Loxton, J. and Levitsky, S. (2018) 'Personalistic authoritarian successor parties in Latin America', in Loxton, J. and Mainwaring, S. (eds.) *Life after dictatorship: Authoritarian successor parties worldwide*. Cambridge: Cambridge University Press, pp. 113–142.

Lührmann, A., Düpont, N., Higashijima, M., Berker Kavasoglu, Y., Marquardt, K.L., Bernhard, M., Döring, H., Hicken, A., Laebens, M., Lindberg, S.I., Medzihorsky, J., Neundorf, A., John Reuter, O., Ruth-Lovell, S.P., Weghorst, K.R., Wiesehomeier, N., Wright, J., Alizada, N., Bederke, P., Gastaldi, L., Grahn, S., Hindle, G., Ilchenko, N., von Römer, J., Wilson, S., Pemstein, D. and Seim, B. (2020) *Varieties of party identity and organization (V-Party) dataset V1*. Gothenburg: The V-Dem Institute.

Luna, J.P. (2014) *Segmented representation: Political party strategies in unequal democracies* (1st ed.). Oxford: Oxford University Press.

Luna, J.P., Rodriguez, R.P., Rosenblatt, F. and Vommaro, G. (2021) 'Political parties, diminished subtypes, and democracy', *Party Politics*, 27(2), p294–307.

Luna, J.P. and Rovira Kaltwasser, C. (2014) *The resilience of the Latin American right*. Baltimore: Johns Hopkins University Press.

Lupu, N. (2015) 'Partisanship in Latin America', in Carlin, R.E., Singer, M.M. and Zechmeister, E.J. (eds.) *The Latin American voter: Pursuing representation and accountability in challenging contexts*. Ann Arbor: University of Michigan Press, pp. 226–245.

Lupu, N. (2016a) 'Building party brands in Argentina and Brazil', in Levitsky, S., Loxton, J., Van Dyck, B. and Domínguez, J.I. (eds.) *Challenges of party-building in Latin America*. Cambridge: Cambridge University Press, pp. 76–99.

Lupu, N. (2016b) *Party brands in crisis: Partisanship, brand dilution, and the breakdown of political parties in Latin America*. Cambridge: Cambridge University Press.

Magaloni, B., Diaz-Cayeros, A. and Estévez, F. (2007) 'Clientelism and portfolio diversification: A model of electoral investment with application to Mexico', in Kitschelt, H.H. and Wilkinson, S. (eds.) *Patrons, clients, and policies: Patterns of democratic accountability and political competition*. Cambridge: Cambridge University Press, pp. 182–205.

Mainwaring, S. (2018a). 'Introduction', in Mainwaring, S. (ed.) *Party systems in Latin America: Institutionalization, Decay, and Collapse*. Cambridge: Cambridge University Press, pp. 1–14.

Mainwaring, S. (2018b) *Party systems in Latin America: institutionalization, decay, and collapse*. Cambridge: Cambridge University Press.

Mainwaring, S. and Scully, T.R. (1995) *Building democratic institutions. Party systems in Latin America*. Stanford: Stanford University Press.

Mainwaring, S. and Zoco, E. (2007) 'Political sequences and the stabilization of interparty competition – Electoral volatility in old and new democracies', *Party Politics*, 13(2), p155–178.

Mair, P. and van Biezen, I. (2001) 'Party membership in twenty European democracies, 1980–2000', *Party Politics*, 7(1), p5–21.

Meléndez, C. and Umpierrez de Reguero, S. (2021) *Party members and activists in Latin America*. Oxford: Oxford University Press.

Moreno, E., Crisp, B.F. and Shugart, M.S. (2003) 'The accountability deficit in Latin America', in Mainwaring, S. and Welna, C. (eds.) *Democratic accountability in Latin America*. Oxford: Oxford University Press, pp. 79–131.

Morgan, J. and Meléndez, C. (2016) 'Parties under stress: Using a linkage decay framework to analyze the Chilean party system', *Journal of Politics in Latin America*, 8(3), p25–59.

Mustillo, T.J. (2009) 'Modeling new party performance: A conceptual and methodological approach for volatile party systems', *Political Analysis*, 17(3), p311–332.

Nichter, S. (2008) 'Vote buying or turnout buying? Machine politics and the secret ballot', *The American Political Science Review*, 102(1), p19–31. www.jstor.org/stable/27644495

Nichter, S. (2018) *Votes for survival: Relational clientelism in Latin America*. Cambridge: Cambridge University Press.

Pribble, J. (2013) *Welfare and party politics in Latin America*. Cambridge: Cambridge University Press.

Rhodes-Purdy, M. and Madrid, R.L. (2020) 'The perils of personalism', *Democratization*, 27(2), p321–339.

Roberts, K.M. (2002) 'Party-society linkages and democratic representation in Latin America', *Canadian Journal of Latin American and Caribbean Studies/Revue canadienne des études latino-américaines et caraïbes*, 27(53), p9–34. https://doi.org/10.1080/08263663.2002.10816813

Roberts, K.M. (2016) 'Historical timing, political cleavages, and party-building in Latin America', in Levitsky, S., Loxton, J., Van Dyck, B. and Domínguez, J.I. (eds.) *Challenges of party-building in Latin America*. Cambridge: Cambridge University Press, pp. 51–75.

Rosenblatt, F. (2018) *Party vibrancy and democracy in Latin America*. Oxford: Oxford University Press.

Ruth-Lovell, S.P. and Spirova, M. (2019) *Clientelism and democratic representation in comparative perspective*. Lanham: ECPR Press, Rowman Littlefield.

Samuels, D.J. (2002) 'Presidentialized parties: The separation of powers and party organization and behavior', *Comparative Political Studies*, 35(4), p461–483.

Singer, M. (2016) 'Elite polarization and the electoral impact of left-right placements: Evidence from Latin America, 1995–2009', *Latin American Research Review*, 51(2), p174–194.

Stokes, S.C. (2001) *Mandates and democracy: Neoliberalism by surprise in Latin America*. Cambridge: Cambridge University Press.

Stokes, S.C. (2005) 'Perverse accountability: A formal model of machine politics with evidence from Argentina', *American Political Science Review*, 99(3), p315–325.

Stokes, S.C. (2007) 'Political clientelism', in Boix, C. and Stokes, S.C (eds.) *The Oxford handbook of comparative politics*. Oxford: Oxford University Press.

Strom, K. (1990) 'A behavioral theory of competitive political parties', *American Journal of Political Science*, 34(2), p565–598.

Szwarcberg, M. (2012) 'Revisiting clientelism: A network analysis of problem-solving networks in Argentina', *Social Networks*, 34(2), p230–240.

Van Dyck, B. (2016) 'The Paradox of adversity: New left party Survival and Collapse in Brazil, Mexico, and Argentina', in Van Dyck, B., Loxton, J., Domínguez, J.I. and Levitsky, S. (eds.) *Challenges of party-building in Latin America*. Cambridge: Cambridge University Press, pp. 133–158.

Van Dyck, B. (2018) 'External appeal, internal dominance: How party leaders contribute to successful party building', *Latin American Politics and Society*, 60(1), p1–26.

van Haute, E. and Gauja, A. (2015) *Party members and activists*. London: Routledge.

Weghorst, K.R. and Bernhard, M. (2014) 'From formlessness to structure? The institutionalization of competitive party systems in Africa', *Comparative Political Studies*, 47(12), p1707–1737.

Weyland, K. (1999) 'Neoliberal populism in Latin America and Eastern Europe', *Comparative Politics*, 31(4), p379–401.

Wiesehomeier, N., Singer, M. and Ruth-Lovell, S.P. (2021) *Political representation, executives, and political parties survey: Data from expert surveys in Latin American countries, 2018–2019*, Harvard Dataverse, UNF:6:tVgxOYC2L9vl8fAFMFjNkA== [fileUNF] (Version V1). https://doi.org/doi.org/10.7910/DVN/JLOYIJ

Wills-Otero, L. (2016) 'The electoral performance of Latin American traditional parties, 1978–2006: Does the internal structure matter?', *Party Politics*, 22(6), p758–772.

34
POLITICAL PARTIES IN SUB-SAHARAN AFRICA

Matthijs Bogaards

In 2010, the Electoral Institute for Sustainable Democracy in Africa (EISA) organised a series of workshops with parties and experts to come up with benchmarks for political parties. The aim was 'to enhance the capacity of political parties in Africa to be effective, accountable, responsive, transparent, and internally democratic' (Fakir and Lodge 2015a, 196). The resulting document contains over 100 dos and don'ts that range from the general ('political parties should be well anchored in society'), to the specific ('there should be no use of state resources for campaigning purposes'). With such high expectations, it is little wonder that 'very few African parties . . . come close to fulfilling all these criteria' (Fakir and Lodge 2015b, xvii). Or indeed very few parties anywhere, as there is little specifically African about EISA's expectations of how political parties should organise and behave.

While not neglecting the normative dimension, the focus of this chapter on political parties in Sub-Saharan Africa is empirical and analytical. It asks what political parties in Africa are actually like and how we can study them. The answers are sought with the help of the cartel party thesis, one of the most influential frameworks for the study of contemporary political parties (Bogaards 2013). The cartel party thesis was originally developed to capture the latest stage in West European party development. It describes the transformation of political parties from representatives of society into agents of the state. However, there are 'many paths to a cartel-like situation' (Katz and Mair 2018, 124). In Africa, with few exceptions, political parties have always been closer to the state than to society. Bleck and van de Walle (2019, 109), for example, note how 'political parties were on the whole not well rooted in society'. Thus, although political parties in Africa followed a different trajectory from those in Western Europe, they are expected to exhibit many of the same features of the cartel party: dependence on the state for critical resources, low membership, weak ties to civil society, lack of intraparty democracy, weak programmatic profiles and collusive behaviour. This is not an attractive list of features and it is no surprise that Katz and Mair's (2009, 762) complaint that 'modern democracy has somehow been hollowed out' is paralleled in concerns about the discrepancy between the form and content of democracy in the region (Adejumobi 2000, 66).

The heart of this chapter consists of the first systematic application of the seven features of the cartel party (state funding, state capture, state regulation of parties, members and affiliates, intraparty organisation, competition, and collusion) to Africa. This is preceded by a brief overview of recent literature on African political parties and followed by a conclusion that seeks to situate the findings into the broader literature.

The state of African parties

After decades of no-party and single-party regimes, almost all African countries now allow political parties, which fulfil crucial functions of articulation, recruitment, representation and government (Gunther and Diamond 2001; Bogaards 2013). Still, there is little reason for optimism. What Carothers (2006, 4) calls the 'standard lament' about parties sounds eerily familiar to observers of African party politics: party leaders are power-hungry elites, parties themselves are corrupt, do not offer policy choice, are only active around election time and do a bad job at governing the country. Already around the time of independence, scholars cautioned that parties in the developing world failed to live up to Western expectations (Bogaards 2013). In addition to being organisationally weak, African parties have often been seen as ethnic, reflecting socio-cultural diversity rather than programmatic differences, though recent research reveals a more nuanced picture (Elischer 2013).

The third wave of democratisation has, with some delay, led to a revival of interest in political parties in Africa. Important new books include LeBas (2011), Osei (2012), Elischer (2013), Southall (2013), Riedl (2014), Morse (2019) and Kelly (2020). Recent research has challenged the conventional wisdom. This includes 'the many simplistic claims of weak parties in Africa' (Riedl 2018, 43), the assumption of low degrees of party nationalisation (Wahman 2017), a lack of local party presence (Krönke, Lockwood and Mattes 2022) and informal relationships dominating formal relationship within parties (Osei 2016). What these studies show, instead, is that party strength varies and depends on authoritarian legacies, that incumbent parties are more nationalised than opposition parties, that new data reveal a surprising degree of grassroots activity and that new methods demonstrate the importance of party organisation. Although party institutionalisation in Africa remains low in comparison to other parts of the world, there has been a noticeable increase over time (Bizzarro et al. 2017, 11). Moreover, Nuvunga and Sitoe's (2015) case study of party institutionalisation in Mozambique shows that generalisations can be tricky: comparing the ruling Frelimo, the former rebel movement turned opposition party RENAMO, and the new challenger the Democratic Movement of Mozambique (MDM), they find the first is highly institutionalised, the second de-institutionalising and the third institutionalising. Finally, party identification is on the rise, with 56 per cent of African respondents saying they 'feel close' to a party in their country (Afrobarometer 2018, 1).

Early typologies of African parties were largely simplifications of the European literature from the 1950s that sought to distinguish between mass and elite parties. They were subsequently criticised for failing to note that genuine mass parties were largely absent in Africa.[1] The African National Congress (ANC) in South Africa is an exception (Lodge 2014). Most scholars working on party politics in Sub-Saharan Africa agree that standard typologies of political parties as developed in the comparative politics literature are suitable for research on African parties, provided certain adjustments are made (Erdmann 2004; Carbone 2007). Katsina (2016), for example, explicitly analyses Nigeria's Peoples Democratic Party as a catch-all party.

One of the most influential modern typologies of parties was developed by Katz and Mair (1995, 2009, 2018). They introduce the 'cartel party' as the next in a long line of party models in the Western world since the emergence of effective parliaments, following on from the elite party of the nineteenth century, the mass party and the catch-all party, to the emergence of the cartel party in the 1970s (see Chapters 1 and 4). The cartel party relies increasingly on the state for its income, uses mass communication techniques to reach supporters and voters, creates autonomy for the party leadership within the party organisation, has even less need for members and competes on the basis of managerial competence rather than policy positions. If the party is seen as an intermediary between society and the state, the development of parties over time resembles a move away from society and towards the state. Whereas the mass party still fulfilled an important linkage function, the cartel party has become part of the state rather than society. Moreover, as the name suggests, the cartel party does not exist in isolation. To protect their position within the state and access to resources, cartel parties form a cartel that tries to make it more difficult for new entrants. The driving force behind the emergence of cartel parties is the self-interest of politicians and the collective interest of the political class (Blyth and Katz 2005). If parties are seen as pursuing votes, policies, or office, then the cartel party is clearly a variant of the office-seeking party (Wolinetz 2002).

The cartel party thesis has been highly influential and has been applied to most countries in Western and Eastern Europe (Aucante and Dézé 2008) and the old Commonwealth. Though contested (Koole 1996), the cartel party continues to dominate academic analysis of contemporary party politics. Its impact on the study of non-Western politics has been more limited, despite occasional case studies of countries like Israel (Yishai 2001), South Korea (Kwak 2003) and Indonesia (Mietzner 2013; Slater 2018). Although the promise of the cartel party thesis for an analysis of party politics in Africa has been noted (Kopecký and Mair 2003), no such study exists.

Despite the different trajectories, there are strong reasons to believe that the cartel party thesis has something important to say about the organisation and behaviour of contemporary parties in Africa. First, parties in the so-called third-wave of democratisation skipped some of the stages that Western parties went through (Carothers 2006). Most African parties are new and do not carry the legacy of previous party types. Second, the nature of the state in Africa has historically provided parties with rich opportunities for patronage, clientelism and corruption (Erdmann and Engel 2007). Ironically, 'even weak states have an astonishing capacity to function, namely in controlling the flow of foreign funds, especially aid payments' (Welz 2021, 145). Third, elite parties are expected to use patronage to make up for their organisational deficiencies (Shefter 1994). The following sections will show how, though in a different context and with different origins, African parties today exhibit many of the features of the cartel party and can usefully be analysed through this framework.

State funding

According to Katz and Mair (2018) the financial dependence of modern parties on the state is the key factor behind the emergence of the cartel party. There is no denying that state subsidies to political parties have become increasingly common around the world (Pinto-Duschinsky 2002). Africa is no exception, as figures from the International IDEA Database on Political Party Finance and from the Electoral Institute for the Sustainability of Democracy in Africa show.[2] South African parties receive more state funding than in any other African country, a practice that is hotly debated (Pottie 2003; Sarakinsky 2007). Even so, 'private funding still exceeds public funding by far' (Uwem Umoh 2018, 463). Worse, 'informal and often illegal public-sector funding of parties and candidates is at least as important as legislated public funding mechanisms' (Butler 2010: 7).

Southall and Wood (1998) identify three stages in African party funding. Whereas the early mass-based political parties were said to be funded in considerable part by members, the ruling parties after independence utilised state resources. This has continued after the return of multiparty politics in the 1990s, while challengers look for grassroots financing and foreign donors.

Indeed, some observers have warned about 'donor dependence' of political parties in Africa (Pottie 2003, 9). There is a structural problem: 'the general level of poverty means that setting membership fees at levels that would produce respectable incomes for the parties would also put them beyond the reach of most people' (Saffu 2003, 27).

Shale's (2018) description of political party funding in Lesotho and Mozambique makes direct reference to the cartel party thesis, though the origins of party funding in both countries were very different from those in Western Europe. In Lesotho, it was the political crisis of 1998, when South African forces had to restore democracy, and in Mozambique the 1992 peace agreement between the ruling Frelimo liberation movement and the RENAMO rebel group, an agreement that ended a long-term civil war. Perhaps the violent origins of party funding, and the need to placate the main contestants, explain why in both countries opposition parties receive at least the same or even more state funding than the election winner/ruling party. Noting how parties in Lesotho and Mozambique influence the state rather than the other way around, Shale (2018, 485) concludes that 'the cartel party thesis propounded by Richard Katz and Peter Mair does not apply to Africa'. However, this juxtaposition of state and parties ignores the blending of the two that Katz and Mair (2018, 103) see as typical for the emergence of the cartel party: 'If the state has been increasingly entered by the parties, however, the parties have also become increasingly entered by the state'.

Observers have lamented the influence of 'godfathers' and their 'client parties' in countries like Nigeria (Kura 2014). While 'the public funding of political parties in Africa would help prevent parties from soliciting funds from dubious sources that may jeopardise the credibility and authenticity of the democratic process' (International IDEA 2019, 16), it also bears the danger of making parties in Africa even more dependent on the state. The application of the cartel party thesis to Africa thus reveals the potential for counterproductive state involvement with parties, a tension highly relevant for the many governmental and non-governmental agencies and programmes that seek to assist parties and multi-party democracy in Africa (Ashiagbor 2005).

State capture

In the original formulation of the cartel party thesis, state capture does not play a role. However, any account of the relationship between the state and political parties is incomplete which does not include rent-seeking, defined as 'the extent to which parties penetrate and control the state and use public offices for their own advantage, as opposed to the general public good' (van Biezen and Kopecký 2007, 240). In Africa, accounts of patronage (Arriola 2009), clientelism (Lindberg 2003) and political corruption (Mwangi 2008) are frequent. Yildirim and Kitschelt (2020) observe that, compared to parties in Latin America and post-communist Europe, African parties have a low tendency for what they call 'relational clientelism' and are more prone to 'single-shot clientelism', characterised by more personalistic exchanges targeting individuals, based on private rather than public resources. Van Biezen and Kopecký (2007, 245) posit that 'a particular type of state–party linkage may be prevalent in Africa, which is one where the sizeable benefits that parties amass from the state are almost solely derived from patronage and clientelistic practices and corruption'. Much to the dismay of the people who remember its crucial role in establishing inclusive democracy in South Africa and the inspiring figure of Nelson Mandela, the ANC in contemporary South Africa provides an example. In his analysis of the ANC, Beresford (2015, 228) invents the term 'gatekeeper politics' to describe 'how political leaders in positions of authority within the ruling party or in public office control access to resources and opportunities in order to forward their own political and economic ends'.

State regulation

There is a clear trend towards the constitutionalisation of parties (Bogaards 2008). For Western and Eastern Europe, van Biezen's project on the constitutionalisation of political parties has mapped the extent of party regulation and its development over time.[3] The best overview of party regulation in Africa remains the project on ethnic party bans in Africa (Bogaards et al. 2013). It found that

> [P]olitical parties are mentioned in nearly all African constitutions; only Rwanda is using the expression 'political organisation' while Eritrea and Swaziland do not have a multiparty-system. Thirty-five countries have a political party law, eight countries regulate political parties in their election law, while Zimbabwe has a 'Political Parties (Finance) Act'. Only Botswana does not have a specific party legislation at all; it treats parties like other associations.
>
> *(Moroff 2010, 619)*

Internationally, Sub-Saharan Africa stands out by its ban on ethnic parties. No less than 40 countries on the continent have a provision to ban particularistic parties in their constitution, party law and/or election law. A particularly good example can be found in the Constitution of Sierra Leone from 1991. Article 35(5) denies registration as a political party on the following grounds: first, when 'membership or leadership of the party is restricted to members of any particular tribal or ethnic group or religious faith'; second, in case 'the name, symbol, colour or motto of the party has exclusive or particular significance or connotation to members of any particular tribal or ethnic group or religious faith'; third, when 'the party is formed for the sole purpose of securing or advancing the interests and welfare of a particular tribal or ethnic group, community, geographical area or religious faith'; fourth, in case 'the party does not have a registered office in each of the Provincial Headquarter towns and the Western Area' (cited in Bogaards et al. 2010, 600). In Sierra Leone, these provisions were never implemented, but other countries did. Moroff (2010, 628) counts 138 parties in Africa that were denied registration, were suspended or were dissolved because of their particularistic nature.

Members and affiliates

The decline of party membership in industrialised nations is well documented. Being new, electoralist parties from the start, African parties are supposed to have few members, though this may be different for older parties and parties that used to be at the helm of one-party states. Surprisingly, even dominant parties in democracies may seek to expand membership. The Botswana Democratic Party (BDP) has ruled Botswana since independence and its close relationship with the state, described by Good (2010, 90) as 'a near fusion of the BDP with the bureaucracy', would seem to obviate the need for party members, as the party can comfortably rely on all the advantages of incumbency. Still, in 2009, it boasted a membership of 471,000, up from 306,000 five years earlier. This amounts to three-quarters of all registered voters and clearly surpasses the number of votes for the BDP in the 2009 elections (290,099)!

As a mass movement, the ANC always had sizeable membership, but even so, the increase from 400,000 in 2002 to 620,000 in 2007 was remarkable. For an explanation, Butler (2015) looks at internal party competition inside the ANC, where voting power in the five-yearly conferences that, among others, elect the next secretary-general and thereby de facto the next president of South Africa, depends on the number of delegates, which in turn depends on the number of members. This gives ANC leaders 'incentives to increase audited "membership" in regions and provinces in which they are popular (and in which their factional allies enjoy organisational control) and to minimise delegate numbers from areas controlled by their opponents' (Butler 2015, 25).

When it comes to the role of ethnicity in African party politics, the literature on the cartel party points in two, opposite, directions. Against the claim of Katz and Mair (2018) that cartel parties have moved decisively away from society, Poguntke (2002) demonstrates the remarkable resilience of this type of linkage in Western Europe. Yishai (2001) provides a possible explanation. As parties never have enough money and are never safe from electoral competitors, cartel parties always seek additional ways to protect themselves. One way is to (re-)connect with civil society and especially with identity groups. In an African context, this points to the continuing value of links between parties and socio-cultural groups (Widner 1997).

Intraparty organisation

Katz and Mair's (1992) collaborative research project on party organisation collected data on the three faces of parties: the party as a membership organisation, the party as a governing organisation and the party as a bureaucracy. They concentrated on what they call the 'official story': the party constitution and party records, in the belief that 'a reading of the party rules and statutes . . . offers a fundamental and indispensable guide to the character of a given party' (Katz and Mair 1992, 7). This may not necessarily be true for African parties. For example, Ikeanyibe (2014) shows how the formal requirement for internal party democracy is habitually flouted in Nigeria. Also writing about Nigeria, Basiru (2019, 111) complains about the 'pervasiveness of intra-party conflicts'. Fortunately for party researchers, Nigerian politicians seem to have a habit of accusing each other in public through lengthy letters. Here is an excerpt from a rebuttal by the chairman of the All Progressive Congress (APC) in Ondo State:

> Nobody has the kind of money that can buy my conscience or makes me do injury to an innocent man. In all the primaries conducted under my watch as National Chairman, I have strived to ensure a free, fair, transparent and credible process. The 2016 Ondo State APC Governorship Primary Elections was not an exception.
> *(quoted in Basiru 2019, 117)*

Unfortunately, systematic data on the rise of the party in public office, the centralisation and professionalisation of the party bureaucracy and the 'disempowering of activists' that Katz and Mair (2009, 759) observe in cartel parties, is lacking for Africa. For example, Bob-Milliar (2019, 3) notes that 'few studies have examined the electoral behaviour of party activists in Africa'.

Competition

Fiscal crisis and globalisation have limited the policy space for parties in the industrialised West. Cartel parties reacted by downsizing the expectations of voters so as to make them less vulnerable to criticism about delivering on electoral promises they well knew they could not keep (Blyth and Katz 2005). The restriction of policy competition took two forms. First, competition became increasingly about competence instead of content. This is even more true for developing countries where globalisation, the end of the Cold War, and neo-liberalism have constrained policy choices, changing the big political questions from one of 'what' to one of 'how' (Carothers 2006, 61–63). Second, decisions were deliberately taken out of politics by delegating authority to lower levels of government or to higher (international) bodies. In Sub-Saharan Africa, the scope of decision-making in many countries is restricted by financial dependence on donors and international organisations such as the International Monetary Fund (IMF) and the World Bank (Van de Walle 1999).

Empirical evidence comes from Bleck and van de Walle (2019, 185) who challenge the 'long-standing conventional wisdom' that African elections are about identity and money. Because of the uncertainty faced by both politicians and voters in the relatively new and changeable circumstances of electoral politics in Africa, Bleck and van de Walle (2019, 189) expect valence appeals to be 'particularly pronounced in sub-Saharan Africa', whereby 'partisan rhetoric focuses on proving competence with regard to the issue rather than on the rightness of a specific position or policy objectives' (Bleck and van de Walle, 188). This is indeed what they find, with development the favourite theme of incumbents, and democracy the rallying cry for the opposition. Though the salience of specific themes varies over time and across countries, 'in every country, valence appeals are employed more frequently than position appeals', with Nigeria showing the biggest gap (Bleck and van de Walle 2019, 212).

Collusion

Cartel parties collude to protect their collective interests. They use the state as 'an institutionalised structure of support, sustaining insiders while excluding outsiders' (Katz and Mair 1995, 16). In a democracy, it is parties themselves who decide on state funding and state regulation of parties, providing them with a unique opportunity to manipulate the rules of the game to their advantage. It comes as no surprise then that 'political financing is relatively under-regulated in Africa' (Saffu 2003, 21), which is explained with reference to the partisan interests of ruling parties and the weakness of opposition parties.

Across Sub-Saharan Africa, 'neopatrimonialism perverts or distorts the very motive of creating political parties', resulting in what Katulondi (2015, 160) calls 'self-benefiting parties'. These are parties that only serve the interests of the party founder, interests that can be summed up as either joining or replacing the existing presidential coalition. Either way, the party will share a piece of the pie, preferably in the form of a plum position in the cabinet. The founders/leaders 'literally own these parties', directing them 'by their personal calculations based on opportunities that present themselves for access to state positions' (Katulondi 2015, 161). This logic explains the often startlingly high number of registered parties in Africa, with over 300 in Cameroon and 554 in the Democratic Republic of Congo.[4] Rather than a sign of the health and vibrancy of party politics, these numbers reflect 'degenerated multipartism' (Katulondi 2015, 155), a party system in which most parties play none of the roles usually ascribed to them, but serve only as the vehicles for the advancement of the private interest of their founder and leader.

Another illustration comes from Mozambique. When Nuvanga and Sitoe (2015, 34) classify parties by their origins, they also have a category 'parties formed by political entrepreneurs in pursuit of personal fortunes'. The description of one such party, the Mozambique Independent Congress (Coinmo) is too revealing not to quote in full: 'Founder: Victor Marcos Saene. History: Coinmo became the second opposition party to hold its founding congress inside the country, but there were only five delegates plus Saene's wife and the man in whose house the couple was living'.

Is there any evidence from Sub-Saharan Africa that parties seek 'to mitigate the risks of electoral misfortune by reducing the disparity of resources available to those in and out of government at any particular moment, in both respects by turning to the coffers of the state' (Katz and Mair 2009, 758)? There is. Gottlieb's (2015, 10) study of local politics in Mali shows that 'parties have incentives not to maximise vote share because colluding and sharing rents is preferable to competing and being held accountable'. She also shows the consequences of this collusive behaviour: in communes where there is opposition outside the local elected body, public goods provision is better than in communes without a credible outsider with an incentive to expose poor performance. Research on the effect of collusion in other regions raises additional concerns. Slater and Simmons (2012) warn that what they call 'promiscuous powersharing' has produced populist backlashes and threatened democratic stability in Bolivia and Indonesia. In post-communist Eastern Europe, cartelisation has been associated with de-democratisation (Susánszky et al. 2020).

Conclusions and avenues for further research

The past decade has seen a revival of scholarly interest in African political parties, especially in the context of democratisation and electoral authoritarianism. Unfortunately, the literature continues to suffer from at least three problems: first, a focus on a handful of countries, most prominently Ghana, Kenya, Nigeria, Senegal and South Africa; second, a lack of comparative data; third, a disconnect with the latest theorising about political parties in the broader, mostly Western and more specifically West European, literature.

The heart of the chapter provided preliminary evidence that African political parties look like cartel parties in their relation to the state and society, internal organisation and interparty behaviour. This is bad news. The inventors of the cartel party thesis have always been highly critical of this development, seeing it as weakening democracy. In Africa, there are indications that the damage is even greater, because of the prevalence of collusion and state capture. Still, easy generalisations should be avoided. For one, the post-colonial state in Africa differs from the Westphalian, Weberian, states found in Western Europe. In Africa, even more so than elsewhere, 'the state is the product of complex processes of negotiation that occur at the interface between the public and the private, the informal and the formal, the illegal and the legal' (Hagmann and Péclard 2010, 552). Second, empirical variation is expected. Even in Europe, only a minority of parties correspond to the cartel party model (Webb et al. 2017) and there are reasons to expect the party landscape in Africa to be even more diverse than in Europe. One reason is the variation in regime type. Kelly's (2020) research on the proliferation of opposition parties in Senegal directly links the country's competitive authoritarian regime to incentives to form parties with an eye to joining the ruling coalition.[5] Another reason is variation in party origin, especially as rebel groups, former authoritarian ruling parties, or liberation movements. Many rebel groups have transformed into political parties (Manning and Smith 2016), and when rebel groups become ruling parties, they display characteristic (authoritarian) features (Lyons 2016). Likewise, authoritarian successor parties are shaped by past choices (Riedl 2014; Morse 2019). Former liberation movements also have a distinct way of organising themselves and of governing as ruling parties (Southall 2013). Moreover, European studies show that parties are not static. Bolleyer and Weeks (2017) document how a party can move away from the cartel party model, especially if a former dominant party succumbs to electoral defeat. And some parties are more susceptible to cartelisation than others (Koskimaa 2020). All of these suggest that there is nothing mechanical about the application of the cartel party thesis to Africa.

Notes

1 For a review of the older literature, see Bogaards (2013).
2 See www.idea.int/parties/finance/db/ and www.eisa.org.za/WEP/comparties.htm.
3 See www.partylaw.leidenuniv.nl.

4 Source: https://aceproject.org/electoral-advice/archive/questions/replies/995291925.
5 For more on competitive authoritarianism in Africa, see Bogaards and Elischer (2016). For more on electoral alliances in Africa, see Bogaards (2014).

References

Adejumobi, S. (2000) 'Elections in Africa: A fading shadow of democracy?', *International Political Science Review*, 21(1), p59–73.

Afrobarometer (2018) *News release: Africans increasingly support multiparty democracy, but trust in parties remains low* Accra: Afrobarometer. Available from: https://www.afrobarometer.org/articles/africans-increasingly-support-multiparty-democracy-trust-political-parties-remains-low/

Arriola, L. (2009) 'Patronage and political stability in Africa', *Comparative Political Studies*, 42(10), p1339–1362.

Ashiagbor, S. (2005) *Party finance reform in Africa: Lessons learned from four countries: Ghana, Kenya, Senegal and South Africa*. Washington, DC: National Democratic Institute for International Affairs.

Aucante, Y. and Dézé, A. (2008) (eds.) *Les systèmes de partis dans les dèmocraties occidentales: Le modèle du parti-cartel en question*. Paris: Sciences Po, Les Presses.

Basiru, A.S. (2019) 'Pervasive intra-party conflicts in a democratising Nigeria: Terrains, implications, drivers and options for resolution', *African Journals Online*, 19(1), p109–130.

Beresford, A. (2015) 'Power, patronage, and gatekeeper politics in South Africa', *African Affairs*, 114(455), p226–248.

Bizzarro, F., Hicken, A. and Self, D. (2017) 'The V-Dem party institutionalization index: A new global indicator', V-Dem Working Paper Series 2017.

Bleck, J. and van de Walle, N. (2019) 'Change and contiuity in African electoral politics since multypartyism', in William Thompson (ed.) *Oxford reserch encyclopedias of politics*. Oxford: Oxford University Press.

Blyth, M. and Katz, R. (2005) 'From catch-all politics to cartelisation: The political economy of the cartel party', *West European Politics*, 28(1), p33–60.

Bob-Milliar, G. (2019) 'Activism of political parties in Africa', *Oxford research encyclopedia of politics*. https://doi.org/10.1093/acrefore/9780190228637.013.1365.

Bogaards, M. (2008) 'Comparative strategies of political party regulation', in Reilly, B., Newman, E. and Nordlund, P. (eds.) *Political party regulation in conflict-prone societies*. Tokyo: United Nations UP, pp. 48–66.

Bogaards, M. (2013) 'Political parties', in Cheeseman, N. Anderson, D. and Scheibler, A. (eds.) *Routledge handbook of African politics*. London: Routledge, pp. 265–274.

Bogaards, M. (2014) 'Electoral alliances in Africa: What do we know, what can we do?', *Journal of African Elections*, 13(1), p25–42.

Bogaards, M., Basedau, M. and Hartmann, C. (2010) 'Ethnic party bans in Africa: An introduction', *Democratization*, 17(4), p599–617.

Bogaards, M., Basedau, M. and Hartmann, C. (2013) (eds.) *Ethnic party bans in Africa*. London: Routledge.

Bogaards, M. and Elischer, S. (2016) (Eds.) 'Special issue on competitive authoritarianism and democratization in Africa', *Zeitschrift für Vergleichende Politikwissenschaft*, 10(1).

Bolleyer, N. (2017) 'From cartel party to traditional membership organisation: The organisational evolution of Fianna Fáil', *Irish Political Studies*, 32(1), p96–117.

Butler, A. (2010) 'Introduction: Money and politics', in Butler, A. (ed.) *Party funding and political change in South Africa and the Global South*. Auckland Park: Jacana, pp. 1–19

Butler, A. (2015) 'The politics of Numbers: National membership growth and subnational power competition in the African National Congress', *Transformation*, 87, p13–31.

Carbone, G. (2007) 'Political parties and party systems in Africa: Themes and research perspectives', *World Political Science Review*, 3(3), p1–29.

Carothers, T. (2006) *Confronting the weakest link: Aiding political parties in new democracies*. Washington, DC: Carnegie Endowment for International Peace.

Elischer, S. (2013) *Political parties in Africa: Ethnicity and party formation*. Cambridge: Cambridge University Press.

Erdmann, G. (2004) 'Party research: Western European bias and the "African Labyrinth"', *Democratization*, 11(3), p63–87.

Erdmann, G. and Engel, U. (2007) 'Neopatrimonialism reconsidered: Critical review and elaboration of an elusive concept', *Commonwealth & Comparative Politics*, 45(1), p95–119.

Fakir, E. and Lodge, T. (2015a) (eds.) *Political parties in Africa*. Auckland Park: Jacana.

Fakir, E. and Lodge, T. (2015b) 'Introduction', in Fakir, E. and Lodge, T. (Eds.), *Political parties in Africa*. Auckland Park: Jacana, pp. xvii-xxxi.

Good, K. (2010) 'Predominance and private party funding in Botswana', in Butler, A. (ed.) *Party funding and political change in South Africa and the Global South*. Auckland Park: Jacana, pp. 81–95.

Gottlieb, J. (2015) 'The logic of party collusion in a democracy: Evidence from Mali', *World Politics*, 67(1), p1–36.

Gunther, R. and Diamond, L. (2001) 'Types and functions of parties', in Diamond, L. and Gunther, R. (eds.) *Political parties and democracy*. Baltimore: Johns Hopkins UP, pp. 3–39.

Hagmann, T. and Péclard, D. (2010) 'Negotiating statehood: Dynamics of power and domination in Africa', *Development and Change*, 41(4), p539–562.

Ikeanyibe, O. (2014) 'Internal party democracy, party candidature, and democratic consolidation in Nigeria's Fourth Republic', *Politics & Policy*, 42(5), p769–804.

International IDEA (2019) *The integrity of political finance systems in Africa: Tackling political corruption*. Stockholm: International IDEA Policy Paper No. 20.

Katsina, A.M. (2016) 'Peoples democratic party in the fourth republic of Nigeria: Nature, structure, and ideology', *SAGE Open*, 6(2), p1–11.

Katulondi, K.B. (2015) 'Neopatrimonial multipartism as an obstacle to the sustainability of democracy in Central Africa', in Fakir, E. and Lodge, T. (eds.) *Political parties in Africa*. Auckland Park: Jacana, pp. 154–171.

Katz, R. and Mair, P. (1992) 'Introduction: The cross-national study of party organizations', in Katz, R. and Mair, P. (eds.) *Party organizations: A data handbook*. London: Sage Publishers.

Katz, R. and Mair, P. (1995) 'Changing models of party organization and party democracy: The emergence of the cartel party', *Party Politics*, 1(1), p5–28.

Katz, R. and Mair, P. (2009) 'The cartel party thesis: A restatement', *Perspectives on Politics*, 7(4), p753–766.

Katz, R. and Mair, P. (2018) *Democracy and the cartelization of political parties*. Oxford: Oxford University Press.

Kelly, C. (2020) *Party proliferation and political contestation in Africa: Senegal in comparative perspective*. Cham: Palgrave Macmillan.

Koole, R. (1996) 'Cadre, catch-all or cartel? A comment on the notion of the cartel party', *Party Politics*, 2(4), p507–523.

Kopecký, P. and Mair, P. (2003) 'Political parties in government', in Salih, M. (ed.) *African political parties: Evolution, institutionalisation and governance*. London: Pluto Press, pp. 275–292.

Koskimaa, V. (2020) 'The "genetic" effect: Can parties' past organizational choices condition the development of their internal distribution of power in the cartel party era? Evidence from Finland, 1983–2017', *Politics*, 40(3), p313–331.

Krönke, M., Lockwood, S. and Mattes, R. (2022) 'Party footprints in Africa: Measuring local party presence across the continent', *Party Politics*, 28(2), p208–222.

Kura, S.B. (2014) '"Clientele democracy": Political party funding and candidate selection in Nigeria', *African Journal of Political Science and International Relations*, 8(5), p124–137.

Kwak, J.Y. (2003) 'The party-state liaison in Korea: Searching for evidence of the cartelized system', *Asian Perspective*, 27(1), p109–135.

LeBas, A. (2011) *From protest to parties: Party-building and democratization in Africa*. Oxford: Oxford University Press.

Lindberg, S. (2003) 'It's our time to "chop"': Do elections in Africa feed neo-patrimonialism rather than counteract it?', *Democratization*, 10(2), p121–140.

Lodge, T. (2014) 'Neo-patrimonial politics in the ANC', *African Affairs* 113(450), p1–23.

Lyons, T. (2016) 'From victorious rebels to strong authoritarian parties: Prospects for post-war democratization', *Democratization*, 23(6), p1026–1041.

Manning, C. and Smith, I. (2016) 'Political party formation by former armed opposition groups after civil war', *Democratization*, 23(6), p972–989.

Mietzner, M. (2013) *Money, power and ideology: Political parties in post-authoritarian Indonesia*. Singapore: National University of Singapore Press.

Moroff, A. (2010) 'Party bans in Africa: An empirical overview', *Democratization*, 17(4), p618–641.

Morse, Y. (2019) *How autocrats compete: Parties, patrons, and unfair elections in Africa*. Cambridge: Cambridge University Press.

Mwangi, O.G. (2008) 'Political corruption, party financing and democracy in Kenya', *Journal of Modern African Studies*, 46(2), p267–285.

Nuvunga, A. and Sitoe, E. (2015) 'Party institutionalization in Mozambique: "The Party of the state" vs the opposition', in Fakir, E. and Lodge, T. (eds.) *Political parties in Africa*. Auckland Park: Jacana, pp. 20–62.

Osei, A. (2012) *Party-voter linkage in Africa: Ghana and Senegal in comparative perspective*. Wiesbaden: Springer.

Osei, A. (2016) 'Formal party organisation and informal relations in African parties: Evidence from Ghana', *Journal of Modern African Studies*, 54(1), p37–66.

Pinto-Duschinsky, M. (2002) 'Financing politics: A global view', *Journal of Democracy*, 13(4), p69–85.

Poguntke, T. (2002) 'Zur empirischen evidenz der kartellparteien-these', *Zeitschrift für Parlamentsfragen*, 33(4), p790–806.

Pottie, D. (2003) 'Party finance and the politics of money in Southern Africa', *Journal of Contemporary African Studies*, 21(1), p7–26.

Riedl, R. (2014) *Authoritarian origins of democratic party systems in Africa*. Cambridge: Cambridge University Press.

Riedl, R. (2018) 'Institutional legacies: Understanding multiparty politics in historical perspective', in Cheeseman, N. (ed.) *Institutions and democracy in Africa: How the rules of the game shape political development*. Cambridge: Cambridge University Press, pp. 41–60.

Saffu, Y. (2003) 'The funding of political parties and election campaigns in Africa', in Austin, R. and Tjernström, M. (eds.) *Funding of political parties and election campaigns*. Stockholm: International IDEA, pp. 21–30.

Sarakinsky, I. (2007) 'Political party finance in South Africa: Disclosure versus secrecy', *Democratization*, 14(1), p111–128.

Shale, V. (2018) 'Political party funding in Lesotho and Mozambique', in Mendilow, J. and Phélippeau, E. (2018) (eds.) *Handbook of political party funding*. Cheltenham: Edward Elgar, pp. 470–486.

Shefter, M. (1994) *Political parties and the state: The American historical experience*. Princeton: Princeton University Press.

Slater, D. (2018) 'Party cartelization, Indonesian-style: Presidential power-sharing and the contingency of democratic opposition', *Journal of East Asian Studies*, 18(1), p23–46.

Slater, D. and Simmons, E. (2012) 'Coping by colluding: Political uncertainty and promiscuous power-sharing in Indonesia and Bolivia', *Comparative Political Studies*, 46(11), p1366–1393.

Southall, R. (2013) *Liberation movements in power: Party and state in Southern Africa*. Woodbridge: James Currey.

Southall, R. and Wood, G. (1998) 'Political party funding in Southern Africa', in Burnell, P. and Ware, A. (eds.) *Funding democratization*. New York: Manchester University Press, pp. 202–228.

Susánszky, P., Unger, A. and Kopper, Á (2020) 'Hungary's over-powerful government party and the desperate opposition', *European Review*, 28(5), p761–777.

Uwem Umoh, S. (2018) 'Party funding in South Africa', in Mendilow, J. and Phélippeau, E. (2018) (eds.) *Handbook of political party funding*. Cheltenham: Edward Elgar, pp. 451–469.

van Biezen, I. and Kopecký, P. (2007) 'The state and the parties: Public funding, public regulation and rent-seeking in contemporary democracies', *Party Politics*, 13(2), p235–254.

van de Walle, N. (1999) 'Globalization and African democracy', in Joseph, R. (ed.) *State, conflict, and democracy in Africa*. Boulder: Lynne Rienner, pp. 95–118.

Wahman, M. (2017) 'Nationalized incumbents and regional challengers: Opposition- and incumbent-party nationalization in Africa', *Party Politics*, 23(3), p309–322.

Webb, P., Poguntke, T. and Scarrow, S. (2017) 'Conclusion', in Scarrow, S., Webb, P. and Poguntke, T. (eds.) *Organizing political parties: Representation, participation, and power*. Oxford: Oxford University Press, pp. 307–312.

Welz, M. (2021) *Africa since decolonization: The history and politics of a diverse continent*. Cambridge: Cambridge University Press.

Widner, J. (1997) 'Political parties and civil societies in Sub-Saharan Africa', in Ottaway, M. (ed.) *Democracy in Africa: The hard road ahead*. Boulder: Lynne Rienner, pp. 65–81.

Wolinetz, S. (2002) 'Beyond the catch-all party: Approaches to the study of parties and party organization in contemporary democracies', in Gunther, R., Montero, J.R. and Linz, J. (eds.) *Political parties: Old concepts and new challenges*. Oxford: Oxford University Press, pp. 136–165.

Yildirim, K. and Kitschelt, H. (2020) 'Analytical perspectives on varieties of clientelism', *Democratization*, 27(1), p20–43.

Yishai, Y. (2001) 'Bringing society back in: Post-cartel parties in Israel', *Party Politics*, 7(6), p667–687.

35
POLITICAL PARTIES IN NORTH AFRICA

Lise Storm[1]

Political parties have existed across the North Africa region since well before the post-independence period, even if the majority of the parties that operated in Algeria, Egypt, Libya, Mauritania, Morocco and Tunisia during the colonial era were barred from contesting elections or excluded from formal politics and thus had to operate clandestinely. That said, there was – and still is – enormous variation within North Africa, with political parties having existed for over 100 years in the case of Egypt, while they are a much more recent phenomenon in Libya, where they were a brief experiment at the time of the 2012 elections. In every North African state, save for Libya, which has consequently been excluded from the analysis here, parties have played a central role within the political system, although they were often far from powerful, either because the party system was fragmented and/or because they were instruments of a more powerful actor. This reality has led some to call into question the relevance of the region's parties, but it is not the case that these parties are irrelevant, but rather that they are differently relevant – their role and functions simply differ from those of their Western counterparts and the Western-centric ideal types identified by academia (Willis 2002a; 2002b; Storm and Cavatorta 2018).

The role and functions of the North African parties are an aspect that has shaped the parties' structure and relationship with society, that is, rootedness. Most notably, the weak ideological basis of most of the region's parties, the virtual absence of programmatic parties, the predominance of machine parties and – in particular – patronage parties, have all contributed to political apathy among the electorate and an increasing preference for horizontal engagement and issue-based politics among the youth, which in turn is proving a threat to party politics and, by extension, the prospects for democracy in North Africa.

This chapter analyses dynamics of party politics in North Africa focusing in particular on the main factors that divide the parties into different groups (or families), as well as the role of parties when assessing the prospects for democracy versus authoritarian resilience. The analysis is organised chronologically, as the lines dividing the parties have tended to reflect changes to the political environment over the years.

Until the eruption of the Arab Uprisings in 2010, most North African states had in place political systems that could best be characterised as cases of competitive authoritarianism, that is, systems 'in which the coexistence of meaningful democratic institutions and serious incumbent abuse yields electoral competition that is real but unfair' (Levitsky and Way 2020, 51). Given the authoritarian nature of the regimes, regardless of their specific variations, political power was rooted outside the electoral arena as habitually is the case in such settings (Reilly 2002; Lyons 2004; Storm 2020b). And thus, while parties existed in the region without interruption for the entire post-independence period, a tradition of resolving political conflict and disagreements at the polls did not develop, largely because politics was seen as a zero-sum game anchored in coercive power and the control of resources.

Although power was located outside the electoral arena, elections continued to take place for much of the post-independence era, but the role they played differed from that in the West. Elections were a means for the regime to legitimise itself, even if the contest was neither free nor fair and mainly for show. Furthermore, they were an important instrument deployed by the regime in order to divide the co-opted opposition and distribute spoils to the various parties and/or candidates, which in turn would distribute these among their supporters. Elections and parties therefore served two primary functions: to provide clientelistic and directive linkage (Hinnebusch 2006, 2017; Heydemann 2007; Cavatorta and Storm 2018). In contrast to the West, where the emphasis has long been on participatory and electoral linkage, the North African parties largely faced the regime as opposed to the electorate following independence. The regime set the parameters and held the parties accountable, and party families, if one can refer to them as such, were consequently primarily centred on issues relating to the regime, rather than societal cleavages. Parties that became adept at navigating regime politics survived, while parties that sought to appeal to the general population and build up a large support base were seen as a potential threat to the *status quo* and thus stifled as evidenced most recently in the treatment of the region's Islamist parties (Hinnebusch 2017; Rivetti and Kraetzschmar 2018; Storm 2020b).

The subsequent sections chart the establishment and development of the North African party systems in the period from independence until late 2020, that is, almost exactly ten years after the eruption of the Arab Uprisings, comparing and contrasting the multi-party Moroccan experience with that of Algeria, Egypt, Mauritania and Tunisia, which long operated with single-party systems. The analysis covers the relationship between parties within the respective party systems as well as the parties' relationship with other powerful political actors, most notably presidents, militaries and the police, illustrating how parties, while central to the region's political systems, have largely been powerless in the post-independence era due to their subjugation. The analysis also highlights the importance of historical-political context in accounting for variation in outcomes on both the party and regime fronts and thus also in assessing the prospects for democracy.

The early post-independence years and the one-party states

The party systems of contemporary North Africa trace their development back to the independence period, that is, the mid-1950s and early 1960s.[2] Several of the parties, which were to play a key role in politics in the newly independent states and, in many instances, which continue to take up a central position within North African party systems today, established themselves politically *qua* their role in the struggle for independence, but the process and outcomes varied across the region.

Party mergers and subsequent subjugation in the one-party states of Algeria, Egypt, Morocco and Mauritania

In Algeria, Egypt, Mauritania and Tunisia, the period leading up to independence saw the presence of several parties representing different segments of the population, and while some parties were arguably much more prominent than others, choice was offered, often between parties labelling themselves as leftist, Islamist, liberal or centrist. Over the years, however, as these four states gained independence and the new institutional set-up began to take shape and consolidate, the role of the parties changed (Hinnebusch 2017; Koehler 2020; Storm 2020a). Instead of being vehicles for citizen mobilisation and political change anchored in the pro-independence versus pro-colonial cleavage, the parties became instruments of more powerful actors and the party systems shrunk as potential rivals were neutralised. In most states, this change had already begun in the final few years prior to independence as parties merged with a view to creating strong, clear leadership in order to better fight the occupiers (Camau and Geisser 2003; Ojeda 2005; Storm 2014; Hinnebusch 2017). Thus, the streamlining of the party systems at the time did not reflect an absence of cleavages within society, but rather a shared an over-arching goal and nationalist orientation that not only cut across these cleavages but also took precedence over other issues.

Once the one-party systems were introduced, they proved to have longevity. In Algeria, the *Front de Libération Nationale* (FLN) was without formal competition until 1989; in Egypt, the Arab Socialist Union (ASU) was the only recognised party from 1962 until 1977; in Mauritania, the *Parti du People Mauritanien* (PPM) remained the sole legal party during the years 1961–1978; and in Tunisia, the *Parti Socialiste Destourien* (PSD) was uncontested in national elections from 1964 until 1981, when the ban on alternative parties was lifted. Notwithstanding the one-party nature of these four North African states, the regime parties did not find themselves at the centre of power, but were rather subjugated by other institutions as the new leaders solidified their grip on power following independence (Willis 2002a, 2002b; Storm 2013; Cavatorta and Storm 2018).

The parties, which had occupied a powerful position at first, thus eventually transformed into regime tools, used to control, direct and co-opt. Facing other institutions with aspirations of power, such as the military and the police as well as the local tribes, which remained highly influential, the parties served as an instrument to weaken and counter-balance their influence *vis-à-vis* the head of state, while at the same time being kept in check by these as the North African regimes pitted potential rivals against each other in order to preserve the *status quo* at the very top. Facing the populace, the ASU, the FLN, the PPM and the PSD were a means to provide directive linkage between the regime and the citizenry, ensuring cooperation via the diffusion of norms and coercion in tandem with the security apparatus, which had direct ties to the regime party, either because the security apparatus had developed from the independence movement, as in Algeria, Mauritania and Tunisia, or as in the case of Egypt, the military had played a central role in the setting up of the regime party (Albrecht 2005; Ojeda 2005; Blaydes 2010; Storm 2014).

While the regime parties were officially the only legal parties during this period, other parties continued their activities, albeit clandestinely, and sometimes from abroad. These included parties on the left, such as the *Front des Forces Socialistes* (FFS) in Algeria, the Communist Party of Egypt, Mauritania's *Mouvement National Démocratique* (MND) and *Parti des Kadihines de Mauritanie* (PKM), the *Parti Communiste des Ouvriers de Tunisie* (PCOT) and the *Congrès pour la République* (CPR) in Tunisia, many of which were closely affiliated to the trade unions, as well as liberal parties, such as Egypt's *Wafd* party and Islamist entities, such as the *Ikhwan* (Muslim Brotherhood; MB) in Egypt and Tunisia's *Ennahda* as well as their earlier iterations. Although these parties were located on different parts of the political spectrum and therefore represented various segments of the electorate, their ideological differences were not the main driving force behind their mobilisation at the time. Rather, the clandestine parties garnered support primarily *qua* their opposition status and then, secondarily, on the basis of their ideological basis and/or societal roots (Willis 2002a; 2002b; Ojeda 2005; Storm 2014; Hinnebusch 2017).

The Moroccan experience: the establishment of the executive monarchy

In Morocco, like in Algeria and Tunisia, and to some extent also in Egypt and Mauritania, the independence movement fed into the party system, particularly in the form of the *Parti Istiqlal* (PI), the dominant force, and also via other, smaller vehicles (SEC 1948; Storm 2008). In contrast to the experience of what was to become the single-party states elsewhere in North Africa, however, the PI in Morocco did not manage to transform into a single party upon independence. As the weaker force in a power-struggle with the king, the PI eventually had to accept that it would be operating within the confines of a small multi-party system, facing competition most notably from the *Mouvement Populaire* (MP), a Berber-dominated so-called *Makhzen* party, that is, a party closely affiliated with the monarchy (Willis 2002a; 2002b; Storm 2014).

As in the cases of Algeria, Egypt, Mauritania and Tunisia, the Moroccan party system was defined by a regime–opposition binary up until the late 1970s, when the PI won the 1977 legislative elections and was invited to take part in government despite the party's opposition credentials. Unlike the other four states, where the opposition parties operated clandestinely, in Morocco, many of these were legal and thus formally part of the system. This reality was not caused by a more benevolent head of state, but rather a different constellation of power: whereas in Algeria, Egypt, Mauritania and Tunisia the heads of state had strong ties to the security apparatuses, the Moroccan monarch found his powers challenged by the military and was accordingly unable to silence the opposition via the use of force (Gaub 2017). Hence, the monarch adopted a divide and conquer strategy and a reliance on dysfunctional, disjointed, oversized governing coalitions, akin to the post-Arab Uprisings 'governments of national unity' found across the MENA, that contrasted from the more overtly repressive policies of the other four states. Yet, while the strategies differed, the objective was the same: for the head of state to consolidate power with a view to remain at the helm for the *longue durée*.

Parties as a means to an end: the resurgence of electoral competition and co-optation

The Moroccan strategy of a controlled multi-party system became the norm across North Africa with the façade political openings of the late 1970s and early 1980s, but the character of these limited multi-party systems varied within the region, with most, albeit not all, being predominant.

Change of strategy: from repression to co-optation

In Morocco, party growth was encouraged by the monarchy from the late 1970s onwards with the objective of creating a fragmented system in which no single party could rest assured of the monarchy's favour, regardless of whether it found itself within the so-called opposition or *makhzen* camp. The expansion of the party system was consequently a continuation of the strategy in place since independence, although there was somewhat of a shift towards a broader co-optation strategy as a wider array of parties were licensed (Willis 2002a; 2002b; Storm 2008, 2014).

In Mauritania, the controlled opening up of the party system occurred in the wake of changes in the presidency, which saw five military coups before Maaouya Ould Sid'Ahmed Taya took over the presidency in 1984 and consolidated his power. Thus, during the years 1978–1984, Mauritania was arguably plagued by significant levels of political instability, which was firmly anchored in disagreements within the military. The opening up of the political system to allow for opposition parties following the dissolution of the PPM in 1979 was consequently of limited importance given that political power lay outside of the electoral arena, a reality that the military establishment did little to hide as no elections at the national level were held during the years 1976–1992. In 1992, following the war in Iraq, parties and elections were brought back by newly elected President Taya in an effort to appease the international community, neutralise the increasingly powerful tribes and legitimise his regime by dissociating himself from the Ba'athists via the creation of a new party, the *Parti Républicain Démocratique et Social* (PRDS) (Marty 2001; Ojeda 2005). The PRDS cruised to a landslide victory in 1992, and the party continued to dominate the party system during Taya's reign, winning absolute majorities in the nominally competitive elections of 1996 and 2001.

In 2005, Taya was ousted in a military coup, but power was transferred to civilian hands following legislative and presidential elections in 2006 and 2007, only for the military to intervene yet again in 2008, installing General Mohamed Ould Abdel Aziz as president. With Aziz in power – a presidency that was to last until another military coup in 2019 – came a return not only to military rule but also to predominant party politics in Mauritania, this time with the *Union pour la République* (UPR) playing the dominant role in a party system in which the opposition was afforded very limited opportunities beyond the ability to field candidates in heavily engineered elections, and a political system in which they remained largely insignificant from a perspective of power (Ojeda 2018).

In Algeria, Egypt and Tunisia, the expansion of the party system came in the aftermath of heightened civilian unrest – so-called 'bread riots' – which saw the cost of repression increase (Sadiki 2000). In an effort to remain in control and thus in power, presidents Chadli Benjedid in Algeria, Anwar Sadat in Egypt and Tunisia's Habib Bourguiba consequently revised their survival strategies, moving from heavy reliance on repression in favour of a policy emphasising co-optation and thus a stake in the survival of the system (Albrecht 2005; Hinnebusch 2006, 2017; Heydemann 2007; Storm 2020a). It was arguably envisaged that the opening up of the party system would come at a limited cost to the regime as the opposition parties were to be offered only a symbolic share of power in the form of the ability to field candidates for election at the national level as well as a small share of marginal cabinet portfolios in the event that a party should perform well at the polls and/or in reward for good behaviour.

In Egypt, the opening was the most tightly controlled with the only choice offered up in the 1976 elections being three different factions of the ASU, before the formation of the new regime party, the National Democratic Party (NDP) in 1978 and the holding of nominally more competitive elections, including the participation of opposition forces, from 1979 onwards. Right from the outset, the NDP was given such favourable conditions that there was never any question whether it would win the contest, and Egypt thus operated with a predominant party system in which the NDP took centre stage until the outbreak of the Arab Uprisings and the party's subsequent dissolution in 2011 (Albrecht 2005; Blaydes 2010).

Similarly in Tunisia, Bourguiba ran a tight ship, providing for legislative elections that were only nominally competitive from 1981 onwards. Initially, the only opposition parties were splinters from the PSD, none of which won any seats in what was a very hostile environment, a reality that resulted in all opposition forces boycotting the 1986 elections. Opposition parties were accordingly not afforded much of an opportunity to contest elections at the national level until the ascendance to the presidency of Zine el-Abidine Ben Ali in 1987, and the Tunisian experience thus mirrors that of Mauritania to some extent in that the introduction of competitive authoritarianism coincided with changes at the level of the head of state and, furthermore, the system remained predominant until the Arab Uprisings despite the broadening of the party landscape.[3]

Finally, in Algeria, President Benjedid, who had taken over from Boumediène in 1979, embarked on a much less cautious approach to political opening in response to the riots of 1985 and 1988. Convinced that the FLN would emerge victorious, legislative elections were allowed to go ahead in 1991 in an environment that was remarkably free and fair for the region at the time. Only when it was too late, did the regime realise that the FLN was going to be relegated to second place behind the *Front Islamique du Salut* (FIS), and the military eventually intervened to abort the elections, removing Chadli from power and installing in his place General Mohamed Boudiaf, one of the founding fathers of the FLN. Following the military coup, elections were suspended and did not take place again until 1997, when the *Rassemblement National Démocratique* (RND), the recently founded party rooted in the military and headed by newly elected President Liamine Zéroual, won a landslide victory in an election where the regime took no chances. The FLN returned to power shortly after, in 1999, when Zéroual, who had lost confidence within the military, unceremoniously stepped down from the presidency and was replaced by Abdelaziz Bouteflika. Under Bouteflika's reign, the FLN assumed predominant status, a position it maintains to this day (Storm 2014; Volpi 2020).

The North African parties and the Arab Uprisings

Until the Arab Uprisings, save for the case of Libya, parties in North Africa were clearly integral to the political systems in place, yet, despite parties playing a pivotal role in the perpetuation of authoritarianism, most parties were largely powerless as a consequence of the reality that they were subjugated by one or more potent actors. Hence, even after the demise of the single-party states and the controlled openings of the party systems in the late 1970s and early 1980s, parties were still not vying for the affection of the electorate, but rather that of other non-elected institutions. Accordingly, when the Arab Uprisings began to unfold in 2010, the North African parties were not only weak but also not very focused on participatory and electoral linkage. This reality was not only a consequence of the parameters set by the regime but also the result of an active choice made by the parties that accepted the bargain offered up by the regime and thus became co-opted into the formal political system during the post-independence period. Over the years, the predominant multi-party systems became an integral part of the regime fabric across North Africa, and as the regimes grew more comfortable, more parties and party families were gradually and willingly incorporated, including eventually parties on the left as well as Islamist parties, although the invitation only extended to parties that could be trusted to play by the rules of the game (Jebari 2020; Kilavuz 2020; Storm 2020c).

Consequently, by the time the Arab Uprisings erupted, nearly all segments of the North African population were able to find a party with which they shared an affinity: there were leftist parties, conservative parties, liberal parties, Islamist parties and green parties. By virtue of having become co-opted into the system, and by the sheer breadth of choice offered up, these parties lent legitimacy to the system. Nonetheless, the various parties did not represent the electorate, but rather represented the interests of the regime, which largely coincided with their own, and there were thus limited incentives for the parties to change their *modus operandi*, especially as electoral appeal was more likely to translate into prohibition than power.

The Arab Uprisings and the formation of new parties

The lack of rootedness in the electorate and, hence, the virtual absence of participatory and electoral linkage among the North African parties at the time of the Arab Uprisings helps explain why these resulted in so few new parties of substance entering the scene in their wake. Two factors were particularly important.

First, the main driving force behind the Arab Uprisings were youths, many of whom had little trust in the parties that already existed, who saw politicians as corrupt and self-interested, and who consequently did not feel represented and preferred more modern forms of horizontal engagement and issue-based politics (Abbott, Teti and Sapsford 2018). These youths neither had an ambition of becoming politicians themselves nor of assisting in the establishment of new parties. It was not that they were not politically engaged, but rather that they were differently engaged. They sought to set something in motion, to initiate change, but their aspiration was not to become part of the system, whether the old one or a new beginning, and thus the protest movements did not transform into political parties (Resta 2020; Thyen 2020). The protest movement in many instances also incorporated already existing parties, which sought to capitalise on popular sentiment. These parties had no interest in new parties emerging as this would result in further competition, which would not be accompanied by an increase in spoils.

Second, it was not the case that no new parties emerged, but rather that very few new parties of substance were formed, that is, parties, which not only survived more than one election but also performed well in these. The majority of those who did, such as the now defunct *Freedom and Justice Party* (FJP) in Egypt, the *Parti Authenticité et Modernité* (PAM) in Morocco as well as the *Congrès pour la République* (CPR), *Nidaa Tounes* and the *Ennahda* in Tunisia, were new in the sense that the parties were newly licensed, but not in terms of their composition.[4] These parties were internally created as opposed to rooted in the electorate and the popular demands voiced in the uprisings. They were established by career politicians departing other parties in their quest for power, or they were created long ago and had operated clandestinely (Storm 2017; Cimini 2020).

Consequently, the North African party landscape did not alter fundamentally with the advent of the Arab Uprisings, nor did the dynamics of party politics, whether within the party system or the political system more broadly. In Algeria, ailing President Bouteflika managed to cling on to power until 2019, when he was finally forced to resign after pressure from the military as popular protests against his reign intensified. Bouteflika's departure saw a change of president, but the regime remained intact and consequently so did the workings of the political system with the important caveat that the military emerged strengthened *vis-à-vis* the FLN and the new head of state (Cimini 2020; Kilavuz and Greval 2020).[5] Similarly, in Mauritania, the incumbent president remained in power until 2019, although, in contrast to the Algerian scenario, the transfer of power was undramatic, as it coincided with the end of President Aziz's term in office. The new president, the UPR's Mohamed Ould Ghazouani, like most presidents before him, had a military background, a factor which most observers credited for his overwhelming victory in the elections, with some going as far as labelling his ascendance 'another military coup' (Ghanmi 2019).

In Egypt, the situation was akin to that in Algeria and Mauritania, as here the regime also survived despite Mubrarak's departure, again with the military strengthened. However, unlike in Algeria and Mauritania, the Egyptian military's role in politics became more direct in the aftermath of the uprisings following General Abdel Fattah el-Sisi's ascent to the presidency in 2012. Hence, the reality that the party system grew exponentially in the first few years after the end of Mubarak's reign had limited impact upon how politics were conducted in Egypt as power remained located outside of the electoral arena. Furthermore, with the prohibition of the NDP, parties were ironically even less powerful than they had previously been, although they remained central to the system through their regime-legitimising role and as vehicles of directive and clientelistic linkage (Völkel 2020).[6] This was also the case for the parties in Morocco, where the political system retained the *status quo*. The country remains an executive monarchy, in which the king not only rules but also governs, and thus power continues to be located outside the electoral arena (Storm 2020c).

Only in Tunisia, which made the transition from competitive authoritarianism to democracy following the Arab Uprisings, did the situation alter markedly with parties offered more opportunity to prosper in what was naturally a much more open political environment compared to that experienced in the other North African states. In post-uprisings Tunisia, power became located within the electoral arena, yet the parties – whether new or old – did not step up, but rather continued to prioritise clientelistic linkage (Cimini 2020). This reality was to a large extent fuelled by a heavily divided electorate, which favoured either parties with ties to the old regime, which were seen as able to deliver, or the Islamist *Ennahda*, which many saw as a new hope as it represented a clear break with the past (Guazzone 2013).

Thus, with the Arab Uprisings, Tunisian politics became dominated by a so-called 'Islamist-secular divide', in which Islamists and anti-Islamist forces labelling themselves as secular were pitted against each other in a struggle for power, which saw the parties lose sight of their representative functions (Wolf 2018; Szmolka 2020). In the early years of the post-Ben Ali era, the Tunisian political system was accordingly plagued by uncertainty and instability as one government after another collapsed due to political differences in what had become a zero-sum game in many respects. As a consequence, public trust in the political institutions, including the parties, plummeted (Yerkes and Yahmed 2019; Cimini 2020). In an effort to appease the general population, and also to reflect the limited power of the parties within the system, Tunisian presidents – several of them without party affiliation – responded by increasingly relying on experts as independent candidates and technocrats came to dominate cabinets in the wake of the uprisings (Ben Salem 2020).

The growing popularity of presidents and cabinet ministers without party affiliation in the post-Arab Uprisings era is not a uniquely Tunisian phenomenon but is also present in Algeria, Egypt, Libya and Mauritania. In Algeria, the current president is a so-called independent, although his candidature was supported by the FLN. In Egypt, President el-Sisi is without party affiliation, the cabinet of Mostafa Madbouly formed in 2018 was composed exclusively by independents and military figures, while 124 out of 596 seats in the legislature belonged to independent candidates after the 2020 elections. In Libya, 64 out of 200 seats were reserved for independent candidates in the 2012 elections, and when the 2014 elections took place, only independent candidates were allowed to contest. In Mauritania, President Ghazouani, a military man formally affiliated with the UPR, appointed cabinets in which some 50 per cent of the portfolios went to technocrats.

This growing reliance on experts, technocrats and independents as opposed to candidates with party affiliation is perhaps the most worrying political trend in the region at present. Precisely because it is less of a blatant violation of democratic principles than non-civilian rule, it blurs the line between what is acceptable and not, therefore delaying the response, domestically and from the international community, to such tactics by remnants of the old regime and non-elected forces. As the power of the party-affiliated politicians and the parties continues to erode, the biggest challenge facing supporters of democracy in North Africa today is not only how to ensure the region's parties succeed in becoming *more* relevant, but rather how they manage to *remain* relevant.

Conclusion and avenues for further research

Political parties in North Africa have played a central role in political life in the post-independence era. However, unlike in the West, where parties tend to focus on participatory and electoral linkages, North African parties emphasise directive and clientelistic linkages as a consequence of the fact that power is largely rooted outside the electoral arena, chiefly among the head of state and unelected actors such as the military, the police and, at times, tribes. The region's parties are thus, on the one hand, clients of these more powerful actors and, on the other hand, have clients of their own. Consequently, they form an integral part of the system, yet they have limited powers – powers that appear to be diminishing further in the wake of the Arab Uprisings and the return to prominence of technocrats within the North African political systems.

What is clear so far is that even following a shift in the balance of power within some of the region's regimes and the transition to democracy in Tunisia, the main defining characteristic of the parties does not relate to cleavage structures or ideological foundations, but rather to whether a party belongs among the so-called opposition or whether it is located within the regime camp. In tandem with the increasing blurring of lines between the regime and the legal, rather nominal opposition, voter apathy has grown, particularly among the youth, and there is very little appetite for party politics among the electorate at present. This reality has been seized upon by the regimes, which have responded by gradually expanding the role of technocrats and parliamentarians without party affiliation, thereby further marginalising the parties. While this is a relatively recent phenomenon, commencing in earnest in the aftermath of the Arab Uprisings, these developments do, to some extent, mirror events within the political landscape in the early post-independence period when several North African states established single-party systems, and this is thus one area of research that deserves scholarly attention in the near future.

Notes

1. Please note that this chapter was written prior to the coup by Tunisian President Kais Saied on 25 July 2021.
2. Note that Egypt gained independence already in 1922.
3. The PSD became the *Rassemblement Constitutionnel et Démocratique* (RDC) in 1988. Note that Islamist representation was not allowed unlike in Algeria, Mauritania and Morocco. Islamists were also not offered the opportunity to run as independents in contrast to the situation in Egypt.
4. Exceptions to this pattern include *Al-Aridha* in Tunisia and the Salafi *al-Nour* in Egypt.
5. President Abdelmajid Tebboune was viewed by many as a mere puppet of the military and a close ally of Bouteflika.
6. Note that even though the Muslim Brotherhood's *Freedom and Justice Party* (FJP) was banned in 2014, the regime did not object to the existence of Islamist parties per se, but rather Islamist parties that constituted a threat to the regime.

References

Abbott, P.A., Teti. and Sapsford, R. (2018) 'The tide that failed to rise: Young people's politics and social values in and after the Arab Uprisings', *Mediterranean Politics*, 25(1), p1–25.
Albrecht, H. (2005) 'How can opposition support authoritarianism? Lessons from Egypt', *Democratization*, 12(3), p378–397.
Ben Salem, M. (2020) 'The delegitimation of political parties in democratic Tunisia', in Cavatorta, F., Storm, L. and Resta, V. (eds.) *Routledge handbook on political parties in the Middle East and North Africa*. London: Routledge, pp. 165–178.
Blaydes, L. (2010) *Elections and distributive politics in Mubarak's Egypt*. Cambridge: Cambridge University Press.
Camau, M. and Geisser, V. (2003) *Le syndrome autoritaire*. Paris: Presses de Sciences Po.
Cavatorta, F. and Storm, L. (eds.) (2018) *Political parties in the Arab World*. Edinburgh: Edinburgh University Press.
Cimini, G. (2020) 'Personalism in MENA politics', in Cavatorta, F., Storm, L. and Resta, V. (eds.) *Routledge handbook on political parties in the Middle East and North Africa*. London: Routledge, pp. 83–95.
Gaub, F. (2017) *Guardians of the Arab State*. Oxford: Oxford University Press.
Ghanmi, L. (2019) '"Historic" Mauritanian elections contested by opposition', *The Arab Weekly*. Available from: https://thearabweekly.com/historic-mauritanian-elections-contested-opposition

Guazzone, L. (2013) 'Ennahda Islamist and the test of government in Tunisia', *Italian Journal of International Affairs,* 48(4), p30–50.

Heydemann, S. (2007) 'Social pacts and the persistence of authoritarianism in the Middle East', in Schlumberger, O. (ed.) *Debating Arab Authoritarianism.* Pualo Alto: Stanford University Press, pp. 21–38.

Hinnebusch, R. (2006) 'Authoritarian persistence, democratization theory and the Middle East: An overview and critique', *Democratization,* 13(3), p373–95.

Hinnebusch, R. (2017) 'Political parties in MENA: Their functions and development', *British Journal of Middle Eastern Studies,* 44(2), p59–75.

Jebari, I. (2020) 'The rise and fall of the Arab left', in Cavatorta, F., Storm, L. and Resta, V. (eds.) *Routledge handbook on political parties in the Middle East and North Africa.* London: Routledge, pp. 17–32.

Kilavuz, M. (2020) 'The establishment and success of Islamist parties', in Cavatorta, F., Storm, L. and Resta, V. (eds.) *Routledge handbook on political parties in the Middle East and North Africa.* London: Routledge, pp. 33–43.

Kilavuz, M. and Grewal, S. (2020) 'Algerians have been protesting for a year. Here's what you need to know', *The Washington Post.* Available from: https://www.washingtonpost.com/politics/2020/02/22/algerians-have-been-protesting-year-heres-what-you-need-know/

Koehler, K. (2020) 'Inheriting the past: Trajectories of single parties in Arab republics', in Cavatorta, F., Storm, L. and Resta, V. (eds.) *Routledge handbook on political parties in the Middle East and North Africa.* London: Routledge, pp. 57–68.

Levitsky, S. and Way, L. (2020) 'The new competitive authoritarianism', *Journal of Democracy,* 31(1), p51–65.

Lyons, T. (2004) 'Post-conflict elections and the process of demilitarizing politics: The role of electoral administration', *Democratization,* 11, p36–62.

Marty, M. (2001) 'Mauritania: Political parties, neo-patrimonialism and democracy', *ECPR Joint Sessions.* Available from: https://ecpr.eu/Filestore/PaperProposal/00557fd6-9166-4a93-a02d-4a4cf050ee40.pdf (Accessed 23 December 2020)

Ojeda, G. (2005) 'The role of elections in Mauritania: Political and social context', *ECPR Joint Sessions.* Available from: https://ecpr.eu/Filestore/PaperProposal/461433bf-dc90-4544-82d2-50dc2ea6a5c2.pdf (Accessed 23 December 2020)

Ojeda, G. (2018) 'Transformations in the political party system in Mauritania: the case of the Union for the Republic', in Cavatorta, F. and Storm, L. (eds.) *Political parties in the Arab World.* Edinburgh: Edinburgh University Press, pp. 252–275.

Reilly, B. (2002) 'Elections in post-conflict scenarios: Constraints and dangers', *International Peacekeeping,* 9, p118–139.

Resta, V. (2020) 'The terminal. Political parties and identity issues in the Arab world', in Cavatorta, F., Storm, L. and Resta, V. (eds.) *Routledge handbook on political parties in the Middle East and North Africa.* London: Routledge, pp. 331–143.

Rivetti, P. and Kraetzschmar, H. (eds.) (2018) *Islamists and the politics of the Arab uprisings.* Edinburgh: Edinburgh University Press.

Sadiki, L. (2000) 'Popular uprisings and Arab democratization', *International Journal of Middle East Studies,* 32(1), p71–95.

SEC (1948) 'France and Morocco', *The World Today,* 4(3), p125–136.

Storm, L. (2008) *Democratization in Morocco.* London: Routledge.

Storm, L. (2013) 'The fragile Tunisian democracy: What prospects for the future?', in Gana, N. (ed.) *The making of the Tunisian revolution.* Edinburgh: Edinburgh University Press, pp. 270–290.

Storm, L. (2014) *Party politics and the prospects for democracy in North Africa.* Boulder: Lynne Rienner.

Storm, L. (2017) 'Parties and Party System Change', in Szmolka, I. (ed.) *Political change in the Middle East and North Africa after the Arab Spring.* Edinburgh: Edinburgh University Press, pp. 63–88.

Storm, L. (2020a) 'Political Parties in the Middle East', in Hinnebusch, R. and Gani, J. (eds.) *The Routledge handbook to the Middle East and North African state and states system.* London: Routledge, pp. 136–152.

Storm, L. (2020b) 'Exploring post-rebel parties in power: Political space and implications for Islamist inclusion and moderation', *Open Journal of Political Science,* 10, p638–667.

Storm, L. (2020c) 'Political Parties under Competitive Authoritarianism', in Cavatorta, F., Storm, L. and Resta, V. (eds.) *Routledge handbook on political parties in the Middle East and North Africa.* London: Routledge, pp. 99–113.

Storm, L. and Cavatorta, F. (2018) 'Do Arabs not do parties?', in Cavatorta, F. and Storm, L. (eds.) *Political parties in the Arab World.* Edinburgh: Edinburgh University Press, pp. 1–20.

Szmolka, I. (2020) 'Liberal-secular parties in Arab political systems', in Cavatorta, F., Storm, L. and Resta, V. (eds.) *Routledge handbook on political parties in the Middle East and North Africa*. London: Routledge, pp. 69–82.

Thyen, K. (2020) 'Youth activism and political parties', in Cavatorta, F., Storm, L. and Resta, V. (eds.) *Routledge handbook on political parties in the Middle East and North Africa*. London: Routledge, pp. 231–242.

Völkel, J. (2020) 'Pawns in the army's hands: Political parties in military-dominated regimes', in Cavatorta, F., Storm, L. and Resta, V. (eds.) *Routledge handbook on political parties in the Middle East and North Africa*. London: Routledge, pp. 125–136.

Volpi, F. (2020) 'Algeria: When elections hurt democracy', *Journal of Democracy*, 31(2), p152–165.

Willis, M. (2002a) 'Political Parties in the Maghrib: The illusion of significance?', *The Journal of North African Studies*, 7(2), p1–22.

Willis, M. (2002b) 'Political parties in the Maghrib: Ideology and identification. A suggested typology', *The Journal of North African Studies*, 7(3), p1–28.

Wolf, A. (2018) 'What are "secular" parties in the Maghreb? Comparing Tunisia's Nidaa Tounes and Morocco's PAM', in Cavatorta, F. and Storm, L. (eds.) *Political parties in the Arab world*. Edinburgh: Edinburgh University Press, pp. 49–71.

Yerkes, S. and Yahmed, Z. (2019) *Tunisia's political system: From stagnation to competition*. Carnegie Endowment for International Peace, 28 March. Available from: https://carnegieendowment.org/2019/03/28/tunisia-s-political-system-from-stagnation-to-competition-pub-78717

36

POLITICAL PARTIES IN THE ARAB MIDDLE EAST

Hendrik Kraetzschmar and Valeria Resta

The experience of party politics in the Arab Middle East is chequered to say the least. Of the 13 countries that make up this sub-region of the wider Arab World, political parties and party-like organisations[1] remain illegal in four (Oman, Qatar, Saudi Arabia and the United Arab Emirates), illegal yet tolerated in one (Kuwait) and legalised in the remaining eight (Bahrain, Egypt, Iraq, Jordan, Lebanon, Palestine, Syria and Yemen). Among the latter nine, meanwhile, differences in regime type and national trajectories have produced a plethora of distinctive (multi-)party systems, ranging from the pulverised partisan landscapes of Lebanon and Jordan to the *de-facto* Baathist one-party state clinging to power in war-torn Syria (see Table 36.1 for overview).

This chapter offers a critical perspective on the state of political parties' research in the Arab Middle East, focusing on three key disciplinary sub-themes: party families and political ideologies, party functions and organisation, and voters, parties and elections. A cursory glance at this collective body of research presents a mixed picture. On a positive note, it reveals a sub-discipline that is gradually coming into its own, having gained substantially in traction and dynamism over the past two decades. This is particularly noteworthy, of course, within the Middle Eastern studies context, where electoral and party politics have all too often been discarded as inconsequential to our understanding of local political dynamics (Hinnebusch 2017; Storm and Cavatorta 2018). The flip side, however, is that this growing body of research is lopsided on several accounts. Dominated by case study analyses, the political parties' literature of the Arab Middle East remains overwhelmingly preoccupied with the study of Islamist political parties, at the expense of their non-Islamist counterparts (e.g. Hamzawy 2011; Hinnebusch, Cavatorta and Storm 2021) and remains limited in comparative scope. It is also lacking in sustained engagement with the wider theoretical literature, thus inhibiting a fruitful integration of the region into mainstream political parties research. There are, of course, some exceptions to this trend (e.g. Masoud 2014; Kurzman and Türkoğlu 2015; Abduljaber 2018; Wegner and Cavatorta 2019; Resta 2019; Aydogan 2021) whose innovative party research will be discussed in the final section of this chapter.

Party families and political ideologies

Even though in the Arab Middle East, the dimensionality and structure of the ideological space remain contested issues (Ozen 2017), and the role of party programmes rather weak in comparison to ascriptive identities, when it comes to mobilisation, ideology proves critical in

Table 36.1 Political parties and elections in the Arab Middle East

Country	Current status of political parties	(Multi-party) Elections[1]
Bahrain	Legal	Non-partisan (1972–1973) – multi-party (2002–)
Egypt	Legal	Single-party (1964–1976) – multi-party (1979–)
Iraq	Legal	Single party (1980–2000) – multi-party (1933–1958, 2005-)
Jordan	Legal	Non-partisan (1950–1953, 1961–1989[2]) – multi-party (1954–1956, 1993-)
Kuwait	Illegal/tolerated	Non-partisan (1980s–[2])
Lebanon	Legal	Multi-party (1943–)
Oman	Illegal	Non-partisan (1991–)
Palestine	Legal	Multi-party (1996–)
Qatar	Illegal	Non-partisan (1999–)
Saudi Arabia	Illegal	Non-partisan (2005–)
Syria	Legal	Single-party (1973–2007) – multi-party (1947–1961, 2012-)
UAE	Illegal	Non-partisan (2006–)
Yemen (united)	legal	Multi-party (1993–)

[1] Most of these elections are for the lower houses of parliament, except for Qatar and Saudi Arabia where they refer to the municipal councils.
[2] Candidates ran/run formally as independents. Of these, some were/are, however, affiliated to tolerated/clandestine partisan organisations.

Source: Inter-Parliamentary Union (IPU), PARLINE Database on National Parliaments, Available at: http://archive.ipu.org/parline-e/parlinesearch.asp. (Accessed 01 March 2021).

structuring political parties. Providing the basic coordinates for mapping the region's party scene, three broad ideological families can be identified. These are the leftist/communist, the Islamic/Islamist and the liberal/centrist party families (Cavatorta and Storm 2018).

Leftist/communist political parties first appeared in the region during the 1920s, inspired by the Bolshevik Revolution in Russia. From their inception, these parties aligned the Marxist dictum of emancipating the working classes from capital with that of a national struggle against colonial rule, thus providing both ideological justification and material backing to the cause of national independence, especially when it was the result of revolution (Bustani 2014). Examples of such parties include the various communist parties that emerged during this period in Egypt, Iraq, Lebanon, Palestine and Syria (Hilal and Hermann 2014). At the time, these parties enjoyed relative popularity, thus becoming the first ideological mass parties in the Arab Middle East (Salem 1994).

Soon after the establishment of national states in the region, however, the left became increasingly side-lined – and in the case of the Communists widely repressed – by army-backed Arab socialist regimes that had come to power during the 1950s and 1960s with a decidedly leftist agenda (Hinnebusch 2017). Throughout this period, the traditional left faced at times severe repression for their overt criticism of populist authoritarian rule and the perceived weaknesses of their leaders vis-à-vis the state of Israel. Some leftist parties were subsequently banned, including most Communist parties, while others were co-opted into the authoritarian umbrella. The creation of the Syrian National Progressive Front in 1972 – a political alliance of legally permitted parties backing the Ba'ath Party – and the National Progressive Unionist Party in Egypt epitomise this latter scenario.

During the era of political liberalisation of the 1980s and 1990s, those leftist parties that were allowed to resurface found themselves confronted with yet another challenge: the growth and rise in popularity of Islamist movements and parties. Fearful of their ideology and mobilisational capacity, many on the left started to view the secular authoritarian regimes as a lesser of two evils, thus downplaying their oppositional posture and turning effectively into a timid/loyal regime opposition. With the traditional left widely seen as co-opted and discredited, the 2000s witnessed the birth of new forms of leftist activism which, eschewing party politics, sought to advance issues of social justice and reform through non-institutionalised channels, including quiet encroachment, wild cat strikes and the formation of protest networks and movements (Bayat 2002). Nowadays the partisan left is all but annihilated, pulverised into small parties and incapable of building any meaningful linkages with voters, even with those displaying leftist leanings (Tessler 2011; Resta 2018).

Of the three-party families prevalent in the Arab Middle East, the Islamist political family has unquestionably received most scholarly interest, primarily not only due to its growth in popularity and electoral muscle but also because of its troubled relationship with notions of democracy (e.g. Driessen 2014). Making a forceful entrance onto the region's political scene in the 1970s and 1980s, the Islamist political family comprises a variegated galaxy of political parties and movements, including both Sunni and Shi'a Islamist forces (Ozzano 2013).

Critiquing the perceived moral/political decay of authoritarian regimes in the region and their lack of authenticity, these Islamist parties and movements all advocate the revival of an all-encompassing Islam as an ordering device for government and society. When it comes to the dissemination of this message, and the type of activism it entails, scholars have highlighted, however, some key divisions in the degree to which this should be achieved through participatory channels or by violent means. The Islamist movement thus became conventionally divided into those shunning political engagement altogether (also known as quietist Salafis), those advocating political engagement (participatory Islamists) and proponents of violent jihad (e.g. Lacroix 2016). Most Islamist political parties presently operating in the Arab Middle East – including the various Muslim Brotherhood (MB) – affiliated parties – belong to the participatory branch of the Islamist political family. In recent years, however, and particularly in the aftermath of the Arab Spring, numerous hitherto quietist Salafi groupings abandoned their apolitical stances, opting instead for the creation of political parties and their participation in competitive politics (Cavatorta and Merone 2017). In Egypt, for instance, the first post-Spring elections of 2011–2012, saw the emergence of numerous Salafi parties, including the al-Nour party, which went on to win the second largest share of seats in parliament. There are several possible explanations for this dramatic shift in Salafi attitudes towards party politics. For some scholars, Salafi politicisation was chiefly driven by a desire to curb the monopolisation of the Islamist spectrum by the MB in the post-Mubarak era (Utvik 2014). For others, meanwhile, it was the political opening created by the Arab Spring which was seen by many Salafis as an opportunity not only to shape the new politics but also to safeguard the Islamic character of the post-Mubarak political order (Cavatorta and Resta 2020).

Within scholarship on the Islamist political family the so-called 'inclusion-moderation' hypothesis has emerged as a key lens through which to study the ideological positioning and development of Islamist political parties and movements. Essentially, the hypothesis posits that the more Islamists participate in the political arena the more they moderate their stances, particularly on attitudes towards democracy, the role of religion in politics, women's rights and minority rights (Schwedler 2006, 2007; Tepe 2013). Political inclusion thus became widely seen as a gateway to democratisation precisely for its effect on Islamist moderation. Critics of this proposition have noted, however, that the de-radicalisation of Islamist stances on any of the aforementioned issues does not necessarily speak to a process of moderation, but rather a process of skilful adaptation to the (authoritarian) status quo (Lust-Okar 2005; Resta 2019). Following on from this observation, scholars have increasingly turned their attention to how precisely a regime's structure of competition affects Islamist policies, and in fact the politicking of all political parties operating in that system (Lust-Okar 2005; Resta 2019).

The liberal/centrist current in the Arab Middle East, finally, is not only the least widespread but also the most under-researched of the three ideological families. Within the relevant literature, in fact, it is perceived as rather difficult to pin down the key trademarks of this current and what it means to be 'liberal' in the Middle Eastern context, so much so that many scholars simply define the current in contraposition to Islamist parties and groupings (Ottaway and Hamzawy 2009). For many regional experts and practitioners, this contraposition has afforded liberal parties the rather dubious status of 'democracy promoters' (Ottaway and Hamzawy 2009), and their scant presence in the region's electoral and parliamentary politics has often been cited among the causes for the lack of democracy in the Arab Middle East (Carothers and Ottaway 2005). Closer scrutiny of the current in the pre-Spring era reveals, however, that many of the liberal/centrist parties of the region, far from being portents of democratisation, were instead bastions of authoritarian resilience and loyalist pro-regime parties whose leader preferred the authoritarian, yet 'secular', status quo to the perceived perils of an 'Islamist turnover' (Lust-Okar 2005; Boduszyński, Fabbe and Lamont 2015).

In one of the few works on Arab liberal parties post-Spring, Szmolka (2020) presents a useful classification of this genre of parties, stipulating that to be labelled as 'liberal' they ought to fulfil the following criteria: a) hold an affiliation to liberal transnational organisations, b) evidence a decidedly liberal ideology in their party programmes/manifestos and c) be widely classed as such by scholars in the field. Using these criteria, Szmolka identified just five liberal parliamentary parties currently operating in the Arab Middle East: the Free Egyptian Party, the Congress Party, the Freedom Party and the New Wafd party in Egypt and the Future Movement in Lebanon.

In the Arab Middle East political ideology thus matters and presents one fruitful avenue of making sense of the spectre of political parties operating in the region. This, however, is only half the story. Alongside ideology– and at times overshadowing it – there are numerous ascriptive identities that form salient features of identity and politics in the Arab Middle East. These include ethnic, sectarian, tribal and familial identities, all of which remain important markers of individual and collective identity and as such shapers of regional party politics (Hinnebusch 2017; Gao 2021). Indeed, many parties have become associated not only with a specific ideology but also with specific tribal groups, ethnic groups and/or sects. This is the case for instance in Iraq and Lebanon where the parties' ethno-sectarian identity and base overshadow their ideological orientation,[2] or in Yemen and Jordan, where many of the parties are little more than vehicles for the advancement of tribal interests (Yamao 2012; Assi 2016; Alles 2018; Kraetzschmar 2018).

Party functions and organisation

In democratic systems, political parties perform a series of functions that render representative government possible. These include most prominently the selection and aggregation of societal interests into coherent manifestos (thus offering programmatic choice to voters), the nomination of candidates for elections, participation in law-making and governance, as well as the scrutiny of government when in opposition (LaPalombara and Anderson 1992, 393). Across the Arab Middle East, however, none of the regimes can be classed as democratic. Instead, we here encounter varying shades of electoral authoritarianism, ranging from the competitive autocracies of Iraq, Jordan, Lebanon, Palestine and Kuwait to the more full-blown authoritarianism of Egypt and Bahrain, alongside war-torn Syria and Yemen (Schedler 2006). Common to all these authoritarian regimes is the fact that electoral competition, while plural, is not free and fair and power alternation between ruling party/regime and the opposition near impossible. As illustrated among others by Albrecht (2005) and Sassoon (2017) the functions political parties perform under such conditions are intimately tied to the authoritarian logic that underpins these regimes and their survival. For authoritarian incumbents, ruling parties/coalitions serve as vital means to safeguard the regime's predominance over the key executive and legislative institutions of the state, as well as a channel for elite recruitment and a mechanism for wider societal co-optation and control (Sassoon 2017). For opposition parties, meanwhile, their *raison d'être* resides elsewhere. While they may put forward candidates and manifestos in elections, unlike in democratic systems they usually do so knowing they stand little realistic chance of capturing power. If anything, their participation in elections serves as a 'fig leaf' for the regime to shore up its 'democratic legitimacy' at home and abroad, and to channel and monitor dissent in the open as well as co-opt oppositional elites/groupings through the provision of selective access to material spoils (Albrecht 2005; Hamid 2014). For numerous scholars, particularly those writing on the pre-Arab Spring era, this co-optation of the opposition has rendered them unsuitable advocates of democratic change, serving to strengthen rather than undermine authoritarian resilience (Albrecht 2005; Shahin 2010). In the more competitive authoritarian regimes, moreover, particularly in those with prevailing ascriptive societal identities such as exist in Iraq, Jordan, Kuwait and Lebanon, political parties function overwhelmingly as elite vessels for the mobilisation and representation of specific tribal and/or sectarian interests and the provision of clientelistic patronage to members of their respective communities (Edwards 2018; Kraetzschmar 2018; Fakhoury and Al-Fakih 2021).

The singularities thus manifest in some of the functions political parties perform in the Arab Middle East are also evident when it comes to their internal organisation. Here again we can detect distinctive trademarks that, while common to many parties across the region and the wider Arab/Muslim world, find limited empirical equivalence among Western party organisations. One such trademark concerns, for instance, the prevalence of political parties – predominantly (yet not exclusively) within the Islamist spectrum – that emerged out of/were forged by pre-existing civil organisations or social movements, and to which they retain a close ideological, inter-personal and/or structural connect. Examples of such parties abound across the Arab Middle East. They are most widely associated with the various MB societies, but – as Table 36.2 shows – they have also emerged as offshoots of other Islamist organisations, including most notably the Salafi and Shi'a Islamist currents (e.g. Bhasin and Hallward 2013; Lacroix 2016; Kraetzschmar 2018). Interestingly, several of the parent organisations that host such parties also engage in coercive politics, featuring dedicated armed wings alongside their varied charitable, financial, electoral and religious endeavours. Some well-known examples of what Berti succinctly labelled as 'hybrid politico-military organisations' (2011, 942) include Hamas in Palestine and Hezbollah in Lebanon, but they can also be found in Iraq in the form of the Sadrist movement, the Islamic Supreme Council of Iraq or the Al-Sadiqoun Bloc (e.g. Berti 2011; Bhasin and Hallward 2013; Thurber 2014).

Elsewhere, the nexus just highlighted between Islamist parent organisations and their affiliate parties has emerged as a powerful explanation for the comparable advantages these parties enjoy in organisational strength and mobilisational reach over their non-Islamist rivals particularly in the electoral arena. Hence they are often perceived as an elevated political threat by authoritarian incumbents (Grewal et al. 2019).[3] It has also precipitated a set of intriguing analyses into the emergence of Islamist parties from within broader social movements, the precise nature of

Table 36.2 Principal Islamist movement parties in the Arab Middle East[1]

Country	Muslim brotherhood – affiliated parties	Parties affiliated with Shi'a Islamist Associations	Parties affiliated with Salafi Societies
Bahrain	National Islamic Society, Al-Minbar (2002–)	Al-Wefaq National Islamic Society (2001–2016)	Al-Asalah Islamic Society (2002–)
Egypt	Freedom and Justice Party (2011–2014)	-	The Party of Light, Al-Nour (2011–)
Iraq	Iraq Islamic Party (1960–)	Sadrist Movement (2003–) Supreme Council of Iraq (1982–)	-
Jordan	Islamic Action Front (1992–)	-	-
Kuwait	Islamic Constitutional Movement, Hadas (1991–)	Islamic National Alliance (1998–)	Salafi Islamic Gathering (1981–)
Lebanon	Islamic Group (1964–)	Loyalty to the Resistance Bloc, Hezbollah (1992–)	-
Palestine	Change and Reform, Hamas (2006–)	-	-
Yemen	Yemen Congregation of Reform, Ishah (1990–)	The Future of Justice Party (2017–)	Al-Rashad Union (2012–)

[1] This table does not claim to represent an exhaustive list of Islamist movement parties, but a snapshot of its most prominent exponents across the Arab Middle East.

their relationship with the parent organisations as well as the effects of this relationship on their electoral behaviour (e.g. Hamid 2014; Bhasin and Hallward 2013). Adopting a social movement theoretical lens Kuschnitzki (2016) and Bhasin and Hallward (2013), for instance, illustrate how changes in political opportunity structures were key in enticing Hamas in Palestine and the Salafi Al-Rashad Union in Yemen to forge distinctive partisan organisations. For Hamas, these opportunity structures revolved principally around the presence of a permissive electoral law alongside Hamas' growing popularity in the lead up to the 2006 parliamentary elections, while for the Al-Rashad Union they resided primarily in the consequences of the Yemeni uprising of 2011–2012 and its aftermath (Kuschnitzki 2016; Bhasin and Hallward 2013).

When assessing the nature of relations between these types of parties and their parent organisations, meanwhile, the scholarly tenor is near unanimous: although there is variation in the precise nature of this relationship, these parties are regarded as little more than a political arm of their parent organisation, as manifested in the absence of any substantive organisational and decision-making autonomy. As Lacroix (2016) illustrates with regard to the Salafi Al-Nour party in Egypt, sometimes this subordination to the parent organisation has resulted in frictions and conflict between the two, but in most instances, it is holding sway across the Arab Middle East and remains critical in defining the parameters of political activism these movement parties engage in (Hamid 2014).

Not all political parties across the Arab Middle East are, however, in the fortunate position to draw on established parent organisations and their human and financial resources to build up strong internal structures and constituency support. Most of the parties that make up the region's political landscape, and certainly those belonging to the non-Islamist current, are plagued by multiple structural weaknesses that render them into 'cardboard parties' (Hamid 2014). These are parties that, limited in financial means and human resources, struggle to sustain a nationwide network of offices and the complex organisational machinery necessary to run effective election and mobilisation campaigns. In Bahrain, Egypt, Jordan, Kuwait and Palestine, many of the liberal and leftist parties fall into this bracket, featuring poorly funded and understaffed organisations with a limited mass membership and constituency support (Ottaway and Hamzawy 2009; Hanna 2015; Resta 2018). The workings of these parties are often also marked by strong oligarchical tendencies, an ongoing underrepresentation of women in leadership positions[4] and overall limited adherence to, and regard for, internal democratic processes (e.g. El Khazen 2003; Ottaway and Hamzawy 2009; Jamal 2018; Benstead 2021). This latter observation applies to both non-Islamist and Islamist parties and has in the eyes of many of the region's citizens seriously dented the credibility of both sets of parties as viable champions of democratic reform.

Although the anatomy of political parties has thus far received comparatively little systematic scrutiny – certainly when it comes to the region's non-Islamist parties – the relevant literature has produced some insightful pointers as to why many parties remain structurally so underdeveloped. For Ottaway and Hamzawy (2009), for example, these internal weaknesses are partly perpetuated by the prevalence of an often aging and/or divided leadership that is either unable or unwilling to advance the party's organisational and programmatic development as well as its constituency outreach activities. Others, such as Shahin (2010) and Lust and Waldner (2016), meanwhile, highlight the authoritarian context within which these parties operate and which is thought to severely constrain efforts at party building, particularly through restrictive legislation and fraud, but also by means of regime co-optation and divide-and-rule tactics.

Voters, parties and elections

While political parties across the Arab Middle East have participated in plural elections, their fortunes at the ballot box vary greatly. Where they exist, ruling parties tend to win big, not because they carry any popularity or activist membership base, but because they can draw on the mobilisational resources of the state and its ability to dispense clientelist patronage (Hinnebusch 2017, 166–167). The National Democratic Party (NDP) in Mubarak's Egypt and the General People's Congress (GPC) in pre-Spring Yemen are two prominent examples of such ruling parties which during the 1990s and 2000s secured their regimes comfortable majorities in the legislature and the executive, thus playing a key part in the maintenance of authoritarian rule (Resende and Kraetzschmar 2005). Elsewhere the fortunes of political parties are less clear cut. In some of the region's monarchies, for instance, political parties present only a fraction of the candidates running in national elections, with independents dominating the electoral field and subsequently often also the legislature (Kraetzschmar 2018, 2021). This is the case in Bahrain, Kuwait and Jordan, where partisan MPs have generally held fewer than, or barely over, 50 per cent of all elective seats in parliament. This numerical weakness is attributable to several factors. These include most notably the prevalence of candidate-centric electoral rules, widespread popular distrust in the utility and trustworthiness of political parties,[5] and a preponderance on the part of voters to select candidates based on their ability to deliver *wasta* and/or their communal background (e.g. familial, tribal, ethnic or sectarian) rather than due to any partisan affinities. In Kuwait, for instance, proto-parties not only have to contend with widespread societal distrust in parties, but they must also hold their ground in a crowded field of contestants dominated by independent candidates, many of whom are nominated by the country's powerful tribes and hence in an often infinitely better position to mobilise electoral support, particularly in the more tribal constituencies (Kraetzschmar 2021). In Jordan as well, partisan candidates have traditionally faced an uphill struggle in their quest for votes and seats. This electoral weakness is tied to both the specificities of Jordan's political parties and successive electoral laws – which remain heavily gerrymandered in favour of the rural tribal districts – as well as to voting patterns that again favour a candidate's ability to deliver patronage and his/her regional background over his/her party membership and programme (Dietrich 1999; Lust-Okar 2002, 2006).

Across the region, variance in the electoral fortunes of political parties also carries a distinctly ideological flavour. Indeed, a closer look at their electoral performance over time – particularly in the pre-Spring era – reveals that Islamist political parties tend to outperform their non-Islamist rivals by significant margins. Parliamentary elections throughout the 1990s and 2000s in Bahrain, Egypt, Jordan and Kuwait showcase this trend, with both Sunni and Shi'a Islamist parties collectively winning a majority share of the partisan vote, and at times even outnumbering the overall vote and seat totals of all other non-Islamist opposition parties taken together[6] (Kraetzschmar 2018; Grewal et al. 2019). For some scholars, this electoral success is primarily grounded in the superior organisational and mobilisational infrastructure that Islamist parties can draw upon compared to their non-Islamist rivals (e.g. Masoud 2014). More recently, attention has also been paid to the religious character of these parties and how this engenders strong support from voters, particularly from those facing economic hardship, but also from the pious middle class, which is less reliant on state patronage to master everyday life (Grewal et al. 2019).

With regard to partisan electioneering, finally, several noteworthy facts ought to be highlighted about the nature of electoral contestation and the state of political parties in the Arab Middle East. Within the non-Islamist spectrum, for instance, the multiple structural weaknesses of political parties have rendered it incredibly difficult for their leaders to recruit and support sufficiently large numbers of candidates in elections. This in turn has perpetuated the preponderance of highly personalised campaigns, even by party candidates who – confronted with limited financial support from party headquarters and voters little concerned with party manifestos – face few incentives to advocate their partisan affiliation and programmes (Dietrich 1999; Kraetzschmar 2018). For Islamist parties, the challenge presents itself somewhat differently. Indeed, while non-Islamist parties struggle to enhance their visibility in elections, Islamist parties tend to be driven by a reverse calculus whereby they seek to downplay rather than upscale their electoral ambitions. Focusing on Bahrain, Egypt, Kuwait, Jordan and Yemen, for instance, Hamid illustrates how Islamist parties have gone out of their way to limit the number of seats they seek to win – even if they believe they could win more – and doing so not only due to fear of repression, but in order to fit in with the much more weighty grassroots social, educational and *da'wa* activities of their parent organisations (Hamid 2014, 68–75).

Conclusions and avenues for further research

As highlighted earlier, scholarship on Arab political parties has expanded considerably in a relatively short period of time, opening new avenues of enquiry that were unthinkable only a decade ago. While in the early 2000s political parties across the Arab Middle East (and North Africa) were largely disregarded, or simply remained outside the radar of enquiry (Eyadat 2015), there are now several (edited) volumes (e.g. Catusse and Karam 2010; Masoud 2014; Cavatorta and Storm 2018; Cavatorta, Storm and Resta 2021) and countless journal articles that problematise key aspects of party politics in the Arab Middle East.

Arguably, this mushrooming of interest in Arab political parties is underpinned by empirical trends and meta-theoretical concerns brought about by the 2011–2012 uprisings in the region. These have made the region more accessible for data collection, particularly regarding the availability online of manifesto, survey and electoral data. Importantly also, they have triggered a process of soul-searching within the area studies community, enticing scholars to turn away from exceptionalist approaches to the region's politics and towards the 'old toolkit' of political science where political parties stand as fundamental (Valbjørn and Bank 2010; Valbjørn 2015).

Although still in its infancy, this rethink has produced several exciting new avenues of research that draw on quantitative analysis and are much more closely aligned with the wider political parties' literature. This is evident, for instance, in a handful of recent publications that – utilising statistical tools – explore party–voter linkages, party constituents and voting behaviour in the Arab Middle East. One such example is the work of Masoud (2014), who demonstrates that the Islamist success in Egypt's 2011–2012 parliamentary election had more to do with their organisational and mobilisational capabilities than with their programme and voters' religious leanings. Drawing on available survey data, Wegner and Cavatorta (2019) demonstrate that the widely assumed 'Islamist-secular' divide in regional party politics is limited to the role of religion in the public sphere and gender equality, but not, however, to other policy areas.

Another innovative avenue of research is the use of spatial modelling to capture the nature and shape of the region's multi-party systems, thus facilitating broader within and across-regional comparisons. Scholars have drawn on data gathering techniques widely used in research on the dimensionality of Western party systems. Aydogan's (2021) analysis of spatial party politics in the MENA, for instance, utilises expert survey data to identify the central cleavages shaping the region's partisan landscapes. Among others, he reveals that the left-right continuum that (Western) political scientists employ to describe (mostly Western) party systems fails to depict the complexity of the political space in the MENA region and that political parties tend to position themselves on different policy issues in ways that appear incoherent with this ideological spectrum. Other scholars, such as Türkoğlu and Kurzman (2015), Abduljaber (2018) and Resta (2019), in turn, have used party manifesto data to uncover the ideological dimensions informing multi-party competition and debate in the Arab Middle East. Abduljaber (2018), for instance, makes the important observation that in the post-Spring era Islam appears to be no longer the predominant policy domain structuring Arab party politics, with issues of socio-economic well-being and governance topping the agenda.

To be sure, as important as these new areas of research are, particularly in their methodological and theoretical advancement of the field, there remain significant gaps in our understanding of regional party politics that will require future attention. These pertain to a host of subjects in party research and include among others analysis of party and party system institutionalisation, areas of investigation that are far more advanced in the North African context than in the Arab Middle East (e.g. Storm 2014; Yardımcı-Geyikçi 2015; and Chapter 35). Yet the newly found interest in party politics, and the rigour this subject has received in recent scholarship, gives hope that our understanding of the intricacies of the region's multi-party politics will grow rapidly in both stature and sophistication.

Notes

1 In this chapter, we refer to political parties when referring to the entire Arab Middle East, acknowledging that in Bahrain partisan organisations are legally known as political societies and in Kuwait best described as proto-parties, given their non-legalised status (Kraetzschmar 2018).
2 In Iraq, the partisan landscape is broadly divided into Shi'a, Sunni, and Kurdish parties (Yamao 2012).
3 This organisational muscle derives principally from their ability to tap into the financial, human and/or infrastructural resources of their parent organisations for the purpose of voter mobilisation and electioneering (Grewal et al. 2019).
4 See Clark and Schwedler (2003) for a discussion of how female members in Sunni Islamist parties in Jordan and Yemen advanced their inclusion and standing within these parties.

5 In Jordan, Arab Barometer (2018) reported that only 0.7 per cent of those interviewed had a lot of trust in political parties. In Kuwait, a 2013 Arab Barometer survey found that 95.6 per cent of those consulted did not feel close to any proto-party (cited from Kraetzschmar 2018, 245).
6 In the Bahraini elections of 2006 and 2010 non-Islamist political societies failed to secure a single seat in parliament. In the 2005 parliamentary elections in Egypt, MB-affiliated candidates won 88 seats compared to the 9 seats held by the entire non-Islamist opposition (Lange 2005).

References

Abduljaber, M. (2018) 'The dimensionality, type, and structure of political ideology on the political party level in the Arab World', *Chinese Political Science Review*, 3(4), p464–494.

Albrecht, H. (2005) 'How can opposition support authoritarianism? Lessons from Egypt', *Democratization*, 12(3), p378–397.

Alles, L. (2018) 'Tribes and political parties in the contemporary Arab World: A reassessment from Yemen', in Cavatorta, F. and Storm, L. (eds.), *Political parties in the Arab world: Continuity and change*. Edinburgh: Edinburgh University Press, pp. 207–229.

Arab Barometer (2018) *'Jordan' poll*. Available from: www.arabbarometer.org/survey-data/data-analysis-tool/ (Accessed 1 March 2021)

Assi, A. 2016 *Democracy in Lebanon: Political parties and the struggle for power since Syrian withdrawal*. London: Bloomsbury Publishing.

Aydogan, A. (2021) 'Party systems and ideological cleavages in the Middle East and North Africa', *Party Politics*, 27(4), p814–826.

Bayat, A. (2002) 'Activism and social development in the Middle East', *International Journal of Middle East Studies*, 34(1), p1–28.

Benstead, L.J. (2021) 'Women in Arab political parties', in Cavatorta, F., Storm, L. and Resta, V. (eds.) *Routledge handbook on political parties in the Middle East and North Africa*. London: Routledge, pp. 255–270.

Berti, B. (2011) 'Armed groups as political parties and their role in electoral politics: The case of Hizballah', *Studies in Conflict & Terrorism*, 34(12), p942–962.

Bhasin, T. and Hallward, M. (2013) 'Hamas as a political party: Democratization in the Palestinian territories', *Terrorism and Political Violence*, 25(1), p75–93.

Boduszyński, M., Fabbe, K. and Lamont, C. (2015) 'Are secular parties the answer?', *Journal of Democracy*, 26(4), p125–139.

Bustani, H. (2014) 'Dissonances of the Arab Left', *Radical Philosophy*, 184, p35–42.

Carothers, T. and Ottaway, M. (2005) *Uncharted journey: Promoting democracy in the Middle East*. Washington, DC: Carnegie Endowment for International Peace.

Catusse, M. and Karam, K. (2010) 'Back to parties? Partisan logics and transformations of politics in the Arab World', in Catusse, M. and Karam, K. (eds.) *Returning to political parties? Political party development in the Arab Word*. Beirut: Lebanese Center for Policy Studies, pp. 11–59.

Cavatorta, F. and Merone, F. (eds.) (2017) *Salafism after the Arab awakening: Contending with people's power*. Oxford: Oxford University Press.

Cavatorta, F. and Resta, V. (2020) 'Beyond quietism: Party institutionalisation, Salafism, and the economy', *Politics and Religion*, 13(4), p796–817.

Cavatorta, F. and Storm, L. (eds.) (2018) *Political parties in the Arab world: Continuity and change*. Edinburgh: Edinburgh University Press.

Cavatorta, F., Storm, L. and Resta, V. (eds.) (2021) *Routledge handbook on political parties in the Middle East and North Africa*. London: Routledge.

Clark, A. and Schwedler, J. (2003) 'Who opened the window? Women's activism in Islamist parties', *Comparative Politics*, 35(3), p293–312.

Dieterich, R. (1999) *Where authoritarianism and tribalism meet: Conflicting experiences of party activism in Jordan since 1989* (Unpublished paper).

Driessen, M. (2014) *Religion and democratization: Framing religious and political identities in Muslim and Catholic societies*. Oxford: Oxford University Press.

Edwards, S. (2018) 'Sectarian friction and the struggle for power: party politics in Iraq post-2003', in Cavatorta, F. and Storm, L. (eds.) *Political parties in the Arab world: Continuity and change*. Edinburgh: Edinburgh University Press, pp. 164–183.

El Khazen, F. (2003) 'Political parties in postwar Lebanon: Parties in search of partisans', *Middle East Journal*, 57(4), p605–624.

Eyadat, Z. (2015) 'A Transition without players: The role of political parties in the Arab revolutions', *Democracy and Security*, 11(2), p160–175.

Fakhoury, T. and Al-Fakih, F. (2021) 'Consociationalism and political parties in the Middle East', in Cavatorta, F., Storm, L. and Resta, V. (eds.) *Routledge handbook on political parties in the Middle East and North Africa*. London: Routledge, pp. 179–191.

Gao, E. (2021) 'Tribes and political parties in the contemporary Arab world', in Cavatorta, F., Storm, L and Resta, V. (eds.) *Routledge handbook on political parties in the Middle East and North Africa*. London: Routledge, pp. 243–254

Grewal, S., Jamal, A., Masoud, T. and Nugent, E. (2019), 'Poverty and divine rewards: The electoral advantage of Islamist political parties', *American Journal of Political Science*, 63(4), p859–874.

Hamid, S. (2014) 'Political party development before and after the Arab spring' in Kamrava, M. (ed.) *Beyond the Arab Spring: The evolving ruling bargain in the Middle East*. Washington, DC: Brookings, pp. 131–150.

Hamzawy, A. (2011) 'Arab writings on Islamist parties and movements', *International Journal of Middle East Studies*, 43(1), p138–140.

Hanna, M. (2015) 'Egypt's non-Islamist parties', *Adelphi Series*, 55(453–454), p105–130.

Hilal, J. and Hermann, K. (2014) *Mapping of the Arab left: Contemporary leftist politics in the Arab East*. Palestine: Rosa Luxemburg Stiftung Regional Office Palestine.

Hinnebusch, R. (2017) 'Political parties in MENA: Their functions and development', *British Journal of Middle Eastern Studies*, 44(2), p159–175.

Hinnebusch, R., Cavatorta, F. and Storm, L. (2021) 'Political parties in MENA: An introduction', in Cavatorta, F., Storm, L. and Resta, V. (eds.) *Routledge handbook on political parties in the Middle East and North Africa*. London: Routledge, pp. 1–14.

Jamal, M. (2018) 'Party politics in the Palestinian territories', in Cavatorta, F. and Storm, L. (eds.) *Political parties in the Arab world: Continuity and change*. Edinburgh: Edinburgh University Press, pp. 147–163.

Kraetzschmar, H. (2018) 'In the shadows of legality: proto-parties and participatory politics in the Emirate of Kuwait', in Cavatorta, F. and Storm, L. (eds.) *Political parties in the Arab world: Continuity and change*. Edinburgh: Edinburgh University Press, pp. 230–251.

Kraetzschmar, H. (2021) 'Political intermediation in the Arabian Peninsula: Partisan organisations, elections and parliamentary representation in Bahrain, Kuwait and Yemen', in Cavatorta, F., Storm. L. and Resta, V. (eds.) *Routledge handbook on political parties in the Middle East and North Africa*. London: Routledge, pp. 114–124.

Kurzman, C. and Türkoğlu, D. (2015) 'After the Arab spring do Muslims vote Islamic now?', *Journal of Democracy*, 26, p100–109.

Kuschnitzki, J. (2016) 'The establishment and positioning of al-Rashad: A case study of political Salafism in Yemen', in Cavatorta, F. and Merone, F. (eds.) *Salafism after the Arab Awakening: Contending with People's Power*. Oxford: Hurst Publishers, pp. 99–118.

Lacroix, S. (2016) 'Egypt's pragmatic Salafis: The politics of Hizb Al-Nour', Carnegie *Endowment for International Peace*. Available from: https://carnegieendowment.org/2016/11/01/egypt-s-pragmatic-salafis-politics-of-hizb-al-nour-pub-64902 (Accessed 1 March 2021)

Lange, M.A. (2005) 'Die Aegyptischen Parlamentswahlen 2005: III. Wahlgang, 22 December 2005', *Konrad Adenauer Foundation*.

LaPalombara, J. and Anderson, J. (1992) 'Political parties', in Hawksworth, M. and Kogan, M. (eds.) *Encyclopaedia of government and politics*. London: Routledge, pp. 393–412.

Lust, E. and Waldner, D. (2016) 'Parties in transitional democracies: Authoritarian legacy and post-authoritarian challenges in the Middle East and North Africa', in Bermeo, N. and Yashar, D. (eds.) *Parties, movements, and democracy in the developing world*. Cambridge: Cambridge University Press, pp. 157–189.

Lust-Okar, E. (2002) 'The decline of Jordanian political parties: Myth or reality?', *International Journal of Middle East Studies*, 33(4), p545–569.

Lust-Okar, E. (2005) *Structuring conflict in the Arab World: Incumbents, opponents, and institutions*. Cambridge: Cambridge University Press.

Lust-Okar, E. (2006) 'Elections under authoritarianism: Preliminary lessons from Jordan' Jordan', *Democratization*, 13(3), p456–471.

Masoud, T. (2014) *Counting Islam: Religion, class, and elections in Egypt*. Cambridge: Cambridge University Press.

Ottaway, M. and Hamzawy, A. (2009) 'Fighting on two fronts: Secular parties in the Arab World', in Ottaway, M. and Hamzawy, A. (eds.) *Getting to pluralism: Political actors in the Arab World*. Washington, DC: Carnegie Endowment for International Peace, pp. 41–68.

Ozen, H. (2017) 'Egypt's s 2011–2012 parliamentary elections: Voting for religious vs. Secular democracy?', *Mediterranean Politics*, 23(4), p1–26.

Ozzano, L. (2013) 'The many faces of the political god: A typology of religiously oriented parties', *Democratization*, 20(5), p807–830.

Resende, M. and Kraetzschmar, H. (2005) 'Parties of power as roadblocks to democracy: The cases of Ukraine and Egypt', *CEPS Policy Brief*, (81). Brussels: Centre for European Policy Studies.

Resta, V. (2018) 'Leftist parties in the Arab region before and after the Arab uprisings: Unrequited love?', in Cavatorta, F. and Storm, L. (eds.) *Political parties in the Arab World: Continuity and change*. Edinburgh: Edinburgh University Press, pp. 23–48.

Resta, V. (2019) 'The effect of electoral autocracy in Egypt's failed transition: a party politics perspective', *Italian Political Science Review*, 49(2), p157–173.

Salem, P. (1994) *Bitter Legacy: Ideology and politics in the Arab World*. Syracuse: Syracuse University Press.

Sassoon, J. (2017) 'Party and governance in the Arab republics', *British Journal of Middle Eastern Studies*, 44(2), p227–239.

Schedler, A. (ed.) (2006) *Electoral authoritarianism: The dynamics of unfree competition*. Boulder: Lynne Rienner.

Schwedler, J. (2006) *Faith in moderation: Islamist parties in Jordan and Yemen*. Cambridge: Cambridge University Press.

Schwedler, J. (2007) 'Democratization, inclusion and the moderation of Islamist parties', *Development*, 50(1), p56–61.

Shahin, E. (2010) 'Political parties in Egypt: Alive, but not kicking', in Ibrahim, S. and Lawson, K. (eds.) *Political parties and democracy. Volume V: The Arab World*. Westport: Praeger, pp. 3–26.

Storm, L. (2014) *Party politics and prospects for democracy in North Africa*. Boulder: Lynne Rienner Publishers.

Szmolka, I. (2020) 'Liberal-secular parties in Arab political systems', in Cavatorta, F., Storm, L. and Resta, V. (eds.) *Routledge handbook on political parties in the Middle East and North Africa*. London: Routledge, pp. 69–82.

Tepe, S. (2013) 'The perils of polarization and religious parties: The democratic challenges of political fragmentation in Israel and Turkey', *Democratization*, 20(5), p831–856.

Tessler, M. (2011) *Public opinion in the Middle East: Survey research and the political orientations of ordinary citizens*. Bloomington: Indiana University Press.

Thurber, C. (2014) 'Militias as sociopolitical movements: Lessons from Iraq's armed Shia groups', *Small Wars & Insurgencies*, 25(5–6), pp. 900–923.

Utvik, B. (2014) The Ikhwanization of the Salafis: Piety in the politics of Egypt and Kuwait. *Middle East Critique*, 23(1), p5–27.

Valbjørn, M. (2015) 'Reflections on self-reflections – On framing the analytical implications of the Arab uprisings for the study of Arab politics', *Democratization*, 22(2), p218–238.

Valbjørn, M. and Bank, A. (2010) 'Examining the 'post' in post-democratization: The future of Middle Eastern political rule through lenses of the past', *Middle East Critique*, 19(3), p183–200.

Wegner, E. and Cavatorta, F. (2019) 'Revisiting the Islamist – Secular divide: Parties and voters in the Arab world', *International Political Science Review*, 40(4), p558–575.

Yamao, D. (2012) 'Sectarianism twisted: Changing cleavages in the elections of post-war Iraq', *Arab Studies Quarterly*, 34(1), p27–51.

Yardımcı-Geyikçi, Ş. (2015) 'Party institutionalization and democratic consolidation: Turkey and Southern Europe in comparative perspective', *Party Politics*, 21(4), p527–538.

37
POLITICAL PARTIES IN INDIA

Indrajit Roy and *Maya Tudor*

India is often lauded as the world's largest democracy. Among the few consolidated democracies in the developing world, national and provincial elections have been held regularly since 1952, keenly contested by a myriad of political parties that are the key to India's democratic identity. Analysing political parties in India, this chapter first outlines the state of play on the study of political parties followed by assessing key elements of India's electoral system within which the country's political parties operate. A focus on the electoral system allows us to analyse how political parties have competed against each other to gain power. Although the formal rules governing the electoral system have remained the same since India's adoption of a republican constitution in 1950, the substantive contests and outcomes have changed quite significantly. We then reflect on the ideological dimension of political parties in India, challenging oft-repeated claims that party politics in the country is non-ideological. We conclude by reflecting on emerging areas of promising research.

Research on political parties in India: the state of play

Although the scholarship on political parties in India has tended to develop autonomously of the Eurocentric literature, keen observers can easily identify the resonances between the two literatures. One strand explores the importance of social cleavages to the dominance, decline and emergence of political parties. Another highlights the importance of formal party organisation. A third strand emphasises the systemic properties of the parliamentary institutions governed by the first-past-the-post (FPTP) procedure of candidate selection.

Scholars focusing on the growing politicisation of social cleavages illustrate the ways in which regional groups, caste and ethnic communities, and social classes aim to assert their presence in the political arena. Such assertions led them to challenge the dominance of the Indian National Congress (INC) for its neglect of growing aspirations of these groups. Several factors explain the general decline of the INC's dominance and the emergence of rival political parties, including its insensitivity towards concerns vis-à-vis demands for political autonomy and economic development of the country's disparate regions (Manor 2000); the party's unwillingness to accommodate the demands of peasants (Brass 2012), especially from communities stigmatised as 'low caste' (Frankel 1978; Yadav 1999) as well as Dalits, historically oppressed as 'untouchable' (Chandra 2004; Pai 2002); and its inability to meet the aspirations of the burgeoning middle classes (Sridharan 2014). Furthermore, scholars who stress the importance of organisation and functioning of parties as machines to retain and expand their voter base also highlight the growing centralisation within the INC. According to Kohli (1990) such centralisation led to a 'crisis of governability' so that the INC was unable to retain, much less expand, its social base. Traditional voters felt their voices were no longer heeded. Newly ascendant social groups also felt marginalised. Disillusioned, these voters turned to alternative political parties (e.g. Kohli 1990).

Finally, scholars highlighting the systemic properties of India's FPTP electoral procedure within the context of a federal polity, emphasise its inclination towards a two-party system (Duverger 1964). For instance, Sridharan (2014) draws on the insight that the FPTP system produces an imperative to coalesce around a principal rival party that would have a realistic chance of winning against a dominant party. In India, Duverger's Law applies at the constituency level: in a federal system, parties compete to form the government at both national and state levels. As Indian states are linguistic and cultural entities, the consolidation of two-party systems at that level often results in multiple bipolarities made up of different parties in different states nationwide.

Not all studies of Indian political parties fall neatly within one of the aforementioned strands. Early scholars tended to focus on the fortunes of the INC, the party that steered India to Independence in 1947, took power from the departing British colonisers and ruled the country continuously for the first three decades of its post-colonial history (Kothari 1964). With the benefit of hindsight, later scholars have focused on the subsequent decline of the INC, and the emergence of new political parties including the Bharatiya Janata Party (BJP), which currently rules India (e.g. Yadav 1999; Yadav and Palshikar 2003; Chhiber and Verma 2019). Second, the social foundations of the different political parties and their implications for the representation of India's myriad ethnicities in the country's parliament have also been a subject of some attention (e.g. Bailey 1970; Hansen 2001; Jaffrelot 2002; Michelutti 2008). A third area of enquiry has been to highlight the strategies through which political parties recruit and retain support, especially focusing on patronage (Chandra 2004), targeted welfare and vote buying (Heath and Tillin 2017). Partially in response to the last strand, a new promising area of enquiry examines the role of ideology among Indian political parties (e.g. Chhiber and Verma 2019).

India's three party systems

Notwithstanding these diverse perspectives, observers concur that at least three party systems mark post-colonial politics in India (Yadav 1999; Yadav and Palshikar 2003), with some debate on whether a fourth system was inaugurated with Narendra Modi's ascendance to power in 2014 (Vaishnav and Hinston 2019). Therefore, for the purpose of this chapter, we organise the discussion of political parties in India through a discussion of the transforming party system in India since the inaugural 1952 elections. India's party and electoral systems have remained largely unchanged since its first elections held under universal suffrage in 1952 after which India committed to a multi-party democracy in its 1950 republican constitution. It adopted the first-past-the-post procedure to elect candidates in single-member districts who represent their constituencies in the 543-member Lok Sabha, India's lower house of Parliament. Although this procedure has remained unchanged, the contests and outcomes underlying this procedure have transformed substantively.

The first system refers to what was called the Congress system, the era during which the INC dominated Indian politics and lasted from 1952 to 1967. The second system refers to the period of growing opposition to INC from the States: elections became a plebiscite on the INC. In this vein, we refer to this period as the plebiscitary system, which lasted from 1967 to 1989. The third system refers to the dawn of the Coalition system, which ushered in the era of coalition politics.

Coalitions between political parties – forged either prior to or after elections – were indispensable to the formation of governments, both at the centre and in the States. Explanations for the emergence of these systems have tended to map onto three thematic clusters. The first, and most prevalent, centres on the growing politicisation of social cleavages. The second focuses on the importance of the organisation and functioning of political parties as machines to retain and expand their voter base while the third emphasises the systemic properties of the electoral system operating in a federal polity. The following section discusses these in turn, distinguishing each of India's three party systems from 1952 until 2014, when the Narendra Modi-led BJP took power in Delhi. Developments after 2014 will be discussed in the following section.

The fortunes of Congress dominance

The INC dominated national politics between 1952 and 1989. Except for a brief period between 1977 and 1979 of rule by the Janata coalition, stitched together against the imposition of the Emergency, the INC held sway in New Delhi without interruption until 1989, after which its dominance crumbled. Even though it came back to power in 2004, the INC now led a multi-party United Progressive Alliance (UPA) coalition and was constrained to act within its framework. In the states, however, as discussed earlier, the party's fortunes have waxed and waned since the 1960s.

Under the Congress system, the INC dominated national and state-level politics. Despite facing an array of opposition parties, the party's vote shares remained above 45 per cent in the parliamentary elections. India's first-past-the-post procedure ensured that the INC converted these vote shares into thumping majorities in the Lok Sabha. Elections to the national parliament and state assemblies were often held simultaneously, allowing the INC to dominate the latter. However, it did face challenges from regional political parties in Kerala (Communist Party of India) and Jammu and Kashmir (National Conference).

The plebiscitary system saw a diminished significance for the INC in the states despite it continuing to be the pole around which politics revolved. Although continuing to exceed 40 per cent of the vote share in national elections, its fortunes waned in the states. The number of states with INC Chief Ministers dropped from 25 to 16 in the 1967 parliamentary elections. In 1977, the party was routed in the parliamentary elections called by Prime Minister Indira Gandhi in the wake of the Emergency: it barely controlled five states in 1978. Although party fortunes were reinvigorated in 1980, its control over state assemblies became ever more tenuous.

The INC's fortunes waned further under the coalition system that was inaugurated in 1989. Its vote share began to steadily decline to around 30 per cent throughout this period. Losing power once again at the centre, it was relegated to the margins of politics in several states: for example, it became irrelevant to politics in Tamil Nadu and Uttar Pradesh, and relevant only as a junior coalition partner in Bihar. Although the period also saw the gradual ascendance of the BJP, it was state-level parties that shaped the direction of national politics. A coalition of state-level parties ran two short-lived governments between 1996 and 1998, while governments led by both the INC (1991–1996 and 2004–2014) and the BJP (1998–1999 and 1999–2004) relied on state parties for support.

Political fragmentation

As the INC lost its dominance of Indian politics, the number of political parties contesting elections increased. During the first general election held in 1952, 55 parties fielded at least one candidate. By 1989, 117 parties had entered the fray, rising to 370 in the 2009 elections.

Regional and caste-based parties proliferated, reflecting popular disenchantment with the INC. As coalition governments became central to government-formation in Delhi, politicians were incentivised to form new political parties that could potentially emerge as 'king-makers' in Delhi.

INC domination under the first electoral system meant that no more than 20 parties were actually represented in the Lok Sabha until 1967. During the plebiscitary system the number of parties fluctuated from almost 25 in 1971 to under 20 in 1984. After 1989, however, the number of parties with at least one MP proliferated, peaking at 40 in 1998, when the BJP first came to power in Delhi at the head of a 13-party coalition.

A calculation of the *effective* number of political parties undertaken by Vaishnav and Hinston (2017), which weighs parties by the number of votes or seats they earn, suggests a similar, but slightly less dramatic, pattern. The effective number of parties only marginally increased from 1962 to 1967 but *declined* under the second electoral system, before registering a marked increase only after 1989, while remaining below eight under both metrics.

A granular analysis of the political contests cautions against interpreting the increased number of parties as signalling political fragmentation during the third electoral system. Indeed, Yadav (1999) notes that the number of effective political parties at the state or constituency level would suggest a bipolar competition. Duverger's law appeared to operate in India even under the third electoral system, with the twist that it operated as such at the state-level. Rather than producing a simple bipolarity, the electoral procedure resulted in 'multiple bipolarities' in the Indian context during this period.

Political competition

Political competition fluctuated over the three successive electoral systems. An analysis of the margin of victory – the difference in the vote share of the winner and the runner-up – across parliamentary constituencies in general elections shows it ranging from just under 15 per cent in 1962 to over 25 per cent in 1977, before tapering down after 1989 to less than 10 per cent in 2009.

Another way of reflecting on political competition is to examine the vote share of the winning candidate. The average vote share of the winning candidate rose from just under 50 per cent at the end of the first electoral system, to higher than 50 per cent, irrespective of the political party in question, throughout the second period (exceeding 60 per cent during the anti-Congress wave of 1977), before returning below 50 per cent during most of the third electoral system, with a historical low of 44 per cent in 2009.

Federalisation

The electoral patterns across the three electoral systems signalled strengthening federalisation of national elections. Under the Congress system, the INC's dominance was shaped by Jawaharlal Nehru's personal popularity. Although, as we shall show later, votes for the INC were often mediated by village-level 'big men' and the party bosses in the states, national elections were essentially national affairs. The trend was strengthened under the second electoral system when elections became a plebiscite on the INC, especially the persona of Mrs Gandhi.

By contrast, elections were considerably more federalised under the coalition system. National election verdicts were 'derivative' (Yadav and Palshikar 2003) of choices made in the politics of Indian states. Indeed, national verdicts resembled an aggregation of state-level verdicts. National-level political competition in each state reflected the dynamics associated with that state's politics. National elections were indeed influenced by state-level political calendars (Ravishankar 2009). The degree of political participation in Lok Sabha elections largely mirrored participation in state-level politics, although lagging the latter. The performance of state governments was an important determinant of voter behaviour in national elections. Thus, national political choices did not 'duplicate' choices made in the states; rather they were *derivative*.

The social foundation of the three party systems

A salient aspect of post-colonial politics in India has been the politicisation of caste. Caste may be understood as the ranked ethnicities that structure socio-economic life in the country. While the dynamic of 'purity' and 'pollution' associated with caste assumes enormous ritual significance among the country's Hindu majority, members of other religious communities have assimilated several of its features. Following sociologists and anthropologists, political scientists studying India are careful to distinguish between the categories of *varna* and *jati*. *Varna* refers to the umbrella social categories referenced in the canonical literature while *jati* is used to describe the multitude of discrete social groups that reside within each category. Thus, *varna* refers broadly to categories such as the self-styled 'high castes' (Savarnas), the castes stigmatised as 'low castes' (Shudra in the ritual literature and Other Backward Classes in official parlance) and castes discriminated against as 'untouchable' (Dalit in activist circles and Scheduled Castes in official parlance). *Jati*, by contrast, refers to the thousands of specific groups that constitute each of these broad clusters.

Under the Congress system, electoral politics was mobilised along *jati* lines. INC party bosses and village-level 'big men', who were overwhelmingly from 'high caste' backgrounds, mobilised key *jati* leaders in favour of the INC. Despite its electoral dominance, the INC was riven with factions, as politicians of different *jatis* competed for office and official patronage. Much of the factionalism was between leaders of the 'high-caste' *jatis* who, despite their mutual rivalries, aligned with each other to keep out members of *jatis* from among the so-called 'low caste' and 'untouchable' communities.

Jati-level identities retained their importance under the plebiscitary system. However, the growing political awareness among members of the numerically dominant 'low caste' groups meant their demands could no longer be ignored. Modest land reforms, technological advances in agriculture and the crumbling social legitimacy of 'high-caste' landed groups contributed to the emergence of leaders from 'low caste' *jatis* whose political ambitions were frustrated by the 'high-caste' dominance within the INC. The regional and socialist parties that emerged in opposition to the INC crafted alliances between individual *jatis* across the broad *varna* clusters to mobilise electoral support. However, discrimination against 'low castes' and 'untouchables' remained, resulting in their continued exclusion from political office.

Matters came to a head when the government-appointed Mandal Commission recommended protective discrimination for Other Backward Classes (OBCs) that would 'reserve' positions for them in the civil services and higher education. The 'high castes' protested violently against the recommendations. Stunned by their visceral reaction, 'low caste' politicians realised the need to forge cross-*jati* alliances among themselves, lending a new political salience to the OBC cluster. Dalit politicians also realised the need to forge cross-jati alliances across castes discriminated as 'untouchable'. The categories of OBC and Dalit now assumed significance as meaningful categories that could structure social and political life in India under the coalition system. North India's socialist parties reoriented themselves towards espousing the cause of the region's 'low caste' groups. Southern India's regional parties also endorsed 'low caste' demands for protective discrimination: Tamil Nadu's AIADMK party blazed a trail in 1993 by becoming the first political party in power to offer 69 per cent 'reservation' to OBCs in public sector employment and admission to universities in that state. The explicit association of political parties with caste cleavages was a defining feature of India's coalition system.

India under Modi: the dawn of a fourth party system?

Narendra Modi's election in 2014 as India's 14th Prime Minister sparked debate as to whether Indian politics was once again experiencing a paradigm shift. Under Modi, the BJP claimed the first single-party majority in 30 years: the party's victory prompted discussions as to whether India had now left the era of 'multipolarity' and 'fragmentation' that had marked the Coalition system. Some scholars downplayed the magnitude of the 2014 electoral verdict (Heath 2015; Diwakar 2017; Ziegfeld 2020), while others emphasised its heralding a new electoral system (Chhibber and Verma 2019; Sridharan 2014). Following Modi's re-election in 2019 with an even stronger majority, political analysts became convinced that India had indeed entered a new electoral and political system, one defined by the BJP (Chhibber and Verma 2019).

The BJP's electoral supremacy, combined with its legislative dominance across India and her states, suggests a return to the unipolarity that was the hallmark of the Congress system. Although the 37 per cent vote share it won in the 2019 elections fell short of the magnitude of support enjoyed by the INC under the Congress system, there can be little doubt that the BJP has now emerged as the pole around which Indian politics rotates. Support for the BJP increased in eastern and southern India during the 2019 elections, suggesting that the party's footprint across the country was on the rise. Beyond geography, the BJP also expanded its support across Hindu caste groups.

Although, on the face of it, political fragmentation continues (36 parties were represented in the Indian Parliament in 2019), the effective number of parties (ENP) is now much reduced. Based on votes, the ENP in 2019 stood at 5.1, much lower than the eight under the Coalition system. The drop is even more dramatic when considering the ENP based on seats: under the Coalition system, it stood at 6.5, dropping to three by 2019.

India's fourth party system has also witnessed a weakening federalisation of national elections. Specifically, the balance of power between national and regional parties has shifted. Under the third party system, the two national parties between them garnered 50 per cent of the vote share, whereas the plethora of regional parties gained the rest, peaking at 52 per cent in 2009. Since 2014, the vote share of the regional parties has reduced to 43 per cent, whereas the combined vote share of the BJP and the Congress has increased to 57 per cent, suggesting that regional parties with federalising commitments may be losing ground in the country's political landscape.

Finally, the social foundations of the fourth party system appear to have shifted. Whereas the Coalition system was defined by the electoral mobilisation of voters under the rubric of such broad caste clusters as 'OBCs' and 'Dalits', the fourth party system has witnessed a reconfiguration. *Jati*-level alliances across caste clusters have regained prominence, as under the plebiscitary system, so that political parties are increasingly identified with *jati* alliances rather than caste cleavages.

The ideological dimensions of a changing party system in India

The changing party systems in India are entwined with transforming ideological configurations among the country's political parties. Drawing on Yadav's (1999) insights, Chibber and Verma (2018) emphasise the ideological origins of these transformations. They specifically direct attention to the manner in which ideological divisions between the 'politics of redistribution' (what they call 'politics of statism') and the 'politics of recognition' have shaped India's changing party system. Following their lead, we offer here a stylised presentation of the four party systems in India and their ideological contours.

The ideological conflicts around the 'politics of redistribution' and the 'politics of recognition' depart from the four axes of cleavage often presented for Western Europe. The politics of redistribution refers to debates on the extent to which the state should dominate society, regulate social norms and redistribute private property (Fraser 2008). The politics of recognition refers to debates on the ways in which the state should accommodate the needs of marginalised groups and protect minority rights from majoritarian dominance (Honneth 1992). By outlining the parameters of the ideological spaces across the four party systems, Chhibber and Verma challenge the dominant view that party politics and elections in India are far removed from the world of ideas (Kothari 1964; Rudolph and Rudolph 1987; Yadav and Palshikar 2003; Chandra 2004; de Souza and Sridharan 2006; Suri 2013; Thachil 2014).

The ideological divides along the politics of redistribution and the politics of recognition have underpinned party politics, and attendant imaginations of the role of the state, since Independence. According to Khilnani (1997, 41),

> the state was enlarged, its ambitions inflated, and it was transformed from a distant alien object into one that aspired to infiltrate the everyday life of Indians, proclaiming itself responsible for everything they could desire: jobs, ration cards, educational places, security, cultural recognition.

Under the Congress system, the INC favoured a limited politics of redistribution but espoused a politics of recognition vis-à-vis Dalits and Adivasis, among the oppressed sections of Indian society. Opposition to the INC's centrism came from parties that favoured greater redistribution (the communists), greater recognition (the socialists) and less of both (Hindu conservatives). Under the plebiscitary system, the INC espoused greater politics of redistribution but limited its politics of recognition to Dalits and Adivasis instead of recognising such demands for recognition among communities stigmatised as 'lower castes': this demand was now espoused by the socialists who delinked the politics of redistribution from the politics of recognition. Under the coalition system, the INC lost ground to regional and socialist parties who favoured recognition for the Backward Castes but maintained its politics of redistribution. The fourth party system led to the consolidation of forces opposed to the politics of both redistribution and recognition.

The changing politics of redistribution

Debates over the politics of redistribution loomed large during the Congress system. These debates were triggered by the INC's commitment to establish a socialist pattern of society. On its watch, the new state promised to implement land reforms that would restructure hierarchical relations of property and power in the countryside. In practice, however, success was limited, in part due to the state's inability and unwillingness to confront rural elites. The state was arguably more successful in its interventions in industrial policy: it invested in heavy industries, implemented import substitution industrialisation and oversaw the production of goods, issued licences to favoured businesses and controlled prices. While not strictly redistributive, state control over business was clearly established during the first party system.

The emergence of the plebiscitary system witnessed a more activist politics of redistribution. As Prime Minister Gandhi purged the INC of its conservative elements, she enhanced the rhetoric as well as practice of redistribution. Banks and insurance companies were nationalised. Privy purses for 600-odd princes (rulers of native States that had acceded to the Indian Union upon Independence in exchange for monthly payments in perpetuity from the exchequer) were abolished. The resultant access to public savings allowed the state to introduce numerous poverty alleviation schemes, leading to direct transfers from the state to the poor. Statist controls over the economy were tightened. Foreign investments – direct and institutional – were discouraged. Although property relations remained untouched, and state subsidies to middle-class households far exceeded sums spent on poverty-alleviation schemes, Gandhi's political sloganeering of *garibi hatao* (eliminate poverty) conveyed a heightened avowal of a politics of redistribution by the Indian state.

Under the coalition system, India's economy underwent a substantial liberalisation from the statist controls introduced during the plebiscitary system. Privatisation of sectors under statist control was pursued, although significant sectors of the economy – such as the Railways – continued to be run by the public sector. Foreign investments were welcomed. Although the state continued to operate massive social welfare programmes, including the sprawling Mahatma Gandhi National Rural Employment Guarantee Act (NREGA), it aggressively promoted itself and the country as business friendly. However, statist controls remained extensive (though considerably diluted compared to the previous period), leading to corruption and rent-seeking, which alienated the proliferating middle class (Chhibber and Verma 2019). Due to economic reforms, a growing number of Indians no longer relied on the state. As a consequence, they resented its continued influence in the economy, viewing it as a hindrance rather than facilitator of their own aspirations. Thus, even as political parties diluted their commitment to the politics of redistribution under the coalition system, emerging middle classes became increasingly disgruntled with whatever remnants of such policy existed.

The changing politics of recognition

The Congress system also witnessed debates over the politics of recognition. Upon Independence, the Constitution guaranteed protective discrimination for members of communities historically oppressed as 'untouchable' (Scheduled Castes, approximately 16 per cent of the population) and 'primitive' (Scheduled Tribes, approximately 8 per cent of the population). However, the INC was less enthusiastic about similar protections for OBCs, who constitute between 36 per cent and 52 per cent of the Indian population: the report of a commission constituted by its own government was ignored. Implementing protective discrimination for the OBCs quickly became a rallying point for the socialist opposition to the INC.

The demand for protective discrimination for OBCs became the defining feature of the politics of recognition under the plebiscitary system. That power and privilege were being monopolised by the Hindu 'upper castes' irked politicians of OBC origin across political parties. The youth wing of the socialist parties attracted many politicians who went on to fashion the politics of recognition in subsequent decades. At the same time, the INC – despite promising an activist politics of redistribution – distanced itself from any political recognition. The short-lived Janata coalition, which had routed the INC in the wake of the Emergency, appointed a second Backward Classes commission, the Mandal Commission, to look into the feasibility of protective discrimination for the OBCs. When the INC returned to power in 1980, it refused to touch the recommendations of the Commission despite the overwhelming majority it enjoyed in Parliament.

The politics of recognition came of age under the coalition system. The Janata Dal-led coalition government which succeeded the INC attempted to implement the recommendations of the Mandal Commission for protective discrimination of OBCs. The visceral reaction from upper castes, and the relative apathy of the INC, stunned the OBCs. They now consolidated behind socialist parties in northern India and regional parties elsewhere, rallying around broader demands for social justice. The rising pitch for Hindu nationalism by the BJP attracted upper castes away from the INC. The twin pressures from parties advocating social justice and those advancing the agenda of Hindu nationalism sealed the fate of the INC as India's predominant political force. Although it returned to power in 2004, it did so as part of a coalition which now included the socialist, communist and regional parties that had contributed to the diminution of its power. These parties perceived the BJP's politics of Hindu nationalism to be a fatal ideological threat to the politics of redistribution espoused by the INC and its communist allies and the politics of recognition anchored in social justice advocated by the socialists and regional parties.

Conclusions and avenues for further research

Despite enduring as a democracy for most of its post-colonial history, political parties in India have been weak relative to Eurocentric dimensions of party organisation, namely institutions and infrastructure (Duverger 1964; Mainwaring and Scully 1995; Tavits 2013). Institutionally, most parties tend to be highly centralised and autocratically run entities (Hansen 2001; Chandra 2004; Wyatt 2009) in which transparent rules for candidate selection and intra-party promotions tend to be rare (Farooqui and Sridharan 2014). Party infrastructures appear to be quite hollow at least at local levels (Erdman 1967; Kashyap 1970; Kamath 1985; Kohli 1990), although the BJP is clearly an exception (Andersen, Walter and Damle 1987; Graham 1990). Nevertheless, a promising new area of research reiterates and refocuses the role of party organisation (Tudor and Ziegfeld 2019). The scholarship in this vein promises to challenge the widespread tendency to neglect the role of party organisation in India (Chibber, Jensenius and Suryanarayan 2014).

Indeed, much emerging literature has thrown up results that are rather surprising, given the weak party organisation in India. Observers have noted the massive mobilisation of human and financial capital by political parties who have launched vigorous campaigns that often require troops of volunteers on the ground (Banerjee 2014; Björkman 2014; Palshikar, Kumar and Lodha 2017). Others have highlighted the effective ways in which political parties and their representatives mediate between the Indian state and the populations inhabiting its jurisdiction. Voters turn to their elected representatives, and the parties to which they belong, for support in navigating the bureaucracy (Corbridge et al. 2005; Berenschot 2010; Dunning and Nilekani 2013; Kruks-Wisner 2018; Roy 2018; Sircar 2018; Bussell 2019; Auerbach 2020; Roy forthcoming). This emerging literature on 'political parties-as-network' rather than 'political parties-as-organisation' (Auerbach et al. 2021) opens up promising new avenues for further research.

A third emerging area of research outlines the ideational dimension of party politics. Extending, the ideological moorings of political parties noted earlier (Chibber and Verma 2019), this literature highlights the ideas, however inchoate, that motivate voters to support specific political parties and commit to it (Michelutti 2008; Heath, Verniers and Kumar 2015; Chauchard 2016; Vaishnav 2017; Ahuja 2019; Roy 2020). Against widespread assumptions that 'Indians vote by their caste rather than cast their vote', new research highlights the role of social class in shaping support for political parties (Thachil 2014; Anderson, Francois and Kotwal 2015; Huber and Suryanarayan 2016; Power and Ready 2018; Suryanarayan 2019; Roy, forthcoming).

The new directions in the study of political parties in India are encouraging. They not only shed greater light on the complexity of Indian politics but also enrich the broader study of politics in times of economic precarity, social implosion and dilution of formal party institutions. These insights suggest exciting insights for the study of comparative politics in our uncertain times.

References

Ahuja, A. (2019) *Mobilizing the marginalized: Ethnic parties without ethnic movements*. New York: Oxford University Press.
Andersen, W.K. and Damle, S.D. (1987) *The Brotherhood in Saffron: The Rashtriya Swayamsevak Sangh and Hindu Revivalism*. Boulder: Westview Press.
Anderson, S., Francois, P. and Kotwal, A. (2015) 'Clientelism in Indian villages', *American Economic Review*, 105(6), p1780–1816.
Auerbach, A.M. (2020) 'Demanding development: The politics of public goods provision in India's urban slums', in *Cambridge studies in comparative politics*. New York: Cambridge University Press.
Auerbach, A.M., Bussell, J., Chauchard, S., Francesca, R.J., Nellis, G., Schneider, M., Neelanjan, S., Suryanarayan, P., Thachil, T., Vaishnav, M., Verma, R. and Ziegfeld, A. (2021) Rethinking the study of electoral politics in the developing world: Reflections on the Indian case. *Perspectives on Politics*, p1–15.
Bailey, F.G. (1970) *Politics and social change: Orissa in 1959*. Berkeley: University of California Press.
Banerjee, M. (2014) *Why India votes?* London: Routledge.
Berenschot, W. (2010) 'Everyday mediation: The politics of public service delivery in Gujarat, India', *Development and Change*, 45(1), p883–905.
Björkman, L. (2014) "You Can't buy a vote': Meanings of money in a Mumbai election', *American Ethnologist*, 41(4), p617–634.
Brass, P. (2012) *An Indian political life: Charan Singh and congress politics*. Delhi, London and Thousand Oaks: Sage Publications.
Bussell, J. (2019) *Clients and constituents: Political responsiveness in patronage democracies*. New York: Oxford University Press.
Chandra, K. (2004) *Why ethnic parties succeed: Patronage and ethnic head counts in India*. New York: Cambridge University Press.
Chauchard, S. (2016) 'Unpacking ethnic preferences: Theory and micro-level evidence from North India', *Comparative Political Studies*, 49(2), p253–284.
Chhibber, P. and Verma, R. (2019) *Ideology and identity: The changing party systems of India*. New Delhi: Oxford University Press.
Chibber, P., Jensenius, F. and Suryanarayan, P. (2014) 'Party organization and party proliferation in India', *Party Politics*, 20(4), p489–505.
Corbridge, S., Williams, G., Srivastava, M. and Veron, R. (2005) *Seeing the state: Governance and governmentality in eastern India*. New York: Cambridge University Press.
de Souza., P.R. and Sridharan, E. (2006) 'Introduction: The Evolution of political parties in India', in Ronald de Souza, P. and Sridharan, E. (eds.) *India's political parties*. New Delhi: Sage Publications, pp. 15–34.
Diwakar, R. (2017) 'Change and continuity in Indian politics and the Indian party system: Revisiting the results of the 2014 Indian General Election', *Asian Journal of Comparative Politics*, 2(4), p327–346.
Dunning, T. and Nilekani, J. (2013) 'Ethnic quotas and political mobilization: Caste, parties, and distribution in Indian village councils', *American Political Science Review*, 107(1), p35–56.
Duverger, M. (1964) *Political parties: Their organization and activity in the modern state*. London: Methuen.
Erdman, H.L. (1967) *The Swatantra party and Indian conservatism*. London: Cambridge University Press.
Farooqui, A. and Sridharan, E. (2014) 'Incumbency, internal processes and renomination in Indian parties', *Commonwealth & Comparative Politics*, 52(1), p78–108.
Frankel, F. (1978) *India's political economy, 1947–1977*. Princeton: Princeton University Press.
Fraser, N. (2008) *The scales of justice*. Oxford: Polity.
Graham, B. (1990) *Hindu nationalism and Indian politics: The origins and development of the Bharatiya Jana Sangh*. Cambridge: Cambridge University Press.
Hansen, T.B. (2001) *Wages of violence: Naming and identity in postcolonial Bombay*. Princeton, NJ: Princeton University Press.
Heath, O. (2015) 'The BJP's return to power: Mobilisation, conversion and vote swing in the 2014 Indian elections', *Contemporary South Asia* 23(2), p123–35.
Heath, O. and Tillin, L. (2017) 'Institutional performance and vote-buying in India.' *Studies in Comparative International Development*, 53, p90–110.
Heath, O., Verniers, G. and Kumar, S. (2015) 'Do Muslim voters prefer Muslim candidates? Co-religiosity and voting behaviour in India', *Electoral Studies*, 38(6), p10–18.
Honneth, A. (1992) *The struggle for recognition: The moral grammar of social conflicts*. Cambridge: MIT Press.

Huber, J.D. and Suryanarayan, P. (2016) 'Ethnic inequality and the ethnification of political parties', *World Politics*, 68(1), p149–188.
Jaffrelot, C. (2002) *India's silent revolution: The rise of lower castes in north India*. London: Hurst & Co.
Kamath, P.M. (1985) 'Politics of defection in India in the 1980s', *Asian Survey*, 25(10) p1039–1054.
Kashyap, S.C. (1970) 'The politics of defection: The changing contours of the political power structure in state politics in India', *Asian Survey*, 10(3), p195–208.
Khilnani, S. (1997) *The idea of India*. London: Penguin.
Kohli, A. (1990) *Democracy and discontent: India's growing crisis of governability*. New York: Cambridge University Press.
Kothari, R. (1964) 'The congress "system" in India.' *Asian Survey*, 4(12), p1161–1173.
Kruks-Wisner, G. (2018) *Claiming the state: Active citizenship and social welfare in rural India*. New York: Cambridge University Press.
Mainwaring, S. and Scully, Y. (1995) *Building democratic institutions: Party systems in Latin America*. Stanford, CA: Stanford University Press.
Manor, J. (2000) 'Small-time fixers in India's States.' *Asian Survey*, 40(5), 816–35.
Michelutti, L. (2008) *The vernacularisation of democracy: Politics, caste, and religion in India*. New Delhi: Routledge.
Pai, S. (2002) *Dalit assertion and the unfinished democratic revolution: The Bahujan Samaj Party in Uttar Pradesh*. Delhi, London and Thousand Oaks: Sage Publications.
Palshikar, S., Kumar, S. and Lodha, S. (2017) *Electoral politics in India: The resurgence of the Bharatiya Janata Party*. New York: Routledge.
Power, E.A. and Ready, E. (2018) 'Building bigness: Reputation, prominence, and social capital in rural South India', *American Anthropologist*, 120(3) p444–59.
Ravishankar, N. (2009) 'The cost of ruling: Anti-incumbency in Elections', *Economic and Political Weekly*, 44(10), p92–99.
Roy, I. (2018) *Politics of the poor: Negotiating democracy in contemporary India*. Cambridge: Cambridge University Press.
Roy, I. (2020) Dignified development: Democratic deepening in an Indian State. *Commonwealth and Comparative Politics*, 52(1) p2–28.
Roy, I. (forthcoming) 'The passionate politics of the Savarna poor' in Roy, I. (ed.) *Passionate politics: Democracy, development and India's 2019 General Elections*. Manchester: Manchester University Press.
Sircar, N. (2018) 'Money in elections: The role of personal wealth in election outcomes', in Kapur, D. and Vaishnav, M. (Eds.) *Cost of democracy: Political finance in India*. New Delhi: Oxford University Press, pp. 36–73.
Sridharan, E. (2014) 'India's watershed vote: Behind Modi's victory', *Journal of Democracy*, 25(4), p20–33.
Suri, K.C. (2013) 'Party system and party politics in India', in Suri, K.C. and Vanaik, A. (Eds.) *ICSSR research surveys and explorations: Political science, volume 2: Indian democracy*, New Delhi: Oxford University Press, pp. 209–252
Suryanarayan, P. (2019) 'When do the poor vote for the right wing and why: Status hierarchy and vote choice in the Indian States', *Comparative Political Studies*, 52(2), p209–245.
Tavits, M. (2013) *Post-communist democracies and party organization*. New York: Cambridge University Press.
Thachil, T. (2014) *Elite parties, poor voters: How social services win votes in India*. New York: Cambridge University Press.
Tudor, M. and Ziegfeld, A. (2019) Social cleavages, party organisation and the end of single-party dominance: Insights from India. *Comparative Politics*, 52(1), p149–188.
Vaishnav, M. (2017) 'Ethnic identifiability in India: Evidence from a voter survey', *Asian Survey*, 57(4), p738–763.
Vaishnav, M. and Jamie, H. (2019) *The dawn of India's fourth party system*. Washington, DC: Carnegie Endowment for International Peace.
Wyatt, A. (2009) *Party system change in South India: Political entrepreneurs, patterns and processes*. New York: Routledge.
Yadav, Y. (1999) 'Electoral parties in the time of change.' *Economic and Political Weekly*, 34(34–35), p2393–2399.
Yadav, Y. and Palshikar, S. (2003) 'From hegemony to convergence: Party system and electoral politics in the Indian States, 1952–2002', *Journal of the Indian School of Political Economy*, 15(1–2), p5–44.
Ziegfeld, A. (2020) A new dominant party in India? Putting the 2019 BJP victory into comparative and historical perspective, *India Review*, 19(2), p136–152.

PART 7

Methods for estimating party preferences

38
TEXT ANALYSIS OF PARTY MANIFESTOS

Daniela Braun

This chapter analyses the methodological approaches used in research on political parties for estimating parties' policy preferences.[1] Although many approaches are now available (see also Chapter 39 on voting advice applications, and Chapter 40 on expert surveys), the most established method, and one that has been used by scholars of party competition for a long time, consists of estimating party preferences through the text analysis of electoral programmes. This method analyses official party documents issued before a given election. These election manifestos are then coded according to a set of pre-existing guidelines by expert coders, thereby transforming the manifesto texts into data. The datasets, which are publicly available in most cases, can then be analysed by scholars of party politics to study various topics, including party policy positions and the salience of certain political issues.

Election manifestos are provided by political parties themselves and as such are an officially sanctioned and valuable source of information regarding political parties' points of view. In their manifestos, parties explain the policies that they ideally intend to enact when elected to parliament and entering government (Klingemann et al. 1994; Budge et al. 2001). Party manifestos are thus 'unique in being the only authoritative party policy statement approved by an official convention or congress' (Klingemann et al. 2006, 17); the documents represent the collective internal expression of the policy preferences of political parties. Therefore, we can act on the assumption that the content of election manifestos, and thus manifesto data, reflects the official preferences that a party assumes on specific issues (Braun and Schmitt 2020).

The analysis of party manifestos has a long history. Since Robertson's (1976) first analyses of the dynamics of party competition in the UK, the development of this field was mostly driven by the Manifesto Research on Political Representation (MARPOR) project, which continues the work of the Manifesto Research Group (MRG) and the Comparative Manifestos Project (CMP) (Budge et al. 2001; Klingemann et al. 2006; Volkens et al. 2013). The latter projects provide manifesto data on the national level. Since then, several projects have been developed for capturing party policy preferences for different electoral levels: the Euromanifestos (EM) project (Schmitt et al. 2018) for the supranational level, that is, the EU level of governance; sub-national manifesto projects at the regional (Alonso, Gómez and Cabeza 2013) and local (Gross and Jankowski 2020) levels; and projects examining manifestos from the past, such as the Habsburg Manifesto dataset (Howe et al. 2020). Even though the analysis of manifesto data has a long pedigree and has been extensively used by scholars from different academic backgrounds, its methods have also faced criticism, including the (manual) way of coding and measurements by means of positioning along the well-known left-right scale (Laver, Benoit and Garry 2003; Benoit, Laver and Mikhaylov 2009; Benoit et al. 2012; Däubler et al. 2012; Mikhaylov, Laver and Benoit 2012).

Against this backdrop, the aim of this chapter is twofold. First, it seeks to provide an overview of the process of manifesto data generation and the use of manifesto data. Second, it discusses the strengths and weaknesses of this approach. Accordingly, the remainder of the chapter is structured as follows: the following section describes the methodology of text analysis via party manifestos in detail, and the subsequent one offers some examples from the scholarly literature on the analysis of political parties' policy preferences via party manifesto data. The strengths and weaknesses of manifesto data are then summarised, followed by some insights on avenues for future manifesto research.

Methodology of text analysis of party manifestos

Although a number of manifesto projects have emerged to analyse different electoral levels, this chapter mainly focuses on the two most established and widely used data sources – the MARPOR and Euromanifestos (EM) projects. Both projects use a similar coding scheme and coding approach and thus offer a useful starting point for explaining the methodology of text analysis of party manifestos. The main differences lie in the fact that the MARPOR project gathers, codes and analyses parties' manifestos for national elections whereas the EM project does the same in the case of European elections, that is, the elections to the European Parliament (EP).

Data collection, the role of expert coders and reliability checks

How do we arrive from the text that is provided by political parties in their official party documents to empirical data which enables us to study political parties' preferences? To gain a firmer grip on this question, this chapter traces the entire coding procedure starting with the collection of party manifestos (for a more detailed description of each of the steps, see also Braun 2020).

The *collection* of relevant election manifestos is ideally carried out by country-based expert coders who have a deep knowledge of different party systems and their respective political parties. Initially, political parties were considered as relevant when they were represented in the national representative assembly or had coalition or blackmail potential in a given party system (Volkens 2001, 3). This criterion was adapted in subsequent project phases: in the case of national elections (MARPOR), relevant parties are defined as those parties that win seats in their respective election (Werner, Lacewell and Volkens 2014, 2) and, in the case of EP elections (the focus of the EM project), relevant parties 'are those that have been represented in the European Parliament at least once and did not stop being represented for at least two consecutive legislative periods' (Schmitt et al. 2018, 8).

Expert coders play an important role in terms of data collection with regard to the overall quality of data. High-quality coding is guaranteed by hiring native-language speakers as expert coders who are also deeply familiar with the political system and the background of the elections for which they are coding the manifestos. Moreover, the manifesto team trains expert coders in extensive workshops. The aim of these training sessions is to teach and discuss each of the coding steps and coding rules in order to ensure comparability of the overall coding procedure and reliability of the data: 'The training process has proven essential in ensuring a consistent understanding of the categories and coding scheme across countries and over time, and for an acceptable reliability of the coding process' (Lacewell and Werner 2013).

The *reliability* of the data is thus ensured through the training of coders. In addition, coders are supported by the project team if problems emerge in the process of coding (for more information on coders and coding instructions, see Werner, Lacewell and Volkens 2014; Schmitt et al. 2018). In addition to these basic requirements, the reliability of the data is further strengthened as coders undergo a series of training tests which are completed by a final official reliability test before they start coding. This reliability test involves the two main coding steps of a test manifesto: unitising and categorising (see section 'from text to data'). The result of this final coding exercise is then compared with a gold standard, that is, a master coding, to estimate the reliability of the coding exercise (for the model calculation of both inter-coder and intra-coder reliability measures in the case of the EM project, see Schmitt et al. 2018). Although more coders per manifesto would be desirable to enhance data quality, for reasons of costs and time, only one coder per manifesto is usually selected. However, the final coding result of each coder is systematically cross-checked before release of the data.

From text to data: the coding procedure

After collecting the election manifestos, the coding procedure starts with two different tasks. First, coders split the electoral programmes into statements or arguments, the so-called quasi-sentences (i.e. unitising). A quasi-sentence is different from a natural sentence as it only contains a single argument. Second, each of these quasi-sentences is then allocated to one particular coding category which is part of an extensive, pre-established coding scheme (i.e. categorising). In this way, the coding scheme and particular coding instructions become relevant. Although some of the coding instructions in the two manifesto projects have evolved over time to some degree, the basic coding scheme is still very much identical to the first versions of each of the coding schemes (Volkens 2001; Wüst and Volkens 2003). In the case of the MARPOR project, 56 coding categories are available, whereby each coding category captures the most relevant policy issues and goals which are subsumed within seven broader policy domains (Volkens et al. 2015). The EM project includes 69 coding categories within nine broader policy domains for three different electoral levels. Table 38.1 summarises the policy domains used to categorise the identified quasi-sentences at a most general level. In the case of the EM project, in addition to the general policy domain 'Political System', one additional domain has been generated for the particular case of EP elections: 'Political System of the European Union'. Moreover, the policy domain 'Economy' has been separated into two different policy domains, that is, 'Economic Structure' and 'Economic Policies and Goals' to simplify the coding task (see also Section 2.3).

Table 38.1 Policy domains in the MARPOR and EM coding schemes

MARPOR	EM
1 External Relations	1 External Relations
2 Freedom and Democracy	2 Freedom and Democracy
3 Political System	3 Political System (general)
	4 Political System of the European Union
4 Economy	5 Economic Structure
	6 Economic Policies and Goals
5 Welfare and Quality of Life	7 Welfare and Quality of Life
6 Fabric of Society	8 Fabric of Society
7 Social Groups	9 Social Groups

Table 38.2 Coding example (based on the Euromanifestos coding scheme)

Text (quasi-sentences)	Policy domain	Coding category	Evaluation	Level of governance
In the European Union, we will fight for clean air	Welfare and quality of life	Environmental Protection	positive	EU
guarantee the rights of employees	Social groups	Labour Groups	positive	EU
fight against corruption	Political system (in general)	Political Corruption	positive	EU
retain our cultural diversity	Fabric of society	Multiculturalism	positive	EU

Each of these broad policy domains consists of a number of more specific coding categories and in some cases sub-categories. Domain 2, 'Freedom and Democracy', for example, consists of the following categories: Freedom and Human Rights (with the sub-categories 'Freedom' and 'Human Rights'); Democracy (with the sub-categories 'Representative Democracy' and 'Direct Democracy'); and Constitutionalism. Coders need to consider both the broad policy domains and their subordinate coding categories while coding. Table 38.2 illustrates the coding process as carried out in the case of the EM coding scheme.[2]

After the text has been broken down into its quasi-sentences, an initial decision is made in view of the classification of the quasi-sentence with regard to the policy domain. After that, more specific steps of categorisation take place. Our first exemplary quasi-sentence 'In the European Union, we will fight for clean air' can be classified in the policy field 'Welfare and Quality of Life' and more specifically in the coding category 'Environmental Protection'. It is also a positive statement on the subject of environmental protection, which is why the evaluation is positive. In addition, Europe is specified as the political level since the text explicitly mentions the EU as a central actor in the field of environmental protection. The same procedure is then applied to each quasi-sentence: accordingly, 'guarantee the rights of employees' is classified into 'Social Groups'/'Labour Groups', etc.

Major advances, new approaches and technologies

Some major advances have taken place in the two manifesto projects under consideration as digital technologies have begun to replace the traditional, manual, paper-and-pencil coding procedure. In 2009, the coding procedures of the two projects were digitised. Prior to this, the manifestos were coded based on printed copies of the election programmes (paper-and-pencil approach), whereby coders inserted the respective coding category in the margins of each text and then transferred the sum of the frequencies of the different codes to the project team, which constructed the dataset based on this information (for more information, see Volkens 2001; Wüst and Volkens 2003). The 2009 digitising of the coding procedures of the two projects involved two aspects. First, all documents were converted into a machine-readable format and are now publicly available to the academic community. In the case of the MARPOR project, data are 'distributed as the Manifesto Corpus, comprising more than 1800 machine readable documents: among them more than 600 digitally coded documents and more than 600,000 annotated statements' (Merz et al. 2016, 2). In the case of the EM project, all Euromanifestos are available as PDFs and text files and are accessible via the GESIS Data Archive (Schmitt et al. 2021). Second, a digitised and more hierarchical coding procedure has been implemented which is less susceptible to coding error (Braun, Mikhaylov and Schmitt 2010). Altogether, the move to a digitised approach has helped to make the two projects more user-friendly and provides – in particular in the case of MARPOR – the opportunity for researchers to 'easily recode parts of the Manifesto Corpus' (Merz, Regel and Lewandowski 2016, 7).

The study of issue emphasis and party positions via party manifesto data

Manifesto data are mainly exploited to study *issue salience*, which relates to how much emphasis political parties place on particular political issues. This data is also used to investigate the *positioning* of political parties along with policy and ideological dimensions in a large-N comparative perspective by means of quantitative empirical analyses (Budge et al. 2001; Klingemann et al. 2006; Volkens et al. 2013). The following section provides a brief overview of some of these research questions as well as of criticisms raised regarding manifesto data.

Issue emphasis

Salience theory implies that the decision about which topics to talk about and which are perhaps best ignored is highly relevant from the perspective of political parties (see in particular Budge and Farlie 1983; Petrocik 1996; Petrocik, Benoit and Hansen 2003; see also Chapter 18). Salience theory is the starting point of text analysis via parties' manifestos. This entails 'that the only way to analyse the way [parties] vary their appeals is to discover general "issue types" or "issue areas" within policy statements' (Budge and Farlie 1983, 23). Against this theoretical background, manifesto data has been used to map the policy space of party manifestos (McDonald and Mendes 2001), regionalisation of parties and issues (Mazzoleni 2009) or ethnicity of voters (Protsyk and Garaz 2013). Moreover, scholars have investigated changes in issue salience over time (Stoll 2010) as well as growing issue competition (Green-Pedersen 2007; Green-Pedersen and Mortensen 2015), general resistance to change (Walgrave and Nuytemans 2009) and different types of salience strategy (Wagner and Meyer 2014). Alongside this, the study of issue salience explored new areas when researchers in the field of EU politics started to investigate the salience of European issues (Netjes and Binnema 2007; Spoon 2012; Braun, Hutter and Kerscher 2016) as well as a wide range of related research questions drawing on EM data. Among other areas of research to be mentioned are studies investigating the presence of EU symbols in parties' Euromanifestos (Popa and Dumitrescu 2015), the responsiveness of parties on EU issues (Spoon and Williams 2017), the role of *Spitzenkandidaten* or lead candidates in EP elections (Braun and Popa 2018), and the overall reshaping of political conflict over Europe (Schäfer et al. 2021).

Party positions

Research has made use of manifesto data to measure and scrutinise parties' positions such as their positioning on the left-right dimension. Yet a number of scholars have raised doubts about the validity and reliability of the estimates commonly used to measure the left-right positioning of political parties. This strand of literature has for a long time shaped a vibrant debate over the most appropriate method for investigating party positions (see e.g. Laver 2001). Gabel and Huber (2000) propose a simple 'vanilla' method for using manifesto data to estimate party left-right positioning. Franzmann and Kaiser (2006) recommend an additive model based on the distinction between position and valence issues (see also Chapter 17) to study left-right ideology. The latter is known to have different meanings from country to country and over time, leading in turn to inconclusive findings when using traditional left-right scales. Furthermore, other scholars take into account uncertainty measures (Benoit, Laver and Mikhaylov 2009; Meyer and Jenny 2013; McDonald and Budge 2014), whereas Lowe et al. (2011) have proposed an alternative measure based on the logarithm of odds ratios (for even more statistical and methodological refinements, see Benoit et al. 2012; Volkens et al. 2013; Lo et al. 2016; Mölder 2016). These rich and diverse methods can help to make manifesto data more useful for the measurement of parties' positions. Thus, 'through using Manifesto data it is possible to obtain valid left-right values in spite of the numerous critics of the dataset itself' (Franzmann 2013, 827). Nonetheless, we also need to be cautious when using manifesto data and always subject 'the analysis to sensitivity testing' (Dinas and Gemenis 2010, 444).

Strengths and weaknesses of manifesto data

The previous overview shows that manifesto data is an established data source in party research. However, as with every data source, scholars should always carefully weigh and appraise its strengths and weaknesses.

Long-term availability and cross-nation comparability

One major strength of manifesto data lies in its long-term availability and comparability over time and countries. This is particularly true for the national and European level of governance. MARPOR data now covers empirical information on election manifestos from over 1,000 parties from 1945 until today, in over 50 countries on five continents.[3] EM data comprises eight EP elections from 1979 to 2014[4] for each of the EU member states, covering 987 parties overall (including EP party groups).

Objectivity

In addition, the objectivity of manifesto data outweighs other data sources. Manifesto data mirrors official policy statements of political parties. Issues that are emphasised by manifestos are to a large extent consistent with those policies that the respective parties advocate in parliaments and governments (Klingemann et al. 1994; Budge et al. 2001) and can therefore be considered as parties' self-positioning towards, or indeed away from, key policy issues. Manifesto data thus maps the official preferences of parties in terms of political issues deemed to be relevant in an election. This is less clear in the case of other data used to study party politics. For example, media data presents the issue of possible gatekeeping effects since not all issues raised in party manifestos make it into media reports and public debate (Meyer, Haselmeyer and Wagner 2017). Moreover,

> Expert surveys and opinion poll data give us the picture of the party as perceived by political analysts and voters, respectively. Manifestos, on the other hand, provide a more accurate and representative picture of where the parties stand in the policy space, without our requiring further knowledge about their policy record.
>
> *(Dinas and Gemenis 2010, 428)*

Although this speaks in favour of the objectivity of manifesto data, what needs to be taken into account is that these official documents are campaign instruments and are thus written with an eye to strategic considerations.

Reliability

One of the weaknesses of manifesto data is related to the coding procedure: the 'manual coding of text into policy categories is time consuming, boring and potentially unreliable' (Kleinnijenhuis and Pennings 2001, 164). Moreover, the traditional codebooks (which are definitely an asset, as they ensure comparability over time) with their sometimes old-fashioned coding categories make coding occasionally a difficult task and can lead to some of the reliability issues described earlier. Misclassification within the coding procedure has indeed been identified as a serious and systemic problem when it comes to evaluating manifesto data, leading to calls to radically simplify the coding scheme (Mikhaylov, Laver and Benoit 2012). This could be done, for example, through the use of natural sentences instead of quasi-sentences (Däubler et al. 2012). The shift towards a digitised and more hierarchical coding approach in the two manifesto projects is aimed particularly at simplifying the entire coding procedure. The manual coding approach is in general prone to errors, but double or triple coding to ensure better data reliability is expensive and funding for this is hard to come by. Although these are important weaknesses, note that the reliability of manifesto data is still acceptable in terms of statistical criteria.

Documents

Finally, the relevance of manifesto data has been questioned because few people actually read manifesto documents and only a minority of party officials are involved in writing them. It is certainly true that only a fraction of the citizenry actually reads these documents, but it is also the case that policy makers pay attention to this form of elite communication and the media coverage surrounding it (Harmel 2018). Furthermore, although election manifestos are drafted by a relatively small group of experts within a party, they are then largely discussed, amended and approved by party conventions in most cases. However, it is important to note that the official information provided by smaller parties is sometimes scant. In these cases, the document to be coded is often not an official manifesto, but a leaflet, flyer or similarly ephemeral public statement. Nevertheless, this disadvantage applies not only for manifesto data but also for the majority of other data sources used for quantitative data analysis: in the media, smaller parties tend not to be given the same visibility and, in the case of public opinion surveys, respondents do not really know about them and are unable to rate them accordingly; the latter is sometimes even true for the experts consulted in the case of expert surveys. Hence, in the case of transparent manifesto data, users can at least check what type of document has been used and consider this information accordingly in their empirical analysis.

The debates surrounding the strengths and weaknesses of coding manifesto data have endured through the long history of manifesto coding. However, the strengths of this data source far outweigh its weaknesses, since this data enables us to study the official preferences of political parties over a long period of time and across many countries. An additional advantage is that each manifesto data source can be linked to each other – allowing researchers to consider different electoral levels, such as the regional or the local level. Consequently, manifesto data represent an invaluable resource for those investigating party politics, although those using it should remain sensitive to its potential weaknesses.

Conclusions and avenues for further research

One major avenue for future manifesto research relates to the need to increase the reliability of data. Different possibilities can be envisaged: first, reliability could be increased by hiring multiple coders for one single manifesto and by revising the coding procedure (Dolezal et al. 2016), or by applying crowd-coding approaches (Benoit et al. 2016). Second, fully reliable and automated coding approaches could be developed which in the long run might replace expensive and time-consuming manual coding procedures. Numerous automated coding approaches have been developed this century to reduce coding errors by human coders. Starting with a computer-coding scheme (Laver and Garry 2000), Laver et al. (2003) came up with their semi-supervised *Wordscores* technique (Lowe 2008), which was followed by a fully unsupervised *Wordfish* approach (Slapin and Proksch 2008). These two automated coding approaches were more recently supplemented by the R package *quanteda* (Benoit et al. 2018). Although all of these (more) automated coding approaches are not (completely) reliant on human coders and their related human 'deficiencies' in terms of coding errors, none of these approaches has so far been able to replace human manifesto coding entirely. This is mainly because these automated approaches are still of limited help when it comes to more complex coding tasks and to examining manifesto programmes in different languages. Nonetheless, the expectation is that newly developed coding strategies using machine-learning models may be an important next step in this regard (Wiedemann 2019). Finally, it is important to note that such innovative approaches should ideally be systematically developed and monitored in coordination with manual-coding approaches instead of simply replacing traditional manifesto projects. By doing so, one of the major advantages of manifesto data – long-term comparability over time – would be guaranteed.

Beyond these rather technical suggestions for improvement, manifesto scholars should also systematically link different fields of research to one another. There is a growing literature that explores the link between political parties and issue salience. In addition, scholars have started to scrutinise the causes and consequences of party policy shifts, drawing on manifesto data to measure such shifts (Adams et al. 2019; Braun, Schmitt and Popa 2019; Spoon and Klüver 2019; Abou-Chadi and Stoetzer 2020). Given these highly insightful studies, one major avenue for future research drawing on manifesto data would be to systematically link manifesto, media and public opinion data to gain a better understanding of how party politics is linked to the public debate and attitudinal or behavioural changes of citizens. Speaking of data linkage, additional effort should be taken to connect the analysis of different levels of electoral systems and politics – namely the local, regional, national and EU levels (e.g. Braun and Schmitt 2020). Manifesto data for each of these levels is available and awaits linking by researchers interested in comparatively studying the facets of party competition at these different levels of the political system (Deschouwer 2003).

Notes

1 I am very grateful to Sofia Vasilopoulou and Hermann Schmitt for their valuable comments and suggestions on this chapter. Moreover, I would like to thank Tuba Yilmaz and Zeth Isaksson for their excellent research support.
2 It should be noted that the MARPOR and the EM coding schemes display some slight variations in their categories and sub-categories (Werner et al., 2014; Schmitt et al., 2018).
3 See https://manifestoproject.wzb.eu/
4 The 2019 EM study is part of the project ProConEU 'Friends and Foes of the European Union: The Nature of the Gap Between Them, and the Likely Consequences of It', funded by the German Ministry of Education and Research (for a description of the project, see www.mzes.uni-mannheim.de/proconeu/, retrieved 05.10.2021).

References

Abou-Chadi, T. and Stoetzer, L.F. (2020) 'How parties react to voter transitions', *American Political Science Review*, 114(3), p940–945.

Adams, J., Bernhardi, L., Lawrence, E., Gordon, O.B., Liu, T.-P. and Phillips, C. (2019) 'A problem with empirical studies of party policy shifts: Alternative measures of party shifts are uncorrelated', *European Journal of Political Research*, 58(4), p1234–1244.

Alonso, S., Gómez, B. and Cabeza, L. (2013) 'Measuring centre-periphery positions: The Regional Manifestos Project', *Regional and Federal Studies*, 23(2), p189–211.

Benoit, K., Conway, D., Lauderdale, B.E., Laver, M. and Mikhaylov, S. (2016) 'Crowd-sourced text analysis: reproducible and agile production of political data', *American Political Science Review*, 110(2), p278–295.

Benoit, K., Laver, M., Lowe, W. and Mikhaylov, S. (2012) 'How to scale coded text units without bias: A response to Gemenis', *Electoral Studies*, 31, p605–608.

Benoit, K., Laver, M. and Mikhaylov, S. (2009) 'Treating words as data with error: Uncertainty in text statements of policy positions', *American Journal of Political Science*, 53(2), p495–513.

Benoit, K., Watanabe, K., Wang, H., Nulty, P., Obeng, A., Müller, S. and Matsuo, A. (2018) 'quanteda: An R package for the quantitative analysis of textual data', *Journal of Open Source Software*, 3(30), p774.

Braun, D. (2020) 'Inhaltsanalyse', in *Fortgeschrittene Analyseverfahren in den Sozialwissenschaften*. Wiesbaden: Springer VS.

Braun, D., Hutter, S. and Kerscher, A. (2016) 'What type of Europe? The salience of polity and policy issues in European Parliament elections', *European Union Politics*, 17(4), p570–592.

Braun, D., Mikhaylov, S. and Schmitt, H. (2010) 'European Parliament Election Study 2009, Manifesto Study', GESIS Data Archive, Cologne. ZA5057 Data file Version 1.0.0 [online]. https://doi.org/10.4232/1.10204.

Braun, D. and Popa, S.A. (2018) 'This time it was different? The salience of the Spitzenkandidaten system among European parties', *West European Politics*, 41(5), p1125–1145.

Braun, D., Popa, S.A. and Schmitt, H. (2019) 'Responding to the crisis: Eurosceptic parties of the left and right and their changing position towards the European Union', *European Journal of Political Research*, 58(3), p797–819.

Braun, D. and Schmitt, H. (2020) 'Different emphases, same positions? The election manifestos of political parties in the EU multilevel electoral system compared', *Party Politics*, 26(5), p640–650.

Budge, I. and Farlie, D. (1983) *Explaining and predicting elections: Issue effects and party strategies in twenty-three democracies*. London: George Allen and Unwin.

Budge, I., Klingemann, H.-D., Volkens, A., Bara, J. and Tannenbaum, E. (eds.) (2001) *Mapping policy preferences: Estimates for parties, electors, and governments 1945–1998*. Oxford: Oxford University Press.

Däubler, T., Benoit, K., Mikhaylov, S. and Laver, M. (2012) 'Natural sentences as valid units for coded political texts', *British Journal of Political Science*, 42(4), p937–951.

Deschouwer, K. (2003) 'Political parties in multi-layered systems', *European Urban and Regional Studies*, 10(3), p213–226.

Dinas, E. and Gemenis, K. (2010) 'Measuring parties' ideological positions with manifesto data: A critical evaluation of the competing methods', *Party Politics*, 16(4), p427–450.

Dolezal, M., Ennser-Jedenastik, L., Müller, W.C. and Winkler, A.K. (2016) 'Analyzing manifestos in their electoral context a new approach applied to Austria, 2002–2008', *Political Science Research and Methods*, 4(3), p641–650.

Franzmann, S.T. and Kaiser, A. (2006) 'Locating political parties in policy space: A reanalysis of party manifesto data', *Party Politics*, 12(2), p163–188.

Franzmann, S.T. (2013) 'Towards a real comparison of left-right indices: A comment on Jahn', *Party Politics*, 21(5), 821–828.

Gabel, M.J. and Huber, J.D. (2000) 'Putting parties in their place: Inferring party left-right ideological positions from party manifestos' data', *American Journal of Political Science*, 44(1), p94–103.

Green-Pedersen, C. (2007) 'The growing importance of issue competition: The changing nature of party competition in Western Europe', *Political Studies*, 55(3), p607–628.

Green-Pedersen, C. and Mortensen, P.B. (2015) 'Avoidance and engagement: Issue competition in multi-party systems', *Political Studies*, 63(4), p747–764.

Gross, M. and Jankowski, M. (2020) 'Dimensions of political conflict and party positions in multi-level democracies: Evidence from the Local Manifesto Project', *West European Politics*, 43(1), p74–101.

Harmel, R. (2018) 'The how's and why's of party manifestos: Some guidance for a cross-national research agenda', *Party Politics*, 24(3), p229–239.
Howe, P.J., Szöcsik, E. and Zuber, C.I. (2020) *Habsburg manifesto dataset* [unpublished dataset].
Kleinnijenhuis, J. and Pennings, P. (2001) 'Measurement of party positions on the basis of party programmes, media coverage and voter perceptions', in Laver, M. (ed.) *Estimating the Policy Positions of Political Actors*. London: Routledge, pp. 162–182.
Klingemann, H.-D., Hofferbert, R. and Budge, I. (1994) *Parties, policies and democracy*. Boulder: Westview Press.
Klingemann, H.-D., Volkens, A., Bara, J.L., Budge, I. and McDonald, M. 2006. *Mapping policy preferences II: Estimates for parties, electors, and governments in Eastern Europe, European Union, and OECD 1990–2003*. Oxford: Oxford University Press.
Lacewell, O.P. and Werner, A. (2013) 'Coder training: Key to enhancing coding reliability and estimate validity', in Volkens, A., Bara, J., Budge, I., Mcdonald, M.D. and Klingemann, H.-D. (eds.) *Mapping policy preferences from texts. Statistical solutions for manifesto analysts*. Oxford: Oxford University Press, pp. 169–193.
Laver, M. (2001) *Estimating the policy positions of political actors*. New York: Routledge.
Laver, M., Benoit, K. and Garry, J. (2003) 'Extracting policy positions from political texts using words as data', *American Political Science Review*, 97(2), p311–331.
Laver, M. and Garry, J. (2000) 'Estimating policy positions from political texts', *American Journal of Political Science*, 44(3), p619–634.
Lo, J., Proksch, S.-O. and Slapin, J.B. (2016) 'Ideological clarity in multiparty competition: A new measure and test using election manifestos', *British Journal of Political Science*, 46(3), p591–610.
Lowe, W. (2008) 'Understanding wordscores', *Political Analysis*, 16(4), p356–371.
Lowe, W., Benoit, K., Mikhaylov, S. and Laver, M. (2011) 'Scaling policy preferences from coded political texts', *Legislative Studies Quarterly*, 36(1), p123–155.
Mazzoleni, M. (2009) 'The saliency of regionalization in party systems: A comparative analysis of regional decentralization in party manifestos', *Party Politics*, 15(2), p199–218.
McDonald, M.D. and Budge, I. (2014) 'Getting it (approximately) right (and center and left!): Reliability and uncertainty estimates for the comparative manifesto data', *Electoral Studies*, 35, p67–77.
McDonald, M.D. and Mendes, S.M. (2001) 'The policy space of party manifestos', in Laver, M. (ed.) *Estimating the policy position of political actors*. London: Routledge, pp. 90–114.
Merz, N., Regel, S. and Lewandowski, J. (2016) 'The manifesto corpus: A new resource for research on political parties and quantitative text analysis', *Research and Politics*, 3, p1–8.
Meyer, T.M., Haselmayer, M. and Wagner, M. (2017) 'Who gets into the papers? Party campaign messages and the media', *British Journal of Political Science*, 50(1), p281–302.
Meyer, T.M. and Jenny, M. (2013) 'Measuring error for adjacent policy position estimates: Dealing with uncertainty using CMP data', *Electoral Studies*, 32, p174–185.
Mikhaylov, S., Laver, M. and Benoit, K.R. (2012) 'Coder reliability and misclassification in the human coding of party manifestos', *Political Analysis*, 20(1), p78–91.
Mölder, M. (2016) 'The validity of the RILE left–right index as a measure of party policy', *Party Politics*, 22(1), p37–48.
Netjes, C.E. and Binnema, H.A. (2007) 'The salience of the European integration issue: Three data sources compared', *Electoral Studies*, 26, p39–49.
Petrocik, J.R. (1996) 'Issue Ownership in presidential elections, with a 1980 case study', *American Journal of Political Science*, 40(3), p825–850.
Petrocik, J.R., Benoit, W.L. and Hansen, G.J. (2003) 'Issue ownership and presidential campaigning, 1952–2000', *Political Science Quarterly*, 118(4), p599–626.
Popa, S.A. and Dumitrescu, D. (2015) 'National but European? Visual manifestations of Europe in national parties' Euromanifestos since 1979', *Party Politics*, 23(5), p526–537.
Protsyk, O. and Garaz, S. (2013) 'Politicization of ethnicity in party manifestos', *Party Politics*, 19(3), p296–318.
Robertson, D. (1976) *A theory of party competition*. London: Wiley.
Schäfer, C., Popa, S.A., Braun, D. and Schmitt, H. (2021) 'The reshaping of political conflict over Europe: From pre-Maastricht to post-Euro-crisis', *West European Politics*, 44(3), p531–557.
Schmitt, H, Braun, D. and Popa, S.A. (2021) ,European Parliament Elections – Euromanifesto Study (Documents 1979–2014)', *GESIS Data Archive*, Cologne. ZA5163 Data file Version 1.0.0: https://doi.org/10.4232/1.5163.

Schmitt, H., Braun, D., Popa, S.A., Mikhaylov, S. and Dwinger, F. (2018) 'European Parliament Election Study 1979–2014, Euromanifesto Study', GESIS Data Archive, Cologne. ZA5102 Data file Version 2.0.0 [online]. https://doi.org/10.4232/1.12830.

Slapin, J.B. and Proksch, S.-O. (2008) 'A scaling model for estimating time-series party positions from texts', *American Journal of Political Science*, 52(3), p705–722.

Spoon, J. (2012) 'How salient is Europe? An analysis of European election manifestos, 1979–2004', *European Union Politics*, 13(4), p558–579.

Spoon, J. and Klüver, H. (2019) 'Party convergence and vote switching: Explaining mainstream party decline across Europe', *European Journal of Political Research*, 58(4), p1021–1042.

Spoon, J. and Williams, C. (2017) 'It takes two: how Eurosceptic public opinion and party divisions influence party positions', *West European Politics*, 40(4), p741–762.

Stoll, H. (2010) 'Elite-level conflict salience and dimensionality in Western Europe: Concepts and empirical findings', *West European Politics*, 33(3), p445–473.

Volkens, A. (2001) *Manifesto coding instructions*. WZB Berlin [online]. Available from: https://manifestoproject.wzb.eu/down/papers/handbook_2001_version_1.pdf.

Volkens, A., Bara, J., Budge, I., McDonald, M.D. and Klingemann, H.-D. (2013) *Mapping policy preferences from texts III. Statistical solutions for manifesto analysts*. Oxford: Oxford University Press.

Volkens, A., Lehmann, P., Matthieß, T., Merz, N., Regel, S. and Werner, A. (2015) *The manifesto data collection. Manifesto project (MRG/CMP/MARPOR). Version 2015a*. Berlin: Wissenschaftszentrum Berlin für Sozialforschung (WZB).

Wagner, M. and Meyer, T. (2014) 'Which issues do parties emphasise? Salience strategies and party organisation in multiparty systems', *West European Politics*, 37(5), p1019–1045.

Walgrave, S. and Nuytemans, M. (2009) 'Friction and party manifesto change in 25 countries, 1945–98', *American Journal of Political Science*, 53(1), p190–206.

Werner, A., Lacewell, O. and Volkens, A. (2014) *Manifesto coding instructions (5th revised edition)*. WZB Berlin [online]. Available from: https://manifestoproject.wzb.eu/down/papers/handbook_2014_version_5.pdf.

Wiedemann, G. (2019) 'Proportional classification revisited: Automatic content analysis of political manifestos using active learning', *Social Science Computer Review*, 37(2), p135–159.

Wüst, A. and Volkens, A. (2003) 'Euromanifesto coding instructions', MZES Working Paper, 64, 1–45.

39
VOTING ADVICE APPLICATIONS

Frederico Ferreira da Silva and Diego Garzia

Over the last two decades, a novel source of data on party positioning in comparative perspective has been made available to political scientists alongside party manifesto coding exercises and expert survey assessments. Voting Advice Applications (VAAs) are typically non-partisan, online platforms primarily designed to inform and assist citizens navigate the policy proposals of competing political parties, with the ultimate goal of finding the best fit between users' policy preferences and the proposals put forward by the parties running for election.[1] In order to do so, users are prompted to fill in a questionnaire marking their positions on a range of electorally salient policy 'statements' (e.g. 'abortion should be forbidden'). A matching algorithm then compares the user's answers with the position of each party on the various statements, and presents the result in the form of a rank-ordered list or graph displaying the degree to which each political party matches the policy preferences of the user.

While their origins can be traced back to the 1980s, the expansion of VAAs, both geographically and on usage numbers, went hand in hand with the spread of internet connections. As the internet turned into an increasingly relevant source of political information and communication, VAAs gained popularity among the electorate as information-reduction tools in the complex world of politics. For these reasons, VAAs have become integral features of contemporary election campaigns, and their relevance is acknowledged by both citizens and political parties alike. Popular VAAs have been able to attract millions of users over the few weeks of an election campaign, in both domestic and transnational contexts such as European Parliament (EP) elections. Today, according to the global census conducted in 2016 by the ECPR Research Network on Voting Advice Applications, these tools have been fielded in as many as 43 countries worldwide, some even having multiple VAAs simultaneously available (Garzia and Marschall 2016).

But how can VAAs be used to study political parties and, in particular, their positions on the political space? VAA research can be divided into two main strands: the more classic study of VAA users, designs, methods, and concrete effects on electoral participation and patterns of party choice; and a more recent strand looking into party system change, cross-national party system comparisons, and changes in political parties (Garzia and Marschall 2019, 1). The latter set of studies has been using VAA-generated party positions to analyse, for example, the dimensionality of the political space (Ferreira da Silva et al., 2021) – similar to expert surveys and manifesto analysis.

When programming VAAs, designers rely on a variety of sources to retrieve information about party stances, and on diverse methods to ascribe policy positions to political parties (which are subsequently used to match with users' responses to the questionnaire). As this chapter will show, these coding procedures follow strict methods, based on rigorous scientific standards. The ongoing search for a *gold standard* in party positioning has been a priority for political scientists for a long time (Marks 2007), but this goal has concerned VAA designers especially, given the implications of (in)accurate party positioning in the context of VAA development. To be clear, if VAAs reach millions of users, aiming at informing them on parties' positions, and potentially influencing voting decisions and electoral outcomes, designers have an increased responsibility to ensure precision and accuracy in placing political parties. For these reasons, the scientific debate on methods to estimate party positions has been particularly lively among VAA scholars. We believe that this vigorous interchange has put VAAs at the forefront of the methods used to estimate party positions.

Against this background, the aim of this chapter is to provide an exhaustive assessment of the potential of VAAs as instruments to estimate and derive party positions, discussing their respective strengths and limitations in comparison with alternative methodologies. The chapter proceeds as follows. The next section discusses the multiple methodological approaches for party positioning among VAAs. The following section introduces the EU Profiler/euandi transnational VAA project as our case study, describing its contribution to provide party positions comparable across time and countries. Next, we discuss the merits and weaknesses of VAAs in relation to other methods, namely expert surveys and text analysis of party manifestos. In what follows, using data from three of the foremost representatives of these methods – EU Profiler/euandi project, the Chapel Hill Expert Survey, and the Comparative Manifesto Project – we triangulate their estimates to assess their validity and compare their relative performances.

The making of a VAA: competing methodologies for party positioning

Voting Advice Applications are not all alike. They widely differ in their questionnaire design, statement selection, inclusion criteria for political parties, matching algorithms used to calculate the results, and – most importantly for the purposes of this chapter – estimation methods from which party positions are derived (Marschall and Garzia 2014, 5). Therefore, when reflecting on the ability of VAAs to provide dependable data for party positioning, it is important to weigh up the varying methodologies currently employed in VAAs across the globe to place political parties.

The first VAAs relied entirely on parties' self-placement. *StemWijzer* was created as a precursor to current online VAAs in 1989, in the Netherlands, at the time in a paper-and-pencil version containing 60 statements taken from political party programmes. As the Internet-based version released in 1998, and all others since then, it assigned parties' positions exclusively based on their self-placement accompanied by a short justification. The same happens with other VAAs across Europe, such as *smartvote* (Switzerland), *VoteMatch* (UK), and *Wahl-O-Mat* (Germany). Such methods tend to work better in contexts with a more established VAA tradition, where parties are aware of the high usage of these platforms, as well as of their ability to sway voters, motivating higher cooperation rates. According to Gemenis and van Ham (2014, 34), this method may prove problematic for two reasons. First, parties may be selective in the responses to the multiple statements, responding to their core issues and avoiding taking a clear stance on irrelevant or more sensitive issues. Second, in the absence of a verification procedure conducted by experts, parties may take more strategic positions (e.g. closer to the centre), with the intention of manipulating the outcome of the advice and maximising potential electoral gains (van Praag 2007).

Even if intuitively able to counterbalance such weaknesses, expert surveys may not constitute an entirely adequate solution either (see also Chapter 40). We shall discuss more extensively the limitations of expert surveys later in this chapter, but the main weakness of these data sources can be summarised as the high degree of uncertainty or disagreement in experts' estimates. This problem arises particularly with smaller parties and with concrete issue positions, characteristic of VAAs (Krouwel and van Elfrinkhof 2014).

To overcome these limitations, an 'iterative' method merging expert judgements and parties' self-placements has been developed as an attempt to 'maximise the strengths of combining different methodologies while also trying to counterbalance their respective weaknesses' (Garzia and Marschall 2019, 12). Originally designed for the Dutch VAA *Kieskompas*, this method comprises

> two stages: first, both experts and party officials are asked to position the party on each of the issues and, second, these calibrations are compared. At this stage, the academic team enters into a process of deliberation with the parties or candidates to solve possible discrepancies between the self-placement and the expert codings.
>
> *(Krouwel and van Elfrinkhof 2014, 1468)*

Should a disagreement between experts and parties subsist at the end of the calibration phase, the expert team reserves the right to make the final coding decision. All relevant documentation supporting the party placement is accessible to respondents when using the VAA. Notwithstanding any remaining shortcomings,[2] the iterative method advanced by the *Kieskompas* gained notable popularity among designers, spreading into multiple VAAs across Europe. In the next section, we take a case study of one such VAA, the EU Profiler/euandi project, which we shall use as a benchmark for the remainder of the chapter.

The EU Profiler/euandi (euandi) dataset, 2009–2019

The EU Profiler/euandi project is the cumulation of three interdisciplinary, pan-European, multi-lingual VAAs fielded during the election campaign of the European Parliament Elections of 2009, 2014, and 2019. The first of these VAAs, named *EU Profiler*, coded over 270 political parties from the European Union and some neighbouring countries on a total of 30 political issues. Hosted at the European University Institute, in Florence, it was developed also in partnership with *smartvote* (Switzerland) and *Kieskompas* (the Netherlands). This first ever transnational VAA was the recipient of the World e-Democracy Forum Award for its 'commitments to carry out meaningful political change through the use of internet and new technologies'. Aimed at overcoming the shortcomings of standard methods employed in existing VAAs, the EU Profiler introduced two fundamental methodological innovations. Combining expert assessments with textual analysis of relevant information, country teams drawn from more than 100 highly qualified social scientists documented party positions on several political issues, which were subsequently calibrated as a by-product of a direct interaction with the self-placement carried by political parties themselves. Furthermore, the documentation supporting parties' positions on each issue (a total of 8.220 party positions) was made available to citizens upon their usage of the VAA (Trechsel and Mair 2011).

The project was rebooted in 2014 – this time in collaboration with the Berkman Center for Internet and Society, at Harvard University, and LUISS University, in Rome – rebranded into *euandi* (reads: 'EU and I'). To explore the full potential of these repeated cross sections, efforts were developed to provide longitudinal comparability, particularly in what concerns the policy statements used as sources of party placement: from the total of 28 statements, 17 were already present in the 2009 edition (Garzia, Trechsel and De Sio 2017). Regarding personnel, *euandi* kept the backbone of the teams of experts from the *EU Profiler*. Party cooperation rates rose *vis-à-vis* 2009 to over 50 per cent of parties included in the VAA, thus maximising the methodological gains deriving from the iterative method.

The latest version of this project was fielded in the 2019 EP election, in collaboration with the University of Lucerne, in Switzerland (Michel et al. 2019). The 2019 edition peaked with over 1.3 million users across Europe. Maintaining the core of policy statements used in previous editions, euandi2019 further expanded the longitudinal scope of the project, offering up to three data points in parties' positions across one decade.

Given the potential of these repeated cross sections to offer large-scale longitudinal and comparative data on party positions in the European political space, the outputs of these three projects have been recently merged into a pooled dataset (Reiljan et al. 2020a). The 'EU Profiler/euandi (euandi) trend file' compiles the data on political issue-positions of 411 parties across 28 European countries between 2009 and 2019, resulting in more than 20.000 unique party positions (Reiljan et al. 2020b). To date, it is the largest dataset of VAA-based party positions and the first to enable cross-national and longitudinal comparisons. Moreover, as 15 of the 42 different statements included were present across all waves, it allows for a decade-long direct comparison of parties' stances on key issues. These longitudinal policy statements are able to represent the three main dimensions of competition in the European political space: socioeconomic left-right; cultural liberal-conservative; pro-anti EU. Table 39.1 presents the categorisation of the continuous policy statements into the three dimensions.

Based on these dimensions, we can then trace and compare the evolution of parties' positions in the main axes of political competition across this decade. This can be done for each individual party in isolation or, as we present next for simplification purposes, for sets of parties grouped into party families. Relying on the seven party family classification used in the Chapel

Table 39.1 Continuous statements and dimensions of political competition (2009–2019)

Dimension	Policy statement
Socioeconomic left-right	1 Social programmes should be maintained even at the cost of higher taxes.
	2 Government spending should be reduced in order to lower taxes.
Cultural liberal-conservative	1 Immigration into the country should be made more restrictive.
	2 Immigrants from outside Europe should be required to accept our culture and values.
	3 The legalisation of same sex marriages is a good thing.
	4 The legalisation/decriminalisation of the personal use of soft drugs is to be welcomed.
	5 Euthanasia should be legalised.
	6 Criminals should be punished more severely.
	7 Renewable sources of energy (e.g. solar or wind energy) should be supported even if this means higher energy costs.
	8 The promotion of public transport should be fostered through green taxes (e.g. road taxing).
Pro-anti EU	1 The EU should acquire its own tax raising powers.
	2 On foreign policy issues [such as the relationship with Russia], the EU should speak with one voice.
	3 The European Union should strengthen its security and defence policy.
	4 European integration is a good thing.
	5 Individual member states of the EU should have less veto power.

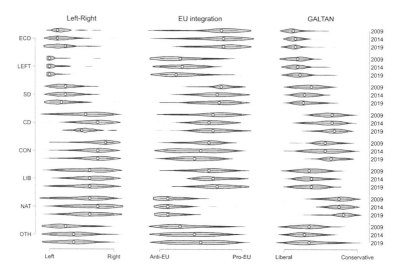

Figure 39.1 Party positions on the socioeconomic left-right, EU integration, and GALTAN dimensions, by party family (2009–2019)

Source: EU Profiler/euandi trend file (2009–2019) (Reiljan et al. 2020a).

Hill Expert Survey (CHES) data (Bakker et al. 2015), we can, for example, analyse the median party family positions for each year of data collection (white dots), the interquartile range, and the distribution of the parties using violin plots (see Figure 39.1). This approach allows us to observe not only the change in average placement but also to get a sense of the internal variation and concentration within the party groups provided by the kernel density estimates.

Strengths and weaknesses of VAAs as methods to estimate party positions

In this section, we discuss the respective merits and weaknesses of VAAs *vis-à-vis* established approaches to deriving estimates of parties' positions, that is, expert surveys and text analysis of party manifestos (see also Chapters 38 and 40). Expert surveys rely on the judgements from a set of academics or other professionals, who use their specialised knowledge to position parties on issues or policy dimensions. A text analysis of party manifestos entails the examination of official party documents made public before an election, and the subsequent coding of such documents by expert coders, usually according to a pre-defined codebook.

As any other method, the use of manifesto and expert survey data to estimate party positions comprises strengths and limitations (for reviews, see Marks 2007; Krouwel and van Elfrinkhof 2014). VAA-generated data on party positions is not necessarily any less problematic than these data sources. In fact, many VAAs rely, to a greater or lesser extent, on expert judgements and manifesto analysis as primary or secondary data sources to ascribe positions to political parties on policy statements. In that sense, they may reproduce the very same biases and shortcomings (along with the merits of these methods), with the aggravation that such estimates are meant to help potential voters navigate the policy proposals of competing political parties and, thus, have potential implications for voting behaviour.

To address these issues, the iterative method (Trechsel and Mair 2011; Krouwel, Vitiello and Wall 2012; Krouwel and van Elfrinkhof 2014; Garzia, Trechsel and De Sio 2017) used by several prominent VAAs combines elements of manifesto and expert data with other data collecting methods such as elite surveying, to overcome the limitations stemming from the use of a single method. For example, the *Kieskompas* combines an expert survey with a documented elite survey of party officials, followed by a calibration phase. The EU Profiler/euandi VAAs was built upon the very same methodology and added a structured, hierarchical text analysis of party manifestos, official party documentation, interviews, and other documentation, on which experts base their judgements. To tackle the problem of inter-coder agreement, the *Preference Matcher* consortium proposes an iterative expert survey approach, in which 'the presence of iteration and anonymity among panellists ensures higher inter-coder/expert agreement compared to both conventional expert surveys and content analysis approaches' (Gemenis 2015, 2302).

While these innovations put forward significant methodological contributions which, in our view, offer increased accuracy compared to the use of a single method in isolation, by no means do they fully respond to the challenge of estimating parties' positions. For as much as we continue to strive to improve accuracy in our measurements, the most fruitful procedure to neutralise the biases and limitations of the multiple methods to estimate party positions is, as Marks (2007, 3) suggests, 'to triangulate, to compare observations derived from *different* experimental designs'. We fully agree with that suggestion and thus take it on board in the empirical analysis that we present in the next section of this chapter.

Comparing party positions across time and space: CHES, CMP, and euandi

In this section, we triangulate party positions derived from the three data sources discussed so far: expert surveys, manifesto analysis, and VAAs. For those purposes, we rely on data from the Chapel Hill Expert Survey (CHES), the Comparative Manifesto Project (CMP), and the EU Profiler/euandi (euandi) longitudinal datasets. We picked the latter, because, among VAAs, it is the data source covering the largest geographical breadth of countries, along the longest time series, allowing for a comparative longitudinal assessment.

The triangulation takes into account the three most significant dimensions of political competition in Western Europe, present in all three data sources under analysis: left-right, Pro-Anti EU integration and GAL-TAN dimensions. For the EU Profiler/euandi dataset, the dimensions were constructed as described in Table 39.1. The conception of the left-right, Pro-Anti EU integration, and GAL-TAN dimensions in the CHES and CMP datasets considered variables measuring the same policy items as in EU Profiler/euandi statements, to maximise comparability across dimensions.[3] For example, in CHES, we used *lrecon* instead of *lrgen*, as the EU Profiler/euandi statements only capture left-right *economic* positioning. Therefore, for CHES, we relied on the original variables *lrecon*, *position*, and *galtan*, respectively.

For CMP, we constructed the three dimensions as follows:

$$CMPLR = \frac{((per\,505 - per\,504) + (per\,401 - per\,403) + (per\,402 - per\,409))}{3}$$

$$CMPEU = per108 - per110$$

$$CMPGALTAN = \frac{((per\,410 - per\,416) + (per\,601 - per\,602) + (per\,603 - per\,604) + (per\,605\_1 - per\,605\_2) + (per\,608 - per\,607))}{5}$$

The dimensions were constructed using a simple additive score, conferring equal weight to all variables used to build the dimensions across all datasets.[4] Further details on the dimensions, the original variables used to build the dimensions, and their description are available in Appendix A.

Figure 39.2 provides a general outlook of the positions of the main party families on the left-right, Pro-Anti EU integration, and GAL-TAN dimensions across the three data sources. It displays the mean values with 95 per cent confidence intervals for the different party families, by data source, across the three dimensions. Whenever the years of publication of CHES and CMP data do not fully coincide with the European Election years featured in the euandi dataset, we have taken the data from the closest year available (details on matching years are available in Appendix B). Again, the party family categorisation corresponds to the one used in the CHES (Bakker et al. 2015). The variables have been standardised to ensure comparability across datasets, and only the parties for which there are observations across all three data sources have been kept for the analysis (N = 146).

The data from Figure 39.2 provides a clear indication of a strong convergence across all dimensions between the EU Profiler/euandi estimates and those from the CMP and, even more so, the CHES. Unsurprisingly, the convergence is stronger in Social Democratic, Conservative, and Christian-Democratic party families (especially between the EU Profiler/euandi and CHES), while incongruences are more evident among smaller and more heterogeneous party families, where measurement error is more substantial. In general, CMP estimates appear to exhibit greater variance and converge more to the centre than the other two datasets, which may be explained by CMP's data collection method, tending to produce party position estimates conforming to a normal distribution. This is particularly visible in the case of Christian-Democratic, Ecologist/Green and Left Socialist party families, especially on the left-right dimension.

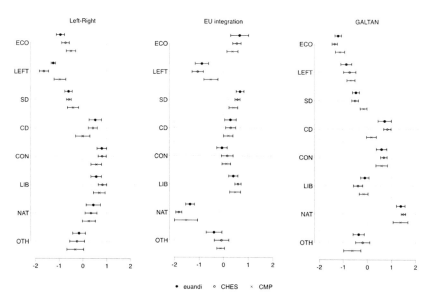

Figure 39.2 Mapping the European political space: Mean party positions by party family/year
Source: EU Profiler/euandi trend file (2009–2019) (Reiljan et al., 2020).

Table 39.2 Paired comparisons by dimension and election year: EU Profier/euandi, CHES, and CMP

	euandi – CHES		euandi – CMP		CHES – CMP	
	r	(N)	r	(N)	r	(N)
Left-right						
2009	.74	(169)	.46	(158)	.51	(140)
2014	.74	(191)	.51	(163)	.57	(150)
2019	.77	(200)	.44	(65)	.52	(58)
GAL-TAN						
2009	.78	(169)	.53	(158)	.64	(140)
2014	.68	(191)	.54	(163)	.66	(150)
2019	.78	(200)	.73	(65)	.72	(58)
Pro-Anti EU integration						
2009	.75	(169)	.41	(158)	.60	(140)
2014	.76	(191)	.56	(163)	.63	(150)
2019	.79	(200)	.67	(65)	.80	(58)

Source: EU Profiler/euandi trend file (2009–2019) (Reiljan et al., 2020a).

But how do these estimates relate across time? Figure 39.1 provides a snapshot of the three datasets but does not provide any information about the estimates across the three timepoints. In Table 39.2, we go beyond mean comparisons and compute correlation coefficients between datasets across time, over the three dimensions. Since these are pairwise comparisons, we have tried to maximise the number of observations across pairs of datasets, so the analysis is no longer restricted to the 146 parties common to all three data sources. The results show a strong correlation between the euandi dataset and the CHES. This correlation has increased between 2009 and 2019 across all dimensions but the longitudinal correlation has grown even stronger between the EU Profiler/euandi dataset and the CMP.

The longitudinal increase in the correlations involving the CMP is greater for euandi dataset than for the CHES. Despite the marked increase in the correlations between CMP and the other two datasets on the Pro-Anti EU integration and the GALTAN dimension, the CMP left-right dimension stands out as an exception, as the relationship with the euandi dataset and the CHES decreases slightly. Previous studies have identified reliability issues associated with CMP data on the left-right dimension, which could help account for this pattern (Laver 2003; Gemenis 2013). Overall, the very high Pearson's correlation coefficients with the two most prominent data sources for party positioning corroborate the validity and reliability of the EU Profiler/euandi longitudinal dataset.

Conclusions and avenues for further research

In this chapter, we have argued for the relevance and usefulness of VAA-generated data to derive reliable estimates of party positions. We have compared the strengths and weaknesses of VAAs vis-à-vis other methods of positioning political parties, namely expert surveys and text analysis of party manifestos. While VAAs overcome several limitations of the two other methods, our conclusions speak in favour of the complementarity of these distinct approaches. The longitudinal triangulation between the three case-studies representing each of the methods – EU Profiler/euandi project, CHES, and CMP – attests the validity of VAA-generated data on party positions. Not only do they largely converge with the expert survey and manifesto data but also such convergence has been increasing over time. While we can only speculate as to why this occurs, we believe it is an interesting research avenue not only for VAA researchers but also for academics generally interested in party positioning methods. Needless to say, the question of gold standards for identifying the party positions remains an obvious avenue for further research and discussion.

Although we have focused primarily on the potential of VAAs for estimating party positions, it should be highlighted that the contributions of VAAs for research on political parties go beyond that. For example, VAAs have been used to analyse party accountability and responsiveness, by comparing parties' prospective policies with actual policy outputs (Ramonaite 2010; Fivaz, Louwerse and Schwarz 2014). Based on clusters of the estimated party positions, VAAs have also been used in several studies to identify dimensions of political competition (Wheatley 2012, 2015; Wheatley et al. 2014; Burean and Popp 2015). Candidate-centred VAAs could also be a useful tool to measure intra-party consensus and cohesiveness, by examining the extent to which candidate positions diverge from the party as a whole (Schwarz, Schädel and Ladner 2010; Hansen and Rasmussen 2013).

VAA-generated data is also promising when it comes to the study of political representation. VAAs are able to attract millions of respondents during an election campaign and, even more importantly, they allow comparisons of the issue positions of voters and parties using the same data source. This results in a facilitated measurement of the extent to which parties and voters are mutually congruent in their issue positions. Furthermore, the rise of supranational VAAs like the EU Profiler and euandi also allows researchers to test theories of supranational representation. For instance, Bright et al. (2016) have identified a 'representative deficit' at the national level and concluded that many European voters could achieve better representation by voting for parties outside of their country in a context of transnational European elections.

As we hope to have shown in this chapter, the contributions of VAA-generated data for the study of political parties and democratic representation are manifold. And while many of their possibilities and research avenues remain largely unexplored, we can expect these tools to be used increasingly as a resource by scholars in the years to come.

Notes

1. In candidate-centred electoral systems such as Switzerland, Finland or Luxembourg, VAAs may also present users with a comparison between their policy preferences and those of individual candidates.
2. Despite its strengths, Gemenis and van Ham (2014, 36–37) maintain that the iterative method still depends on the (often limited) cooperation from political parties, and that the mechanisms to reach consensus in cases of inter-coder disagreement remain suboptimal and potentially biased. To address the latter issue, the *Preference Matcher* consortium proposed an interaction method guaranteeing anonymity and controlled feedback, known as the *Delphi* method (Gemenis 2015).
3. Regardless of this attempt, there are still some dissimilarities in the statements used to build the dimensions in the EU Profiler/euandi dataset, and in the CHES and CMP. For instance, since the left-right socioeconomic positions in the CHES are not disaggregated into policies, it does not directly match the EU Profiler/euandi statements tapping tax policies, social programmes and general government spending. A key strength of the euandi dataset consists in collecting party positions longitudinally not only across dimensions but, especially, on specific policy items. Also for this reason, we resorted to the individual 'content analytical data' items from the CMP instead of the 'programmatic dimensions' variables such as *rile, planeco or markeco*, as the latter do not represent all the policy items comprised in the EU Profiler/euandi dimensions, or may include other absent items.
4. For example, in the euandi dataset, if Party X was coded 4 in the statement 'Social programs should be maintained even at the cost of higher taxes' and 5 in the statement 'Government spending should be reduced in order to lower taxes', it would score 4.5 on the left-right dimension.

References

Bakker, R., de Vries, C., Edwards, E., Hooghe, L., Jolly, S., Marks, G. . . . and Vachudova, M.A. (2015) 'Measuring party positions in Europe: The Chapel Hill expert survey trend file, 1999–2010', *Party Politics*, 21(1), p143–152.

Bright, J., Garzia, D., Lacey, J. and Trechsel, A. (2016) 'Europe's voting space and the problem of second-order elections: A transnational proposal', *European Union Politics*, 17(1), p184–198.

Burean, T. and Popp, R. (2015) 'The ideological mapping of political parties in Romania', *Romanian Journal of Society and Politics*, 10(1), p118–136.

Ferreira da Silva, F.D., Reiljan, A., Cicchi, L., Trechsel, A.H. and Garzia, D. (2021) Three sides of the same coin? comparing party positions in VAAs, expert surveys and manifesto data. *Journal of European Public Policy*. DOI: 10.1080/13501763.2021.1981982

Fivaz, J., Louwerse, T. and Schwarz, D. (2014) 'Keeping promises: Voting advice applications and political representation', in Garzia, D. and Marschall, S. (eds.), *Matching voters with parties and candidates. Voting advice applications in comparative perspective*. Colchester: ECPR Press, pp. 197–215.

Garzia, D. and Marschall, S. (2016) 'Research on voting advice applications: State of the art and future directions'. *Policy and Internet*, 8(4), p376–390.

Garzia, D. and Marschall, S. (2019) 'Voting advice applications', in *Oxford research encyclopedia of politics*, pp. 1–24. https://doi.org/10.1093/acrefore/9780190228637.013.620.

Garzia, D., Trechsel, A. and De Sio, L. (2017) 'Party placement in supranational elections: An introduction to the euandi 2014 dataset', *Party Politics*, 23(4), p333–341.

Gemenis, K. (2013) 'What to do (and not to do) with the comparative manifestos project data', *Political Studies*, 61(1), p3–23.

Gemenis, K. (2015) 'An iterative expert survey approach for estimating parties' policy positions', *Quality & Quantity*, 49(6), p2291–2306.

Gemenis, K. and van Ham, C.T. (2014) 'Comparing methods for estimating parties' positions in Voting Advice Applications', in Garzia, D. and Marschall, S. (eds.), *Matching voters with parties and candidates. Voting advice applications in comparative perspective*. Colchester: ECPR Press, pp. 33–47.

Hansen, M.E. and Rasmussen, N.E. K. (2013) 'Does running for the same party imply similar policy preferences? Evidence from voting advice applications', *Representation*, 49(2), p189–205.

Krouwel, A. and van Elfrinkhof, A. (2014) 'Combining strengths of methods of party positioning to counter their weaknesses: the development of a new methodology to calibrate parties on issues and ideological dimensions', *Quality & Quantity*, 48(3), p1455–1472.

Krouwel, A., Vitiello, T. and Wall, M. (2012) 'The practicalities of issuing vote advice: a new methodology for profiling and matching', *International Journal of Electronic Governance*, 5(3–4), p223–243.

Laver, M. (ed.). (2003) *Estimating the policy position of political actors*. London: Routledge.

Marks, G. (2007) 'Introduction: Triangulation and the square-root law', *Electoral Studies*, 26(1), p1–10.

Marschall, S. and Garzia, D. (2014) 'Voting Advice Applications in a comparative perspective: An introduction', in Garzia, D. and Marschall, S. (eds.), *Matching voters with parties and candidates. Voting advice applications in comparative perspective*. Colchester: ECPR Press, pp. 1–10.

Michel, E., Cicchi, L., Garzia, D., Ferreira da Silva, F. and Trechsel, A. (2019) 'Euandi2019: Project description and datasets documentation', *Robert Schuman Centre for Advanced Studies Research Paper*. RSCAS, 61.

Ramonaite, A. (2010) 'Voting advice applications in Lithuania: Promoting programmatic competition or breeding populism?', *Policy & Internet*, 2(1), p117–147.

Reiljan, A., Ferreira da Silva, F.D., Cicchi, L., Garzia, D. and Trechsel, A.H. (2020a) *EU Profiler/euandi Trend File (2009–2019)*. Available from: https://cadmus.eui.e

Reiljan, A., Ferreira da Silva, F.D., Cicchi, L., Garzia, D. and Trechsel, A.H. (2020b) 'Longitudinal dataset of political issue-positions of 411 parties across 28 European countries (2009–2019) from voting advice applications EU profiler and euandi', *Data in Brief* 31, 105968.

Schwarz, D., Schädel, L. and Ladner, A. (2010) 'Pre-Election Positions and Voting Behaviour in Parliament: Consistency among Swiss MPs', *Swiss Political Science Review*, 16(3), p533–564.

Trechsel, A.H. and Mair, P. (2011) 'When parties (also) position themselves: An introduction to the EU Profiler', *Journal of Information Technology & Politics*, 8(1), p1–20.

Wheatley, J. (2012) 'Using VAAs to explore the dimensionality of the policy space: experiments from Brazil, Peru, Scotland and Cyprus', *International Journal of Electronic Governance*, 5(3–4), p318–348.

Wheatley, J. (2015) 'Restructuring the policy space in England: The end of the Left–Right paradigm?', *British Politics*, 10(3), p268–285.
Wheatley, J., Carman, C., Mendez, F. and Mitchell, J. (2014) 'The dimensionality of the Scottish political space: Results from an experiment on the 2011 Holyrood elections', *Party Politics*, 20(6), p864–878.
van Praag, P. (2007) *De Stemwijzer: hulpmiddel voor de kiezers of instrument van manipulatie*. Amsterdam: Lezing Amsterdamse Academische Club.

Appendix A
CHES AND CMP VARIABLES USED TO CREATE ANALYTICAL DIMENSIONS

Dataset	Dimension	Variable name	Variable description
CHES	Left-right	lrecon	Position of the party in YEAR in terms of its ideological stance on economic issues
	Pro-Anti EU integration	position	Overall orientation of the party leadership towards European integration in YEAR
	GALTAN	galtan	Position of the party in YEAR in terms of of their views on democratic freedoms and rights
CMP	Left-right	Per505	Limiting state expenditures on social services or social security. Favourable mentions of the social subsidiary principle (i.e. private care before state care)
		Per504	Favourable mentions of need to introduce, maintain or expand any public social service or social security scheme
		Per401	Favourable mentions of the free market and free market capitalism as an economic model
		Per402	Favourable mentions of supply side oriented economic policies (assistance to businesses rather than consumers)
		Per403	Support for policies designed to create a fair and open economic market. May include calls for increased consumer protection; increasing economic competition by preventing monopolies and other actions disrupting the functioning of the market; defence of small businesses against disruptive powers of big businesses; social market economy
		Per409	Favourable mentions of demand side oriented economic policies (assistance to consumers rather than businesses)

(Continued)

Dataset	Dimension	Variable name	Variable description
	Pro-Anti EU integration	Per108	European Community/Union: Positive. Favourable mentions of European Community/Union in general. May include the: Desirability of the manifesto country joining (or remaining a member); Desirability of expanding the European Community/Union; Desirability of increasing the ECs/EUs competences; Desirability of expanding the competences of the European Parliament.
		Per110	European Community/Union: Negative. Negative references to the European Community/Union. May include: Opposition to specific European policies which are preferred by European authorities; Opposition to the net-contribution of the manifesto country to the EU budget
	GALTAN	Per410	Economic Growth: Positive. The paradigm of economic growth. Includes: General need to encourage or facilitate greater production; Need for the government to take measures to aid economic growth.
		Per416	Anti-Growth Economy: Positive. Favourable mentions of anti-growth politics. Rejection of the idea that all growth is good growth. Opposition to growth that causes environmental or societal harm. Call for sustainable economic development.
		Per601	National Way of Life: Positive. Favourable mentions of the manifesto country's nation, history, and general appeals.
		Per602	National Way of Life: Negative. Unfavourable mentions of the manifesto country's nation and history.
		Per603	Traditional Morality: Positive. Favourable mentions of traditional and/or religious moral values.
		Per604	Traditional Morality: Negative. Opposition to traditional and/or religious moral values.
		Per605_1	Law and Order: Positive. Favourable mentions of strict law enforcement, and tougher actions against domestic crime. Only refers to the enforcement of the status quo of the manifesto country's law code.
		Per605_2	Law and Order: Negative. Favourable mentions of less law enforcement or rejection of plans for stronger law enforcement. Only refers to the enforcement of the status quo of the manifesto country's law code.
		Per607	Multiculturalism: Positive. Favourable mentions of cultural diversity and cultural plurality within domestic societies. May include the preservation of autonomy of religious, linguistic heritages within the country, including special educational provisions.
		Per608	Multiculturalism: Negative. The enforcement or encouragement of cultural integration. Appeals for cultural homogeneity in society.

Appendix B
MATCHING TIME-SERIES ACROSS DATA SOURCES

Country	EU Profiler/euandi	CHES	CMP
Austria	2009	2010	2008
	2014	2014	2013
	2019	2019	2017
Belgium	2009	2010	2010
	2014	2014	2014
	2019	2019	–
Bulgaria	2009	2010	2007
	2014	2014	2014
	2019	2019	2017
Croatia	2009	–	2011
	2014	2014	2015
	2019	2019	–
Cyprus	2009	–	2011
	2014	2011	2016
	2019	2019	–
Czech Rep.	2009	2010	2010
	2014	2014	2013
	2019	2019	2017
Denmark	2009	2010	2007
	2014	2014	2011
	2019	2019	–
Estonia	2009	2010	2011
	2014	2014	2015
	2019	2019	–
Finland	2009	2010	2007
	2014	2014	2011
	2019	2019	–

(*Continued*)

Country	EU Profiler/euandi	CHES	CMP
France	2009	2010	2007
	2014	2014	2012
	2019	2019	2017
Germany	2009	2009	2009
	2014	2014	2013
	2019	2019	2017
Greece	2009	2010	2009
	2014	2014	2015
	2019	2019	–
Hungary	2009	2010	2010
	2014	2014	2014
	2019	2019	–
Ireland	2009	2010	2011
	2014	2014	2016
	2019	2019	–
Italy	2009	2010	2008
	2014	2014	2013
	2019	2019	2018
Latvia	2009	2010	2010
	2014	2014	2014
	2019	2019	–
Lithuania	2009	2010	2008
	2014	2014	2016
	2019	2019	–
Luxembourg	2009	–	2009
	2014	2014	2013
	2019	2019	–
Malta	2009	–	–
	2014	2014	–
	2019	2019	–
The Netherlands	2009	2010	2010
	2014	2014	2012
	2019	2019	2017
Poland	2009	2010	2007
	2014	2014	2011
	2019	2019	–
Portugal	2009	2010	2005
	2014	2014	2015
	2019	2019	–
Romania	2009	2010	2008
	2014	2014	2016
	2019	2019	–
Slovakia	2009	2010	2010
	2014	2014	2016
	2019	2019	–
Slovenia	2009	2010	2008
	2014	2014	2014
	2019	2019	–

Country	EU Profiler/euandi	CHES	CMP
Spain	2009	2010	2008
	2014	2014	2015
	2019	2019	–
Sweden	2009	2010	2010
	2014	2014	2014
	2019	2019	2018
UK	2009	2010	2010
	2014	2014	2015
	2019	2019	2017

40
EXPERT SURVEYS IN PARTY RESEARCH

Maurits J. Meijers and *Nina Wiesehomeier*

During the last 30 years, the use of expert surveys in political science has become ubiquitous. This is for good reason. Expert surveys allow researchers to collect data in a systematic and comparable way about issues and topics that are otherwise difficult to measure. Compared to other means of data collection, they combine speed and a relatively low cost; particularly with the advent of user-friendly, easy to deploy, and increasingly inexpensive online surveys, the number of expert surveys has accelerated. Expert surveys, however, are not unique to political science and have been applied in a wide variety of academic disciplines, such as cognitive psychology, cultural anthropology, and sociology (Benoit and Wiesehomeier 2009). Within political science, they have perhaps been most widely used to measure countries' level of democracy (Coppedge et al. 2021), the integrity of elections (Norris and Grömping 2019), and especially the characteristics of political parties.

Ever since Castles and Mair applied the first expert survey to measure parties' left-right ideological positions in 1984, the substantive and geographical scope of expert surveys that have been deployed to gauge party characteristics has expanded considerably. While initially limited to political parties in Western democracies (Castles and Mair 1984; Ray 1999), expert surveys have increasingly been used to measure party characteristics also in countries in Central and Eastern Europe (Bakker et al. 2020), Asia (Huber and Inglehart 1995; Benoit and Laver 2006), Latin America (Coppedge 1997; Wiesehomeier and Benoit 2009), and Africa (Huber and Inglehart 1995; Kopecký et al. 2016). In addition, some expert surveys have been repeated regularly – providing researchers with longitudinal data (Szöcsik and Zuber 2015; Wiesehomeier, Singer and Ruth-Lovell 2019; Bakker et al. 2020). Whereas early applications focused on measuring parties' positions on ideological and policy dimensions, scholars have increasingly moved beyond this narrow focus, eliciting expert judgements on additional features such as party organisation, accountability, and non-policy-related ideological characteristics such as populism and authoritarianism (Kitschelt and Kselman 2013; Wiesehomeier 2018; Norris 2020; Meijers and Zaslove 2021). Arguably, the potential of expert surveys for party research is particularly apparent when measuring non-policy-related party characteristics, as these may be especially hard to grasp and subject to fierce debate, requiring the triangulation of different sources of information.

In party research, respondents – the experts in question – are usually academics with a distinct expertise in a given country's party system. These 'country experts' synthesise different strands of information about political parties to cast a qualitative judgement about a party's trait on a predefined scale, which is then typically aggregated to a mean or median score per party (Lindstädt, Proksch and Slapin 2018). Thus, expert surveys are fundamentally an *a priori* approach and can be regarded as an indirect, reputational measure of party characteristics that offer assessments at a higher level of generality than more direct measures of party policy. Textual measures of party manifestos (if available) or press releases, for instance, are prone to suffer from 'contextual bias', as the ideological positions parties communicate often depend strongly on the type of document or text in which they appear (Hawkins and Castanho Silva 2018; Hawkins and Littvay 2019). However, as any measurement tool in the social sciences, expert surveys are also not exempt from criticism, and the proliferation of their use has started to bring challenges to the forefront. The increase in substantive scope, particularly the possibility of eliciting expert judgements across many different countries at the same time, has forced researchers to grapple with ways to account for expert bias and the pitfalls of cross-cultural applications.

In this chapter, we will take stock of the current state of the expert survey methodology to study political parties. We will first trace their development and applications, underscoring how moving beyond the initial confines of Western democracies also brought about considerations of conceptual constructs relevant for party competition elsewhere. The expansion in geographical and substantive terms was concomitant with important methodological advances to alleviate problems arising from such an increased comparative scope. Challenges remain, however, and we will highlight areas that have so far received less attention, but call for more careful consideration in future applications of expert surveys.

Expert surveys in party research

Castles and Mair (1984) were the first to apply the expert survey methodology to measuring ideological positioning of political parties to go beyond idiosyncratic, ad hoc classifications of parties' ideological positions. Based on the responses of 117 experts, their survey resulted in left-right placements for 119 political parties in 17 Western democracies. Table 40.1 provides an overview of the most relevant expert surveys on political parties that have been fielded since then. As this overview highlights, expert surveys have drastically expanded their substantive scope and cover an increasing number of countries, as the regional focus has widened to include non-Western democracies.

Laver and Hunt (1992), for instance, were the first to expand the number of policy issues included. They queried experts about parties' positions on issues such as foreign policy, environmental policy, decentralisation, religion, and urban-rural interests. Huber and Inglehart (1995) kept the focus on the general left-right dimension, but moved beyond the established Western democracies, increasing drastically the coverage of countries that had been surveyed up until that point. The expert survey deployed by Coppedge (1997) was one of the first to venture into eliciting retrospective expert evaluations. Providing respondents with a left-right classification scheme, his survey gathered judgements on about 800 parties that had contested lower-chamber or constituent assembly elections in 11 Latin American countries, yielding information on parties as early as 1912 for Argentina or 1915 for Chile, among others. Similarly, Ray (1999) used the expert survey tool to measure parties' positioning retrospectively, gauging issue positions on European integration of 191 political parties in 17 Western European countries, thereby providing information spanning 1984–1996. While retrospective evaluations may be an attractive possibility, such evaluations may not be unproblematic and prone to bias, a point we will return to later.

Table 40.1 Overview of relevant expert surveys in party research

Expert Survey	Reference	What?	Region	Total Countries	Total Parties	Year(s) covered
Left-Right Political Scales: Some 'Expert' Judgments	Castles and Mair (1984)	General left-right dimension	WE, NA, OCEANIA	17	119	1984
Policy and Party Competition	Laver and Hunt (1992)	Policy positions; salience; party organization	NA, OCEANIA, ME, WE	24	159	1989
Expert Interpretations of Party Space and Party Locations in 42 Societies	Huber and Inglehart (1995)	General left-right dimension, inductively collected country-specific dimensions	WE, CEE, NA, LATAM, SA, ASIA, ME, OCEANIA	42	310	1995
A classification of Latin American Political Parties	Coppedge (1997)	General left-right dimension; secular, Christian, personalist	LATAM	11	ca. 800	Coverage depends on the country (retrospective)
Measuring Party Positions on European Integration: Results from an Expert Survey.	Ray (1999)	General left-right dimension; European integration; salience	WE	17	191	1984, 1988, 1992, 1996 (retrospective)
Chapel Hill Expert Survey (CHES)	Bakker et al. (2020)	Policy positions; European integration; salience; non-policy issues	WE, CEE	32	277	1999, 2002, 2006, 2010, 2014, 2017, 2019
Expert Survey on European Integration	Rohrschneider and Whitefield (2009)	Policy positions; non-policy issues; salience	CEE	13	87	2003–2004
Party Policy in Modern Democracies (PPMD)	Benoit and Laver (2006)	Policy positions; salience	WE, EE, NA, OCEANIA, EA, ME	47	387	2003–2004
Political Representation, Executives, and Political Parties Survey (PREPPS)/Presidents and Parties in Latin America (PPLA)	Wiesehomeier and Benoit (2009); Wiesehomeier et al. (2020)	Policy positions; salience; non-policy issues; party organization; linkages; direct democracy	LATAM, WE, CEE, OCEANIA, ME	61	ca.420 parties. 40 presidents, 38 PMs	2006–2007, 2011, 2015, 2018–2019, 2020

Democratic Accountability and Linkages Project (DALP)	Kitschelt et al. (2009)	Policy positions; party organization; linkages	WE, CEE, LATAM, SA, AS, ME	88	1227	2008–2009; 2020–2021
Ethnonationalism in Party Competition (EPAC)	Szöcsik and Zuber (2015); Zuber and Szöcsik (2018)	Policy positions; ethnonational positions	Europe	22	222	2011; 2017
Global Party Survey (GPS)	Norris (2020)	Policy positions; non-policy issues; populism; authoritarianism	'global coverage'	163	1043	2019
Populism and Political Parties Expert Survey (POPPA)	Meijers and Zaslove (2020)	Policy positions; populism; non-policy issues; party organization	EU	28	250	2018
Varieties of Party Identity and Organization (V-Party)	Lührmann et al. (2020)	Policy positions; party organization; non-policy issues	'global coverage'	169	1,943 (1,759 elections)	1970–2019 (retrospective, coverage depends on country)

Note: When several waves are available, total parties refers to the last survey fielded. No time frame for data collection was given by Castles and Mair (1984). 1984 is the year of publication of the accompanying article.

The work by Ray (1999) on measuring parties' positions with a particular focus on European integration was continued and extended by a team at the University of North Carolina at Chapel Hill in 1999 – founding the Chapel Hill Expert Survey (CHES) (Steenbergen and Marks 2007). Having been fielded seven times so far, CHES has since become an invaluable longitudinal data resource. Initially aimed at measuring the dimensionality of European Union (EU) politics in Western Europe, CHES has over the years expanded its coverage to include multiple policy issues in 32 European countries (Bakker et al. 2020). CHES has also championed the conceptualisation of the cultural dimension as a package of attitudes in line with Inglehart's (1990) distinction between materialist and postmaterialist politics. Conceived as the GAL-TAN continuum, with Green-Alternative-Libertarian (GAL) politics on one endpoint and Traditional/Authoritarian/Nationalist (TAN) politics on the other hand, this dimension bundles party positions on the environment, social lifestyle, law and order, and national identity in a single scale (Hooghe, Marks and Wilson 2002). Cultural politics have without a doubt become increasingly important in party competition over the last 20 years (Kriesi et al. 2012), and being able to place parties on an overarching cultural dimension appears therefore particularly attractive. Yet this level of *a priori* aggregation may run the risk of conflating ideological components (see also Benoit and Wiesehomeier 2009), and other scholars therefore opt for measuring party stances on nativism, immigration, law and order, and social lifestyle separately (Benoit and Laver 2006; Wiesehomeier and Benoit 2009; Rohrschneider and Whitefield 2019; Meijers and Zaslove 2021). The Ethnonationalism in Party Competition (EPAC) expert survey is even more fine-grained and focuses specifically on the ethnonational dimension in a subset of European countries in which the centre-periphery cleavages is politically relevant (Zuber and Szöcsik 2018).

The latter example also speaks to a distinct benefit of expert surveys – their design can be tailored to specific political contexts.[1] The 2003/2004 Rohrschneider-Whitefield expert survey on Central and Eastern Europe (CEE), for example, asked respondents about parties' positions on issues such as the strengthening of democratic institutions, rights of ethnic groups, and parties' perceptions of the communist legacy (Rohrschneider and Whitefield 2009). Benoit and Laver (2006) highlight that their aims was 'to measure party positions on policy on as many separate dimension as our local experts deemed politically relevant for any given country' (2006, 84). Hence, for CEE countries, they provided experts with specific post-communist policy dimensions pertaining to issues such as privatisation, media freedom, and foreign ownership of land. In Cyprus, Malta, Turkey, and Norway, on the other hand, the same authors included dimensions to examine party positions towards European peacekeeping missions. Surveying 18 Latin American countries, Wiesehomeier and Benoit (2009) included questions on globalisation, party regulation, regional cooperation, and the rights of indigenous people and minorities. Taking into account the central role of the executive in presidential systems, their survey also asked experts to place both presidents and their parties on a number of policy scales. Nevertheless, adapting expert surveys to specific local needs should be considered carefully and should not come at the expense of generality, thereby potentially hampering the opportunities for cross-national analyses. In addition, measuring a multiplicity of policy dimensions or including additional actors has important implications for survey complexity and length, risking expert fatigue, and thus affecting data quality.

Given such flexibility, it is no surprise that expert surveys have been increasingly deployed to measure characteristics beyond policy positioning, such as parties' attitudes and behaviour towards broader issues pertaining to democracy and representation. They have been used to examine parties' commitment to democracy in democratising countries (Benoit and Laver 2006; Rohrschneider and Whitefield 2009) and party attitudes towards the functioning of democracy in established democracies (Rohrschneider and Whitefield 2019). With regard to parties' electoral and policy-making strategies, Laver and Hunt (1992) asked experts to assess the influence of party activists, legislators, and leaders over party policy. Similarly, the Democratic Accountability and Linkages Project (DALP) includes information on linkages parties maintain to actors such as interest groups, religious organisations, or trade unions, but is much more far-reaching. Centring on party organisation and linkage strategies understood more broadly, country experts in 88 countries judged parties on an extensive battery of questions relating to issues such as the financing of party staff, the existence of local chapters, and the type of nomination procedures (see Kitschelt and Kselman 2013). In addition to a reduced set of policy positions, DALP also collected detailed data on parties' clientelistic practices, and whether they rely on material benefits, party identification, policy or charismatic appeals for voter mobilisation. Related to this, with the rise of populist actors around the world, a number of expert surveys, including our own, have turned their attention to the measurement of populism (Wiesehomeier 2018; Norris 2020; Meijers and Zaslove 2021). The Varieties of Democracy project, which uses expert surveys to assess the quality of democracy on multiple dimensions across countries, has recently developed the V-Party expert survey. As a true collaborative effort, it builds on several of these previous experiences and combines issues tapping into party identity, such as immigration, religious principles, gender equality, clientelism, or populism, with aspects of party organisation (Lührmann et al. 2020).

Finally, expert surveys have been used not only to establish the *positions* of political parties but also to determine how important or *salient* certain issues are for each party (Laver and Hunt 1992; Benoit and Laver 2006; Wiesehomeier and Benoit 2009; Rohrschneider and Whitefield 2012a; Bakker et al. 2020). Spatial conceptions of party competition assume that political parties compete with one another by taking contrasting positions on the policy issues at hand. Typically, issue competition perspectives consider political conflict to revolve around agenda control, that is, which issues are politically salient (Carmines and Stimson 1986). However, the approaches to measuring salience differ considerably across surveys. They range from asking experts to place parties on salience for each issue dimension asked (Laver and Hunt 1992; Benoit and Laver 2006; Rohrschneider and Whitefield 2009; Wiesehomeier and Benoit 2009) to instructing experts to indicate the two or three most important issue dimensions that inform a party's identity (Bakker et al. 2020). The former approach increases drastically the burden placed on experts, risking expert fatigue or survey satisficing (see later), while the second one may limit the applicability of this data.

Uses of expert survey party data

The uses of expert survey data in party research are manifold and our chapter cannot possibly provide a comprehensive overview of this vast literature. In general, studies have focused on mapping and explaining party positioning. In other words, these studies aim to explain the phenomena of interest for which the data had originally been collected. The main motivation for the first expert survey, for instance, was to empirically assess the distribution of political parties on the left-right continuum (Castles and Mair 1984), and subsequent expert surveys aimed at exploring the dimensionality of party competition in different party systems (Laver and Hunt 1992; Huber and Inglehart 1995; Benoit and Laver 2006). Having collected data on the influence of different actors on policy-making, Laver and Hunt (1992) also assessed the extent to which parties cooperate with interest groups, and whether a party is likely to sacrifice policy objectives for government participation. Rohrschneider and Whitefield (2009) emphasise the distinction between issue position and issue salience and use their data to analyse the cleavage structure in post-communist countries, while Ray (1999) maps parties' positioning on EU integration, the salience of the issue and the extent of intra-party disagreement. Being able to tap into distinct measures of policy positioning of presidents and their own parties, Wiesehomeier and Benoit (2009) assess the institutional and policy incentives for differences between these actors. Kitschelt and Kselman (2013) analyse the impact of a country's democratic experience and its level of economic development on modes of accountability. Meijers and Zaslove (2021) assess whether the components of the ideational populism definition amount to a underlying latent construct of populism, and how populism manifests itself in different forms.

Expert surveys have also been used to assess party strategies. First, scholars have employed expert survey data longitudinally to examine parties' policy change (Meijers 2017). As expert surveys rely on reputational judgements, they are less volatile than other measures of party policy, such as manifesto-based textual measures (see Benoit and Wiesehomeier 2009; see also Chapter 38), reflecting the relative stability of party positions more generally. Policy changes visible in expert survey data then likely reflect perceived substantive changes in parties' positions. Yet the very same property may mean that expert surveys are less amenable to the detection of smaller positional changes. Second, expert survey data has also been used to assess parties' positional clarity. Rovny (2012), for instance, measures 'position blurring' of political parties using the standard deviations of expert placements in CHES.

In addition, expert surveys are regularly used in combination with other data resources. They have been combined, for example, with textual data resources such as manifesto data. Schumacher, de Vries and Vis (2013) use expert surveys questions on party organisation from Laver and Hunt (1992) and Rohrschneider and Whitefield (2012a) to assess the effect of party leaders and activists on parties' policy change. In their study of the European Parliament's issue attention to democratic backsliding in Hungary and Poland, Meijers and van der Veer (2019) combine semi-automated text analysis with party position indicators from the CHES data. More frequently, scholars combine expert survey data with individual-level voter data to study political supply and political demand. In particular, such studies assess the quality of representation by measuring the correspondence between the policy preferences of parties and voters. Rohrschneider and Whitefield (2012b), for instance, fuse their expert survey with European Social Survey (ESS) data to assess the effect of political institutional contexts on ideological congruence. Similarly, Stecker and Tausendpfund (2016) rely on data from CHES and ESS to assess the impact of ideological congruence on satisfaction with democracy. In the Latin American context, Wiesehomeier and Doyle (2013) fuse *Latinobarometro* survey data with expert survey data from Wiesehomeier and Benoit (2009) to explain the electoral success of left parties.

Finally, expert surveys have also been utilised for numerous validation purposes. Most prominently, expert surveys have been used to highlight some of the reliability issues that afflict hand-coded manifesto data (e.g. Benoit and Laver 2007; Benoit, Laver and Mikhaylov 2009; see also Chapters 38 and 39). Di Cocco and Monechi (2021) employ the populism measure from POPPA (Meijers and Zaslove 2021) to validate their measures derived from supervised machine-learning. Similarly, Arnold, Doyle and Wiesehomeier (2017) contrast their left-right positions extracted from presidential state of the union addresses with those from expert surveys.

Methodological challenges

The previous overview shows that expert surveys have become an established method for data gathering in party research. The impressive proliferation of surveys across a variety of political contexts and research contents, not the least driven by the relative ease of implementation due to technological advances, has nevertheless revealed a number of important challenges that afflict expert surveys. Their distinct *a priori* nature calls upon scholars to carefully weigh and appraise decisions about design and operationalisation.

Some of these challenges have been widely noted (see Benoit and Wiesehomeier 2009). Benoit and Wiesehomeier (2009), for instance, warn against using expert surveys for obtaining factual information that can be easily gathered by other means, thus avoiding the overuse of experts and expert fatigue, and advise scholars to carefully balance the goal of generalisation with attention for relevant local political contexts. In the following, we highlight a number of methodological challenges that have not received enough attention so far.

Expert confidence: An inherent feature and advantage of expert surveys is that they provide researchers with direct measures of uncertainty of the estimates of party positions. In other words, expert surveys allow us to quantify the observed variation of different experts' placements. In addition, some expert survey initiatives have tapped into a different notion of confidence and included questions that ask experts to assess their degree of confidence they have in their given answers (e.g. DALP, V-Party, POPPA, and GPS). Respondents are of course called upon for their expertise, that is, for being more knowledgeable in the specific field of interest than others, and experts have been shown to be less prone to overestimating the confidence of their answers (Lichtenstein and Fischhoff 1977). Nevertheless, there are strong indications for gender differences when it comes to such self-assessments, with women typically underestimating their abilities and performances, while the opposite holds for male respondents (Lundeberg, Fox and Puncohar 1994). The extent to which this afflicts expert survey panels is, quite frankly, unknown. There is some indication, however, that female and male experts assess their level of confidence differently. In the POPPA data (Meijers and Zaslove 2021) female experts assessed their overall accuracy at 7.11, whereas the self-reported accuracy of male experts is at 7.48 (significant at $\alpha = 0.05$, one-tailed t-test). But in general, this is an area that warrants more systematic attention, particularly if future applications of expert surveys aim to use such confidence assessments to draw conclusions about data quality.

An important related issue is the overrepresentation of male experts on virtually all expert panels. For instance, only 23 per cent of the experts in the POPPA data (Meijers and Zaslove 2021) were female, in Norris' (2020) GPS 25 per cent of the experts were female, and 30 per cent of the respondents in the 2019 CHES were female (Bakker et al. 2020).

Expert bias: Similarly, there is the possibility that some expert characteristics systematically influence the elicited judgements. Most of the surveys reviewed here include a question aimed at controlling for this potential. Typically, surveys include a 'sympathy question' that had been championed by Laver and Hunt (1992), asking experts to indicate their own closeness to each party's policies (Laver and Hunt 1992; Benoit and Laver 2006; Kitschelt and Kselman 2013). In addition, scholars have started to add ideological self-placement questions (Bakker et al. 2020; Norris 2020; Meijers and Zaslove 2021). While many expert surveys report examining for potential systematic bias, these analyses are not systematically published. It is likely that both authors and editors are not too keen on publishing extensive, rather technical validity tests of already published expert survey data. Yet a careful analysis of possible expert-level biases is necessary and it is important that researchers are transparent about the strengths and weaknesses of the data.

Sympathy or ideological biases may be easier to detect than potential problems related to the use of retrospective evaluations in expert surveys (Coppedge 1997; Ray 1999; Lührmann et al. 2020). For instance, the large-scale V-Party project, like its parent project V-Dem, has asked experts to rank parties as far back as 1970 for many countries included to create an extended time-series dataset (Lührmann et al. 2020). Recall biases are widely reported for self-evaluations in diverse areas such as health, life-satisfaction, or social performance. Although not a self-assessment, when experts are asked to judge placements of individual parties on numerous policy dimensions *throughout time*, such recall biases are not unlikely. So far, such cognitive biases have not received much attention in party research. Nevertheless, Levick and Olavarria-Gambi (2020) highlight that data collected this way could indeed suffer from a number of problems. Analysing disaggregated V-Dem data the authors detect higher disagreement among experts for periods that preceded major crises of democracy. In this sense, policy positions of parties collected retrospectively are also explicitly linked to key events, such as elections, which may cloud the assessment of policy positions.[2] More research on the validity of retrospective expert surveys is therefore called for.

Expert burden and expert fatigue: Scholars using expert surveys face a trade-off between survey scope and length. Although they are relatively inexpensive and comparably quick, carefully fielded expert surveys are still work-intensive. The temptation to gather as much valuable information as possible is therefore understandable. Yet the longer and the more cognitively complex an expert survey is, the higher the respondent burden becomes (see also Benoit and Wiesehomeier 2009). This increases the risk of survey satisficing and lower quality responses. In addition, lengthy and complex surveys can lead to non-response or even survey 'break-off'. However, we are not aware of any systematic research into the effects of survey length and complexity on satisficing and response quality.

A different dimension of expert fatigue is the sheer increase in volume of expert surveys fielded. The more experts are requested to participate in surveys, the higher the overall respondent burden becomes. We should be careful therefore that the success of expert surveys does not precipitate its downfall. It is important that scholars using this tool are cognisant of these challenges. We contend, therefore, that expert surveys start to improve cooperation and coordination in data collection processes. In addition, we advise keeping expert survey length manageable and openly communicating to respondents the expected completion time of surveys.

Comparability: Expert surveys in party research have been devised to systematically measure party characteristics across countries and parties. However, a growing concern is the question of whether expert judgements on policy scales are comparable. It is possible that experts in different political and cultural contexts interpret certain scales differently, which can amount to a problem known as differential item functioning (DIF). Using measurement invariance tests, Castanho Silva and Littvay (2019), for instance, find that cross-regional comparability fails for the country-level 'Perceptions of Electoral Integrity' expert survey data. To assess DIF empirically, bridge experts can be employed, who code parties in multiple countries. While this has been applied in country-level V-Dem estimates (Marquardt and Pemstein 2018), this has not been widely used in party research. A challenge to bridging is that experts are considered to be local specialists and it may be difficult to find experts with in-depth knowledge about several party systems. Anchoring vignettes are also used to assess measurement variance across countries (e.g. CHES and PREPPS). Anchoring vignettes provide scenarios of hypothetical parties' vignettes or internationally known political actors that experts from all countries place on the same policy scales. These allow researchers to assess as well as correct for DIF (Bakker et al. 2014). The Political Representation, Executives, and Political Parties Survey (PREPPS) includes anchoring vignettes for more contentious concepts, such as rhetoric, charisma, and gender equality (Wiesehomeier, Singer and Ruth-Lovell 2019, see also Kitschelt and Kselman 2013). Bakker et al. (2014) find that DIF in the 2010 CHES is limited, which is a promising sign.

Language and academic culture: Related to the issue of comparability is the rather neglected aspect of the language used to field questionnaires in cross-national expert surveys. Some expert surveys are exclusively administered in English (Laver and Hunt 1992; Bakker et al. 2020), others have relied on translations. The codebook for Norris' GPS (2020) notes the survey was available English, French, German, Spanish, Russian, and Mandarin. PREPPS is fielding the survey in the national language(s) unless local expert feedback suggested that an English version would be feasible (Wiesehomeier, Singer and Ruth-Lovell 2019).

The effects on data quality and response rates of using translated or untranslated versions are unknown. It is nevertheless possible that the language of the survey affects the expert-pool. English-only surveys could suffer from self-selection problems as certain scholars may choose to opt out. If such a behaviour is related to some systematic expert characteristic, our remaining expert pool may create biased estimates. Yet there may also be potential problems of translated surveys if not done carefully; hence, English as *lingua franca* may have its advantages. Another possible source of differential interpretation is whether or not the experts are residents in the country in question, as it is possible that non-residents evaluate parties differently than resident experts (e.g. Norris 2020 measures expert residency). Relatedly, initiators of expert surveys should be aware of differences in academic cultures. While political scientists in many countries lean on common research traditions, it is important to be aware that the interpretation of key concepts and methodological practices can be vastly different across countries. We therefore call upon expert survey projects to reflect on questions of academic culture when devising their projects. Future research should also examine whether survey language and expert residency affect expert disagreement.

Conclusions and avenues for further research

This chapter has highlighted how the use of expert surveys in party research has sky-rocketed in the last three decades. Expert surveys cover an increasing number of countries and have been used to empirically measure an ever-broadening array of party characteristics pertaining to policy positions, organisational features, and non-policy-related ideological and stylistic characteristics. In short, expert surveys have become an essential resource in party research that has been used for a rich variety of research endeavours.

As expert surveys are here to stay, it is paramount to tackle the challenges that their implementation may face. In the future, PIs of expert surveys (including this chapter's authors) should do more to address and systematically assess issues related to expert confidence, expert bias, and comparability across different cultural contexts. In particular, future expert surveys should assess whether the (self-reported) confidence of experts' judgements is steered by gender and whether the overrepresentation of male experts affects data quality. We also need more systematic research into the reliability and validity of retrospective expert surveys, which have become increasingly popular to create longitudinal measures of party positioning. In addition, we need to know more about how (academic) cultures and language-use affect the composition of expert pools and data comparability.

Finally, future expert survey research should take the challenges related to expert burden and expert fatigue seriously. These challenges stem particularly from the proliferation of (long and complex) expert surveys. This is in part due to a lack of collaboration between projects using this data collection method. Collaboration *between* various projects could reduce the number of expert surveys fielded. While this means that future projects should overcome potential differences regarding conceptualisation and design, collaboration between projects would also facilitates cross-fertilisation of research ideas.[3]

Notes

1 Expert surveys can also be implemented in different institutional contexts. For instance, McElroy and Benoit (2007) examine the policy positions of European party groups in the European Parliament.
2 V-Party explicitly instructed experts to assess party characteristics 'before a specific election' (Lührmann et al. 2020, 20).
3 We commend the V-Party and V-Dem projects in this regard, as they create a platform that brings together many different scholars.

References

Arnold, C., Doyle, D. and Wiesehomeier, N. (2017) 'Presidents, policy compromise, and legislative success', *Journal of Politics*, 79(2), p380–395.

Bakker, R., Jolly, S., Polk, J. and Poole, K. (2014) 'The European common space: Extending the use of anchoring vignettes', *The Journal of Politics*, 76(4), p1089–1101.

Bakker, R., Hooghe, H., Jolly, S., Marks, G., Polk, J., Rovny, J., Steenbergen, M. and Vachudova, M.A. (2020) *1999 – 2019 Chapel Hill expert survey trend file Version 1.2*. Chapel Hill: University of North Carolina, Chapel Hill. Available at: chesdata.eu.

Benoit, K. and Laver, M. (2006) *Party policy in modern democracies*. London: Routledge.

Benoit, K. and Laver, M. (2007) 'Estimating party policy positions: Comparing expert surveys and hand-coded content analysis', *Electoral Studies*, 26, p90–107.

Benoit, K., Laver, M. and Mikhaylov, S. (2009) 'Treating words as data with error: Uncertainty in text statements of policy positions', *American Journal of Political Science*, 53(2), p495–513.

Benoit, K. and Wiesehomeier, N. (2009) 'Expert judgments' in Pickel, S., Pickel, G., Lauth, H-J. and Jahn, D. (eds.) *Methoden der vergleichenden Politik-und Sozialwissenschaft*. VS Verlag für Sozialwissenschaften, pp. 497–516.

Carmines, E.G. and Stimson, J.A. (1986) 'On the structure and sequence of issue evolution', *The American Political Science Review*, 80(3), p901–920.

Castanho Silva, B. and Littvay, L. (2019) 'Comparative research is harder than we thought: Regional differences in experts' understanding of electoral integrity questions', *Political Analysis*, 27(4), p599–604.

Castles, F.G. and Mair, P. (1984) 'Left-right political scales: Some 'expert' judgements', *European Journal of Political Research*, 12(1), p73–88.

Coppedge, M. (1997) 'A classification of Latin American political parties', Working Paper – Helen Kellogg Institute for International Studies, 244.

Coppedge, M., Gerring, J., Knutsen, C.H., Lindberg, S.I., Teorell, J., Alizada, N., Altman, D., Bernhard, M., Cornell, A., Fish, M.S., Gastaldi, L., Gjerløw, H., Glynn, A., Hicken, A., Hindle, G., Ilchenko, N., Krusell, J., Luhrmann, A., Maerz, S.F., Marquardt, K.L., McMann, K., Mechkova, V., Medzihorsky, J., Paxton, P., Pemstein, D., Pernes, J., von Römer, J., Seim, B., Sigman, R., Skaaning, S-E., Staton, J., Sundström, A., Tzelgov, E., Wang, Y., Wig, T., Wilson, S. and Ziblatt, D. (2021) *V-Dem dataset v11.1 varieties of democracy project*. Available from: https://doi.org/10.23696/vdemds21.

Di Cocco, J. and Monechi, B. (2021) 'How populist are parties? Measuring degrees of populism in party manifestos using supervised machine learning', *Political Analysis*. https://doi.org/https://doi.org/10.1017/pan.2021.29.

Hawkins, K.A. and Castanho Silva, B. (2018) 'Text analysis: Big data approaches', in Hawkins, K.A., Carlin, R.E., Littvay, L. and Rovira Kaltwasser, C. (eds.) *The ideational approach to populism: Concept, theory & analysis*. London: Routledge, pp. 27–48.

Hawkins, K.A. and Littvay, L. (2019) *Contemporary US populism in comparative perspective*. Cambridge: Cambridge University Press.

Hooghe, L., Marks, G. and Wilson, C.J. (2002) 'Does left/right structure party positions on European integration?', *Comparative Political Studies*, 35(8), p965–989.

Huber, J. and Inglehart, R. (1995) 'Expert interpretations of party space and party locations in 42 societies', *Party Politics*, 1(1), p73–111.

Inglehart, R. (1990) *Culture shift in advanced industrial society*. Princeton: Princeton University Press.

Kitschelt, H. and Kselman, D.M. (2013) 'Economic development, democratic experience, and political parties' linkage strategies', *Comparative Political Studies*, 46(11), p1453–1484.

Kopecký, P., Meyer Sahling, J.H., Panizza, F., Scherlis, G., Schuster, C. and Spirova, M. (2016) 'Party patronage in contemporary democracies: Results from an expert survey in 22 countries from five regions', *European Journal of Political Research*, 55(2), p416–431.

Kriesi, H., Grande, E., Dolezal, M., Helbling, M., Höglinger, D., Hutter, S. and Wüest, B. (2012) *Political conflict in western Europe*. Cambridge: Cambridge University Press.

Laver, M. and Hunt, W.B. (1992) *Policy and party competition*. New York: Routledge.

Levick, L. and Olavarria-Gambi, M. (2020) 'Hindsight bias in expert surveys: How democratic crises influence retrospective evaluations', *Politics*, 40(4), p494–509.

Lichtenstein, S. and Fischhoff, B. (1977) 'Do those who know more also know more about how much they know?', *Organizational Behavior and Human Performance*, 20(2), p159–183.

Lindstädt, R., Proksch, S.O. and Slapin, J.B. (2018) 'When experts disagree: Response aggregation and its consequences in expert surveys', *Political Science Research and Methods*, 8(3), p580–588.

Lührmann, A., Düpont, N., Higashijima, M., Kavasoglu, Marquardt, K.L., Bernhard, M., Döring, H., Hicken, A., Laebens, M., Lindberg, S.I., Medzihorsky, J., Neundorf, A., Reuter, O.J., Ruth – Lovell, S., Weghorst, K.R., Wiesehomeier, N., Wright, J., Alizada, N., Bederke, P., Gastaldi, L., Grahn, S., Hindle, G., Ilchenko, N., von Römer, J., Wilson, S., Pemstein, D. and Seim, B., (2020) *Codebook varieties of party identity and organisation (V – Party) V1*. Varieties of Democracy (V – Dem) Project. Available from: https://www.v-dem.net/static/website/img/refs/vparty_codebook.pdf

Lührmann, A., Medzihorsky, J., Hindle, G. and Lindberg, S.I. (2020) New global data on political parties: V-Party. *V-Dem Institute Briefing Paper*, 9. https://www.v-dem.net/documents/8/vparty_briefing.pdf

Lundeberg, M.A., Fox, P.W. and Puncohar, J. (1994) 'Gender differences and similarities in confidence judgements', *American Psychological Association*, 86(1), p114–121.

Marquardt, K.L. and Pemstein, D. (2018) 'IRT models for expert-coded panel data', *Political Analysis*, 26(4), p431–456.

McElroy, G. and Benoit, K. (2007) 'Party groups and policy positions in the European Parliament', *Party Politics*, 13(1), p5–28.

Meijers, M.J. (2017) 'Contagious Euroscepticism? The impact of Eurosceptic support on mainstream party positions on European integration', *Party Politics*, 23(4), p413–423.

Meijers, M.J. and van der Veer, H. (2019) 'MEP responses to 'democratic backsliding' in Hungary and Poland. An analysis of agenda-Setting and voting behaviour', *Journal of Common Market Studies*, 57(4), p838-856.

Meijers, M.J. and Zaslove, A. (2021) 'Measuring populism in political parties: Appraisal of a new approach', *Comparative Political Studies*, 54(2), p372–407.

Norris, P. (2020) 'Measuring populism worldwide', *Party Politics*, 26(6), p697–717.

Norris, P. and Grömping, M. (2019) 'Perceptions of electoral integrity (PEI-7.0)'. Available from: https://doi.org/10.7910/DVN/PDYRWL.

Ray, L. (1999) 'Measuring party orientations towards European integration: Results from an expert survey', *European Journal of Political Research*, 36(2), p283–306.

Rohrschneider, R. and Whitefield, S. (2009) *Understanding cleavages in party systems: Issue position and issue salience in 13 post-communist democracies*, Comparative Political Studies, 42(2), p280–313.

Rohrschneider, R. and Whitefield, S. (2012a) *The strain of representation: How parties represent diverse voters in Western and Eastern Europe*. Oxford: Oxford University Press.

Rohrschneider, R. and Whitefield, S. (2012b) 'Institutional context and representational strain in party – voter agreement in Western and Eastern Europe', *West European Politics*, 35(6), p1320–1340.

Rohrschneider, R. and Whitefield, S. (2019) 'Critical parties: How parties evaluate the performance of democracies', *British Journal of Political Science*, 49(1), p355–379.

Rovny, J. (2012) 'Who emphasizes and who blurs? Party strategies in multidimensional competition', *European Union Politics*, 13(2), p269–292.

Schumacher, G., de Vries, C.E. and Vis, B. (2013) 'Why do parties change position? Party organization and environmental incentives', *Journal of Politics*, 75(2), p464–477.

Stecker, C. and Tausendpfund, M. (2016) 'Multidimensional government-citizen congruence and satisfaction with democracy', *European Journal of Political Research*, 55(3), p492–511.

Steenbergen, M.R. and Marks, G. (2007) 'Evaluating expert judgments', *European Journal of Political Research*, 46(3), p347–366.

Szöcsik, E. and Zuber, C.I. (2015) 'EPAC – a new dataset on ethnonationalism in party competition in 22 European democracies', *Party Politics*, 21(1), p153–160.

Wiesehomeier, N. (2018) 'Expert Surveys', in Hawkins, K.A., Carlin, R.E., Littvay, L. and Rovira Kaltwasser, C. (eds.) *The ideational approach to populism: Concept, theory & analysis*. London: Routledge, pp. 90–111.

Wiesehomeier, N. and Benoit, K. (2009) 'Presidents, parties, and policy competition', *Journal of Politics*, 71(4), p1435–1447.

Wiesehomeier, N. and Doyle, D. (2013) 'Discontent and the left turn in Latin America', *Political science research and methods*, 1(2), p201–221.

Wiesehomeier, N., Singer, M. and Ruth-Lovell, S.P. (2019) 'Political representation, executives, and political parties survey: Data from expert surveys in 18 Latin American countries, 2018–2019'. *Harvard Dataverse*. https://doi.org/ 10.7910/DVN/Z5DESA.

Zuber, C.I. and Szöcsik, E. (2018) 'The second edition of the EPAC expert survey on ethnonationalism in party competition – Testing for validity and reliability', *Regional and Federal Studies*, 29(1), p91–113.

INDEX

Note: Page numbers in *italics* indicate a figure and page numbers in **bold** indicate a table on the corresponding page.

activist(s) 90, 168, 350, 384–386, 397; amateur-activist 191; anti-nuclear 368; feminist 182; grassroots 60; green 193; left-wing 63; networks 93; niche party 224–228; party 50, 63–64, 203–207, 245, 420, 471–472; politics of redistribution 432–433; RLP 165, 174, 181; women party activists 145
adaptation (party) 1, 10–13, 53
Afrobarometer 393
agency 1, 17, 46, 97, 270, 308; causal 26; citizen 23, 25; democratic 14; elite 31; participatory 21, 27; party 25, 131, 164, 238–239; political 270, 308; women's 105
agenda setting 211
ambition gap 106, 284
anchoring vignettes 474
anti-capitalism 173–175
anti-elitism 128, 180, 271
anti-establishment (parties) 11, 156, 176, 360, 367–369
anti-nuclear 94, 186–188, 368
anti-party sentiment 9, 71, 384
Arab Barometer 423n5
Arab socialism 405, 415
Arab Spring 416–418; uprising 403–411
arena 80–81, 90, 102; behavioural 255–262; institutional 11, 30–37, 235–239, 312, 357, 386
assimilation 293–295
asylum 292–297, 304
austerity 74, 94–95, 163, 165–168, 173–181, 227, 306, 337, 368
authoritarianism 14, 418, 466, **469**; competitive 400n5, 403, 407–410; democracy *vs.* 117; democratisation under 95; electoral 349, 399, 417; far right classification 127; parties 120, 357–358; and populism 272, 276
authoritarian states: governance 109, 127; legacies 393; political parties 80
automated text analysis 282, 285, 472

bias 5, 70, 102–109, 200, 341, 454–455, 458n2, 467–475
Brexit 131–133, 144, 156, 277, 330
business firm parties 354, 358, 365, 377

cadre parties 46, 71
calibration 452, 455
campaigning 47, 49, 63, 73–74, 207, 258, 316, 324, 377, 392; online 48, 52, 60, 63, 73
candidate selection 12, 48–50, 57, 255–257, 384, 426, 434; gender 101–103, 105–107, 145, 317
canvassing 60, 63
capitalism 162, 166, 174–175, 179, 274, 304, 354, **461**
cartel parties 2, 10–11, 15, 46–47, 68, 71, 91–92, 392–399; cartelized parties 356
catch-all party(ies) 10, 14, 46–47, 71, 244, 247, 372, 393
Catholic church 116, 139
centre-left 152–155, 236, 291, 361; communist embrace of 174, 178; compared with the centre-right 137–143; decline 133, 161, 176; and European integration 304–307; failure of 142; green parties 186, 192; immigration 291–298; parties 92, 162–168, *163*
centre-right 3, 137–146, 226, 236, 283; compared with the centre-left 137–146; competition 161, 164–165, 179, 283, 306; ideology 152,

304; immigration 291–298; non-cooperative game theory 236; parties 154–155, 166, 226, 306–307; vote share *163*, 167
chain of equivalence 270
challenger parties 165, 168, 223–224, 227, 307, 368–369
challenger parties 165–168, 223–224, 227, 307, 368–369
Chapel Hill Expert Survey (CHES) 202, 212, 248, 455, **468**, 470
Chinese Civil War 362
Christian democracy 94, 138–139
Christian democratic parties 27, 137–145, 153, *163*, 167, 295, 304, 313, 319
Citizens' Assemblies 20
civil wars 4, 323–324, 327, 331
clans 83, 371, 374–377
class politics 187
class-voting 117, 163
cleavage(s) 2, 32, 470–471; cleavage theory 4, 115–121; cultural 198, 352, 431–432; immigration policy 291–297; new cleavages 9, 23, 151, 154; party system 221, 371, 374–376; regional 367; religious 372–373; social 363, 404, 426–428; societal 31; socio-economic 5, 94, 151; socio-political 31, 162, 176, 301–306, 372; structural 116, 150, 329, 411; transnational 129, 150; wartime 327, 329–330
clientelism 4–5, 334–342, 376, 379n1, 394–395, 471; electoral 334–336; linkages 334–335, 336–338, 374, 386–387; organisational 4, 328, 334, 338–340, 363, 371, 376
climate change 4–5, 96–97, 164, 167, 189, 192–194, 213, 250, 280–287
climate change adaptation 281, 285–286
climate change mitigation 283, 286
climate policy 4, 281–287
climate policy preferences 4, 281–287
climate sceptics 283
coalition 4, 11; agreements 132, 297, 357–358; agreement variation 237; Arab Middle East 418; behaviour 232–238; building 15, 35–37, 51, 155–156, 178; centre-right 139–144; Chilean 386; conflict 179; Conservative-led 27; cross-class 162–169; electoral 93, 387; EU integration 304–306; far right 125–132; formation 139, 354; government 245–247; grand coalitions 372–378; green parties 185–193, 228, 283; Indian 427–433; LDP 361, 369n2; maintaining 260; North African 406; parties 37, 215–216, 232–238, 440; Sub-Saharan 398–399
coding 212, 248, 440–446, 450–454
Cold War 30, 32, 36, 323, 330–331, 360, 362, 397
collective action 4, 78, 143, 232, 234–235
collusion 392, 398–399
colour revolutions 354

communism/ist: East Asia 364–365; fear of 141; former 274; ideology 12; labour movement 94; legacy 470; regimes 118; transition 14, 58, 151, 173–180
communist parties: Arab Middle East 415; East Asia 360; EU 303–307; India 432–434; niche **222**, 223; North Africa 405; post-conflict parties 323–328; radical left 173–180; Russia and post-Soviet states 350–578; South-East Asia 371–377
Comparative Agendas Project (CAP) 212, 281
Comparative Campaign Dynamics Dataset 202, 248
Comparative Manifesto Project (CMP) 211–212, 439, 455–456, **457**, 458n3
comparative research 3, 46, 125, 133, 140–142, 180, 284, 286
Comparative Study of Electoral Systems (CSES) 202, 248, 250n2, 313
competition: analysis of party competition 34, 260, 439, 446; binding party competition 21, 24; cleavage 116–121; and climate change 282, 286; in East Asia 363–369; electoral 46, 403, 406, 418; electoral competition change 12; electoral funding 69–73; and European integration 303–304; external/internal party 46; far right 125, 129–134; green party 187, 190; and immigration 291, 298; inter-party 30, 36–37, 341; in Latin America 387; multi-party 422; niche party 221–229; party 2, 4–5, 12–17, 211–217; party personalisation 262; party strategy 199–108; party system 78, 83; and populism 269; post-conflict 324–330; radical left parties 176; representation 244–246; in Southeast Asia 371; in Sub-Saharan Africa 396–397
conceptual stretching 118
conflict 4, 25–26, 115–117; in Arab Middle East 419; class-conflict 141; and European integration 303–306; future 237; ideological 165, 385, 432; internal 191, 214, 247; intra-party 397; leadership 61; in North Africa 404; partisan 308; party 31–33, 46, 96, 140, 152; political 247–249, 274, 283, 291–292, 443, 471; post-conflict 323–327; in Russa and post-Soviet states 358; social 31, 116, 120, 211
congruence 207, 243–249, 286, 472
conservatism 138–140, 143, 151
conservative parties 118, 139; and climate change 281; conservative-liberals 152–153, 293; in East Asia 360; and gender 312–316; and immigration 292–293; mainstream 221; in North Africa 408; and patterns of behaviour 141–144; women's representation 145
conspiracy theory 277
constraining dissensus 307
contagion 133–134, 224–226, 296, 307
co-optation 406–407, 418–420

Index

cordon sanitaire 126, 132, 226, 298
corporatist 139, 141
corruption 354–355, 433, **442**; allegations 328; creation 14; GRECO 75n2; Italian 142; political 68–70; populist 274; private sector 337; scandals 317, 368; Sub-Saharan 394–395
Covid-19 96, 134, 214–215, 250, 297, 315
crisis 96, 274, 292, 388n3, 395, 427; climate 97, 280; economic 245–246, 364, 386, 397; euro 119, 368; global 91, 280; leadership 358–386; organisational 152–153, 427; parties 9, 14; party leaders 12, 21; and populism 27; SDPs 161, 164
critical juncture 31, 116–117, 119–121, 304, 375
culture 101, 115, 130–131, 139, 155, 182, 304, **453**, 475

dealignment 31, 118, 121, 259, 274, 372–373, 385
decline, party 13, 85, 152
de-industrialisation 163
deliberation 4, 22–27, 261, 452
deliberative democracy: intra-party deliberation 26
demand(s) 22, 46, 176, 276; class 426, 430–434; electoral politics 328; elite(s) 357; and far right parties 125–126, 129–134; and gender 105–108; and ideology 152; and left-wing parties 273–274; management 164, 168; multi-party 34–37; organisational 79, 324; political 472; popular 409; responding to 190; social justice 434; societal 26–27, 270; voter 187, 341
democracy(ies): and clientelism 4; consolidated 85; diversity 120; funding 70; and institutionalisation 78–85; new 2, 9, 326, 331–334, 337; new democracies and party change 14–16
Democratic Accountability and Linkages Project (DALP) 388, **469**, 471, 473
democratic backsliding 95, 472
democratic centralism 175, 177, 181
democratic legitimacy 22, 27, 418
democratic theory 20–21, 23–27, 46
democratic transition(s) 95, 366
democratisation 16, 94–95; Arab Middle East 416–417; cleavages 115; East Asia 361–629; intraparty 16; Latin America 382; liberal democratisation 155–157; party systems 120; promoting 330; route to 358; Southeast Asia 371–372; trend(s) 1, 5
descriptive representation 109, 243, 317; strategic 108, 312, 316–319
differential item functioning (DIF) 474
digital parties 3, 11, 16, 47–48, 97
dimensions of competition 453; cultural liberal-conservative 120, 453; economic dimension 305; pro-anti EU integration 453; socio-economic left-right 453
discursive opportunities 131
divide-and-rule 420

donations 71–72, 337–338
dynamic representation 249–250

economic crisis 94, 133, 134n1, 245, 246, 364, 386
economic inequality 71
electoral competition 12, 51, 367–368, 403, 406; adaption to 282; in authoritarian regimes 418; funding 69–73; leadership 324–330; and party competition 246
electoral costs 237–238, 316
electoral decline 12, 319
Electoral Institute for Sustainable Democracy in Africa (EISA) 392, 399n2
electoral performance 3, 325, 341, 421; electoral pledges 237; electoral promises 4, 233, 238, 397; and the far right 126–131; gender 318; green parties 185–191; party promises 17, 232–233, 238, 397; RLP 176–178
electoral professional parties 47
electoral systems 5, 73, 107, 156, 256, 260, 427–429, 458n1; majoritarian 131, 189, 368; mixed 352; PR fragmentation 168; PR and gender 107; proportional representation 25, 69, 139, 145, 189, 378; PR systems 60, 145, 368; restrictive 168; single non-transferable vote (SNTV) 365
electoral volatility 15, 35–36, 117, 120, 247, 378, 382
elite politicians 224, 375
elites 130, 280, 373, 378, 418, 432; communist party 350–358; competing 24; corrupt 269, 276; and the economy 176, 180; EU elites 308; liberal 155–157, 273; minority 23; national 115; party 52, 78–82, 144–145, 317, 339–340; political 46, 117, 140, 383–387, 393; recruitment 50, 334; religious 31
employment 162–163, 166–168, 217, 236–237, 314–315, 335–341, 377, 431–433
environmental linkage 92
environmental policy 236, 280–285, 287, 304, 467
ethnicity 10, 25, 107, 243, 379, 443; cleavages 120, 373, 397; intersections 319; and language 154; and party support 376; and RLPs 182
ethnic minority(ies) 50, 109, 115, 273, 294–295, 319
EU profiler/euandi (EUP&I) trend file **457**
European Election Study (EES) 202, 313
European integration 5, 155, 211–212, 301–309, **453**, 470; backlash 164, 368; challenges to nation-state 12; embrace of 150, **461**; new issue 221; opposition to 179; politicisation 32, 117, 248–249, 467, **468–469**; response to 245; wedge issue 216, 227
European Parliament 450–452, 472, 475n1; affiliations 150, 174; elections 131–133, 247, 440, 452; and gender 109; green party 185, 190; party membership 58
European Social Survey (ESS) 227

European Union 4, 26, 149, **452–453**, 470; Brexit 140; identity 139; international cooperation 301; policies 441–442, 446n4; SDPs 168
Euroscepticism 173, 176, 179, 245, 301–308; conditional 179; definitions of 301–302; disobedient 179, 302; equivocal 303; expansionist/integrationist 302; hard-soft 302; rejectionist 302; touchstone of dissent 304
expert: bias 467, 473, 475; burden 474–475; coders 439–440, 454; confidence 473; disagreement 475; fatigue 470–475; surveys 5, 186, 202, **222**, 228, 249, 271, 282, 303, 306–307, 444–445, 450–457, 466–475, 475n1

factions/factionalism 169, 191, 328, 379n1; elite factions 349–350, 354, 357; Eurosceptic 305; party change 51; party faction(s) 341, 407; party systems 371–378; power seeking 272; socio-economic 292, 430
family reunification 292, 293, 296–297
far right 3, 95–96, 161, 185, 187, 308
far right parties 52, 125–134, 144, 281, 303–305
federalism/federalisation 152, 190, 429, 431
Federal systems 190
femonationalism 315–316
formalisation 95, 105, 384
formal model 200–201, 206, 232–233
frames 15, 24–25, 302
franchise party model 156
freezing hypothesis 31, 116
fundraising 71, 74, 368

gender: action plans 103, 108; difference in support 314–319; equality 74, 103–110, 110n3, 182, 312, 314–319, 422, 471–474; power relations 101; quotas 102–104, 107–108, 110n1, 182, 314–316, 318–319; voting gap 141
gendered hierarchies 102
gendered horizontal segregation 104
gendered rules of the game 102, 108–109
gendered vertical segregation 104
General Incentives Model (GIM) 61–62, 64
Global Financial Crisis 163, 165, 168
globalisation 1, 31, 301, 309, 397, 470; anti-globalisation 94, 307; attitudes toward 117–121, 129–131, 211; impact of 12, 176–179, 315; Latin America 470; liberal parties 156; responses to 3, 164–168; socio-economic 94, 153, 245–246, 377
grassroots democracy 177, 185–187, 191
Great Recession 74, 142, 165, 168, 368
green/alternative/libertarian (GAL) – traditional/authoritarian/nationalist (TAN) dimension [GALTAN] 186, 188, *454*, 455, 457, **461**, **462**
greenhouse gas emissions 192, 280
green parties 49, 119, 185–194, 244, 293; in global south 377, 408; issue competition 205, 214–216, 281–284; migration 293; as niche party 221–227; and rival parties 156, 161, 174; women's representation 104, 318

hegemonic parties 357
hierarchical text analysis 455
hybrid regime(s) 79, 375

IDEA 69, 75n1, 394–395
identity politics 25, 108, 397–398, 417, 471; gender 108, 319; liberal 151, 157
ideology: centrist 186; left 107, 176, 284; party 2–3, 232; right 284, 364, 444
immigrants 126, 128, 130, 192, 273, **453**
immigration 4–5, 32, 229, 290–298, 315, 470–471; attention to 215–216; attitudes toward 117, 137, **453**; demand-side 121, 142–144; European 119; the far right 126–132, 134, 178; liberal parties 154, 186; niche parties 225–229; UK 140
inclusion-moderation hypothesis 324, 416
individualisation 31, 254, 256, 259, 261
industrialisation 115, 138, 324, 432
informal networks 80, 86, *106*, 109, 339
informal politics 373
informal rules 3, 102, 109
institutionalisation 5, 11, 15, 79–85, 86n9, 379n1; African 393; clientelism 339; consequences of 79, 86n11; and gender 102; Latin American 382–387; party politics 30–31; party system 36, 86n1–2, 116, 120, 378, 422; and post-rebel parties 324, 327, 331; and RLPs 181
institutionalism 101
institutionally sexist' organisations 102
integration 328, 414, 456–457; economic 10, 354, 363; and immigration 291–298; political community 21; social integration 24, 26, 104
interest groups 48, 71–72, 216–217, 283, 286, 471; party 51, 282, 386
International Monetary Fund (IMF) 398
international organisations 68, 70, 303, 398
intersectionality 109
intra-party democracy 14, 27, 46, 181, 328; advocates 25, 155; commitment to 74, 155; and gender 101–103
intra-party politics 233, 239, 260, 286
invariance tests 474
Islamist parties 404, 408, 416, 418, 420, 422n4; Islamist-secular divide 411n5, 417, 421
issue: characteristics 217; competition 4, 211–218, 471; emphasis 214–215, 225, 243–244, 246–248, 249, 250n1, 443; engagement 213; entrepreneurs 215, 223, 227, 306; evolution 360–363; overlap 213; ownership 141, 185–186, 192, 204, 212–213, 226, 293; position 11, 203, 223, 248–250, 305, 308, 314, 452, 458, 467, 471; preference 212–214, 243;

priority 248; salience 223, 238, 248, 305, 308, 443, 446, 471; yield 212
iterative method 452–453, 454, 458n2

junior coalition partner 179, 192, 247, 428
junior minister 237, 239

knowledge society 164
Korean War 364

labour migration 292–293
labour movement 94, 161–162, 166
law of curvilinear disparity 60
leadership 10–15, 143, 247, 258, 315, 383; alternative(s) 46; charismatic 81, 128, 272; dissenters 27; far right 132–133; funding 72; gender balance 104–107, 133; in Latin America 80; parliamentary 233–235; party 270, 337, 357–358, 394, 396, 405; post-conflict 326–328; restriction 60; SDPs 165–169; selection 51, 86n9, 153–155; tension of/between 16, 61–63, 82, 128, 206, 420; training 106
leadership selection 49–51, 103–104, 234, 235
leftist parties 14, 165, 189, 312–313, 372, 375–377, 415–416, 420; left-right continuum 34, 199, 201, *201*, 206, 422, 471
left-libertarian parties 190
left-right (positions) 206, 246, 249
left-wing populism 275
legitimacy 92–93, 325, 354, 357–358, 408; benefits 60; crisis 9–10; democratic 9–10, 22, 27, 418; participation 49; party systems 86n2; social 25, 103, 430; statutory legitimacy 108; undermine 35, 71
liberal democracy 4, 149, 156, 180, 272, 274–276
liberalism 24, 138, 149–156; market liberalism 14; socio-economic 118; undemocratic liberalism 276
liberal parties 138–145, 149–157, 164, 216, 277n2, 353, 405, 408, 417
libertarian 186–194, 211, 247, 293, 304; GAL 470; green-libertarian 165–167; left-libertarian(s) 32, 118–119
life cycle 11
linkage 47, 60, 92, 224, 243, 249–250, 261; clientelist(ic) 243, 250, 386–388, 395, 404, 409–410; directive 405; electoral 404, 408; environmental 92; Latin American 385–387; linkage mass-party system 394–397; organisations 243; participatory 47, 243, 404; party 395; separate spheres 92
localisation 256
loyalty (party) 24, 81, 193, 340–342

Maastricht treaty 301
mainstream left 226–228
mainstream parties 3, 306–307; and anti-system parties 11, 131–134, 367–369; assessment of 9, 206; cleavages 119; decline of 1, 15, 168; and green parties 190–194, 205; immigration 291–298; issue engagement 5, 179, 215; niche parties 221–229, 245, 315; responsiveness 275–276; and RLPs 179; vote-seeking 216, 244, 247
mainstream right 14–15, 94, 216, 227–228
male-female voter ratio(s) 312–313, *313*
manifesto(s): Euromanifestos project (EM) 307, 439–443; manifesto data 152, 422, 439–440, 443–446, 458, 472; party manifestos 93, 108, 212–216, **222**, 228, 439–445, 451, 454–457, 467
MARPOR project 248, 439–440, **441**, 442–444, 446n2, **461**, **463–465**
Marxism 179
masculinity 101–102
mass party(ies) 10, 13, 16, 46–49, 71, 78–82, 151, 161, 393–394, 415
matching algorithm 450–451
measurement: climate policy 285–286; electoral 33; expert surveys 467; gender 319; innovative 262; party salience and position 229; populism 471; responsiveness 244, 249; valence 204, 207–208; voting 455–458
media: agenda 216; attention 128, 211, 216, 225, 260; coverage 11, 107, 207, 246, 248–249, 444–446; freedom 470; and gender 103; migrant media 295; new media 15; oligarchs 377; outlets 26, 63, 217; party organisation 45, 53; personalisation 254–258, 261–262; RLPs 177; Russia 354–356; salience 119
mediatisation 1, 254, 259
memberless parties 3, 47
Members and Activists of Political Parties (MAPP) 56
#MeToo 102
Middle-class 128, 164, 166, 168, 192, 319n1
mobilisation 23, 354; of capital 434; clientelism 334–337, 386–387; cognitive 118; electoral 52, 56, 341, 431; employment 338; ethnic 350; extra-parliamentary 47–49, 175; forms of 20; function 25; interest group(s) 217; Islamist parties 405, 414–422; party 12, 301; personalisation 255; political 121, 270, 330, 349; popular 324, 375; populist 181, 269, 271, 273, 379; social 96; voter 339, 471
money 68–74, 102, 105, 204, 335, 338–339, 371, 397–398
multiculturalism 132, 137, 142, 274, 294–295, **442**, **462**

nationalism 4, 32, 127, 131; Catalan 153; Euroscepticism 179, 303; Hindu nationalism 434; 'new politics' 304
nation-state 12, 115–116, 294–296, 303
neighbouring portfolios 237
neo-conservatism 140
neo-liberalism 140, 143, 179, 273, 397

New Left 107, 167, 175, 181, 190, 313
new middle class 188
new party 9, 16, 37, 70, 351–355, 362–368, 383–384, 407
new politics 187, 304, **361**, 416
new social movements 94–96, 188
niche parties 221–229, **222**, 244–245; behaviour 245; coalition 216; electoral fortunes 214, 307; new niche parties 211; rise of 143, 315; SDPs 169

one-party dominance 363, 369
opposition parties 245–247, 337; agenda setting 215; alliance building 356; Arab Middle East 418, 421; East Asia 360–369; India 428; influence 286, 326; issue emphasis 203, 307; North Africa 406–407; office seeking 245–247; Southeast Asia 373, 378; Sub Saharan Africa 393–399; suppression 350
organisational change 51, 83

Paris Agreement 280
parliamentary rules 233–239
participation: electoral 78–79, 85, 323–324, 327, 331, 450
partisan networks 15
partisanship 13, 20–27, 243, 285–286, 385
party accountability 458
party branches 79–80, 350
party change 3, 9–13, 16–17, 50–51, 91, 180, 323, 327
party competition: inter-party competition 30, 37, 341; intra-party competition 26–27, 61, 207; multidimensionality 79, 85, 229; two-party competition 199, 201, 365; unidimensional 32, 199–203, 249, 304, 364, 368
party de-institutionalisation 79
party democracy 9, 14, 21–22, 26, 143–144, 173, 181, 254, 397
party family 3, 453–456; centre-right 137, 143–145; EU integration 301–304; the far right 126–127; green 185–194; immigration 292; legitimise 297; liberal 149–157; niche **222**, 223; populist 270–273; RLPs 173–174; and social democracy 161–162, *163*, 166–169; women's representation 312–313, *317*
party financing 355, 376–377
party following 24
party formation 4–5, 11, 186, 323–324, 383–384
party fragmentation 140
party friends 58
party functions 48, 51, 57, 243, 414
party funding 51, 68–75, 394–395; regimes 69, 74, 75n4; regulation 68–69, 75n2; transparency 68
party government 232–236, 238–239, 261–262, 280, 284–285
party identification 24, 81, 118, 154, 193, 204, 258, 374, 376, 393, 471

party ideology 2–3, 113, 232
party institutionalisation 5, 15, 78–85, 82, 86n2, 378, 385, 393
party leader(s) 11–16; charismatic 128, 177, 243, 255, 262, 374, 377; clientelism 335–341; coercion 27; communist 350, **351**, 358; and gender 107–108, 316–318; in governments and coalitions 233–235; green parties 191–193; Latin America 384, 387; membership 60–63; organisation 48–52, 165; partisanship 26; perceptions 11; personalisation 256–263; popular 204; post-conflict 326; radical 168; selection 86n9, 104; Southeast Asia 374–374; Sub-Saharan Africa 393
party members 81, 255, 377
party membership 1, 56–59, 64, 71, 103, 192, 373, 384, 396, 421; costs 57; joining 57, 64, 192; leaving 64
party models 2, 10–3, 15, 46–50, 68, 78–80, 156, 186, 191, 393, 399
partyness 255–256, 261–262
party officials 80, 165, 261, 445, 452, 455
party organisation 1–3, 45–53, 155, 157, 466, 471–472; centre right 137, 144–145; change beyond classical models 10, 14–16; changes in women's representation 318; cleavage beyond Europe 120; clientelism 335–337; climate change mitigation policy 284; faces of 47, 80, 397; far right 125–128, 131–133; finance 71–72; gender 101, 109; India 426, 434; institutionalisation 78–86; Latin America 382–388; membership 64; personalisation 260; populism 270–276; radical left 177, 180; Russia and post-Soviet states 349, 356; Southeast Asia 375–376; Sub-Saharan Africa 392–394, 397; systems and change 36
party policy preferences 439
party positions 27, 443, **468**, 470–473, 475; competition and agenda setting 211–214; EU integration 302–304, 307; government, legislative power 235; mainstream party responses 226; measurement 248–249; niche parties 223; party strategies *201*, 202; VAAs 450–458
party programme(s) 228, 255, 312, 414, 417, 451
party reification 84
party resources 68
party responsiveness 245–246, 248
party rules 80, 107–108, 239, 397
party sorting 285
party spending 73, 75
party strategy 190, 199, 200, 203, 205, 213, 319, 384, 386
party supporters 45, 245, 257, 275, 308, 337, 384
party survival 274, 384
party system: agenda 213–217; change 5, 10, 30–37, 117–118, 142, 149, 363, 450; dominant

362, 407; fragmentation (of) 34, 131, 168–169, 297, 350, 358, 372, 374; legitimacy (of) 9–10, 35, 71, 86n2, 93, 103, 120, 357, 408; nationalisation 360, 366–369, 393; transition 31, 79, 157, 324, 331, 334, 342
party systemness 79–80
party transformation 9, 15–16, 330–331
party women's organisations 104–105, 108
patronage: African parties and state capture 394–395; Arab Middle East 418–421; clientelism 335, 341–342; East Asia 363; India 427, 430; North Africa 403; Russia and post-Soviet states 375; Southeast Asia 375–377
patrons 334–336, 338–340, 386
peacebuilding 323–325, 328
permissive consensus 307
personalisation: behavioural personalisation 254, 255, 258, 262; centralised personalisation 256, 258; decentralised personalisation 256, 258; institutional personalisation 255–257; media personalisation 255, 257, 261–262; personalisation of politics 254, 259, 261, 379; self-personalisation 258
personalised politics 254–262
personalism 139, 225, 259–260, 358, 386
Plebiscitarian parties 58
pluralism 21, 24, 26, 35, 70, 354
polarisation 11, 38, 82, 95; cleavage 115; climate change 282, 285–286; East Asia 365–367; EU integration 305–308; explanations of electoral success 153; Latin America 385; liberal party origins 151; niche party aims and strategies 224; party spatial strategies 200; representation 245–247; Russia and post-Soviet states 352–353; Sartorian tradition 34–35; Southeast Asia 374–379
policy: climate change 281; East Asia 365–366; EU integration 306; far right 132; gender 312–316, 319; governments and coalition 232; green parties 186; immigration 292; liberal parties 152; party strategies 199–207; personalisation 256; populism 275; positions 46, 60, 439, **468–469**, 471, 474–475, 475n1; radical left 178; representation 245–246, 249; statements 246, 439, 443–444, 452–454, **453**; Sub-Saharan Africa 394; VAAs 450
policy agenda setting 213–217
policy entrepreneur 283
policy-making 244, 470–471; centre right 143; climate change 280–281; EU integration 302; gender 109; government and coalitions 232–239; group representation 104; party change 12; party competition 190; party membership 57
policy problems 287
political cleavages 31, 301, 303
political competition 4, 21, 275, 429; cleavage theory 117–118; clientelism 342; convergence on authoritarianism 354; party finance 71; party organisation 46–47; responses to European integration 304–305; VAAs 453–455, **453**, 458
political corruption 68, 395, **442**
political opportunities 104, 131
political outsider(s) 106, 163, 331, 398
Political Party Database (PPDB) 276, 302, 342
political regime(s) 276, 302, 342; democratic 14, 16, 103, 276, 357; hybrid 79, 96
political representation 1, 25, 96–97, 317, 355, 388, 439, 458, **468**, 474
Political Representation, Parties, and Presidents Survey (PREPPS) 388, **468**, 474
political space 32, 131, 169, 304, 352, 422, 450, 453, *456*
politicisation 32, 117, 224–226, 339, 379, 416, 426, 428, 430
politico-military organisations 418
populism: attitudes 274–277; exclusionary 273; inclusionary 273, 275, 277n2
populist parties 4, 32, 156, 177–181, 269, 271–277
portfolio allocation 4, 155, 236–239
portfolio model 236
positional competition 211–214, 218
position blurring 472
post-communism 14
post-industrial economies 10
postmaterial(ism/ist) 118, 151, 187–189, 193, 227
poverty 314, 339–340, 386, 395, 433
preferences 21, 31; climate policy 4; conflict(ing) 165; far right voting 128–131; ideological 244; individual 238; leader 239; liberal party 154; party 2, 5, 31, 59, 69, 137, 225–227, 280–287, 308; party behaviour 141; party influence 235; party systems 36–37; policy 1, 200–207, 280–286, 314–316; stabilising 30; voter/voting 201–207, 224–225, 247, 258, 319, 383
preferential: access 335; treatment 72
presidentialism 350, 352
presidential systems 234, 272, 365, 387, 470
private companies 337
private funding 69–71, 74, 394
private sector 337
privatisation 132, 151, 179, 256, 261, 433, 470
problem indicators 216–217
procurement 337
professional (party) 47
'project parties' 355–356
protest(s) 416, 430; centre right 139, 141; East Asia 368; far right 129–130; green parties 190; niche party success 227; North Africa 409; parties and deliberation 23; post conflict parties 325; radical left 173, 176, 178; responses to EU integration 303–305; Russia and post-Soviet states 354; social movements 90–94; Southeast Asia 376; voting 129–130, 178, 190, 227
public agenda 217

public attitudes to climate change 285
public funding 15, 47, 69–71, 74, 103, 295, 394–395
public institutions 335, 340, 342
public opinion 26–27, 35, 46, 445–446; climate change 286; climate policy preferences 282; Europe as a threat/opportunity 305; far right 131; green parties 193; issue competition 217; niche party aims/strategies 225; party strategies 203; representation 244–246; voters and EU integration 307
public sector 166, 168, 314, 336, 431, 433

quantitative analysis 422

radical left party 3, 302
radical right party(ies) 104, 127, 165, 177–178, 221–224, 247, 271–273, 308
radical right populism 133, 181, 287n1
realignment 32, 118, 164, 167–168, 274, 385
rebel groups 323–327, 331, 399
rebel group successor parties 324–326
recruitment 49–50, 80, 105, *106*, 108, 155, 292, 382, 393, 418
refugees 293, 297, 308
regionalism 329, 360, 365–367, 369
regionalist parties 221, 228, 304
reliability (of the data)/reliability (test) 440–441
religion 25, 31, 154, 467; Arab Middle East 416, 422; Christian democrats 141–142; Cleavage politics 118; gender 319; radical left 178; representation 243; Southeast Asia 376
renewable energy 192–193, 284
representation: crisis of 385; legislative 83; political 1, 25, 96–97, 317, 335, 388, 439, 458, **468**, 474
resistance 51, 107, 374, 376, **419**, 443
responsiveness 4, 17, 243–250, 301, 309, 443, 458; clarity of responsibility 247; coalition government 245, 247; economic conditions 246; governing status 4, 243–247; intra-party dynamics 245; leadership change 247; party competition 4, 17, 244–246; party size 246; party type 4, 244–246; polarisation 245–247; voters 4, 17, 243–250, 309, 443, 458
rhetoric 23, 26, 108, 206, 474; centre right 140; far right 127, 131; India 433; niche parties 228; populism 271; re-gendering political parties 108; Sub-Saharan Africa 398
right-left index (RILE) 248
routinisation 80–85, 86nn2, 9, 10, 383–884, 388n1

salience/saliency 439, 443, 446, **468**, 471; cleavage 119–120; climate change 281–287; European integration 305–308; far right 143; gender 315–316; government and coalition 238; green parties 189–190; immigration and integration 292, 295; India 430; liberal parties 151–153, 156; niche parties 223–225, 229; party organisation 51; representation 245–249; SDPs 164, 167; Sub-Saharan Africa 398
Second World War 126; post-era 312
secularisation 12, 31, 139, 153
self-placement 154, 248, 250n2, 451–452, 473
sexual harassment 103, 109
single-issue parties 186, 221, 223, 305, 315
sleeping giant thesis 307–308
social and attitudinal aspect 32
social democracy 94, 161–169, 174–177
social democratic parties 46, 83, 92, 144, 161–162, 216; centre right 137; European integration 306; gender 313; immigration 293; radical left parties 174
social investment 164, 168, 192
socialist 12, 31, 50, 61, 403, 456; Arab Middle East 415; centre right 138; East Asia 360, 365; European integration 302, 304, 306; green parties 186, 189–190; ideology and policy 152; India 430–434; Latin America 387; niche parties 221; North Africa 405; populism 272–273; radical left parties 174–180; Russia and post-Soviet States **351**, 353; social democracy 161–163, 167, 168; Southeast Asia 371, 377
social media 3, 63–64, 97, 255; Cleavage 118; digitalisation of politics 48–49; media personalisation 257–258, 261; populism 269, 277; Southeast Asia 378
social movement(s) 3, 90–97, 371; Arab Middle East 418–419; gender 110, 318; green parties 186–188, 191–193; parties and partisanship 20, 27; party organisation 45, 53; populism 269; post conflict parties 326; radical left 181; SDPs 167; Southeast Asia 375, 378
spatial model 199–200, 202, 204–205, 244, 422; Nash equilibrium 200–202; policy preferences/issues 200, 203; proximity voting 199–200, 205
state capture 15, 342, 392, 395, 399
state funding 73–74, 82–83, 392, 394–395, 398
state regulation of parties 392
state subsidies 14, 69–70, 377–378, 394, 433
strategy 14–15, 33, 92–93, 108, 190, 443; CEE democracies 15; centre right 141, 144; clientelism 334, 337–338, 341; east Asia 363; European integration 305–308; far right 132–133; gender 316–319; green parties 193–194; impact on mainstream politics 156; issue competition 212–213; Latin America 384–387; niche party strategies 224–227; parties in North Africa 406; party strategies 199–207; personalisation 258–260; populism 271; representation 247; size and balance in party politics 33; substantive representation 109, 145, 243
supply 61, 130, 204, 262, 352–353, 472; centre right 143; cleavage 121; closure approach

37; competition 34; electoral performance 176–177; far right 125–130, 133–134; green parties 185, 187; ideational resources 385; non-programmatic linkages 386; populism and parties 274, 276; representation 105–106; Russia and Ukraine 352–353; SDPs 165, 168; volatility approach 36
supranational representation 458
Supreme Court 26
survey satisficing 471, 474

technocrat 96, 223, 239, 372, 410–411
technological change 132, 163
territorial branches 341
third wave of democratisation 371, 382, 393
third way 138, 142, 164–165, 167–168
trade unions 60, 92, 107, 130, 162, 166–167, 372, 405, 471
transnational affiliation 149–151, 185, 417, 451–452
triangulation 455, 457, 466
tribes 318, 405–407, 411, 420, 433
Trotskyism 175
two-party system 31, 33, 35, 140, 153, 245, 360, 366, 369, 427

valence competition 281
valence model 199, 203
value infusion 80–86, 86n2, 86n10, 385
veto player 236
vote-buying 335, 337–339, 377, 427

voter behaviour 17, 262, 378, 430
voter turnout 9–10, 116, 319n1
vote-seeking strategy 205, 216, 225, 246, 282, 318
vote switching 35, 247
Voting Advice Applications (VAAs) 5, 450–455, 457–459, 465
voting behaviour 103, 117, 119, 169, 204, 235, 258; Arab Middle East 422; centre right 137; far right 125; issues and gender 312–313; parties in East Asia 365; post conflict parties 331; VAAs 454

wedge issue 305
welfare state 162, 221, 302, 386–387; coalitions 236; gender 312, 314, 316; green parties 186, 190; Latin America 386–387; niche parties 221; retrenchment 140, 164, 167; SDPs 186, 190
women candidates 106–109
Women Members of Parliament (MPs) 108, 318–319
women's issue positions 314
women's parties 110
women's representation 107, 144–145, 312, 317–318
women's rights 94, 186, 221, 312, 315–316, 416
work-family policies 316
working-class 31, 162, 164–168
World Bank 398
World Values Survey 59, *59*, 188–189

xenophobia 95, 269, 275